A Quarterly
Author-Subject
Index to the
International
Periodical Literature
of Film and
Television/Video

film literature index

Section One: Film
Section Two: Television/Video

Volume 24 Number 1 1996

Editors
Linda Provinzano
Deborah Sternklar

Managing Editors
Vincent J. Aceto
Fred Silva

Film and Television Documentation Center
Richardson 390C
State University of New York at Albany
Albany, New York 12222

Printed quarterly with annual cumulations
Printed in the United States of America

CONTRIBUTING INDEXERS

Chris Barbour
Hilde De Bruyne
Inka Heiler
Denisa Krzystyniak
Susan Malbin
Dorothea Mantis
Judith Panitch
Colleen E. Parks
Peggie Partello
Asta Roberts
Yelizaveta Rudneva-Salters
Ulla Sattinger
Fred Silva
Richard Sloma
Mari Sorri

COMPUTER PROGRAMMER

I-far Lin

TECHNICAL ASSISTANTS

Meredith Case
Katherine Moss
Colleen E. Parks
Suzanne Winkler
Deborah J. Woodworth

Type and design: University Computing Center,
    University at Albany

ISBN 0–8352–0954–7
ISSN 0093–6758
Library of Congress Catalog Card Number: 74–642396
Copyright© 1996 by:
    Film and Television Documentation Center
    State University of New York at Albany
    1400 Washington Avenue
    Albany, New York 12222
    U.S.A.

ANNUAL SUBSCRIPTION RATES

United States and Canada
$375.00 - Three quarterly issues, with annual bound cumulation.

All other countries
$400.00 - Three quarterly issues, with annual bound cumulation.

PREFACE

Film Literature Index is a quarterly subject, author index to the international film and television/video literature appearing in periodicals. The list of film periodicals indexed is based on an examination of over three hundred titles from around the world. While periodicals of purely fan interest, totally technical data and extremely short pieces of press release information have been eliminated, *Film Literature Index* does include both well-known established film journals and the specialized, exotic or fugitive film publications.

Recognizing the increased periodical coverage of television as a cultural and economic force, *Film Literature Index* has greatly expanded its inclusion of television/video material. This coverage will be found in a separate alphabet in Section Two.

Designed for use by either the specialist or the general reader interested in film and television/video, *Film Literature Index* provides the most comprehensive survey available of the entire spectrum of current periodical writing on film.

In addition to the author's name and over one thousand subject headings, articles are indexed under the names of individual screenwriters, performers, directors, cinematographers, professional societies, and corporations.

Article entries indicate the presence of filmography, credits, biographical data or interviews.

Film title and television/video program entries include original language title, American release title, director's name, original release date, and country of production.

Book reviews appear under subject and author entries.

Film Literature Index acknowledges the institutional support of the State University of New York at Albany.

INTRODUCTION

In order to provide some historical background on the
development of *Film Literature Index*, the following introduction
is reprinted from the Prototype Issue published April 1973.

Recognizing the necessity for interested scholars and the general public to gain access to the rapidly increasing flow of film information in periodicals, The New York State Council on the Arts awarded a grant to The Upper Hudson Library Federation, Albany, New York, in 1971 to investigate the feasibility of creating an index to this material. This prototype issue of the *Film Literature Index* represents the completion of that study as well as the initiation of a larger project, the publication of a quarterly index to film literature appearing in periodicals.

We isolated two major problems: the inadequate range and lack of specificity of film subject heading terms in the existing indexes (e.g., *Reader's Guide to Periodical Literature*); and the limited number of periodicals listed in these sources. First, we developed a comprehensive and precise set of subject headings based on an analysis of film glossaries, dictionaries, and indexes from standard texts as well as an intensive reading of film scholarship. From this process and discussions with film scholars emerged a basic list of over one thousand subject headings and an authority list of individuals, film titles, organizations and institutions. This list meets the needs of film scholars and the general public. The continual addition of subject headings will insure the list's status as the most complete collection of such terms available.

Wishing to expand the inclusion of periodicals beyond the core of recognized serious film periodicals (e.g. *Sight & Sound*), we located those publications covering the sometimes neglected popular culture dimension of film activity. To arrive at this core we examined the standard international periodical directories (e.g., *Ulrich's*) and identified several hundred international film periodicals from which we eliminated those with purely fan interest, totally technical data, and those that consisted entirely of either extremely short pieces or press release information. What remained were approximately one hundred twenty-five international periodicals which we called the core. In addition, we included approximately one hundred non-film publications presenting film material with some frequency. From this combined list we selected twenty-eight periodicals to test the adequacy of the subject headings and to develop the policies which determine the format of this prototype issue of the *Film Literature Index*.

In the full *Index* we will include the entire core of specialist film periodicals as well as the non-film publications to provide the most complete access to film literature available.

We wish to acknowledge the people who made the study feasible: Jane Graves, Art Librarian, Skidmore College, Saratoga Springs, New York, whose contribution in time, commitment, and knowledge to this *Index* equals our own; Florence Kretzschmar, Editor-in-Chief, *The Music Index*, whose wide experience and sympathetic understanding saved us repeatedly; Peter Bradley, Film Program Director, New York State Council on the Arts; Edgar Tompkins, Director, The Upper Hudson Library Federation, Albany, New York; Diane Hack and Bill O'Connor, Graduate Assistants; Linda Welch, secretary; Alfred Dascher, Assistant to the Dean, School of Library and Information Science, State University of New York at Albany. The help was theirs; the errors are ours.

VINCENT J. ACETO
Professor, Library Science, SUNYA

FRED SILVA
Associate Professor American Literature and Film, SUNYA

State University of New York at Albany
April 1973

PERIODICAL ABBREVIATIONS

In alphabetical order according to the abbreviations used to identify them.
An asterisk following a title indicates selective indexing.

AFRICA MEDIA REV—Africa Media Review*
AFTERIMAGE—Afterimage*
AM ANTHRO—American Anthropologist*
AM IMAGO—American Imago*
AM JEWISH HIST—American Jewish History*
AM JOUR REV—American Journalism Review*
AM SCHOL—American Scholar*
AMCIN—American Cinematographer
AMER HIST R—American Historical Review*
AMER PREM—American Premiere
AMERASIA J—Amerasia Journal*
AMERICA—America*
AMERICAN QUARTERLY—American Quarterly*
ANGLES—Angles
ANIMATION J—Animation Journal
ANIMATOR—Animator
ANIMATRIX—Animatrix
ANTIOCH R—Antioch Review*
ARACHNE—Arachne*
ARCHIVES—Archives: Institut Jean Vigo
ARMCHAIR DET—Armchair Detective*
ART IN AM—Art in America*
ARTF—Artforum*
ASIAN—Asian Cinema
ATL —Atlantic, The*
AVANT-SCENE—Avant-Scene Cinema, L'
BLACK CAMERA—Black Camera
BLACK F REV—Black Film Review
BLIMP—Blimp. Film Magazine
BOMB—Bomb*
BOUNDARY 2—Boundary 2*
BOXOFFICE—Boxoffice
BREF—Bref: le magazine du court metrage
BULLETIN FIAF—Bulletin FIAF
C & MEDIA—Cine & Media
C ACTION—Cineaction
C BUL—Cine-Bulles
C CUBANO—Cine Cubano
C FANTAS—Cinefantastique
C FOCUS—Cinefocus
C FORUM—Cineforum
C NUOVO—Cinema Nuovo
C PAPERS—Cinema Papers
C SUD—Cinema Sud
C TECH—Cinema Technology
C92—Cinema 92
C&C—Cinema & Cinema
CAHIERS—Cahiers du Cinema
CAHIERS CINEMATHEQUE—Cahiers de la Cinematheque, Les
CAHIERS SCENARIO—Cahiers du Scenario, Les
CAM OBS—Camera Obscura
CAM STYLO—Camera/Stylo

CAN J COM—Canadian Journal of Communication*
CAN J F STUD—Canadian Journal of Film Studies
CANTRILL'S FMNTS—Cantrill's Filmnotes
CARDOZO—Cardozo Arts & Entertainment Law Journal*
CASTORO CIN—Castoro Cinema, II
CHAPLIN—Chaplin
CHINA SCREEN—China Screen
CHR CENT—Christian Century*
CICIM—CICIM: Revue Pour le Cinema Francais
CINEASTE—Cineaste
CINE-BULLETIN—Cine-Bulletin
CINEFEX—Cinefex
CINEMACTION—CinemAction
CINEMAS—Cinemas
CINEMATOGRAPH—Cinematograph
CINEMAYA—Cinemaya
CIRCA—CIRCA: Art Magazine*
CJ—Cinema Journal
CLASSIC—Classic Images
COL JOUR REV—Columbia Journalism Review*
COMM & LAW—Communications and the Law*
COMM RES—Communication Research*
COMMENTARY—Commentary*
COMMONWEAL—Commonweal*
COMMUNICATION—Communication*
CONS REP—Consumer Reports*
CONS RES MAG—Consumers' Research Magazine*
CONT R—Contemporary Review*
CONTINUUM—Continuum*
COSA VISTA—Cosa Vista, La
CRF—Current Research in Film
CRIT INQ—Critical Inquiry*
CRIT Q—Critical Quarterly*
C(SWITZ)—Cinema (Switzerland)
CUE SHEET—Cue Sheet
CULT CRIT—Cultural Critique*
CVA REVIEW—CVA Review*
DANCE MAG—Dance Magazine*
DIACRITICS—Diacritics*
DICINE—Dicine
DIFFERENCES—Differences*
DISCOURSE—Discourse
DISCOURSE & SOC—Discourse & Society*
DISSENT—Dissent*
DOC BOX—Documentary Box
EAST-WEST FJ—East-West Film Journal
EBONY—Ebony*
EKRAN—Ekran
EMPIRICAL STUD ARTS—Empirical Studies of the Arts*
ENGL J—English Journal*
EPD—EPD Film

ESQUIRE—Esquire*
EYEPIECE—Eyepiece
F BUL—Filmbulletin
F COM—Film Comment
F CRITICISM—Film Criticism
F CUL—Film Culture
F DOPE—Film Dope
F ECHANGE—Film Echange
F FAUST—Filmfaust
F FAX—Filmfax
F HAFTET—Filmhaftet
F HIST—Film History
F KULTURA—Filmkultura
F KUNST—Filmkunst
F NEWS—Filmnews
F SCORE MONTHLY—Film Score Monthly
F THREAT—Film Threat
F VILAG—Filmvilag
F WAERTS—Filmwaerts
F & FAKTEN—Film & Fakten
F & FERNSEHEN—Film und Fernsehen
F-HISTORIA—Film-Historia
FATAL VISIONS—Fatal Visions
FCR—Filmcritica
FIHUL—Filmihullu
FILM—Film
FILM (ITALY)—Film: tutti i film della stagione
FILMMAKER—Filmmaker: the Magazine of Independent Film
FIR—Films in Review
FJ—Film Journal
FKT—Fernseh- und Kino-Technik
FQ—Film Quarterly
FRAMEWORK—Framework
FRAME-WORK—Frame-Work: the Journal of Images and
    Culture*
FRAUEN & F—Frauen und Film
FSP—Filmowy Serwis Prasowy
F&HIST—Film & History
F&K—Film & Kino
F&TV—Film en Televisie + Video
F&TV KAM—Film & TV Kameramann
GENDERS—Genders*
GENRE—Genre*
GEORGIA R—Georgia Review*
GRAND ANGLE—Grand Angle
GRAPHIS—Graphis*
GRIFFITHIANA—Griffithiana
HARPER'S—Harper's Magazine*
HIST JFR&TV—Historical Journal of Film, Radio and Television
HITCHCOCK ANN—Hitchcock Annual
HUDSON R—Hudson Review*
HUMANIST—Humanist*
HUMANITIES—Humanities*
IKON—Ikon
ILLUSIONS—Illusions
IMAGE TECH—Image Technology
IMMAGINE—Immagine
INDEP—Independent Film & Video Monthly, The
INDEP SPIRIT—Independent Spirit
INTERV—Interview*
INTL DOC—International Documentary
IRIS—Iris

ISKUS K—Iskusstvo Kino
J AESTH & ART C—Journal of Aesthetics and Art Criticism*
J AESTH EDUC—Journal of Aesthetic Education*
J AM CUL—Journal of American Culture*
J AM STUDIES—Journal of American Studies*
J COMM—Journal of Communication*
J COMM INQUIRY—Journal of Communication Inquiry*
J DURASSIAN STUD—Journal of Durassian Studies*
J F PRES—Journal of Film Preservation
J MOD LIT—Journal of Modern Literature*
J POP CUL—Journal of Popular Culture*
J WOMEN'S HIST—Journal of Women's History*
JEUNE C—Jeune Cinema
JOURNAL WGA—The Journal: Writers Guild of America, West
JPF—Journal of Popular Film and Television
JUMP CUT—Jump Cut
KINO—Kino
KINO (BRD)—Kino; Filme der Bundesrepublik Deutschland
KINO (GF)—Kino; German Film
KOSMORAMA—Kosmorama
LATIN AM RES REV—Latin American Research Review*
LIT IMAG—Studies in the Literary Imagination*
LIT/FQ—Literature/Film Quarterly
LITERATURE & PSYCHOLOGY—Literature and Psychology*
LONDON MAG—London Magazine*
MASS R—Massachusetts Review*
MEDIA—Media
MEDIA CUL & SOC—Media Culture and Society*
MEDIA INFO AUSTRALIA—Media Information Australia*
MEDIEN—Medien + Erziehung
MEDIEN PRAKTISCH—Medien Praktisch
MEDIUM—Medium
MENSUEL C—Mensuel du Cinema, Le
MICHIGAN ACADEMICIAN—Michigan Academician*
MIDNIGHT MARQUEE—Midnight Marquee
MIDSTREAM—Midstream*
MILLENNIUM—Millennium Film Journal
MINN R—Minnesota Review*
MOD DRAMA—Modern Drama*
MOD LANG R—Modern Language Review, The*
MONITEUR—Moniteur du Film en Belgique, Le
MOVIE—Movie
MOVIELINE—Movieline
MQR—Michigan Quarterly Review*
MS—MS*
NAT R—National Review*
NATION—Nation*
NDQ—North Dakota Quarterly*
NEW GERMAN CRITIQUE—New German Critique*
NEW HUNGARIAN Q—New Hungarian Quarterly, The*
NEW LIT HIST—New Literary History*
NEW MAGIC LANTERN J—New Magic Lantern Journal
NEW ORLEANS REV—New Orleans Review*
NEW REPUB—New Republic*
NEW STATESM—New Statesman and Society*
NEW YORK—New York Magazine*
NEW YORKER—New Yorker*
NEWSWK—Newsweek*
NOSFERATU—Nosferatu
NY R BKS—New York Review of Books*
NY TIMES—New York Times, The*
OCTOBER—October*

ON PRODUCTION—On Production and Post-Production
ONFILM—Onfilm
PART R—Partisan Review*
PEILI—Peili
PERF ARTS J—Performing Arts Journal*
PICTURE HOUSE—Picture House
PLATEAU—Plateau
PLAYBOY—Playboy*
POETICS TODAY—Poetics Today*
POP CUL LIB—Popular Culture in Libraries*
POP PHOT—Popular Photography*
POSITIF—Positif
POV—Persistence of Vision
PREM—Premiere
PRESENCE—Presence du cinema francais
PRINT—Print*
PROJECTIONS—Projections
PS—Post Script
PSYCH R—Psychoanalytic Review*
PUBLIC CULT—Public Culture*
QUADERNI—Quaderni di Cinema
Q REV F & VIDEO—Quarterly Review of Film and Video
R BELG—Revue Belge du Cinema
R CINEMATHEQUE—Revue de la Cinematheque, La
R CINEMATOGRAFO—Rivista del Cinematografo
RADICAL AMERICA—Radical America*
RADICAL HIST REV—Radical History Review*
RARITAN—Raritan*
RECTANGLE—Rectangle
REEL WEST—Reel West Magazine
REIDS F INDX—Reid's Film Index
REPRESENTATIONS—Representations*
RES AFRICAN LIT—Research in African Literatures*
RETHINKING MARXISM—Rethinking Marxism*
REZYSER—Rezyser
ROLLING STONE—Rolling Stone*
S&S—Sight & Sound
SALMAGUNDI—Salmagundi*
SAQ—South Atlantic Quarterly, The*
SCARLET STREET—Scarlet Street*
SCN—Soundtrack!: the Collector's Quarterly
SCORE—Score
SCREEN—Screen
SCREEN ACTOR—Screen Actor
SEGNO—Segnocinema
SEMIOTICA—Semiotica*
SEQUENCES—Sequences
SF JUNG INST LIB J—San Francisco Jung Institute Library
    Journal*
SGTL—Sightlines
SHAKESPEARE Q—Shakespeare Quarterly*
SINEMA—Andere Sinema
SKRIEN—Skrien
SMPTE J—SMPTE Journal
SOCIAL POLICY—Social Policy*
SOCIETY—Society*
SOUTHERN HUM R—Southern Humanities Review*
SPECTATOR—Spectator
SPETTACOLO—Spettacolo, Lo*
SQ—Southern Quarterly*
STANFORD HUMANITIES R—Stanford Humanities Review*
STARS—Stars

STRATEGIES—Strategies*
STUD POP CULT—Studies in Popular Culture*
STUDIES HUM—Studies in the Humanities*
STYLE—Style*
SUBSTANCE—Substance*
TAKE ONE—Take One
TCI—TCI*
TELEVISION Q—Television Quarterly
THEATER—Theater*
THEORY CUL & SOC—Theory, Culture & Society*
THIRD TEXT—Third Text*
TIJD THEATERWETENSCHAP—Tijdschrift voor
    Theaterwetenschap*
TIME—Time*
UFAJ—Journal of Film and Video
USA TODAY—USA Today*
VANITY FAIR—Vanity Fair*
VARIETY—Variety
VEL LT TRAP—Velvet Light Trap, The
VERTIGO (FRANCE)—Vertigo
VERTIGO (UK)—Vertigo
VIDEOGRAPHY—Videography
VILLAGE VOICE—Village Voice, The*
24 IMAGES—24 Images
VISUAL ANTHRO R—Visual Anthropology Review*
VISUAL SOC—Visual Sociology*
WAR LIT & ARTS—War, Literature & the Arts*
WESTERN AM LIT—Western American Literature*
WESTERN FOLKLORE—Western Folklore*
WESTERN HUM REV—Western Humanities Review*
WIDE ANGLE—Wide Angle
WOMEN—Women: a Cultural Review*
WOMEN'S STUD—Women's Studies*
WOMEN'S STUD COMM—Women's Studies in Communication*
YALE J CRIT—Yale Journal of Criticism*
YALE R—Yale Review*
Z—Z Filmtidsskrift

FILM AND TELEVISION PERIODICALS INDEXED

All data as of latest issue received.
Abbreviations for frequency of issues:

a	annual	m	monthly
bi-m	bi-monthly	q	quarterly
bi-w	bi-weekly	w	weekly
irreg	irregular	yr	year

AMERICAN CINEMATOGRAPHER m ASC Holding Corporation, 1782 North Orange Drive, Hollywood, California 90028 (AMCIN)

AMERICAN PREMIERE; The Magazine of the Film Industry q 8421 Wilshire Boulevard, Penthouse, Beverly Hills, California 90211 (AMER PREM)

ANDERE SINEMA bi-m Ommeganckstraat 21, 2018 Antwerp, Belgium (SINEMA)

ANGLES q P.O. Box 11916, Milwaukee, Wisconsin 53211 (ANGLES)

ANIMATION JOURNAL 2/yr AJ Press, 2011 Kingsboro Circle, Tustin, California 92680-6733 (ANIMATION J)

ANIMATOR irreg The Filmcraft Association, 13 Ringway Road, Park Street, St. Albans, Herts, AL2 2RE, Great Britain (ANIMATOR)

ANIMATRIX a UCLA Animation Workshop, Department of Theater Arts, UCLA, 405 Hilgard Avenue, Los Angeles, California 90024 (ANIMATRIX)

ARCHIVES: INSTITUT JEAN VIGO 5/yr Institut Jean Vigo, 21, rue Mailly, 66000 Perpignan, France (ARCHIVES)

ASIAN CINEMA 2/yr Asian Cinema Studies Society, Cynthia Contreras, Film Department, Brooklyn College, Brooklyn, New York 11210 (ASIAN)

AVANT-SCENE CINEMA, L' m 6, rue Git-le-Coeur, 75006 Paris, France (AVANT-SCENE)

BLACK CAMERA 2/yr Black Film Center/Archive, Smith Research Center, Suite 180-81, 2805 East 10th Street, Indiana University, Bloomington, Indiana 47408 (BLACK CAMERA)

BLACK FILM REVIEW q P.O. Box 18665, Washington, D.C. 20036 (BLACK F REV)

BLIMP. Film Magazine q Muchargasse 12/III/10, A-8010 Graz, Austria (BLIMP)

BOXOFFICE 10/yr RLD Communications, Inc., 203 North Wabash Avenue, Suite 800, Chicago, Illinois 60601 (BOXOFFICE)

BREF: le magazine du court metrage 3yr 2, rue de Tocqueville, 75017 Paris, France (BREF)

CICIM: REVUE POUR LE CINEMA FRANCAIS q Centre d'information Cinematographique de l'Institut Francais de Munich, Kaulbachstrasse 13, 8000 Munich 22, Germany (CICIM)

CAHIERS DE LA CINEMATHEQUE, LES irreg Institut Jean Vigo, 21, rue Mailly, 66000 Perpignan, France (CAHIERS CINEMATHEQUE)

CAHIERS DU CINEMA m 9 passage de la Boule-Blanche, 75012 Paris, France (CAHIERS)

CAHIERS DU SCENARIO, LES irreg IEE, 30 avenue A. Bertrand, 1190 Bruxelles, Belgium (CAHIERS SCENARIO)

CAMERA OBSCURA 3/yr Journals Division, Indiana University Press, 601 North Morton Street, Bloomington, Indiana 47404 (CAM OBS)

CAMERA/STYLO irreg 18, rue des Fosses-Saint-Jacques, 75005 Paris, France (CAM STYLO)

CANADIAN JOURNAL OF FILM STUDIES 3/yr School for Studies in Art and Culture, Film Studies, Carleton University, 1125 Colonel By Drive, Ottawa, Ontario, Canada K1S 5B6 (CAN J F STUD)

CANTRILL'S FILMNOTES irreg Box 1295L, G.P.O., Melbourne, Victoria 3001, Australia (CANTRILL'S FMNTS)

CASTORO CINEMA, IL bi-m Editrice Il Castoro, Via Paisiello, 6, 20131 Milan, Italy (CASTORO CIN)

CHAPLIN 6/yr Box 27126, 102 52 Stockholm, Sweden (CHAPLIN)

CHINA SCREEN q Guoji Shudian, POB 399, Beijing, China (CHINA SCREEN)

CINE & MEDIA bi-m OCIC, rue de l'Orme, 8, 1040 Brussels, Belgium (C & MEDIA)

CINE CUBANO irreg Calle 23 No. 1166, entre 10 y 12, Vedado, C.P. 10400, Havana 4, Cuba (C CUBANO)

CINEACTION 3/yr 40 Alexander Street, Suite 705, Toronto, Ontario M4Y 1B5, Canada (C ACTION)

CINEASTE q P.O. BOX 2242, New York, New York 10009-8917 (CINEASTE)

CINE-BULLES; Revue de cinema q l'Association des cinemas paralleles du Quebec, 4545, av. Pierre-de-Coubertin, CP1000 Succursale M, Montreal, Quebec H1V 3R2, Canada (C BUL)

CINE-BULLETIN m Redaktion Cine-Bulletin, Pruntruterstrasse 6, Postfach, 4008 Basel, Switzerland (CINE-BULLETIN)

CINEFANTASTIQUE bi-m 7240 West Roosevelt Road, Forest Park, Illinois 60130 (C FANTAS)

CINEFEX q P.O. Box 20027, Riverside, California 92516 (CINEFEX)

CINEFOCUS a c/o Department of Comparative Literature, Ballantine Hall 402, Indiana University, Bloomington, Indiana 47405 (C FOCUS)

CINEFORUM m via Pascoli 3, 24121 Bergamo, Italy (C FORUM)

CINEMA & CINEMA irreg Editrice Clueb Bologna, via Marsala 24, 40126 Bologna, Italy (C&C)

CINEMA 93, CINEMA 94 m BP 544, 75667 Paris, Cedex 14, France (C93, C94)

CINEMA JOURNAL q University of Texas Press, Journals Department, 2100 Comal, Austin, Texas 78722-2550 (CJ)

CINEMA NUOVO bi-m Via Giacinta Pezzana 110, 00197 Rome, Italy (C NUOVO)

CINEMA PAPERS bi-m MTV Publishing Limited, 116 Argyle Street, Fitzroy, Victoria, Australia 3065 (C PAPERS)

CINEMA SUD bi-m Galleria Via Mancini, 83100 Avellino, Italy (C SUD)

CINEMA (SWITZERLAND) a Postfach 79, CH-4007 Basel, Switzerland (C(SWITZ))

CINEMA TECHNOLOGY q British Kinematograph Sound and Television Society, M6-M14 Victoria House, Vernon Place, London WC1B 4DJ, England (C TECH)

CINEMACTION q Editions Corlet, route de Vire, 14110 Conde-sur-Noireau, France (CINEMACTION)

CINEMAS 3/yr Secteur des etudes cinematographiques, Departement d'histoire de l'art, Universite de Montreal, C.P. 6128, succursale Centre-Ville, Montreal, Quebec, Canada H3C 3J7 (CINEMAS)

CINEMATOGRAPH; a Journal of the San Francisco Cinematheque a Foundation for Arts in Cinema, 480 Potrero Avenue, San Francisco, California 94110 (CINEMATOGRAPH)

CINEMAYA q B90 Defence Colony, New Delhi, 110024 India (CINEMAYA)

CLASSIC IMAGES m Muscatine Journals, P.O. Box 809, Muscatine, Iowa 52761 (CLASSIC)

COSA VISTA, LA q Centro Universitario Cinematografico, Dipartimento di Scienze Politiche, Universita degli Studi di Trieste, Piazzale Europa, 1, 34127 Trieste, Italy (COSA VISTA)

CUE SHEET, THE q Society for the Preservation of Film Music, P.O. Box 93536, Hollywood, California 90093-0536 (CUE SHEET)

CURRENT RESEARCH IN FILM a Ablex Publishing Corporation, 355 Chestnut Street, Norwood, New Jersey 07648 (CRF)

DICINE bi-m Leonardo de Vinci 161-A, 03700 Mexico D.F., Mexico (DICINE)

DISCOURSE 3/yr Indiana University Press, 601 North Morton Street, Bloomington, Indiana 47404 (DISCOURSE)

DOCUMENTARY BOX q Yamagata International Documentary Film Festival, Kitagawa Building, Fourth Floor, 6-42 Kagurazaka, Shinjuku-ku, Tokyo 162, Japan

EPD FILM m Gemeinschaftswerk der Evangelischen Publizistik e.V., Postfach 50 05 50, 60394 Frankfurt/Main, Germany (EPD)

EAST-WEST FILM JOURNAL 2/yr Journals Department, University of Hawaii Press, 2840 Kolowalu Street, Honolulu, Hawaii 96822 (EAST-WEST FJ)

EKRAN 10/yr Ulica talcev 6/II, p.p. 14, 61104 Ljubljana, Yugoslavia (EKRAN)

EYEPIECE bi-m The Guild of British Camera Technicians, 5-11 Taunton Road, Metropolitan Centre, Greenford, Middlesex UB6 8UQ, Great Britain (EYEPIECE)

FATAL VISIONS irreg P.O. Box 133, Northcote, Victoria 3070, Australia (FATAL VISIONS)

FERNSEH- UND KINO-TECHNIK m Huethig GmbH, 69018 Heidelberg, Postfach 10 28 69, Germany (FKT)

FILM bi-m British Federation of Film Societies, 21 Stephen Street, London W1P 1PL Great Britain (FILM)

FILM & HISTORY q Historians Film Committee, Popular Culture Center, Route 3 Box 80, Cleveland, Oklahoma 74020 (F&HIST)

FILM COMMENT bi-m Film Society of Lincoln Center, 70 Lincoln Center Plaza, New York, New York 10023-6595 (F COM)

FILM CRITICISM 3/yr Allegheny College, Meadville, Pennsylvania 16335 (F CRITICISM)

FILM CULTURE q 32 Second Avenue, New York, New York 10003 (F CUL)

FILM DOPE irreg 74 Julian Road, Nottingham NG2 5AN, England (F DOPE)

FILM ECHANGE q 6, Git-le-Coeur, 75006 Paris, France (F ECHANGE)

FILM EN TELEVISIE + VIDEO 10/yr Haachtsesteenweg 35, 1210 Brussels, Belgium (F&TV)

FILM HISTORY q John Libbey & Company, Ltd., 13 Smiths Yard, Summerley Street, London SW18 4HR, England (F HIST)

FILM JOURNAL m Pubsun Corp., 244 West 49th Street, Suite 200, New York, New York 10019 (FJ)

FILM & KINO 10/yr Kongensgaten 23, 0153 Oslo, Norway (F&K)

FILM QUARTERLY q University of California Press, 2120 Berkeley Way, Berkeley, California 94720 (FQ)

FILM SCORE MONTHLY m Box 1554, Amherst College, Amherst, Massachusetts 01002-5000

FILM THREAT bi-m 9171 Wilshire Boulevard, Suite 300, Beverly Hills, California 90210 (F THREAT)

FILM: TUTTI I FILM DELLA STAGIONE bi-m Centro Studi Cinematografici, Via Gregorio VII, 6, 00165 Rome, Italy (FILM (ITALY))

FILM & FAKTEN m Spitzenorganisation der Filmwirtschaft e.v., Postfach 51 29, 65041 Wiesbaden, Germany (F & FAKTEN)

FILM UND FERNSEHEN m Filmverband Brandenburg e.V., Am Bassinplatz 4, 14467 Potsdam, Germany (F & FERNSEHEN)

FILM & TV KAMERAMANN m Ohmstrasse 15, 80802 Munich, Germany (F&TV KAM)

FILM-HISTORIA 3/yr Centro de Investigaciones Cinematograficas, Apartado 12109, 08080 Barcelona, Spain (F-HISTORIA)

FILMBULLETIN bi-m Postfach 137 Hard 4, CH-8408 Winterthur, Switzerland (F BUL)

FILMCRITICA 10/yr Piazza del Grillo 5, 00184 Rome, Italy (FCR)

FILMFAUST: Internationale Filmzeitschrift bi-m Filmfaust Verlag, Bion Steinborn, Liebigstrasse 44, 60323 Frankfurt am Main, Germany (F FAUST)

FILMFAX: The Magazine of Unusual Film and Television bi-m Filmfax Subscriptions, P.O. Box 1900, Evanston, Illinois 60204 (F FAX)

FILMHAFTET: kritisk tidskrift for analys av rorliga bilder q Box 101 56, 100 55 Stockholm, Sweden (F HAFTET)

FILMIHULLU 8/yr Malminkatu 36, 00100 Helsinki, Finland (FIHUL)

FILMKULTURA m Solymar u. 8, 1032 Budapest, Hungary (F KULTURA)

FILMKUNST; Zeitschrift fuer Filmkultur und Filmwissenschaft q Rauhensteingasse 5, 1010 Vienna, Austria (F KUNST)

FILMMAKER: The Magazine of Independent Film q 1625 Olympic Boulevard, Santa Monica, California 90404-3822 (FILMMAKER)

FILMNEWS m P.O. Box 341, Kings Cross, New South Wales 2011, Australia (F NEWS)

FILMOWY SERWIS PRASOWY m Dom Wydawniczy ABC, ul. Zamenhofa 1, Warsaw, Poland (FSP)

FILMS IN REVIEW bi-m National Board of Review of Motion Pictures, Films in Review Subscriptions Department, P.O. Box 3000, Denville, New Jersey 07834-3000 (FIR)

FILMVILAG m Filmvilag Alapitvany, Hollan Erno utca 38/a, 1136 Budapest XIII., Hungary (F VILAG)

FILMWAERTS q Rolf Aurich, Uhdestrasse 2, 30171 Hannover, Germany (F WAERTS)

FRAMEWORK irreg Sankofa Film & Video Ltd, Unit K, 32-34 Gordon House Road, London NW5 1LP, England (FRAMEWORK)

FRAUEN UND FILM 2/yr Jahnstrasse 19, D-6000 Frankfurt am Main 1, Germany (FRAUEN & F)

GRAND ANGLE m rue d'Arschot, 29, 5660 Mariembourg, Belgium (GRAND ANGLE)

GRIFFITHIANA 3/yr La Cineteca del Friuli, via Osoppo, 26, 33013 Gemona (Udine), Italy; North American distributor: The Johns Hopkins University Press, 2715 North Charles Street, Baltimore, Maryland 21218-4319 (GRIFFITHIANA)

HISTORICAL JOURNAL OF FILM, RADIO AND TELEVISION q Carfax Publishing Company, P.O. Box 25, Abingdon, Oxfordshire OX14 3UE, United Kingdom (HIST JFR&TV)

HITCHCOCK ANNUAL a P.O. Box 540, Gambier, Ohio 43022 (HITCHCOCK ANN)

IKON irreg Instituto di ricerca sulla communicazione, via le Piceno 60, 20129 Milan, Italy (IKON)

ILLUSIONS 3/yr P.O. Box 6476, Te Aro, Wellington, New Zealand (ILLUSIONS)

IMAGE TECHNOLOGY m British Kinematograph Sound and Television Society, M6-M14 Victoria House, Vernon Place, London WC1B 4DJ, England (IMAGE TECH)

IMMAGINE q Associazione Italiana per le Ricerche di Storia del Cinema, via Villafranca, 20, 00185, Rome, Italy (IMMAGINE)

INDEPENDENT FILM & VIDEO MONTHLY, THE 10/yr Foundation for Independent Video and Film, Inc., 304 Hudson Street, New York, New York 10013 (INDEP) [Supersedes INDEPENDENT, THE]

INDEPENDENT SPIRIT q South Carolina Arts Commission, Media Arts Center, 1800 Gervais Street, Columbia, South Carolina 29201 (INDEP SPIRIT)

INTERNATIONAL DOCUMENTARY m International Documentary Association, 1551 South Robertson Boulevard, Suite 201, Los Angeles, California 90035-4233 (INTL DOC)

IRIS 2/yr Institute for Cinema and Culture, 162 Communications Studies Building, University of Iowa, Iowa City, IA 52242 (IRIS)

ISKUSSTVO KINO m Ulitsa Usievicha 9, 125319 Moscow A-319, Russia (ISKUS K)

JEUNE CINEMA bi-m 12, impasse Mousset, 75012 Paris, France (JEUNE C)

JOURNAL OF FILM AND VIDEO q University Film and Video Association, Department of Communication, Georgia State University, University Plaza, Atlanta, Georgia 30303-3080 (UFAJ)

JOURNAL OF FILM PRESERVATION bi-a FIAF Secretariat, rue Franz Merjay190, 1180 Brussels, Belgium (J F PRES)

JOURNAL OF POPULAR FILM AND TELEVISION q Heldref Publications, 4000 Albemarle Street, N.W., Washington, D.C. 20016 (JPF)

JOURNAL: WRITERS GUILD OF AMERICA, WEST, THE m 8955 Beverly Boulevard, West Hollywood, California 90048 (JOURNAL WGA)

JUMP CUT a P.O. Box 865, Berkeley, California 94701 (JUMP CUT)

KINO m ul. Chelmska 19/21, 00-724 Warsaw, Poland (KINO)

KINO; FILME DER BUNDESREPUBLIK DEUTSCHLAND 3/yr Export-Union des Deutschen Films e.V., Tuerkenstrasse 93, D-80799 Munich, Germany (KINO(BRD))

KINO; GERMAN FILM 3/yr Helgolaender Ufer 6, 10557 Berlin, Germany (KINO (GF))

KOSMORAMA q Danske Film Museum, Store Sondervoldestraede, 1419 Copenhagen K, Denmark (KOSMORAMA)

LITERATURE/FILM QUARTERLY q Salisbury State University, Salisbury, Maryland 21801 (LIT/FQ)

MEDIA 2/yr Holde Lhoest, Managing Editor; Media Programme, Commission of the European Community, Directorate General AV Information, Communication and Culture; 120 rue de Treves, B-1040 Bruxellex, Belgium (MEDIA)

MEDIEN PRAKTISCH q Gemeinschaftswerk der Evangelischen Publizistik e.V., Postfach 50 05 50, 60394 Frankfurt am Main, Germany (MEDIEN PRAKTISCH)

MEDIEN + ERZIEHUNG 6/yr Pfaelzer-Wald-Strasse 64, 81539 Munich, Germany (MEDIEN)

MEDIUM q Postfach 50 05 50, 60394 Frankfurt am Main, Germany (MEDIUM)

MENSUEL DU CINEMA, LE m Subscriptions Department, 38, rue des Blancs, Manteaux, 75004 Paris, France (MENSUEL C)

MIDNIGHT MARQUEE 2/yr Gary J. Svehla, Subscriptions, 4000 Glenarm Avenue, Baltimore, Maryland 21206 (MIDNIGHT MARQUEE)

MILLENNIUM FILM JOURNAL 3/yr 66 East 4th Street, New York, New York 10003 (MILLENNIUM)

MONITEUR DU FILM EN BELGIQUE, LE m Rue de Framboisier 35, 1180 Brussels, Belgium (MONITEUR)

MOVIE irreg P.O. Box 1, Moffat, Dumfriesshire, DG10 9SU England (MOVIE)

MOVIELINE m P.O. Box 469004, Escondido, California 92046-9982 (MOVIELINE)

NEW MAGIC LANTERN JOURNAL irreg Magic Lantern Society 'Prospect', High Street, Nutley, East Sussex TN22 3NH, Great Britain (NEW MAGIC LANTERN J)

NOSFERATU: revista de cine 3/yr Patronato Municipal de Cultura de San Sebastian, Republica Argentina, 2, 20004 Donostia-San Sebastian, Spain (NOSFERATU)

ON PRODUCTION AND POST-PRODUCTION bi-m Cahners Publishing Company, 5700 Wilshire Boulevard, Suite 120, Los Angeles, California 90036-3659 (ON PRODUCTION)

ONFILM 11/yr Onfilm Magazine Ltd., P.O. Box 37-193, Parnell, Auckland, New Zealand (ONFILM)

PEILI q Elokuva-ja televisio-kasvatuksen keskus ry; Annankatu 13B11, 00120 Helsinki, Finland (PEILI)

PERSISTENCE OF VISION irreg c/o Tony Pipolo 53-24 63rd Street, Maspeth, New York 11378 (POV)

PICTURE HOUSE q William Wren, Membership Secretary, Flat 30, Cambridge Court, Cambridge Road, Southend-on-Sea, Essex SS1 1EJ, England (PICTURE HOUSE)

PLATEAU q Bondgenotenstraat 52, B-1190 Brussels, Belgium (PLATEAU)

POSITIF m 3 rue Lhomond, 75005 Paris, France (POSITIF)

POST SCRIPT 3/yr Literature and Languages Department, East Texas State University, Commerce, Texas 75429 (PS)

PREMIERE m P.O. Box 55389, Boulder, Colorado 80323-5389 (PREM)

PRESENCE DU CINEMA FRANCAIS bi-m Les editions de l'Expression, 22, rue Plumet, 75015 Paris, France (PRESENCE)

PROJECTIONS a Faber & Faber Ltd., 3 Queen Square, London WCIN 3AU, Great Britain (PROJECTIONS)

QUADERNI DI CINEMA irreg Via Benedetto Varchi, 57, 50132 Florence, Italy (QUADERNI)

QUARTERLY REVIEW OF FILM AND VIDEO q Harwood Academic Publishers GmbH, 820 Town Center Drive, Langhorne, Pennsylvania 19047 (Q REV F & VIDEO)

RECTANGLE q CAC-Voltaire, rue General-Dufour 16, 1204 Geneva, Switzerland (RECTANGLE)

REEL WEST MAGAZINE bi-m Reel West Productions Inc., 1106 Boundary Road, Burnaby, British Columbia, Canada V5K 4T5 (REEL WEST)

REID'S FILM INDEX q Rastar Pty. Limited, 26 Casey Drive, Wyong, New South Wales 2259, Australia (REIDS F INDX)

REVUE BELGE DU CINEMA q 73, avenue des Coccinelles, 1170 Brussels, Belgium (R BELG)

REVUE DE LA CINEMATHEQUE, LA bi-m Cinematheque Quebecoise, 335, boulevard de Maisonneuve est, Montreal, Quebec, H2X 1K1 Canada (R CINEMATHEQUE)

REZYSER m ul. Chelmska, 00-724 Warsaw, Poland (REZYSER)

RIVISTA DEL CINEMATOGRAFO m G. Palombini. 6, 00165 Rome, Italy (R CINEMATOGRAFO)

SMPTE JOURNAL m Society of Motion Picture and Television Engineers, Inc., 595 West Hartsdale Avenue, White Plains, New York 10607 (SMPTE J)

SCORE q Stichting Cinemusica, Postbus 406, 8200 Ak Lelystad, Netherlands (SCORE)

SCREEN q Journals Subscriptions Department, Oxford University Press, Walton Street, Oxford OX2 6DP, Great Britain (SCREEN)

SCREEN ACTOR q Screen Actors Guild, 5757 Wilshire Boulevard, Los Angeles, California 90036-3600 (SCREEN ACTOR)

SEGNOCINEMA bi-m via G. Prati, 34-36100 Vicenza, Italy (SEGNO)

SEQUENCES bi-m Jacques Belanger, C.P. 609, Haute-Ville, Quebec, Quebec, G1R 4S2, Canada (SEQUENCES)

SIGHT AND SOUND m British Film Institute, 21 Stephen Street, London W1P 1PL, England (S&S)

SIGHTLINES q The American Film and Video Association, Inc., 8050 Milwaukee Avenue, P.O. Box 48659, Niles, Illinois 60714 (SGTL)

SKRIEN 8/yr Stichting Skrien, Vondelpark 3, 1071, AA Amsterdam, Netherlands (SKRIEN)

SOUNDTRACK!: THE COLLECTOR'S QUARTERLY q Luc Van de Ven, Astridlaan 171, 2800 Mechelen, Belgium (SCN)

SPECTATOR bi-a Division of Critical Studies of the School of Cinema-Television, University of Southern California, University Park, Los Angeles, California 90089-2211 (SPECTATOR)

STARS q Rue d'Arschot 29, 5660 Mariembourg, Belgium (STARS)

TAKE ONE q 2255B Queen Street East, P.O. Box 151, Toronto, Ontario M4E 1G3, Canada (TAKE ONE)

TELEVISION QUARTERLY q National Academy of Television Arts & Sciences, 111 West 57th Street, New York, New York 10019 (TELEVISION Q)

VARIETY w 249 West 17th Street, 4th Floor, New York, New York 10016 (VARIETY)

VELVET LIGHT TRAP, THE 2/yr University of Texas Press, 2100 Comal, Austin, Texas 78722-2550 (VEL LT TRAP)

VERTIGO 2/yr Editions Jean-Michel-Place, 12 rue Pierre-et-Marie Curie, 75005 Paris, France (VERTIGO (FRANCE))

VERTIGO q Registered Office, Vertigo UK Ltd., 7-9 Earlham Street, London WC2H 9LL, Great Britain (VERTIGO (UK))

VIDEOGRAPHY m Miller Freeman PSN Inc., 460 Park Avenue South, 9th Floor, New York, New York 10016 (VIDEOGRAPHY)

24 IMAGES: La revue quebecoise du cinema bi-m 3962, rue Laval, Montreal, Quebec H2W 2J2, Canada (24 IMAGES)

WIDE ANGLE q The Johns Hopkins University Press, Journals Division, 2715 North Charles Street, Baltimore Maryland 21218-4319 (WIDE ANGLE)

Z FILMTIDSSKRIFT q Teatergate 3, 0180 Oslo, Norway (Z)

NONFILM AND TELEVISION PERIODICALS SELECTIVELY INDEXED

INTERVIEW (INTERV)
JOURNAL OF AESTHETIC EDUCATION (J AESTH EDUC)
JOURNAL OF AESTHETICS AND ART CRITICISM (J AESTH & ART C)
JOURNAL OF AMERICAN CULTURE (J AM CUL)
JOURNAL OF AMERICAN STUDIES (J AM STUDIES)
JOURNAL OF COMMUNICATION (J COMM)
JOURNAL OF COMMUNICATION INQUIRY (J COMM INQUIRY)
JOURNAL OF DURASSIAN STUDIES (J DURASSIAN STUD)
JOURNAL OF MODERN LITERATURE (J MOD LIT)
JOURNAL OF POPULAR CULTURE (J POP CUL)
JOURNAL OF WOMEN'S HISTORY (J WOMEN'S HIST)
LATIN AMERICAN RESEARCH REVIEW (LATIN AM RES REV)
LITERATURE AND PSYCHOLOGY (LITERATURE & PSYCHOLOGY)
LONDON MAGAZINE (LONDON MAG)
MASSACHUSETTS REVIEW (MASS R)
MEDIA CULTURE AND SOCIETY (MEDIA CUL & SOC)
MEDIA INFORMATION AUSTRALIA (MEDIA INFO AUSTRALIA)
MICHIGAN ACADEMICIAN (MICHIGAN ACADEMICIAN)
MICHIGAN QUARTERLY REVIEW (MQR)
MIDSTREAM (MIDSTREAM)
MINNESOTA REVIEW (MINN R)
MODERN DRAMA (MOD DRAMA)
MODERN LANGUAGE REVIEW, THE (MOD LANG R)
MS (MS)
NATION (NATION)
NATIONAL REVIEW (NAT R)
NEW GERMAN CRITIQUE (NEW GERMAN CRITIQUE)
NEW HUNGARIAN QUARTERLY, THE (NEW HUNGARIAN Q)
NEW LITERARY HISTORY (NEW LIT HIST)
NEW ORLEANS REVIEW (NEW ORLEANS REV)
NEW REPUBLIC (NEW REPUB)
NEW STATESMAN & SOCIETY (NEW STATESM & SOC)
NEW YORK MAGAZINE (NEW YORK)
NEW YORK REVIEW OF BOOKS (NY R BKS)
NEW YORK TIMES, THE (NY TIMES)
NEW YORKER (NEW YORKER)
NEWSWEEK (NEWSWK)
NORTH DAKOTA QUARTERLY (NDQ)
OCTOBER (OCTOBER)
PARTISAN REVIEW (PART R)
PERFORMING ARTS JOURNAL (PERF ARTS J)
PLAYBOY (PLAYBOY)
POETICS TODAY (POETICS TODAY)
POPULAR CULTURE IN LIBRARIES (POP CUL LIB)
POPULAR PHOTOGRAPHY (POP PHOT)
PRINT (PRINT)
PSYCHOANALYTIC REVIEW (PSYCH R)
PUBLIC CULTURE (PUBLIC CULT)
RADICAL AMERICA (RADICAL AMERICA)
RADICAL HISTORY REVIEW (RADICAL HIST REV)
RARITAN (RARITAN)
REPRESENTATIONS (REPRESENTATIONS)
RESEARCH IN AFRICAN LITERATURES (RES AFRICAN LIT)
RETHINKING MARXISM (RETHINKING MARXISM)
ROLLING STONE (ROLLING STONE)
SALMAGUNDI (SALMAGUNDI)
SAN FRANCISCO JUNG INSTITUTE LIBRARY JOURNAL (SF JUNG INST LIB J)
SCARLET STREET (SCARLET STREET)

SEMIOTICA (SEMIOTICA)
SHAKESPEARE QUARTERLY (SHAKESPEARE Q)
SOCIAL POLICY (SOCIAL POLICY)
SOCIETY (SOCIETY)
SOUTH ATLANTIC QUARTERLY, THE (SAQ)
SOUTHERN HUMANITIES REVIEW (SOUTHERN HUM R)
SOUTHERN QUARTERLY (SQ)
SPETTACOLO, LO (SPETTACOLO)
STANFORD HUMANITIES REVIEW (STANFORD HUMANITIES R)
STRATEGIES (STRATEGIES)
STUDIES IN POPULAR CULTURE (STUDIES POP CULT)
STUDIES IN THE HUMANITIES (STUDIES HUM)
STUDIES IN THE LITERARY IMAGINATION (LIT IMAG)
STYLE (STYLE)
SUBSTANCE (SUBSTANCE)
TCI (TCI) [Supersedes THEATRE CRAFTS]
THEATER (THEATER)
THEATRE CRAFTS [Superseded by TCI]
THEORY, CULTURE & SOCIETY (THEORY CUL & SOC)
THIRD TEXT (THIRD TEXT)
TIJDSCHRIFT VOOR THEATERWETENSCHAP (TIJD THEATERWETENSCHAP)
TIME (TIME)
USA TODAY (USA TODAY)
VANITY FAIR (VANITY FAIR)
VILLAGE VOICE, THE (VILLAGE VOICE)
VISUAL ANTHROPOLOGY REVIEW (VISUAL ANTHRO R)
VISUAL SOCIOLOGY (VISUAL SOC)
WAR, LITERATURE & THE ARTS (WAR LIT & ARTS)
WESTERN AMERICAN LITERATURE (WESTERN AM LIT)
WESTERN FOLKLORE (WESTERN FOLKLORE)
WESTERN HUMANITIES REVIEW (WESTERN HUM REV)
WOMEN: A CULTURAL REVIEW (WOMEN)
WOMEN'S STUDIES (WOMEN'S STUD)
WOMEN'S STUDIES IN COMMUNICATION (WOMEN'S STUD COMM)
YALE JOURNAL OF CRITICISM (YALE J CRIT)
YALE REVIEW (YALE R)

Section One: Film

USE OF TERM *FILM*	The term *FILM* is not used if it can be inferred from the subject heading.
Example	FILM STUDY AND TEACHING entered under: STUDY AND TEACHING
USE OF TERMS *TELEVISION/VIDEO*	Articles on these subjects appear in a separate alphabetical index in Section Two: Television/Video.
TITLES OF FILMS	Articles which discuss films appear under the original language titles with the following information, if available, in parentheses: American release title for foreign language films, director's name, date of first public showing and country of production. An *f* is found directly after the title of films to denote film titles, and d is used to indicate director.
Example	RAYON VERT, LE f (Summer d Rohmer, Eric 1986 Fr)
	Cross references appear from the American release titles and directors to their respective film titles.
Examples	Summer See RAYON VERT, LE ROHMER, ERIC See also RAYON VERT, LE
REVIEWS OF FILMS	All film reviews appear together under the titles of films with the subheading Reviews.
FESTIVALS	Festivals appear under the general subject heading *FESTIVALS* arranged by country, state or province, city, and date.

Example	FESTIVALS
	  United States
	    New York, New York 1986

GEOGRAPHIC NAMES	Geographic names appear as subheadings under specific subject headings following all other subheadings.

Example	CINEMATOGRAPHY
	  History
	  Australia

ABBREVIATIONS

Arg	Argentina	bet	between
Belg	Belgium	bibliog	bibliography
Bulg	Bulgaria	biog	biography
Can	Canada	credits	credits
China	China (People's Republic)	d	director
CIS	Commonwealth of Independent States	diag(s)	diagram(s)
Czech	Czech and Slovak Federative Republic	discog(s)	discography(s)
Denmk	Denmark	f	film
E Ger	Germany (Democratic Republic)	filmog(s)	filmography(s)
Finl	Finland	glos	glossary
Fr	France	graph(s)	graph(s)
FR Ger	Germany (Federal Republic)	il	illustrations
Ger	Germany (before 1949)	interv(s)	interview(s)
Gt Br	Great Britain	map(s)	map(s)
It	Italy	n	number
Mex	Mexico	obit	obituary
Neth	Netherlands	p	page(s)
N Korea	Korea (Democratic People's Republic)	port(s)	portrait(s)
N Vietnam	Vietnam (Democratic Republic)	prod	produced/producer
Norw	Norway	pt	part
Phil	Philippines	scenario	scenario(s)/scenario excerpt(s)
Port	Portugal	score	musical score(s)
S Afr	South Africa	sec	section
S Korea	Korea (Republic)	specs	specifications
S Vietnam	Vietnam (Republic)	stat	statistics
Sp	Spain	sup	supplement
Swed	Sweden	table(s)	table(s)
Switz	Switzerland		
Taiwan	China (Republic)		
Thai	Thailand		
USA	United States		
USSR	Union of Soviet Socialist Republics		
W Ger	Germany (Federal Republic) [1949-1990]		
Yugo	Yugoslavia		

SUBHEADINGS

The following terms appear only as subheadings.

Adults	Product Guides
Amateur	Professional Activities
Applications	Public
Black and White	Recollections
Children	Rental
Comparison With Television	Retrospectives
Digital	Review Excerpts
Effects of Television/Video	Social Aspects
Film Lists	Sociological Aspects
International Aspects	Sound Track Reviews
Maintenance	Technical Aspects
Membership Lists	Techniques
Men	Testing and Measurement
Nitrate	Tributes
Nonprofessional Activities	Videocassettes
Personal Lives	Women
Personnel	Youth

In addition, most subject headings also appear as subheadings.

CALVERT, FRANCES For film reviews see author under the following titles: DEAD, THE

Camera accessories [Prior to V16, 1988 use CAMERA ACCESSORIES] See CAMERA EQUIPMENT

CAMERA EQUIPMENT [Prior to V16, 1988 use CAMERA ACCESSORIES] See also LENSES **FORMER SUBJECT HEADINGS**
  Computer Applications
  Lusznat, H.A. Samuelsons Computerprogramm 37:72 May 1988
  United States
  What's new: image compositing made easy. il AMCIN 69:18+ [5p] Jul 1988

CAMERA MOUNTS
  Amateur
  Knight, G. Between ourselves: a dolly good idea to get steady filming. diags MBM 4:2 Jun 1988
  United States
  Cooy, k. Motorbike cameras a smooth ride. il AMCIN 69:82-84 Aug 1988

CAMERA SPEED **SUBJECT HEADING ENTRIES**
  Germany (Federal Republic)
  Technical Aspects
  Fromm, G. Torpedoboot attackiert Schlachtschiff. F&TV KAM 37:14 May 1988

Cameramen See CINEMATOGRAPHERS **SEE REFERENCES**

CAMERAS See also CAMERA EQUIPMENT **SEE ALSO REFERENCES**
  Focusing
  Standards and Recommended Practices
  Motion-picture cameras - zero point for focus [American National Standard]. SMPTE J 97:516 Jun 1988
  Standards and Recommended Practices **SUBHEADING ENTRIES**
  Measurement methods for motion-picture camera [SMPTE engineering guideline]. SMPTE J 97:516-517 Jun 1988
  Super-eight mm Film
  Chinon 60SM XL
  "MBM" vintage test report: Chinon 60SM XL super 8 sound camera. il MBM 4:20-21 Jun 1988
  Germany (Federal Republic) **GEOGRAPHIC SUBHEADING ENTRIES**
  History
  Lusznat, H.A. Die Arriflex-Story (8): 50 Jahre Werden und Wirken einer Filmkamera. il F&TV KAM 37:58+ [4p] Jun 1988
  Germany (until 1949)
  History. Technical Aspects
  Lusznat, H.A. Die Arriflex-Story (7): 50 Jahre Werden und Wirken einer Filmkamera. il port F&TV KAM 37:58+ [5p]

CAMERON, JAMES See ALIENS; TERMINATOR, THE **FILM CROSS REFERENCES**
CAMERON, KIRK
  Jewett, D. Lite lit: all beef patsies [Book Reviews]. il port VILLAGE VOICE 33:Literary Supplement n67:6-7 Jul 12 1988
CAMERON-WILSON, JAMES
  Cameron-Wilson, J. The changing faces of Streep. il stills PHOTOPLAY 39:40-43 Jul 1988
  Cameron-Wilson, J. Theresa Russell: versatility of a Californian beauty. ports stills PHOTOPLAY 39:13-15 Sep 1988
CAMILLE f (d Cukor, George 1936 USA)
  Matthews, P. Garbo and phallic motherhood: a "homosexual" visual economy. port stills SCREEN 29:14-39 n3 1988
CAMINITO, AUGUSTO See NOSFERATU A VENEZIA
CAMINO DEL SUR, EL f (d Stagnaro, Juan Bautista 1988 Arg/Yugo)
  Reviews
  Meyer, N.E. "El camino del sur" ("The Road South"). credits VARIETY 332:16 Aug 31 1988
CAMINO, JAIME See LUCES Y SOMBRAS
CAMMELL, DONALD See WHITE OF THE EYE
CAMMELLI, I f (d Bertolucci, Giuseppe 1988 It)
  Reviews
  Young, D. "I cammelli" ("The Camels"). credits VARIETY 332:21 Sep 28 1988
CAMOMILLE f (d Charef, Mehdi 1987 Fr)
  Danglades, V. "Camomille": a boire et a rever. still C88 n440:8 May 4/10 1988
  Reviews
  Magny, J. Too much. credits still CAHIERS n407/408:135-136 May 1988
CAMORRISTA, IL f (d Tornatore, Giuseppe 1986 It)
  Reviews
  Loiselle, M.-C. "Le maitre de la Camorra." 24 IMAGES n39/40:110 Fall 1988
CAMP, JOE See BENJI THE HUNTED
CAMPARI, ROBERTO
  Campari, R. Cinema e pittura in America. stills C&C n50:54-56 Dec 1987
CAMPBELL, GRAEME See MURDER ONE
CAMPBELL, MARTIN See CRIMINAL LAW
CAMPBELL, PEG
  Wharton, C. Faces behind the camera: a **COUNTRY SEE REFERENCES**
  C CAN n151:11-15 Apr 1988
CAMUS, MARIO See RUSA, LA
Canada See as a subheading under individual subject headings; See CANADIAN FILM INSTITUTE; FRASER COMMITTEE; NATIONAL FILM BOARD OF CANADA; SOCIETE GENERALE DES INDUSTRIES CULTURELLES QUEBEC (SOGIC, Canada)
CANADIAN CENTRE FOR ADVANCED FILM STUDIES (North York, Canada)
  Changing the guard at the Advanced Centre. C CAN n154:56 1988
CANADIAN FILM INSTITUTE (Ottawa)
  Losique establishes Ottawa base with Cinematheque. C CAN n154:52 1988
  Losique picks up Canadian Film Institute. C CAN n151:36 Apr 1988
CANBY, VINCENT For film reviews see author under the following titles: AMI DE MON AMI, L'; ARTHUR 2: ON THE ROCKS; BEAST, THE; COCKTAIL; COR DO SEU DESTINO, A; DEAD POOL, THE; DEAR AMERICA: LETTERS HOME FROM VIETNAM; DISTANT VOICES, STILL LIVES; FISH CALLED WANDA, A; LOOSE CONNECTIONS; [LOVE SUICIDES AT SONEZAKI, THE]; MAMA CUMPLE 100 ANOS; MATADOR; MIDNIGHT RUN; (MISTER) MR. NORTH; MUJERES AL BORDE DE UN ATAQUE DE NERVIOS; NILOUHE NUER; PATTY HEARST; PELLE EROBREREN; PUNCHLINE; SANTA-FE; SEVEN HOURS TO JUDGMENT; SHORT AND THE CURLIES, THE; SHORT CIRCUIT 2; SHY PEOPLE; AN UNS GLAUBT GOTT NICHT MEHR
  Canby, V. Film view: "Die Hard" calls to the kidult. still NY TIMES 137:19-20 sec 2 Jul 31 1988
  Canby, V. Film view: in the theaters, an American harvest. stills NY TIMES 137:23+ [2p] sec 2 Sep 25 1988

Canby, V. Stardom seen in light of the 80's. still NY TIMES 137:1+ [2p] sec 2 Jul 17 1988
Canby, V. Toons and bushers fly high. still NY TIMES 137:1+ [2p] sec 2 Jul 3 1988
Watters, J. and [...]it." still NY TIMES 137:24 sec 2 **FILM TITLE ENTRIES**
Aug 21 1988
CANDY MOUNTAIN f (d Frank, Robert/Wurlitzer, Rudy 1987 Switz/Can/Fr)
  "Candy Mountain." credits COPIE ZERO n36:18 Aug 1988
  Gehrig, C. Robert Frank (2). interv still BLIMP n9:35 Spring 1988
  Hoberman, J. Film: off the road. still VILLAGE VOICE 33:67 Jun 14 1988
  Trenczak, H. Robert Frank (1): (kein) Zuckerschlecken. credits still BLIMP n9:34 Spring 1988
  Reviews **FILM REVIEW ENTRIES**
  Allen, M. "Candy Mountain."
CANE TOADS: AN UNNATURAL HISTORY f (d Lewis, Mark 1987 Australia)
  Reviews
  Lee, R. "Cane Toads." SIGHTLINES 21:20 n4 1988
  Maslin, J. Review/film: "Cane Toads," irreverent documentary. NY TIMES 137:C19 Sep 30 1988
CANI DI GERUSALEMME f (d Malerba, Luigi It)
  Carpi, F. Le fatalita dei "'Cani' di Gerusalemme." stills C NUOVO 37:5-6 Mar/Apr (n312) 1988
CANIBAIS, OS f (d Oliveira, Manoel de 1988 Port)
  Bergala, A. "Les cannibales." still CAHIERS n409:60 Jun 1988
  Reviews
  Grugeau, G. "Les cannibales." credits stills 24 IMAGES n39/40:14-15 Fall 1988
  "Les cannibales." SEQUENCES n135/136:24 Sep 1988
CANNIERE, PATRICK
  Canniere, P. Isabella Rossellini sur les traces de sa mere. port C88 n440:21 May 4/10 1988
  Canniere, P. Noir c'est noir [Book Review]. stills C88 n437:11-13 Apr 13/19 1988
CANNON ENTERTAINMENT GROUP **CORPORATE BODY ENTRIES**
  Adams, M. Cannon sells venerable Elstree VARIETY 331:3+ [2] Jul 6 1988
  Adams, M. Move on to save Cannon's Elstree. VARIETY 331:5 Jul 20 1988
  Avton's offer to buy Elstree meets surprise and skepticism. VARIETY 332:5 Jul 27 1988
  Cannon shutters London prod. unit; Kagan going solo. VARIETY 332:3 Sep 28 1988
  Groves, D. Cannon's on the mend and reloading. stat VARIETY 332:3+ [2p] Sep 21 1988
  Werba, H. Berlusconi uninvolved in Pathe. VARIETY 332:2 Sep 28 1988
  Economic Aspects
  Cannon continues financial recovery. stat VARIETY 332:3 Aug 24 1988
  Lawsuits
  Quinn hits Cannon for pact breach. VARIETY 332:3 Aug 3 1988
CANNON FRANCE
  Borger, L. Cannon France gets okay for buyout of GTC-CTM film labs. VARIETY 331:7 Jul 13 1988
  Four pictures by Kieslowski taken by Cannon **FILM REVIEWER ENTRIES**
  1988
CANOVA, GIANNI For film reviews see author under the following titles: BELIEVERS, THE; EMPIRE OF THE SUN; KAMIKAZEN - ULTIMA NOTTE A MILANO; SOMEONE TO WATCH OVER ME; VISIONE DEL SABBA, LA
  Canova, G. Inside Hollywood. il SEGNO n31:58 Jan 1988
  Canova, G. Schegge di '68. stills SEGNO n33:16-20 May 1988
CAN'T BUY ME LOVE f (d Rash, Steve 1987 USA)
  "Can't Buy Me Love." stills C REVUE n26:22-25 Jun 30 1988
  Reviews
  Caputo, R. "Can't Buy Me Love." credits il C PAPERS n68:46-47 Mar 1988
  Newman, K. "Can't Buy Me Love." credits still MFB 55:166-167 Jun 1988
CANTRILL, ARTHUR **AUTHOR ENTRIES**
  Cantrill, A. Even Orchestra film [...] stills CANTRILL'S FMNTS n55/56:16-17 May 1988
  Cantrill, A. Speaking through colour, form and movement - the work of Ivor Cantrill. il stills CANTRILL'S FMNTS n55/56:67-71 May 1988
CANTRILL, IVOR
  Cantrill, A. Speaking through colour, form and movement - the work of Ivor Cantrill. il stills CANTRILL'S FMNTS n55/56:67-71 May 1988
CAPELIER, MARGOT
  Ostria, V. Vampires, pygmalions, conseillers ou amis. il still CAHIERS n407/408:66-69 May 1988
CAPPONI, MARIA
  Capponi, M. Regiestuehle international [Book Review]. EPD 5:13 Jun 1988
CAPRA, FRANK
  Browne, N. American vision: the films of Frank Capra by Raymond Carney [Book Review]. WIDE ANGLE 10:63-64 n3 1988
  Magny, J. Le realisme de l'utopie [Book Review]. stills CAHIERS n405:Journal n81:XV Mar 1988
  Sklar, R. Film: American sadness. still VILLAGE VOICE 33:70 May 10 1988
CAPUTO, RAFFAELE For film reviews see author under the following titles: CAN'T BUY ME LOVE; HOUSE OF GAMES
  Caputo, R. Jim McBride tells it like it is. il interv still C PAPERS n68:52-55 Mar 1988
CARAVAGGIO f (d Jarman, Derek 1986 Gt Br)
  Diana, M. "Caravaggio": la luce della verita. stills C&C n50:73-74 Dec 1987
CARAX, LEOS See MAUVAIS SANG
CARAYANNIS, P.A.
  Carayannis, P.A. Al St. John (additions and corrections to the Al St. John filmography). CLASSIC n159:bet p32 and 33 [pC1] Sep 1988
CARDELLO, JOHN A.
  Cardello, J.A. John A. Cardello's observation post: "Star Trek - the Motion Picture." il still CLASSIC n157:25 Jul 1988
CARDOZE, MICHEL For film reviews see author under the following titles: OEUVRE AU NOIR, L'
  Cardoze, M. "Corentin (ou les infortunes conjugales)." credits stills C88 n438:3-5 Apr 20/26 1988
  Cardoze, M. "Mes amours de 68": plaisir garanti. still C88 n438:8-9 Apr

AIDS [Prior to V18, 1990 use HEALTH]
    Festivals
    Bo, F. Tempo de vivere, tempo di morire. still FCR 45:349-353 Jun/Jul
        (n446/447) 1994
        Canada
            Historical Analysis
    Cagle, R.L. "Tell the story of my life...": the making of meaning,
        "Monsters," and music in John Greyson's "Zero Patience." il stills VEL LT
        TRAP n35:69-81 Spring 1995
        United States
    Juhasz, A. So many alternatives. stills CINEASTE 21:37-39 n1/2 1995
        Effects on Film
    Green, J. The bug. il PREM 8:20-21 Feb 1995
AIDS FILMS
    Juhasz, A. So many alternatives. stills CINEASTE 21:37-39 n1/2 1995
A.K.A. DON BONUS f (d Nakasako, Spencer/Ny, Sokly 1995 USA)
    Reviews
    Harvey, D. "A.K.A. Don Bonus." credits VARIETY 358:53 Mar 13/19 1995
A CAUSA SECRETA f (d Bianchi, Sergio 1994 Brazil)
    Reviews
    Stratton, D. "The Secret Cause" ("A causa secreta"). credits VARIETY
        357:74 Jan 2/8 1995
A CAUSE D'ELLE f (d Hubert, Jean-Loup 1993 Fr)
    Reviews
    Mockler, J. "Egy lany miatt." credits F VILAG 38:64 n1 1995
A CRAN f (d Martin, Solange 1995 Fr)
    Reviews
    Cheshire, G. "On the edge" ("A cran"). credits VARIETY 358:77 Mar 27/Apr 2
        1995
A LA BELLE ETOILE f (d Desrosieres, Antoine 1993 Fr/Switz)
    Reviews
    Rousseau, Y. "A la belle etoile." still 24 IMAGES n75:72-73 Dec/Jan
        1994/95
...A LA CAMPAGNE f (d Poirier, Manuel 1995 Fr)
    Reviews
    Nesselson, L. "Out in the Country" ("A la campagne"). credits VARIETY
        358:53 Feb 13/19 1995
A LA FOLIE f (Six Days, Six Nights d Kurys, Diane 1994 Fr)
    Reviews
    Causo, M. "A la folie." still C FORUM 34:17 Sep (n337) 1994
AALMUHAMMED, JEFRI See also BROTHER MINISTER: THE ASSASSINATION OF MALCOLM X
AARDMAN ANIMATIONS
    Codelli, L. Creative discomfort. stills POSITIF n407:22-23 Jan 1995
    Herpe, N. "Wallace et Gromit." credits still POSITIF n407:24 Jan 1995
    Sifianos, G. Aardman Animations. il interv stills POSITIF n407:25-28 Jan
        1995
AAS, NILS KLEVJER
    Ottmar, T.W. Fritt fram a soke ef-stotte. il interv port F&K n7:34-35 1993
AASAROD, PAULINE
    Aasarod, P. Derek Jarman. il Z n4:26-27 (n46) 1993
    Og alle var der... ports Z n4:36-38 (n46) 1993
ABASHIDZE, DODO See also ASHIK-KERIB
ABBE, ELFRIEDA
    Abbe, E. Michelle Crenshaw. il interv ANGLES 2:12-16 n4 1995
ABBOTT AND COSTELLO GO TO MARS f (d Lamont, Charles 1953 USA)
    Production
    Palumbo, R. and Furmanek, B. This island mirth. il stills F FAX n48:56-63
        Jan/Feb 1995
ABBOTT, BUD
    Catsos, G. J.M. Children of the corn. il intervs F FAX n48:64-65+ [3p]
        Jan/Feb 1995
    Morlan, D.B. Slapstick contributions to WWII propaganda: The Three Stooges
        and Abbott and Costello. bibliog STUDIES POP CULT 17:29-43 n1 1994
ABBOTT, BUD, JR.
    Catsos, G. J.M. Children of the corn. il intervs F FAX n48:64-65+ [3p]
        Jan/Feb 1995
ABBOTT, GEORGE
    Gerard, J. George Abbott. obit VARIETY 358:84-85 Feb 6/12 1995
    Lentz, H., III. Obituaries. biogs filmogs obits ports CLASSIC n237:57-59
        Mar 1995
ABBRESCIA-RATH, SILVANA See also WIEDERKEHR
ABDRASHITOV, VADIM See also P'ESA DLIA PASSAZHIRA
ABE, MARK NORNES
    Abe, M.N. Documentarists of Japan (first in a series). biog filmog port
        stills DOC BOX 1:9-13 1992
    Abe, M.N. Documentarists of Japan (fourth in a series). biog interv port
        stills DOC BOX 4:8-12 1993
    Abe, M.N. Documentarists of Japan (second in a series). biog il interv
        stills DOC BOX 2:9-16 1993
ABEL, RICHARD
    Cantrill, A. French film theory and criticism, volume 1: 1907-1929; volume
        2: 1929-1939. By Richard Abel [Book Reviews]. CANTRILL'S FMNTS n73/74:41
        May 1994
    Cherchi Usai, P. The cine goes to town: French cinema, 1896-1914. By Richard
        Abel [Book Review]. J F PRES n49:69 Oct 1994
    Codelli, L. The cine goes to town. French cinema, 1896-1914. Di Richard Abel
        [Book Review]. GRIFFITHIANA n51/52:252-253 Oct 1994
    Turner, G. The cine goes to town. By Richard Abel [Book Review]. AMCIN
        76:85 Jan 1995
ABERG, ANDERS
    Aberg, A. "Askadaren" vid glipan: Maaret Koskinen om Ingmar Bergman [Book
        Review]. F HAFTET 22:59-60 n3 (n87) 1994
ABITTAN, GAD
    Abittan, G. (Onzieme) XIeme Festival de films de Jerusalem. AVANT-SCENE
        n437:88-89 Dec 1994
ABORIGINES IN FILM
    Australia
    McFarlane, B. Crofts, Stephen. Identification, gender and genre in film: the
        case of "Shame" [Book Reviews]. MEDIA INFO AUSTRALIA n75:159-160 Feb 1995

    Canada
        Cultural Context
    Fraser, F. The participation of Aboriginal and other cultural minorities in
        cultural development. bibliog CAN J COM 19:477-493 n3/4 1994
ABORIGINES IN FILM INDUSTRY
    Australia
    Dutchak, P. Wal Saunders. port stat C PAPERS n102:44+ [2p] Dec 1994
        Ethnographic Film. History
    Long, C. Australia's first films: facts and fables, part eleven: Aborigines
        and actors. filmogs il map ports C PAPERS n102:52-57+ [8p] Dec 1994
ABRAHAMS, JIM See also HOT SHOTS! PART DEUX
ABRAMSON, NEIL See also WITHOUT AIR
Academy Awards See AWARDS - United States - Academy of Motion Picture Arts and
    Sciences
ACADEMY OF MOTION PICTURE ARTS AND SCIENCES (Beverly Hills, California)
    Weiner, R. Visual F/X morphs its own Acad wing. VARIETY 358:22 Feb 13/19
        1995
Accidental Hero See HERO
ACE VENTURA, PET DETECTIVE f (d Shadyac, Tom 1994 USA)
    Reviews
    De Marinis, G. "Ace Ventura: L'acchiappanimali." credits still C FORUM
        34:84-85 Sep (n337) 1994
    Meyers, R. The crime screen. port stills ARMCHAIR DET 27:320-321 n3 1994
ACHESON, KEITH
    Acheson, K. and Maule, C.J. Copyright and related rights: the international
        dimension. bibliog CAN J COM 19:423-446 n3/4 1994
    Acheson, K. and Maule, C.J. International regimes for trade, investment, and
        labour mobility in the cultural industries. bibliog CAN J COM 19:401-421
        n3/4 1994
ACHTERNBUSCH, HERBERT See also HADES
ACKERMAN, ROBERT ALLAN See also SAFE PASSAGE
Acquired Immune Deficiency Syndrome See AIDS
ACTING
    France
    Aude, F. Entretien avec Nicole Garcia. il interv stills POSITIF n407:15-20
        Jan 1995
    Poland
    Lubelski, T. Seweryn. il interv KINO 27:10-15 Jul 1993
    Sobolewski, T. Krysia is the best. interv ports still KINO 27:20-23+ [5p]
        May 1993
    United States
    Lilley, J. Jan Murray. il interv stills SCARLET STREET n17:90+ [4p] Winter
        1995
        History
    Bawden, J. Rhonda Fleming. biog filmog il ports stills FIR 45:6-17 Nov/Dec
        1994
    Randisi, S. Lifetime contract. il port stills F FAX n48:76-81+ [8p]
        Jan/Feb 1995
        Study and Teaching
    Midding, G. Lee Strasberg: Ein Traum der Leidenschaft [Book Review]. il F
        BUL 37:7 n1 (n198) 1995
        Style. History
    Creekmur, C.K. Roberta Pearson. Eloquent gestures: the transformation of
        performance style in the Griffith Biograph films [Book Review]. ARACHNE
        1:266-269 n2 1994
ACTION FILM
    United States
        Gender Roles
    Vahtera, H. Toimivatko toimintaleffojen roolimallit? still PEILI 18:26-27
        n4 1994
ACTORS AND ACTRESSES See also names of actors and actresses; CHILDREN AS ACTORS;
    STAR SYSTEM; SUPPORTING ROLES
        Professional Activities
    Kamp, D. The importance of being Hamlet. il stills VANITY FAIR 58:74+ [3p]
        Mar 1995
        France
    Bonneville, L. Gueules d'atmosphere: les acteurs du cinema francais
        (1929-1959). Par Olivier Barrot et Raymond Chirat [Book Review]. il
        SEQUENCES n174:59 Sep/Oct 1994
        Dubbing. Strikes
    Williams, M. Unions suspend dubbing strike. VARIETY 357:49 Jan 9/15 1995
        Great Britain
        Spectatorship
    Stacey, J. Hollywood memories. SCREEN 35:317-335 n4 1994
        Scandinavia
        History
    Turner, G. Strangers in Hollywood. By Hans J. Wollstein [Book Review].
        AMCIN 76:86 Feb 1995
    Wagenknecht, E. "Strangers in Hollywood: the history of Scandinavian actors
        in American films from 1910 to World War II." By Hans J. Wollstein [Book
        Review]. CLASSIC n236:49 Feb 1995
        United States
    Bellafante, G. Generation X-cellent. ports TIME 145:62-64 Feb 27 1995
    Lahr, J. The great Guskin. il NEW YORKER 71:44-49 Mar 20 1995
        Awards
    Dwyer, E. A night to remember. ports stills VARIETY 357:59+ [2p] Jan 2/8
        1995
    Hindes, A. Industryites choose favorites. ports stills VARIETY 357:59+
        [2p] Jan 2/8 1995
        Awards. History
    Dwyer, E. Long history of protest, controversy. il VARIETY 357:60+ [2p]
        Jan 2/8 1995
    Hindes, A. Surprise endings highlight actress award competition. port
        VARIETY 357:60+ [2p] Jan 2/8 1995
        Casting and Casting Directors
    Campbell, V. and Margulies, E. More great moments in miscasting. stills
        MOVIELINE 6:62-66+ [8p] Mar 1995
        Comedy Film. History
    Caslavsky, K. Comedians. filmogs il stills GRIFFITHIANA n51/52:60-169 Oct
        1994

ACTORS AND ACTRESSES
  United States
  (continued)
    Contracts
Cox, D. SAG, producers settle in a cliffhanger deal. VARIETY 358:16 Mar
  27/Apr 2 1995
Seigel, R.L. Wanted: Guild actors at a discount. il INDEP 18:38-41 Jan/Feb
  1995
    Employment, Foreigners. History
Wagenknecht, E. "Strangers in Hollywood: the history of Scandinavian actors
  in American films from 1910 to World War II." By Hans J. Wollstein [Book
  Review]. CLASSIC n236:49 Feb 1995
    Photography
Nangle, J. Heavies/drag/lovers/weddings. Edited by J.C. Suares [Book
  Review]. FIR 45:69 Nov/Dec 1994
    Professional Activities
Peyser, M. No experience necessary: can celebrities save Broadway? graph
  ports NEWSWK 125:66 Mar 6 1995
    Silent Film
Katchmer, G. Remembering the great silents. biogs filmogs port CLASSIC
  n236:50-53 Feb 1995
Katchmer, G. Remembering the great silents. biogs filmogs port CLASSIC
  n237:35+ [3p] Mar 1995
    Strikes
Cox, D. Studios running scared. VARIETY 358:6 Mar 13/19 1995
    Wages and Salaries
Brodie, J. Stars' double standards. il stat VARIETY 358:13-14 Feb 27/Mar 5
  1995
    Women
Atkinson, M. Girls! Girls! Girls! il MOVIELINE 6:56-60+ [6p] Mar 1995
ADAGIO, CARMELO For film reviews see author under the following titles: AMATEUR;
  GO FISH; I LOVE A MAN IN UNIFORM; LOVE AND HUMAN REMAINS; POSTINO, IL;
  PULP FICTION; PURA FORMALITA, UNA; SOMEBODY TO LOVE; TORO, IL; VELENO;
  WOLF; WYATT EARP
Adagio, C. Per un sano e urgente rilancio del cinema europeo. stills C
  NUOVO 43:25-27 Nov/Dec (n352) 1994
ADAMEK, PAULINE
Adamek, P. "The Crow." il interv stills FATAL VISIONS n17:33-34 1994
ADAMS, JOEY LAUREN
Fuller, G. Parker's party. ports INTERV 25:79-81 Feb 1995
ADAMSON, JOE
Adamson, J. and others. Forgotten laughter. credits port stills
  GRIFFITHIANA n51/52:170-197 Oct 1994
Adamson, J. and others. La fabbrica della risata. credits port stills
  GRIFFITHIANA n51/52:170-197 Oct 1994
ADAPTATIONS See also names of authors; PROPERTIES, LITERARY
Frey, M. International guide to literature on film [Book Review]. F KUNST
  n144:70-71 1994
Gruber, E. Une reprise impossible? "Effi Briest" et la question de ses
  reecritures filmiques. CINEMAS 4:59-71 n1 1993
    Drama
Las peliculas del ciclo. bibliog credits stills NOSFERATU n8:56-73 Feb 1992
Latorre, J.M. Shakespeare segun Zeffirelli. il stills NOSFERATU n8:48-55
  Feb 1992
Miguez, M. No pongais vuestras sucias manos sobre Shakespeare! stills
  NOSFERATU n8:14-19 Feb 1992
Riambau, E. Shakespeare y Welles. stills NOSFERATU n8:32-39 Feb 1992
    Bibliographies
Bibliografia y fuentes iconograficas. bibliog NOSFERATU n8:74 Feb 1992
    History
Aldarondo, R. La tentacion de Shakespeare. stills NOSFERATU n8:20-27 Feb
  1992
    Literature
Andersson, L.G. Ricoeur och film [Book Review]. F HAFTET 22:58 n3 (n87)
  1994
Breen, J.L. Hubin, Allen J. Crime fiction II: a comprehensive bibliography
  1749-1990 [Book Review]. ARMCHAIR DET 28:197 n2 1995
Comuzio, E. Michele Serra (a cura di:) Letteratura e cinema. Testi e
  linguaggi [Book Review]. C FORUM 34:94 Nov (n339) 1994
Laster, A. Les miserables sur les ecrans de cinema et de television.
  credits filmog il stills AVANT-SCENE n438/439:81-91 Jan/Feb 1995
Savater, F. La palabra imaginaria (notas sobre cine y literatura). stills
  NOSFERATU n8:4-7 Feb 1992
    Canada
    Literature
Viswanathan, J. L'un(e) dort, l'autre pas: la scene de la veille dans les
  scenarios et quelques romans de Rejean Ducharme. bibliog scenario still
  table CINEMAS 5:189-209 n1/2 1994
    France
    Literature
Benard, J. Un cinema zazique? bibliog still CINEMAS 4:135-154 n3 1994
Gardies, A. Narration et temporalite dans "Moderato cantabile." bibliog
  still CINEMAS 4:88-102 n1 1993
Sommier, J.-C. "La salle de bain": l'immobilite cinetique. bibliog CINEMAS
  4:103-114 n1 1993
    Germany (Democratic Republic, 1949-1990)
    Literature
Graef, C. Erfahrungen im Spielfilm-Studio. il F & FERNSEHEN 22:12-25 n6
  1994
    Germany (Federal Republic, 1949-1990)
    Drama
Plater, E.M.V. Helmut Kaeutner's film adaptation of "Des Teufels General."
  bibliog LIT/FQ 22:253-264 n4 1994
    Germany (until 1949)
    Literature
Vernet, M. Le voir-dire. CINEMAS 4:35-47 n1 1993
    Great Britain
    Short Story
Jensen, P.M. Inside "The Skull." il stills SCARLET STREET n17:26-28+ [6p]
  Winter 1995

  Hong Kong
  Literature
Hoare, S. Romance du livre et du film: l'adaptation de la "Romance du livre
  et de l'epee" par Ann Hui. bibliog glos stills CINEMAS 3:141-155 n2/3 1993
  Hungary
  Literature
Gothar, P. "Reszleg" - reszletek. il interv stills F VILAG 38:6-9 n2 1995
  India
  Literature
Longfellow, B. "The Bandit Queen." stills C ACTION n36:10-16 1995
  Italy
  Literature
Rooney, D. Italo helmers try novel ideas. il VARIETY 358:7+ [2p] Mar 20/26
  1995
  Mexico
Toledo, T. "Fresa y chocolate." interv stills DICINE n59:4-6 Nov/Dec 1994
  New Zealand
  Literature
Lewis, B. Lee Tamahori's "Once Were Warriors." port stills C PAPERS
  n102:4-8 Dec 1994
  United States
Bradley, M.R. Nolan's "Run." biog il interv stills F FAX n48:42-48+ [8p]
  Jan/Feb 1995
Weiner, R. Vidgames won't play by Hollywood's rules. VARIETY 358:1+ [2p]
  Mar 20/26 1995
  Drama
Pipolo, T. Making "Antigone/Rites of Passion." interv stills MILLENNIUM
  n26:34-55 Fall 1992
  Literature
Birdsall, E. Interpreting Henry James: Bogdanovich's "Daisy Miller."
  bibliog still LIT/FQ 22:272-277 n4 1994
Gabbard, K. The circulation of sadomasochistic desire in the "Lolita" texts.
  bibliog still UFAJ 46:19-30 n2 1994
Gallagher, B. It's a print!: detective fiction from page to screen. Edited
  by William Reynolds and Elizabeth A. Trembley [Book Review]. MICHIGAN
  ACADEMICIAN 27:229-231 n2 1995
Helman, A. Kaleb potomek Kaina. il stills KINO 27:22-25 Jun 1993
Helman, A. Swiat wedlug Hilla. il stills KINO 27:24-26 Jul 1993
Nuernberg, S.M. Jack London - the movies, an historical survey. By Tony
  Williams [Book Review]. WESTERN AM LIT 28:173-174 n2 1993
Parker, H. The waiting game. interv port MOVIELINE 6:66-67 Apr 1995
Ropars-Wuilleumier, M.-C. L'oubli du texte. bibliog CINEMAS 4:11-22 n1
  1993
Sallis, J. David Goodis: life in black and white. il ARMCHAIR DET
  26:16-22+ [12p] n2 1993
Slide, A. The Slide area film book notes [Book Reviews]. CLASSIC n236:47-49
  Feb 1995
Stewart, J. The street side of the game. interv ports still INTERV
  25:98-99 Apr 1995
Terry, P. A Chinese woman in the west: "Thousand Pieces of Gold" and the
  revision of the heroic frontier. bibliog still LIT/FQ 22:222-226 n4 1994
Vidal, J.-P. La Berlue et le mythe: S/K, ou de Stephen King a Stanley
  Kubrick. still CINEMAS 4:115-129 n1 1993
Walker, J. Deconstructing an American myth: Hollywood and "The Last of the
  Mohicans." bibliog still F&HIST 23:104-116+ [14p] n1/4 1993
    Literature. History
Scalera, B. Over my dead body. Lee Server [Book Review]. SCARLET STREET
  n17:99 Winter 1995
    Radio
Breen, J.L. Harmon, Jim. Radio mystery and adventure and its appearances in
  film, television and other media [Book Review]. ARMCHAIR DET 26:78-79 n3
  1993
    Short Story
Montesano, A.P. "Johnny Mnemonic." stills C FANTAS 26:44+ [2p] n3 1995
Singer, R. One against all: the New England past and present
  responsibilities in "The Devil and Daniel Webster." bibliog still LIT/FQ
  22:265-271 n4 1994
ADDICTION, THE f (d Ferrara, Abel 1995 USA)
  Reviews
Greene, R. "The Addiction." BOXOFFICE 131:bet p125 and 144 [pR22] Apr 1995
McCarthy, T. "The Addiction." credits still VARIETY 358:73-74 Feb 6/12
  1995
ADDISON, ERIN
Addison, E. Saving other women from other men: Disney's "Aladdin." stills
  CAM OBS n31:4-25 Jan/May 1993
ADJANI, ISABELLE
Webster, A. Filmographies. biogs filmogs stills PREM 8:100 Feb 1995
ADKINSON, ROBERT
Harrison, S. House of horror: the complete Hammer Films story. By Allen
  Eyles, Robert Adkinson & Nicholas Fry with additional revisions by Jack
  Hunter [Book Review]. il FATAL VISIONS n17:30 1994
ADMISSIONS
  Belgium
Balans van de bioscoopuitbating in Belgie in 1993. stat tables MONITEUR
  n128:5-9 Feb 1995
Bilan de l'exploitation en Belgique en 1993. stat tables MONITEUR n128:5-9
  Feb 1995
L'appreciation des spectateurs. stat table MONITEUR n127:24-25 Jan 1995
  Italy
I 50 film di maggiore successo della stagione. stat table SEGNO n63:26
  Sep/Oct 1993
  Norway
Kinoenes Adelskalender 1993. stat table F&K n1:44 1994
ADMISSIONS EQUIPMENT
  United States
  Computer Applications
Bumbieris, N. Don't underestimate the humble ticket. il FJ 98:54+ [2p] Mar
  1995
  Omniterm Data Technology
Coman, E. Theatre point-of-sale automation: innovation, evolution,

integration. il FJ 98:84+ [2p] Mar 1995
   Ticketpro
  Shaw, J. Ticketpro staff applies theatre experience. FJ 98:86+ [2p] Mar 1995
Adolescents in film See YOUTH IN FILM
ADVENTURE FILM
  United States
    Historical Film
  Cantrill, A. The romance of adventure: the genre of historical adventure movies. By Brian Taves [Book Review]. CANTRILL'S FMNTS n73/74:42 May 1994
  Codelli, L. The romance of adventure: the genre of historical adventure movies. Di Brian Taves [Book Review]. GRIFFITHIANA n51/52:265 Oct 1994
ADVENTURES OF PRISCILLA, QUEEN OF THE DESERT, THE f (d Elliott, Stephan 1994 Australia)
  Noel, P. "Les aventures de Priscilla, folle du desert." bibliog credits stills GRAND ANGLE n177:7-8 Dec 1994
    Reviews
  Castiel, E. "The Adventures of Priscilla, Queen of the Desert." still SEQUENCES n174:44 Sep/Oct 1994
  Hamilton, A. "The Adventures of Priscilla, Queen of the Desert." credits still FILM 4:19 n1 [1995]
  Pearson, H., Jr. "The Adventures of Priscilla: Queen of the Desert." FIR 45:61-62 Nov/Dec 1994
ADVERTISING See also POSTERS; TRAILERS
  United States
    Animation. History
  Kaufman, J.B. Good mousekeeping: family-oriented publicity in Disney's golden age. il ANIMATION J 3:78-85 n2 1995
AELITA f (Aelita: Queen of Mars d Protazanov, Iakov 1924 USSR)
    Reviews
  Hogan, D.J. "Aelita." stills F FAX n49:20 Mar/Apr 1995
Aelita: Queen of Mars See AELITA
AESTHETICS See also CLASSICISM; EMOTION; LETTRISM; PERCEPTION; PHILOSOPHY; STYLE; THEORY
  Kremski, P. Film als Schule des Sehens. il interv stills F BUL 36:53-59 n6 (n197) 1994
    Silent Film
  Codelli, L. Seductive cinema: the art of silent film. Di James Card [Book Review]. GRIFFITHIANA n51/52:265-266 Oct 1994
    Canada
      Quebec. Documentary Film
  Lockerbie, I. Le documentaire autoreflexif au Quebec. "L'emotion dissonante" et "Passiflora." still CINEMAS 4:118-132 n2 1994
    Italy
  Loesche, C.-D. Antonioni [Book Review]. F KUNST n144:73-75 1994
    United States
      Computer Animation
  Bishko, L. Expressive technology: the tool as metaphor of aesthetic sensibility. il stills ANIMATION J 3:74-91 n1 1994
AF GEIJERSTAM, EVA
  Af Geijerstam, E. Inte bara for kalenderbitare [Book Review]. il CHAPLIN 36:61 n6 (n255) 1994/95
AFFAIRE NORMAN WILLIAM, L' f (d Godbout, Jacques 1994 Can)
    Reviews
  Landry, G. "L'affaire Norman William." still 24 IMAGES n75:72 Dec/Jan 1994/95
AFRICAN QUEEN, THE f (d Huston, John 1952 USA)
  Brill, L. "The African Queen" and John Huston's filmmaking. CJ 34:3-21 n2 1995
AFRIQUE, MON AFRIQUE... f (d Ouedraogo, Idrissa 1995 Fr/Burkina Faso)
    Reviews
  Stratton, D. "Africa, My Africa..." ("Afrique, mon Afrique..."). credits VARIETY 358:83 Feb 20/26 1995
Afro-Americans in film [Prior to V21, 1993 use AFRO-AMERICANS IN FILM] See BLACKS IN FILM
AG IGAZI MAO f (d Siklosi, Szilveszter 1995 Hungary)
    Reviews
  Elley, D. "Mao, the Real Man." credits VARIETY 358:86 Feb 20/26 1995
AGE D'OR, L' f (d Bunuel, Luis 1930 Fr)
  Suleiman, S.R. Between the street and the salon: the dilemma of surrealist politics in the 1930's. il stills VISUAL ANTHRO R 7:39-50 n1 1991
AGE OF INNOCENCE, THE f (d Scorsese, Martin 1993 USA)
    Sound Track Reviews
  Carrocino, J. "The Age of Innocence." F SCORE MONTHLY n40:11 Dec 1993
AGENTS See also names of agents
  United States
  Brodie, J. and O'Steen, K. Antsy agents make mutant managers. il VARIETY 358:1+ [3p] Mar 20/26 1995
    Screenwriters
  Hoag, D. A match made in Hollywood. il JOURNAL WGA 7:14-20 Feb 1994
AGHED, JAN
  Aghed, J. Entretien avec James Gray. interv stills POSITIF n407:8-11 Jan 1995
AGONIE DE JERUSALEM, L' f (d Duvivier, Julien 1926 Fr)
  Pedler, G. Garth's vintage viewing: Julien Duvivier's "Revelation." biogs il stills CLASSIC n237:30+ [3p] Mar 1995
AGRICULTURE IN FILM
  Italy
  Masala, F. Il ritorno di De Seta autore non "pacificato." interv stills C FORUM 34:63-66 Nov (n339) 1994
AGUILAR, CARLOS
  Aguilar, C. "S.O.S., el mundo en peligro." credits stills NOSFERATU n6:96-97 Apr 1991
AGUILAR MENDEZ, SERGIO For film reviews see author under the following titles: EUROPA
AGUILAS NO CAZAN MOSCAS f (d Cabrera, Sergio 1994 Colombia/It)
    Reviews
  Fadda, M. "Aguilas no cazan moscas." still C FORUM 34:21 Sep (n337) 1994

AHARE HAHAGIM f (d Rubinstein, Amnon 1995 Isreal)
    Reviews
  Stratton, D. "On the Edge" ("Ahare hahagim"). credits VARIETY 358:54 Mar 13/19 1995
AHLIN, PER See also RESAN TILL MELONIA
AHLUND, JANNIKE
  Ahlund, J. Filmens historia ar Runes historia. il interv ports CHAPLIN 36:42-45 n6 (n255) 1994/95
  Ahlund, J. Nordlig rutt genom filmhistorien. interv port CHAPLIN 36:57 n6 (n255) 1994/95
AIDIN TYTTO f (d Paljakka, Kari 1993 Finl)
    Reviews
  Nygren, A. Angelican kosto. credits still PEILI 17:31 n3 1993
AINSI SOIENT-ELLES f (d Alessandrin, Patrick 1995 Fr/Sp)
    Reviews
  Nesselson, L. "Femmes" ("Ainsi soient-elles"). credits VARIETY 358:70 Feb 27/Mar 5 1995
  Vasse, C. "Ainsi soient-elles." POSITIF n409:41 Mar 1995
AIQING WANSUI f (d Tsai, Ming-liang 1994 Taiwan)
  Causo, M. "Vive l'amour." credits stills C FORUM 34:76-78 Nov (n339) 1994
  Gariazzo, G. Quel raro equilibrio di sospensione. still C FORUM 34:78-79 Nov (n339) 1994
  Roberti, B. and others. La lingua interiore degli spazi. interv FCR 45:425-428 Sep (n448) 1994
    Reviews
  Catelli, D. "Vive l'amour." credits stills SEGNO n71:36-37 Jan/Feb 1995
  Loffreda, P. "Aiquing wansui"/"Vive l'amour." still C FORUM 34:13 Sep (n337) 1994
  Sanzone, D. "Vive l'amour." credits still FILM (ITALY) 3:15-16 n13 1995
AIRBORNE EXPRESS
  Airborne/Technicolor system tracks prints. FJ 98:94 Jan/Feb 1995
AIRHEADS f (d Lehmann, Michael 1994 USA)
    Reviews
  Cloutier, M. "Airheads." SEQUENCES n174:47 Sep/Oct 1994
AKERMAN, CHANTAL See also CONTRE L'OUBLI; TOUTE UNE NUIT
AKOMFRAH, JOHN See also WHO NEEDS A HEART?
AKUMULATOR 1 f (d Sverak, Jan 1994 Czech R)
    Reviews
  Gandini, L. "Akumulator 1." still C FORUM 34:34-35 Sep (n337) 1994
ALADDIN f (d Musker, John/Clements, Ron 1992 USA)
  Johnsen, F. Disneys nye flaggskip. stills F&K n7:4-6 1993
    Characterization
  Griffin, S. The illusion of "identity": gender and racial representation in "Aladdin." ANIMATION J 3:64-73 n1 1994
    Feminist Analysis
  Addison, E. Saving other women from other men: Disney's "Aladdin." stills CAM OBS n31:4-25 Jan/May 1993
    Reviews
  Salakka, M. Totuuden henki - johda sina meita. stills PEILI 18:30-31 n1 1994
ALBANESE, ALEX For film reviews see author under the following titles: INTO THE DEEP; MINA TANNENBAUM
  Albanese, A. The shape of things to come? il BOXOFFICE 131:bet p82 and 83 [pSW16-SW18] Apr 1995
Albania See as a subheading under individual subject headings
ALBERSMEIER, FRANZ-JOSEF
  Mueller, J.E. Albersmeier, Franz-Josef. Theater, Film, Literatur in Frankreich. Medienwechsel und Intermedialitat [Book Review]. CINEMAS 5:223-228 n1/2 1994
ALBERT, MITCH
  Albert, M. Solo flyers. il stills INDEP 18:24-28 Mar 1995
  Albert, M. There's no business at Showbiz. il INDEP 18:35 Apr 1995
ALBERTI, IRENE VON See also PAUL BOWLES - HALBMOND
  "Paul Bowles - Halbmond." biogs credits still KINO(BRD) n1:24-25 1995
ALBIN, ANDY
  Lentz, H., III. Obituaries. biogs filmogs obits ports CLASSIC n237:57-59 Mar 1995
ALBRECHT, RICHARD
  Albrecht, R. Knights of the roundtable. il JOURNAL WGA 8:51 Dec/Jan 1995
ALCOTT, LOUISA MAY
  Lurie, A. She had it all. il still NY R BKS 42:3-5 Mar 2 1995
ALDARONDO, RICARDO
  Aldarondo, R. "Chantaje criminal." credits still NOSFERATU n6:77 Apr 1991
  Aldarondo, R. "El presidente." credits stills NOSFERATU n5:44-45 Jan 1991
  Aldarondo, R. "El sueno de una noche de verano." credits still NOSFERATU n8:58-59 Feb 1992
  Aldarondo, R. "Enrique V." credits il NOSFERATU n8:73 Feb 1992
  Aldarondo, R. "Extrano suceso." credits still NOSFERATU n6:76 Apr 1991
  Aldarondo, R. "Hamlet." credits NOSFERATU n8:71 Feb 1992
  Aldarondo, R. "La Fierecilla domada." credits still NOSFERATU n8:72 Feb 1992
  Aldarondo, R. La tentacion de Shakespeare. stills NOSFERATU n8:20-27 Feb 1992
  Aldarondo, R. "Las hijas del cervecero"; "Romeo y Julia en la nieve." credits stills NOSFERATU n8:57-58 Feb 1992
  Aldarondo, R. "Los motivos de Berta." credits still NOSFERATU n9:91-92 Jun 1992
  Aldarondo, R. and Ma Latorre, J. "Dracula." credits stills NOSFERATU n6:78-80 Apr 1991
ALDRIDGE, KAY
  Lentz, H., III. Obituaries. biogs filmogs obits ports CLASSIC n237:57-59 Mar 1995
Alea, Tomas Gutierrez See GUTIERREZ ALEA, TOMAS
ALEKSANDR NEVSKII f (Alexander Nevsky d Eisenstein, Sergei Mikhailovich 1938 USSR)
    Music
  Merritt, R. Recharging "Alexander Nevsky." il musical scores stills FQ 48:34-47 n2 1994/95
ALEKSANDROV, GRIGORII See also OKTIABR'
ALESSANDRIN, PATRICK See also AINSI SOIENT-ELLES

ALEXANDER, JANE
O'Steen, K. Jane tells it plain. stat VARIETY 358:12 Feb 27/Mar 5 1995
Ramos, D. Jane's addiction. port NEW REPUB 212:23+ [2p] Jan 9/16 1995
ALEXANDER, MAX
Alexander, M. "Siege" the day. port VARIETY 358:6 Feb 13/19 1995
Alexander, M. The auteurist trap. port VARIETY 358:8 Feb 6/12 1995
Alexander, M. The determined dilettante. port VARIETY 358:10 Mar 27/Apr 2 1995
Alexander, M. The men behind the "King." ports VARIETY 357:10 Jan 9/15 1995
ALEXANDER, MIRIYAMA
Alexander, M. Kung-fu flick feels the heat. ONFILM [12]:5 n1 1995
Alexander Nevsky See ALEKSANDR NEVSKII
ALEXANDER, PAUL
Queenan, J. St. James? [Book Review]. il MOVIELINE 6:20-21 Mar 1995
ALEXANDER, PERRY
Alexander, P. "Vicar," "Space Case," "Killer" and "The Night City." filmogs il stills CANTRILL'S FMNTS n73/74:12-14 May 1994
Ball, S. The Alexander enigma. il stills CANTRILL'S FMNTS n73/74:15-18 May 1994
ALGRANT, DANIEL See also NAKED IN NEW YORK
Ali See ANGST ESSEN SEELE AUF
ALIA
Li, W. A pearl reveals its splendor. port stills CHINA SCREEN n4:24-25 1994
ALICE'S RESTAURANT f (d Penn, Arthur 1969 USA)
   Reviews
Elia, M. "Alice's Restaurant." credits still SEQUENCES n175:28 Nov/Dec 1994
ALIEN f (d Scott, Ridley 1979 Gt Br)
   Feminist Analysis
Torry, R. Awakening to the other: feminism and the ego-ideal in "Alien." bibliog WOMEN'S STUD 23:343-363 n4 1994
ALIEN3 f (d Fincher, David 1992 USA)
   Psychoanalytic Analysis
Bick, I.J. "Well, I guess I must make you nervous": woman and the space of "Alien3" bibliog stills PS 14:45-58 n1/2 1994/95
ALIGHIERO MANACORDA, MARIO
Alighiero Manacorda, M. La scuola nel cinema, il cinema nella scuola. il still C NUOVO 43:7-10 Nov/Dec (n352) 1994
All Night Long See TOUTE UNE NUIT
ALL THAT MONEY CAN BUY f (d Dieterle, William 1941 USA)
   Adaptations
Singer, R. One against all: the New England past and present responsibilities in "The Devil and Daniel Webster." bibliog still LIT/FQ 22:265-271 n4 1994
ALL THIS AND HEAVEN TOO f (d Litvak, Anatole 1940 USA)
   Feminist Analysis
McKee, A.L. "L'affaire praslin" and "All This, and Heaven Too": gender, genre, and history in the 1940s woman's film. VEL LT TRAP n35:33-51 Spring 1995
ALLAN QUATERMAIN AND THE LOST CITY OF GOLD f (d Nelson, Gary 1987 USA)
   Sound Track Reviews
Hirsch, D. "Allan Quatermain and the Lost City of Gold." F SCORE MONTHLY n38:12 Oct 1993
ALLE JAHRE WIEDER f (d Hoentsch, Andreas 1983 E Ger)
Graef, C. Hochschulfilme. il F & FERNSEHEN 22:30-35 n6 1994
ALLEMAGNE ANNEE 90 NEUF ZERO f (Germany Year 90 Nine Zero d Godard, Jean-Luc 1991 Fr)
   Ethics
Leutrat, J.-L. Ah! les salauds! bibliog CINEMAS 4:73-84 n3 1994
   Reviews
Rafferty, T. Double Godard. il NEW YORKER 70:92-95 Feb 6 1995
ALLEN, IOAN
Allen, I. Winds of change. il port BOXOFFICE 131:bet p82 and 83 [pSW14] Apr 1995
ALLEN, JOHN F.
Allen, J.F. Maintaining legends. il port BOXOFFICE 131:bet p82 and 83 [pSW46-SW50] Apr 1995
ALLEN, MIKE
Allen, M. and others. Exposure to pornography and acceptance of rape myths. bibliog stat tables J COMM 45:5-26 n1 1995
ALLEN, WOODY See also ANNIE HALL; BULLETS OVER BROADWAY; LOVE AND DEATH; MANHATTAN; SHADOWS AND FOG; STARDUST MEMORIES
Amiel, V. Woody Allen et les pieges de la scene. il stills POSITIF n408:24-25 Feb 1995
Ciment, M. and Tobin, Y. Entretien avec Woody Allen. il interv stills POSITIF n408:26-32 Feb 1995
Deleyto, C. The narrator and the narrative: the evolution of Woody Allen's film comedies. bibliog F CRITICISM 19:40-54 n2 1994/95
Dixon, W.W. American-Jewish filmmakers: traditions and trends. By David Desser and Lester D. Friedman [Book Review]. F CRITICISM 19:108-113 n2 1994/95
Harris, J.B. Radiographie de Woody Allen. il still POSITIF n408:33-35 Feb 1995
ALLERS, ROGER See also LION KING, THE
Alexander, M. The men behind the "King." ports VARIETY 357:10 Jan 9/15 1995
ALLEVA, RICHARD For film reviews see author under the following titles: LITTLE WOMEN; MADNESS OF KING GEORGE, THE; NOBODY'S FOOL; TOM & VIV
Alleva, R. Correspondence: the reviewer replies. COMMONWEAL 122:29 Mar 10 1995
Conner, D.M. Correspondence: Alleva on "Vampire." COMMONWEAL [122]:22-23 Feb 10 1995
Donohue, W.A. Correspondence: "Voice" vs. Alleva. COMMONWEAL 122:29 Mar 10 1995
ALLIANCE COMMUNICATIONS CORPORATION
Weiner, R. Alliance, MDP ink feature film joint venture. VARIETY 358:24 Mar 6/12 1995

   Economic Aspects
Enchin, H. Royal credits for Alliance. stat VARIETY 358:26 Feb 27/Mar 5 1995
ALLIANCE OF MOTION PICTURE AND TELEVISION PRODUCERS (AMPTP, United States)
Cox, D. SAG, producers settle in a cliffhanger deal. VARIETY 358:16 Mar 27/Apr 2 1995
   Contracts
Cox, D. WGA, producers' pact "groundbreaking." VARIETY 358:17 Feb 6/12 1995
Cox, D. Writers Guild gains ground with new pact. VARIETY 358:18 Feb 13/19 1995
Cox, D. and Busch, A.M. Producers draw battle lines over credit order. ports VARIETY 358:28+ [2p] Feb 20/26 1995
ALLIANCE-MDP WORLDWIDE
Weiner, R. Alliance, MDP ink feature film joint venture. VARIETY 358:24 Mar 6/12 1995
ALLINGTON, ROBERT
Menashe, L. Requiem for Soviet cinema 1917-1991 [Book Reviews]. stills CINEASTE 21:23-27 n1/2 1995
ALLIO, RENE See also CAMISARDS, LES; CONTRE L'OUBLI
ALLOUACHE, MERZAK See also BAB EL-OUED CITY
ALLULLO DROM f (d Zangardi, Tonino 1993 It)
   Reviews
Emiliani, S. "Allullo drom." credits still FILM (ITALY) 3:27-28 n13 1995
Allusion [Prior to V20, 1992 use ALLUSION] See REFERENCES TO LITERATURE IN FILM
Allusion [Prior to V20, 1992 use also ALLUSION] See REFERENCES TO FILMS IN FILM
ALMASI, MIKLOS For film reviews see author under the following titles: MEGINT TANU
Almasi, M. Europa megszallasa. F VILAG 38:4-5 n3 1995
ALMODOVAR, PEDRO See also KIKA
ALNAES, KARSTEN
Alnaes, K. Pliktens blinde oyne. stills F&K n1:6-7 1994
ALONSO, MARIA CONCHITA
A new spider woman. il NEW YORKER 70:30 Jan 16 1995
ALONZO, JOHN
Beeler, M. John Alonzo. il C FANTAS 26:27 n2 1995
Alternative cinema See INDEPENDENT FILM
ALTMAN, RICK
Altman, R. Deep-focus sound: "Citizen Kane" and the radio aesthetic. diag scenario Q REV F & VIDEO 15:1-34 n3 1994
Altman, R. Film Studies, Inc.: lessons from the past about the current institutionalization of film studies. F CRITICISM 17:22-30 n2/3 1992/93
Altman, R. The sound of sound. diags il CINEASTE 21:68-71 n1/2 1995
Chateauvert, J. Altman, Rick (direction). Sound theory. Sound practice [Book Review]. CINEMAS 4:157-166 n3 1994
ALTMAN, ROBERT See also IMAGES; READY TO WEAR (PRET-A-PORTER)
ALTRA ESTATE, UN' f (d Piersanti, Umberto/Peticca, Sandro 1986 It)
Loffreda, P. Immagini, parole e suoni. credits stills C FORUM 34:57-58 Oct (n338) 1994
ALTRA VITA, UN' f (d Mazzacurati, Carlo 1992 It)
Vecchi, P. Un western mitteleuropeo. il interv still C FORUM 34:71-72 Oct (n338) 1994
ALVARADO, MANUEL
Sinclair, J. King, John, Lopez, Ana M and Alvarado, Manuel, eds. Mediating two worlds: cinematic encounters in the Americas [Book Review]. MEDIA INFO AUSTRALIA n75:166-167 Feb 1995
ALWYN, WILLIAM
Vallerand, F. Anthologies. il obit SEQUENCES n175:56-57 Nov/Dec 1994
AM ENDE DER SCHIENEN f (d Kiss, Marianna/Honegger, Andreas 1993 FR Ger)
   Reviews
Lachat, P. "Am Ende der Schienen." credits C(SWITZ) 40:212 1994
AMAR, DENIS See also CONTRE L'OUBLI
AMATEUR f (d Hartley, Hal 1994 Fr/Gt Br/USA)
Chiacchiari, F. and De Marinis, G. "Amateur." credits stills C FORUM 34:60-62 Sep (n337) 1994
De Marinis, G. Pu(ri)tain de film! stills C FORUM 34:62-63 Sep (n337) 1994
Derryberry, D. Have you seen Elina? interv ports INTERV 25:32+ [2p] Apr 1995
Dupagne, M.-F. "Amateur." bibliog credits stills GRAND ANGLE n177:3-4 Dec 1994
Neff, R. Hartley's "Amateur" defies movie thriller conventions. il interv still FJ 98:18+ [2p] Mar 1995
   Reviews
Adagio, C. "Amateur"; "La natura ambigua dell'amore." credits still C NUOVO 43:47-48 Nov/Dec (n352) 1994
Brownlie, T. "Amateur." credits still FILM 4:19 n1 [1995]
Kemp, P. "Amateur." credits still S&S 5:42 Jan 1995
AMATEUR FILM AND FILMMAKING [Prior to V16, 1988 use also FILMMAKING]
   History
Huet, A. On n'a pas tous les jours cent ans...: ou de l'interet du cinema amateur. il J F PRES n49:40-42 Oct 1994
   Hungary
      Documentary Film
A tizenotezredik pillanat. interv stills F VILAG 38:18-23 n1 1995
AMBER PRODUCTION TEAM See also EDEN VALLEY
AMEERIKA MAED f (d Simm, Peeter 1995 Estonia/Fr/Hungary)
   Reviews
Stratton, D. "Big Dipper" ("Ameerika maed"). credits VARIETY 358:87 Feb 20/26 1995
AMELIO, GIANNI See also LAMERICA
Gili, J.A. Entretien avec Gianni Amelio. il interv stills POSITIF n406:25-31 Dec 1994
Siciliani de Cumis, N. Ecce Lamelio alla scoperta della "Merica." C NUOVO 43:2-3 Nov/Dec (n352) 1994
AMERICAN DREAM f (d Kopple, Barbara 1990 USA)
   Rhetorical Analysis
Orvell, M. Documentary film and the power of interrogation. il stills FQ 48:10-18 n2 1994/95
American Film Institute. National Center for Film and Video Preservation (Hollywood, California)

See NATIONAL CENTER FOR FILM AND VIDEO PRESERVATION (Hollywood, California)

AMERICAN FILM MARKETING ASSOCIATION
   History
   Saperstein, P. and Klady, L. Fifteen seasons of sun & sums. il ports VARIETY 358:bet p88 and 173 [pA2+ (2p)] Feb 20/26 1995

American Indians in film See INDIANS, AMERICAN, IN FILM

AMERICAN NATIONAL ENTERPRISES
   Wasser, F. Four walling exhibition: regional resistance to the Hollywood film industry. CJ 34:51-65 n2 1995

AMERICAN SOCIETY OF CINEMATOGRAPHERS
   Membership Lists
   American Society of Cinematographers. AMCIN 76:94 Mar 1995

AMES, CAROL
   Ames, C. Reaching for a star: writing for actors' production companies. il JOURNAL WGA 8:14-18 Feb 1995

AMICO ARABO, L' f (d Fornari, Carmine 1991 It)
   Reviews
   Emiliani, S. "L'amico arabo." credits FILM (ITALY) 3:25 n13 1995

AMICO IMMAGINARIO, L' f (d D'Alessandria, Nico 1994 It)
   Reviews
   Young, D. "The Imaginary Friend" ("L'amico immaginario"). credits VARIETY 357:75 Jan 2/8 1995

AMIEL, VINCENT For film reviews see author under the following titles: TZEDEK
   Amiel, V. Liberte d'esprit [Book Review]. still POSITIF n407:59 Jan 1995
   Amiel, V. "Vous ne savez pas, en France, ce qu il en coute de vivre dans un monde sans representation." filmog il stills POSITIF n409:58-60 Mar 1995
   Amiel, V. Woody Allen et les pieges de la scene. il stills POSITIF n408:24-25 Feb 1995
   Amiel, V. and Masson, A. Entretien avec Marcel Ophuls. il interv POSITIF n406:15-21 Dec 1994

AMIGUET, JEAN-FRANCOIS See also ECRIVAIN PUBLIC, L'

AMIRI, NOUSHABEH
   Amiri, N. Daughters of the revolution. filmog il port stills CINEMAYA n25/26:36-41 Autumn/Winter 1994/95
   Amiri, N. Rakhshan Bani'etemad. il stills CINEMAYA n25/26:42-43 Autumn/Winter 1994/95

AMIS, MARTIN
   Amis, M. Travolta's second act. il NEW YORKER 71:212-216+ [6p] Feb 20/27 1995

AMNESIA f (d Justiniano, Gonzalo 1994 Chile)
   Reviews
   Bozza, G. "Amnesia." still C FORUM 34:20-21 Sep (n337) 1994

AMONGST FRIENDS f (d Weiss, Rob 1993 USA)
   Economic Aspects
   Jackson, D. Never do business with "Friends." il port PREM 8:36 Apr 1995

AMOUR A MORT, L' f (d Resnais, Alain 1984 Fr)
   Cremonini, G. AA vari (sotto la direzione di Jean-Louis Leutrat): L'amour a mort di A. Resnais [Book Review]. C FORUM 34:92-93 Oct (n338) 1994

AMOUREUX, LES f (d Corsini, Catherine 1994 Fr)
   Reviews
   Grugeau, G. "Les amoureux." still 24 IMAGES n75:46 Dec/Jan 1994/95

AMRAM, DAVID
   Camunas, C.R. David Amram: a reluctant film composer. F SCORE MONTHLY n36/37:24 Aug/Sep 1993

Analysis See COGNITIVE ANALYSIS; CONTEXTUAL ANALYSIS; CROSS-CULTURAL ANALYSIS; DECONSTRUCTIVE ANALYSIS; FEMINIST ANALYSIS; HISTORICAL ANALYSIS; IDEOLOGICAL ANALYSIS; IMAGE ANALYSIS; INTERTEXTUAL ANALYSIS; MARXIST ANALYSIS; NARRATIVE ANALYSIS; POLITICAL ANALYSIS; POSTCOLONIAL ANALYSIS; PSYCHOANALYTIC ANALYSIS; PSYCHOLOGICAL ANALYSIS; QUEER THEORY ANALYSIS; RHETORICAL ANALYSIS; SEMIOTIC ANALYSIS; SOCIOLOGICAL ANALYSIS; STRUCTURAL ANALYSIS; TEXTUAL ANALYSIS; THEMATIC ANALYSIS

ANATA GA SUKI DESU, DAI SUKI DES f (d Oki, Hiroyuki 1995 Japan)
   Reviews
   Harvey, D. "I Like You, I Like You Very Much" (Anata ga suki desu, dai suki des"). credits VARIETY 358:53 Mar 13/19 1995

ANCHORESS f (d Newby, Chris 1993 Gt Br/Belg)
   Murphy, K. Nativity scenes. stills F COM 31:12-16 Jan/Feb 1995

AND THE BAND PLAYED ON f (d Spottiswoode, Roger 1993 USA)
   Reviews
   Cieutat, M. "Les soldats de l'esperance." still POSITIF n406:48-49 Dec 1994

Andalusian Dog, An See CHIEN ANDALOU, UN

ANDANTE CON MOTO f (d Hoentsch, Andreas 1981 E Ger)
   Graef, C. Hochschulfilme. il F & FERNSEHEN 22:30-35 n6 1994

ANDERE GESCHICHTE, EINE f (d Roy, Tula 1994 Switz)
   Reviews
   Geiser, R. "Eine andere Geschichte." credits C(SWITZ) 40:219-221 1994

ANDERS, ALLISON See also FOUR ROOMS; MI VIDA LOCA
   Rich, B.R. Slugging it out for survival. stills S&S 5:14-17 Apr 1995

ANDERSEN, ELGA
   Lentz, H., III. Obituaries. biogs filmogs il obits ports CLASSIC n236:57-59 Feb 1995

ANDERSON, LINDSAY See also IS THAT ALL THERE IS?
   Anderton, J. Lindsay Anderson notes. il port VERTIGO (UK) 1:59-60 n4 1994/95
   John Ford. Par Lindsay Anderson [Book Review]. il GRAND ANGLE n176:40 Nov 1994
   Manuelli, M. Lindsay Anderson anticonformismo e rabbia. still C NUOVO 43:38-39 Nov/Dec (n352) 1994
   McFarlane, B. Lindsay Anderson. biog il obit C PAPERS n102:20-21 Dec 1994

ANDERSON, MICHAEL See also LOGAN'S RUN

ANDERSSON, LARS GUSTAF
   Andersson, L.G. Ricoeur och film [Book Review]. F HAFTET 22:58 n3 (n87) 1994

ANDERTON, JOHN
   Anderton, J. Lindsay Anderson notes. il port VERTIGO (UK) 1:59-60 n4 1994/95

ANDRAS, FERENC See also TORVENYTELEN

ANDREW, DUDLEY
   Andrew, D. Appraising French images. WIDE ANGLE 16:53-65 n3 1995

ANEZ, NICHOLAS
   Anez, N. Westerns. stills FIR 45:18-27 Nov/Dec 1994

ANGE NOIR, L' f (d Brisseau, Jean-Claude 1994 Fr)
   Broeck, C.V. and Noel, J. "L'ange noir." credits stills GRAND ANGLE n177:5-6 Dec 1994
   Reviews
   Grugeau, G. D'entre les ombres. credits stills 24 IMAGES n76:56-57 Spring 1995

ANGELO, YVES See also COLONEL CHABERT, LE

ANGELOPOULOS, THEODOROS See also TOPIO STIN OMIHLI; VLEMMA TOU ODYSSEA, TO
   Trenczak, H. Walter Ruggle. Theo Angelopoulos: Filmische Landschaft [Book Review]. BLIMP n30:74 Winter 1994

ANGERAME, DOMINIC See also DECONSTRUCTION SIGHT

ANGIARI, LUISELLA
   Giuffrida, S. and Angiari, L. Sitges: al supermarket dell'orrore quotidiano. stills C FORUM 34:7-9 Nov (n339) 1994

ANGLADE, JEAN-HUGUES
   Millea, H. All the Queen's men. biogs il intervs ports still PREM 8:76-79 Feb 1995

ANGST ESSEN SEELE AUF f (Ali d Fassbinder, Rainer Werner 1974 W Ger)
   Ideological Analysis
   Sharma, S. Fassbinder's "Ali" and the politics of subject-formation. bibliog stills PS 14:104-116 n1/2 1994/95

ANGULO, JESUS
   Angulo, J. "El rey Lear." credits NOSFERATU n8:66-67 Feb 1992
   Angulo, J. "El sueno de una noche de verano." credits still NOSFERATU n8:63-64 Feb 1992
   Angulo, J. "La pasion de Juana de Arco." credits stills NOSFERATU n5:60-61 Jan 1991
   Angulo, J. "Otelo." credits NOSFERATU n8:65-66 Feb 1992
   Angulo, J. "Romeo y Julieta." credits still NOSFERATU n8:70-71 Feb 1992
   Angulo, J. Terence Fisher, revisitador de mitos. biog il stills NOSFERATU n6:22-43 Apr 1991
   Angulo, J. and others. Entrevista: Garay, Guerin, Jorda y Portabella. il interv stills NOSFERATU n9:68-87 Jun 1992

ANIMALS IN FILM
   United States
   Slide, A. The Slide area film book notes [Book Reviews]. CLASSIC n237:42-44+ [4p] Mar 1995

ANIMATION See also CLAY ANIMATION; COMPUTER ANIMATION
   Sifianos, G. and McLaren, N. The definition of animation: a letter from Norman McLaren. il ANIMATION J 3:62-66 n2 1995
   Conferences, Institutes, Workshops, etc.
   Dumala, P. Wlochy. il KINO 27:38 Jul 1993
   Festivals
   Gizycki, M. Pan uwalnia sie spod wladzy slugi. il KINO 27:35 Jul 1993
   Sharman, L.F. International Animation Festival, Cardiff, 16-22 May 1994. SCREEN 35:397-399 n4 1994
   History
   Pilling, J. The greatest art condensed [Book Review]. still FILM 4:25 n1 [1995]
   Markets
   Isto, K. Cartoon Forum 1993. il PEILI 17:36-37 n4 1993
   Estonia (since 1992)
   Niskanen, E. Tallinnassa tehdaan taidokasta animaatiota. il still PEILI 17:6-7 n4 1993
   Europe, Eastern
   Socialist Realism
   Lawrence, A. Masculinity in Eastern European animation. stills ANIMATION J 3:32-43 n1 1994
   Finland
   Dubbing
   Salakka, M. Puhumme Suomea. il port still PEILI 18:6-7 n1 1994
   Study and Teaching
   Lehtonen, V.-p. Nimekkaat opettajat ja kova innostus. il PEILI 17:4-5 n4 1993
   Great Britain
   Herpe, N. "Wallace et Gromit." credits still POSITIF n407:24 Jan 1995
   Kemppinen, P. Saarivaltion kummajaiset. still PEILI 17:16 n4 1993
   Sifianos, G. Aardman Animations. il interv stills POSITIF n407:25-28 Jan 1995
   Japan
   Jerrman, T. Splatteria animaation keinoin. stills PEILI 17:17-19 n4 1993
   Merchandising Spin-offs
   Niskanen, E. Pienia pyoreakasvoisia tyttoja. il stills PEILI 17:20-21 n4 1993
   Music
   Larson, R.D. Music for Japanese animation: interview with Hiroshi Miyagawa. il interv port SCN 14:28-31 Mar 1995
   Norway
   Iversen, J. Regissor eller ikke regissor? il interv Z n4:23-25 (n46) 1993
   Jurgens, J.H. Tegnefilmcompagniet. il Z n4:20-22 (n46) 1993
   Poland
   Gizycki, M. Chcialem zatytulowac swoj film "Piotr Dumala." interv port stills KINO 27:36 Jul 1993
   United States
   Advertising. History
   Kaufman, J.B. Good mousekeeping: family-oriented publicity in Disney's golden age. il ANIMATION J 3:78-85 n2 1995
   History
   Canemaker, J. Vladimir Tytla - master animator. biog il ANIMATION J 3:4-30 n1 1994
   Industry
   Brodie, J. Disney wannabes play copycat-and-mouse. il still VARIETY 357:1+ [2p] Jan 2/8 1995
   Narrative Analysis
   Schaffer, W. Klein, Norman. Seven minutes: the life and death of the

ARGENTO, DARIO See also GATTO A NOVE CODE, IL
Boswell, S. Neither Mozart nor Hendrix. il still S&S 5:37 Apr 1995
Gass, L.H. "Ich freue mich ja in dem Sterbenden zu sterben." C(SWITZ)
40:135-152 1994
Retrospectives
Stein, E. Dear Dario. still VILLAGE VOICE 40:60 Feb 7 1995
ARISHA, DER BAR UND DER STEINERNE RING f (d Wenders, Wim 1994 FR Ger)
Reviews
Gandini, L. "Arisha, der Baer und der steinerne Ring." still C FORUM
34:30-31 Sep (n337) 1994
ARISTOPOULOS, KOSTAS See also ENASTROS THOLOS
ARISTOV, VIKTOR See also DOZHDI V OKEANE
ARIZONA COLT f (Man From Nowhere, The d Lupo, Michele 1966 Fr/It/Sp)
Mansell, J. Francesco De Masi. il SCN 14:25-27 Mar 1995
Sound Track Reviews
Deutsch, D.C. "Arizona Colt"; "Johnny Yuma." SCN 14:16 Mar 1995
ARMATAGE, KAY
Armatage, K. "Les silences du palais." still C ACTION n36:24-27 1995
ARMSTRONG, GILLIAN See also LITTLE WOMEN
Francke, L. What are you girls going to do? stills S&S 5:28-29 Apr 1995
ARSENEAULT, BETTIE See also DE RETOUR POUR DE BON
ART AND ARTISTS See also names of artists; DANCE; DRAMA; FILM AND THE ARTS;
LETTRISM; MODERNISM; MUSIC; PHOTOGRAPHY; POSTMODERNISM; REALISM; SOCIALIST
REALISM; SURREALISM
Hanet, K. Walker, John A. Art and artists on screen [Book Review]. MEDIA
INFO AUSTRALIA n75:171 Feb 1995
France
Calle-Gruber, M. La chimere du modele. bibliog still CINEMAS 4:72-87 n1
1993
Italy
Comuzio, E. AA. VV. (Auditorium du Louvre): Histoire de l'art et cinema. Les
critofilms de C.L. Ragghianti [Book Review]. C FORUM 34:92 Oct (n338) 1994
ART CINEMA
China (People's Republic, since 1949)
Huang, S. The resurrection of Chinese art films. port CHINA SCREEN n4:33
1994
Lo, Y. Obsession or expectation. port CHINA SCREEN n4:32 1994
Teng, J. A new light on Chinese film. il CHINA SCREEN n4:32 1994
Yu, Q. An escape from desperation. il CHINA SCREEN n4:33 1994
ART FOR TEACHERS OF CHILDREN f (d Montgomery, Jennifer 1995 USA)
Reviews
Cheshire, G. "Art for Teachers of Children." credits VARIETY 358:76-77 Mar
27/Apr 2 1995
ARTHUR, PAUL For film reviews see author under the following titles: FREEDOM ON
MY MIND
[ARTILLERY MAJOR] f (d Zhao, Weiheng 1994 China)
"Artillery Major." credits il stills CHINA SCREEN n4:4-5 1994
ARTISTE, UNE f (d Cournoyer, Michele 1994 Can)
Dionne, M.-C. Droits au coeur. SEQUENCES n175:12 Nov/Dec 1994
Reviews
Blois, M. de. "Une artiste." credits still 24 IMAGES n76:49 Spring 1995
ARTISTS RIGHTS FOUNDATION (United States)
Yonover, N.S. and others. Artists Rights Symposium: three days of
discussion. DGA NEWS 19:26-27+ [3p] n3 1994
Arts and film See FILM AND THE ARTS
ASBOTH, EMIL For film reviews see author under the following titles: HUDSUCKER
PROXY, THE; JUNIOR
Asboth, E. Quentin es John ma este balba mennek. il interv still F VILAG
38:28-29 n4 1995
ASCIONE, GIUSEPPE For film reviews see author under the following titles: DROP
ZONE; JUNIOR; MASK, THE
Ascione, G. The end. still SEGNO n71:57 Jan/Feb 1995
ASHIK-KERIB f (d Paradzhanov, Sergei/Abashidze, Dodo 1989 USSR)
"Asik-Kerib." Ed: Gianroberto Scarcia [Book Review]. il KINO(GF) n56:29 Nov
1994
ASIA IN FILM
United States
Marchetti, G. Pass och forforelse. bibliog stills F HAFTET 22:4-12 n3
(n87) 1994
ASIAN-AMERICANS See also CHINESE-AMERICANS
United States
A recommended filmography of contemporary Asian American titles. filmog
CINEASTE 21:36 n1/2 1995
Feng, P. In search of Asian American cinema. stills CINEASTE 21:32-35 n1/2
1995
ASMARA f (d Poloni, Paolo 1993 Switz)
Reviews
Sauvaget, D. "Asmara." credits still C(SWITZ) 40:217-218 1994
ASPDEN, PETER For film reviews see author under the following titles: FIORILE
ASPHAUG, MARTIN
Og alle var der... ports Z n4:36-38 (n46) 1993
Assassin, The See POINT OF NO RETURN
ASSASSINAT DU DUC DE GUISE, L' f (d Le Bargy, Charles/Calmettes, Andre 1908 Fr)
Cosandey, R. Wo ist die grosse Treppe hingekommen? il stills C(SWITZ)
40:51-74 1994
ASSELBERGHS, HERMAN
Asselberghs, H. "Mediamatic" [Book Review]. il interv BLIMP n30:48-50
Winter 1994
ASSOCIATION OF INDEPENDENT VIDEO AND FILMMAKERS (AIVF, New York, New York)
Lobbying
Wallner, M. Chicago mediamakers get organized. INDEP 18:58 Apr 1995
ASSOCIATION PROFESSIONNELLE DE LA PRESSE CINEMATOGRAPHIQUE BELGE (Belgium)
Membership Lists
Association Professionnelle de la Presse Cinematographique Belge (1995).
table MONITEUR n128:26-27 Feb 1995
ASSOCIAZIONE AUTORI CINEMATOGRAFICI ITALIANI (ANAC, Italy)
Manuelli, M. L'ANAC e lo stato delle cose. il still C NUOVO 43:30-31
Nov/Dec (n352) 1994
ASSOCIAZIONE INSEGNANTI LINGUAGGI CINE-AUDIOVISUALI
Codella, L. and Scalzo, D. Una ipotesi di lavoro per il centenario del

cinema. still C NUOVO 43:58-60 Nov/Dec (n352) 1994
ATALANTE, L' f (d Vigo, Jean 1934 Fr)
Ciment, M. BFI film classics [Book Reviews]. stills POSITIF n408:75-77 Feb
1995
Cultural Context
Faulkner, C. Affective identities: French national cinema and the 1930s.
CAN J F STUD 3:3-23 n2 1994
ATKINS, IRENE KAHN
Codelli, L. David Butler. Interviewed by Irene Kahn Atkins [Book Review].
GRIFFITHIANA n51/52:254 Oct 1994
ATKINSON, MICHAEL For film reviews see author under the following titles:
SPECIALIST, THE
Atkinson, M. Frames of mind. port VILLAGE VOICE 40:74 Feb 28 1995
Atkinson, M. Girls! Girls! Girls! il MOVIELINE 6:56-60+ [6p] Mar 1995
Atkinson, M. Into the underground. VILLAGE VOICE 40:66+ [2p] Mar 28 1995
Atkinson, M. Jane Fonda in "Klute." still MOVIELINE 6:82 Apr 1995
Atkinson, M. Mel Gibson in "Gallipoli." still MOVIELINE 6:80 Mar 1995
ATTALI, JACQUES
Attali, J. Hollywood vs. Europe: the next round. il JOURNAL WGA 7:26-27
Feb 1994
ATTENBOROUGH, RICHARD See also GANDHI; SHADOWLANDS
Mazierska, E. "Cienista dolina." biog credits filmog FSP 40:10 n3 (n757)
1994
Richard Attenborough. biog filmog il port still STARS n21:[3-6] Winter 1995
AU NOM DU CHRIST f (d Gnoan, M'Bala Roger 1994 Ivory Coast)
Reviews
Thirard, P.L. "Au nom du Christ." POSITIF n408:56 Feb 1995
AU PAYS DES ORANGES f (d Gitai, Amos 1994 Fr)
Reviews
Loffreda, P. "Au pays des oranges." still C FORUM 34:33 Sep (n337) 1994
AUBERT, ELISABETH See also REGARDE-MOI
AUBIER, PASCAL See also FILS DE GASCOGNE, LE
AUCTIONS
United States
Music. Sound Tracks
Murray, R.M. The adventures of Recordman. il F SCORE MONTHLY n38:5-6 Oct
1993
Posters
Vintage items sold at auction. stat CLASSIC n237:12 Mar 1995
AUDE, FRANCOISE For film reviews see author under the following titles: LOU N'A
PAS DIT NON; PISTE DU TELEGRAPHE, LA
Aude, F. Creteil. still POSITIF n409:64 Mar 1995
Aude, F. Des films pendant 40 ans [Book Reviews]. il POSITIF n409:69-71
Mar 1995
Aude, F. (Deux) 250 cineastes europeens d'aujourd'hui. Sous la direction de
Gilles Garcia [Book Review]. POSITIF n409:73 Mar 1995
Aude, F. Entretien avec Nicole Garcia. il interv stills POSITIF n407:15-20
Jan 1995
Aude, F. Entretien avec Noemie Lvovsky. il interv stills POSITIF
n408:39-42 Feb 1995
Aude, F. "Les cent et une nuits" d'Agnes Varda: chronique d'un tournage. Par
Bernard Bastide [Book Review]. il POSITIF n409:71 Mar 1995
AUDERLITZKY, CHRISTA
Auderlitzky, C. Vom netten Mariandl zur schamlosen Annabella. F KUNST
n144:50-55 1994
AUDIENCE See also POPULAR CULTURE; SPECTATORSHIP
Recollections
Masson, A. Le spectateur nocturne. Les ecrivains au cinema. Par Jerome
Prieur [Book Review]. POSITIF n408:79 Feb 1995
Austria
Frey, M. Kulturstatistik 1992 [Book Review]. F KUNST n144:75-76 1994
Psychoanalytic Analysis
Reichert, H. Film und Kino. Die Maschinerie des Sehens. F KUNST n144:23-34
1994
Hungary
Kovacs, A.B. Krem torta nelkul. still F VILAG 38:4-5 n2 1995
United States
Recollections
Zemeckis, R. Guilty pleasures. port stills F COM 31:66-69 Jan/Feb 1995
AUDIENCE, CHILDREN
Finland
Comedy Film. Research
Vaisanen, M. Koululaisnaytoksessa laulettiin Dannya. il still PEILI 18:29
n2 1994
AUDIENCE RESEARCH
Canada
Jeffrey, L. Rethinking audiences for cultural industries: implications for
Canadian research. bibliog stat tables CAN J COM 19:495-522 n3/4 1994
Great Britain
Theory
Stacey, J. Hollywood memories. SCREEN 35:317-335 n4 1994
India
Stern, J. Sara Dickey. Cinema and the urban poor in South India [Book
Review]. STUDIES POP CULT 17:102 n1 1994
United States
Effects of Film. Pornography and Obscenity
Allen, M. and others. Exposure to pornography and acceptance of rape myths.
bibliog stat tables J COMM 45:5-26 n1 1995
Gunther, A.C. Overrating the X-rating: the third-person perception and
support for censorship of pornography. bibliog stat tables J COMM 45:27-38
n1 1995
Exhibition
Austin, B.A. Audience research for exhibitors. il BOXOFFICE 131:114-117
Apr 1995
AUDIENCE, WOMEN
Austria
Hass, F. Der weibliche Blick - Der Blick aufs Weib. F KUNST n144:43-49 1994
United States
Feminism
Petzall, J. Want to see more work by independents? still ANGLES 2:6-7 n4

AUDIENCE, WOMEN
  United States
  (continued)
    1995
AUDIENCE, YOUTH
  Effects of Film
    Violence in Film
Peretie, O. Kell-e gyilkossaggal vadolnunk Hollywoodot? stills F VILAG
38:37-39 n1 1995
  Europe, Western
    Government Regulation
Brudny, W. Jugendmedienschutz in Europa. table MEDIEN 38:376-377 n6 1994
Audio See subject headings beginning with SOUND (e.g. SOUND RECORDERS AND
RECORDING)
AUDLEY, PAUL
Audley, P. Cultural industries policy: objectives, formulation, and
evaluation. bibliog CAN J COM 19:317-352 n3/4 1994
AUERSALO, TEEMU
Hanninen, S. and Auersalo, T. Animaatiota Italialaisittain. still PEILI
17:39 n4 1993
AUGUST, BILLE See also HOUSE OF THE SPIRITS, THE
AULETTA, KEN
Auletta, K. Redstone's secret weapon. il NEW YORKER 70:46-52+ [17p] Jan 16
1995
AUMONT, JACQUES
Jaubert, J.-C. Sous la direction de J. Aumont, A. Gaudreault, M. Marie.
Histoire du cinema, nouvelles approaches [Book Review]. CAN J F STUD
1:91-92 n1 1990
AUNE, KINE
Iversen, J. Regissor eller ikke regissor? il interv Z n4:23-25 (n46) 1993
AUSTER, PAUL See also BLUE IN THE FACE
AUSTIN, BRUCE A.
Austin, B.A. Audience research for exhibitors. il BOXOFFICE 131:114-117
Apr 1995
AUSTIN, MICHAEL See also PRINCESS CARABOO
Australia See as a subheading under individual subject headings See AUSTRALIAN
FILM COMMISSION; FILM AUSTRALIA PTY LTD.
AUSTRALIAN FILM COMMISSION
Murray, S. Australian Film Commission. stat table C PAPERS n102:24-25 Dec
1994
Murray, S. Cathy Robinson. interv port C PAPERS n102:26-31+ [7p] Dec 1994
Murray, S. Tim Read. interv port stat C PAPERS n102:36-39+ [6p] Dec 1994
  Aborigines in Film Industry
Dutchak, P. Wal Saunders. port stat C PAPERS n102:44+ [2p] Dec 1994
  Marketing
Urban, A.L. Sue Murray. interv port C PAPERS n102:40-43 Dec 1994
Austria See as a subheading under individual subject headings
AUTEUR THEORY
  Europe
Adagio, C. Per un sano e urgente rilancio del cinema europeo. stills C
NUOVO 43:25-27 Nov/Dec (n352) 1994
  Italy
Ellero, R. Fuochi di paglia? still SEGNO n63:22 Sep/Oct 1993
AUTHORSHIP THEORY
Russell, C. The life and death of authorship in Wim Wenders' 'The State of
Things." scenario CAN J F STUD 1:15-28 n1 1990
  United States
Brill, L. "The African Queen" and John Huston's filmmaking. CJ 34:3-21 n2
1995
Polan, D. Reflections in a male eye: John Huston and the American
experience. Edited by Gaylyn Studlar and David Desser [Book Review]. F
CRITICISM 19:103-108 n2 1994/95
  Cinematographers
Storaro, V. The right to sign ourselves as "authors of cinematography."
AMCIN 76:96 Feb 1995
AUTOBIOGRAPHY
  Documentary Film
Odin, R. Le documentaire interieur. Travail du JE et mise en phase dans
"Lettres d'amour en Somalie." bibliog still CINEMAS 4:82-100 n2 1994
AUTOMOBILES IN FILM
  United States
Hogan, D.J. Races, chases & crashes. By Dave Mann and Ron Main [Book
Review]. il F FAX n48:12 Jan/Feb 1995
AVANT-GARDE FILM See also EXPERIMENTAL FILM; INDEPENDENT FILM
  Screenplays
The script issue. MILLENNIUM n25:5-7 Summer 1991
  Poland
    Festivals
Antal, I. A szem es a ful. stills F VILAG 38:60-61 n1 1995
  United States
Higgins, G. and others. Grisled roots. interv ports MILLENNIUM n26:56-66
Fall 1992
    History
Porton, R. Review of David James: allegories of cinema [Book Review]. il
MILLENNIUM n25:114-120 Summer 1991
AVARY, ROGER See also KILLING ZOE
AVATI, PUPI See also DICHIARAZIONI D'AMORE
AVNET, JON See also WAR, THE
AVONDOLA, CARLO For film reviews see author under the following titles:
PROFESSIONAL, THE
Avondola, C. Una faccia splatter. stills SEGNO n72:30-31 Mar/Apr 1995
AVVENTURA, L' f (d Antonioni, Michelangelo 1960 Fr/It)
Schenk, I. Natur und Anti-Natur in den Filmen von Michelangelo Antonioni.
C(SWITZ) 40:175-193 1994
AWARDS See also COMMENDATIONS; FESTIVALS; POLLS AND SURVEYS
  Belgium
    Prix Joseph Plateau 1994
Prix Joseph Plateau. MONITEUR n126:26 Dec 1994

  Canada
    Quebec. Prix Albert-Tessier 1994
Elia, M. Le Prix Albert-Tessier a Pierre Perrault. port SEQUENCES n175:5
Nov/Dec 1994
  Europe
    European Film Academy 1994
(Siebente) 7. Europaeischer Filmpreis - FELIX. still KINO(GF) n56:2 Nov
1994
  France
    Academie des Arts et Techniques du Cinema 1995
Les nominations aux Cesar. MONITEUR n127:27-28 Jan 1995
Williams, M. "Sauvages" snatches the Cesar top pic title. VARIETY 358:34
Mar 6/12 1995
  Great Britain
    British Academy of Film and Television Arts 1995
Dawtrey, A. "Weddings" waltzes away with 11 BAFTA noms. VARIETY 358:66 Feb
20/26 1995
  Italy
    Cinema Nuovo 1994
Premio "Cinema Nuovo"-Pasinetti 1992/1993. port C NUOVO 43:3 Nov/Dec (n352)
1994
  New Zealand
    New Zealand Film & Television Awards Society 1995
May, S. Film & TV awards date confirmed. ONFILM [12]:20 n2 1995
  Poland
    Komitet Kinematografii 1993
Laterna Magica. REZYSER n15:1 1993
  United States
Bart, P. Of laurels and lepers. il VARIETY 358:6+ [2p] Mar 6/12 1995
O'Steen, K. Even psychic friends can't help predict Oscar winners. table
VARIETY 358:7+ [2p] Mar 20/26 1995
    Academy of Motion Picture Arts and Sciences
Dwyer, E. Hollywood's emotional high. ports VARIETY 357:63+ [2p] Jan 9/15
1995
Gaydos, S. Oscar's prop. 187. still VARIETY 357:68+ [2p] Jan 9/15 1995
Jones, M.F. "From where I sit..." il port BOXOFFICE 131:94-96 Apr 1995
Levy, E. How to win the Oscar. still VARIETY 357:62+ [2p] Jan 2/8 1995
Moore, D.S. Foreign influence is felt at Oscars. still VARIETY 357:68-69
Jan 9/15 1995
O'Steen, K. The sound and the jury. VARIETY 358:13+ [2p] Mar 6/12 1995
Pond, S. Paltry pleasures. il MOVIELINE 6:32 Apr 1995
Pond, S. Putting it together. il PREM 8:109+ [24p] Apr 1995
    Academy of Motion Picture Arts and Sciences. History
Bona, D. Boys' night out. il ports PREM 8:98-101 Apr 1995
Dwyer, E. Long history of protest, controversy. il VARIETY 357:60+ [2p]
Jan 2/8 1995
Hindes, A. Surprise endings highlight actress award competition. port
VARIETY 357:60+ [2p] Jan 2/8 1995
Moore, D.S. Oscars reflect, record history. still VARIETY 357:64 Jan 9/15
1995
Oscar is not strictly made in good ol' USA. still VARIETY 357:71 Jan 2/8
1995
Winner rarely takes all. stat table VARIETY 358:18 Feb 20/26 1995
    Academy of Motion Picture Arts and Sciences 1944
Ellenberger, A.R. Journey for Margaret's Oscar. il ports stills CLASSIC
n237:bet p32 and 33 [pC12-C13] Mar 1995
    Academy of Motion Picture Arts and Sciences 1995
Ansen, D. Why did Oscar drop the ball on "Hoop Dreams"? stills NEWSWK
125:71-72 Mar 27 1995
Corliss, R. How the winner lost. still TIME 145:66 Feb 27 1995
Evans, G. Oscar rings in new era of indie chic. stills VARIETY 358:1+ [2p]
Feb 20/26 1995
Goldman, W. Anything but "Gump." stills NEW YORK 28:32-33 Jan 30 1995
Goldman, W. What should win Best Picture? il PREM 8:96-97 Apr 1995
Klady, L. Foreign-language Oscar speaks tongue of its own. stat VARIETY
358:11+ [2p] Feb 6/12 1995
Klady, L. Oscar's gold standards. il VARIETY 358:11+ [2p] Feb 20/26 1995
(Nineteen) 1995 Academy Award nomination checklist. il port stills FJ
98:46-47 Mar 1995
Oscar predix. il F COM 31:7 Mar/Apr 1995
O'Steen, K. Even psychic friends can't help predict Oscar winners. table
VARIETY 358:7+ [2p] Mar 20/26 1995
O'Steen, K. Kodak, Vlahos honored with tech Oscars. VARIETY 357:28 Jan 9/15
1995
O'Steen, K. Oscar night hits the Internet. VARIETY 358:26 Feb 13/19 1995
O'Steen, K. and Brodie, J. Acad rebounds after "Hoop" airball. il VARIETY
358:11+ [2p] Feb 20/26 1995
Russo, T. Unsung Oscars. il ports still PREM 8:108 Apr 1995
Travers, P. Controversy in three colors. stills ROLLING STONE n702:80 Feb
23 1995
Weiner, R. Behind the illusion. VARIETY 358:6-7 Feb 13/19 1995
Weiner, R. F/X Oscar pits rookie vs. veteran. VARIETY 358:14 Feb 20/26 1995
    Academy of Motion Picture Arts and Sciences 1995. Film Lists
Acad sees the "Forrest" for the Oscars. VARIETY 358:18+ [2p] Feb 20/26 1995
    American Cinema Editors 1995
Cox, D. "Hoop," "Forrest" make the film editors' cut. VARIETY 358:24 Mar
27/Apr 2 1995
Eddie Award nominations out. VARIETY 358:38 Feb 13/19 1995
    Chicago Film Critics Circle 1995
Klady, L. "Dreams" takes Chi crix nod. VARIETY 358:19 Mar 20/26 1995
    Directors Guild of America 1994
Deutsch, J. Meet the nominees: theatrical motion pictures. ports DGA NEWS
19:19-23 n2 1994
Klady, L. DGA fetes Ivory with Griffith. port VARIETY 358:18 Feb 6/12 1995
    Gay & Lesbian Alliance Against Defamation 1995
Evans, G. GLAAD honcho blasts talkers at awards. VARIETY 358:10 Mar 20/26
1995
    Hollywood Foreign Press Association 1995
O'Steen, K. "Gump," "Fiction" take over Globes. il stills VARIETY 357:32+
[2p] Jan 2/8 1995

International Documentary Association 1994
Heuring, D. Real life through the lens. AMCIN 76:28-30 Jan 1995
        Mystery Writers of America 1993
The 1993 Edgar Awards. il ARMCHAIR DET 26:86 n3 1993
        Mystery Writers of America 1994
The 1994 Edgar Awards. il ports ARMCHAIR DET 27:318-319 n3 1994
        National Association of Theatre Owners 1995
The 1995 honorees. ports BOXOFFICE 131:bet p82 and 83 [pSW20-SW22] Apr 1995
        National Society of Film Critics 1995
McCarthy, T. Nat'l Society crix fall for "Fiction." VARIETY 357:30 Jan 9/15
        1995
        New York Film Critics' Circle 1994
Godard, J.-L. Award-winning correspondence. port F COM 31:2 Mar/Apr 1995
        Writers Guild of America 1995
And the nominees for the 47th Annual WGA Awards are... JOURNAL WGA 8:41 Mar
        1995
Cox, D. Eclectic pic mix makes the Writers Guild grade. still VARIETY
        358:6 Feb 13/19 1995
Evans, G. "Gump's" glory continues. VARIETY 358:24 Mar 27/Apr 2 1995
AWFULLY BIG ADVENTURE, AN f (d Newell, Mike 1995 Gt Br)
        Reviews
Kemp, P. "An Awfully Big Adventure." credits S&S 5:38 Apr 1995
AXELROD, NATHAN
The Nathan Axelrod collection, volume 1: Moledet Productions, 1927-1934,
        Carmel newsreels, series 1, 1935-1948. Ed: Amy Kronish, Edith Falk and Paula
        Weiman-Kelman [Book Review]. il KINO(GF) n56:31 Nov 1994
AXELSSON, SUN
Axelsson, S. I filmfralsta poeters sallskap [Book Review]. il CHAPLIN
        36:62 n6 (n255) 1994/95
AZZALIN, CLAUDIA For film reviews see author under the following titles: NO
        SMOKING; SMOKING
Azzalin, C. L'amore di molti. stills SEGNO n71:65-66 Jan/Feb 1995
Azzalin, C. Storie adolescenti. stills SEGNO n71:60-61 Jan/Feb 1995
BMG Entertainment See BERTELSMANN MUSIC GROUP (BMG)
B MOVIE
        United States
                History
Muscio, G. The commerce of classicism [Book Review]. Q REV F & VIDEO
        15:57-69 n3 1994
Scalera, B. Over my dead body. Lee Server [Book Review]. SCARLET STREET
        n17:99 Winter 1995
                Western Film
Anez, N. Westerns. stills FIR 45:18-27 Nov/Dec 1994
BAB EL-OUED CITY f (d Allouache, Merzak 1994 Fr/Algeria/FR Ger/Switz)
        Reviews
Derobert, E. "Bab el-Oued City." credits stills POSITIF n407:38-39 Jan
        1995
BABY I WILL MAKE YOU SWEAT f (d Hein, Birgit 1995 FR Ger)
        Reviews
Stratton, D. "Baby I Will Make You Sweat." credits VARIETY 358:66 Mar 6/12
        1995
BABY'S DAY OUT f (d Johnson, Patrick Read 1994 USA)
Noel, P. "Bebe part en vadrouille." bibliog credits stills GRAND ANGLE
        n176:3-4 Nov 1994
BACCARO, SALVATORE
Avondola, C. Una faccia splatter. stills SEGNO n72:30-31 Mar/Apr 1995
BACH, JEAN See also GREAT DAY IN HARLEM, A
BACH, STEVEN
Bach, S. "Legend to leper" [Book Review]. port F COM 31:82-83+ [3p]
        Mar/Apr 1995
Back lighting See LIGHTING
BACK OF BEYOND f (d Robertson, Michael 1995 Australia)
        Cinematography
Urban, A.L. Michael Robertson's "Back of Beyond." il stills C PAPERS
        n102:12-18 Dec 1994
BACK STREET f (d Stahl, John M. 1932 USA)
        Psychoanalytic Analysis
White, S. I burn for him: female masochism and the iconography of melodrama
        in Stahl's "Back Street" (1932). bibliog stills PS 14:59-80 n1/2 1994/95
BACKBEAT f (d Softley, Iain 1993 Gt Br)
        Reviews
Loffreda, P. "Backbeat." credits still C FORUM 34:76 Sep (n337) 1994
BACON, HENRY
Andersson, L.G. Ricoeur och film [Book Review]. F HAFTET 22:58 n3 (n87)
        1994
BACON, KEVIN
Sorensen, H. Kevin Bacon wants to be the guy. il ports stills PREM 8:70-73
        Mar 1995
BACON, LLOYD See also (FORTY-SECOND) 42ND STREET
BACSO, PETER See also MEGINT TANU; TANU, A
Zsugan, I. Pelikan ladikjan. il interv stills F VILAG 38:26-28 n1 1995
BAD BOY BUBBY f (d Heer, Rolf de 1993 Australia/It)
        Reviews
"Bad Boy Bubby." still FATAL VISIONS n17:9 1994
BAD COMPANY f (d Harris, Damian 1995 USA)
        Reviews
Coleman, B. "Bad Company." VILLAGE VOICE 40:55 Jan 31 1995
McDonagh, M. "Bad Company." credits FJ 98:66-67 Mar 1995
Williams, E. "Bad Company." still BOXOFFICE 131:bet p125 and 144 [pR36]
        Apr 1995
BAD GIRLS f (d Kaplan, Jonathan 1994 USA)
Dowell, P. The mythology of the western: Hollywood perspectives on race and
        gender in the nineties. stills CINEASTE 21:6-10 n1/2 1995
        Sound Track Reviews
Pugliese, R. Segnodischi. stills SEGNO n71:71 Jan/Feb 1995
        Reviews
Molinari, M. "Bad Girls." credits stills SEGNO n71:54+ [2p] Jan/Feb 1995

BADGLEY, CHRISTINE See also BLACK IS... BLACK AIN'T
BADHAM, JOHN See also ANOTHER STAKEOUT; DROP ZONE; POINT OF NO RETURN
BADIR, SEMIR
Badir, S. "India Song" ou le temps tragique. bibliog scenario still
        CINEMAS 5:123-133 n1/2 1994
BAER, GREGOIRE See also FAITS DIVERS
BAERT, RENEE
Baert, R. Skirting the issue. stills SCREEN 35:354-373 n4 1994
BAGH, PETER VON
Bagh, P. von. Memories of Bologna. J F PRES n49:43-45 Oct 1994
BAGLEY, CHRISTOPHER
Bagley, C. The pursuit of happiness. il PREM 8:64-67 Apr 1995
BAILEY, JOHN
Bailey, J. Bangbangbangbang, ad nauseum. il DGA NEWS 19:12+ [3p] n6
        1994/95
Fisher, B. and Pizzello, C. "In the Line of Fire": an action film for
        existentialists. il stills AMCIN 74:36-40+ [7p] Sep 1993
BAIRD, ROBERT
Baird, R. "Going Indian" through "Dances With Wolves." bibliog still
        F&HIST 23:92-102+ [12p] n1/4 1993
Bait, The See APPAT, L'
BAJON, FILIP See also LEPIEJ BYC PIEKNA I BOGATA
BAKACS, TIBOR SETTENKEDO
Bakacs, T.S. Csaladi vallalkozas. interv still F VILAG 38:46-47 n3 1995
Bakacs, T.S. Es a vonat megy... interv port stills F VILAG 38:14-16 n4
        1995
BAKER, FORREST
Campbell, C. Screen sex & violence? Just say none. il port stills
        BOXOFFICE 131:46+ [4p] Apr 1995
BAKER, JOSEPHINE
Stuart, A. Looking at Josephine Baker. WOMEN 5:137-143 n2 1994
BAKER, ROY WARD
Dixon, W.W. Twilight of the empire: the films of Roy Ward Baker part III.
        interv stills CLASSIC n236:bet p32 and 33 [pC12+ (4p)] Feb 1995
BAKER, WILLIAM
Meisel, M. Baker leads MPA into new era of growth. port FJ 98:16+ [2p]
        Jan/Feb 1995
BAKERMAN, JANE S.
Bakerman, J.S. Midnight baby. By Wendy Hornsby [Book Review]. il ARMCHAIR
        DET 27:120 n1 1994
BAKHTIN, MIKHAIL
Sallmann, B. Karl Sierek. Ophuels: Bachtin. Versuch mit Film zu reden [Book
        Review]. BLIMP n30:73 Winter 1994
BAKISH, DAVID
Slide, A. The Slide area film book notes [Book Reviews]. CLASSIC
        n237:42-44+ [4p] Mar 1995
BALABAN, BOB See also LAST GOOD TIME, THE
BALASKO, JOSIANE See also GAZON MAUDIT
BALDONI, SANDRO See also STRANE STORIE - RACCONTI DI FINE SECOLO
Santucci, E. Obiettivo festival. il SEGNO n71:19-23 Jan/Feb 1995
BALDWIN, ALEC
"Ucieczka gangstera." biogs credits filmogs FSP 40:11 n4 (n758) 1994
BALIO, TINO
Muscio, G. The commerce of classicism [Book Review]. Q REV F & VIDEO
        15:57-69 n3 1994
BALL, STEVEN
Ball, S. The Alexander enigma. il stills CANTRILL'S FMNTS n73/74:15-18 May
        1994
BALLAD OF LITTLE JO, THE f (d Greenwald, Maggie 1993 USA)
Dowell, P. The mythology of the western: Hollywood perspectives on race and
        gender in the nineties. stills CINEASTE 21:6-10 n1/2 1995
BALLARD, BAMBI
Ballard, B. I sat glued to the screen. still VERTIGO (UK) 1:43 n4 1994/95
BALLARD, CARROLL See also WIND
Ballet See DANCE
BALLET f (d Wiseman, Frederick 1995 USA)
        Reviews
Cheshire, G. "Ballet." credits VARIETY 358:76 Mar 27/Apr 2 1995
Tobias, T. "Ballet." still VILLAGE VOICE 40:66+ [2p] Mar 28 1995
BALLON D'OR, LE f (d Doukoure, Cheik 1994 Fr/Guinea)
        Reviews
Bloech, M. Merz-Kinderfilm. credits still MEDIEN 38:374-375 n6 1994
BALSMEYER, JEFF
Berthome, J.-P. and Kohn, O. Entretien avec Jeff Balsmeyer. il interv still
        POSITIF n407:85-89 Jan 1995
BALZAC, HONORE DE
Calle-Gruber, M. La chimere du modele. bibliog still CINEMAS 4:72-87 n1
        1993
BANDIT QUEEN f (d Kapur, Shekhar 1994 India/Gt Br)
Cunha, U. da. "Bandit" set for Indian pic screens. VARIETY 358:32 Mar 20/26
        1995
Longfellow, B. "The Bandit Queen." stills C ACTION n36:10-16 1995
Prasad, U. Woman on the edge. stills S&S 5:14-17 Feb 1995
        Reviews
Kemp, P. "Bandit Queen." credits S&S 5:40 Feb 1995
Padgaonkar, L. "The Bandit Queen." credits CINEMAYA n25/26:86
        Autumn/Winter 1994/95
BANG-HANSEN, PAL
Og alle var der... ports Z n4:36-38 (n46) 1993
Bangladesh See as a subheading under individual subject headings
BANI'ETEMAD, RAKHSHAN See also NARGESS
Amiri, N. Rakhshan Bani'etemad. il stills CINEMAYA n25/26:42-43
        Autumn/Winter 1994/95
BANN, RICHARD W.
Adamson, J. and others. Forgotten laughter. credits port stills
        GRIFFITHIANA n51/52:170-197 Oct 1994
Adamson, J. and others. La fabbrica della risata. credits port stills
        GRIFFITHIANA n51/52:170-197 Oct 1994
BANYERA, LA f (d Garay, Jesus 1989 Sp)
Casas, Q. Jesus Garay: la linea de sombra. biog il stills NOSFERATU

n9:26-37 Jun 1992
Garay, J. "La banera." credits stills NOSFERATU n9:90 Jun 1992
BARANSKI, ANDRZEJ   See also DWA KSIEZYCE
BARBER, LYNN
Barber, L. Mad about Nigel. il VANITY FAIR 58:102-105 Jan 1995
BARCELONA   f (d Stillman, Whit 1994 USA)
   Marketing
Brodie, J. Distribs' marketing debate becomes tale of 3 cities. stat
   VARIETY 358:9+ [2p] Feb 13/19 1995
   Reviews
Elia, M. "Barcelona." SEQUENCES n174:44 Sep/Oct 1994
James, N. "Barcelona." credits still S&S 5:41 Feb 1995
Kissin, E.H. "Barcelona." FIR 45:59-60 Nov/Dec 1994
Vasse, C. "Barcelona." POSITIF n408:56 Feb 1995
BARDOT, BRIGITTE
Elia, M. Sacres monstres! il ports SEQUENCES n175:58-59 Nov/Dec 1994
BARER, BURL
Breen, J.L. Barer, Burl. The Saint: a complete history in print, radio, film
   and television of Leslie Charteris' Robin Hood of crime, Simon Templar,
   1928-1992 [Book Review]. ARMCHAIR DET 27:222-223 n2 1994
BARKER, CLIVE   See also LORD OF ILLUSIONS
Beeler, M. Clive Barker's "Lord of Illusions." il stills C FANTAS 26:23-26
   n3 1995
Beeler, M. Horror visionary. il port stills C FANTAS 26:16-17+ [9p] n3
   1995
Beeler, M. Producing horror in Hollywood. il stills C FANTAS 26:28-29 n3
   1995
Beeler, M. Surrealist artist. il C FANTAS 26:18 n3 1995
Beeler, M. "The Thief of Always." il C FANTAS 26:20-21 n3 1995
McDonagh, M. Barker works horrific magic with UA's "Lord of Illusions." il
   still FJ 98:14+ [2p] Jan/Feb 1995
BARKERS
      Canada
         Quebec. History
Gaudreault, A. and Lacasse, G. Fonctions et origines du bonimenteur du
   cinema des premiers temps. bibliog il CINEMAS 4:132-147 n1 1993
BARLOW, HELEN
Barlow, H. Pur ekstase. stills F&K n7:20-21 1993
Barlow, H. Slik er det a vaere barnestjerne. stills F&K n1:16-18 1994
BARNABO DELLE MONTAGNE   f (d Brenta, Mario 1994 It/Switz/Fr)
   Reviews
Gili, J.A. "Barnabo des montagnes." credits still POSITIF n409:39-40 Mar
   1995
Barnabo of the Mountains   See BARNABO DELLE MONTAGNE
BARON, GYORGY
Baron, G. A kerdezo [Book Review]. il F VILAG 38:44-45 n3 1995
BAROTANYI, ZOLTAN   For film reviews see author under the following titles:
   PUPPET MASTERS, THE; RENAISSANCE MAN
BARRAULT, JEAN-LOUIS
Dodsfall. obits F&K n1:34 1994
BARRETT, KAY BROWN
Transition. obit NEWSWK 125:45 Jan 30 1995
BARROT, OLIVIER
Bonneville, L. Gueules d'atmosphere: les acteurs du cinema francais
   (1929-1959). Par Olivier Barrot et Raymond Chirat [Book Review]. il
   SEQUENCES n174:59 Sep/Oct 1994
BARRY LYNDON   f (d Kubrick, Stanley 1975 Gt Br)
Fitzgerald, L. and Keep, C.J. "Barry Lyndon" demembre: la perte de
   l'histoire dans le film de Stanley Kubrick. bibliog still CINEMAS 4:23-33
   n1 1993
BARSON, MICHAEL
Barson, M. Hollywood censored: morality codes, Catholics and movies. By
   Gregory D. Black [Book Review]. DGA NEWS 19:59 n6 1994/95
Barson, M. Hollywood's first choices: how the greatest casting decisions
   were made. By Jeff Burkhart & Bruce Stuart [Book Review]. DGA NEWS 20:42-43
   n1 1995
Barson, M. Step right up! I'm gonna scare the pants off America. By William
   Castle [Book Review]. DGA NEWS 19:34+ [2p] n2 1994
Barson, M. The films of John Cassavetes: pragmatism, modernism, and the
   movies. By Ray Carney [Book Review]. DGA NEWS 19:29-30 n3 1994
Barson, M. Turnaround: a memoir. By Milos Forman and Jan Novak [Book
   Review]. DGA NEWS 19:32 n2 1994
BART, PETER
Bart, P. Building bridges. il VARIETY 358:4+ [2p] Mar 13/19 1995
Bart, P. H'wood's slow shooters. il VARIETY 358:9+ [2p] Feb 13/19 1995
Bart, P. Newtering the arts. il VARIETY 358:6+ [2p] Feb 6/12 1995
Bart, P. Of laurels and lepers. il VARIETY 358:6+ [2p] Mar 6/12 1995
Bart, P. Squirmy over sex. il VARIETY 358:6+ [2p] Feb 20/26 1995
Bart, P. Suiting up. il VARIETY 358:4+ [2p] Mar 20/26 1995
Bart, P. The Roth regimen. il VARIETY 358:8+ [2p] Feb 27/Mar 5 1995
BARTALOTTA, GIANFRANCO
Bartalotta, G. Gli esercizi teatrali di Mario Verdone. C SUD 33:58
   Jul/Aug/Sep (n113) 1994
BARTHOLOMEW, DAVID   For film reviews see author under the following titles:
   FARINELLI: IL CASTRATO; OKNO V PARIZH; PAODA SHUANG DENG
BARYLLI, GABRIEL   See also HONIGMOND
BASE, GIULIO   See also POLIZIOTTI
BASIC INSTINCT   f (d Verhoeven, Paul 1992 USA)
   Semiotic Analysis
Namaste, K. Le deplacement et la crise du reel: la socio-semiotique et la
   biphobie de "Basic Instinct." bibliog scenario CINEMAS 3:223-238 n2/3 1993
BASINGER, KIM
"Ucieczka gangstera." biogs credits filmogs FSP 40:11 n4 (n758) 1994
   Lawsuits
O'Steen, K. Settlement seen in "Boxing" case. VARIETY 358:20 Mar 13/19 1995
BASKETBALL DIARIES, THE   f (d Kalvert, Scott 1995 USA)
Frankel, M. The young lion. il port stills MOVIELINE 6:42-46+ [8p] Mar
   1995
Neff, R. Kalvert shoots and scores in "Basketball Diaries' debut. il interv
   FJ 98:14+ [2p] Mar 1995

   Adaptations
Stewart, J. The street side of the game. interv ports still INTERV
   25:98-99 Apr 1995
   Reviews
Farber, S. Teen tales. still MOVIELINE 6:42-43 Apr 1995
Greene, R. "The Basketball Diaries." still BOXOFFICE 131:bet p125 and 144
   [pR22-R23] Apr 1995
McCarthy, T. "The Basketball Diaries." credits still VARIETY 358:74 Feb
   6/12 1995
Travers, P. He shoots, he scores. il still ROLLING STONE n704:127-128 Mar
   23 1995
BASSA, JOAN
Freixas, R. and Bassa, J. Frankenstein: cadenas a la Creacion? il stills
   NOSFERATU n6:56-65 Apr 1991
BASSETTI, SERGIO
Bassetti, S. E. John - H. Zimmer - T. Rice: "The Lion King." C FORUM
   34:95-96 Nov (n339) 1994
Bassetti, S. James Newton Howard: "Wyatt Earp." C FORUM 34:95-96 Oct (n338)
   1994
BASSOLI, VINCENZO
Bassoli, V. Alla Ventiduesima Mostra Internazionale del Cinema Libero di
   Bologna. C SUD 33:17-18 Jul/Aug/Sep (n113) 1994
BASTIDE, BERNARD
Aude, F. "Les cent et une nuits" d'Agnes Varda: chronique d'un tournage. Par
   Bernard Bastide [Book Review]. il POSITIF n409:71 Mar 1995
BASTONE, WILLIAM
Bastone, W. La cosa nostra 90210. il stills VILLAGE VOICE 40:27-30 Feb 7
   1995
BATAILLE, SYLVIA
Pagliano, J.-P. Entretien avec Sylvia Bataille. il interv still POSITIF
   n408:90-93 Feb 1995
BATARD DE DIEU, LE   f (d Fechner, Christian 1993 Fr)
   Reviews
Horguelin, T. "Le batard de Dieu." still 24 IMAGES n75:73 Dec/Jan 1994/95
BATTERSBY, MARK E.
Battersby, M.E. Buying the competition. il BOXOFFICE 131:60+ [3p] Apr 1995
BATTIATO, GIACOMO   See also CRONACA DI UN AMORE VIOLATO
BATTIS, JEREMY
Battis, J. Czech film production rests on shaky ground. VARIETY 358:62 Feb
   6/12 1995
BATTLE OF THE RIVER PLATE, THE   f (Pursuit of the Graf Spee d Powell, Michael
   1956 Gt Br)
Combs, R. "Battle of the River Plate." il stills F COM 31:20-22+ [4p]
   Mar/Apr 1995
Battleship Potemkin, The   See BRONENOSETS POTEMKIN
BATTY, LINDA
Batty, L. Index to volume 30, 1994. F COM 31:insert [5p] Mar/Apr 1995
BAUMGOLD, JULIE
Baumgold, J. A graveyard smash. stills ESQUIRE 123:120+ [2p] Jan 1995
Baumgold, J. Midnight in the garden of good and Elvis. il ports ESQUIRE
   123:92-102 Mar 1995
Baumgold, J. Tough guys don't wear underwear. ports ESQUIRE 123:83-87 Feb
   1995
BAUR, GABRIELLE   See also BETTKOENIGIN, DIE
BAUR, PHILIPP JACQUES
Baur, P.J. Ich tue, also bin ich! il C(SWITZ) 40:97-104 1994
BAWDEN, JAMES
Bawden, J. Rhonda Fleming. biog filmog il ports stills FIR 45:6-17 Nov/Dec
   1994
BAXTER, JACK   See also BROTHER MINISTER: THE ASSASSINATION OF MALCOLM X
BAZELON, IRWIN
Hubbard, R. Book reviews [Book Reviews]. F SCORE MONTHLY n40:9 Dec 1993
BAZZONI, ALESSANDRO
Bazzoni, A. Al 46 Festival Internazionale di Locarno due retrospettive.
   stills C SUD 33:20-21 Jul/Aug/Sep (n113) 1994
BEACHAM, FRANK
Beacham, F. Digital artists: reinventing electronic media. il AMCIN
   76:59-60+ [3p] Mar 1995
BEAL, JOHN
Kendall, L. John Beal. interv port F SCORE MONTHLY n36/37:18-19 Aug/Sep
   1993
BEALE, ALISON
Beale, A. Framing culture: criticism and policy in Australia. By Stuart
   Cunningham [Book Reviews]. CAN J COM 19:556-559 n3/4 1994
BEALS, JENNIFER
Hooper, J. Dances with devils. port ESQUIRE 123:42-43 Mar 1995
BEAM, BARBARA
James, C. Barbara Beam and the American dream. il port BOXOFFICE 131:74-77
   Apr 1995
BEAN, JENNIFER M.
Bean, J.M. Couching resistance: women, film and psychoanalytic psychiatry.
   By Janet Walker [Book Review]. VEL LT TRAP n35:85-87 Spring 1995
BEAR, LIZA   For film reviews see author under the following titles: EXOTICA
BEARD, WILLIAM
Beard, W. Cronenberg, flyness, and the other-self. bibliog still CINEMAS
   4:153-173 n2 1994
Beard, W. "Unforgiven" and the uncertainties of the heroic. CAN J F STUD
   3:41-62 n2 1994
BEATTY, WARREN
Brown, C. No love affair. ports PREM 8:46-47+ [3p] Feb 1995
BEAUCHEMIN, ERIC   For film reviews see author under the following titles:
   NAUFRAGOS, LOS; NORTH
BEAUCHEMIN, SERGE
Jean, M. and Loiselle, M.-C. A l'ombre du 7e art. il interv stills 24
   IMAGES n76:4-7+ [7p] Spring 1995
BEAUDRY, DIANE   See also REVE AVEUGLE
BEAULIEU, JANICK   For film reviews see author under the following titles: GRANDE
   COCOMERO, IL; OCTOBRE; ONLY YOU; REVE AVEUGLE; SECRET DE JEROME, LE
Beaulieu, J. Entrevue avec Charles Biname. il interv SEQUENCES n174:15
   Sep/Oct 1994

Beaulieu, J. Le nouveau cinema francais. stills SEQUENCES n174:22-24
    Sep/Oct 1994
BEAUTE DES FEMMES, LA f (d Menard, Robert 1994 Can)
    Reviews
    Elia, M. "La beaute des femmes." SEQUENCES n175:44 Nov/Dec 1994
BEAUTY IN FILM
    Pezzotta, A. La fragilita del brutto. il stills SEGNO n72:24-26 Mar/Apr
    1995
    Italy
    Comuzio, E. Roberto Campari: Il fantasma del bello. Iconologia del cinema
    italiano [Book Review]. il C FORUM 34:93 Nov (n339) 1994
BEAUX SOUVENIRS, LES f (d Mankiewicz, Francis 1981 Can)
    Adaptations
    Viswanathan, J. L'un(e) dort, l'autre pas: la scene de la veille dans les
    scenarios et quelques romans de Rejean Ducharme. bibliog scenario still
    table CINEMAS 5:189-209 n1/2 1994
BEAVER, FRANK
    Oliver Stone: wakeup cinema. Edited by Frank Beaver [Book Review]. il FATAL
    VISIONS n17:32 1994
BEAVER, FRANK E.
    Slide, A. The Slide area film book notes [Book Reviews]. CLASSIC n236:47-49
    Feb 1995
BECK, HENRY CABOT For film reviews see author under the following titles: GREAT
    DAY IN HARLEM, A
    Beck, H.C. A wild one. interv still VILLAGE VOICE 40:60-61 Mar 14 1995
BECKER, HAROLD See also MALICE
BECKER, JACQUES See also VIE EST A NOUS, LA
BECKER, JEAN See also CONTRE L'OUBLI; ELISA
BEDEUR, MICHEL
    Noel, J. Cinema de Verviers (1896-1993). Par Michel Bedeur et Paolo Zagaglia
    [Book Review]. il GRAND ANGLE n177:49-50 Dec 1994
BEELER, MICHAEL
    Beeler, M. Clive Barker's "Lord of Illusions." il stills C FANTAS 26:23-26
    n3 1995
    Beeler, M. El-Aurian heavy. il still C FANTAS 26:23 n2 1995
    Beeler, M. Feature vs. series. il still C FANTAS 26:24-25 n2 1995
    Beeler, M. "Hellraiser IV: Bloodline." il stills C FANTAS 26:10-11+ [3p]
    n2 1995
    Beeler, M. "Hellraiser IV: Bloodline." il stills C FANTAS 26:32-33+ [4p]
    n3 1995
    Beeler, M. Horror visionary. il port stills C FANTAS 26:16-17+ [9p] n3
    1995
    Beeler, M. John Alonzo. il C FANTAS 26:27 n2 1995
    Beeler, M. Kevin Yagher, director. il C FANTAS 26:34 n3 1995
    Beeler, M. "Lord of Illusions." il stills C FANTAS 26:6-7 n2 1995
    Beeler, M. Makeup effects. il still C FANTAS 26:39 n3 1995
    Beeler, M. Pin Head speaks! il port stills C FANTAS 26:36-37 n3 1995
    Beeler, M. Producing horror in Hollywood. il stills C FANTAS 26:28-29 n3
    1995
    Beeler, M. Spock speaks. il stills C FANTAS 26:20-21 n2 1995
    Beeler, M. "Star Trek Generations." il port stills C FANTAS 26:16-17+
    [10p] n2 1995
    Beeler, M. Surrealist artist. il C FANTAS 26:18 n3 1995
    Beeler, M. "The Thief of Always." il C FANTAS 26:20-21 n3 1995
    Beeler, M. Two captains. il still C FANTAS 26:18 n2 1995
BEERY, NOAH, SR.
    Katchmer, G. Remembering the great silents. biogs filmogs port CLASSIC
    n237:35+ [3p] Mar 1995
BEFORE SUNRISE f (d Linklater, Richard 1995 USA)
    Fuller, G. and Linklater, R. Truer than romance? il interv ports INTERV
    25:118-121 Feb 1995
    Horton, R. Offhand enchantment. stills F COM 31:4-5+ [3p] Jan/Feb 1995
    Taubin, A. A sense of place. il VILLAGE VOICE 40:56-57 Feb 7 1995
    Marketing
    Brodie, J. Distribs' marketing debate becomes tale of 3 cities. stat
    VARIETY 358:9+ [2p] Feb 13/19 1995
    Reviews
    Brown, G. Midsummer lite dreams. still VILLAGE VOICE 40:50 Jan 31 1995
    Corliss, R. Slack jawing. still TIME 145:88 Jan 30 1995
    Giles, J. A fine romance. still NEWSWK 125:58 Feb 6 1995
    James, C. "Before Sunrise." BOXOFFICE 131:bet p89 and 96 [pR16] Mar 1995
    Lane, A. Up all night. il NEW YORKER 70:93-95 Jan 30 1995
    Travers, P. Sex and the single slacker. il stills ROLLING STONE n702:79-80
    Feb 23 1995
    Weinstein, W. "Before Sunrise." credits still FJ 98:67 Mar 1995
    Wrathall, J. "Before Sunrise." credits still S&S 5:39 Apr 1995
BEFORE THE RAIN f (d Manchevski, Milcho 1994 It/Gt Br/Fr/Macedonia)
    Ascione, G. The end. still SEGNO n71:57 Jan/Feb 1995
    Crespi, A. "Prima della pioggia." credits stills C FORUM 34:77-79 Oct
    (n338) 1994
    Woodward, R.B. Slav of New York. still VILLAGE VOICE 40:50 Feb 21 1995
    Reviews
    Conforti, A. "Before the Rain." still C FORUM 34:13-14 Sep (n337) 1994
    Hoberman, J. Deepest darkest Europe. still VILLAGE VOICE 40:63 Feb 28 1995
    Lane, A. Balkan homecoming. il NEW YORKER 71:109-111 Mar 13 1995
    Matsumoto, J. "Before the Rain." BOXOFFICE 131:bet p89 and 96 [pR18] Mar
    1995
    Meisel, M. "Before the Rain." credits still FJ 98:63-64 Mar 1995
    Schickel, R. Hollow pity, empty terror. still TIME 145:71-72 Mar 20 1995
    Taggi, P. "Prima della pioggia." credits stills SEGNO n71:56-57 Jan/Feb
    1995
    Travers, P. "Before the Rain." port still ROLLING STONE n704:128 Mar 23
    1995
BEFREIER UND BEFREITE f (Liberators Take Liberties d Sander, Helke 1992 FR Ger)
    Liebman, S. There should be no scissors in your mind. interv port stills
    CINEASTE 21:40-42 n1/2 1995
BEHAR, ANDREW See also TIE-DYED: ROCK 'N ROLL'S MOST DEADICATED FANS
BEHI, RIDHA See also HIRONDELLES NE MEURENT PAS A JERUSALEM, LES
BEHIND THE LENS (United States)
    Krasilovsky, A. A sharper image. il port ANGLES 2:10-11 n4 1995

BEHLMER, RUDY
    Behlmer, R. Directors' paper trails. table DGA NEWS 19:50+ [3p] n6 1994/95
    Turner, G. Memo from Darryl F. Zanuck. By Rudy Behlmer [Book Review]. AMCIN
    74:95 Sep 1993
BEHREND, JEAN
    Behrend, J. ADs, UPMs, directors explain it all at Expo. il DGA NEWS 20:22
    n1 1995
    Behrend, J. DGA goes indie at IFFM. il DGA NEWS 19:24-25 n6 1994/95
BEHRENS, ALFRED See also [UNKNOWN WAR, AN]
    A tizenotezredik pillanat. interv stills F VILAG 38:18-23 n1 1995
BEI KAO BEI, LIAN DUI LIAN f (d Huang, Jianxin 1994 Hong Kong/China)
    Reviews
    Cheng, S. "Bei kao bei, lian dui lian." credits still CINEMAYA
    n25/26:81-82 Autumn/Winter 1994/95
BEINEIX, JEAN-JACQUES See also IP5: L'ILE AUX PACHYDERMS
    Berthome, J.-P. Le "storyboard" en livres [Book Reviews]. POSITIF n407:90+
    [2p] Jan 1995
BELACH, HELGA
    Codelli, L. "Greed." Di Jonathan Rosenbaum [Book Reviews]. GRIFFITHIANA
    n51/52:260 Oct 1994
    "Das Wachsfigurenkabinett." Drehbuch von Henrik Galeen zu Paul Lenis film von
    1923/Waxworks: screenplay by Henrik Galeen for Paul Leni's film in 1923
    [Book Review]. il KINO(GF) n56:31 Nov 1994
BELANGER, FERNAND See also EMOTION DISSONANTE, L'; PASSIFLORA
BELFRAGE, JULIAN
    Obituaries. obits VARIETY 358:188-189 Feb 20/26 1995
Belgium See as a subheading under individual subject headings
BELL, DAVID
    Redman, N. Competing composers [Book Reviews]. DGA NEWS 19:56-57 n6 1994/95
BELL, MONTA
    Birchard, R.S. Monta Bell. biog filmog il stills GRIFFITHIANA n51/52:198+
    [7p] Oct 1994
    Birchard, R.S. Monta Bell. biog filmog il stills GRIFFITHIANA n51/52:199+
    [7p] Oct 1994
    Lodato, N. I quattro figli di Willy Wyler con le gemelle di Monta Bell. il
    stills C FORUM 34:10-12 Oct (n338) 1994
BELLA VITA, LA f (d Virzi, Paolo 1994 It)
    Reviews
    Gandini, L. "La bella vita." credits still C FORUM 34:78-79 Sep (n337)
    1994
BELLAFANTE, GINIA
    Bellafante, G. Generation X-cellent. ports TIME 145:62-64 Feb 27 1995
    Bellafante, G. The inventor of bad TV. ports TIME 145:111 Mar 13 1995
BELLE AL BAR f (d Benvenuti, Alessandro 1994 It)
    Reviews
    Fittante, A. "Belle al Bar." credits stills SEGNO n72:44-45 Mar/Apr 1995
    Rooney, D. "Belle al bar." credits VARIETY 357:73 Jan 2/8 1995
BELLE NOISEUSE, LA f (d Rivette, Jacques 1991 Fr)
    Time
    Calle-Gruber, M. La chimere du modele. bibliog still CINEMAS 4:72-87 n1
    1993
BELLE OF THE NINETIES f (d McCarey, Leo 1934 USA)
    Sjogren, O. Kan en antilady sjunga blues? bibliog port stills F HAFTET
    22:38-47 n3 (n87) 1994
BELLION, CORALIE
    Bellion, C. "Les braqueuses." bibliog credits stills GRAND ANGLE n178:3-4
    Jan 1995
    Bellion, C. "Les gens de la riziere." bibliog credits stills GRAND ANGLE
    n176:13-14 Nov 1994
    Bellion, C. "Petit Pierre au pays des reves." credits stills GRAND ANGLE
    n177:33-34 Dec 1994
    Bellion, C. "Petits arrangements avec la mort." bibliog credits still
    GRAND ANGLE n178:23-24 Jan 1995
BELLOCCHIO, MARCO See also SOGNO DELLA FARFALLA, IL
    Bellocchio, M. and Petraglia, S. Due testimonianze di Marco Bellocchio e
    Sandro Petraglia su Vittorio Mezzogiorno strappato per un male inguaribile
    al cinema che aveva bisogno della sua preparazione artisticae severita
    morale. il C SUO 33:15-16 Jul/Aug/Sep (n113) 1994
    Roberti, B. and others. Lavorare sulla bellezza del "niente." interv stills
    FCR 45:322-328 Jun/Jul (n446/447) 1994
BELTON, JOHN
    Cherchi Usai, P. Widescreen cinema. By John Belton [Book Review]. J F PRES
    n49:75 Oct 1994
    Cherchi Usai, P. Widescreen cinema. By John Belton [Book Review].
    GRIFFITHIANA n51/52:266-267 Oct 1994
BELTZ, JEFF VON
    Beltz, J. von. The neverending story. JOURNAL WGA 7:37 Feb 1994
BELVAUX, REMY See also C'EST ARRIVE PRES DE CHEZ VOUS
BEMBERG, MARIA LUISA See also DE ESO NO SE HABLA
BEN MING NIAN f (d Xie, Fei 1990 China)
    Political Analysis
    Berry, C. "Ce qui meritait le plus d'etre puni etait son penis":
    postsocialisme, distopie et la mort du heros. bibliog glos still CINEMAS
    3:38-59 n2/3 1993
BENARD, JOHANNE
    Benard, J. Un cinema zazique? bibliog still CINEMAS 4:135-154 n3 1994
BENDAZZI, GIANNALBERTO
    Bendazzi, G. The first Italian animated feature film and its producer: "La
    Rosa di Bagdad" and Anton Gino Domeneghini. biogs il stat stills ANIMATION
    J 3:4-18 n2 1995
    Pilling, J. The greatest art condensed [Book Review]. still FILM 4:25 n1
    [1995]
BENET, STEPHEN VINCENT
    Singer, R. One against all: the New England past and present
    responsibilities in "The Devil and Daniel Webster." bibliog still LIT/FQ
    22:265-271 n4 1994
BENGTS, ULRIKA
    (Sju) 7 debutanter. ports CHAPLIN 36:6-7 n6 (n255) 1994/95

BENIGNI, ROBERTO See also MOSTRO, IL
BENJAMIN, DOMINIQUE
    Benjamin, D. Sur le plateau de "Kabloonak." il still SEQUENCES n174:7-8
        Sep/Oct 1994
BENJAMIN, RICHARD See also MILK MONEY
BENJAMIN, WALTER
    McKinley, A. Anne Friedberg. Window shopping: cinema and the postmodern
        [Book Review]. ARACHNE 1:270-274 n2 1994
BENNETT, ALAN
    Buruma, I. The great art of embarrassment. il still NY R BKS 42:15-18 Feb
        16 1995
    Corliss, R. Bard of embarrassment. biog il port still TIME 145:65-66 Feb
        27 1995
BENNETT, BILL See also SPIDER & ROSE
BENNETT, RONAN
    Bennett, R. Lean mean and cruel. interv stills S&S 5:34-36 Jan 1995
    Bennett, R. Telling the truth about Ireland. il stills VERTIGO (UK)
        n1:24-29 n4 1994/95
BENOIT, MARIUSZ
    Slodowski, J. Mariusz Benoit. filmog still FSP 40:12 n11 (n765) 1994
BENOIT, PEETERS
    Berthome, J.-P. Le "storyboard" en livres [Book Reviews]. POSITIF n407:90+
        [2p] Jan 1995
BENSMAIA, REDA
    Bensmaia, R. De l'"automate spirituel" ou le temps dans le cinema moderne
        selon Gilles Deleuze. bibliog CINEMAS 5:167-186 n1/2 1994
BENSON, SHEILA
    Benson, S. Laurence Fishburne: the actor who puts risk before reputation.
        interv ports stills INTERV 25:62-67 Jan 1995
BENTLEY, MICHAEL For film reviews see author under the following titles: ROUGE
BENTON, ROBERT See also NOBODY'S FOOL
    Keathley, C. Robert Benton. il interv stills F COM 31:36-43+ [12p] Jan/Feb
        1995
    Lally, K. Benton returns with tale of smalltown redemption. il still FJ
        98:10+ [2p] Jan/Feb 1995
BENVENUTI, ALESSANDRO See also BELLE AL BAR
BERCZES, LASZLO
    Berczes, L. Mozi van. still F VILAG 38:17 n4 1995
    Berczes, L. Nem mas. il interv stills F VILAG 38:10-13 n2 1995
BERDEL f (d Yilmaz, Atif 1991 Turkey)
        Reviews
    Emiliani, S. "Berdel." credits still FILM (ITALY) 3:39-40 n13 1995
BERG, ELLEN K.
    Berg, E.K. "Rebecca." bibliog stills Z n1:26-29 (n47) 1994
BERG, LENE
    (Sju) 7 debutanter. ports CHAPLIN 36:6-7 n6 (n255) 1994/95
BERGALA, ALAIN
    Thirard, P.L. Une encyclopedie du nu au cinema. Ouvrage reuni par Jacques
        Deniel et Patrick Leboutte, sur une idee d'Alain Bergala [Book Review].
        still POSITIF n408:78-79 Feb 1995
BERGER, CATHERINE
    Berger, C. Das Panorama - Paradigma eines Perspektivenwechsels. F KUNST
        n144:4-13 1994
BERGER, LAUREL
    Berger, L. On the waterfront. stills INDEP 18:38-41 Mar 1995
BERGER, THOMAS
    Kasdan, M. and Tavernetti, S. The Hollywood Indian in "Little Big Man": a
        revisionist view. still F&HIST 23:70-80 n1/4 1993
BERGERY, BENJAMIN
    Bergery, B. Reflections: Vilmos Zsigmond, ASC. il specs stills AMCIN
        74:74-78 Sep 1993
BERGLUND, BO
    Adamson, J. and others. Forgotten laughter. credits port stills
        GRIFFITHIANA n51/52:170-197 Oct 1994
    Adamson, J. and others. La fabbrica della risata. credits port stills
        GRIFFITHIANA n51/52:170-197 Oct 1994
BERGMAN, ANDREW See also IT COULD HAPPEN TO YOU; STRIPTEASE
BERGMAN, INGMAR See also SJUNDE INSEGLET, DET
    Aberg, A. "Askadaren" vid glipan: Maaret Koskinen om Ingmar Bergman [Book
        Review]. F HAFTET 22:59-60 n3 (n87) 1994
BERGRAEBNIS UND DIE AUFERSTEHUNG DER VIER FAEUSTE, EIN f (d Clucher, E.B. 1994
    FR Ger/It/Sp)
    Ein Begraebnis und die Auferstehung der vier Faeuste. credits filmog still
        KINO(BRD) n1:12-13 1994
BERLIN APARTMENT, THE f (d Cantrill, Arthur/Cantrill, Corinne 1994 prod 1985-
    Australia)
    Cantrill, A. and Cantrill, C. "The Berlin Apartment." filmog scenario
        excerpts stills CANTRILL'S FMNTS n73/74:32-39 May 1994
BERLIN IN BERLIN f (d Cetin, Sinan 1993 Turkey/FR Ger)
    Slodowski, J. "Obcy w Berlinie." biog credits filmog FSP 40:9 n5 (n759)
        1994
BERNARDI, SANDRO
    Bernardi, S. Letture per un anno. bibliog still SEGNO n63:75-78 Sep/Oct
        1993
BERNARDINI, ALDO
    Codelli, L. Il cinema muto italiano: i film degli anni d'oro, 1913, prima
        parte. Di Aldo Bernardini e Vittorio Martinelli [Book Review]. GRIFFITHIANA
        n51/52:253 Oct 1994
    Comuzio, E. Aldo Bernardini (a cura di): Il cinema sonoro 1930-1969 [Book
        Reviews]. il C FORUM 34:95-96 Sep (n337) 1994
BERNARDO, JOSE MANUEL
    Bernardo, J.M. "Dracula, Principe de las Tinieblas." credits il still
        NOSFERATU n6:94-95 Apr 1991
    Bernardo, J.M. "El cerebro de Frankenstein." credits stills NOSFERATU
        n6:98-99 Apr 1991
    Bernardo, J.M. "El collar de la muerte." credits il NOSFERATU n6:90-91 Apr
        1991
    Bernardo, J.M. El perro de Baskerville. credits stills NOSFERATU n6:82-83
        Apr 1991
    Bernardo, J.M. "La leyenda de Vandorf." credits stills NOSFERATU n6:92-93

Apr 1991
    Bernardo, J.M. "Las dos caras del Doctor Jekyll." credits still NOSFERATU
        n6:84-85 Apr 1991
    Bernardo, J.M. "Las novias de Dracula." credits il still NOSFERATU
        n6:86-87 Apr 1991
BERNARDO, MARIO
    Bernardo, M. Il "primo piano luminoso" del nostro Michele. il port C NUOVO
        43:37-38 Nov/Dec (n352) 1994
BERNINK, MIEKE
    Bernink, M. "Skrien" [Book Review]. il BLIMP n30:57-58 Winter 1994
BERNSTEIN, ELMER
    Handzo, S. The golden age of film music. il ports stills CINEASTE 21:46-55
        n1/2 1995
    MacLean, P.A. Elmer Bernstein. il interv F SCORE MONTHLY n36/37:14-15
        Aug/Sep 1993
    MacLean, P.A. The fantasy film music of Elmer Bernstein. il F SCORE
        MONTHLY n36/37:15-17 Aug/Sep 1993
BERNSTEIN, MATTHEW
    Bernstein, M. "Roger and Me": documentaphobia and mixed modes. bibliog
        stills UFAJ 46:3-20 n1 1994
    Turner, G. Walter Wanger, Hollywood independent. By Matthew Bernstein [Book
        Review]. AMCIN 76:85 Feb 1995
BERNSTEIN, STEVEN
    Frey, M. Film production [Book Review]. F KUNST n144:67-68 1994
BERRI, CLAUDE See also GERMINAL
    Slodowski, J. "Germinal." biogs credits filmogs FSP 40:10 n4 (n758) 1994
BERRY, CHRIS For film reviews see author under the following titles: KEU SOME
    GAGO SIPTA
    Berry, C. A turn for the better? - genre and gender in "Girl From Hunan" and
        other recent mainland Chinese films. bibliog stills PS 14:81-103 n1/2
        1994/95
    Berry, C. "Ce qui meritait le plus d'etre puni etait son penis":
        postsocialisme, distopie et la mort du heros. bibliog glos still CINEMAS
        3:38-59 n2/3 1993
    Berry, C. Pauline Chan. il interv stills CINEMAYA n25/26:65-67
        Autumn/Winter 1994/95
    Wark, M. Berry, Chris. A bit on the side: East-West topographies of desire
        [Book Review]. MEDIA INFO AUSTRALIA n75:157 Feb 1995
BERRY, HALLE
    Kelly, C. No more tears. il ports PREM 8:78-84 Apr 1995
    Rebello, S. Halle terror. ports MOVIELINE 6:52-56+ [7p] Apr 1995
BERRY, JOANNA For film reviews see author under the following titles: RAPA NUI
BERRYMAN, KEN
    Berryman, K. Cecil Holmes. biog il obit C PAPERS n102:19 Dec 1994
BERTELSMANN AG
    Dawtrey, A. Bertelsmann grows new arm. stat VARIETY 358:36 Feb 27/Mar 5
        1995
BERTELSMANN MUSIC GROUP (BMG)
    Molner, D. Zelnick looking to boost BMG's RCA label, pump up core business.
        port VARIETY 357:47-48 Jan 9/15 1995
BERTETTO, PAOLO
    Bluemlinger, C. Bernard Eisenschitz & Paolo Bertetto (Hg.): Fritz Lang, La
        mise en scene [Book Review]. BLIMP n30:70 Winter 1994
BERTHOME, JEAN-PIERRE
    Berthome, J.-P. Le "storyboard." il POSITIF n407:76-84 Jan 1995
    Berthome, J.-P. Le "storyboard" en livres [Book Reviews]. POSITIF n407:90+
        [2p] Jan 1995
    Berthome, J.-P. "Storyboard" et bande dessinee. il POSITIF n407:90-91 Jan
        1995
    Berthome, J.-P. Voir un peu d'herbe avant de mourir... il POSITIF
        n408:84-89 Feb 1995
    Berthome, J.-P. and Kohn, O. Entretien avec Jeff Balsmeyer. il interv still
        POSITIF n407:85-89 Jan 1995
BERTHOMIEU, PIERRE For film reviews see author under the following titles:
    CLERKS; I LIKE IT LIKE THAT; KEU SOME GAGO SIPTA; SIRENS; SLEEP WITH ME
BERTIN, CELIA
    Bonneville, L. Jean Renoir. Par Celia Bertin [Book Review]. il SEQUENCES
        n174:59 Sep/Oct 1994
BERTOLUCCI, BERNARDO See also LITTLE BUDDHA; SHELTERING SKY, THE; ULTIMO TANGO
    A PARIGI
    Lori, S. I films di Bernardo Bertolucci. Di Jefferson Kline [Book Review].
        C SUD 33:37 Jul/Aug/Sep (n113) 1994
BESAS, PETER For film reviews see author under the following titles: WIEDERKEHR
BESSON, LUC See also PROFESSIONAL, THE
    Filmografie. biogs filmogs SEGNO n72:40 Mar/Apr 1995
Best films See COMMENDATIONS
Better Tomorrow, A See YINGXIONG BENSE
Better Tomorrow II, A See YINGXIONG BENSE II
BETTETINI, GIANFRANCO
    Santucci, E. Obiettivo festival. il SEGNO n71:19-23 Jan/Feb 1995
BETTKOENIGIN, DIE f (d Baur, Gabrielle 1993 Switz)
        Reviews
    Senn, D. "Die Bettkoenigin." credits C(SWITZ) 40:205 1994
BEWEGTE MANN, DER f (d Wortmann, Soenke 1994 FR Ger)
        Reviews
    Holloway, D. "Der bewegte Mann." credits still KINO(GF) n56:19-20 Nov 1994
BEZ KONCA f (No End d Kieslowski, Krzysztof 1984 Poland)
    Falkowska, J. "The political" in the films of Andrzej Wajda and Krzysztof
        Kieslowski. CJ 34:37-50 n2 1995
BHAJI ON THE BEACH f (d Chadha, Gurinder 1994 Gt Br)
    "Bhaji on the Beach." biog credits filmog il still CINEMAYA n25/26:107
        Autumn/Winter 1994/95
    Robbins, H. "Bhaji" a lark in Blackpool. ANGLES 2:8 n4 1995
BIANCA f (d Moretti, Nanni 1984 It)
    Dusi, N. Il geloso a rotelle. bibliog still SEGNO n71:3-7 Jan/Feb 1995
BIANCHI, SERGIO See also A CAUSA SECRETA
BIBLIOGRAPHIES See also INDEXES
    France
    Gauteur, C. Un an de lecture. bibliog AVANT-SCENE n437:90-92 Dec 1994

BLEYS, JEAN-PIERRE
Bleys, J.-P. Angers. POSITIF n406:62 Dec 1994
BLINK f (d Apted, Michael 1994 USA)
Ciapara, E. "Blink." biog credits filmogs still FSP 40:8 n4 (n758) 1994
    Reviews
Canova, G. "Occhi nelle tenebre." credits stills SEGNO n72:37-38 Mar/Apr 1995
BLISS, MICHAEL
Redman, N. A Siegel film: an autobiography. By Don Siegel [Book Reviews]. il DGA NEWS 19:33-34 n2 1994
Redman, N. Peckinpah and Sidney reconsidered [Book Reviews]. il DGA NEWS 20:40-41 n1 1995
Williams, T. Justified lives: morality and narrative in the films of Sam Peckinpah. By Michael Bliss [Book Review]. il FQ 48:62-63 n2 1994/95
BLOCH, ROBERT
Jensen, P.M. Inside "The Skull." il stills SCARLET STREET n17:26-28+ [6p] Winter 1995
BLOECH, MICHAEL For film reviews see author under the following titles: BALLON D'OR, LE
BLOIS, MARCO DE For film reviews see author under the following titles:
ARTISTE, UNE; C'ETAIT LE 12 DU 12 ET CHILI AVAIT LES BLUES;
DISCLOSURE; FAUST; ROAD TO WELLVILLE, THE; RUTH; WES CRAVEN'S NEW
NIGHTMARE; WINDIGO
Blois, M. de. Entretien avec Robert Morin. il interv stills 24 IMAGES n75:6-11 Dec/Jan 1994/95
Blois, M. de. La douleur en soi. interv port still 24 IMAGES n76:47-48 Spring 1995
Blois, M. de. Richard Lavoie. il R CINEMATHEQUE n33:6-7 Mar/Apr 1995
BLOMKVIST, MARTEN
Blomkvist, M. Mot filmhistorien - med sprang! port CHAPLIN 36:72 n6 (n255) 1994/95
BLOOD IN FILM
Taubin, A. Bloody tales. stills S&S 5:8-11 Jan 1995
BLOOD MEMORY f (d Dennison, Deborah 1995 USA)
Zibart, R. "Blood Memory." port INDEP 18:22 Apr 1995
BLORE, ERIC
Van Neste, D. Eric Blore. biog il CLASSIC n236:24+ [3p] Feb 1995
BLOWN AWAY f (d Hopkins, Stephen 1994 USA)
    Special Effects
Stalter, K. Explosive close-ups trigger "Blown Away." diag il AMCIN 76:72-74 Feb 1995
    Reviews
Ciment, M. "Blown Away." still POSITIF n407:40-41 Jan 1995
Blue See BLEU
BLUE CHIPS f (d Friedkin, William 1994 USA)
    Reviews
Borroni, M. "Basta vincere." credits still C FORUM 34:83-84 Sep (n337) 1994
BLUE IN THE FACE f (d Wang, Wayne/Auster, Paul 1995 USA)
    Reviews
Stratton, D. "Blue in the Face." credits still VARIETY 358:76 Feb 20/26 1995
Blue Light, The See BLAUE LICHT, DAS
BLUE, MONTE
Katchmer, G. Remembering the great silents. biogs filmogs port CLASSIC n237:35+ [3p] Mar 1995
BLUE STEEL f (d Bigelow, Kathryn 1990 USA)
    Psychoanalytic Analysis
Self, R.T. Redressing the law in Kathryn Bigelow's "Blue Steel." bibliog stills UFAJ 46:31-43 n2 1994
BLUE VELVET f (d Lynch, David 1986 USA)
    Oedipal Narrative
Layton, L. "Blue Velvet": a parable of male development. SCREEN 35:374-393 n4 1994
BLUEMLINGER, CHRISTA
Bluemlinger, C. Ansichten aus Lussas. stills BLIMP n30:36-38 Winter 1994
Bluemlinger, C. Bernard Eisenschitz & Paolo Bertetto (Hg.): Fritz Lang, La mise en scene [Book Review]. BLIMP n30:70 Winter 1994
Bluemlinger, C. "Trafic" [Book Review]. il BLIMP n30:62-63 Winter 1994
Bluemlinger, C. Varda par Agnes [Book Review]. BLIMP n30:70 Winter 1994
BLUM, FREDERIC See also FAUSSAIRES, LES
BLUM, GABRIELE CLERMONT
Blum, G.C. In memory of... Georges Delerue. il F SCORE MONTHLY n36/37:25 Aug/Sep 1993
BLUMENBERG, HANS-CHRISTOPH See also ROTWANG MUSS WEG!
"Rotwang muss weg!" biog credits filmog still KINO(BRD) n1:40-41 1995
BLUMENLAND f (d Foth, Joerg 1976 E Ger)
Graef, C. Hochschulfilme. il interv F & FERNSEHEN 22:50-53 n6 1994
BLUTH, DON See also HANS CHRISTIAN ANDERSEN'S THUMBELINA
BLYTH, ANN
Ghulam, L.E. Ann Blyth: Ann of a thousand smiles. biog il interv ports CLASSIC n236:18+ [4p] Feb 1995
BO, FABIO
Bo, F. Impassibilita quieta, impassibilita inquieta. still FCR 45:405-407 Sep (n448) 1994
Bo, F. Tempo di vivere, tempo di morire. still FCR 45:349-353 Jun/Jul (n446/447) 1994
BO, FINN See also TO LIV
Boards See FILM COMMISSIONS
BOBER, PHILIPPE
Molner, D. October buys rights to Danish "Kingdom." VARIETY 358:27 Mar 13/19 1995
BOCHICCHIO, GISELLA
Bochicchio, G. Mostri. stills FCR 45:354-358 Jun/Jul (n446/447) 1994
BOCK, HANS-MICHAEL
Codelli, L. Das Ufa-Buch. A cura di Hans-Michael Bock e Michael Toeteberg [Book Review]. GRIFFITHIANA n51/52:267 Oct 1994
"Das Wachsfigurenkabinett." Drehbuch von Henrik Galeen zu Paul Lenis film von 1923/Waxworks: screenplay by Henrik Galeen for Paul Leni's film in 1923 [Book Review]. il KINO(GF) n56:31 Nov 1994

Grbic, B. Hans-Michael Bock (Hrsg.): "Cinegraph" [Book Review]. BLIMP [n1]:65 Mar 1985
BODIES IN FILM
Thomson, D. Really a part of me. stills F COM 31:17-18+ [8p] Jan/Feb 1995
BODIES, REST & MOTION f (d Steinberg, Michael 1993 USA)
    Reviews
Candeloro, L. "Desideri smarriti." credits FILM (ITALY) 3:20 n13 1995
BODOR, ADAM
Gothar, P. "Reszleg" - reszletek. il interv stills F VILAG 38:6-9 n2 1995
BODY MELT f (d Brophy, Philip 1993 Australia)
    Reviews
Caputo, R. "Body Melt." credits still C PAPERS n102:66-67 Dec 1994
BODY OF EVIDENCE f (d Edel, Uli 1992 USA)
    Reviews
Meyers, R. The crime screen. ports still ARMCHAIR DET 26:63-64 n3 1993
BODY SNATCHERS f (d Ferrara, Abel 1993 USA)
    Reviews
Cherchi Usai, P. "Ultracorpi - l'invasione continua." credits still SEGNO n63:98-99 Sep/Oct 1993
BOGANI, GIOVANNI
Comuzio, E. Giovanni Bogani: Good morning, San Gimignano. Il cinema fra le torri [Book Review]. il C FORUM 34:93 Oct (n338) 1994
BOGART, HUMPHREY
Martin, A. Performing the city [Book Review]. Q REV F & VIDEO 15:71-76 n3 1994
BOGDANOVICH, PETER See also DAISY MILLER; TEXASVILLE; THING CALLED LOVE, THE
Gariazzo, G. Bogdanovich inedito. il C FORUM 34:88-90 Sep (n337) 1994
Koppold, R. Das Genie und das Scheitern [Book Review]. MEDIEN 38:379-380 n6 1994
Kremski, P. "Die Musik soll nicht das ausdruecken, was in der Szene zu sehen ist." credits il interv stills F BUL 37:33-38 n1 (n198) 1995
BOILING POINT f (d Harris, James B. 1993 USA/Fr)
    Reviews
Meyers, R. The crime screen. port stills ARMCHAIR DET 26:59-61 n4 1993
BOLT, ROBERT
Elley, D. Robert Bolt. obit VARIETY 358:78 Feb 27/Mar 5 1995
Hodson, J. Who wrote "Lawrence of Arabia"? il port stills JOURNAL WGA 8:16-20 Mar 1995
Milestones. obits ports TIME 145:31 Mar 6 1995
Transition. obit NEWSWK 125:55 Mar 6 1995
BOLZ, EVELYN
    Recollections
Wehrbein, J. A special movie fan. il BOXOFFICE 131:102+ [2p] Apr 1995
BOLZONI, FRANCESCO
Serravalli, L. "Dies irae" un revival dei film dell'anno 1943 nel catalogo curato da Francesco Bolzoni e Guido Fink per conto della Mostra del Cinema di Venezia (93) [Book Review]. C SUD 33:40-42 Jul/Aug/Sep (n113) 1994
BOMBA, ENRICO See also JEZEBEL
BONA, DAMIEN
Bona, D. Boys' night out. il ports PREM 8:98-101 Apr 1995
BONA, LASZLO
Bona, L. Jakob oszlopa. stills F VILAG 38:18-19 n4 1995
BOND, JEFF
Bond, J. Concert report. F SCORE MONTHLY n36/37:5 Aug/Sep 1993
BOND, SCOTT
Bond, S.R. and Bond, S. Report form 221B Baker Street. il ARMCHAIR DET 26:70-71 n4 1993
Bond, S.R. and Bond, S. Report from 221B Baker Street. biog il still ARMCHAIR DET 28:184-185 n2 1995
BOND, SHERRY ROSE
Bond, S.R. and Bond, S. Report form 221B Baker Street. il ARMCHAIR DET 26:70-71 n4 1993
Bond, S.R. and Bond, S. Report from 221B Baker Street. biog il still ARMCHAIR DET 28:184-185 n2 1995
BONDI, CLAUDIO See also RICHIAMO, IL
BONNET, JEAN-CLAUDE
Bonnet, J.-C. Le XVIIIe siecle a l'ecran. bibliog still CINEMAS 4:48-58 n1 1993
BONNET, MICHEL
Obituaries. obits VARIETY 358:58-59 Mar 20/26 1995
BONNEVILLE, LEO
Bonneville, L. Entrevue avec Andre Forcier. filmog interv still SEQUENCES n174:10-13 Sep/Oct 1994
Bonneville, L. Gueules d'atmosphere: les acteurs du cinema francais (1929-1959). Par Olivier Barrot et Raymond Chirat [Book Review]. il SEQUENCES n174:59 Sep/Oct 1994
Bonneville, L. Jean Renoir. Par Celia Bertin [Book Review]. il SEQUENCES n174:59 Sep/Oct 1994
Bonneville, L. (Trente) 30. SEQUENCES n174:1 Sep/Oct 1994
BONO, FRANCESCO
Bono, F. "Segnocinema" [Book Review]. il BLIMP n30:53-54 Winter 1994
Bono, F. Stillhet og landskap i nordisk film. stills F&K n7:24-28 1993
BONS DEBARRAS, LES f (d Mankiewicz, Francis 1980 Can)
    Adaptations
Viswanathan, J. L'un(e) dort, l'autre pas: la scene de la veille dans les scenarios et quelques romans de Rejean Ducharme. bibliog scenario still table CINEMAS 5:189-209 n1/2 1994
BONZEL, ANDRE See also C'EST ARRIVE PRES DE CHEZ VOUS
BOOK REVIEWS
    Italy
Bernardi, S. Letture per un anno. bibliog still SEGNO n63:75-78 Sep/Oct 1993
Booking [Prior to V17, 1989 use BOOKING] See DISTRIBUTION
Books about film See FICTION ABOUT FILM
BOON, PHILIPPE See also LUC & MARIE: LE FILM
BORDEN, LIZZIE
Borden, L. Blood and redemption. still S&S 5:61 Feb 1995
BORDOWITZ, GREGG See also FAST TRIP, LONG DROP
Nolan, A.M. Double dare. il still VILLAGE VOICE 40:50 Jan 10 1995

BORDWELL, DAVID
  Bordwell, D. Film interpretation revisited. bibliog F CRITICISM 17:93-119
    n2/3 1992/93
  Branigan, E. On the analysis of interpretive language: Part I. bibliog F
    CRITICISM 17:4-21 n2/3 1992/93
  Cherchi Usai, P. Cent'anni da riscrivere [Book Review]. still SEGNO n72:71
    Mar/Apr 1995
  Cherchi Usai, P. Film history: an introduction. By Kristin Thompson and
    David Bordwell [Book Review]. J F PRES n49:70-72 Oct 1994
  Cook, D.A. Making sense. bibliog F CRITICISM 17:31-39 n2/3 1992/93
  Eagle, H. The cinema of Eisenstein. By David Bordwell [Book Review]. FQ
    48:58-60 n2 1994/95
  Kaplan, E.A. Disorderly disciplines. bibliog F CRITICISM 17:48-52 n2/3
    1992/93
  Livio, L. The cinema of Eisenstein. Di David Bordwell [Book Review].
    GRIFFITHIANA n51/52:253-254 Oct 1994
  Testa, B. Out of theory [Book Reviews]. CAN J F STUD 1:49-65 n2 1991
  Turconi, D. Film history: an introduction. Di Kristin Thompson e David
    Bordwell [Book Review]. GRIFFITHIANA n51/52:255-258 Oct 1994
BORGER, LENNY
  Borger, L. Sisyphian struggles [Book Review]. S&S 5:37-38 Feb 1995
BORGHI, LORENA
  Zappoli, G. Cosi vicino cosi lontano. il intervs SEGNO n71:24-27 Jan/Feb
    1995
BORI, ERZSEBET For film reviews see author under the following titles: LAMERICA;
    OMBRE DU DOUTE, L'; SIMPLE MEN
  Bori, E. Elet a dobozban. still F VILAG 38:58-59 n1 1995
  Bori, E. Itt lapatol a kommunista part! still F VILAG 38:24-25 n1 1995
BORN, ADOLF
  Saija, P. Adolf Born on kuuluisimpia animaation tekijoita Tsekinmaassa.
    port still PEILI 18:17-18 n3 1994
BORRONI, MARCO For film reviews see author under the following titles: BLUE
    CHIPS
BORSOS, PHILLIP See also FAR FROM HOME: THE ADVENTURES OF YELLOW DOG
  Kelly, B. Phillip Borsos. obit VARIETY 358:85 Feb 6/12 1995
BORUSZKOWSKI, LILLY ANN
  Boruszkowski, L.A. An interview with documentary filmmaker Jim Klein.
    filmog interv port UFAJ 46:34-42 n1 1994
BORZAGE, FRANK See also FAREWELL TO ARMS, A
BOSE, SUDHIR
  Bose, S. Pesaro. CINEMAYA n24:61-62 Summer 1994
  Bose, S. The contemporaries. il port stills CINEMAYA n25/26:20-23
    Autumn/Winter 1994/95
BOSNA! f (d Levy, Bernard-Henri/Ferrari, Alain 1994 Fr)
    Reviews
  Grugeau, G. "Bosna!": "Veillees d'armes - histoire du journalisme en temps
    de guerre." still 24 IMAGES n75:47-48 Dec/Jan 1994/95
BOSTON, RICHARD
  Ciment, M. BFI film classics [Book Reviews]. stills POSITIF n408:75-77 Feb
    1995
BOSWELL, SIMON
  Boswell, S. Neither Mozart nor Hendrix. il still S&S 5:37 Apr 1995
  Kermode, M. Simon Boswell: filmography. filmog still S&S 5:62 Apr 1995
BOSZORMENYI, ZSUZSA See also VOROS COLIBRI
  Bakacs, T.S. Csaladi vallalkozas. interv still F VILAG 38:46-47 n3 1995
BOTELHO, JOAO See also AQUI NA TERRA; TRES PALMEIRAS
  Pastor, A. and Maudente, F. Preservare le cose importanti... interv still
    FCR 45:329-338 Jun/Jul (n446/447) 1994
BOTTE DI NATALE f (d Hill, Terence 1994 FR Ger)
  "Die Troublemaker." biog credits filmog il KINO(BRD) n1:50-51 1995
BOTTIROLI, GIOVANNI
  Bottiroli, G. Il bello del brutto. stills SEGNO n72:21-23 Mar/Apr 1995
BOTTOMORE, STEPHEN
  Adamson, J. and others. Forgotten laughter. credits port stills
    GRIFFITHIANA n51/52:170-197 Oct 1994
  Adamson, J. and others. La fabbrica della risata. credits port stills
    GRIFFITHIANA n51/52:170-197 Oct 1994
BOUDU SAUVE DES EAUX f (Boudu Saved From Drowning d Renoir, Jean 1932 Fr)
  Ciment, M. BFI film classics [Book Reviews]. stills POSITIF n408:75-77 Feb
    1995
Boudu Saved From Drowning See BOUDU SAUVE DES EAUX
BOUKHRIEF, NICOLAS See also VA MOURIRE
BOULTON, LAURA
  McMillan, R. Ethnology and the N.F.B.: the Laura Boulton mysteries. CAN J F
    STUD 1:67-82 n2 1991
BOURELLY, ROBERT
  Bourelly, R. The European documentary: second in a three-part series. il
    stills DOC BOX 3:8-11 1993
BOURGET, JEAN-LOUP For film reviews see author under the following titles:
    GETTYSBURG; KABLOONAK
  Bourget, J.-L. Correspondances 1890-1953. Par Auguste et Louis Lumiere [Book
    Review]. POSITIF n409:72-73 Mar 1995
  Bourget, J.-L. L'American Center sur le chemin de Hollywood. still POSITIF
    n409:63 Mar 1995
BOURGUIGNON, THOMAS
  Bourguignon, T. "Exotica." il still POSITIF n406:78 Dec 1994
BOUSE, DEREK
  Bouse, D. True life fantasies: storytelling traditions in animated features
    and wildlife films. stat ANIMATION J 3:19-39 n2 1995
BOUTONNAT, LAURENT See also GIORGINO
BOUTROY, PASCAL For film reviews see author under the following titles:
    PAMIETNIK ZNALEZIONY W GARBIE; PERSONNE NE M'AIME; ROAD TO WELLVILLE,
    THE
BOVANI, RENATO
  Bovani, R. and Bovani, R. Le prime proiezioni in Italia: Firenze. il still
    IMMAGINE n28:20-23 Autumn 1994
BOVANI, ROSALIA
  Bovani, R. and Bovani, R. Le prime proiezioni in Italia: Firenze. il still
    IMMAGINE n28:20-23 Autumn 1994

BOWMAN, DAVID K.
  Bowman, D.K. The great Gildersleeve. il port stills F FAX n49:69-72
    Mar/Apr 1995
BOWMAN, DURRELL S.
  Bowman, D.S. Mail bag: I wish to respond to several points raised by
    Douglass Fake. F SCORE MONTHLY n38:16 Oct 1993
BOWSER, EILEEN
  Adamson, J. and others. Forgotten laughter. credits port stills
    GRIFFITHIANA n51/52:170-197 Oct 1994
  Adamson, J. and others. La fabbrica della risata. credits port stills
    GRIFFITHIANA n51/52:170-197 Oct 1994
Box-office (grosses) See GROSSES
BOXOFFICE (periodical)
  Barometer '95: 1994 in review. stat table BOXOFFICE 131:20-21 Mar 1995
    History
  Greene, R. Second sight: "Boxoffice" remembers 75 films from 75 years at the
    movies. il stills BOXOFFICE 131:36-38+ [28p] Mar 1995
  Leyendecker, F. The "Boxoffice" story. il port BOXOFFICE 131:24-25 Mar
    1995
  Shlyen, S. Jesse's song. il ports BOXOFFICE 131:30-31 Mar 1995
  The people who make "Boxoffice." il ports BOXOFFICE 131:34-35 Mar 1995
  Williamson, K. Our man Morrie. ports BOXOFFICE 131:26+ [2p] Mar 1995
BOY CALLED HATE, A f (d Marcus, Mitch 1995 USA)
    Reviews
  Levy, E. "A Boy Called Hate." credits VARIETY 358:80 Feb 20/26 1995
BOY MEETS GIRL f (d Brady, Ray 1994 Gt Br)
    Reviews
  Lipman, A. "Boy Meets Girl." credits S&S 5:57 Feb 1995
BOYCE, MARTIN For film reviews see author under the following titles: CROW, THE;
    GETAWAY, THE
  Boyce, M. (Forty-third) 43rd Melbourne Film Festival. il stills FATAL
    VISIONS n17:20 1994
BOYLE, DANNY See also SHALLOW GRAVE
  Bennett, R. Lean mean and cruel. interv stills S&S 5:34-36 Jan 1995
  Shacter, S. Sundance: Antonia Bird & Danny Boyle. intervs port stills BOMB
    n51:36-41 Spring 1995
BOYS LIFE f (d Sloan, Brian/O'Connell, Raoul/King, Robert Lee 1994 USA)
    Reviews
  Cheshire, G. "Boys Life." credits VARIETY 357:72 Jan 9/15 1995
  Noh, D. "Boys Life." credits FJ 98:58 Jan/Feb 1995
BOYS OF ST. VINCENT, THE f (d Smith, John N. 1993 Can)
  Alleva, R. Correspondence: the reviewer replies. COMMONWEAL 122:29 Mar 10
    1995
  Donohue, W.A. Correspondence: "Voice" vs. Alleva. COMMONWEAL 122:29 Mar 10
    1995
BOYS ON THE SIDE f (d Ross, Herbert 1995 USA)
    Reviews
  Giles, J. and Schoemer, K. Hear me roar. stills NEWSWK 125:72 Feb 20 1995
  Hoberman, J. Two weddings and two funerals. still VILLAGE VOICE 40:49 Feb
    14 1995
  Lally, K. "Boys on the Side." credits still FJ 98:65-66 Mar 1995
  Travers, P. "Boys on the Side." still ROLLING STONE n702:80-81 Feb 23 1995
  Williamson, K. "Boys on the Side." still BOXOFFICE 131:bet p89 and 96
    [pR16] Mar 1995
BOZZA, GIANLUIGI For film reviews see author under the following titles:
    AMNESIA; LIMITA; PIGALLE; YANGGUANG CANLAN DE RIZI
BRABIN, CHARLES J. See also MASK OF FU MANCHU, THE; RAVEN, THE
BRACH, GERARD
  Brach, G. Gespraech mit Gerard Brach ueber Otar Iosseliani. biog filmog il
    still BLIMP [n2]:52-53 Winter 1985
BRADBURY, RAY
  Bradbury, R. How did I get here from there? JOURNAL WGA 8:32-33 Feb 1995
BRADLEY, DOUG
  Beeler, M. Pin Head speaks! il port stills C FANTAS 26:36-37 n3 1995
BRADLEY, MATTHEW R.
  Bradley, M.R. Nolan's "Run." biog il interv stills F FAX n48:42-48+ [8p]
    Jan/Feb 1995
  Bradley, M.R. "The Haunting" and other Wise tales... il interv port stills
    F FAX n49:50-55+ [9p] Mar/Apr 1995
BRADY BUNCH MOVIE, THE f (d Thomas, Betty 1995 USA)
  Handelman, D. The birth of the uncool. il stills PREM 8:84-88 Mar 1995
  Marin, R. and Chang, Y. A wildly successful Bunch. stills NEWSWK 125:71
    Mar 6 1995
    Reviews
  Coleman, B. "The Brady Bunch Movie." VILLAGE VOICE 40:74 Feb 28 1995
  Klady, L. "The Brady Bunch Movie." credits VARIETY 358:73-74 Feb
    20/26 1995
  Noh, D. "The Brady Bunch Movie." credits still FJ 98:57-58 Mar 1995
  Schickel, R. Sons of "Wayne's World." stills TIME 145:100 Mar 6 1995
  Silberg, J. "The Brady Bunch." BOXOFFICE 131:bet p125 and 144 [pR30] Apr
    1995
BRADY, RAY See also BOY MEETS GIRL
BRAENDLI, SABINA For film reviews see author under the following titles:
    ENFANTS JOUENT A LA RUSSIE, LES; MOUVEMENTS DU DESIR; PUNCH
BRAGG, MELVYN
  Ciment, M. BFI film classics [Book Reviews]. stills POSITIF n408:75-77 Feb
    1995
  Cremonini, G. Sam Rohdie: Rocco and his bothers (Rocco e i suoi fratelli) di
    L. Visconti [Book Reviews]. C FORUM 34:93 Sep (n337) 1994
BRAKHAGE, STAN See also VISIONS IN MEDITATION #1
  Brakhage, S. Gertrude Stein: meditative literature and film. il MILLENNIUM
    n25:100-107 Summer 1991
  Higgins, G. and others. Grisled roots. interv ports MILLENNIUM n26:56-66
    Fall 1992
  Testa, B. The two religions of avant-garde film, or maybe three. CAN J F
    STUD 3:89-100 n2 1994
BRAMBILLA, MARCO See also DEMOLITION MAN
BRAMKAMP, ROBERT See also EROBERUNG DER MITTE, DIE
  Die Eroberung der Mitte. biog credits filmog still KINO(BRD) n1:16-17 1995

BRANAGH, KENNETH   See also MARY SHELLEY'S FRANKENSTEIN
Calderale, M. Filmografie. biogs filmogs il SEGNO n71:40 Jan/Feb 1995
Elrick, T. Kenneth Branagh re-creates the classics. filmog interv ports
   DGA NEWS 19:32-33+ [4p] n6 1994/95
Thomas, M.R. Mary Shelley's Frankenstein. Kenneth Branagh [Book Review]. il
   SCARLET STREET n17:97 Winter 1995
BRANCO, IL f (d Risi, Marco 1994 It)
   Reviews
   Causo, M. "Il branco." credits still C FORUM 34:78 Sep (n337) 1994
   Picchi, M. "Il branco." credits still C NUOVO 43:57 Nov/Dec (n352) 1994
BRANDENBOURGER, LAURENT   See also LUC & MARIE: LE FILM
BRANDO, JOCELYN
   Marlon Brando. biogs filmogs il port stills STARS n21:[7-10] Winter 1995
BRANDO, MARLON
   Elia, M. Sacres monstres! il ports SEQUENCES n175:58-59 Nov/Dec 1994
   Marlon Brando. biogs filmogs il port stills STARS n21:[7-10] Winter 1995
   Mitchell, L. Dueling Brandos [Book Reviews]. still DGA NEWS 19:55-56 n6
      1994/95
   Murray, S. Songs my mother taught me. Marlon Brando, with Robert Lindsey
      [Book Review]. il C PAPERS n102:73-74 Dec 1994
   Naremore, J. Brando: songs my mother taught me. By Marlon Brando, with
      Robert Lindsey [Book Reviews]. CINEASTE 21:92-94 n1/2 1995
BRANDT, JAMES B.
   Brandt, J.B. "Street Fighter." il stills C FANTAS 26:56-57 n2 1995
BRANIGAN, EDWARD
   Branigan, E. On the analysis of interpretive language: Part I. bibliog F
      CRITICISM 17:4-21 n2/3 1992/93
   Odin, R. Narrative comprehended [Book Review]. Q REV F & VIDEO 15:35-46 n3
      1994
   Rothschild, W. Branigan, Edward. Narrative comprehension and film [Book
      Review]. CINEMAS 4:177-182 n3 1994
BRANNAGH, KENNETH
   Aldarondo, R. La tentacion de Shakespeare. stills NOSFERATU n8:20-27 Feb
      1992
BRAQUEUSES, LES f (d Salome, Jean-Paul 1994 Fr)
   Bellion, C. "Les braqueuses." bibliog credits stills GRAND ANGLE n178:3-4
      Jan 1995
BRASELL, R. BRUCE
   Brasell, R.B. Queer nationalism and the musical fag bashing of John
      Greyson's "The Making of 'Monsters'." il stills WIDE ANGLE 16:26-36 n3
      1995
BRASHINSKY, MICHAEL
   Menashe, L. Requiem for Soviet cinema 1917-1991 [Book Reviews]. stills
      CINEASTE 21:23-27 n1/2 1995
BRAUDEL, FERNAND
   Lagny, M. Le film et le temps braudelien. bibliog stills CINEMAS 5:15-39
      n1/2 1994
BRAUNBERGER, PIERRE
   Berthome, J.-P. Voir un peu d'herbe avant de mourir... il POSITIF
      n408:84-89 Feb 1995
Brazil   See as a subheading under individual subject headings
BRAZZI, ROSSANO
   Lentz, H., III. Obituaries. biogs filmogs il obits ports CLASSIC
      n236:57-59 Feb 1995
   Milestones. obit port TIME 145:19 Jan 9 1995
   Obituaries. biog obits VARIETY 357:83-84 Jan 2/8 1995
   Transition. obits ports NEWSWK 125:66 Jan 9 1995
BREAMER, SYLVIA
   Katchmer, G. Remembering the great silents. biogs filmogs port CLASSIC
      n237:35+ [3p] Mar 1995
BREATHLESS f (d McBride, Jim 1983 USA)
   Loffreda, P. Primi sguardi nella scuola: dalla descrizione al racconto. il
      stills C FORUM 34:3-7 Oct (n338) 1994
BREDIN, ROBERT
   Bredin, R. Fail-safe device prevents polyester film breakdowns. il FJ
      98:95 Jan/Feb 1995
BREEN, JON L.
   Breen, J.L. Barer, Burl. The Saint: a complete history in print, radio, film
      and television of Leslie Charteris' Robin Hood of crime, Simon Templar,
      1928-1992 [Book Review]. ARMCHAIR DET 27:222-223 n2 1994
   Breen, J.L. Cocchiarelli, Joseph J. Screen sleuths: a filmography [Book
      Review]. ARMCHAIR DET 27:92 n1 1994
   Breen, J.L. Cutler, Stan. Shot on location [Book Review]. il port ARMCHAIR
      DET 26:74 n3 1993
   Breen, J.L. Gerald, Marc, ed. Murder plus: true crime stories from the
      masters of detective fiction [Book Review]. ARMCHAIR DET 28:78 n1 1995
   Breen, J.L. Hanke, Ken. Charlie Chan at the movies: history, filmography,
      and criticism [Book Review]. still ARMCHAIR DET 26:78 n3 1993
   Breen, J.L. Harmon, Jim. Radio mystery and adventure and its appearances in
      film, television and other media [Book Review]. ARMCHAIR DET 26:78-79 n3
      1993
   Breen, J.L. Hubin, Allen J. Crime fiction II: a comprehensive bibliography
      1749-1990 [Book Review]. ARMCHAIR DET 28:197 n2 1995
   Breen, J.L. Kincaid, D., Pseudonym of Bert Fields. The lawyer's tale [Book
      Review]. ARMCHAIR DET 26:74-75 n3 1993
   Breen, J.L. Langman, Larry, and David Ebner. Encyclopedia of American spy
      films [Book Review]. ARMCHAIR DET 27:93-94 n1 1994
BREEN, MARCUS   For film reviews see author under the following titles: MY COUNTRY
BREER, EMILY   See also DOG, POPE, AND JOE
   Breer, E. "Dog, Pope and Joe." il scenario stills MILLENNIUM n26:68-77
      Fall 1992
BRENTA, MARIO   See also BARNABO DELLE MONTAGNE
BRESCIA, ANTONIO
   Brescia, A. "Sotto il vecchio berso'." Di Giacomo D'Onofrio [Book Review].
      biog C SUD 33:40 Jul/Aug/Sep (n113) 1994
BRESLO, ROBERT PAUL
   Obituaries. biogs obits VARIETY 358:86-87 Mar 27/Apr 2 1995
BREST, MARTIN   See also SCENT OF A WOMAN
BRIAN, MARY
   Ankerich, M. Reel stars: a chat with Mary Brian. biog il interv port stills

CLASSIC n236:14-16 Feb 1995
BRIDE OF FRANKENSTEIN f (d Whale, James 1935 USA)
   Sound Track Reviews
   Larson, R.D. Review spotlight: "The Bride of Frankenstein" - at last! il F
      SCORE MONTHLY n39:15 Nov 1993
Bride of Glomdal, The   See GLOMDALSBRUDEN
BRIDES OF DRACULA, THE f (d Fisher, Terence 1960 Gt Br)
   Bernardo, J.M. "Las novias de Dracula." credits il still NOSFERATU
      n6:86-87 Apr 1991
BRIDGES, JIM
   Bridges, J. Cinematic interruptus. il stills CANTRILL'S FMNTS n73/74:20-31
      May 1994
BRIEF ENCOUNTER f (d Lean, David 1945 Gt Br)
   Ciment, M. BFI film classics [Book Reviews]. stills POSITIF n408:75-77 Feb
      1995
BRILL, LESLEY
   Brill, L. "The African Queen" and John Huston's filmmaking. CJ 34:3-21 n2
      1995
BRILL, LOUIS M.
   Brill, L.M. Las Vegas: mega-movie mecca. il table BOXOFFICE 131:24-25+
      [3p] Apr 1995
BRILL, STEVEN   See also HEAVYWEIGHTS
BRINKMOELLER-BECKER, HEINRICH
   Brinkmoeller-Becker, H. Kino und die Wahrnehmung von Filmen. il MEDIEN
      38:327-332 n6 1994
BRISSEAU, JEAN-CLAUDE   See also ANGE NOIR, L'
BRITISH BOARD OF FILM CLASSIFICATION
   Dean, P. Wind up. still S&S 5:70 Jan 1995
   Mathews, T.D. Strictly classified. il S&S 5:5 Jan 1995
BRITISH FEDERATION OF FILM SOCIETIES
   Brownlie, T. David Phillips BFFS Chair. il ports FILM 4:16-18 n1 [1995]
      Conferences, Institutes, Workshops, etc.
   Clay, B. "To Live" is tops in South West. port stat still table FILM 4:7+
      [2p] n1 [1995]
   Currie, R. Glasgow Copthorne all aglow. stat still table FILM 4:6 n1
      [1995]
   Dempster, J. Stabilising the ship. il table FILM 4:5 n1 [1995]
   Robson, P. Autumn viewing sessions. still FILM 4:4 n1 [1995]
BRITISH FILM INSTITUTE (London)
   Brownlie, T. David Phillips BFFS Chair. il ports FILM 4:16-18 n1 [1995]
      Distribution
   New from BFI. still table FILM 4:29 n1 [1995]
BRITISH FILM INSTITUTE. NATIONAL FILM AND TELEVISION ARCHIVE (London)
   Borger, L. Sisyphian struggles [Book Review]. S&S 5:37-38 Feb 1995
   Pollock, N. McKernan, Luke and Terris, Olwen, eds. Walking shadows:
      Shakespeare in the National Film and Television Archive [Book Review].
      MEDIA INFO AUSTRALIA n75:168 Feb 1995
      History
   Cosandey, R. Keepers of the frame: the film archives. Edited by Penelope
      Houston [Book Review]. J F PRES n49:67-68 Oct 1994
BROCA, PHILIPPE DE   See also JARDIN DE PLANTES
BROCHMANN, KRISTIN
   Brochmann, K. "Hodet over vannet." credits still F&K n7:38-39 1993
   Brochmann, K. "Koloss." still F&K n7:38 1993
BROCHU, DOMINIQUE
   Brochu, D. Marques d'un cinema moderne: "Le roi des enfants." bibliog glos
      still CINEMAS 3:8-22 n2/3 1993
BRODIE, JOHN
   Brodie, J. Disney wannabes play copycat-and-mouse. il still VARIETY 357:1+
      [2p] Jan 2/8 1995
   Brodie, J. Distribs' marketing debate becomes tale of 3 cities. stat
      VARIETY 358:9+ [2p] Feb 13/19 1995
   Brodie, J. Hapless helmers torn by tensions. il ports VARIETY 358:1+ [3p]
      Feb 6/12 1995
   Brodie, J. Managers pounding at the studio gates. VARIETY 358:15-16 Mar
      27/Apr 2 1995
   Brodie, J. Rysher sets to make splash into pic pool. stat VARIETY 358:13+
      [2p] Mar 6/12 1995
   Brodie, J. Stars' double standards. il stat VARIETY 358:13-14 Feb 27/Mar 5
      1995
   Brodie, J. and O'Steen, K. Antsy agents make mutant managers. il VARIETY
      358:1+ [3p] Mar 20/26 1995
   O'Steen, K. and Brodie, J. Acad rebounds after "Hoop" airball. il VARIETY
      358:11+ [2p] Feb 20/26 1995
BRODKEY, HAROLD
   Brodkey, H. The last word on Winchell. il NEW YORKER 70:70-78 Jan 30 1995
BROECK, CHRISTOPHE VANDEN
   Broeck, C.V. and Noel, J. "Farinelli." bibliog credits stills GRAND ANGLE
      n177:15-16 Dec 1994
   Broeck, C.V. and Noel, J. "La separation." credits stills GRAND ANGLE
      n176:23-24 Nov 1994
   Broeck, C.V. and Noel, J. "L'ange noir." credits stills GRAND ANGLE
      n177:5-6 Dec 1994
   Broeck, C.V. and Noel, J. "Les nouvelles aventures de Croc Blanc - le mythe
      du loup." bibliog credits stills GRAND ANGLE n176:17-18 Nov 1994
BROKEN ARROW f (d Daves, Delmer 1950 USA)
   Manchel, F. Cultural confusion: a look back at Delmar Daves's "Broken
      Arrow." bibliog stills F&HIST 23:58-69+ [13p] n1/4 1993
BROKEN CHAIN, THE f (d Johnson, Lamont 1993 USA)
   Dowell, P. The mythology of the western: Hollywood perspectives on race and
      gender in the nineties. stills CINEASTE 21:6-10 n1/2 1995
BROLLEY, MARIA
   Brolley, M. Shallow graves. By William Jefferies [Book Reviews]. ARMCHAIR
      DET 26:104 n3 1993
BROMBERG, SERGE
   Adamson, J. and others. Forgotten laughter. credits port stills
      GRIFFITHIANA n51/52:170-197 Oct 1994
   Adamson, J. and others. La fabbrica della risata. credits port stills
      GRIFFITHIANA n51/52:170-197 Oct 1994

83 [pSW1O] Apr 1995
BURTON, RICHARD See also DOCTOR FAUSTUS
BURTON, TIM See ED WOOD
 Coursodon, J.-P. "Ed Wood." credits stills POSITIF n406:8-11 Dec 1994
BURUMA, IAN
 Buruma, I. The great art of embarrassment. il still NY R BKS 42:15-18 Feb
  16 1995
BUSCH, ANITA M.
 Busch, A. M. and Laski, B. Hughes hightails it back to CAA. VARIETY 357:8
  Jan 9/15 1995
 Busch, A.M. Hughes and Mestres team in Disney-based Great Oaks Ent. port
  VARIETY 358:22 Feb 20/26 1995
 Busch, A.M. Oliver Stone, New Regency on the rocks? stat VARIETY 358:14+
  [2p] Feb 20/26 1995
 Busch, A.M. ShoWest's growing pains. VARIETY 358:7+ [2p] Mar 13/19 1995
 Busch, A.M. Summer pix get a fast food fix. il VARIETY 358:1+ [2p] Feb
  20/26 1995
 Busch, A.M. and Peers, M. Troika has its eyes on $1 bil prize. stat
  VARIETY 358:13 Feb 27/Mar 5 1995
 Busch, A.M. and Weiner, R. Gates joins DreamWorks team. il VARIETY 358:15+
  [2p] Mar 27/Apr 2 1995
 Cox, D. and Busch, A.M. Producers draw battle lines over credit order.
  ports VARIETY 358:28+ [2p] Feb 20/26 1995
 Cox, D. and Busch, A.M. Producers piqued. VARIETY 358:8-9 Feb 27/Mar5 1995
 Klady, L. and Busch, A.M. Wintry b.o. chills ShoWest's sizzle. stat
  VARIETY 358:1+ [2p] Mar 6/12 1995
BUSCOMBE, EDWARD
 Buscombe, E. Classical Hollywood narrative: the paradigm wars. Edited by
  Jane Gaines [Book Review]. FQ 48:60-61 n2 1994/95
 Ciment, M. BFI film classics [Book Reviews]. stills POSITIF n408:75-77 Feb
  1995
 Cremonini, G. Sam Rohdie: Rocco and his bothers (Rocco e i suoi fratelli) di
  L. Visconti [Book Reviews]. C FORUM 34:93 Sep (n337) 1994
 Hendrykowski, M. BFI Film Classics [Book Review]. il KINO 27:39-40 May
  1993
BUTLER, DAVID
 Codelli, L. David Butler. Interviewed by Irene Kahn Atkins [Book Review].
  GRIFFITHIANA n51/52:254 Oct 1994
BUTTERFLY KISS f (d Winterbottom, Michael 1995 Gt Br)
  Reviews
 Elley, D. High-octane mayhem elevates "Butterfly." credits still VARIETY
  358:73+ [2p] Feb 20/26 1995
BUVOS VADASZ f (d Enyedi, Ildiko 1994 Hungary/Switz/Fr)
  Reviews
 Comuzio, E. "Buvos vadasz." still C FORUM 34:17 Sep (n337) 1994
 La Rochelle, R. "Magic Hunter." still 24 IMAGES n75:44-45 Dec/Jan 1994/95
BYARS, JACKIE
 McKee, A.L. Negotiating gender in post-World War II America [Book Reviews].
  Q REV F & VIDEO 15:47-56 n3 1994
BYE BYE, LOVE f (d Weisman, Sam 1995 USA)
 Lally, K. "Bye Bye Love" sees funny side of divorce. il still FJ 98:16+
  [2p] Mar 1995
  Reviews
 Finnegan, C. "Bye Bye, Love." VILLAGE VOICE 40:68 Mar 28 1995
 Klady, L. "Bye Bye, Love." credits still VARIETY 358:49-50 Mar 13/19 1995
BYUN, YOUNG-JOO
 Byun, Y.-j. Recent movements in the Korean documentary scene. biog il DOC
  BOX 3:19-20 1993
CAM
 Carriou, A. and Radovich, G. The wonderful world of CAM. F SCORE MONTHLY
  n36/37:36-37 Aug/Sep 1993
CBS See COLUMBIA BROADCASTING SYSTEM, INC.
CABEZA DE VACA f (d Echevarria, Nicolas 1991 Mex/Sp)
 Hershfield, J. Assimilation and identification in Nicholas Echeverria's
  "Cabeza de vaca." bibliog WIDE ANGLE 16:6-24 n3 1995
CABO BLANCO f (d Thompson, J. Lee 1980 USA)
  Sound Track Reviews
 Kendall, L. "Caboblanco." F SCORE MONTHLY n40:12 Dec 1993
CABRERA INFANTE, GUILLERMO
 Cabrera Infante, G. Cinema paradiso [Book Review]. NEW REPUB 212:40-42 Jan
  23 1995
 Cabrera Infante, G. Laurence Olivier, un actor de teatro en el cine. stills
  NOSFERATU n8:28-31 Feb 1992
CABRERA, SERGIO See also AGUILAS NO CAZAN MOSCAS
CAGLE, ROBERT L.
 Cagle, R.L. On the irresponsibility of a certain film critic: a note to an
  "outsider." stills C ACTION n36:3-8 1995
 Cagle, R.L. "Tell the story of my life...": the making of meaning,
  "Monsters," and music in John Greyson's "Zero Patience." il stills VEL LT
  TRAP n35:69-81 Spring 1995
CAGNEY, JAMES
 Martin, A. Performing the city [Book Review]. Q REV F & VIDEO 15:71-76 n3
  1994
CAHN, EDWARD L. See also IT!: THE TERROR FROM BEYOND SPACE
CAIXA, A f (d Oliveira, Manoel de 1994 Port/Fr)
  Reviews
 Gili, J.A. "La cassette." still POSITIF n409:41-42 Mar 1995
 Jean, M. "La cassette." still 24 IMAGES n75:42-43 Dec/Jan 1994/95
CALAVITA, MARCO For film reviews see author under the following titles: COBB
CALDERALE, MARIO For film reviews see author under the following titles: SIRENS
 Calderale, M. Filmografie. biogs filmogs il SEGNO n71:40 Jan/Feb 1995
 Calderale, M. Piccola guida allo special. stills SEGNO n63:18 Sep/Oct 1993
CALENDAR f (d Egoyan, Atom 1993 Can/FR Ger/Armenia)
 Egoyan, A. "Calendar." il still POSITIF n406:93-94 Dec 1994
 Rouyer, P. "Calendar." credits stills POSITIF n406:91-92 Dec 1994
CALENDARS
  Germany (Federal Republic, since 1990)
 (Hundert) 100 Jahre Filmgeschichte. il KINO(GF) n56:27 Nov 1994
CALLAN, MICHAEL FEENEY
 Nangle, J. Anthony Hopkins, the unauthorized biography. By Michael Feeney

Callan [Book Review]. FIR 45:70-71 Nov/Dec 1994
CALLE-GRUBER, MIREILLE
 Calle-Gruber, M. La chimere du modele. bibliog still CINEMAS 4:72-87 n1
  1993
CALLEJON DE LOS MILAGROS, EL f (d Fons, Jorge 1995 Mex)
  Reviews
 Leydon, J. "Midaj alley" ("El callejon de los milagros"). credits VARIETY
  358:51 Mar 20/26 1995
CALMETTES, ANDRE See also ASSASSINAT DU DUC DE GUISE, L'
CALPARSORO, DANIEL See also SALTO AL VACIO
CALVINO, ITALO
 Calvino, I. Voyage en camion. POSITIF n408:62-64 Feb 1995
Camera accessories [Prior to V16, 1988 use CAMERA ACCESSORIES] See CAMERA
  EQUIPMENT
CAMERA EQUIPMENT [Prior to V16, 1988 use CAMERA ACCESSORIES]
  United States
   Cinema Products Vidiflex viewfinder
 Solman, G. Hollywood's high-fiber diet. il DGA NEWS 19:18 n6 1994/95
CAMERAMAN, THE f (d Sedgwick, Edward 1928 USA)
 Parshall, P.F. Buster Keaton and the space of farce: "Steamboat Bill, Jr."
  versus "The Cameraman." bibliog diag stills UFAJ 46:29-46 n3 1994
Cameramen See CINEMATOGRAPHERS
CAMERIERI f (d Pompucci, Leone 1995 It)
  Reviews
 Maerini, O. "Camerieri." credits still FILM (ITALY) 3:8-9 n13 1995
 Molinari, M. "Camerieri." credits stills SEGNO n72:47-49 Mar/Apr 1995
 Rooney, D. "Waiters" ("Camerieri"). credits VARIETY 358:48 Feb 13/19 1995
CAMERON, EVAN WILLIAM
 Cameron, E.W. Kant's station; the Lumieres' train: seeing things by means of
  film. CAN J F STUD 1:36-56 n1 1990
CAMERON, JAMES See also TERMINATOR 2: JUDGMENT DAY; TRUE LIES
CAMHI, LESLIE For film reviews see author under the following titles:
  FARINELLI: IL CASTRATO; KKK BOUTIQUE AIN'T JUST REDNECKS, THE
CAMILLA f (d Mehta, Deepa 1994 Can/Gt Br)
  Reviews
 Nagy, G. "Camilla." credits still F VILAG 38:56 n4 1995
 Porter, B. "Camilla." credits FJ 98:57-58 Jan/Feb 1995
CAMISARDS, LES f (d Allio, Rene 1971 Fr)
  Time
 Lagny, M. Le film et le temps braudelien. bibliog stills CINEMAS 5:15-39
  n1/2 1994
CAMP
 Canova, G. L'unica igiene del cinema. still SEGNO n72:26 Mar/Apr 1995
CAMPANADAS A MEDIANOCHE f (Chimes at Midnight d Welles, Orson 1966 Sp/Switz)
 Riambau, E. "Campanadas a medianoche." credits stills NOSFERATU n8:61-62
  Feb 1992
 Riambau, E. Shakespeare y Welles. stills NOSFERATU n8:32-39 Feb 1992
CAMPARI, ROBERTO
 Comuzio, E. Roberto Campari: il fantasma del bello. Iconologia del cinema
  italiano [Book Review]. il C FORUM 34:93 Nov (n339) 1994
CAMPBELL, CAROLYN
 Campbell, C. Screen sex & violence? Just say none. il port stills
  BOXOFFICE 131:46+ [4p] Apr 1995
CAMPBELL, DON See also YOUNG AT HEARTS
CAMPBELL, MARTIN See also GOLDENEYE; NO ESCAPE
CAMPBELL, VIRGINIA
 Campbell, V. Open secret. port MOVIELINE 6:70-71 Apr 1995
 Campbell, V. and Margulies, E. More great moments in miscasting. stills
  MOVIELINE 6:62-66+ [8p] Mar 1995
CAMPION, ANNA See also LOADED
 Pryor, I. Loaded ...with talent. port ONFILM [12]:12 n1 1995
CAMPION, JANE
 Comuzio, C. Garage n. 1: Jane Campion [Book Review]. il C FORUM 34:94 Oct
  (n338) 1994
CAMUNAS, CARLOS RAFAEL
 Camunas, C.R. David Amram: a reluctant film composer. F SCORE MONTHLY
  n36/37:24 Aug/Sep 1993
 Camunas, C.R. Film music in Puerto Rico. F SCORE MONTHLY n40:4 Dec 1993
Canada See as a subheading under individual subject headings See CINEMATHEQUE
  QUEBECOISE, LA (Montreal, Canada); NATIONAL FILM BOARD OF CANADA
CANADIAN FILMMAKERS' DISTRIBUTION CENTRE (CFMDC)
 Fothergill, R. Canadian Film-makers' Distribution Centre: a founding memoir.
  CAN J F STUD 3:81-85 n2 1994
CANDELORO, LAURA For film reviews see author under the following titles:
  BODIES, REST & MOTION; TRIAL BY JURY
CANDYMAN f (d Rose, Bernard 1992 USA)
 kydd, E. Guess who else is coming to dinner: racial/sexual hysteria in
  "Candyman." stills C ACTION n36:63-72 1995
CANDYMAN: FAREWELL TO THE FLESH f (d Condon, Bill 1995 USA)
 French, T. "Candyman 2." stills C FANTAS 26:40-41+ [3p] n3 1995
 French, T. "Candyman 2." stills C FANTAS 26:8-9 n2 1995
  Reviews
 Klady, L. "Candyman: Farewell to the Flesh." credits VARIETY 358:49 Mar
  20/26 1995
CANEMAKER, JOHN
 Canemaker, J. Vladimir Tytla - master animator. biog il ANIMATION J 3:4-30
  n1 1994
CANNON, DANNY See also JUDGE DREDD
CANOSA, MICHELE
 Montanaro, C. Henri Storck: il litorale belga. A cura di Michele Canosa
  [Book Review]. GRIFFITHIANA n51/52:260 Oct 1994
CANOVA, GIANNI For film reviews see author under the following titles: BLINK;
  NAKED
 Canova, G. L'unica igiene del cinema. still SEGNO n72:26 Mar/Apr 1995
 Canova, G. "Melo." filmog il stills SEGNO n72:72-73 Mar/Apr 1995
 Poggi, E. Il critico al festival ovvero lo spettatore indiscreto. intervs
  SEGNO n71:19-33 Jan/Feb 1995
CANOVAS BELCHI, JOAQUIN T.
 Livio, J. Catalogo del cine espanol volumen F2: peliculas de ficcion
  1921-1930. Di Palmira Gonzalez Lopez e Joaquin T. Canovas Belchi [Book

still C SUD 33:8-9 Jul/Aug/Sep (n113) 1994
CASLAVSKY, KAREL
Caslavsky, K. American comedy series: filmographies 1914-1930. filmog il
stills GRIFFITHIANA n51/52:9+ [50p] Oct 1994
Caslavsky, K. Comedians. filmogs il stills GRIFFITHIANA n51/52:60-169 Oct
1994
Caslavsky, K. Le serie comiche americane: filmografie 1914-1930. filmog il
stills GRIFFITHIANA n51/52:8+ [50p] Oct 1994
CASSANDRA, ELLIS For film reviews see author under the following titles: IN
DARKEST HOLLYWOOD: CINEMA & APARTHEID
CASSAVETES, JOHN
Barson, M. The films of John Cassavetes: pragmatism, modernism, and the
movies. By Ray Carney [Book Review]. DGA NEWS 19:29-30 n3 1994
Cantrill, A. The films of John Cassavetes: pragmatism, modernism and the
movies. By Ray Carney [Book Review]. CANTRILL'S FMNTS n73/74:40 May 1994
CASTIEL, ELIE For film reviews see author under the following titles:
ADVENTURES OF PRISCILLA, QUEEN OF THE DESERT, THE; HUEVOS DE ORO;
KABLOONAK; MUSTARD BATH
Castiel, E. Festival international du cinema en Abitibi-Temiscamingue. il
still SEQUENCES n175:7-8 Nov/Dec 1994
Castiel, E. Jean-Daniel Lafond. interv still SEQUENCES n175:8 Nov/Dec 1994
Castiel, E. Robert Morin. filmog il interv SEQUENCES n175:13-16 Nov/Dec
1994
Castiel, E. Sylvie Vartan. interv still SEQUENCES n175:9 Nov/Dec 1994
Castiel, E. Toronto International Film Festival. il stills SEQUENCES
n175:6-7 Nov/Dec 1994
CASTILLO DURANTE, DANIEL
Castillo Durante, D. Noriega, Chon A. (ed). Chicanos and film.
Representation and resistance [Book Review]. CINEMAS 4:177-181 n2 1994
CASTING AND CASTING DIRECTORS See also names of casting directors
United States
Actors and Actresses
Campbell, V. and Margulies, E. More great moments in miscasting. stills
MOVIELINE 6:62-66+ [8p] Mar 1995
History
Barson, M. Hollywood's first choices: how the greatest casting decisions
were made. By Jeff Burkhart & Bruce Stuart [Book Review]. DGA NEWS 20:42-43
n1 1995
CASTLE, ANTONY
Castle, A. Ghosts in the kingdom. il stills BLIMP n30:4-11 Winter 1994
CASTLE, NICK See also DENNIS THE MENACE; MAJOR PAYNE
CASTLE, WILLIAM
Barson, M. Step right up! I'm gonna scare the pants off America. By William
Castle [Book Review]. DGA NEWS 19:34+ [2p] n2 1994
CASTORO CINEMA, IL
Michele Picchi. Sergei Paradzanov [Book Review]. il KINO(GF) n56:29 Nov
1994
CATELLI, DANIELA For film reviews see author under the following titles: AIQING
WANSUI; SHAWSHANK REDEMPTION, THE
Catelli, D. Il falso e i falsi. stills SEGNO n63:91-92 Sep/Oct 1993
Catelli, D. Un diluvio di film. stills SEGNO n71:58-59 Jan/Feb 1995
CATERERS AND CATERING
France
History
La cantiniere du cinema. Par Henriette Marello [Book Review]. il GRAND
ANGLE n176:39 Nov 1994
CATES, JOSEPH See also WHO KILLED TEDDY BEAR?
CATON-JONES, MICHAEL See also ROB ROY
CATSOS, GREGORY J.M.
Catsos, G.J.M. Children of the corn. il intervs F FAX n48:64-65+ [3p]
Jan/Feb 1995
Catsos, G.J.M. Disney's folly! il interv stills F FAX n48:49-53 Jan/Feb
1995
CAUSO, MASSIMO For film reviews see author under the following titles: A LA
FOLIE; BRANCO, IL; LITTLE ODESSA; MOVING THE MOUNTAIN; ONCE WERE
WARRIORS; TETA I LA LUNA, LA; UNO A TE, UNO A ME, E UNO A RAFFAELE;
VEJA ESTA CANCAO; WORDS UPON THE WINDOW PANE
Causo, M. "Vive l'amour." credits stills C FORUM 34:76-78 Nov (n339) 1994
CAVALCANTI, ALBERTO See also WENT THE DAY WELL?
CAZALS, PATRICK
Patrick Cazals: Serguei Paradjanov [Book Review]. il KINO(GF) n56:29 Nov
1994
CD [author]
CD [author]. "Kraj swiata." biog credits filmog still FSP 40:13 n4 (n758)
1994
CD [author]. "Mieso." biog credits filmog FSP 40:7 n6 (n760) 1994
CECCHI GORI, VITTORIO
Zecchinelli, C. Cecchi Gori deal thrusts producer onto b'cast map. VARIETY
358:47 Mar 13/19 1995
CEDERNA, GIUSEPPE
Santucci, E. Obiettivo festival. il SEGNO n71:19-23 Jan/Feb 1995
CELINSKA, STANISLAWA
Pelka, B. Stanislawa Celinska. filmog still FSP 40:10 n11 (n765) 1994
CENSORSHIP See also MORALITY; POLITICS AND GOVERNMENT; PORNOGRAPHY AND OBSCENITY;
PUBLIC ATTITUDES
International Aspects
Lochen, K. Eksisterer det ufarlige? stat stills table F&K n1:28-30 1994
Great Britain
Dean, P. Wind up. still S&S 5:70 Jan 1995
Mathews, T.D. Strictly classified. il S&S 5:5 Jan 1995
Sweden
Lovlund, B.-F. Guidet tur gjennom voldelig subkultur [Book Review]. il Z
n4:41 (n46) 1993
United States
White, S. I burn for him: female masochism and the iconography of melodrama
in Stahl's "Back Street" (1932). bibliog stills PS 14:59-80 n1/2 1994/95
History
Barson, M. Hollywood censored: morality codes, Catholics and movies. By
Gregory D. Black [Book Review]. DGA NEWS 19:59 n6 1994/95
McLane, B.A. Hollywood censored [Book Review]. DGA NEWS 19:58-59 n6

1994/95
Muscio, G. The commerce of classicism [Book Review]. Q REV F & VIDEO
15:57-69 n3 1994
Turner, G. Hollywood censored. By Gregory D. Black [Book Review]. AMCIN
76:85 Mar 1995
Vowe, K.W. Political Correctness und Hollywood. still MEDIEN 38:356-359 n6
1994
Ohio, Cincinnati
Kaufman, B.L. Cincinnati's morality squad targets Pasolini. il INDEP
18:9-11 Jan/Feb 1995
CENT ET UNE NUITS, LES f (d Varda, Agnes 1995 Fr/Gt Br)
Production
Aude, F. "Les cent et une nuits" d'Agnes Varda: chronique d'un tournage. Par
Bernard Bastide [Book Review]. il POSITIF n409:71 Mar 1995
Reviews
Herpe, N. "Les cent et une nuits." credits still POSITIF n408:44-45 Feb
1995
CENTURY f (d Poliakoff, Stephen 1993 Gt Br)
Reviews
Meisel, M. "Century." credits FJ 98:71 Mar 1995
Cesars See AWARDS - France - Academie des Arts et Techniques du Cinema
C'EST ARRIVE PRES DE CHEZ VOUS f (Man Bites Dog d Belvaux, Remy/Bonzel,
Andre/Poelvoorde, Benoit 1992 Belg)
Lochen, K. Aggressiv satire. stills F&K n7:18-19 1993
C'ETAIT LE 12 DU 12 ET CHILI AVAIT LES BLUES f (d Biname, Charles 1994 Fr/Can)
Beaulieu, J. Entrevue avec Charles Biname. il interv SEQUENCES n174:15
Sep/Oct 1994
Reviews
Blois, M. de. "C'etait le 12 du 12, et Chili avait les blues." still 24
IMAGES n75:73-74 Dec/Jan 1994/95
CETIN, SINAN See also BERLIN IN BERLIN
Slodowski, J. "Obcy w Berlinie." biog credits filmog FSP 40:9 n5 (n759)
1994
CHA FORTE CON LIMAO f (d Macedo, Antonio de 1994 Port)
Reviews
Gili, J.A. "The noir au citron." POSITIF n406:49 Dec 1994
CHADHA, GURINDER See also BHAJI ON THE BEACH
"Bhaji on the Beach." biog credits filmog il still CINEMAYA n25/26:107
Autumn/Winter 1994/95
Kent, M. Gurinder Chadha. stills CINEMAYA n25/26:24-25 Autumn/Winter
1994/95
Robbins, H. "Bhaji" a lark in Blackpool. ANGLES 2:8 n4 1995
CHADWICK, HELENE
Katchmer, G. Remembering the great silents. biogs filmogs port CLASSIC
n237:35+ [3p] Mar 1995
CHAHINE, YOUSSEF See also MOHAGER, AL
CHAMBERS, LISA
Chambers, L. Fade in. il scenario JOURNAL WGA 8:43 Dec/Jan 1995
CHAMPAGNE, JOHN
Champagne, J. Psychoanalysis and cinema studies: a "queer" perspective.
bibliog PS 14:33-44 n1/2 1994/95
Chan, Charlie See CHARLIE CHAN (fictional character)
CHAN, JACKIE See also [RUMBLE IN THE BRONX]
Corliss, R. Jackie can! il TIME 145:82-83 Feb 13 1995
Giltz, M. Hi-yaaaah! still NEW YORK 28:89 Jan 30 1995
Jackie Chan. biog port FJ 98:86 Jan/Feb 1995
Retrospectives
Katz, A. Super Jackie. il VILLAGE VOICE 40:52 Jan 31 1995
CHAN, PAULINE See also TRAPS
Berry, C. Pauline Chan. il interv stills CINEMAYA n25/26:65-67
Autumn/Winter 1994/95
"Traps." biog credits port still CINEMAYA n25/26:98 Autumn/Winter 1994/95
CHANAN, MICHAEL
Chanan, M. The European documentary: third in a three-part series. stills
DOC BOX 4:13-16 1993
Chanan, M. "The Maltese Double Cross": Allan Francovich's film on Lockerbie
and the CIA. il port VERTIGO (UK) 1:30-32 n4 1994/95
Petley, J. and Chanan, M. Henri Storck interviewed for "Vertigo." interv
stills VERTIGO (UK) 1:34-36 n4 1994/95
CHANEY, LON
Turner, G. Lon Chaney: the man behind the thousand faces. By Michael F.
Blake [Book Review]. AMCIN 74:96 Sep 1993
CHANG, CHRIS
Chang, C. Disordinately absolute. stills F COM 31:8-10 Jan/Feb 1995
Chang, Sun-Woo See JANG, SUN-WOO
CHANG, SYLVIA See also ZUI AI
Sylvia Chang. il CINEMAYA n25/26:49 Autumn/Winter 1994/95
CHANG, YAHLIN
Marin, R. and Chang, Y. A wildly successful Bunch. stills NEWSWK 125:71
Mar 6 1995
CHANNEL 4 TELEVISION CO. LTD.
Dawtrey, A. Sky moves into movies. stat VARIETY 358:9 Mar 27/Apr 2 1995
Chaplin, Charles Spencer See CHAPLIN, CHARLIE
CHAPLIN, CHARLIE [Prior to V13, 1985 use CHAPLIN, CHARLES SPENCER] See also
CITY LIGHTS; COUNT, THE; EASY STREET; IMMIGRANT, THE; KID, THE
Lieberman, E.A. Charlie the trickster. bibliog stills UFAJ 46:16-28 n3
1994
Livio, J. "Limelight," the quarterly newsletter of the Charlie Chaplin Film
Company [Book Review]. GRIFFITHIANA n51/52:263 Oct 1994
Woal, M. and Woal, L.K. Chaplin and the comedy of melodrama. bibliog stills
UFAJ 46:3-15 n3 1994
CHAPLIN PUZZLE, THE f (d McGlynn, Don Denmk)
Sound Track Reviews
Larson, R.D. ...And by "Bride" producer Soren Hyldgaard: "The Chaplin
Puzzle." F SCORE MONTHLY n39:15 Nov 1993
CHAPLIN, SAUL
Redman, N. The golden age of movie musicals and me. By Saul Chaplin [Book
Review]. DGA NEWS 20:42 n1 1995
CHARLIE CHAN (fictional character)
Breen, J.L. Hanke, Ken. Charlie Chan at the movies: history, filmography,

and criticism [Book Review]. still ARMCHAIR DET 26:78 n3 1993
CHARMANT, GILLES See also IRON HORSEMEN
CHARME DISCRET DE LA BOURGEOISIE, LE f (Discreet Charm of the Bourgeoisie, The
  d Bunuel, Luis 1972 Fr/Sp/It)
    Pauly, R. A revolution is not a dinner party: "The Discrete Charm" of
      Bunuel's "Bourgeoisie." bibliog LIT/FQ 22:232-237 n4 1994
CHARTERIS, LESLIE
    Breen, J.L. Barer, Burl. The Saint: a complete history in print, radio, film
      and television of Leslie Charteris' Robin Hood of crime, Simon Templar,
      1928-1992 [Book Review]. ARMCHAIR DET 27:222-223 n2 1994
CHASE, CHARLEY
    Hogue, P. Charley with a y. il stills F COM 31:76-81 Mar/Apr 1995
    Roberts, R.M. Past humor, present laughter: the comedy film industry
      1914-1945. credits filmog il CLASSIC n236:41-46+ [7p] Feb 1995
    Roberts, R.M. Past humor, present laughter the comedy film industry
      1914-1945: Charley Chase filmography, part III: 1931-1940. credits filmog
      CLASSIC n237:36+ [5p] Mar 1995
CHASE SCENES IN FILM
    United States
    Hogan, D.J. Races, chases & crashes. By Dave Mann and Ron Main [Book
      Review]. il F FAX n48:12 Jan/Feb 1995
CHASE, THE f (d Rifkin, Adam 1994 USA)
    Reviews
    Emiliani, S. "Sesso e fuga con l'ostaggio." credits still FILM (ITALY)
      3:7-8 n13 1995
CHASERS f (d Hopper, Dennis 1994 USA)
    Reviews
    Hasted, N. "Chasers." credits S&S 5:43 Jan 1995
    Martini, E. "Una bionda sotto scorta." credits still C FORUM 34:81-82 Sep
      (n337) 1994
CHASING THE DEER f (d Holloway, Graham 1994 Gt Br)
    Reviews
    Elley, D. "Chasing the Deer." credits VARIETY 357:72 Jan 9/15 1995
    Macnab, G. "Chasing the Deer." credits S&S 5:43-44 Jan 1995
CHATEAUVERT, JEAN
    Chateauvert, J. Altman, Rick (direction). Sound theory. Sound practice [Book
      Review]. CINEMAS 4:157-166 n3 1994
    Chateauvert, J. Metz, Christian. L'enonciation impersonnelle ou le site du
      film [Book Review]. bibliog CINEMAS 3:241-246 n2/3 1993
CHATTERJEE, PARTHA
    Chatterjee, P. Over the years. il still CINEMAYA n25/26:18-19
      Autumn/Winter 1994/95
CHBOSKY, STEVE See also FOUR CORNERS OF NOWHERE, THE
    Spines, C. This boy's film. il PREM 8:33-34 Apr 1995
CHEAH, PHILIP
    Cheah, P. The NETPAC Asian Film Conference. il CINEMAYA n24:29 Summer 1994
    Cheah, P. Tokyo. il CINEMAYA n25/26:92-93 Autumn/Winter 1994/95
CHEANG, SHU LEA See also FRESH KILL
CHECHIK, JEREMIAH See also TALL TALE: THE UNBELIEVABLE ADVENTURES OF PECOS BILL
    French, L. "Tall Tale." il stills FANTAS 26:8-9 n3 1995
CHEN, GUOXING See also ["REDUNDANT" HUSBAND]
CHEN, KAIGE See also HAIZI WANG
    Huot, M.C. Deux poles yang du nouveau cinema chinois: Chen Kaige et Zhang
      Yimou. bibliog glos stills CINEMAS 3:103-125 n2/3 1993
CHEN, PEISI See also [FINAL WISH]
CHEN, RIXIN
    Chen, R. Jiang Shan, a rising star in music and film. il ports CHINA
      SCREEN n4:36-37 1994
CHEN, RU-SHOU ROBERT For film reviews see author under the following titles:
    DULI SHIDAI
CHEN, XIHE
    Yang, M.-Y. Film in contemporary China: critical debates, 1979-1989. Edited
      by George S. Semsel, Chen Xihe, and Xia Hong [Book Review]. FQ 48:61-62 n2
      1994/95
CHENG, SCARLET For film reviews see author under the following titles: BEI KAO
    BEI, LIAN DUI LIAN; CHUNGHING SAMLAM
    Cheng, S. Tran Anh Hung and the scents of Vietnam. stills CINEMAYA n24:4-7
      Summer 1994
CHERCHI USAI, PAOLO For film reviews see author under the following titles:
    BLADE RUNNER; BODY SNATCHERS; INTERVIEW WITH THE VAMPIRE: THE VAMPIRE
    CHRONICLES; LOVE AFFAIR; READY TO WEAR (PRET-A-PORTER); WHITE MEN
    CAN'T JUMP
    Adamson, J. and others. Forgotten laughter. credits port stills
      GRIFFITHIANA n51/52:170-197 Oct 1994
    Adamson, J. and others. La fabbrica della risata. credits port stills
      GRIFFITHIANA n51/52:170-197 Oct 1994
    Cherchi Usai, P. Catalogue Pathe des annees 1896 a 1914 [Book Review]. J F
      PRES n49:68-69 Oct 1994
    Cherchi Usai, P. Cent'anni da riscrivere [Book Review]. still SEGNO n72:71
      Mar/Apr 1995
    Cherchi Usai, P. El rescate de un camarografo: las imagenes perdidas de
      Eustasio Montoya. By Fernando del Moral Gonzalez [Book Review]. J F PRES
      n49:75 Oct 1994
    Cherchi Usai, P. El rescate de un camarografo: las imagenes perdidas de
      Eustasio Montoya. By Fernando del Moral Gonzalez [Book Review].
      GRIFFITHIANA n51/52:265 Oct 1994
    Cherchi Usai, P. Film history: an introduction. By Kristin Thompson and
      David Bordwell [Book Review]. J F PRES n49:70-72 Oct 1994
    Cherchi Usai, P. Film um 1910: Aus der Sammlung Joseph Joye (London). By
      Roland Cosandey [Book Review]. GRIFFITHIANA n51/52:258 Oct 1994
    Cherchi Usai, P. Film um 1910: Aus der Sammlung Joseph Joye (London). By
      Roland Cosandey [Book Review]. J F PRES n49:73 Oct 1994
    Cherchi Usai, P. Il cinema ritrovato: teoria e metodologia del restauro
      cinematografico. Edited by Gian Luca Farinelli and Nicola Mazzanti [Book
      Review]. J F PRES n49:69 Oct 1994
    Cherchi Usai, P. La mediocrita al potere. il still SEGNO n72:33-34 Mar/Apr
      1995
    Cherchi Usai, P. The cine goes to town: French cinema, 1896-1914. By Richard
      Abel [Book Review]. J F PRES n49:69 Oct 1994
    Cherchi Usai, P. The films of D.W. Griffith. By Scott Simmon [Book Reviews].

GRIFFITHIANA n51/52:259 Oct 1994
    Cherchi Usai, P. The films of D.W. Griffith. By Scott Simmon [Book Reviews].
      J F PRES n49:72-73 Oct 1994
    Cherchi Usai, P. The Library of Congress video collection: rare silent films
      with piano scores composed and performed by Philip Carli. GRIFFITHIANA
      n51/52:262-263 Oct 1994
    Cherchi Usai, P. The Library of Congress video collection: rare silent films
      with piano scores composed and performed by Philip Carli. J F PRES
      n49:74-75 Oct 1994
    Cherchi Usai, P. Widescreen cinema. By John Belton [Book Review]. J F PRES
      n49:75 Oct 1994
    Cherchi Usai, P. Widescreen cinema. By John Belton [Book Review].
      GRIFFITHIANA n51/52:266-267 Oct 1994
    Crossley, P. Catching silent cinema, - before it's too late [Book Review].
      il FILM 4:26 n1 [1995]
CHEREAU, PATRICE See also CONTRE L'OUBLI; REINE MARGOT, LA
CHESHIRE, GODFREY For film reviews see author under the following titles: A
    CRAN; ART FOR TEACHERS OF CHILDREN; BALLET; BOYS LIFE; LEONA'S SISTER
    GERRI; MANGLER, THE
CHEUNG, TAMMY
    Cheung, T. and Gilson, M. Gender trouble in Hongkong cinema. bibliog glos
      stills CINEMAS 3:181-201 n2/3 1993
CHIACCHIARI, FEDERICO
    Chiacchiari, F. "Go Fish." credits stills C FORUM 34:74-76 Oct (n338) 1994
    Chiacchiari, F. "Il mostro." credits stills C FORUM 34:68-71 Nov (n339)
      1994
    Chiacchiari, F. and De Marinis, G. "Amateur." credits stills C FORUM
      34:60-62 Sep (n337) 1994
CHIAO, PEGGY HSIUNG-PING
    Chiao, P. H. P. Stan Lai: "illusions, lies and reality." interv stills
      CINEMAYA n24:48-54 Summer 1994
CHIBANE, MALIK See also PANNE DE SENS
CHIEN ANDALOU, UN f (Andalusian Dog, An d Bunuel, Luis 1928 Fr)
    Jay, M. The disenchantment of the eye: surrealism and the crisis of
      ocularcentrism. il stills VISUAL ANTHRO R 7:15-38 n1 1991
CHIENNE, LA f (d Renoir, Jean 1931 Fr)
    Jeancolas, J.-P. Geraniums [Book Reviews]. stills POSITIF n408:94-95 Feb
      1995
Children See as a subheading under individual subject headings [Prior to
    V17, 1989 use as a subject heading]
CHILDREN AS ACTORS See also names of child actors and actresses
    United States
    Barlow, H. Slik er det a vaere barnestjerne. stills F&K n1:16-18 1994
Children's audience See AUDIENCE, CHILDREN
CHILDREN'S FILM
    Festivals
    Kantola, M. Oulun kansainvalinen lastenelokuvafestivaali. still PEILI
      17:40-41 n4 1993
    Uggeldahl, K. Sandnesin Kinossa elokuvissa. stills PEILI 18:36-37 n3 1994
    Finland
    Naranen, P. Reunamerkintoja Ronnbergin lapsikuvasta. bibliog il PEILI
      18:14-15 n2 1994
    Short Film
    Juurikkala, K. Lyhyt johdatus lyhytelokuvan sielunmaisemaan. stills PEILI
      17:4-5 n3 1993
Chimes at Midnight See CAMPANADAS A MEDIANOCHE
China (People's Republic, since 1949) See as a subheading under individual
    subject headings
China (Republic, since 1949) See as a subheading under individual subject
    headings
CHINA SCREEN
    To our readers. CHINA SCREEN n4:34 1994
CHINESE-AMERICANS
    United States
    History
    Terry, P. A Chinese woman in the west: "Thousand Pieces of Gold" and the
      revision of the heroic frontier. bibliog still LIT/FQ 22:222-226 n4 1994
CHION, MICHEL
    Rosenbaum, J. Audio-vision: sound on screen. By Michael Chion. Edited and
      translated by Claudia Gorbman [Book Review]. CINEASTE 21:94-95 n1/2 1995
CHIRAT, RAYMOND
    Bonneville, L. Gueules d'atmosphere: les acteurs du cinema francais
      (1929-1959). Par Olivier Barrot et Raymond Chirat [Book Review]. il
      SEQUENCES n174:59 Sep/Oct 1994
CHISHOLM, DAVID
    Chisholm, D. Letters: arbitrary arbitrations... JOURNAL WGA 8:5 Dec/Jan
      1995
    Lawton, J.F. Letters: crediting a response... JOURNAL WGA 8:5 Feb 1995
CHISNALL, KEVIN
    Chisnall, K. Get reel, Thornten. ONFILM [12]:15 n1 1995
CHITEN, LAUREL See also TWITCH AND SHOUT
CHITI, ROBERTO
    Chiti, R. Le tragicomiche disavventure del film "Jezebel" o "Muro
      d'asfalto." il stills IMMAGINE n28:24-27 Autumn 1994
CHOO, MEILEEN
    Choo, M. Cinemas will always have a place in Singapore! FJ 98:88+ [2p]
      Jan/Feb 1995
CHOW, REY
    Chow, R. Un souvenir d'amour. bibliog glos scenario still CINEMAS
      3:156-180 n2/3 1993
CHOY, CHRISTINE See also WHO KILLED VINCENT CHIN?
CHRISTEN, THOMAS
    Christen, T. Die Praesenz der Dinge und die Absenz der Protagonisten.
      bibliog C(SWITZ) 40:9-19 1994
CHRISTIAN, ROGER See also NOSTRADAMUS
CHRISTIE, IAN
    Christie, I. Really the most important art. stills F COM 31:41-44 Mar/Apr
      1995
CHRISTMAS CAROL, A f (d Collins, John H. 1910 USA)
    Guida, F. Merry Christmas from Charles Dickens... and Thomas Edison. il

FIR 45:2-5 Nov/Dec 1994

CHRISTOPHERSEN, BIRGIT SEMB
Christophersen, B.S. Latinske folelser med dansk aksent. stills F&K n7:8-10 1993

CHRYSALIS FILMS PRODUCTIONS
Dawtrey, A. Chrysalis deal leads to U.K. pic ventures. VARIETY 358:14 Mar 13/19 1995

CHU, HAI
Chu, H. Wang Zhiwen, a new star bursts onto the scene. il ports CHINA SCREEN n4:14-15 1994

CHUJI TABI NIKKI f (Diary of Chuji's Travels, A d Ito, Daisuke 1927 Japan)
Yamane, S. Schon bald hundert Jahre Film. stills C(SWITZ) 40:163-174 1994

CHUNG, JI-YOUNG See also HOLLYWOOD KID EU SAENG-AE

CHUNGGAMSUK f (d Leung, Siu-hung (Alex) 1994 Hong Kong)
Thorne, A. The Chinatown beat. il stills FATAL VISIONS n17:14-16 1994

CHUNGHING SAMLAM f (d Wong, Kar-wai 1994 Hong Kong)
Morrison, S. John Woo, Wong Kar-wai, and me: an ethnographic mediation. stills C ACTION n36:37-41 1995
> Reviews
Cheng, S. "Chongqing senlin." credits still CINEMAYA n24:33-34 Summer 1994

Chungking Express See CHUNGHING SAMLAM

CHUTE, DAVID
Chute, D. Gods walk the earth. il stills F COM 31:50-53 Jan/Feb 1995

CHUVSTVITEL'NYI MILITSIONER f (d Muratova, Kira 1992 Ukraine/Fr)
> Reviews
Kolodynski, A. Apokalipsa wedlug Muratowej. credits still KINO 27:32-33 Jul 1993

CIAPARA, ELZBIETA
Ciapara, E. Anthony Hopkins. filmog stills FSP 40:11-12 n6 (n760) 1994
Ciapara, E. "Blink." biog credits filmogs still FSP 40:8 n4 (n758) 1994
Ciapara, E. "Niebezpieczna kobieta." biog credits filmog FSP 40:14 n3 (n757) 1994
Ciapara, E. "Niewinni." biogs credits filmogs still FSP 40:6 n10 (n764) 1994
Ciapara, E. "Surfujacy Ninja." credits filmogs still FSP 40:9 n4 (n758) 1994

CIBLE EMOUVANTE f (d Salvadori, Pierre 1993 Fr)
Slodowski, J. "Czuly cel." biogs credits filmogs stills FSP 40:7 n10 (n764) 1994

CIECHOMSKA, MARIA
Ciechomska, M. Prokrustowe loze. KINO 27:38-39 Jul 1993

CIEUTAT, MICHEL For film reviews see author under the following titles: AND THE BAND PLAYED ON; CORRINA, CORRINA; FLESH AND BONE; IT COULD HAPPEN TO YOU; SPECIALIST, THE; WIDOWS' PEAK
Cieutat, M. L'espace au cinema. Par Andre Gardies [Book Reviews]. POSITIF n409:72 Mar 1995
Cieutat, M. Strasbourg. stills POSITIF n409:67-68 Mar 1995

CIMENT, MICHEL For film reviews see author under the following titles: BLOWN AWAY; DISCLOSURE; INDIEN DANS LA VILLE, UN; ROAD TO WELLVILLE, THE
Ciment, M. BFI film classics [Book Reviews]. stills POSITIF n408:75-77 Feb 1995
Ciment, M. Locarno, 47e edition. stills POSITIF n408:68-69 Feb 1995
Ciment, M. and Goudet, S. Entretien avec Abbas Kiarostami. il interv stills POSITIF n408:14-19 Feb 1995
Ciment, M. and Rouyer, P. Entretien avec Atom Egoyan. il interv stills POSITIF n406:79-83 Dec 1994
Ciment, M. and Tobin, Y. Entretien avec Woody Allen. il interv stills POSITIF n408:26-32 Feb 1995
Noel, J. Elia Kazan, une odyssee americaine. Par Michel Ciment [Book Review]. il GRAND ANGLE n177:50 Dec 1994

CINEASTE
> Indexes
Ohmer, S. Index to "Cineaste," vol. XX. CINEASTE 21:89+ [2p] n1/2 1995

CINEMA RECORDS
These boots were made for hawkin': part I - Cinema Records. il F SCORE MONTHLY n36/37:12 Aug/Sep 1993

Cinema studies See FILM STUDIES

CINEMA SUD
Brescia, A. "Sotto il vecchio berso'." Di Giacomo D'Onofrio [Book Review]. biog C SUD 33:40 Jul/Aug/Sep (n113) 1994

CINEMACTION
Histoire du cinema. Abrege pedagogique par Rene Predal [Book Review]. il GRAND ANGLE n176:39-40 Nov 1994
Holmlund, C. "CinemAction," no. 67 (1993), 200pp. "Vingt ans de theories feministes sur le cinema." Eds Ginette Vincendeau and Berenice Reynaud [Book Review]. SCREEN 35:407-410 n4 1994

CINEMARK USA, INC.
> Mergers
Peers, M. Cinemark, Cineplex merge ops. VARIETY 358:22 Mar 6/12 1995

CINEMATECA PORTUGUESA (Lisbon, Portugal)
Costa, J.B. de. Lisboa. J F PRES n49:25-28 Oct 1994

CINEMATHEQUE AFRICAINE, LA (Ouagadougou, Burkina Faso)
La Cinematheque Africaine de Ouagadougou. J F PRES n49:21-22 Oct 1994

CINEMATHEQUE DE CORSE, LA (Porto-Vecchio, France)
Mattei, J.-P. La Cinematheque de Corse. J F PRES n49:17-18 Oct 1994

CINEMATHEQUE QUEBECOISE, LA (Montreal, Canada)
Jean, M. Des restes d'images non identifies. il interv stills 24 IMAGES n75:26-32+ [8p] Dec/Jan 1994/95
Jean, M. Entretien avec Real La Rochelle. il interv 24 IMAGES n75:32-33 Dec/Jan 1994/95

CINEMATOGRAPHERS See also names of cinematographers; WOMEN CINEMATOGRAPHERS
> Canada
>> Quebec, Montreal. History
Montreal cinematographie en debut de siecle. il port still 24 IMAGES n75:51-54 Dec/Jan 1994/95
> United States
>> Authorship Theory
Storaro, V. The right to sign ourselves as "authors of cinematography." AMCIN 76:96 Feb 1995

CINEMATOGRAPHY See also COLOR; DEEP FOCUS CINEMATOGRAPHY; LIGHTING; LONG TAKE; PHOTOGRAPHY; SPECIAL EFFECTS
> Japan
Burch, N. Flaeche und Tiefe. BLIMP [n2]:24-27 Winter 1985
> United States
Comer, B. Rafting down "The River Wild." il AMCIN 76:52-56 Feb 1995
Fisher, B. Creating another "Miracle on 34th Street." il stills AMCIN 76:50-52+ [6p] Mar 1995
Fisher, B. and Pizzello, C. "In the Line of Fire": an action film for existentialists. il stills AMCIN 74:36-40+ [7p] Sep 1993
Heuring, D. Gordon Willis to receive ASC Lifetime Achievement Award. filmog interv port AMCIN 76:44-46+ [5p] Feb 1995
Heuring, D. "The Secret of Roan Inish" revealed. il interv stills AMCIN 76:34-42 Feb 1995
Pizzello, S. "Interview With the Vampire" taps new vein. il stills AMCIN 76:43-52 Jan 1995
Pizzello, S. "Legends of the Fall" exploits scenic locale. il stills AMCIN 76:30-38 Mar 1995
Scharres, B. The hard road to "Hard Target." il still AMCIN 74:62-64+ [10p] Sep 1993
>> Techniques
Bergery, B. Reflections: Vilmos Zsigmond, ASC. il specs stills AMCIN 74:74-78 Sep 1993

Cinematology See HISTORY OF THE FILM

CINEPLEX INTL.
Peers, M. Cinemark, Cineplex merge ops. VARIETY 358:22 Mar 6/12 1995

CINEPLEX ODEON CORPORATION
> Mergers
Peers, M. Cinemark, Cineplex merge ops. VARIETY 358:22 Mar 6/12 1995

Cinerama [Prior to V16, 1988 use also CINERAMA] See WIDE SCREEN

CINERGI PRODUCTIONS
Cinema + energy = Andy Vajna. interv port BOXOFFICE 131:11 Apr 1995

CIRCLE OF FRIENDS f (d O'Connor, Pat 1995 Ireland/USA)
> Reviews
Farber, S. Teen tales. still MOVIELINE 6:42-43 Apr 1995
Greenman, B. "Circle of Friends." VILLAGE VOICE 40:58 Mar 21 1995
James, C. "Circle of Friends." BOXOFFICE 131:bet p125 and 144 [pR30] Apr 1995
Levy, E. "Circle of Friends." credits still VARIETY 358:51+ [2p] Mar 13/19 1995
Schickel, R. Ruffled duckling. still TIME 145:74 Mar 27 1995
Travers, P. "Circle of Friends." still ROLLING STONE n704:129 Mar 23 1995

CITIES IN FILM See also names of cities
> Italy
Verdone, M. L'immaginario urbano e le avanguardie "storiche." C SUD 33:34-36 Jul/Aug/Sep (n113) 1994
> Switzerland
Wendt, U. Decor. stills C(SWITZ) 40:20-36 1994
> United States
Gandini, L. La citta della malavita. stills C FORUM 34:43-45 Sep (n337) 1994
>> History
Martin, A. Performing the city [Book Review]. Q REV F & VIDEO 15:71-76 n3 1994

CITIZEN KANE f (d Welles, Orson 1941 USA)
Altman, R. Deep-focus sound: "Citizen Kane" and the radio aesthetic. diag scenario Q REV F & VIDEO 15:1-34 n3 1994
Ciment, M. BFI film classics [Book Reviews]. stills POSITIF n408:75-77 Feb 1995

CITIZEN LANGLOIS f (d Cozarinsky, Edgardo 1995 Fr)
> Reviews
Nesselson, L. "Citizen Langlois." credits VARIETY 358:54 Mar 13/19 1995

CITRAN, ROBERTO
Vecchi, P. Recitare con Corinto. interv stills C FORUM 34:73 Oct (n338) 1994

CITY LIGHTS f (d Chaplin, Charlie 1931 USA)
Woal, M. and Woal, L.K. Chaplin and the comedy of melodrama. bibliog stills UFAJ 46:3-15 n3 1994

CITY OF GOLD f (d Low, Colin/Koenig, Wolf 1957 Can)
Tibbetts, J. All that glitters. il stills F COM 31:52-55 Mar/Apr 1995

CIVIL RIGHTS See also INTEGRATION; MINORITIES
> United States
Lucia, C. Progress and misgivings in Mississippi. interv port stills CINEASTE 21:43-45 n1/2 1995

CIVIL WAR, THE f (d Burns, Ken 1990 USA)
> Ideological Analysis
McPherson, T. "Both kinds of arms": remembering the Civil War. bibliog il VEL LT TRAP n35:3-18 Spring 1995

Civil War (United States) See UNITED STATES - CIVIL WAR, 1861-1865

CLAIR, RENE
Cremonini, G. Il fascino discreto dell'intelligenza. stills C FORUM 34:28-35 Oct (n338) 1994

CLANCY, TOM
Cohen, R. Master of war. il ROLLING STONE n696:114-116+ [5p] Dec 1 1994

CLARK, JOHN
Clark, J. A list is still a list [Book Review]. stills PREM 8:93 Feb 1995
Clark, J. Renny Harlin gets the girl. il port still PREM 8:56-64 Mar 1995
Clark, J. Some of Sam. il stills PREM 8:74-78 Mar 1995

CLARK, LARRY See also KIDS

CLARK, PAUL
Clark, P. Chronicles of Chinese life. port stills CINEMAYA n25/26:4-6+ [4p] Autumn/Winter 1994/95

CLARKE, JEREMY
Clarke, J. Jan Svankmajer: puppetry's dark poet. il stills C FANTAS 26:54-57 n3 1995

CLARKE, SHIRLEY
Bruyn, O. de. Belfort 1993. POSITIF n406:60 Dec 1994

CLARKE, STEVE
Clarke, S. Carlton bids for MGM Cinemas. VARIETY 358:44 Mar 13/19 1995

COLLECTIONS AND COLLECTING
    United States
    (continued)
            Cowboys in Film
    Slide, A. The Slide area film book notes [Book Reviews]. CLASSIC
        n237:42-44+ [4p] Mar 1995
            Directors
    Behlmer, R. Directors' paper trails. table DGA NEWS 19:50+ [3p] n6 1994/95
            History
    Guida, F. Merry Christmas from Charles Dickens... and Thomas Edison. il
        FIR 45:2-5 Nov/Dec 1994
            Music. Sound Tracks
    Murray, R.M. The adventures of Recordman. il F SCORE MONTHLY n39:4-5 Nov
        1993
    Murray, R.M. The adventures of Recordman. il F SCORE MONTHLY n40:4-5 Dec
        1993
            Silent Film. Films Shown on Television/Video
    Cherchi Usai, P. The Library of Congress video collection: rare silent films
        with piano scores composed and performed by Philip Carli. GRIFFITHIANA
        n51/52:262-263 Oct 1994
    Cherchi Usai, P. The Library of Congress video collection: rare silent films
        with piano scores composed and performed by Philip Carli. J F PRES
        n49:74-75 Oct 1994
COLLEGES AND UNIVERSITIES See also names of colleges and universities
    United States
        History
    Slide, A. The Slide area film book notes [Book Reviews]. CLASSIC
        n237:42-44+ [4p] Mar 1995
COLLINS, JOAN
    Joan Collins. port VANITY FAIR 58:152 Jan 1995
COLLINS, JOHN H. See also CHRISTMAS CAROL, A
COLLINS, NANCY
    Collins, N. Michael's full disclosure. il ports VANITY FAIR 58:68-75+
        [12p] Jan 1995
COLON, ALEX
    Lentz, H., III. Obituaries. biogs filmogs obits ports CLASSIC n237:57-59
        Mar 1995
COLONEL CHABERT, LE f (d Angelo, Yves 1994 Fr)
        Reviews
    Desjardins, D. "Le Colonel Chabert." credits still SEQUENCES n175:37-38
        Nov/Dec 1994
    Horguelin, T. "Le Colonel Chabert." still 24 IMAGES n75:74 Dec/Jan 1994/95
    Neff, R. "Colonel Chabert." credits FJ 98:50-51 Jan/Feb 1995
COLONIALISM
    Asia
    Sutton, G. Colonialism and nationalism in Asian cinema. Edited by Wimal
        Dissanayake [Book Review]. il AFTERIMAGE 22:15 Jan 1995
COLOR CORRECTION
    United States
    Roland, F. Embracing the concept of color correction. AMCIN 76:22+ [3p] Jan
        1995
COLOR OF NIGHT f (d Rush, Richard 1994 USA)
        Reviews
    O'Neill, E. "Color of Night." POSITIF n406:45 Dec 1994
COLPO DI LUNA f (d Simone, Alberto 1995 It/Fr/Neth)
        Reviews
    Rooney, D. "Moon Shadow" ("Colpo di luna"). credits still VARIETY 358:83
        Feb 20/26 1995
COLUMBIA BROADCASTING SYSTEM, INC.
    Zoglin, R. Kicked while it's down. graph port still TIME 145:71 Mar 6 1995
COLUMBIA PICTURES INDUSTRIES INC.
    Hagopian, K.J. Columbia Pictures: portrait of a studio. Edited by Bernard F.
        Dick [Book Review]. F CRITICISM 19:95-99 n2 1994/95
        History
    Keenan, R. Hail, Columbia! a studio odyssey [Book Review]. still LIT/FQ
        22:278-279 n4 1994
COLUMBUS, CHRIS See also MRS. DOUBTFIRE
COMAN, ED
    Coman, E. Theatre point-of-sale automation: innovation, evolution,
        integration. il FJ 98:84+ [2p] Mar 1995
COMBS, RICHARD
    Combs, R. "Battle of the River Plate." il stills F COM 31:20-22+ [4p]
        Mar/Apr 1995
COMEAU, PHIL See also SECRET DE JEROME, LE
COMEDY See also FARCE; HUMOR; PARODY; SATIRE; SLAPSTICK
    Italy
    Garofalo, M. Slapstick all'italiana. il interv stills SEGNO n72:3-9
        Mar/Apr 1995
    United States
    Parshall, P.F. Buster Keaton and the space of farce: "Steamboat Bill, Jr."
        versus "The Cameraman." bibliog diag stills UFAJ 46:29-46 n3 1994
        Psychoanalytic Analysis
    Bick, I.J. "That hurts!": humor and sadomasochism in "Lolita." bibliog
        stills UFAJ 46:3-18 n2 1994
    Lieberman, E.A. Charlie the trickster. bibliog stills UFAJ 46:16-28 n3
        1994
COMEDY FILM
    Finland
        Military. Women
    Laine, K. Vaapeli Kormy ja naiset. stills PEILI 18:16-17 n4 1994
    United States
    Comuzio, E. Edoardo Bruno: "Pranzo alle otto" - Forme e figure della
        sophisticated comedy [Book Review]. C FORUM 34:95 Sep (n337) 1994
    Woal, M. and Woal, L.K. Chaplin and the comedy of melodrama. bibliog stills
        UFAJ 46:3-15 n3 1994
        Actors and Actresses. History
    Caslavsky, K. Comedians. filmogs il stills GRIFFITHIANA n51/52:60-169 Oct
        1994
        Screenwriting
    Seipp, C. A season of love and laughter: writing romantic comedy. stills

JOURNAL WGA 8:16-19 Dec/Jan 1995
        Series. History. Film Lists
    Caslavsky, K. American comedy series: filmographies 1914-1930. filmog il
        stills GRIFFITHIANA n51/52:9+ [50p] Oct 1994
    Caslavsky, K. Le serie comiche americane: filmografie 1914-1930. filmog il
        stills GRIFFITHIANA n51/52:8+ [50p] Oct 1994
COMER, BROOKE
    Comer, B. "A Great Day in Harlem" evokes the jazz age. AMCIN 76:83-84 Feb
        1995
    Comer, B. Behind the counter and the camera: Manhattan Video Center's owner
        produces feature film. AMCIN 76:83-84 Jan 1995
    Comer, B. "Eat Drink Man Woman": a feast for the eyes. il still AMCIN
        76:62-67 Jan 1995
    Comer, B. "New Jersey Drive" puts Kimmel behind the wheel. still AMCIN
        76:83-84 Mar 1995
    Comer, B. Rafting down "The River Wild." il AMCIN 76:52-56 Feb 1995
Comic book and strip characters See names of comic book and strip characters
    (e.g. BATMAN)
COMINO, JO For film reviews see author under the following titles: EDEN VALLEY;
    LOVE CHEAT & STEAL; ONLY YOU
COMMENDATIONS
    Canada
            (Quatre-vingt) 24 Images
    Les dix meilleurs films de 1994. still 24 IMAGES n76:29 Spring 1995
    Italy
            Segnocinema
    I 5 film dell'anno di "Segnocinema." stills SEGNO n63:25-26 Sep/Oct 1993
    Norway
            Film & Kino
    Kritikernes valg. stills F&K n1:31-33 1994
    United States
    Critics choice. table PREM 8:106-107 Apr 1995
    Zemeckis, R. Guilty pleasures. port stills F COM 31:66-69 Jan/Feb 1995
            Boxoffice
    "Boxoffice's" eighth annual miscellaneous film awards! il BOXOFFICE 131:bet
        p82 and 83 [pSW32-SW37] Apr 1995
            Film Comment
    Moments out of time. stills F COM 31:54-59 Jan/Feb 1995
            Rolling Stone
    Travers, P. Great performances: the year's best. stills ROLLING STONE
        n700:68 Jan 26 1995
    Travers, P. The year in movies. il stills ROLLING STONE n698/699:193-194+
        [5p] Dec 29/Jan 12 1994/95
            The Film Journal
    "FJ" editors' top '94 films. FJ 98:100 Jan/Feb 1995
            Village Voice, The
    Brown, G. Pulp dreams. stills VILLAGE VOICE 40:57+ [2p] Jan 3 1995
    Hoberman, J. Pulp dreams. stills VILLAGE VOICE 40:57+ [2p] Jan 3 1995
    Taubin, A. The ten best films of 1994. il stills VILLAGE VOICE 40:62-63
        Jan 3 1995
COMMERCIALS
    France
        Special Effects
    Magid, R. Perrier ad employs latest whistles and bells. stills AMCIN
        74:26-28+ [5p] Sep 1993
COMMISSION OF THE EUROPEAN COMMUNITIES
    Protection du patrimoine cinematographique Europeen. MONITEUR n126:30 Dec
        1994
    Williams, M. and Stern, A. EC wants to double financial support for film,
        TV. VARIETY 358:43-44 Feb 13/19 1995
        Lobbying
    Dawtrey, A. Euro majors gather in lobby. VARIETY 358:34 Feb 6/12 1995
COMMISSIONED FILM
    Festivals
    Sendecka, M. Swieto reklamy. interv REZYSER n18:4-5 1993
    Denmark
        History
    Miguez, M. Cortometrajes. stills NOSFERATU n5:72-73 Jan 1991
Commissions See FILM COMMISSIONS
COMMUNICATION See also COMMUNICATIONS INDUSTRY; LANGUAGE; POPULAR CULTURE
    Germany (Federal Republic, since 1990)
    Schaar, E. Kommunikation und Leben. MEDIEN 38:321 n6 1994
COMMUNICATIONS INDUSTRY See also RADIO
    Television (broadcast) and Video (non-broadcast)
        United States
    Greenwald, J. Battle for remote control. il TIME 145:69-71 Spring 1995
COMMUNISM See also ANTI-COMMUNISM
    Union of Soviet Socialist Republics
    Casiraghi, U. Per Ejzenstein resto solo un sogno filmare il "capitale." il
        still C SUD 33:8-9 Jul/Aug/Sep (n113) 1994
Companies See INDUSTRY
COMPANY OF STRANGERS, THE f (Strangers in Good Company d Scott, Cynthia 1990
    Can)
        Feminist Analysis
    Russell, C. Mourning the woman's film: the dislocated spectator of "The
        Company of Strangers." stills CAN J F STUD 3:25-40 n2 1994
COMPLAINTS OF A DUTIFUL DAUGHTER f (d Hoffmann, Deborah 1994 USA)
    Blackwell, E. "Complaints of a Dutiful Daughter." still INDEP 18:14-15 Mar
        1995
COMPLETE OUTSIDER, THE f (d Warnow, Catherine/Weinrich, Regina 1994? USA)
    Tanner, L. Accents and umlauts. FIR 45:38-39 Nov/Dec 1994
COMPLETE POST
    Case, D. Flame at Complete Post. il interv port still C PAPERS n102:60-62+
        [4p] Dec 1994
COMPOSERS See also names of composers; MUSIC
    Hommages posthumes. biogs il obits port SEQUENCES n174:56-58 Sep/Oct 1994
    Hubbard, R. Film score: the art and craft of movie music. Tony Thomas [Book
        Review]. F SCORE MONTHLY n36/37:22 Aug/Sep 1993
    United States
    Hubbard, R. Book reviews [Book Reviews]. F SCORE MONTHLY n40:9 Dec 1993

CONFERENCES, INSTITUTES, WORKSHOPS, ETC.
    United States
(continued)
            California, Los Angeles 1995
Weiner, R. Market & post/LA seminars. il still VARIETY 358:bet p88 and 173 [pA20] Feb 20/26 1995
            California, San Francisco 1995
Fox, M. Looking for funds in some of the right places. il INDEP 18:40-41 Apr 1995
Klady, L. Indie prods targeted at Int'l Film Finance confab. VARIETY 357:30 Jan 9/15 1995
            Massachusetts, Cambridge 1994
Beacham, F. Digital artists: reinventing electronic media. il AMCIN 76:59-60+ [3p] Mar 1995
            Nevada, Las Vegas 1995
Burton, H. Welcome to NATO/ShoWest '95! il port BOXOFFICE 131:bet p82 and 83 [pSW10] Apr 1995
Busch, A.M. ShoWest's growing pains. VARIETY 358:7+ [2p] Mar 13/19 1995
Kartozian, W.F. ShoWest achieves its majority. il port BOXOFFICE 131:bet p82 and 83 [pSW6] Apr 1995
Klady, L. and Busch, A.M. Wintry b.o. chills ShoWest's sizzle. stat VARIETY 358:1+ [2p] Mar 6/12 1995
Warner, T. A magical journey. il port BOXOFFICE 131:bet p82 and 83 [pSW4] Apr 1995
            New York, New York 1994
Behrend, J. DGA goes indie at IFFM. il DGA NEWS 19:24-25 n6 1994/95
Orbanz, E. Domitor '94 - cinema turns 100. il J F PRES n49:56-63 Oct 1994
            Texas, Austin 1995
Leydon, J. Soderbergh pic preems at Southwest arts confab. VARIETY 358:22 Mar 13/19 1995
CONFORTI, ANGELO For film reviews see author under the following titles: BEFORE THE RAIN; WOODSTOCK: 3 DAYS OF PEACE AND MUSIC: THE DIRECTOR'S CUT
Congress of Penguins, The See KONGRESS DER PINGUINE, DER
CONGRESSIONAL ARTS CAUCUS (United States)
Sutton, G. Stript-o-caucus neA. AFTERIMAGE 22:3 Jan 1995
CONNER, DEBORAH MATTINGLY
Conner, D.M. Correspondence: Alleva on "Vampire." COMMONWEAL [122]:22-23 Feb 10 1995
CONNICK, THOMAS
Higgins, G. and others. Grisled roots. interv ports MILLENNIUM n26:56-66 Fall 1992
CONNORS, ROBIN
Connors, R. and others. Letters: the king and us. MS 5:8 n4 1995
CONSEIL DES ARTS ET DES LETTRES (Quebec, Canada)
Racine, C. and Loiselle, M.-C. Partie de ping-pong. 24 IMAGES n76:2-3 Spring 1995
CONSENTEMENT MUTUEL f (d Stora, Bernard 1994 Fr)
    Reviews
Bruyn, O. de. "Consentement mutuel." POSITIF n407:41 Jan 1995
CONSORTIUM DE REALISATION
Williams, M. Credit Lyonnais ankles the biz. VARIETY 358:4 Mar 20/26 1995
CONSUMERISM
McKinley, A. Anne Friedberg. Window shopping: cinema and the postmodern [Book Review]. ARACHNE 1:270-274 n2 1994
CONTEXTUAL ANALYSIS
    United States
hooks, b. Dreams of conquest. still S&S 5:22-23 Apr 1995
CONTRACTS
    Australia
        Techniques
Hart, L. Negotiation: "I hear what you say, but..." il C PAPERS n102:78-79 Dec 1994
    New Zealand
Bisset, B. Letters: Blue Book piece was half right. ONFILM 11:10-11 n11 1994/95
Drinnan, J. Blue Book blues dog TVC shoots. ONFILM 11:3 n11 1994/95
Drinnan, J. Letters: John Drinnan responds. ONFILM 11:11 n11 1994/95
Dryburgh, S. Letters: open letter from a film technician on the subject of lunch. ONFILM 11:11 n11 1994/95
Howard, C. Letters: get your act together. ONFILM 11:12 n11 1994/95
    United States
Cox, D. WGA, producers' pact "groundbreaking." VARIETY 358:17 Feb 6/12 1995
        Actors and Actresses
Cox, D. SAG, producers settle in a cliffhanger deal. VARIETY 358:16 Mar 27/Apr 2 1995
Seigel, R.L. Wanted: Guild actors at a discount. il INDEP 18:38-41 Jan/Feb 1995
        Merchandising Spin-offs
O'Steen, K. Interactive rights give studios clause. VARIETY 358:18 Mar 20/26 1995
        Producers
Cox, D. and Busch, A.M. Producers draw battle lines over credit order. ports VARIETY 358:28+ [2p] Feb 20/26 1995
        Screenwriters
Cox, D. Writers Guild gains ground with new pact. VARIETY 358:18 Feb 13/19 1995
Petrie, D., Jr. The long and winding road. port JOURNAL WGA 8:2 Mar 1995
Young, P.F. Writing tip. VARIETY 358:10 Mar 27/Apr 2 1995
        Theater Management
Battersby, M.E. Buying the competition. il BOXOFFICE 131:60+ [3p] Apr 1995
CONTRE L'OUBLI f (d Deville, Michel/Moon, Sarah/Depardon, Raymond/Cartier-Bresson, Henri/Doillon, Jacques/Chereau, Patrice/Hubert, Jean-Loup/Corneau, Alain/Becker, Jean/Girod, Francis/Carre, Jean-Michel/Muyl, Philippe/Dante, Dominique/Mieville, Anne-Marie/Godard, Jean-Luc/Deray, Jacques/Frot-Coutaz, Gerard/Amar, Denis/Leconte, Patrice/Denis, Claire/Allio, Rene/Goupil, Romain/Kramer, Robert/Resnais, Alain/Akerman, Chantal/Trintignant, Nadine/Costa-Gavras/Tavernier, Bertrand/Serreau, Coline 1991 Fr)
        Emotion
Gardies, R. Vers l'emotion documentaire. bibliog CINEMAS 4:49-60 n2 1994

CONWAY, GARY
Lilley, J. How to make a movie star. il interv ports stills SCARLET STREET n17:72-76 Winter 1995
CONWAY, JACK See also LADY OF THE TROPICS
COOK, DAVID A.
Cook, D.A. Making sense. bibliog F CRITICISM 17:31-39 n2/3 1992/93
COOK, PETER
Lahr, J. Bedazzled ports NEW YORKER 70:80-85 Jan 23 1995
Lentz, H., III. Obituaries. biogs filmogs obits ports CLASSIC n237:57-59 Mar 1995
Milestones. obit still TIME 145:13 Jan 23 1995
Transition. obit port NEWSWK 125:55 Jan 23 1995
COOLIDGE, MARTHA
Zeitlin, M. Martha, I says. filmog il DGA NEWS 19:24-25+ [3p] n2 1994
COOPER, JAMES FENIMORE
Walker, J. Deconstructing an American myth: Hollywood and "The Last of the Mohicans." bibliog still F&HIST 23:104-116+ [14p] n1/4 1993
COPPENS, FREDDY See also MAX
COPPOLA, ANTONIO
Comuzio, E. Nessuno nasce "imparato." interv still C FORUM 34:28-30 Nov (n339) 1994
COPPOLA, FRANCIS FORD See also COPPOLA, FRANCIS See also ON THE ROAD
CO-PRODUCTION
    Australia
Woods, M. Co-prods high on the Aussie agenda. VARIETY 358:62 Feb 27/Mar 5 1995
        China (People's Republic, since 1949)
Groves, D. Aussie film scales walls of China. VARIETY 358:17 Mar 13/19 1995
    Norway
        Audience
Jensen, J.R. Nordisk film pa det naere marked. stat stills tables F&K n7:29-31 1993
COPYRIGHT
    Archives
Henry, M. Copyright, neighbouring rights and film archives. J F PRES n49:2-9 Oct 1994
        Conferences, Institutes, Workshops, etc.
Monty, I. Symposium on legal rights, Bologna, 1994. J F PRES n49:10 Oct 1994
    Canada
Acheson, K. and Maule, C.J. Copyright and related rights: the international dimension. bibliog CAN J COM 19:423-446 n3/4 1994
    China (People's Republic, since 1949)
Elley, D. China: trick or treaty? VARIETY 358:1+ [2p] Mar 6/12 1995
    United States
Greene, J. Rights squabble begins over new media explosion. VARIETY 357:4+ [2p] Jan 2/8 1995
        Laws and Legislation
Wharton, D. Copyright extension on the House table. port VARIETY 358:18 Feb 6/12 1995
Wharton, D. House bills aim to add 20 years to copyrights. port VARIETY 358:30 Feb 20/26 1995
        Properties, Literary
Evans, G. Random act opens can of bookworms. il VARIETY 358:1+ [3p] Mar 6/12 1995
        Screenplays
Harris, L.E. A roadmap for writers' rights on the information superhighway. il JOURNAL WGA 8:20-23 Feb 1995
CORBIAU, GERARD See also FARINELLI: IL CASTRATO
CORDEAU, ARIANE
J'irai comme un cheval fou. filmogs il SEQUENCES n175:10-11 Nov/Dec 1994
CORLISS, RICHARD For film reviews see author under the following titles: BEFORE SUNRISE; LADYBIRD LADYBIRD; ONCE WERE WARRIORS; OUTBREAK
Corliss, R. Bard of embarrassment. biog il port still TIME 145:65-66 Feb 27 1995
Corliss, R. Hey, let's put on a show! il ports TIME 145:54-60 Mar 27 1995
Corliss, R. How the winner lost. still TIME 145:66 Feb 27 1995
Corliss, R. Jackie can! il TIME 145:82-83 Feb 13 1995
Corliss, R. Take a bow, Winona. il ports still TIME 145:64-66 Jan 9 1995
Corliss, R. That sinking feeling. stills table TIME 145:70-72 Feb 20 1995
Corliss, R. The first angry man. port TIME 145:75 Jan 9 1995
CORMAN, ROGER See also MASQUE OF THE RED DEATH, THE; TALES OF TERROR
CORNEAU, ALAIN See also CONTRE L'OUBLI; NOUVEAU MONDE, LE
CORONADO, CELESTINO See also HAMLET
CORPORATE OWNERSHIP
    Germany (Federal Republic, since 1990)
Molner, D. Germans making a public appearance. VARIETY 358:31-32 Mar 20/26 1995
Corporations See INDUSTRY
CORPS ET AMES f (d Vermeil, Aude 1994 Switz)
    Reviews
Perret, J. "Corps et Ames." credits C(SWITZ) 40:226 1994
CORRENTE, MICHAEL See also FEDERAL HILL
CORRINA, CORRINA f (d Nelson, Jessie 1994 USA)
    Reviews
Cieutat, M. "Corinna, Corinna." still POSITIF n408:56-57 Feb 1995
CORSINI, CATHERINE See also AMOUREUX, LES
COSANDEY, ROLAND
Cherchi Usai, P. Film um 1910. Aus der Sammlung Joseph Joye (London). By Roland Cosandey [Book Review]. GRIFFITHIANA n51/52:258 Oct 1994
Cherchi Usai, P. Film um 1910: Aus der Sammlung Joseph Joye (London). By Roland Cosandey [Book Review]. J F PRES n49:73 Oct 1994
Cosandey, R. Keepers of the frame: the film archives. Edited by Penelope Houston [Book Review]. J F PRES n49:67-68 Oct 1994
Cosandey, R. Le retour de l'Abbe Joye ou la cinematheque, l'historien et le cinema communal. il J F PRES n49:46-55 Oct 1994
Cosandey, R. Wo ist die grosse Treppe hingekommen? il stills C(SWITZ) 40:51-74 1994

CRITICS See also names of critics
   New Zealand
   Coutts, D. Hire me and I'll tosh in a free aphorism. il ONFILM [12]:15 n1 1995
CROFTS, STEPHEN
   McFarlane, B. Crofts, Stephen. Identification, gender and genre in film: the case of "Shame" [Book Reviews]. MEDIA INFO AUSTRALIA n75:159-160 Feb 1995
CROMBIE, DONALD See also ROUGH DIAMONDS
CRONACA DI UN AMORE VIOLATO f (d Battiato, Giacomo 1995 It/Fr/Sp)
   Reviews
   Young, D. "Diary of a Rapist" ("Cronaca di un amore violato"). credits VARIETY 358:72 Feb 27/Mar 5 1995
CRONENBERG, DAVID See also FLY, THE; VIDEODROME
   Beard, W. Cronenberg, flyness, and the other-self. bibliog still CINEMAS 4:153-173 n2 1994
   Tanzi-Mira, F. L'immagine virale di David Cronenberg. C SUD 33:18-19 Jul/Aug/Sep (n113) 1994
CROSBY, BING
   Slide, A. The Slide area film book notes [Book Reviews]. CLASSIC n236:47-49 Feb 1995
CROSS-CULTURAL ANALYSIS See also CULTURAL CONTEXT
   Italy
   Mariniello, S. Techniques audiovisuelles et reecriture de l'histoire. De la representation a la production du temps au cinema. bibliog still CINEMAS 5:41-56 n1/2 1994
CROSSLEY, PHIL
   Crossley, P. Catching silent cinema, - before it's too late [Book Review]. il FILM 4:26 n1 [1995]
CROW, THE f (d Proyas, Alex 1994 USA)
   Adamek, P. "The Crow." il interv stills FATAL VISIONS n17:33-34 1994
   Reviews
   Boyce, M. "The Crow." credits FATAL VISIONS n17:9 1994
   Martini, E. "Il corvo." credits still C FORUM 34:76-77 Sep (n337) 1994
CROWDUS, GARY
   Burlingame, J. and Crowdus, G. Music at the service of the cinema. il interv port stills CINEASTE 21:76-80 n1/2 1995
CRUEL SEA, THE f (d Frend, Charles 1953 Gt Br)
   Deighton, L. Sand and sea. stills S&S 5:30-33 Jan 1995
CRUMB f (d Zwigoff, Terry 1994 USA)
   Hoberman, J. Notes from the underground. il PREM 8:44-45 Feb 1995
   Reviews
   Greene, R. "Crumb." BOXOFFICE 131:bet p125 and 144 [pR24] Apr 1995
   Head, G. "Crumb": a comic-strip review. il INTERV 25:30 Apr 1995
CRYING GAME, THE f (d Jordan, Neil 1992 Gt Br)
   Murphy, K. Nativity scenes. stills F COM 31:12-16 Jan/Feb 1995
   Reviews
   Meyers, R. The crime screen. ports still ARMCHAIR DET 26:63-64 n3 1993
[CRYSTAL FORTUNE RUN] f (d Sang, Li Kin 1994 Hong Kong)
   Thorne, A. The Chinatown beat. il stills FATAL VISIONS n17:14-16 1994
CSALA, KAROLY
   Gyorffy, M. Ha en filmlexikont szerkesztenek [Book Review]. F VILAG 38:53-54 n4 1995
CSOKKAL ES KOROMMEL f (d Szomjas, Gyorgy 1995 Hungary)
   Reviews
   Elley, D. "Kisses and Scratches" ("Csokkal es korommel"). credits VARIETY 358:87 Feb 20/26 1995
Cuba See as a subheading under individual subject headings
CUDOWNE MIEJSCE f (d Kolski, Jan Jakub 1995 Poland)
   Reviews
   Elley, D. "Miraculous Place" ("Cudowne miejsce"). credits VARIETY 358:64 Mar 6/12 1995
CUKOR, GEORGE See also DINNER AT EIGHT; MY FAIR LADY
   Aldarondo, R. La tentacion de Shakespeare. stills NOSFERATU n8:20-27 Feb 1992
   Turner, G. George Cukor, master of elegance. By Emanuel Levy [Book Review]. AMCIN 76:86 Jan 1995
CULT FILM
   Noel, J. Le petit livres des films-cultes. Par Christophe Goffette [Book Review]. il GRAND ANGLE n177:50 Dec 1994
CULTURAL CONTEXT
   Africa
      Ideological Analysis
   Mulvey, L. "Xala," Ousmane Sembene (1974): the carapace that failed. stills CAM OBS n31:48-71 Jan/May 1993
   Australia
   Beale, A. Framing culture: criticism and policy in Australia. By Stuart Cunningham [Book Reviews]. CAN J COM 19:556-559 n3/4 1994
   Canada
      Aborigines in Film
   Fraser, F. The participation of Aboriginal and other cultural minorities in cultural development. bibliog CAN J COM 19:477-493 n3/4 1994
      Economic Aspects
   Hoskins, C. and others. The environment in which cultural industries operate and some implications. bibliog CAN J COM 19:353-376 n3/4 1994
      Government Support
   Audley, P. Cultural industries policy: objectives, formulation, and evaluation. bibliog CAN J COM 19:317-352 n3/4 1994
      Popular Culture
   Knight, G. The Beaver bites back? American popular culture in Canada. Edited by David H. Flaherty & Frank E. Manning [Book Review]. CAN J COM 19:560-561 n3/4 1994
   China (People's Republic, since 1949)
   Yang, M.-Y. Film in contemporary China: critical debates, 1979-1989. Edited by George S. Semsel, Chen Xihe, and Xia Hong [Book Review]. FQ 48:61-62 n2 1994/95
   France
      History
   Cantrill, A. French national cinema. By Susan Hayward [Book Review]. CANTRILL'S FMNTS n73/74:42-43 May 1994

   Germany (Federal Republic, 1949-1990)
   Sharma, S. Fassbinder's "Ali" and the politics of subject-formation. bibliog stills PS 14:104-116 n1/2 1994/95
   Germany (Federal Republic, since 1990)
   Linville, S.E. "Europa, Europa": a test case for German national cinema. stills WIDE ANGLE 16:38-51 n3 1995
   Hong Kong
   Chow, R. Un souvenir d'amour. bibliog glos scenario still CINEMAS 3:156-180 n2/3 1993
      Gangster Film
   Williams, T. To live and die in Hong Kong. bibliog stills C ACTION n36:42-52 1995
   India
   Ganguly, S. No moksha: Arcadia lost in Satyajit Ray's "Days and Nights in the Forest." bibliog still F CRITICISM 19:75-85 n2 1994/95
   Latin America
   Richardson, D. Communication, culture and hegemony: from the media to mediations. By Jesus Martin-Barbero [Book Review]. CAN J COM 19:562-563 n3/4 1994
   Poland
   Falkowska, J. "The political" in the films of Andrzej Wajda and Krzysztof Kieslowski. CJ 34:37-50 n2 1995
   United States
   Kasdan, M. and Tavernetti, S. The Hollywood Indian in "Little Big Man": a revisionist view. still F&HIST 23:70-80 n1/4 1993
   Martin, A. Performing the city [Book Review]. Q REV F & VIDEO 15:71-76 n3 1994
   Russett, M. The "Caraboo" hoax: romantic woman as mirror and mirage. bibliog il DISCOURSE n17.2:26-47 Winter 1994/95
   Swann, P. International conspiracy in and around "The Iron Curtain." VEL LT TRAP n35:52-60 Spring 1995
      Immigrants in Film
   Lieberman, E.A. Charlie the trickster. bibliog stills UFAJ 46:16-28 n3 1994
      Pornography and Obscenity
   Heffernan, K. A social poetics of pornography [Book Review]. Q REV F & VIDEO 15:77-83 n3 1994
   Venezuela
   Schwartzman, K. National cinema in translation: the politics of exhibition culture. il stills WIDE ANGLE 16:66-99 n3 1995
Cultural identity See NATIONAL CONSCIOUSNESS
CULTURAL STUDIES
   Great Britain
   Cantrill, A. Like a film: ideological fantasy on screen, camera and canvas. By Timothy Murray [Book Review]. CANTRILL'S FMNTS n73/74:43 May 1994
CUNDIEFF, RUSTY See also FEAR OF A BLACK HAT
CUNHA, UMA DA
   Cunha, U. da. "Bandit" set for Indian pic screens. VARIETY 358:32 Mar 20/26 1995
   Cunha, U. da. India Film Fest features tributes to Fellini, Elvis. VARIETY 357:24 Jan 2/8 1995
   Cunha, U. da. Local "Mammo" launches Int'l Film Fest of India. VARIETY 357:28 Jan 9/15 1995
   Cunha, U. da. UA Theaters to build in India. VARIETY 358:14 Feb 20/26 1995
CUNNINGHAM, STUART
   Beale, A. Framing culture: criticism and policy in Australia. By Stuart Cunningham [Book Reviews]. CAN J COM 19:556-559 n3/4 1994
CURCHOD, OLIVIER
   Curchod, O. Autour de "Partie de campagne." il still POSITIF n408:82-83 Feb 1995
   Jeancolas, J.-P. Geraniums [Book Reviews]. stills POSITIF n408:94-95 Feb 1995
CURI, UMBERTO
   Roberti, B. and Suriano, F. La Biennale, la Mostra e l'archivio. interv still FCR 45:371-381 Sep (n448) 1994
CURIEL, HERBERT See also KRIMA-KERIME: NOAH'S ARK
CURRAN, WILLIAM See also LOVE CHEAT & STEAL
CURRIE, RONALD
   Currie, R. Glasgow Copthorne all aglow. stat still table FILM 4:6 n1 [1995]
CURRY, JO-ANNE For film reviews see author under the following titles: KALIFORNIA
CURSE OF FRANKENSTEIN, THE f (d Fisher, Terence 1957 Gt Br)
   Eriksen, F. Taste of fear. il stills Z n1:14-19 (n47) 1994
CURTIS, JAMIE LEE
   De Marinis, G. Il debole di Jamie Lee Curtis: a volte sorride. filmog stills C FORUM 34:31-34 Nov (n339) 1994
   Jamie Lee Curtis. biog filmog port stills STARS n21:[11-12] Winter 1995
CURTIS, RICHARD
   Katz, S.B. A conversation with... Richard Curtis. il interv JOURNAL WGA 8:24-27 Mar 1995
CURTIS, TONY
   Tony Curtis. biog filmog il stills STARS n21:[13-18] Winter 1995
CURTIZ, MICHAEL See also FRANCIS OF ASSISI; MILDRED PIERCE
CUSACK, CYRIL
   Dodsfall. biogs obits ports F&K n7:37 1993
CUSHING, PETER
   Bond, S.R. and Bond, S. Report from 221B Baker Street. biog il still ARMCHAIR DET 28:184-185 n2 1995
   Eriksen, F. Leksikal Peter Cushing biografi [Book Review]. il Z n4:40 (n46) 1993
   Ma Latorre, J. Retrato de Peter Cushing. il stills NOSFERATU n6:70-73 Apr 1991
   Schiller, R. Christopher Lee and Peter Cushing and horror cinema: a filmography of their 22 collaborations. By Mark A. Miller [Book Review]. F FAX n48:12+ [2p] Jan/Feb 1995
   Slide, A. The Slide area film book notes [Book Reviews]. CLASSIC n236:47-49 Feb 1995
CUSTEN, GEORGE F.
   Greenspan, C. Custen, George F. Bio/pics: how Hollywood constructed public

history [Book Review]. stat UFAJ 46:47-49 n3 1994
CUTLER, JANET
  Arthur, P. and Cutler, J. "Freedom on My Mind." credits still CINEASTE
    21:81-82 n1/2 1995
CUTLER, R.J. See also SEMPER FI
CUTLER, STAN
  Breen, J.L. Cutler, Stan. Shot on location [Book Review]. il port ARMCHAIR
    DET 26:74 n3 1993
CUTTHROAT ISLAND f (d Harlin, Renny 1995 USA)
  Clark, J. Renny Harlin gets the girl. il port still PREM 8:56-64 Mar 1995
CYCLO f (d Tran, Anh Hung 1995 Fr/Hong Kong/Vietnam)
  Rayns, T. Here and now. biog stills S&S 5:18-20 Apr 1995
CYNICISM See also IRONY
  Paquette, J.-M. Tarkovski, cineaste cynique. bibliog CINEMAS 4:15-23 n3
    1994
Czech Republic (since 1993) See as a subheading under individual subject
  headings
Czechoslovakia (1918-1990) See as a subheading under individual subject
  headings
CZLOWIEK Z ZELAZA f (Man of Iron d Wajda, Andrzej 1981 Poland)
  Falkowska, J. "The political" in the films of Andrzej Wajda and Krzysztof
    Kieslowski. CJ 34:37-50 n2 1995
D2: THE MIGHTY DUCKS f (d Weisman, Sam 1994 USA)
  Reviews
  Tunney, T. "D2: the Mighty Ducks." credits still S&S 5:44-45 Jan 1995
DEFA See DEUTSCHE FILM-AKTIEN-GESELLSCHAFT (DEFA)
D.W. Griffith Award See AWARDS - United States - Directors Guild of America
DA QUALCHE PARTE IN CITTA f (d Sordillo, Michele 1994 It)
  Reviews
  Loffreda, P. "Da qualche parte in citta." still C FORUM 34:26-27 Sep
    (n337) 1994
DABROWSKI, WALDEMAR
  Dabrowski, W. Krakow '93. REZYSER n18:1 1993
DAFOE, WILLEM
  Fuller, G. and Dafoe, W. Two chums who see eye to eye. il INTERV 25:38+
    [2p] Feb 1995
DAHL, JOHN See also LAST SEDUCTION, THE; RED ROCK WEST
DAISY MILLER f (d Bogdanovich, Peter 1974 USA)
  Adaptations
  Birdsall, E. Interpreting Henry James: Bogdanovich's "Daisy Miller."
    bibliog still LIT/FQ 22:272-277 n4 1994
DAJANI, NADIA
  Fuller, G. Parker's party. ports INTERV 25:79-81 Feb 1995
D'ALATRI, ALESSANDRO See also SENZA PELLE
D'ALESSANDRIA, NICO See also AMICO IMMAGINARIO, L'
DALLAS DOLL f (d Turner, Ann 1994 Australia/Gt Br)
  Reviews
  Francke, L. "Dallas Doll." credits still S&S 5:43-44 Feb 1995
DALMOLIN, ELIANE
  DalMolin, E. A voice in the dark: feminine figuration in Truffaut's "Jules
    and Jim." bibliog still LIT/FQ 22:238-245 n4 1994
DAMME, CHARLIE VAN See also JOUEUR DE VIOLON, LE
DAMNED IF YOU DON'T f (d Friedrich, Su 1987 USA)
  Homosexuals in Film
  Holmlund, C. Fractured fairytales and experimental identities: looking for
    lesbians in and around the films of Su Friedrich. bibliog stills DISCOURSE
    n17.1:16-46 Fall 1994
DAMPIER, MICHAEL For film reviews see author under the following titles: DARK
  SUMMER
DANA, VIOLA
  Rolick, J.M. Viola Dana: one of the silent screen's shining stars. il port
    CLASSIC n236:28+ [2p] Feb 1995
DANCE
  Sorenson, E. Bjud upp till dans! port CHAPLIN 36:69 n6 (n255) 1994/95
  Comparison With Film
  Hadj-Moussa, R. Le corps dansant au cinema. bibliog CINEMAS 3:205-221 n2/3
    1993
DANCES WITH WOLVES f (d Costner, Kevin 1990 USA)
  Baird, R. "Going Indian" through "Dances With Wolves." bibliog still
    F&HIST 23:92-102+ [12p] n1/4 1993
DANES, CLAIRE
  Marvel, M. Claire Danes: start remembering her name - you're going to need
    to know it. interv ports INTERV 25:68-71 Jan 1995
DANEY, SERGE
  Douchet, J. Serge Daney and Yamagata. biogs il obit port DOC BOX 2:1 1993
DANG, NHAT MINH
  Dang, N.M. Good cinema gasps for breath. CINEMAYA n24:55 Summer 1994
DANGEROUS WOMAN, A f (d Gyllenhaal, Stephen 1993 USA)
  Ciapara, E. "Niebezpieczna kobieta." biog credits filmog FSP 40:14 n3
    (n757) 1995
DANIEL, FERENC
  Daniel, F. Dosztojevszkij-mutatvany. stills F VILAG 38:31-33 n2 1995
  Daniel, F. Megszallott az utolso centig. il stills F VILAG 38:14-17 n3
    1995
DANITZ, BRIAN See also ECOLOGICAL DESIGN: INVENTING THE FUTURE
DANSE INDIENNE f (d Veyre, Gabriel 1898 Can)
  Gaudreault, A. and Lacasse, G. "Danse indienne": film Lumiere: no 1000: le
    premier film tourne au Quebec? stills 24 IMAGES n76:17-21 Spring 1995
DANTE, DOMINIQUE See also CONTRE L'OUBLI
DANTE, JOE See also GREMLINS
DANTE NO ES UNICAMENTE SEVERO f (d Esteva, Jacinto/Jorda, Joaquin 1967 Sp)
  Jorda, J. "Dante no es unicamente severo." credits stills NOSFERATU
    n9:97-99 Jun 1992
  Vidal, N. Joaquin Jorda: el circulo del perverso. biog il stills NOSFERATU
    n9:48-55 Jun 1992
DARABONT, FRANK See also SHAWSHANK REDEMPTION, THE
  Filmografie. biogs filmogs SEGNO n72:40 Mar/Apr 1995
  Katz, S.B. A conversation with... Frank Darabont. filmog interv port
    JOURNAL WGA 8:28-31 Feb 1995

DARBY, WILLIAM
  Hubbard, R. Book reviews [Book Reviews]. F SCORE MONTHLY n40:9 Dec 1993
DARGIS, MANOHLA
  Dargis, M. O solo Mia. port VILLAGE VOICE 40:58 Mar 14 1995
  Dargis, M. Reworking "Women." port still VILLAGE VOICE 40:70-71 Jan 3 1995
DARK EYES OF LONDON, THE f (Human Monster, The d Summers, Walter 1939 Gt Br)
  Senn, B. Bela's dark triad. stills F FAX n48:71-75+ [7p] Jan/Feb 1995
DARK HALF, THE f (d Romero, George A. 1993 USA)
  Reviews
  Garofalo, M. "La meta oscura." credits still SEGNO n63:99-100 Sep/Oct 1993
DARK SUMMER f (d Teton, Charles 1993 Gt Br)
  Reviewing
  Teton, C. Don't let the bastards grind you down! VERTIGO (UK) 1:60-61 n4
    1994/95
  Reviews
  Dampier, M. "Dark Summer." still VERTIGO (UK) 1:61 n4 1994/95
  Yates, R. "Dark Summer." credits S&S 5:64 Jan 1995
DARKE, CHRIS For film reviews see author under the following titles: DUMB AND
  DUMBER; REINE MARGOT, LA; SUTURE
DARKER SIDE OF BLACK f (d Julien, Isaac 1994 Gt Br)
  Grundmann, R. Black nationhood and the rest in the West. interv port
    CINEASTE 21:28-31 n1/2 1995
  Nolan, A.M. Double dare. il still VILLAGE VOICE 40:50 Jan 10 1995
DARNBOROUGH, ANTONY See also SO LONG AT THE FAIR
D'Artagnan's Daughter See FILLE DE D'ARTAGNAN, LA
DASTE, JEAN
  Du Bus, O.L. Les capitaines de "L'Atalante" ont leve l'ancre... filmog
    still SEQUENCES n175:50 Nov/Dec 1994
DAUDELIN, ROBERT
  Jean, M. Des restes d'images non identifies. il interv stills 24 IMAGES
    n75:26-32+ [8p] Dec/Jan 1994/95
DAUPHIN, GARY For film reviews see author under the following titles: BROTHER
  MINISTER: THE ASSASSINATION OF MALCOLM X; FILS DU REQUIN, LE; HIGHER
  LEARNING; LOSING ISAIAH; MURDER IN THE FIRST; ONCE WERE WARRIORS;
  TALES FROM THE CRYPT PRESENTS DEMON KNIGHT; ZIRE DARAKHTAN ZEYTON
DAVES, DELMER See also BROKEN ARROW
DAVID f (d Lilienthal, Peter 1979 W Ger)
  Cultural Context
  Linville, S.E. "Europa, Europa": a test case for German national cinema.
    stills WIDE ANGLE 16:38-51 n3 1995
DAVID, PIERRE See also SCANNER COP
DAVIDOFF, SOLOMON
  Davidoff, S. Kathy Merlock Jackson, Walt Disney: a bio-bibliography [Book
    Review]. ANIMATION J 3:92 n1 1994
DAVIDSON, SALLY For film reviews see author under the following titles: NATURAL
  BORN KILLERS
DAVIS, ANDREW See also DEAD DROP; FUGITIVE, THE; UNDER SIEGE
DAVIS, DON
  Hirsch, D. The film music of Don Davis: "Hyperspace." F SCORE MONTHLY
    n36/37:33 Aug/Sep 1993
DAVIS, GEENA
  Clark, J. Renny Harlin gets the girl. il port still PREM 8:56-64 Mar 1995
DAVIS, MARK H.
  In memoriam. biog il obit AMCIN 76:94 Feb 1995
DAVIS, PETER See also IN DARKEST HOLLYWOOD: CINEMA & APARTHEID
DAVIS, TAMRA See also BILLY MADISON
DAVIS, TOM
  Weiner, R. Partner at the periphery. port VARIETY 358:5 Mar 20/26 1995
DAWSON, ANTHONY M. See also MONDO DI YOR, IL
DAWTREY, ADAM
  Dawtrey, A. AFM enjoys late rush. il VARIETY 358:13+ [3p] Mar 6/12 1995
  Dawtrey, A. Bertelsmann grows new arm. stat VARIETY 358:36 Feb 27/Mar 5
    1995
  Dawtrey, A. Chrysalis deal leads to U.K. pic ventures. VARIETY 358:14 Mar
    13/19 1995
  Dawtrey, A. Costner's Tig set for "Water" remake. VARIETY 358:175 Feb 20/26
    1995
  Dawtrey, A. Euro majors gather in lobby. VARIETY 358:34 Feb 6/12 1995
  Dawtrey, A. Euros go on screen-building spree. graph VARIETY 358:1+ [2p]
    Feb 6/12 1995
  Dawtrey, A. Exim dives deeper into film biz. VARIETY 358:36 Mar 6/12 1995
  Dawtrey, A. For McGuiness, film is a long way from rock 'n' roll. VARIETY
    358:36 Mar 6/12 1995
  Dawtrey, A. Fox's Elstree plan dealt setback. VARIETY 358:43 Feb 13/19 1995
  Dawtrey, A. Gilbert, Samuelsons ink Miramax pic pact. il ports VARIETY
    358:14+ [2p] Mar 20/26 1995
  Dawtrey, A. Miramax Intl. takes a world view. VARIETY 358:24 Mar 6/12 1995
  Dawtrey, A. Sky moves into movies. stat VARIETY 358:9 Mar 27/Apr 2 1995
  Dawtrey, A. "Weddings" waltzes away with 11 BAFTA noms. VARIETY 358:66 Feb
    20/26 1995
  Dawtrey, A. and Cox, D. Days of "Dredd" at AFM. VARIETY 358:1+ [2p] Feb
    27/Mar 5 1995
  Dawtrey, A. and Williams, M. To dub or not to dub. VARIETY 358:10 Mar
    27/Apr 2 1995
  Williams, M. and Dawtrey, A. Brits, Euros finally get the big picture.
    graph il stat VARIETY 357:1+ [2p] Jan 2/8 1995
Day in the Country, A See PARTIE DE CAMPAGNE, UNE
Day of Wrath See VREDENS DAG
Days and Nights in the Forest See ARANYER DIN RAATRI
DAZED AND CONFUSED f (d Linklater, Richard 1993 USA)
  Reviews
  Brownlie, T. "Dazed and Confused." credits still FILM 4:20 n1 [1995]
  Reed, T. "Dazed and Confused." still FATAL VISIONS n17:7 1994
DE BERNARDINIS, FLAVIO For film reviews see author under the following titles:
  PARFUM D'YVONNE, LE; QUIZ SHOW; VANYA ON 42ND STREET; WYATT EARP
  De Bernardinis, F. Flashback. filmog stills SEGNO n63:94-95 Sep/Oct 1993
  De Bernardinis, F. Sex & flash. stills SEGNO n63:20-21 Sep/Oct 1993

DE BONT, JAN See also SPEED
DE ESO NO SE HABLA f (I Don't Want to Talk About It d Bemberg, Maria Luisa 1993 Arg/It)
    Reviews
    Jaehne, K. "I Don't Want to Talk About It." credits stills FQ 48:52-55 n2 1994/95
DE GAETANO, ROBERTO
    De Gaetano, R. "Gia vola il fiore magro." credits stills C FORUM 34:80-81 Nov (n339) 1994
DE GRAZIA, EDWARD
    De Grazia, E. Sex de jure [Book Reviews]. NATION 260:242-249 Feb 20 1995
DE MARINIS, GUALTIERO For film reviews see author under the following titles: ACE VENTURA, PET DETECTIVE; CLIENT, THE; PRESTAZIONE STRAORDINARIA; SPEED; VISITEURS, LES
    Chiacchiari, F. and De Marinis, G. "Amateur." credits stills C FORUM 34:60-62 Sep (n337) 1994
    De Marinis, G. Il debole di Jamie Lee Curtis: a volte sorride. filmog stills C FORUM 34:31-34 Nov (n339) 1994
    De Marinis, G. Pu(ri)tain de film! stills C FORUM 34:62-63 Sep (n337) 1994
    De Marinis, G. Un nez qui voque. stills C FORUM 34:49-56 Oct (n338) 1994
DE MASI, FRANCESCO
    Mansell, J. Francesco De Masi. il SCN 14:25-27 Mar 1995
De Mille, Cecil B. See DEMILLE, CECIL B.
DE NIRO, ROBERT See also BRONX TALE, A
DE PALMA, BRIAN See also CARLITO'S WAY
    Bruno, M.W. Brian De Hitchcock. port stills SEGNO n63:9-13 Sep/Oct 1993
    Mazierska, E. "Zycie Carlita." biog credits filmog FSP 40:8 n6 (n760) 1994
DE PASCALE, GOFFREDO
    Mancino, A.G. Goffredo De Pascale: Fernando Birri, l'altramerica [Book Review]. C FORUM 34:93-94 Nov (n339) 1994
DE RETOUR POUR DE BON f (d Arseneault, Bettie 1994 Can)
    Reviews
    El Yamani, M. L'Acadie des "etranges" et des secrets. credits still 24 IMAGES n75:69 Dec/Jan 1994/95
DE SANTI, GUALTIERO
    De Santi, G. Cinema e donne: la grande barriera corallina. stills C FORUM 34:21-23 Oct (n338) 1994
    De Santi, G. Soviet melodies. stills C FORUM 34:16-17 Oct (n338) 1994
DE SETA, VITTORIO See also IN CALABRIA
    Masala, F. Il ritorno di De Seta autore non "pacificato." interv stills C FORUM 34:63-66 Nov (n339) 1994
DE SICA, CHRISTIAN See also UOMINI UOMINI UOMINI
DE SICA, VITTORIO
    Comuzio, E. Giancarlo Governi: Vittorio De Sica. Parlami d'amore Mariu [Book Review]. il C FORUM 34:93-94 Sep (n337) 1994
DE SOUZA, STEVEN E. See also STREET FIGHTER
DE SUEUR ET DU SANG f (d Vecchiali, Paul 1994 Fr)
    Reviews
    Derobert, E. "Wonder Boy." still POSITIF n407:45 Jan 1995
DE TOTH, ANDRE
    Codelli, L. Fragments. Portraits from the inside. Par Andre De Toth [Book Reviews]. POSITIF n407:73 Jan 1995
    Henry, M. Entretien avec Andre De Toth. il interv stills POSITIF n407:68-73 Jan 1995
    Tavernier, B. Andre De Toth: eblouissement et zones d'ombre. il stills POSITIF n407:64-67 Jan 1995
    Tobin, Y. Andre De Toth. il stills POSITIF n407:60-63 Jan 1995
DEAD DROP f (d Davis, Andrew project 1995- USA)
    Laski, B. Reeves, Davis ring up "Dead" cash. stat VARIETY 357:13+ [2p] Jan 9/15 1995
DEALEY CENTER THEATRE (Groton, Connecticut)
    Allen, J.F. Maintaining legends. il port BOXOFFICE 131:bet p82 and 83 [pSW46-SW50] Apr 1995
DEAN, JAMES
    Noel, J. James Dean. De Barney Hoskyns [Book Review]. il GRAND ANGLE n177:49 Dec 1994
    Queenan, J. St. James? [Book Review]. il MOVIELINE 6:20-21 Mar 1995
    Rees, R.R. Vampira remembers Jimmy. il interv SCARLET STREET n17:40 Winter 1995
    Sullivan, D. The mysteries of James Dean. il still SCARLET STREET n17:37-41+ [6p] Winter 1995
DEAN, PETER
    Dean, P. Wind up. still S&S 5:70 Jan 1995
DEAR BABE f (d Ehrlich, Rosanne 1995 USA)
    Reviews
    Levy, E. "Dear Babe." credits VARIETY 358:52 Mar 13/19 1995
Dear Diary See CARO DIARIO
DEATH AND THE MAIDEN f (d Polanski, Roman 1994 USA/Fr/Gt Br)
    Heilpern, J. Roman's tortured holiday. il VANITY FAIR 58:88-91+ [5p] Jan 1995
    Thompson, D. I make films for adults. biog filmog interv port stills S&S 5:6-11 Apr 1995
    Reviews
    Denby, D. Deaf and the maidens. stills NEW YORK 28:48-49 Jan 9 1995
    James, N. "Death and the Maiden." credits still S&S 5:40 Apr 1995
    Lane, A. Power mad. il NEW YORKER 70:86-88 Jan 16 1995
    Meisel, M. "Death and the Maiden." credits FJ 98:46-47 Jan/Feb 1995
    Porton, R. "Death and the Maiden." CINEASTE 21:104 n1/2 1995
    Rousseau, Y. "Death and the Maiden." still 24 IMAGES n76:60 Spring 1995
    Travers, P. "Death and the Maiden." still ROLLING STONE n700:68 Jan 26 1995
DEATH IN FILM
    Killing for culture: an illustrated history of death film from mondo to snuff. By David Kerekes & David Slater [Book Review]. il still FATAL VISIONS n17:29 1994
    United States
    Marocco, P. Giocare il tempo. filmog port stills SEGNO n71:8-11 Jan/Feb 1995
DEATH LINE f (Raw Meat d Sherman, Gary 1972 Gt Br)
    Kraniauskas, J. Notes from the underground. still S&S 5:41 Jan 1995

DEBARTOLO, JOHN For film reviews see author under the following titles: BLAUE LICHT, DAS; MAN FROM BEYOND, THE; RAVEN, THE; STEAMBOAT BILL, JR.
DEBNEY, JOHN
    Rixman, J. John Debney. il interv F SCORE MONTHLY n38:8-9 Oct 1993
DECAMERON NO. 2 - LE ALTRE NOVELLE DEL BOCCACCIO f (d Guerrini, Mino 1971 It)
    Garofalo, M. Scult movie. credits il still SEGNO n71:78-79 Jan/Feb 1995
DECKNAME: ROSA f (d Specogna, Heidi 1993 Switz/W Ger)
    Reviews
    Wendt, U. "Deckname: Rosa." credtis C(SWITZ) 40:224-225 1994
DECONSTRUCTION SIGHT f (d Angerame, Dominic 1990 USA)
    Voorhees, B.J. The endless loop of the human continuum: Dominic Angerame's "Deconstruction Sight." stills MILLENNIUM n25:108-113 Summer 1991
DECONSTRUCTION ANALYSIS
    Great Britain
    Cantrill, A. Deconstruction and the visual arts: art, media, architecture. Edited by Peter Brunette and David Wills [Book Review]. CANTRILL'S FMNTS n73/74:40-41 May 1994
DEEP FOCUS CINEMATOGRAPHY
    United States
        Sound Design and Designers
        Altman, R. Deep-focus sound: "Citizen Kane" and the radio aesthetic. diag scenario Q REV F & VIDEO 15:1-34 n3 1994
Definitions and terms See TERMINOLOGY
DEGOUDENNE, LAURENCE
    Degoudenne, L. "Harcelement." credits still GRAND ANGLE n178:13-14 Jan 1995
    Degoudenne, L. "Max." credits stills GRAND ANGLE n176:15-16 Nov 1994
    Degoudenne, L. "Suture." bibliog credits stills GRAND ANGLE n178:33-34 Jan 1995
DEIGHTON, LEN
    Deighton, L. Sand and sea. stills S&S 5:30-33 Jan 1995
DEJA S'ENVOLE LA FLEUR MAIGRE f (d Meyer, Paul 1960 Belg)
    De Gaetano, R. "Gia vola il fiore magro." credits stills C FORUM 34:80-81 Nov (n339) 1994
    Fava, I. Intervista a Paul Meyer. interv stills C FORUM 34:81-83 Nov (n339) 1994
    Reviews
    Bruciamonti, A. "Gia vola il fiore magro." credits C NUOVO 43:54 Nov/Dec (n352) 1994
    Coco, A. "Gia vola il fiore magro." credits stills SEGNO n71:49-50 Jan/Feb 1995
DEKKER, FRED See also ROBOCOP 3
DEL RE, GIANMARCO
    Del Re, G. Londra: periferie, castelli e bandiere che bruciano. stills C FORUM 34:3-6 Nov (n339) 1994
DEL TORO, GUILLERMO
    Paxman, A. Del Toro latest H'wood recruit. il VARIETY 358:54+ [2p] Mar 27/Apr 2 1995
DEL VECCHIO, DEBORAH
    Eriksen, F. Leksikal Peter Cushing biografi [Book Review]. il Z n4:40 (n46) 1993
DELERUE, GEORGES
    Blum, G.C. In memory of... Georges Delerue. il F SCORE MONTHLY n36/37:25 Aug/Sep 1993
    Upton, R. Truffaut and Delerue on the screen. F SCORE MONTHLY n39:12 Nov 1993
DELEUZE, GILLES
    Bensmaia, R. De l'"automate spirituel" ou le temps dans le cinema moderne selon Gilles Deleuze. bibliog CINEMAS 5:167-186 n1/2 1994
DELEYTO, CELESTINO
    Deleyto, C. The narrator and the narrative: the evolution of Woody Allen's film comedies. bibliog F CRITICISM 19:40-54 n2 1994/95
DELISLE, FRANCOIS See also RUTH
    Jean, M. Francois Delisle. il interv stills 24 IMAGES n76:24-26+ [4p] Spring 1995
DELISLE, MARTIN For film reviews see author under the following titles: ETE INOUBLIABLE, UN; WAR, THE; YINSHI NAN NU
DELLA CASA, STEFANO For film reviews see author under the following titles: MAVERICK; NO ESCAPE
    Della Casa, S. Tutti colpevoli. il stills SEGNO n72:31-32 Mar/Apr 1995
DELLAMORTE DELLAMORE f (d Soavi, Michele 1994 It/Fr/FR Ger)
    Sound Track Reviews
    Deutsch, D.C. "Dellamorte dell'amore." il SCN 14:22 Mar 1995
DELON, ALAIN
    Alain Delon. biog filmog il stills STARS n21:[19-24] Winter 1995
DELPY, JULIE
    Fuller, G. and Linklater, R. Truer than romance? il interv ports INTERV 25:118-121 Feb 1995
DELVAL, DANIEL
    Delval, D. "Un indien dans la ville." credits stills GRAND ANGLE n177:17-18 Dec 1994
    Delval, D. and Noel, J. "Only You." credits stills GRAND ANGLE n178:21-22 Jan 1995
    Delval, D. and Noel, J. "Sirenes." bibliog credits stills GRAND ANGLE n178:25-26 Jan 1995
DEMARCO, MARIO
    DeMarco, M. A real all-American. il CLASSIC n237:63 Mar 1995
    DeMarco, M. Colonel Tim McCoy. il CLASSIC n236:8 Feb 1995
DEMILLE, CECIL B. See also SAMSON AND DELILAH
DEMME, JONATHAN See also PHILADELPHIA; SILENCE OF THE LAMBS, THE
    Weis, E. Sync tanks. il CINEASTE 21:56-61 n1/2 1995
DEMOLITION MAN f (d Brambilla, Marco 1993 USA)
    Reviews
    Meyers, R. The crime screen. port stills ARMCHAIR DET 27:207-209 n2 1994
DEMPSEY, JOHN
    Dempsey, J. Family feature films get a familiar ring. il VARIETY 358:1+ [2p] Mar 27/Apr 2 1995
DEMPSTER, JIM
    Dempster, J. Stabilising the ship. il table FILM 4:5 n1 [1995]

DENBY, DAVID For film reviews see author under the following titles: DEATH AND
  THE MAIDEN; DISCLOSURE; DUMB AND DUMBER; I.Q.; IMMORTAL BELOVED; LITTLE
  WOMEN; MADNESS OF KING GEORGE, THE; NOBODY'S FOOL; READY TO WEAR
  (PRET-A-PORTER)

DENIEL, JACQUES
  Thirard, P.L. Une encyclopedie du nu au cinema. Ouvrage reuni par Jacques
    Deniel et Patrick Leboutte, sur une idee d'Alain Bergala [Book Review].
    still POSITIF n408:78-79 Feb 1995

DENIS, CLAIRE See also CONTRE L'OUBLI

DENISE CALLS UP f (d Salwen, Hal 1995 USA)
  Reviews
  Levy, E. "Denise Calls up." credits VARIETY 358:52 Mar 13/19 1995

Denmark See as a subheading under individual subject headings

Dennis See DENNIS THE MENACE

DENNIS THE MENACE f (d Castle, Nick 1993 USA)
  Reviews
  Lampelto, R. "Ville Vallaton" on muuttunut herttaiseksi pikkuviikariksi.
    credits PEILI 17:45 n4 1993

DENNISON, DEBORAH See also BLOOD MEMORY
  Zibart, R. "Blood Memory." port INDEP 18:22 Apr 1995

DENTI, JOSEPH
  Bastone, W. La cosa nostra 90210. il stills VILLAGE VOICE 40:27-30 Feb 7
    1995

DEOCAMPO, NICK
  Deocampo, N. From revolution to revolution. biog il stills DOC BOX 5:15-18
    1994

DEPARDIEU, GERARD
  Slodowski, J. "Germinal." biogs credits filmogs FSP 40:10 n4 (n758) 1994

DEPARDON, RAYMOND See also CONTRE L'OUBLI

DEPP, JOHNNY
  Millea, H. Ghost in the machine. il port PREM 8:50-55+ [8p] Feb 1995

DERAY, JACQUES See also CONTRE L'OUBLI; ORSO DI PELUCHE, L'

DERNIER GLACIER, LE f (d Frappier, Roger/Leduc, Jacques 1984 Can)
  Lockerbie, I. Le documentaire autoreflexif au Quebec. "L'emotion dissonante"
    et "Passiflora." still CINEMAS 4:118-132 n2 1994

DERNIER STADE f (d Zerbib, Christian 1994 Fr/Switz/Belg/FR Ger)
  Reviews
  Nesselson, L. "Dernier Stade." credits VARIETY 357:74 Jan 2/8 1995

DEROBERT, ERIC For film reviews see author under the following titles: BAB
  EL-OUED CITY; DE SUEUR ET DU SANG; KASPAR HAUSER; KATIA ISMAILOVA;
  KUROCHKA RIABA; MACHINE, LA; MOTS PERDUS, LES; PECHE VENIEL... PECHE
  MORTEL...

DERRER, JAN CHRISTIAN For film reviews see author under the following titles:
  GROSSE FATIGUE; MURIEL'S WEDDING
  Derrer, J.C. "Liebe Luegen": Drehtag am Zuerichsee. il F BUL 37:9 n1
    (n198) 1995

DERRIDA, JACQUES
  Cantrill, A. Deconstruction and the visual arts: art, media, architecture.
    Edited by Peter Brunette and David Wills [Book Review]. CANTRILL'S FMNTS
    n73/74:40-41 May 1994

DERRYBERRY, JIL
  Derryberry, J. Have you seen Elina? interv ports INTERV 25:32+ [2p] Apr
    1995

DERTENO, ROBERT C. See also PIN-DOWN GIRL

DERUDDERE, DOMINIQUE See also SUITE 16

DESBARATS, CAROLE
  Rollet, S. Atom Egoyan. Par Carole Desbarats, Daniele Riviere et Jacinto
    Lageira; lettres-video de Paul Virilio et Atom Egoyan [Book Review]. il
    POSITIF n406:86 Dec 1994

DESERTO ROSSO f (Red Desert d Antonioni, Michelangelo 1964 It/Fr)
  Elder, R.B. Antonioni's tragic vision. CAN J F STUD 1:1-34 n2 1991
  Schenk, I. Natur und Anti-Natur in den Filmen von Michelangelo Antonioni.
    C(SWITZ) 40:175-193 1994

DESIERTOS MARES f (d Garcia Agraz, Jose Luis 1994 Mex)
  Torres San Martin, P. El cine por sus creadores Jose Luis Garcia Agraz. il
    interv still DICINE n59:26-27 Nov/Dec 1994

Design See PRODUCTION DESIGN AND DESIGNERS

DESIO, GIOVANNI For film reviews see author under the following titles:
  POSTINO, IL

DESJARDINS, DENIS For film reviews see author under the following titles:
  COLONEL CHABERT, LE; HISTOIRE DU GARCON QUI VOULAIT QU'ON
  L'EMBRASSE, L'

DESPERATE REMEDIES f (d Main, Stewart/Wells, Peter 1993 New Zealand)
  Barlow, H. Pur ekstase. stills F&K n7:20-21 1993

DESROSIERES, ANTOINE See also A LA BELLE ETOILE

DESSAU, MAXIM See also ERSTER VERLUST; RADI; SCHNAUZER; STILLEBEN
  Richter, E. Maxim Dessau. biog filmog il F & FERNSEHEN 22:6-7 n6 1994

DESSER, DAVID
  Dixon, W.W. American-Jewish filmmakers: traditions and trends. By David
    Desser and Lester D. Friedman [Book Review]. F CRITICISM 19:108-113 n2
    1994/95
  Polan, D. Reflections in a male eye: John Huston and the American
    experience. Edited by Gaylyn Studlar and David Desser [Book Review]. F
    CRITICISM 19:103-108 n2 1994/95

D'ESTATE f (d Soldini, Silvio 1994 It)
  Reviews
  Gandini, L. "Miracoli. Storie per corti": "Antonio Mastronunzio, pittore
    sannita"; "Dov'e Yankel?"; "D'estate." C FORUM 34:33 Sep (n337) 1994

DESTINY IN SPACE f (d Neihouse, James 1994 USA/Can)
  Reviews
  Williamson, K. "Destiny in Space." still BOXOFFICE 131:bet p125 and 144
    [pR37] Apr 1995

DETASSIS, PIERA
  Poggi, E. Il critico al festival ovvero lo spettatore indiscreto. intervs
    SEGNO n71:19-33 Jan/Feb 1995

DETECTIVE FILM See also GANGSTER FILM; MYSTERY FILM; SUSPENSE FILM
  Breen, J.L. Cocchiarelli, Joseph J. Screen sleuths: a filmography [Book
    Review]. ARMCHAIR DET 27:92 n1 1994

  United States
    Adaptations
  Gallagher, B. It's a print!: detective fiction from page to screen. Edited
    by William Reynolds and Elizabeth A. Trembley [Book Review]. MICHIGAN
    ACADEMICIAN 27:229-231 n2 1995
    History
  Farrell, S. The American detective: an illustrated history. Jeff Siegel
    [Book Review]. SCARLET STREET n17:99 Winter 1995

DETOUR f (d Ulmer, Edgar G. 1945 USA)
  Music
  Creekmur, C.K. Strains of utopia: gender, nostalgia, and Hollywood music.
    Caryl Flinn [Book Review]. DISCOURSE n17.1:172-175 Fall 1994

DEUS PINHEIRO, JOAO DE
  Protection du patrimoine cinematographique Europeen. MONITEUR n126:30 Dec
    1994

DEUTSCH, ANDRE
  Strick, P. Fresh slogans [Book Review]. still S&S 5:34-35 Apr 1995

DEUTSCH, DIDIER C.
  Deutsch, D.C. "Anni rebelli"; "Il postino." SCN 14:22 Mar 1995
  Deutsch, D.C. "Arizona Colt." SCN 14:16 Mar 1995
  Deutsch, D.C. Comedy, Italian style. SCN 14:20 Mar 1995
  Deutsch, D.C. "Dellamorte dell'amore." il SCN 14:22 Mar 1995
  Deutsch, D.C. "Doctor Faustus"; "Francis of Assisi." il SCN 14:16-17 Mar
    1995
  Deutsch, D.C. "I pugni in tasca"/"I basilischi"/"Gente di rispetto." SCN
    14:20-21 Mar 1995
  Deutsch, D.C. "Lamerica." SCN 14:21 Mar 1995
  Deutsch, D.C. "Senza pelle." SCN 14:20 Mar 1995
  Deutsch, D.C. Spaghetti Western encyclopedia. SCN 14:17-18 Mar 1995

DEUTSCH, JOEL
  Deutsch, J. Meet the nominees: theatrical motion pictures. ports DGA NEWS
    19:19-23 n2 1994

DEUTSCHE FILM-AKTIEN-GESELLSCHAFT (DEFA)
  History
  Das zweite Leben der Filmstadt Babelsberg DEFA-Spielfilme 1946-1992 [Book
    Review]. il KINO(GF) n56:28 Nov 1994

DEVAUX, FREDERIQUE
  Cantrill, A. Le cinema Lettriste (1951-1991). By Frederique Devaux [Book
    Review]. CANTRILL'S FMNTS n73/74:42 May 1994

DEVEAU, VINCENT
  DeVeau, V. Honoring the artistry of Fred Zinnemann. filmog il DGA NEWS
    19:18-24 n3 1994
  DeVeau, V. Michael Apted and the documentary heartbeat. filmog il interv
    DGA NEWS 19:36-37+ [6p] n6 1994/95

DEVERS, CLAIRE See also MAX ET JEREMIE

Devil and Daniel Webster, The See ALL THAT MONEY CAN BUY

DEVILLE, MICHEL See also CONTRE L'OUBLI

DEVINE, JEREMY M.
  Slide, A. The Slide area film book notes [Book Reviews]. CLASSIC n236:47-49
    Feb 1995

DEWASSE, GUY
  Dewasse, G. "Sugar Hill." bibliog credits stills GRAND ANGLE n176:27-28
    Nov 1994

DEY, TOM
  Dey, T. ASC hails career of Gabriel Figueroa. il port stills AMCIN
    76:40-44+ [8p] Mar 1995

DI GIORGI, SERGIO
  Di Giorgi, S. Donne senza storia. stills FCR 45:301-307 Jun/Jul (n446/447)
    1994

DI LUZIO, ALESSANDRA For film reviews see author under the following titles:
  CRACKING UP; JASON'S LYRIC; METAL SKIN; OUBLIE-MOI
  Di Luzio, A. Montecatini: il cinema "corto" va riscoprendo il racconto.
    stills C FORUM 34:18-20 Oct (n338) 1994

DI MARINO, BRUNO
  Comuzio, E. Bruno Di Marino e Giovanni Spagnoletti (a cura di): Friedrich
    Wilhelm Murnau [Book Review]. il C FORUM 34:93 Nov (n339) 1994

DI NOVI, DENISE
  Cox, D. Di Novi inks with Turner. VARIETY 358:36 Mar 6/12 1995

DI NUBILA, DOMINGO
  Di Nubila, D. Abel Santa Cruz. obit VARIETY 358:54 Feb 13/19 1995
  Di Nubila, D. Argentine gov't OKs aid. stat VARIETY 358:54 Mar 27/Apr 2
    1995

DI PALMA, CARLO
  Oppenheimer, J. "Team Woody" fires "Bullets Over Broadway." il stills
    AMCIN 76:66-70 Feb 1995

DIA DE LOS MUERTOS, EL f (d Jorda, Joaquin 1960 Sp)
  Jorda, J. Numax presenta... y otras cosas. still NOSFERATU n9:56-59 Jun
    1992

DIABLO NUNCA DUERME, EL f (d Portillo, Lourdes 1994 USA/Mex)
  Thompson, A. "The Devil Never Sleeps." il INDEP 18:20-22 Apr 1995

DIAGULUDE YAOLAN f (d Mi, Jiashan 1994 China)
  "Cradle on Wheels." credits il stills CHINA SCREEN n4:before p1-1 [2p] 1994

DIAL M FOR MURDER f (d Hitchcock, Alfred 1954 USA)
  Sound Track Reviews
  Larson, R.D. "Dial M for Murder." F SCORE MONTHLY n39:12 Nov 1993

DIALOGUES WITH MADWOMEN f (d Light, Allie 1993 USA)
  Milvy, E. Allie Light tells all. ANGLES 2:5 n4 1995
  Reviews
  Warren, S. A frank "Dialogue" on mental illness. port still ANGLES 2:4 n4
    1995

DIANA, MARIOLINA
  Diana, M. Prima del silenzio. stills SEGNO n71:62-64 Jan/Feb 1995

DIARY FILM
  Italy
  Porton, R. and Ellickson, L. Comedy, communism, and pastry: an interview
    with Nanni Moretti. interv port stills CINEASTE 21:11-15 n1/2 1995

Diary of Chuji's Travels, A See CHUJI TABI NIKKI

DIAWARA, MANTHIA
  Harrow, K.W. Diawara, Manthia. African cinema: politics and culture [Book
    Review]. CINEMAS 4:183-185 n2 1994

DIAZ, CAMERON
D'Souza, C. Cameron comes on. ports ESQUIRE 123:130-133 Feb 1995
Hensley, D. Buenos Díaz. interv port MOVIELINE 6:18 Mar 1995
DICAPRIO, LEONARDO
Frankel, M. The young lion. il port stills MOVIELINE 6:42-46+ [8p] Mar
1995
DICHIARAZIONI D'AMORE f (d Avati, Pupi 1994 It)
   Reviews
Comuzio, E. "Dichiarazioni d'amore." credits still C FORUM 34:77-78 Sep
(n337) 1994
DICK, BERNARD F.
Hagopian, K.J. Columbia Pictures: portrait of a studio. Edited by Bernard F.
Dick [Book Review]. F CRITICISM 19:95-99 n2 1994/95
Keenan, R. Hail, Columbia! a studio odyssey [Book Review]. still LIT/FQ
22:278-279 n4 1994
DICK TRACY (fictional character)
Hoppenstand, G. Dick Tracy and American culture: morality and mythology,
text and context. By Garyn G. Roberts [Book Review]. ARMCHAIR DET
27:236-237 n2 1994
DICKERSON, ERNEST See also TALES FROM THE CRYPT PRESENTS DEMON KNIGHT
DICKEY, SARA
Stern, J. Sara Dickey. Cinema and the urban poor in South India [Book
Review]. STUDIES POP CULT 17:102 n1 1994
DICTIONARIES AND ENCYCLOPEDIAS See also TERMINOLOGY
Brown, G. The birds (and a book) [Book Review]. stills VILLAGE VOICE 40:48
Jan 10 1995
Clements, M. The medium needs a message. il PREM 8:52-53 Mar 1995
   Europe
Aude, F. (Deux) 250 cineastes europeens d'aujourd'hui. Sous la direction de
Gilles Garcia [Book Review]. POSITIF n409:73 Mar 1995
   Hungary
Gyorffy, M. Ha en filmlexikont szerkesztenek [Book Review]. F VILAG
38:53-54 n4 1995
   Italy
Francesco Vedovati: Dizionario dei termini cinematografici [Book Review].
IMMAGINE n28:31 Autumn 1994
Thirard, P.L. Dizionario dei film. Sous la direction de Paolo Mereghetti
[Book Review]. POSITIF n409:73 Mar 1995
   Norway
Fonn, E.B. Filmen i HHH 94 [Book Review]. F&K n1:39 1994
Lochen, K. Filmleksikon pa diskett [Book Review]. still F&K n7:41 1993
   United States
Af Geijerstam, E. Inte bara for kalenderbitare [Book Review]. il CHAPLIN
36:61 n6 (n255) 1994/95
Blomkvist, M. Mot filmhistorien - med sprang! port CHAPLIN 36:72 n6 (n255)
1994/95
Cabrera Infante, G. Cinema paradiso [Book Review]. NEW REPUB 212:40-42 Jan
23 1995
Dykyj, O. Cinemania 1995. il SEQUENCES n175:55-56 Nov/Dec 1994
Kemp, P. Discworld [Book Review]. still S&S 5:34 Apr 1995
Rosenburg, J. Motion picture guide on CD-ROM. CLASSIC n237:bet p32 and 33
[pC15] Mar 1995
Strick, P. Fresh slogans [Book Review]. still S&S 5:34-35 Apr 1995
Thal, O. Cinemania '94 - der interaktive Kinofuehrer. MEDIEN 38:369-373 n6
1994
Turner, G. The first century of film. By Martin S. Quigley [Book Review].
AMCIN 76:85-86 Mar 1995
Webster, E. The motion picture guide [Book Review]. il VARIETY 358:42-43
Mar 13/19 1995
DIDEROT, DENIS
Bonnet, J.-C. Le XVIIIe siecle a l'ecran. bibliog still CINEMAS 4:48-58 n1
1993
DIEGUES, CARLOS See also VEJA ESTA CANCAO
Dieterle, Wilhelm See DIETERLE, WILLIAM
DIETERLE, WILLIAM See also ALL THAT MONEY CAN BUY; MIDSUMMER NIGHT'S DREAM, A
DIETL, HELMUT See also SCHTONK
DIETMEIER, PAT For film reviews see author under the following titles: NEW
JERSEY DRIVE
DIETRICH, MARLENE
Longfellow, B. Gaylyn Studlar. In the realm of pleasure: Von Sternberg,
Dietrich and the masochistic aesthetic [Book Review]. CAN J F STUD 1:83-89
n2 1991
DIEULEVEULT, BRUNO DE
Berthome, J.-P. Le "storyboard" en livres [Book Reviews]. POSITIF n407:90+
[2p] Jan 1995
DIEXIE JIETOU f (Bullet in the Head d Woo, John 1990 Hong Kong)
Williams, T. To live and die in Hong Kong. bibliog stills C ACTION
n36:42-52 1995
DIEXUE SHUANG XIONG f (Killer, The d Woo, John 1989 Hong Kong)
Williams, T. To live and die in Hong Kong. bibliog stills C ACTION
n36:42-52 1995
DIGEH CHE KHABAR? f (d Milani, Tahmineh 1992 Iran)
"Digeh che khabar?" biog credits filmog il still CINEMAYA n25/26:100
Autumn/Winter 1994/95
Digital See as a subheading under individual subject headings (e.g. SOUND
SYSTEMS - Digital)
DILLMAN, BRADFORD
Weiner, R. Dillman takes Giants step. port VARIETY 357:4 Jan 2/8 1995
DIMARCO, STEVE See also SPIKE OF LOVE
DIMITROVSKI, DUSKO
Dimitrovski, D. "Sineast" [Book Review]. il BLIMP n30:56 Winter 1994
DINAMITE (NURAXI FIGUS, ITALIA) f (d Segre, Daniele 1994 It)
   Reviews
Fadda, M. "Dinamite (Nuraxi Figus, Italia)." still C FORUM 34:28-29 Sep
(n337) 1994
DINDO, RICHARD See also ERNESTO "CHE" GUEVARA: DAS BOLIVIANISCHE TAGEBUCH
DINH, THUY For film reviews see author under the following titles: MUI DU DU
XANH
DINNER AT EIGHT f (d Cukor, George 1934 USA)
Comuzio, E. Edoardo Bruno: "Pranzo alle otto" - Forme e figure della

sophisticated comedy [Book Review]. C FORUM 34:95 Sep (n337) 1994
DIONNE, MARIE-CLAUDE
Dionne, M.-C. Droits au coeur. SEQUENCES n175:12 Nov/Dec 1994
DIRECTING
   Canada
Blois, M. de. Entretien avec Robert Morin. il interv stills 24 IMAGES
n75:6-11 Dec/Jan 1994/95
   France
Aude, F. Entretien avec Nicole Garcia. il interv stills POSITIF n407:15-20
Jan 1995
Aude, F. Entretien avec Noemie Lvovsky. il interv stills POSITIF
n408:39-42 Feb 1995
Carroll, T. From "Knife" to "Death" with Roman Polanski. filmog il interv
DGA NEWS 19:38-39+ [5p] n6 1994/95
Sineux, M. and Vachaud, L. Entretien avec Bertrand Tavernier. il interv
stills POSITIF n409:25-30 Mar 1995
      Ethnographic Film
Taylor, L. A conversation with Jean Rouch. biog interv port VISUAL ANTHRO
R 7:92-102 n1 1991
   Great Britain
Bennett, R. Lean mean and cruel. interv stills S&S 5:34-36 Jan 1995
Elrick, T. Kenneth Branagh re-creates the classics. filmog interv ports
DGA NEWS 19:32-33+ [4p] n6 1994/95
      Horror Film. History
Ma Latorre, J. Terence Fisher: notas a la sombra de un estilo. il stills
NOSFERATU n6:44-49 Apr 1991
   Iran
Ciment, M. and Goudet, S. Entretien avec Abbas Kiarostami. il interv stills
POSITIF n408:14-19 Feb 1995
Euvrard, J. Retrouver l'enfance. interv stills 24 IMAGES n75:14-16 Dec/Jan
1994/95
   Italy
Fofi, G. and Volpi, G. Entretien avec Federico Fellini. il interv stills
POSITIF n409:76-92 Mar 1995
Garofalo, M. Slapstick all'italiana. il interv stills SEGNO n72:3-9
Mar/Apr 1995
   United States
DeVeau, V. Michael Apted and the documentary heartbeat. filmog il interv
DGA NEWS 19:36-37+ [6p] n6 1994/95
Elrick, T. Gump becomes him. il interv port DGA NEWS 20:26-27+ [6p] n1
1995
Henry, M. Entretien avec John Carpenter. il interv stills POSITIF
n409:10-18 Mar 1995
Keathly, C. Robert Benton. il interv stills F COM 31:36-43+ [12p] Jan/Feb
1995
Kremski, P. "Die Musik soll nicht das ausdruecken, was in der Szene zu sehen
ist." credits il interv stills F BUL 37:33-38 n1 (n198) 1995
Krolikowska-Avis, E. Alan Parker. il interv KINO 27:10-13 Jun 1993
Smith, G. Barbet Schroeder. il interv stills F COM 31:64-75 Mar/Apr 1995
Yonover, N.S. Mick Garris takes "The Stand." filmog il interv port DGA
NEWS 19:26-28 n2 1994
Zeitlin, M. Martha, I says. filmog il DGA NEWS 19:24-25+ [3p] n2 1994
DIRECTORIES
What's for sale at the market. stills VARIETY 358:bet p88 and 173 [pA25+
(26p)] Feb 20/26 1995
   Austria
Frey, M. Oesterreichischer forschungsstaettenkatalog [Book Review]. F KUNST
n144:76-77 1994
   Poland
Kaplinska, A. Edukacja filmowa. REZYSER n19:6 1993
DIRECTORS See also names of directors; WOMEN DIRECTORS
Trente heritiers d'un siecle de cinema. il ports 24 IMAGES n76:30-42 Spring
1995
   France
Williams, M. Pic biz sees French resistance: helmers eschew H'wood way. il
VARIETY 358:44-45 Mar 13/19 1995
   Festivals
Azzalin, C. L'amore di molti. stills SEGNO n71:65-66 Jan/Feb 1995
   United States
Brodie, J. Hapless helmers torn by tensions. il ports VARIETY 358:1+ [3p]
Feb 6/12 1995
Klady, L. Directors with seasoning. VARIETY 358:87 Feb 6/12 1995
Slide, A. The Slide area film book notes [Book Reviews]. CLASSIC
n237:42-44+ [4p] Mar 1995
      Collections and Collecting
Behlmer, R. Directors' paper trails. table DGA NEWS 19:50+ [3p] n6 1994/95
      Credit
Reynolds, G. Credits where they're due. port DGA NEWS 19:5 n6 1994/95
      Health
Elrick, T. Stamina on the set. DGA NEWS 19:10-11+ [3p] n3 1994
      Horror Film
Nangle, J. The fearmakers: the screen's directorial masters of suspense and
terror. By John McCarty [Book Review]. FIR 45:69-70 Nov/Dec 1994
DIRECTOR'S CONTROL
   United States
      Conferences, Institutes, Workshops, etc.
Behrend, J. DGA goes indie at IFFM. il DGA NEWS 19:24-25 n6 1994/95
DIRECTORS GUILD OF AMERICA
   Conferences, Institutes, Workshops, etc.
Behrend, J. DGA goes indie at IFFM. il DGA NEWS 19:24-25 n6 1994/95
Director's Place, The See IS THAT ALL THERE IS?
DIRIGIDO POR
Lassacher, M. Spanische Schriften [Book Review]. il BLIMP n30:58-60 Winter
1994
DISCLOSURE f (d Levinson, Barry 1994 USA)
Degoudenne, L. "Harcelement." credits still GRAND ANGLE n178:13-14 Jan
1995
   Reviews
Blois, M. de. "Disclosure." still 24 IMAGES n76:60-61 Spring 1995
Ciment, M. "Harcelement." still POSITIF n409:43-44 Mar 1995

DOESCHERS f (d Schoenemann, Hannes 1977 E Ger)
Graef, C. Hochschulfilme. il F & FERNSEHEN 22:73-81 n6 1994
DOG, POPE, AND JOE f (d Breer, Emily 1992 USA)
    Storyboards
Breer, E. "Dog, Pope and Joe." il scenario stills MILLENNIUM n26:68-77
Fall 1992
DOHERTY, THOMAS For film reviews see author under the following titles: QUIZ
SHOW
Turner, G. Projections of war. By Thomas Doherty [Book Review]. AMCIN 76:85
Feb 1995
DOILLON, JACQUES See also CONTRE L'OUBLI; DU FOND DU COEUR: GERMAINE ET
BENJAMIN; JEUNE WERTHER, LE
DOLLAR, STEVE
Dollar, S. Music documentarian. il INDEP 18:18-19 Jan/Feb 1995
DOLORES CLAIBORNE f (d Hackford, Taylor 1995 USA)
    Reviews
Lowry, B. "Dolores Claiborne." credits still VARIETY 358:48 Mar 20/26 1995
Schickel, R. Woman under the influence. still TIME 145:73 Mar 27 1995
DOM KALLAR OSS MODS f (d Jarl, Stefan/Lindqvist, Jan 1969 Swed)
Vahtera, H. Kapinallisten perinto. still PEILI 18:31 n4 1994
DOMENEGHINI, ANTON GINO See also ROSA DI BAGDAD, LA
Bendazzi, G. The first Italian animated feature film and its producer: "La
Rosa di Bagdad" and Anton Gino Domeneghini. biogs il stat stills ANIMATION
J 3:4-18 n2 1995
DOMITOR
    Conferences, Institutes, Workshops, etc.
Orbanz, E. Domitor '94 - cinema turns 100. il J F PRES n49:56-63 Oct 1994
DON JUAN DEMARCO f (d Leven, Jeremy 1995 USA)
    Reviews
Levy, E. "Don Juan DeMarco." credits still VARIETY 358:75 Mar 27/Apr 2
1995
DON JUAN HEIMKEHR f (d Hoentsch, Andreas 1984 E Ger)
Graef, C. Hochschulfilme. il F & FERNSEHEN 22:30-35 n6 1994
DONAGGIO, ADRIANO
Zappoli, G. Cosi vicino cosi lontano. il intervs SEGNO n71:24-27 Jan/Feb
1995
DONALDSON, ROGER See also GETAWAY, THE
"Ucieczka gangstera." biogs credits filmogs FSP 40:11 n4 (n758) 1994
DONDUREI, DANIIL
Film, TV, video in Russia - 1994. Ed: Daniil Dondurei [Book Review]. il
KINO(GF) n56:30 Nov 1994
DONEN, STANLEY See also SINGIN' IN THE RAIN
DONMEZ COLIN, GONUL
Donmez Colin, G. Kazakh new wave: post perestroika, post Soviet Union. il
stat stills table BLIMP n30:12-15 Winter 1994
Donmez Colin, G. Sema Poyraz: contending with an alien land. il CINEMAYA
n25/26:60-61 Autumn/Winter 1994/95
DONMEZ, GONUL
Donmez, G. International Izmir Film Festival. CINEMAYA n24:63 Summer 1994
DONNER, RICHARD See also MAVERICK
D'ONOFRIO, GIACOMO
Brescia, A. "Sotto il vecchio berso'." Di Giacomo D'Onofrio [Book Review].
biog C SUD 33:40 Jul/Aug/Sep (n113) 1994
D'ONOFRIO, VINCENT
Hooper, J. Playing the heavy. port ESQUIRE 123:36 Feb 1995
DONOHUE, WILLIAM A.
Alleva, R. Correspondence: the reviewer replies. COMMONWEAL 122:29 Mar 10
1995
Donohue, W.A. Correspondence: "Voice" vs. Alleva. COMMONWEAL 122:29 Mar 10
1995
DONOVAN, MARTIN See also APARTMENT ZERO
DON'T GET ME STARTED f (d Ellis, Arthur 1994 Gt Br/FR Ger)
    Reviews
Fadda, M. "Don't Get Me Started." still C FORUM 34:36-37 Sep (n337) 1994
DOOLE, KERRY
Doole, K. Welcome mat out for NZ. ONFILM [12]:4 n1 1995
DOOM GENERATION, THE f (d Araki, Gregg 1995 USA/Fr)
    Reviews
Levy, E. "Araki's 'Doom' a dazzling machine. credits still VARIETY
358:73-74 Feb 6/12 1995
DOP, PETER See also SCHADUWLOPERS, DE
DORAN, ANN
Randisi, S. Lifetime contract. il port stills F FAX n48:76-81+ [8p]
Jan/Feb 1995
Valley, R. Ann Doran. il interv port stills SCARLET STREET n17:42+ [9p]
Winter 1995
DORLAND, MICHAEL
Dorland, M. The war machine: American culture, Canadian cultural sovereignty
& film policy. CAN J F STUD 1:35-48 n2 1991
DOROGA V RAI f (d Moskalenko, Vitalii 1994 Russia/FR Ger)
Fornara, B. "Doroga v ray." still C FORUM 34:37 Sep (n337) 1994
DOROTHEA LANGE: A VISUAL LIFE f (d Partridge, Meg 1995 USA)
    Reviews
Levy, E. "Dorothea Lange: a Visual Life." credits VARIETY 358:76 Feb 6/12
1995
DORSAY, ATILLA For film reviews see author under the following titles: BIR
SONBAHAR HIKAYESI
Dorsay, A. Alexandria. still CINEMAYA n25/26:87-88 Autumn/Winter 1994/95
Dorsay, A. Before tomorrow after yesterday. stills CINEMAYA n25/26:56-58
Autumn/Winter 1994/95
Dorsay, A. The stubborn ambition of Bilge Olgac. stills CINEMAYA
n25/26:59-60 Autumn/Winter 1994/95
DOSTOEVSKII, FEDOR
Dumala, P. "Zbrodnia i kara" - epilog. il KINO 27:14-17 Jun 1993
Dostoyevsky, Fyodor See DOSTOEVSKII, FEDOR
DOTY, ALEXANDER
Bronski, M. Queer looks: perspectves on lesbian and gay film and video.
Edited by Martha Gever, John Greyson and Pratibha Parmar [Book Reviews].
still CINEASTE 21:90-92 n1/2 1995

DOUBLE INDEMNITY f (d Wilder, Billy 1944 USA)
Ciment, M. BFI film classics [Book Reviews]. stills POSITIF n408:75-77 Feb
1995
Cremonini, G. Sam Rohdie: Rocco and his bothers (Rocco e i suoi fratelli) di
L. Visconti [Book Reviews]. C FORUM 34:93 Sep (n337) 1994
Hendrykowski, M. BFI Film Classics [Book Review]. il KINO 27:39-40 May
1993
Double Life of Veronique, The See DOUBLE VIE DE VERONIQUE, LA
DOUBLE VIE DE VERONIQUE, LA f (Double Life of Veronique, The d Kieslowski,
Krzysztof 1991 Fr/Poland)
    Reviews
Carro, N. "La doble vida de Veronica." credits stills DICINE n59:34-35
Nov/Dec 1994
DOUCHET, JEAN
Douchet, J. Serge Daney and Yamagata. biogs il obit port DOC BOX 2:1 1993
DOUGLAS, MICHAEL
Collins, N. Michael's full disclosure. il ports VANITY FAIR 58:68-75+
[12p] Jan 1995
Hoberman, J. Victim victorious. stills VILLAGE VOICE 40:31-33 Mar 7 1995
DOUKOURE, CHEIK See also BALLON D'OR, LE
DOUSI CHINGYUN f (d Lau, Jeff 1995 Hong Kong)
    Reviews
Rooney, D. "Love and the City" ("Dousi chingyun"). credits VARIETY 358:52
Feb 13/19 1995
DOV'E YANKEL? f (d Rosa, Paolo 1994 It)
    Reviews
Gandini, L. "Miracoli. Storie per corti": "Antonio Mastronunzio, pittore
sannita"; "Dov'e Yankel?"; "D'estate." C FORUM 34:33 Sep (n337) 1994
DOWELL, PAT
Dowell, P. The mythology of the western: Hollywood perspectives on race and
gender in the nineties. stills CINEASTE 21:6-10 n1/2 1995
DOWLING, KEVIN See also SUM OF US, THE
DOWNING, TAYLOR
Ciment, M. BFI film classics [Book Reviews]. stills POSITIF n408:75-77 Feb
1995
DOZHDI V OKEANE f (d Aristov, Viktor/Mamin, Iurii 1995 Russia)
    Reviews
Rooney, D. "Rains in the Ocean" ("Dozhdi v okeane"). credits VARIETY
358:85 Feb 20/26 1995
DRACULA f (Horror of Dracula d Fisher, Terence 1958 Gt Br)
Aldarondo, R. and Ma Latorre, J. "Dracula." credits stills NOSFERATU
n6:78-80 Apr 1991
Lee, C. Extracto de una carta de Christopher Lee sobre "Dracula." still
NOSFERATU n6:81 Apr 1991
DRACULA - PRINCE OF DARKNESS f (d Fisher, Terence 1965 Gt Br)
Bernardo, J.M. "Dracula, Principe de las Tinieblas." credits il still
NOSFERATU n6:94-95 Apr 1991
DRAGON: THE BRUCE LEE STORY f (d Cohen, Rob 1993 USA)
Norcen, L. Le 7 vite del drago. stills SEGNO n63:7-8 Sep/Oct 1993
DRAMA See also TRAGEDY
    Germany (Federal Republic, 1949-1990)
        Adaptations
Plater, E. M.V. Helmut Kaeutner's film adaptation of "Des Teufels General."
bibliog LIT/FQ 22:253-264 n4 1994
    Great Britain
        Influence on Film
Vidal Estevez, M. William Akira Shakespeare Kurosawa. il stills NOSFERATU
n8:40-47 Feb 1992
Drama into film See ADAPTATIONS
Dramatic re-enactments See HISTORICAL FILM
DRAPER, ROBERT
Draper, R. The Tao of Dennis. ports PREM 8:70-75+ [7p] Feb 1995
DREAMWORKS SKG
Busch, A.M. and Weiner, R. Gates joins DreamWorks team. il VARIETY 358:15+
[2p] Mar 27/Apr 2 1995
Corliss, R. Hey, let's put on a show! il ports TIME 145:54-60 Mar 27 1995
    Economic Aspects
Busch, A.M. and Peers, M. Troika has its eyes on $1 bil prize. stat
VARIETY 358:13 Feb 27/Mar 5 1995
DREI ROSEN UND EIN LUFTBALLON f (d Schoenemann, Sibylle unrealized project 1983
E Ger)
Graef, C. Startversuche im Spielfilm-Studio. il interv F & FERNSEHEN
22:107-111 n6 1994
DREYER, CARL THEODOR See also BLADE AF SATANS BOG; DU SKAL AERE DIN HUSTRU;
GERTRUD; GEZEICHNETEN, DIE; GLOMDALSBRUDEN; MIKAEL; ORDET; PASSION DE JEANNE
D'ARC, LA; PRAESIDENTEN; PRASTANKEN; TVA MANNISKOR; VAMPYR: DER TRAUM DES
ALLAN GRAY; VAR ENGANG, DER; VREDENS DAG
Las peliculas del ciclo. filmog il still NOSFERATU n5:42-71 Jan 1991
Masoni, T. Carl Theodor Dreyer: l'assoluto e il dubbio. stills C FORUM
34:14-17 Nov (n339) 1994
Miguez, M. Aproximacion bibliografica. il NOSFERATU n5:74-75 Jan 1991
Miguez, M. Cortometrajes. stills NOSFERATU n5:72-73 Jan 1991
Miguez, M. La mirada Dreyer. il stills NOSFERATU n5:24-37 Jan 1991
Minguet Batllori, J.M. Carl Theodor Dreyer: clasicismo y cine. il port
stills NOSFERATU n5:12-23 Jan 1991
Monty, I. Vida y obras de Carl Theodor Dreyer. biog il port stills
NOSFERATU n5:4-11 Jan 1991
DRIDI, KARIM See also PIGALLE
DRINNAN, JOHN
Bisset, B. Letters: Blue Book piece was half right. ONFILM 11:10-11 n11
1994/95
Drinnan, J. Blue Book blues dog TVC shoots. ONFILM 11:3 n11 1994/95
Drinnan, J. Letters: John Drinnan responds. ONFILM 11:11 n11 1994/95
Drinnan, J. Mates rates fade on shorts shoots. ONFILM 11:5 n11 1994/95
DROP ZONE f (d Badham, John 1994 USA)
    Reviews
Ascione, G. "Omicidio nel vuoto." credits stills SEGNO n72:57-58 Mar/Apr
1995
Macnab, G. "Drop Zone." credits still S&S 5:41 Apr 1995
McDonagh, M. "Drop Zone." credits FJ 98:55-56 Jan/Feb 1995

Snee, P. "Halalugras." credits F VILAG 38:57 n4 1995
DROUIN, JACQUES See also EX-ENFANTS
DROWNING BY NUMBERS f (d Greenaway, Peter 1988 Gt Br)
Modrzejewska, E. "Wyliczanka." credits still FSP 40:8 n3 (n757) 1994
DRUKER, MIKAEL
(Sju) 7 debutanter. ports CHAPLIN 36:6-7 n6 (n255) 1994/95
DRYBURGH, STUART
Dryburgh, S. Letters: open letter from a film technician on the subject of lunch. ONFILM 11:11 n11 1994/95
DSCHUNGELZEIT f (d Tran, Vu/Foth, Joerg 1988 E Ger/Vietnam)
Graef, C. Der Weg zum ersten Spielfilm. il interv F & FERNSEHEN 22:54-69 n6 1994
D'SOUZA, CHRISTA
D'Souza, C. Cameron comes on. ports ESQUIRE 123:130-133 Feb 1995
DU BRINGST MICH NOCH UM f (d Paulus, Wolfram 1994 Austria)
Reviews
Rauzi, P. "Du bringst mich noch um." still C FORUM 34:21-22 Sep (n337) 1994
DU BUS, OLIVIER LEFEBURE
Du Bus, O.L. Les capitaines de "L'Atalante" ont leve l'ancre... filmog still SEQUENCES n175:50 Nov/Dec 1994
DU FOND DU COEUR: GERMAINE ET BENJAMIN f (d Doillon, Jacques 1994 Fr)
Reviews
Fornara, B. "Du fond du coeur 'Germaine et Benjamin'." still C FORUM 34:19-20 Sep (n337) 1994
DU SKAL AERE DIN HUSTRU f (Master of the House d Dreyer, Carl Theodor 1925 Denmk)
Miguez, M. "El amo de la casa." credits stills NOSFERATU n5:56-57 Jan 1991
DUBBING
Finland
Animation
Salakka, M. Puhumme Suomea. il port still PEILI 18:6-7 n1 1994
DUBEAU, ALAIN For film reviews see author under the following titles: ED WOOD; EXOTICA; LAST SUPPER, THE; MI VIDA LOCA; TOEDLICHE MARIA, DIE
DUBOIS, JACK
Hubbard, R. Book reviews [Book Reviews]. F SCORE MONTHLY n40:9 Dec 1993
DUCHARME, REJEAN
Viswanathan, J. L'un(e) dort, l'autre pas: la scene de la veille dans les scenarios et quelques romans de Rejean Ducharme. bibliog scenario still table CINEMAS 5:189-209 n1/2 1994
DUCKENFIELD, MARK
Duckenfield, M. "Terminator 2": a call to economic arms? bibliog STUDIES POP CULT 17:1-16 n1 1994
DUFF, ALAN
Lewis, B. Lee Tamahori's "Once Were Warriors." port stills C PAPERS n102:4-8 Dec 1994
Dufresne, Isabelle See ULTRA VIOLET
DUGOWSON, MARTINE See also MINA TANNENBAUM
DUIGAN, JOHN See also SIRENS
Filmografie. biogs filmogs SEGNO n72:40 Mar/Apr 1995
DULI SHIDAI f (d Yang, Edward 1994 Taiwan)
Reviews
Chen, R.-S. R. "Du li shi dai." credits CINEMAYA n24:36-37 Summer 1994
DUMALA, PIOTR See also ZBRODNIA I KARA
Dumala, P. Indianin. KINO 27:34 May 1993
Dumala, P. Wlochy. il KINO 27:38 Jul 1993
Dumala, P. "Zbrodnia i kara" - epilog. il KINO 27:14-17 Jun 1993
Lawrence, A. Masculinity in Eastern European animation. stills ANIMATION J 3:32-43 n1 1994
DUMAS, DANIELLE
Dumas, D. Alambic et vieilles querelles. AVANT-SCENE n437:85-87 Dec 1994
DUMB AND DUMBER f (d Farrelly, Peter 1994 USA)
Reviews
Darke, C. "Dumb and Dumber." credits still S&S 5:42 Apr 1995
Denby, D. "Fool's" gold. still NEW YORK 28:56-57 Jan 16 1995
Giles, J. Nobody does dumb better. still NEWSWK 125:67 Jan 16 1995
Robertson, V. "Dumb and Dumber." credits FJ 98:48 Jan/Feb 1995
Schickel, R. Grossing out. still TIME 145:66 Jan 9 1995
DUMITRESCU, BOGDAN See also THALASSA, THALASSA. RUCKKEHR ZUM MEER
"Thalassa, Thalassa - Rueckkehr zum Meer." biog credits filmog still KINO(BRD) n1:46-47 1995
DUNCAN, JAMES
Fry, K. Place/culture/representation. By James Duncan & David Ley (eds.) [Book Review]. bibliog J COMM 45:173-177 n1 1995
DUNCAN, PETRIE
Hanet, K. Petrie, Duncan, ed. Cinema and the realms of enchantment: lectures, seminars and essays by Marina Warner and others [Book Review]. MEDIA INFO AUSTRALIA n75:169 Feb 1995
Routt, W.D. Petrie, Duncan, ed. New questions of British cinema [Book Review]. MEDIA INFO AUSTRALIA n75:169 Feb 1995
DUNG CHE SAI DUK f (d Wong, Kar-wai 1994 Hong Kong)
Morrison, S. John Woo, Wong Kar-wai, and me: an ethnographic mediation. stills C ACTION n36:37-41 1995
Reviews
Grosoli, F. "Dongxie xidu." still C FORUM 34:14 Sep (n337) 1994
DUNNE, JOHN GREGORY
Eaton, M. Casino trades [Book Review]. S&S 5:37 Feb 1995
DUPAGNE, MARIE-FRANCE
Dupagne, M.-F. "Amateur." bibliog credits stills GRAND ANGLE n177:3-4 Dec 1994
Dupagne, M.-F. "Frankenstein." bibliog credits stills GRAND ANGLE n178:9-10 Jan 1995
Dupagne, M.-F. "I Like It Like That." bibliog credits still GRAND ANGLE n178:15-16 Jan 1995
Dupagne, M.-F. "Killing Zoe." bibliog credits stills GRAND ANGLE n177:21-22 Dec 1994
Dupagne, M.-F. "Pulp Fiction." bibliog credits stills GRAND ANGLE n177:35-36 Dec 1994
Dupagne, M.-F. "Soleil trompeur." bibliog credits il still GRAND ANGLE n176:25-26 Nov 1994

DUPE OD MRAMORA f (d Zilnik, Zelimir 1995 Yugo)
Reviews
Stratton, D. "Marble Ass" ("Dupe od Mramora"). credits VARIETY 358:72 Feb 27/Mar 5 1995
DUPEYRON, FRANCOIS See also MACHINE, LA
DURAN, PAUL See also FLESH SUITCASE
DURANTE, JIMMY
Slide, A. The Slide area film book notes [Book Reviews]. CLASSIC n237:42-44+ [4p] Mar 1995
DURAS, MARGUERITE See also INDIA SONG
Gardies, A. Narration et temporalite dans "Moderato cantabile." bibliog still CINEMAS 4:88-102 n1 1993
DURNFORD, MARK J.
Durnford, M.J. The art of borrowing: reasons why a composer chooses to plagiarize, part I. il F SCORE MONTHLY n36/37:22-23 Aug/Sep 1993
DURSIN, ANDY
Dursin, A. Andy reviews more new CDs. F SCORE MONTHLY n40:12 Dec 1993
Dursin, A. "Gremlins." F SCORE MONTHLY n36/37:32 Aug/Sep 1993
Dursin, A. Vampire circus: the essential vampire theme collection. F SCORE MONTHLY n36/37:33 Aug/Sep 1993
Dursin, A. and Kendall, L. Soundtrack watchdogs!: Andy and Lukas review lots of new CDs. il F SCORE MONTHLY n38:14-15 Oct 1993
Dursin, A. and others. Four by Basil Poledouris. F SCORE MONTHLY n36/37:32 Aug/Sep 1993
DUSI, NICOLA
Dusi, N. Il geloso a rotelle. bibliog stills SEGNO n71:3-7 Jan/Feb 1995
DUTCHAK, PHILIP
Dutchak, P. Multimedia and the cultural statement. il stat stills C PAPERS n102:32-35 Dec 1994
Dutchak, P. Wal Saunders. port stat C PAPERS n102:44+ [2p] Dec 1994
DUVIVIER, JULIEN See also AGONIE DE JERUSALEM, L'
DWA KSIEZYCE f (d Baranski, Andrzej 1993 Poland)
Reviews
Meils, C. "Two Moons" ("Dwa ksiezyce"). credits VARIETY 357:74 Jan 2/8 1995
DWYER, ED
Dwyer, E. A night to remember. ports stills VARIETY 357:59+ [2p] Jan 2/8 1995
Dwyer, E. Hollywood's emotional high. ports VARIETY 357:63+ [2p] Jan 9/15 1995
Dwyer, E. Long history of protest, controversy. il VARIETY 357:60+ [2p] Jan 2/8 1995
DYBCZYNSKI, JAN
Sendecka, M. Oryginalnosc wyroznia. interv REZYSER n18:6-7 1993
DYER, RICHARD
Ciment, M. BFI film classics [Book Reviews]. stills POSITIF n408:75-77 Feb 1995
Dyer, R. Varldens ljus. bibliog il ports stills F HAFTET 22:13-22 n3 (n87) 1994
Hendrykowski, M. R jak Routledge [Book Reviews]. il KINO 27:41-42 Jul 1993
Kaltenecker, S. Richard Dyer: The matter of images. Essays on representations [Book Review]. BLIMP n30:71 Winter 1994
DYJA, TOM
Clark, J. A list is still a list [Book Review]. stills PREM 8:93 Feb 1995
DYKYJ, OKSANA
Dykyj, O. Cinemania 1995. il SEQUENCES n175:55-56 Nov/Dec 1994
DYMNA, ANNA
Slodowski, J. Anna Dymna. filmog still FSP 40:11 n11 (n765) 1994
EAGLE, HERBERT
Eagle, H. The cinema of Eisenstein. By David Bordwell [Book Review]. FQ 48:58-60 n2 1994/95
EAST OF EDEN f (d Kazan, Elia 1955 USA)
Adaptations
Helman, A. Kaleb potomek Kaina. il stills KINO 27:22-25 Jun 1993
EASTBURN, JOSEPH
McDonald, T.L. Kiss them goodbye. By Joseph Eastburn [Book Review]. ARMCHAIR DET 27:107 n1 1994
EASTWOOD, CLINT See also PERFECT WORLD, A; UNFORGIVEN
Beard, W. "Unforgiven" and the uncertainties of the heroic. CAN J F STUD 3:41-62 n2 1994
Grieveson, L. Steven Cohan and Ina Rae Hark (eds). Screening the male: exploring masculinities in Hollywood cinema [Book Reviews]. SCREEN 35:400-406 n4 1994
Slide, A. The Slide area film book notes [Book Reviews]. CLASSIC n237:42-44+ [4p] Mar 1995
EASY STREET f (d Chaplin, Charlie 1917 USA)
Psychoanalytic Analysis
Lieberman, E.A. Charlie the trickster. bibliog stills UFAJ 46:16-28 n3 1994
Eat Drink Man Woman See YINSHI NAN NU
EATON, MICHAEL
Eaton, M. Casino trades [Book Review]. S&S 5:37 Feb 1995
EBNER, DAVID
Breen, J.L. Langman, Larry, and David Ebner. Encyclopedia of American spy films [Book Review]. ARMCHAIR DET 27:93-94 n1 1994
EBREDES f (d Elek, Judit 1995 Hungary/Fr/Poland)
Berczes, L. Nem mas. il interv stills F VILAG 38:10-13 n2 1995
Reviews
Stratton, D. "Awakening" ("Ebredes"). credits VARIETY 358:86 Feb 20/26 1995
EBY, DOUGLAS
Eby, D. "Demon Knight." stills C FANTAS 26:12-13 n2 1995
ECHEVARRIA, NICOLAS See also CABEZA DE VACA
ECHTE, BERNHARD
Echte, B. Dieses graziose Vorueberhuschen der Bedeutungen. C(SWITZ) 40:153-162 1994
ECKHARDT, JOSEPH P.
Adamson, J. and others. Forgotten laughter. credits port stills GRIFFITHIANA n51/52:170-197 Oct 1994
Adamson, J. and others. La fabbrica della risata. credits port stills

GRIFFITHIANA n51/52:170-197 Oct 1994
Eclipse See ECLISSE, L'
ECLIPSE f (d Podeswa, Jeremy 1994 Can/FR Ger)
  Harcourt, P. "Eclipse." stills C ACTION n36:17-19 1995
    Reviews
  Nagy, E. "Eclipse." BOXOFFICE 131:bet p125 and 144 [pR28] Apr 1995
ECLISSE, L' f (Eclipse d Antonioni, Michelangelo 1962 Fr/It)
  Christen, T. Die Praesenz der Dinge und die Absenz der Protagonisten.
    bibliog C(SWITZ) 40:9-19 1994
ECOLOGICAL DESIGN: INVENTING THE FUTURE f (d Danitz, Brian 1995 USA)
    Reviews
  Levy, E. "Ecological Design: Inventing the Future." credits VARIETY 358:51
    Feb 13/19 1995
ECONOMIC ASPECTS See also ADMISSIONS; COPYRIGHT; EMPLOYMENT; FINANCING; GROSSES;
  INDUSTRY; TAXES
    Asia
  Gianopulos, J. Asia's economic expansion creates big opportunities. FJ
    98:92 Jan/Feb 1995
    Austria
  Frey, M. Kulturstatistik 1992 [Book Review]. F KUNST n144:75-76 1994
    Brazil
  Hoineff, N. Brazilian prod'n gets real. il VARIETY 358:54+ [2p] Mar 27/Apr
    2 1995
    Canada
      Marketing
  Finn, A. and others. Marketing, management, and competitive strategy in the
    cultural industries. bibliog CAN J COM 19:523-550 n3/4 1994
    Italy
  Calderale, M. Piccola guida allo special. stills SEGNO n63:18 Sep/Oct 1993
    United States
  Klady, L. H'wood: land of the rising sum. stat VARIETY 358:14 Mar 13/19
    1995
  Peers, M. Is Milken mulling moguldom? VARIETY 358:1+ [2p] Mar 13/19 1995
  Weiner, R. Pirates up, profits are down in '94. graph stat VARIETY 358:bet
    p88 and 173 [pA2+ (2p)] Feb 20/26 1995
      Export Market
  Klady, L. Earth to H'wood: you win. il stat VARIETY 358:1+ [2p] Feb 13/19
    1995
  Wharton, D. Intellectual property no. 2 in export sales. stat VARIETY
    358:30 Feb 20/26 1995
ECRIVAIN PUBLIC, L' f (d Amiguet, Jean-Francois 1993 Fr/Switz/Greece)
    Reviews
  Schaub, M. "L'ecrivain public." credits C(SWITZ) 40:203-204 1994
ED WOOD f (d Burton, Tim 1994 USA)
  Coursodon, J.-P. "Ed Wood." credits stills POSITIF n406:8-11 Dec 1994
    Sound Track Reviews
  Larson, R.D. "Ed Wood." SCN 14:17 Mar 1995
    Reviews
  Dubeau, A. "Ed Wood." credits stills SEQUENCES n175:24-25 Nov/Dec 1994
  Jean, M. Orson Welles et moi. credits stills 24 IMAGES n75:60-61 Dec/Jan
    1994/95
  Persons, D. "Ed Wood." C FANTAS 26:59 n3 1995
Eddies See AWARDS - United States - American Cinema Editors
EDEL, ULI See also BODY OF EVIDENCE
EDELMAN, ROB
  Edelman, R. "Jupiter's Wife." port INDEP 18:14-15 Jan/Feb 1995
EDEN VALLEY f (d Amber Production Team 1995 Gt Br/Fr)
    Reviews
  Comino, J. "Eden Valley." credits still S&S 5:54 Apr 1995
Edgar Awards See AWARDS - United States - Mystery Writers of America
EDITING, ELECTRONIC
    United States
  Heuring, D. Editing continues to evolve with "Needful Things." il AMCIN
    74:55-56+ [5p] Sep 1993
EDITING, ELECTRONIC, EQUIPMENT
    United States
  Solman, G. Sound advice for editing, playback. il DGA NEWS 20:12-13 n1
    1995
EDMUNDS, MARLENE
  Edmunds, M. Belgium may back VT4. VARIETY 358:176 Feb 20/26 1995
  Edmunds, M. Blazing trails in exhib biz. port still VARIETY 358:38 Mar
    20/26 1995
  Edmunds, M. Distribber freezes out its competish. still VARIETY 358:40+
    [2p] Mar 20/26 1995
  Edmunds, M. Island's exhibition arena proves cutthroat. il VARIETY 358:42+
    [2p] Mar 20/26 1995
  Edmunds, M. Leading the pack. il still VARIETY 358:37 Mar 20/26 1995
  Edmunds, M. (Nineteen ninety-five) 1995 could well be dandy for Scandi
    filmmakers. VARIETY 358:55 Feb 6/12 1995
EDWARDS, SANNA
  (Sju) 7 debutanter. ports CHAPLIN 36:6-7 n6 (n255) 1994/95
EFFECTS OF FILM See also INFLUENCE OF FILM
    Violence in Film
  Lochen, K. Eksisterer det ufarlige? stat stills table F&K n1:28-30 1994
    Youth
      Violence in Film
  Peretie, O. Kell-e gyilkossaggal vadolnunk Hollywoodot? stills F VILAG
    38:37-39 n1 1995
    Finland
      Youth
  Pimenoff, M. Laulavat lantiot ja suositut salat. il still PEILI 17:31-33
    n4 1993
    United States
      Pornography and Obscenity. Audience Research
  Allen, M. and others. Exposure to pornography and acceptance of rape myths.
    bibliog stat tables J COMM 45:5-26 n1 1995
  Gunther, A.C. Overrating the X-rating: the third-person perception and
    support for censorship of pornography. bibliog stat tables J COMM 45:27-38
    n1 1995

EFFECTS ON FILM See also INFLUENCE ON FILM
    United States
      AIDS
  Green, J. The bug. il PREM 8:20-21 Feb 1995
      Networks and Networking
  Ehrlich, E.M. Virtual companies, walled cities, and the right-brained
    economy: cinematographers on the information highway. AMCIN 76:96 Mar 1995
EFFI BRIEST f (d Fassbinder, Rainer Werner 1974 W Ger)
  Gruber, E. Une reprise impossible? "Effi Briest" et la question de ses
    reecritures filmiques. CINEMAS 4:59-71 n1 1993
EGOYAN, ATOM See also CALENDAR; EXOTICA; SPEAKING PARTS
  Ciment, M. and Rouyer, P. Entretien avec Atom Egoyan. il interv stills
    POSITIF n406:79-83 Dec 1994
  Egoyan, A. "Calendar." il still POSITIF n406:93-94 Dec 1994
  Egoyan, A. Tension en surface. il still POSITIF n406:88-90 Dec 1994
  Rollet, S. Atom Egoyan. Par Carole Desbarats, Daniele Riviere et Jacinto
    Lageira; lettres-video de Paul Virilio et Atom Egoyan [Book Review]. il
    POSITIF n406:86 Dec 1994
  Rollet, S. Le cinema d'Atom Egoyan. stills POSITIF n406:84-87 Dec 1994
  Seibel, A. "The ground is always shifting." interv stills BLIMP n30:32-35
    Winter 1994
  Winters, L. Atom Egoyan is watching us. il interv stills INTERV 25:58+
    [2p] Mar 1995
    Retrospectives
  Hoberman, J. Ghost story. still VILLAGE VOICE 40:49 Mar 7 1995
Egypt See as a subheading under individual subject headings
EHRLICH, EVERETT M.
  Ehrlich, E.M. Virtual companies, walled cities, and the right-brained
    economy: cinematographers on the information highway. AMCIN 76:96 Mar 1995
EHRLICH, LINDA C.
  Ehrlich, L.C. Interior gardens: Victor Erice's "Dream of Light" and the
    Bodegon tradition. il stills CJ 34:22-36 n2 1995
EHRLICH, ROSANNE See also DEAR BABE
EHRMANN, HANS
  Ehrmann, H. Conate tops Chilean distrib'n. VARIETY 358:50 Mar 27/Apr 2 1995
EI IST EINE GESCHISSENE GOTTESGABE, DAS f (d Wagner, Dagmar 1993 FR Ger)
    Reviews
  Holloway, D. "Das Ei ist eine geschissene Gottesgabe." KINO(GF) n56:18 Nov
    1994
Eight mm film See SUPER-EIGHT MM FILM
EINER MEINER AELTESTEN FREUNDE f (d Kaufmann, Rainer 1994 FR Ger)
  Einer meiner aeltesten Freunde. biog credits filmog still KINO(BRD)
    n1:18-19 1995
EISENSCHITZ, BERNARD
  Bluemlinger, C. Bernard Eisenschitz & Paolo Bertetto (Hg.): Fritz Lang, La
    mise en scene [Book Review]. BLIMP n30:70 Winter 1994
  Frank Tashlin, sous la direction de Roger Garcia e Bernard Eisenchitz [Book
    Review]. IMMAGINE n28:30-31 Autumn 1994
EISENSTEIN, SERGEI MIKHAILOVICH See also ALEKSANDR NEVSKII; BRONENOSETS
  POTEMKIN; OKTIABR'
  Casiraghi, U. Per Ejzenstein resto solo un sogno filmare il "capitale." il
    still C SUD 33:8-9 Jul/Aug/Sep (n113) 1994
  Eagle, H. The cinema of Eisenstein. By David Bordwell [Book Review]. FQ
    48:58-60 n2 1994/95
  Livio, J. The cinema of Eisenstein. Di David Bordwell [Book Review].
    GRIFFITHIANA n51/52:253-254 Oct 1994
  Sorensen, J. "Lef," Eisenstein, and the politics of form. bibliog F
    CRITICISM 19:55-74 n2 1994/95
EISMEER RUFT, DAS f (d Foth, Joerg 1984 E Ger)
  Graef, C. Der Weg zum ersten Spielfilm. il interv F & FERNSEHEN 22:54-69
    n6 1994
Eizenshtein, Sergei See EISENSTEIN, SERGEI MIKHAILOVICH
EKBERG, ANITA
  Errata/addenda. STARS n21:[2] Winter 1995
EL SANTO (fictional character)
  Rhodes, S. El Santo. biog filmog il stills F FAX n49:44-49 Mar/Apr 1995
EL YAMANI, MYRIAME For film reviews see author under the following titles: DE
  RETOUR POUR DE BON; SECRET DE JEROME, LE
EL-BAHR BI-YEDHAK LEY f (d El-Kalyoubi, Mohamed Kamel 1994 Egypt)
    Reviews
  Young, D. "Why Does the Sea Laugh?" ("El-bahr bi-yedhak ley"). credits
    VARIETY 357:74 Jan 2/8 1995
ELDER, R. BRUCE
  Elder, R.B. Antonioni's tragic vision. CAN J F STUD 1:1-34 n2 1991
ELDORADO f (d Biname, Charles 1995 Can)
    Reviews
  Kelly, B. "Eldorado." credits VARIETY 358:50 Mar 13/19 1995
Electronic editing See EDITING, ELECTRONIC
Electronic editing equipment See EDITING, ELECTRONIC, EQUIPMENT
ELEK, JUDIT See also EBREDES
  Berczes, L. Nem mas. il interv stills F VILAG 38:10-13 n2 1995
[ELEPHANT SONG] f (d Riju, Go 1995 Japan)
    Reviews
  Elley, D. "Elephant Song." credits VARIETY 358:54 Mar 13/19 1995
ELIA, MAURICE For film reviews see author under the following titles: ALICE'S
  RESTAURANT; BARCELONA; BEAUTE DES FEMMES, LA; BULLETS OVER BROADWAY;
  IT COULD HAPPEN TO YOU; PARFUM D'YVONNE, LE; ROSEAUX SAUVAGES, LES;
  ROUGE; SHAWSHANK REDEMPTION, THE; SIMPLE TWIST OF FATE, A; UTOMLENNYE
  SOLNTSEM; VENT DU WYOMING, LE
  Elia, M. Le Prix Albert-Tessier a Pierre Perrault. port SEQUENCES n175:5
    Nov/Dec 1994
  Elia, M. Les bonnes (et parfois les dernieres) repliques de ceux qui nous
    ont quittes. biogs il obits port stills SEQUENCES n175:6 Nov/Dec 1994
  Elia, M. Sacres monstres! il ports SEQUENCES n175:58-59 Nov/Dec 1994
  Elia, M. The Vermont International Film Festival. still SEQUENCES n175:10
    Nov/Dec 1994
  Elia, M. Tommy Lee Jones. filmog port stills SEQUENCES n174:26-28 Sep/Oct
    1994

ELISA f (d Becker, Jean 1995 Fr)
      Reviews
   Nesselson, L. "Elisa." credits VARIETY 358:78 Feb 20/26 1995
   Rouyer, P. "Elisa." still POSITIF n409:42 Mar 1995
ELISBERG, ROBERT J.
   Elisberg, R.J. Coming soon to a desktop near you. JOURNAL WGA 8:37 Dec/Jan
      1995
EL-KALYOUBI, MOHAMED KAMEL See also EL-BAHR BI-YEDHAK LEY
ELLENBERGER, ALLAN R.
   Ellenberger, A.R. Journey for Margaret's Oscar. il ports stills CLASSIC
      n237:bet p32 and 33 [pC12-C13] Mar 1995
ELLERO, ROBERTO
   Ellero, R. Fuochi di paglia? still SEGNO n63:22 Sep/Oct 1993
ELLEY, DEREK For film reviews see author under the following titles: AG IGAZI
      MAO; BRUIT QUI REND FOU, UN; BUTTERFLY KISS; CHASING THE DEER; CSOKKAL
      ES KOROMMEL; CUDOWNE MIEJSCE; [ELEPHANT SONG]; ELSKER, ELSKER IKKE;
      EN MAI...FAIS CE QU'IL TE PLAIT; ESTI KORNEL CSODALATOS UTAZASA;
      EUROPA MESSZE VAN; GIOT LE HA LONG; GUI TU; HONG MEIGUI BAI MEIGUI;
      JARDIN DE PLANTES; LEVELEK PERZSIABOL; LIVRE DE CRISTAL, LE;
      MEDIOCREN, DIE; MEGINT TANU; NUIYAN, SEISAP; NUREN HUA; SOLITAIRE FOR
      TWO; SPIKE OF LOVE; TAMEN ZHENG NIANQING; THIN ICE; WELCOME II THE
      TERRORDOME; WHEN NIGHT IS FALLING; WITHOUT AIR; YOUNG AT HEARTS;
      ZABRANENIAT PLOD
   Elley, D. Anne Tasker. obit VARIETY 358:87 Mar 27/Apr 2 1995
   Elley, D. Buying search on for Chinese fare. VARIETY 358:60 Feb 6/12 1995
   Elley, D. China: trick or treaty? VARIETY 358:1+ [2p] Mar 6/12 1995
   Elley, D. Christopher Palmer. biog obit VARIETY 358:59 Feb 20/26 1995
   Elley, D. Derek York. biog obit VARIETY 358:87 Mar 27/Apr 2 1995
   Elley, D. Donald Pleasence. obit VARIETY 358:85 Feb 6/12 1995
   Elley, D. Film archivist Van Leer heads festival jury of 11. VARIETY 358:62
      Feb 6/12 1995
   Elley, D. Fresh, spiffy Berlinale. still VARIETY 358:49+ [2p] Feb 6/12
      1995
   Elley, D. Jeanette Lin Tsui. biog obit VARIETY 358:56 Mar 13/19 1995
   Elley, D. Nigel Finch. obit VARIETY 358:58 Mar 20/26 1995
   Elley, D. Robert Bolt. obit VARIETY 358:78 Feb 27/Mar 5 1995
   Elley, D. and Stratton, D. "Bait" lures Berlin's top bear. VARIETY 358:30
      Feb 27/Mar 5 1995
   Elley, D. and Williams, M. Going, going, gong? il VARIETY 358:9 Feb 27/Mar
      5 1995
ELLICKSON, LEE
   Porton, R. and Ellickson, L. Comedy, communism, and pastry: an interview
      with Nanni Moretti. interv port stills CINEASTE 21:11-15 n1/2 1995
ELLIOTT, STEPHAN See also ADVENTURES OF PRISCILLA, QUEEN OF THE DESERT, THE
ELLIS, ARTHUR See also DON'T GET ME STARTED
ELLIS, JOHN
   Hendrykowski, M. R jak Routledge [Book Reviews]. il KINO 27:41-42 Jul 1993
ELLISON, JOE
   Ellison, J. A taxing encounter. JOURNAL WGA 8:30 Mar 1995
ELLROY, JAMES
   Pelecanos, G. Hollywood nocturnes. By James Ellroy [Book Review]. ARMCHAIR
      DET 27:361 n3 1994
ELRICK, TED
   Elrick, T. Gump becomes him. il interv port DGA NEWS 20:26-27+ [6p] n1
      1995
   Elrick, T. Kenneth Branagh re-creates the classics. filmog interv ports
      DGA NEWS 19:32-33+ [4p] n6 1994/95
   Elrick, T. Matters of light & depth. By Ross Lowell [Book Review]. DGA NEWS
      20:43 n1 1995
   Elrick, T. Scott Brothers' work showcased for UK/LA. il DGA NEWS 19:26 n6
      1994/95
   Elrick, T. Stamina on the set. DGA NEWS 19:10-11+ [3p] n3 1994
   Yonover, N.S. and others. Artists Rights Symposium: three days of
      discussion. DGA NEWS 19:26-27+ [3p] n3 1994
ELSAESSER, THOMAS
   Elsaesser, T. Film studies in search of the object. F CRITICISM 17:40-47
      n2/3 1992/93
ELSKER, ELSKER IKKE f (d Sonder, Carsten 1995 Denmk)
      Reviews
   Elley, D. "Love Me, Love Me Not" ("Elsker, elsker ikke"). credits VARIETY
      358:74 Feb 27/Mar 5 1995
ELSTREE STUDIOS
   Dawtrey, A. Fox's Elstree plan dealt setback. VARIETY 358:43 Feb 13/19 1995
ELSWIT, ROBERT
   Comer, B. Rafting down "The River Wild." il AMCIN 76:52-56 Feb 1995
ELVIS, DER f (d Moritsugu, Jon 1987 USA)
   Moritsugu, J. Plans for "Der Elvis" (1987). il MILLENNIUM n25:37-41 Summer
      1991
EMHARDT, ROBERT
   Lentz, H., III. Obituaries. biogs filmogs obits ports CLASSIC n237:57-59
      Mar 1995
EMILIANI, SIMONE For film reviews see author under the following titles:
      ALLULLO DROM; AMICO ARABO, L'; BERDEL; CHASE, THE; I'LL DO ANYTHING;
      QUIZ SHOW
EMMERICH, ROLAND See also STARGATE
   Filmografie. biogs filmogs SEGNO n72:40 Mar/Apr 1995
EMMERS, TARA
   Allen, M. and others. Exposure to pornography and acceptance of rape myths.
      bibliog stat tables J COMM 45:5-26 n1 1995
EMOTION See also INNOCENCE
      France
   Gardies, R. Vers l'emotion documentaire. bibliog CINEMAS 4:49-60 n2 1994
      United States
         Screenwriters
   Palumbo, D. Jealousy. JOURNAL WGA 8:32 Mar 1995
EMOTION DISSONANTE, L' f (d Belanger, Fernand 1984 Can)
   Lockerbie, I. Le documentaire autoreflexif au Quebec. "L'emotion dissonante"
      et "Passiflora." still CINEMAS 4:118-132 n2 1994

Emperor's Naked Army Marches On, The See YUKI YUKI TE SHINGUN
EMPLOYMENT, FOREIGNERS [Prior to V16, 1988 use FOREIGNERS IN FILM INDUSTRY]
      See also EXILE FILMMAKERS
      United States
         Actors and Actresses. History
   Turner, G. Strangers in Hollywood. By Hans J. Wollstein [Book Review].
      AMCIN 76:86 Feb 1995
   Wagenknecht, E. "Strangers in Hollywood: the history of Scandinavian actors
      in American films from 1910 to World War II." By Hans J. Wollstein [Book
      Review]. CLASSIC n236:49 Feb 1995
EN EL AIRE f (d Llaca, Juan Carlos de 1995 Mex)
      Reviews
   Paxman, A. "On the Air" ("En el aire"). credits VARIETY 358:76 Feb 27/Mar
      5 1995
EN MAI...FAIS CE QU'IL TE PLAIT f (d Grange, Pierre 1995 Fr)
      Reviews
   Elley, D. "Mayday" ("En mai... fais ce qu'il te plait"). credits VARIETY
      358:65 Mar 6/12 1995
ENASTROS THOLOS f (d Aristopoulos, Kostas 1994 Greece)
      Reviews
   Rauzi, P. "Enastros tholos." C FORUM 34:32 Sep (n337) 1994
ENCARGO DEL CAZADOR, EL f (d Jorda, Joaquin 1990 Sp)
   Jorda, J. "El encargo del cazador." credits still NOSFERATU n9:100-102 Jun
      1992
ENCHIN, HARVEY
   Enchin, H. Royal credits for Alliance. stat VARIETY 358:26 Feb 27/Mar 5
      1995
Encyclopedias See DICTIONARIES AND ENCYCLOPEDIAS
ENDINGS
      United States
         Humorous Essays
   Thonson, T. The happiness of an unhappy ending. JOURNAL WGA 8:46 Dec/Jan
      1995
ENFANTS JOUENT A LA RUSSIE, LES f (d Godard, Jean-Luc 1993 Switz)
      Reviews
   Braendli, S. "Les enfants jouent a la Russie." credits C(SWITZ) 40:209-210
      1994
ENGER, L.L.
   Miller, R.C. The sinners' league. By L.L. Enger [Book Review]. ARMCHAIR DET
      28:219 n2 1995
ENGLISHMAN WHO WENT UP A HILL BUT CAME DOWN A MOUNTAIN, THE f (d Monger,
      Christopher 1995 Gt Br)
      Production
   Porter, B. How "The Englishman" dazzled a Welsh village. il FJ 98:20+ [2p]
      Mar 1995
ENYEDI, ILDIKO See also BUVOS VADASZ
EPHRON, NORA See also MIXED NUTS
EPIC FILM See also SPECTACLE FILM
      Italy
         History
   Garofalo, M. Peplum. filmog stills SEGNO n71:74-75 Jan/Feb 1995
EPSTEIN, MEL
   Lentz, H., III. Obituaries. biogs filmogs obits ports CLASSIC n237:57-59
      Mar 1995
EQUIPMENT See also specific kinds of equipment (e.g. ANIMATION EQUIPMENT); types
      of equipment (e.g. CAMERAS)
      History
   Heusala, A. Kuvahistorian keksintojen sarjakuva-albumi [Book Review]. il
      PEILI 18:30 n2 1994
      France
         History
   Wyss, S. Korrekte Darstellung technischer Zusammenhaenge. F BUL 37:5 n1
      (n198) 1995
Equipment exhibitions See TRADE FAIRS
ERDOSS, PAL See also FENYERZEKENY TORTENET
   Slodowski, J. "Swiatloczula historia." biog credits filmog FSP 40:6 n11
      (n765) 1994
ERGAS, JOSEPH
   Obituaries. biogs obits VARIETY 358:86-87 Mar 27/Apr 2 1995
ERGAS, MORIS
   Rooney, D. Moris Ergas. biog obit VARIETY 358:74-75 Mar 6/12 1995
   Rooney, D. Moris Ergas. obit VARIETY 358:56 Mar 13/19 1995
ERICE, VICTOR See also ESPIRITU DE LA COLMENA, EL; SOL DEL MEMBRILLO, EL; SUR,
      EL
   Ehrlich, L.C. Interior gardens: Victor Erice's "Dream of Light" and the
      Bodegon tradition. il stills CJ 34:22-36 n2 1995
ERIKSEN, FREDRIK
   Eriksen, F. Leksikal Peter Cushing biografi [Book Review]. il Z n4:40
      (n46) 1993
   Eriksen, F. Taste of fear. il stills Z n1:14-19 (n47) 1994
ERIKSEN, OLAV LIND
   Gjestland, R. Maendene bag i biffen [Book Review]. still F&K n1:35 1994
ERIKSEN, SOLVEJG
   Dodsfall. biogs obits ports F&K n7:37 1993
ERNESTO "CHE" GUEVARA: DAS BOLIVIANISCHE TAGEBUCH f (d Dindo, Richard 1994
      Switz)
      Reviews
   Perret, J. "Ernesto 'Che' Guevara: Das bolivianische Tagebuch." credits
      still C(SWITZ) 40:205-206 1994
ERNROOTH, ALBERT
   Ernrooth, A. Filmproducenter gor det tillbakalutade [Book Review]. still
      CHAPLIN 36:60 n6 (n255) 1994/95
EROBERUNG DER MITTE, DIE f (d Bramkamp, Robert 1994 FR Ger)
   Die Eroberung der Mitte. biog credits filmog still KINO(BRD) n1:16-17 1995
EROE BORGHESE, UN f (d Placido, Michele 1995 It/Fr/Belg)
      Reviews
   Rooney, D. "Un eroe borghese." credits VARIETY 358:50-51 Mar 13/19 1995
EROE DEI DUE MONDI, L' f (d Manuli, Guido 1994 It)
      Reviews
   Zappoli, G. "L'eroe dei due mondi." credits FILM (ITALY) 3:30-31 n13 1995

ERSTER VERLUST f (d Dessau, Maxim 1991 FR Ger)
  Graef, C. "Erster Verlust." il F & FERNSEHEN 22:26-27 n6 1994
ES LEBE UNSERE DDR f (d Hausner, Thomas 1994 FR Ger)
  "Es lebe unsere DDR." biog credits filmog still KINO(BRD) n1:20-21 1995
ESBJORNSON, MARY
  Esbjornson, M. Media arts madness. il stills INDEP 18:6-7+ [3p] Jan/Feb
    1995
ESCAPISM
      India
  Stern, J. Sara Dickey. Cinema and the urban poor in South India [Book
    Review]. STUDIES POP CULT 17:102 n1 1994
ESPIRITU DE LA COLMENA, EL f (Spirit of the Beehive, The d Erice, Victor 1973
    Sp)
  Ehrlich, L.C. Interior gardens: Victor Erice's "Dream of Light" and the
    Bodegon tradition. il stills CJ 34:22-36 n2 1995
ESTATE DI BOBBY CHARLTON, L' f (d Guglielmi, Massimo 1995 It)
      Reviews
  Stratton, D. "The Summer of Bobby Charlton" ("L'estate di Bobby Charlton").
    credits VARIETY 358:72 Feb 27/Mar 5 1995
ESTEVA, JACINTO See also DANTE NO ES UNICAMENTE SEVERO
ESTI KORNEL CSODALATOS UTAZASA f (d Pacskovszky, Jozsef 1995 Hungary)
  Bakacs, T.S. Es a vonat megy... interv port stills F VILAG 38:14-16 n4
    1995
      Reviews
  Elley, D. "The Wondrous Voyage of Kornel Esti" ("Esti Kornel csodalatos
    utazasa"). credits VARIETY 358:53 Feb 13/19 1995
Estonia (since 1992) See as a subheading under individual subject headings
ETE INOUBLIABLE, UN f (Unforgettable Summer, An d Pintilie, Lucian 1994
    Fr/Romania)
  Faber, A. Mozarttol keletre. il interv still F VILAG 38:50-52 n4 1995
      Reviews
  Delisle, M. "Un ete inoubliable." credits still SEQUENCES n174:39-40
    Sep/Oct 1994
ETHICS See also MORALITY
  Gardies, A. Le genre co-operateur. CINEMAS 4:43-55 n3 1994
  Roy, L. Presentation. bibliog CINEMAS 4:7-14 n3 1994
  Warren, P. Pour une ethique cinematographique. bibliog CINEMAS 4:25-42 n3
    1994
      Canada
  Roy, L. Langage cinematographique et faillibilite. bibliog CINEMAS
    4:99-118 n3 1994
      France
  Lacasse, A. Considerations sur la portee ethique des propositions de
    Christian Metz pour une enonciation impersonnelle au cinema. bibliog
    CINEMAS 4:85-97 n3 1994
  Leutrat, J.-L. Ah! les salauds! bibliog CINEMAS 4:73-84 n3 1994
ETHNICITY See also MINORITIES
      Sociological Analysis
  Geber, N.-H. Krigarkulturen och popularfilmens etniska strategier. bibliog
    diag il stills F HAFTET 22:23-37 n3 (n87) 1994
      United States
        Gangster Film
  Winokur, M. Marginal marginalia: the African-American voice in the nouvelle
    gangster film. stills VEL LT TRAP n35:19-32 Spring 1995
ETHNOGRAPHIC FILM
  Forsman, M. Antropologi och rorliga bilder [Book Reviews]. F HAFTET
    22:60-62 n3 (n87) 1994
      Festivals
  Appert, M. Le Reel 94, ou l'eloge de la culture du pauvre. stills POSITIF
    n409:65-66 Mar 1995
      Australia
        Aborigines in Film Industry. History
  Long, C. Australia's first films: facts and fables, part eleven: Aborigines
    and actors. filmogs il map ports C PAPERS n102:52-57+ [8p] Dec 1994
      Canada
  McMillan, R. Ethnology and the N.F.B.: the Laura Boulton mysteries. CAN J F
    STUD 1:67-82 n2 1991
      France
        Directing
  Taylor, L. A conversation with Jean Rouch. biog interv port VISUAL ANTHRO
    R 7:92-102 n1 1991
EUE, RALPH
  Eue, R. Begegnungen mit Alexandre Trauner. biog il C(SWITZ) 40:87-96 1994
EURASIATICA
  "Asik-Kerib." Ed: Gianroberto Scarcia [Book Review]. il KINO(GF) n56:29 Nov
    1994
EUROPA f (Zentropa d Trier, Lars von 1991 Denmk/Fr/FR Ger)
      Reviews
  Aguilar Mendez, S. "Europa." credits stills DICINE n59:32-33 Nov/Dec 1994
EUROPA EUROPA f (d Holland, Agnieszka 1990 Fr/W Ger/Poland)
      Cultural Context
  Linville, S. E. "Europa, Europa": a test case for German national cinema.
    stills WIDE ANGLE 16:38-51 n3 1994
EUROPA MESSZE VAN f (d Kabay, Barna/Petenyi, Katalin 1995 FR Ger/Hungary)
      Reviews
  Elley, D. "Europe Is Far Away" ("Europa messze van"). credits VARIETY
    358:87 Feb 20/26 1995
Europaeischer Filmpreis See AWARDS - Europe - European Film Academy
European Community Commission See COMMISSION OF THE EUROPEAN COMMUNITIES
European Film Award See AWARDS - Europe - European Film Academy
EUROPEAN PRODUCTION OFFICE
  Stern, A. Thomas Halaczinsky. port INDEP 18:20-21 Jan/Feb 1995
EUVRARD, JANINE
  Euvrard, J. Anne-Marie Mieville. il interv stills 24 IMAGES n76:12-14+
    [4p] Spring 1995
  Euvrard, J. Retrouver l'enfance. interv stills 24 IMAGES n75:14-16 Dec/Jan
    1994/95
EVANS, GREG
  Evans, G. Confirmation of new N.Y. pic commish still pending. VARIETY
    358:36 Feb 27/Mar 5 1995

Evans, G. Disney dishes new look for "Fantasia" in 1998. VARIETY 358:21 Feb
    6/12 1995
Evans, G. GLAAD honcho blasts talkers at awards. VARIETY 358:10 Mar 20/26
    1995
Evans, G. "Gump's" glory continues. VARIETY 358:24 Mar 27/Apr 2 1995
Evans, G. IFP sets cutoff for Cannes. VARIETY 358:32 Mar 6/12 1995
Evans, G. Miramax shifts "Priest's" date. VARIETY 358:25-26 Mar 27/Apr 2
    1995
Evans, G. Miramax to urge Acad to see "Red" as Swiss. VARIETY 357:20 Jan
    9/15 1995
Evans, G. "Oblivion" opens new director series. VARIETY 358:14 Feb 27/Mar 5
    1995
Evans, G. Oscar rings in new era of indie chic. stills VARIETY 358:1+ [2p]
    Feb 20/26 1995
Evans, G. "Pocahontas" bows in the park. VARIETY 358:21 Feb 6/12 1995
Evans, G. Random act opens can of bookworms. il VARIETY 358:1+ [3p] Mar
    6/12 1995
Evans, G. Sands shifts to Miramax Int'l prexy. port VARIETY 358:26 Feb
    13/19 1995
Evans, G. Showbiz is psyched for cybermalls. VARIETY 358:1+ [2p] Mar 27/Apr
    2 1995
Evans, G. Sony Classics finds place for "Sun." VARIETY 358:28 Feb 13/19
    1995
Evans, G. Sony spreads its "Wings." stat VARIETY 358:7+ [2p] Mar 13/19
    1995
Evans, G. and Fleming, M. Location police's Gotham beat may die. VARIETY
    358:36 Feb 27/Mar 5 1995
Evans, G. and McCarthy, T. Will "Kids" be too hot for Harvey? VARIETY
    358:1+ [2p] Feb 6/12 1995
EVANS, ROBERT
  Bach, S. "Legend to leper" [Book Review]. port F COM 31:82-83+ [3p]
    Mar/Apr 1995
EVEN COWGIRLS GET THE BLUES f (d Van Sant, Gus 1993 USA)
  Mazierska, E. "I kowbojki moga marzyc." biogs credits filmogs still FSP
    40:8 n5 (n759) 1994
      Reviews
  Thompson, B. "Even Cowgirls Get the Blues." credits still S&S 5:45-46 Jan
    1995
EVERAERT-DESMEDT, NICOLE
  Everaert-Desmedt, N. L'eternite au quotidien: la representation des temps
    dans "Les ailes du desir" de Wim Wenders. bibliog diag CINEMAS 5:105-122
    n1/2 1994
Every Man for Himself and God Against All See JEDER FUER SICH UND GOTT GEGEN
    ALLE
EVERYNIGHT... EVERYNIGHT f (d Tsilimidos, Alkinos 1994 Australia)
      Reviews
  Nazzaro, G.A. "Everynight... Everynight." C FORUM 34:31 Sep (n337) 1994
EVSTIGNEEV, DENIS See also LIMITA
EVTUSHENKO, EVGENII
  Hoberman, J. Mea Cuba II. il VILLAGE VOICE 40:49+ [2p] Mar 14 1995
EXCESS
  Fitzgerald, L. and Keep, C.J. "Barry Lyndon" demembre: la perte de
    l'histoire dans le film de Stanley Kubrick. bibliog still CINEMAS 4:23-33
    n1 1993
EX-ENFANTS f (d Drouin, Jacques 1994 Can)
  Dionne, M.-C. Droits au coeur. SEQUENCES n175:12 Nov/Dec 1994
EXHIBITION
      Asia
  Hammond, S. Eyeball on Asia. il FATAL VISIONS n17:17-19 1994
      Austria
        History
  Kubo, C. Institution Wanderkino. F KUNST n144:14-22 1994
      Belgium
        Brussels. Economic Aspects
  L'annee 1994 a Bruxelles. stat tables MONITEUR n127:10-15 Jan 1995
      Brazil
  Paxman, A. A Latin screen play. stat VARIETY 358:59-60 Feb 27/Mar 5 1995
      China (People's Republic, since 1949)
  Elley, D. China: trick or treaty? VARIETY 358:1+ [2p] Mar 6/12 1995
      France
        Verviers
  Noel, J. Cinema de Verviers (1896-1993). Par Michel Bedeur et Paolo Zagaglia
    [Book Review]. il GRAND ANGLE n177:49-50 Dec 1994
      Germany (Federal Republic, since 1990)
  Brinkmoeller-Becker, H. Kino und die Wahrnehmung von Filmen. il MEDIEN
    38:327-332 n6 1994
      Iceland
  Edmunds, M. Blazing trails in exhib biz. port still VARIETY 358:38 Mar
    20/26 1995
  Edmunds, M. Distribber freezes out its competish. still VARIETY 358:40+
    [2p] Mar 20/26 1995
  Edmunds, M. Island's exhibition arena proves cutthroat. il VARIETY 358:42+
    [2p] Mar 20/26 1995
  Edmunds, M. Leading the pack. il still VARIETY 358:37 Mar 20/26 1995
      Italy
        Film Lists
  Tuttofilm dalla A alla zeta. credits il stills SEGNO n63:27-73 Sep/Oct 1993
      Norway
        Government Support
  Fonn, E.B. Regjeringen prioriterer kultur. il F&K n7:32-33 1993
      Senegal
  Thurston, C. Ein Wanderkino in Senegal. il C(SWITZ) 40:199-202 1994
      United States
  Klady, L. Exhibs forecast bleak outlook for 1st-qtr. pix. il VARIETY
    357:11+ [2p] Jan 2/8 1995
  Klady, L. Summer pix: swords and sequels. il still VARIETY 358:1+ [2p] Mar
    13/19 1995
  Klady, L. and Busch, A.M. Wintry b.o. chills ShoWest's sizzle. stat
    VARIETY 358:1+ [2p] Mar 6/12 1995
  Klawans, S. Year-end celluloid wrap-up. NATION 260:106-108 Jan 23 1995

FANTASY FILM
(continued)
United States
Music
MacLean, P.A. The fantasy film music of Elmer Bernstein. il F SCORE
MONTHLY n36/37:15-17 Aug/Sep 1993
FAR FROM HOME: THE ADVENTURES OF YELLOW DOG f (d Borsos, Phillip 1995 USA)
Reviews
Gray, L. "Far From Home: the Adventures of Yellow Dog." credits still S&S
5:43 Apr 1995
Klady, L. "Far From Home: the Adventures of Yellow Dog." credits VARIETY
357:71+ [2p] Jan 9/15 1995
Williamson, K. "Far From Home." BOXOFFICE 131:bet p89 and 96 [pR19] Mar
1995
FARBER, STEPHEN For film reviews see author under the following titles:
BASKETBALL DIARIES, THE; CIRCLE OF FRIENDS; ONCE WERE WARRIORS;
ROSEAUX SAUVAGES, LES; SHALLOW GRAVE
FARCE
United States
Parshall, P.F. Buster Keaton and the space of farce: "Steamboat Bill, Jr."
versus "The Cameraman." bibliog diag stills UFAJ 46:29-46 n3 1994
FAREWELL TO ARMS, A f (d Borzage, Frank 1933 USA)
Censorship
Leff, L.J. "A Farewell to Arms." stills F COM 31:70-71+ [3p] Jan/Feb 1995
FARICCIOTTI, CARLO
Fariciotti, C. Il diario di un regista "viaggiatore" e vincitore della
"Palma d'Oro" per la regia a Cannes (94). C SUD 33:10-11 Jul/Aug/Sep (n113)
1994
FARIDA, IDA
Sen, K. Women directors but whose films? il CINEMAYA n25/26:10-13
Autumn/Winter 1994/95
FARINELLI, GIAN LUCA
Cherchi Usai, P. Il cinema ritrovato: teoria e metodologia del restauro
cinematografico. Edited by Gian Luca Farinelli and Nicola Mazzanti [Book
Review]. J F PRES n49:70 Oct 1994
Montanaro, C. Il cinema ritrovato: teoria e metodologia del restauro
cinematografico. A cura di Gianluca Farinelli e Nicola Mazzanti [Book
Review]. GRIFFITHIANA n51/52:254 Oct 1994
Montanaro, C. Il cinematografo al campo: l'arma nuova nel primo conflitto
mondiale. A cura di Renzo Renzi con la collaborazione di Gianluca Farinelli
e Nicola Mazzanti [Book Review]. GRIFFITHIANA n51/52:254 Oct 1994
FARINELLI: IL CASTRATO f (d Corbiau, Gerard 1994 Fr/Belg/It/FR Ger)
Broeck, C.V. and Noel, J. "Farinelli." bibliog credits stills GRAND ANGLE
n177:15-16 Dec 1994
"Farinelli il castrato." credits still MONITEUR n126:6-7 Dec 1994
Reviews
Bartholomew, D. "Farinelli." credits FJ 98:68-69 Mar 1995
Camhi, L. "Farinelli." VILLAGE VOICE 40:56 Mar 21 1995
Tobin, Y. "Farinelli." still POSITIF n407:42 Jan 1995
Travers, P. "Farinelli." still ROLLING STONE n704:129 Mar 23 1995
FARIS, JOCELYN
Slide, A. The Slide area film book notes [Book Reviews]. CLASSIC
n237:42-44+ [4p] Mar 1995
Farms and farming See AGRICULTURE IN FILM
FARQUHAR, MARY ANN
Farquhar, M.A. Oedipality in "Red Sorghum" and "Judou." bibliog glos
scenario stills CINEMAS 3:60-86 n2/3 1993
FARR, ROBERT
Adamson, J. and others. Forgotten laughter. credits port stills
GRIFFITHIANA n51/52:170-197 Oct 1994
Adamson, J. and others. La fabbrica della risata. credits port stills
GRIFFITHIANA n51/52:170-197 Oct 1994
FARRELL, SEAN
Farrell, S. Ghostmasters. Mark Walker [Book Review]. il SCARLET STREET
n17:98-99 Winter 1995
Farrell, S. The American detective: an illustrated history. Jeff Siegel
[Book Review]. SCARLET STREET n17:99 Winter 1995
FARRELLY, PETER See also DUMB AND DUMBER
FASSBINDER, RAINER WERNER See also ANGST ESSEN SEELE AUF; EFFI BRIEST; MARTHA
FAST TRIP, LONG DROP f (d Bordowitz, Gregg 1994 USA)
Nolan, A.M. Double dare. il still VILLAGE VOICE 40:50 Jan 10 1995
FASTER, PUSSYCAT! KILL! KILL! f (d Meyer, Russ 1965 USA)
Giltz, M. John Waters on "Faster, Pussycat! Kill! Kill!" stills NEW YORK
28:66 Jan 16 1995
Reviews
Rich, B.R. What's new, "Pussycat?" il VILLAGE VOICE 40:56 Jan 17 1995
FATON, JACQUES
Berthome, J.-P. Le "storyboard" en livres [Book Reviews]. POSITIF n407:90+
[2p] Jan 1995
FAULKNER, CHRISTOPHER
Faulkner, C. Affective identities: French national cinema and the 1930s.
CAN J F STUD 3:3-23 n2 1994
FAUSSAIRES, LES f (d Blum, Frederic 1994 Fr)
Majois, I. "Les faussaires." bibliog credits still GRAND ANGLE n178:7-8
Jan 1995
Reviews
Thirard, P.L. "Les Faussaires." POSITIF n407:42 Jan 1995
FAUST f (d Svankmajer, Jan 1994 Czech R/Gt Br/FR Ger/Fr)
Reviews
Blois, M. de. Bienvenue en enfer. credits still 24 IMAGES n75:70 Dec/Jan
1994/95
FAUST: EINE DEUTSCHE VOLKSSAGE f (d Murnau, F.W. 1926 Ger)
Music
Comuzio, E. "Il Faust" di Murnau con la musica di Gianfranco Plenizio -
registrazione live del reparto fonico dell'Istituto Cine TV "Roberto
Rossellini." C FORUM 34:96 Nov (n339) 1994
FAUST (legendary character)
Singer, R. One against all: the New England past and present
responsibilities in "The Devil and Daniel Webster." bibliog still LIT/FQ
22:265-271 n4 1994

FAVA, ISABELLA
Fava, I. Intervista a Paul Meyer. interv stills C FORUM 34:81-83 Nov
(n339) 1994
FAVORIS DE LA LUNE, LES f (Favorites of the Moon d Ioseliani, Otar 1984 Fr/It)
Zach, P. (Sieben) 7 1/2 beziehungen und bestimmungen des Guenstlingen des
mondes. credits il stills BLIMP [n2]:48-51 Winter 1985
Favorites of the Moon See FAVORIS DE LA LUNE, LES
FAWCETT, FARRAH
Mizrahi, I. A Fawcett that's tapped into our times. il interv ports INTERV
25:88-93 Feb 1995
Fear Eats the Soul See ANGST ESSEN SEELE AUF
FEAR OF A BLACK HAT f (d Cundieff, Rusty 1993 USA)
Reviews
Hamilton, A. "Fear of a Black Hat." credits still FILM 4:20 n1 [1995]
FEATURE FILMS FOR FAMILIES
Campbell, C. Screen sex & violence? Just say none. il port stills
BOXOFFICE 131:46+ [4p] Apr 1995
FECHNER, CHRISTIAN See also BATARD DE DIEU, LE
Federal aid See GOVERNMENT SUPPORT
FEDERAL BUREAU OF INVESTIGATION (United States)
Cohen, K. The importance of the FBI's "Walt Disney File" to animation
scholars. ANIMATION J 3:67-77 n2 1995
FEDERAL HILL f (d Corrente, Michael 1994 USA)
Reviews
Noh, D. "Federal Hill." credits FJ 98:53-54 Jan/Feb 1995
Travers, P. "Federal Hill." still ROLLING STONE n696:134 Dec 1 1994
FEDERATION INTERNATIONALE DES ARCHIVES DU FILM (FIAF)
Conferences, Institutes, Workshops, etc.
Bagh, P. von. Memories of Bologna. J F PRES n49:43-45 Oct 1994
Polls and Surveys
Survey and other activities of the Commission for Programming and Access.
stat J F PRES n49:11-14 Oct 1994
FEDERATION INTERNATIONALE DES SYNDICATS DES TRAVAILLEURS DE L'AUDIOVISUEL
Conferences, Institutes, Workshops, etc.
Gradowski, K. O zgromadzeniu europejskiej sekcji FISTAV, porozumieniu z
Dunczykami i projekcie ustawy o kinematografii. REZYSER n15:5 1993
FEIGELSON, ROGER
Feigelson, R. "Wes Craven's New Nightmare." SCN 14:17 Mar 1995
FEINGOLD, MICHAEL
Feingold, M. Crash course. still VILLAGE VOICE 40:60 Feb 14 1995
FEINSTEIN, HOWARD For film reviews see author under the following titles:
HIRONDELLES NE MEURENT PAS A JERUSALEM, LES; JUNIOR
Feinstein, H. Francesco Rosi. il interv F COM 31:64 Jan/Feb 1995
FEIXIA AHDA f (d Lai, Stan 1994 Taiwan)
Chiao, P. H.-P. Stan Lai: "illusions, lies and reality." interv stills
CINEMAYA n24:48-54 Summer 1994
FELD, BRUCE For film reviews see author under the following titles: IMMORTAL
BELOVED; NELL
FELDMAN, BRUCE
Kuhn, E. Marketing executives. il ports table PREM 8:38 Mar 1995
Felix See AWARDS - Europe - European Film Academy
FELLINI, FEDERICO See also CASANOVA DI FEDERICO FELLINI, IL
Comuzio, E. Gianfranco Miro Gori e Giuseppe Ricci (a cura di): Io F.F. il re
del cine [Book Review]. C FORUM 34:96 Sep (n337) 1994
Comuzio, E. Renzo Renzi: L'ombra di Fellini. Quarant'anni di rapporti con il
grande regista e uno Stupidario degli anni Ottanta [Book Review]. il C
FORUM 34:94-95 Sep (n337) 1994
Dodsfall. biogs obits ports F&K n7:37 1993
Federico Fellini. Designi anni '30-'70 [Book Review]. il KINO(GF) n56:30
Nov 1994
Fellini, F. and Pinelli, T. "Utazas Tulumba." il F VILAG 38:44-51 n2 1995
Fofi, G. and Volpi, G. Entretien avec Federico Fellini. il interv stills
POSITIF n409:76-92 Mar 1995
Lori, S. Un sincero ricordo di Federico Fellini al Festival Cinematografico
di Cannes 94. biog il C SUD 33:3-5 Jul/Aug/Sep (n113) 1994
Mariniello, S. Fellini: un humaniste anarchiste. il port R CINEMATHEQUE
n32:6-7 Jan/Feb 1995
Tributes
Niccoli, V. Fellini: i costumi e le mode. il C NUOVO 43:40-41 Nov/Dec
(n352) 1994
Fellini's Casanova See CASANOVA DI FEDERICO FELLINI, IL
FELPERIN, LESLIE For film reviews see author under the following titles: MI VIDA
LOCA; (ONE HUNDRED AND ONE) 101 DALMATIANS; PAGEMASTER, THE; ROUGH
DIAMONDS; UNENDLICHE GESCHICHTE III, DIE
FEMINISM
United States
Torry, R. Awakening to the other: feminism and the ego-ideal in "Alien."
bibliog WOMEN'S STUD 23:343-363 n4 1994
Audience, Women
Petzall, J. Want to see more work by independents? still ANGLES 2:6-7 n4
1995
Pornography and Obscenity
Kershaw, S. Against pornophobia. port NEW YORK 28:20+ [2p] Jan 16 1995
FEMINIST ANALYSIS
Studlar, G. Seduced and abandoned? Feminist film theory and psychoanalysis
in the 1990s. bibliog PS 14:5-13 n1/2 1994/95
Gender Roles
Horror Film
Harris, J. Clover, Carol J. Men, women, and chain saws: gender in the modern
horror film [Book Review]. MEDIA INFO AUSTRALIA n75:158-159 Feb 1995
History
Holmlund, C. "CinemAction," no. 67 (1993), 200pp. "Vingt ans de theories
feministes sur le cinema." Eds Ginette Vincendeau and Berenice Reynaud [Book
Review]. SCREEN 35:407-410 n4 1994
Horror Film
Women in Film
Cantrill, A. The monstrous-feminine: film, feminism, psychoanalysis. By
Barbara Creed [Book Review]. CANTRILL'S FMNTS n73/74:42 May 1994
Women in Film
Niessen, S. Gaines, Jane, Herzog, Charlotte (eds). Fabrications: costume and

the female body [Book Review]. CINEMAS 3:247-251 n2/3 1993
  Austria
Hass, F. Der weibliche Blick - Der Blick aufs Weib. F KUNST n144:43-49 1994
  Canada
    Woman's Film
Russell, C. Mourning the woman's film: the dislocated spectator of "The
  Company of Strangers." stills CAN J F STUD 3:25-40 n2 1994
  Great Britain
Williams, L.R. Women can only misbehave. still S&S 5:26-27 Feb 1995
    Clothes in Film
Baert, R. Skirting the issue. stills SCREEN 35:354-373 n4 1994
    Spectatorship
Stacey, J. Hollywood memories. SCREEN 35:317-335 n4 1994
  India
Longfellow, B. "The Bandit Queen." stills C ACTION n36:10-16 1995
  United States
Berry, C. A turn for the better? - genre and gender in "Girl From Hunan" and
  other recent mainland Chinese films. bibliog stills PS 14:81-103 n1/2
  1994/95
Longfellow, B. Gaylyn Studlar. In the realm of pleasure: Von Sternberg,
  Dietrich and the masochistic aesthetic [Book Review]. CAN J F STUD 1:83-89
  n2 1991
McKee, A.L. Negotiating gender in post-World War II America [Book Reviews].
  Q REV F & VIDEO 15:47-56 n3 1994
Torry, R. Awakening to the other: feminism and the ego-ideal in "Alien."
  bibliog WOMEN'S STUD 23:343-363 n4 1994
  Gaze in Film
Hinton, L. A "woman's" view: the "Vertigo" frame-up. bibliog still F
  CRITICISM 19:2-22 n2 1994/95
  Gender Roles
Addison, E. Saving other women from other men: Disney's "Aladdin." stills
  CAM OBS n31:4-25 Jan/May 1993
  Independent Production. Women Directors
Ouellette, L. Reel women. stills INDEP 18:28-34 Apr 1995
  Pornography and Obscenity
Heffernan, K. A social poetics of pornography [Book Review]. Q REV F &
  VIDEO 15:77-83 n3 1994
  Spectatorship
Hastie, A. Window shopping: cinema and the postmodern. Anne Friedberg [Book
  Reviews]. DISCOURSE n17,2:171-176 Winter 1994/95
  Woman's Film
McKee, A.L. "L'affaire praslin" and "All This, and Heaven Too": gender,
  genre, and history in the 1940s woman's film. VEL LT TRAP n35:33-51 Spring
  1995
FENG, PETER
  Feng, P. In search of Asian American cinema. stills CINEASTE 21:32-35 n1/2
  1995
FENYERZEKENY TORTENET f (d Erdoss, Pal 1994 Hungary)
  Slodowski, J. "Swiatloczula historia." biog credits filmog FSP 40:6 n11
  (n765) 1994
FERGUSON, ALLYN
  Theiss, K. The film music of Allyn Ferguson, vol. 1. il SCN 14:18 Mar 1995
FERNANDEZ L'HOESTE, HECTOR D. For film reviews see author under the following
  titles: RODRIGO D. - NO FUTURO
FERNGULLY... THE LAST RAINFOREST f (d Kroyer, Bill 1992 USA/Australia)
  Reviews
Salakka, M. Keijut ja ilkea heksus. PEILI 17:43 n4 1993
FERRAN, PASCALE See also PETITS ARRANGEMENTS AVEC LES MORTS
FERRANTE, ENEA
  Ferrante, E. Ad Agrigento si e tenuto il trentunesimo Convegno
  Internazionale sul linguaggio di Pirandello. C SUD 33:30 Jul/Aug/Sep (n113)
  1994
FERRARA, ABEL See also ADDICTION, THE; BODY SNATCHERS; NEW ROSE HOTEL
FERRARA, GIUSEPPE See also SEGRETO DI STATO
FERRARI, ALAIN See also BOSNA!
FERRARIO, DAVIDE See also ANIME FIAMMEGGIANTI
  Comuzio, E. Davide Ferrario: Dissolvenza al nero [Book Review]. il C FORUM
  34:91-92 Oct (n338) 1994
FERREIRA BARBOSA, LAURENCE See also GENS NORMAUX N'ONT RIEN D'EXCEPTIONNEL, LES
FESTIVALS See also AWARDS; MARKETS
  Prudente, I. Diario di un vizio. il SEGNO n71:31-33 Jan/Feb 1995
  Zappoli, G. Come e per chi? il port SEGNO n71:16-18 Jan/Feb 1995
  Zappoli, G. Cosi vicino cosi lontano. il intervs SEGNO n71:24-27 Jan/Feb
  1995
  Zappoli, G. Intervista col festival. il SEGNO n71:15 Jan/Feb 1995
  Conferences, Institutes, Workshops, etc.
Mantegazza, I. L'unione fa i bei festival, o no? il stat SEGNO n71:34
  Jan/Feb 1995
  Australia
    Melbourne 1994
Boyce, M. (Forty-third) 43rd Melbourne Film Festival. il stills FATAL
  VISIONS n17:20 1994
Teo, S. Melbourne. CINEMAYA n24:60-61 Summer 1994
    Sydney 1994
Pattison, B. The 39th Asia-Pacific Film Festival. il stills C PAPERS
  n102:22-23 Dec 1994
    Sydney 1995
Woods, M. Gay fest pic riles Oz censors. VARIETY 358:20 Feb 6/12 1995
Woods, M. Oz censors uphold "Cage" ban. VARIETY 358:24 Feb 13/19 1995
  Austria
    Salzburg 1994
Diagonale. il KINO(GF) n56:14 Nov 1994
  Belgium
Circulation des films de la Comunaute francaise dans les festivals en 1994.
  MONITEUR n126:22-26 Dec 1994
Liste des films de la Communaute Francaise primes dans les festivals en 1994.
  MONITEUR n127:26-27 Jan 1995
    Brussels 1995
Festival du Film Brussels. MONITEUR n126:28 Dec 1994
Le Festival du Dessin Anime et du Film d'Animation. MONITEUR n126:27 Dec

1994
(Treizieme) XIIIeme Festival International du Film Fantastique, de
  Science-Fiction & Thriller de Bruxelles. MONITEUR n128:32 Feb 1995
  Canada
    British Columbia, Vancouver
Reynaud, B. Vancouver. CINEMAYA n25/26:95-96 Autumn/Winter 1994/95
    Ontario, Ottawa 1993
Gizycki, M. Pan uwalnia sie spod wladzy slugi. il KINO 27:35 Jul 1993
    Ontario, Toronto 1967
Gilmour, C. Movies by Clyde Gilmour: the underground is here. CAN J F STUD
  3:87-88 n2 1994
    Ontario, Toronto 1994
Castiel, E. Toronto International Film Festival. il stills SEQUENCES
  n175:6-7 Nov/Dec 1994
Marks, L.U. Your fest of fests. stills INDEP 18:22-24 Jan/Feb 1995
Vasudev, A. Toronto. still CINEMAYA n25/26:94-95 Autumn/Winter 1994/95
    Quebec, Montreal 1994
Beaulieu, J. Le nouveau cinema francais. stills SEQUENCES n174:22-24
  Sep/Oct 1994
Cloutier, M. Le 18e FFM. il stills SEQUENCES n174:6-9 Sep/Oct 1994
Girard, M. Sur quelques exercices de style au FFM. stills SEQUENCES
  n174:16-18 Sep/Oct 1994
Haim, M. Amerique autre et meme. stills 24 IMAGES n75:49-50 Dec/Jan
  1994/95
Larue, J. Erotique? stills SEQUENCES n174:18-19 Sep/Oct 1994
Larue, J. L'autre cinema americain. stills SEQUENCES n174:20-22 Sep/Oct
  1994
Lucia, C. Montreal's feminist edge. stills CINEASTE 21:96-97 n1/2 1995
Roy, A. Festival des films du monde. stills 24 IMAGES n75:40-48 Dec/Jan
  1994/95
Tessier, M. Montreal. still CINEMAYA n25/26:89-90 Autumn/Winter 1994/95
    Quebec, Montreal 1995
Grugeau, G. Images du monde arabe. 24 IMAGES n76:46 Spring 1995
    Quebec, Rimouski 1994
Cloutier, M. Le Carrousel international du film de Rimouski. il SEQUENCES
  n175:9 Nov/Dec 1994
    Quebec, Rouyn-Noranda 1994
Castiel, E. Festival international du cinema en Abitibi-Temiscamingue. il
  still SEQUENCES n175:7-8 Nov/Dec 1994
Jean, M. La force des films brefs. still 24 IMAGES n76:46 Spring 1995
  China (People's Republic, since 1949)
    Shanghai 1994
Robbins, H. "Bhaji" a lark in Blackpool. ANGLES 2:8 n4 1995
  Czech Republic (since 1993)
    Karlovy Vary
Gaydos, S. Karlovy Vary impacted by proposed rival fest. il VARIETY 357:24
  Jan 2/8 1995
Williams, M. Czech fests fight for A list. VARIETY 357:36 Jan 9/15 1995
  Egypt
    Alexandria 1994
Dorsay, A. Alexandria. still CINEMAYA n25/26:87-88 Autumn/Winter 1994/95
  Europe
Repetto, M. Tutti in gara. il SEGNO n71:28-30 Jan/Feb 1995
  Finland
    Oulu 1993
Kantola, M. Oulun kansainvalinen lastenelokuvafestivaali. still PEILI
  17:40-41 n4 1993
    Tampere 1995
Young, D. Finnish fest comes up shorts. VARIETY 358:19 Mar 20/26 1995
  France
    Amiens 1993
Bruyn, O. de. Peckinpah, encore et toujours, a Amiens. still POSITIF
  n406:59-60 Dec 1994
    Angers 1994
Bleys, J.-P. Angers. POSITIF n406:62 Dec 1994
    Annecy 1993
Kohn, O. Annecy 1993. still POSITIF n406:61-62 Dec 1994
    Belfort 1993
Bruyn, O. de. Belfort 1993. POSITIF n406:60 Dec 1994
    Cannes 1994
Bruno, E. Il gran teatro dell'allegoria. il stills FCR 45:276-285 Jun/Jul
  (n446/447) 1994
Cappabianca, A. Finestre infrante. stills FCR 45:292-297 Jun/Jul
  (n446/447) 1994
Di Giorgi, S. Donne senza storia. stills FCR 45:301-307 Jun/Jul (n446/447)
  1994
Gariazzo, G. Cortocircuito mentale. FCR 45:298-300 Jun/Jul (n446/447) 1994
Lori, S. Un sincero ricordo di Federico Fellini al Festival Cinematografico
  di Cannes 94. biog il C SUD 33:3-5 Jul/Aug/Sep (n113) 1994
Marino, C. A Cannes "Veillees d'Armes" di Marcel Ophuls girato sul
  sacrificio encomiabile e sulla generosa morte di tanti corrispondenti di
  guerra in Bosnia. C SUD 33:2 Jul/Aug/Sep (n113) 1994
Pastor, A. Accadde, a maggio. stills FCR 45:286-291 Jun/Jul (n446/447)
  1994
Tessier, M. Cannes. CINEMAYA n24:56-57 Summer 1994
    Clermont-Ferrand 1994
Niel, P. Clermont-Ferrand. still POSITIF n408:73-74 Feb 1995
    Creteil 1993
Wiese, I. Evas dotre. il ports Z n4:28-33 (n46) 1993
    Creteil 1994
Aude, F. Creteil. still POSITIF n409:64 Mar 1995
Fowler, C. and Kueppers, P. Creteil International Women's Film Festival,
  18-27 March 1994. SCREEN 35:394-397 n4 1994
    Dunkerque 1994. Awards
Palmares des Huitiemes rencontres de Dunkerque. AVANT-SCENE n437:89 Dec 1994
    La Baule 1994
Touati, J.-P. Cinema voyage. AVANT-SCENE n437:89 Dec 1994
    La Rochelle 1994
Tessier, M. La Rochelle. CINEMAYA n24:59-60 Summer 1994

FESTIVALS
France
(continued)
Lussas 1994
Bluemlinger, C. Ansichten aus Lussas. stills BLIMP n30:36-38 Winter 1994
Montpellier 1993
Masson, A. Montpellier. still POSITIF n407:56-57 Jan 1995
Montpellier 1994
Masson, A. Montpellier. still POSITIF n407:56-57 Jan 1995
Paris 1994
Appert, M. Le Reel 94, ou l'eloge de la culture du pauvre. stills POSITIF n409:65-66 Mar 1995
Bourget, J.-L. L'American Center sur le chemin de Hollywood. still POSITIF n409:63 Mar 1995
Perpignan 1994
Veronneau, P. Confrontation 30 a Perpignan: dans la duree et la difference. J F PRES n49:63-66 Oct 1994
Rennes 1994
Kohn, O. Rennes 1994. POSITIF n407:57-58 Jan 1995
Strasbourg 1994
Cieutat, M. Strasbourg. stills POSITIF n409:67-68 Mar 1995
Germany (Federal Republic, since 1990)
Berlin 1985
Berlinale 85. il BLIMP [n1]:34-39 Mar 1985
Berlin 1993
Plazewski, J. Kryzys w branzy biografow. stills KINO 27:28-29 Jun 1993
Sobolewski, T. Zycie na moscie. interv port KINO 27:20-21+ [3p] Jun 1993
Tuominen, S. Huoli eurooppalaisesta elokuvasta Berliinissa. il stills PEILI 18:22-23 n1 1994
Berlin 1995
Crawley, T. Gallic films rely on proven star power. VARIETY 358:56 Feb 6/12 1995
Elley, D. Film archivist Van Leer heads festival jury of 11. VARIETY 358:62 Feb 6/12 1995
Elley, D. Fresh, spiffy Berlinale. still VARIETY 358:49+ [2p] Feb 6/12 1995
Elley, D. and Stratton, D. "Bait" lures Berlin's top bear. VARIETY 358:30 Feb 27/Mar 5 1995
Hansen, E. German filmmaking takes commercial turn. VARIETY 358:50 Feb 6/12 1995
Kelly, B. Canuck pix make a hefty contribution. still VARIETY 358:55 Feb 6/12 1995
Kemp, P. Count on solid British presence. VARIETY 358:55-56 Feb 6/12 1995
Molner, D. Berlin festival bows with record crowds. VARIETY 358:9+ [2p] Feb 13/19 1995
Molner, D. "Kiss" seduces Berlin, stirring sluggish mood. stills VARIETY 358:11+ [2p] Feb 20/26 1995
Rayns, T. A few sparks of flair. il S&S 5:5 Apr 1995
Taubin, A. Berlin's bear market. ports VILLAGE VOICE 40:54 Mar 14 1995
Berlin 1995. Awards
Berlin Film Festival winners. VARIETY 358:30 Feb 27/Mar 5 1995
Berlin 1995. Film Lists
Films in competition. VARIETY 358:50 Feb 6/12 1995
Films in panorama. VARIETY 358:54 Feb 6/12 1995
International forum of young cinema. table VARIETY 358:58 Feb 6/12 1995
Hannover 1993
Koskinen, K. Hannoverin Eurooppalaisfestari. PEILI 17:38-39 n4 1993
Hof 1994
Koehler, M. (Fuenf) 5415 Minuten Kino. still MEDIEN 38:362-363 n6 1994
Leipzig 1994
Holloway, D. and Holloway, R. (Sieben und dreissigste) 37. DOKfilm Festival Leipzig. KINO(GF) n56:3-4 Nov 1994
Potsdam 1994
Rust, R. (Fuenfte) V. Filmfestival Potsdam. KINO(GF) n56:24 Nov 1994
Saarbruecken 1995
Max-Ophuels-Preis. KINO(GF) n56:14 Nov 1994
Great Britain
Bradford 1993
Salli, O.-P. Festivaalivieraan paivakirjasta. il PEILI 17:25-26 n3 1993
Cardiff 1994
Sharman, L.F. International Animation Festival, Cardiff, 16-22 May 1994. SCREEN 35:397-399 n4 1994
London 1993
Lovlund, B.-F. Mord og vanvidd i London. stills Z n1:12-13 (n47) 1994
London 1994
Del Re, G. Londra: periferie, castelli e bandiere che bruciano. stills C FORUM 34:3-6 Nov (n339) 1994
London 1995
Porter, B. Wide-ranging London festival has its eye on box office. FJ 98:18 Jan/Feb 1995
Hong Kong
Hong Kong 1994
Reynaud, B. HongKong. still CINEMAYA n24:57-59 Summer 1994
Hungary
Budapest 1993
Bikacsy, G. Fragments. NEW HUNGARIAN Q 34:159-162 n130 1993
Budapest 1994
Antal, I. A szem es a ful. stills F VILAG 38:60-61 n1 1995
Bori, E. Elet a dobozban. still F VILAG 38:58-59 n1 1995
Budapest 1995
Ardai, Z. Lassu hajo Kina fele. stills F VILAG 38:7-9 n4 1995
Mikola, D. Napilapok zselleref. stills F VILAG 38:4-6 n4 1995
Nadler, J. Hungarian pix now slimmer but stronger. stat VARIETY 358:27 Feb 13/19 1995
Budapest 1995. Awards
A 26. Magyar Filmszemle dijai. F VILAG 38:11 n4 1995
India
Bombay 1995
Cunha, U. da. India Film Fest features tributes to Fellini, Elvis. VARIETY 357:24 Jan 2/8 1995

Cunha, U. da. Local "Mammo" launches Int'l Film Fest of India. VARIETY 357:28 Jan 9/15 1995
Israel
Jerusalem 1994
Abittan, G. (Onzieme) XIeme Festival de films de Jerusalem. AVANT-SCENE n437:88-89 Dec 1994
Italy
I festival: tra politica e cultura. FCR 45:382-383 Sep (n448) 1994
Poggi, E. Il critico al festival ovvero lo spettatore indiscreto. intervs SEGNO n71:19-33 Jan/Feb 1995
Santucci, E. Obiettivo festival. il SEGNO n71:19-23 Jan/Feb 1995
Bergamo 1993
Hanninen, S. and Auersalo, T. Animaatiota Italialaisittain. still PEILI 17:39 n4 1993
Bologna 1993
Bassoli, V. Alla Ventiduesima Mostra Internazionale del Cinema Libero di Bologna. C SUD 33:17-18 Jul/Aug/Sep (n113) 1994
Cattolica 1993
Catelli, D. Il falso e i falsi. stills SEGNO n63:91-92 Sep/Oct 1993
Cattolica 1994
Bochicchio, G. Mostri. stills FCR 45:354-358 Jun/Jul (n446/447) 1994
Zagari, P. Dracula e serial-killer per "cinetalpe" incallite. still C NUOVO 43:20-21 Nov/Dec (n352) 1994
Florence 1994
Azzalin, C. L'amore di molti. stills SEGNO n71:65-66 Jan/Feb 1995
Giffoni Valle Piana 1994
Picchi, M. Futuro con lotteria nel sogno fatto di spot. stills C NUOVO 43:11-15 Nov/Dec (n352) 1994
Milan 1994
Lori, S. La sessantesima manifestazione del Mifed organizzata dalla Fiera di Milano. C SUD 33:31 Jul/Aug/Sep (n113) 1994
Montecatini Terme 1994
Di Luzio, A. Montecatini: il cinema "corto" va riscoprendo il racconto. stills C FORUM 34:18-20 Oct (n338) 1994
Pesaro 1993
Gottardi, M. Cinema arabo. stills SEGNO n63:88-89 Sep/Oct 1993
Speciale, A. La speranza e tutta nella donna. still SEGNO n63:90 Sep/Oct 1993
Pesaro 1994
Bose, S. Pesaro. CINEMAYA n24:61-62 Summer 1994
Pesaro 1994
Morsiani, A. Il sogno americano. stills SEGNO n72:69-70 Mar/Apr 1995
Pordenone
Merritt, R. Pordenone Film Festival. CLASSIC n237:9 Mar 1995
Pordenone 1993
Serravalli, L. Dal 9 al 16 ottobre 1993 a Pordenone si e svolta la XII Edizione della Settimana del Cinema Muto. C SUD 33:12-14 Jul/Aug/Sep (n113) 1994
Pordenone 1994
Kasten, J. Slapstick, Indien, Wyler und die Garbo. il stills F BUL 36:10-13 n6 (n197) 1994
Kovacs, A.B. Az elfeledett nevetes. F VILAG 38:56-57 n1 1995
Lodato, N. I quattro figli di Willy Wyler con le gemelle di Monta Bell. il stills C FORUM 34:10-12 Oct (n338) 1994
Lodato, N. Pordenone: luci dell'Asia e fabbriche di risate. stills C FORUM 34:8-10 Oct (n338) 1994
Tryster, H. Due belle scoperte. il ports stills SEGNO n71:72-73 Jan/Feb 1995
Pordenone 1994. Film Lists
Adamson, J. and others. Forgotten laughter. credits port stills GRIFFITHIANA n51/52:170-197 Oct 1994
Adamson, J. and others. La fabbrica della risata. credits port stills GRIFFITHIANA n51/52:170-197 Oct 1994
Prato 1994
Niccoli, V. Fellini: i costumi e le mode. il C NUOVO 43:40-41 Nov/Dec (n352) 1994
Rimini 1994
Pioppo, M. Rimini: cronache e storie di mondi separati. stills C FORUM 34:13-14 Oct (n338) 1994
Preziosi, A. Americani, oggi. stills SEGNO n71:70 Jan/Feb 1995
Preziosi, A. Finestre sul mondo. stills SEGNO n71:67-69 Jan/Feb 1995
Preziosi, A. Soviet melodies. il SEGNO n71:68-69 Jan/Feb 1995
Rome 1994
Martani, M. Fantafestival: l'orrore riciclato mortifica il fantastico. stills C FORUM 34:24-26 Oct (n338) 1994
Taormina 1994
Bruno, E. Classicita e trasgressione. still FCR 45:384-385 Sep (n448) 1994
Oldani, M.T. Kazakhistan: la nuova ondata. still FCR 45:386-389 Sep (n448) 1994
Oldani, M.T. Taormina. still CINEMAYA n25/26:90-91 Autumn/Winter 1994/95
Trento 1994
Diciassette nazioni sono state ammesse dopo una scrupolosa selezione mirata. C SUD 33:32 Jul/Aug/Sep (n113) 1994
Trieste 1995
Gottardi, M. Vicina, lontana. stills SEGNO n72:66-68 Mar/Apr 1995
Turin 1994
Azzalin, C. Storie adolescenti. stills SEGNO n71:60-61 Jan/Feb 1995
Bo, F. Tempo de vivere, tempo di morire. still FCR 45:349-353 Jun/Jul (n446/447) 1994
Catelli, D. Un diluvio di film. stills SEGNO n71:58-59 Jan/Feb 1995
Diana, M. Prima del silenzio. stills SEGNO n71:62-64 Jan/Feb 1995
Preziosi, A. Cerimonie segrete. stills SEGNO n71:61-64 Jan/Feb 1995
Terrazzan, S. Il festival ritrovato: l'undicesima edizione del Festival del Cinema Giovani. C SUD 33:27-28 Jul/Aug/Sep (n113) 1994
Turin 1995
Zalan, V. Keleti szel. stills F VILAG 38:34-35 n3 1995
Venice
Roberti, B. and Suriano, F. La Biennale, la Mostra e l'archivio. interv still FCR 45:371-381 Sep (n448) 1994

FETISHISM
Africa
Ideological Analysis

FEW GOOD MEN, A f (d Reiner, Rob 1992 USA)
Reviews

FICTION ABOUT FILM See also HOLLYWOOD IN LITERATURE
Italy

United States

FISHER, BOB
    Fisher, B. Amassing digital crowds (and snowflakes) for "Miracle on 34th
        Street." il AMCIN 76:54-55 Mar 1995
    Fisher, B. Creating another "Miracle on 34th Street." il stills AMCIN
        76:50-52+ [6p] Mar 1995
    Fisher, B. Off to work we go: the digital restoration of "Snow White." il
        stills AMCIN 74:48-50+ [6p] Sep 1993
    Fisher, B. and Pizzello, C. "In the Line of Fire": an action film for
        existentialists. il stills AMCIN 74:36-40+ [7p] Sep 1993
FISHER, MARK
    Fisher, M. Why is it so hard to enjoy? VERTIGO (UK) 1:42-43 n4 1994/95
FISHER, TERENCE See also BRIDES OF DRACULA, THE; CURSE OF FRANKENSTEIN, THE;
        DRACULA; DRACULA - PRINCE OF DARKNESS; FRANKENSTEIN MUST BE DESTROYED; GORGON,
        THE; HOUND OF THE BASKERVILLES, THE; ISLAND OF TERROR; LAST PAGE, THE; PHANTOM
        OF THE OPERA; SHERLOCK HOLMES UND DAS HALSBAND DES TODES; SO LONG AT THE FAIR;
        TWO FACES OF DR. JEKYLL, THE
    Angulo, J. Terence Fisher, revisitador de mitos. biog il stills NOSFERATU
        n6:22-43 Apr 1991
    Las peliculas del ciclo. credits filmog il stills NOSFERATU n6:74-80+ [25p]
        Apr 1991
    Ma Latorre, J. Terence Fisher: notas a la sombra de un estilo. il stills
        NOSFERATU n6:44-49 Apr 1991
    Molina Foix, J.A. Hammer Films: una herencia de miedo. il stills NOSFERATU
        n6:4-21 Apr 1991
FITTANTE, ALDO For film reviews see author under the following titles: BELLE AL
        BAR; DISCLOSURE; PORTAMI VIA
FITZGERALD, LARA
    Fitzgerald, L. and Keep, C.J. "Barry Lyndon" demembre: la perte de
        l'histoire dans le film de Stanley Kubrick. bibliog still CINEMAS 4:23-33
        n1 1993
FITZGERALD, MICHAEL
    Fitzgerald, M. Gary Gray: the former child star is heading for Memphis.
        biog credits filmog il ports stills CLASSIC n236:bet p32 and 33 [pC10-C11+
        (3p)] Feb 1995
FLAHERTY, DAVID H.
    Knight, G. The Beaver bites back? American popular culture in Canada. Edited
        by David H. Flaherty & Frank E. Manning [Book Review]. CAN J COM 19:560-561
        n3/4 1994
FLASHBACK
    De Bernardinis, F. Flashback. filmog stills SEGNO n63:94-95 Sep/Oct 1993
Flaubert Dreams of Travel See GUSTAVE FLAUBERT DREAMS OF TRAVEL BUT THE ILLNESS
        OF HIS MOTHER PREVENTS IT
FLECHE, MANUEL See also MARIE-LOUISE OU LA PERMISSION
FLEET, PRESTON
    Lentz, H., III. Obituaries. biogs filmogs obits ports CLASSIC n237:57-59
        Mar 1995
FLEISCHER, ALAIN See also TOURNAGE A LA CAMPAGNE, UN
FLEMING, ANDREW See also THREESOME
    Margulies, E. It's just movies. il interv MOVIELINE 6:68-69 Mar 1995
FLEMING, ANN MARIE See also NEW SHOES; PIONEERS OF X-RAY TECHNOLOGY; WAVING;
        YOU TAKE CARE NOW
    Fleming, A.M. "You Take Care Now." scenario MILLENNIUM n25:10-13 Summer
        1991
    Hoolboom, M. The queen of disaster. stills MILLENNIUM n26:26-32 Fall 1992
FLEMING, MICHAEL
    Evans, G. and Fleming, M. Location police's Gotham beat may die. VARIETY
        358:36 Feb 27/Mar 5 1995
    Fleming, M. Propaganda buys "Sleepers." VARIETY 358:4 Feb 20/26 1995
FLEMING, RHONDA
    Bawden, J. Rhonda Fleming. biog filmog il ports stills FIR 45:6-17 Nov/Dec
        1994
FLEMING, VICTOR See also WIZARD OF OZ, THE
FLESH AND BONE f (d Kloves, Steve 1994 USA)
        Reviews
    Bruyn, O. de. "Flesh and Bone." POSITIF n407:42-43 Jan 1995
    Cieutat, M. "Flesh and Bone." credits still POSITIF n409:36-37 Mar 1995
FLESH SUITCASE f (d Duran, Paul 1995 USA)
        Reviews
    Klady, L. "Flesh Suitcase." credits VARIETY 358:52 Mar 13/19 1995
FLINN, CARYL
    Creekmur, C.K. Strains of utopia: gender, nostalgia, and Hollywood music.
        Caryl Flinn [Book Review]. DISCOURSE n17.1:172-175 Fall 1994
FLINTSTONES, THE f (d Levant, Brian 1994 USA)
        Reviews
    Hannula, M. Kultaista keskinkertaisuutta. credits il still PEILI 18:14-15
        n3 1994
FLITTERMAN-LEWIS, SANDY
    Kalaga, W. Stam, Robert, Burgoyne, Robert, Flitterman-Lewis, Sandy. New
        vocabularies in film semiotics: structuralism, post-structuralism, and
        beyond [Book Review]. CINEMAS 4:167-175 n3 1994
FLOOD, JAMES See also SHANGHAI
FLORENCE, PENNY
    Florence, P. "Screen" [Book Review]. il BLIMP n30:53 Winter 1994
FLORODORA f (d Mason, Clement 1901 Australia)
    Long, C. Australia's first films: facts and fables, part eleven: Aborigines
        and actors. filmogs il map ports C PAPERS n102:52-57+ [8p] Dec 1994
FLUETSCH, JOHANNES See also PUNCH
FLY, THE f (d Cronenberg, David 1986 USA)
        Thematic Analysis
    Beard, W. Cronenberg, flyness, and the other-self. bibliog still CINEMAS
        4:153-173 n3 1994
FLYNDRA f (d Jorfald, Oivind S. 1993 Norw)
    Jurgens, J.H. Tegnefilmcompagniet. il Z n4:20-22 (n46) 1993
Focus Awards See AWARDS - United States - Directors Guild of America
FOFI, GOFFREDO
    Fofi, G. and Volpi, G. Entretien avec Federico Fellini. il interv stills
        POSITIF n409:76-92 Mar 1995

FOKKEMA, FROUKE See also WILDGROEI
Foley process See SOUND RECORDERS AND RECORDING
FOLK TALES
    Torres, S. Sombra y asombro de los vampiros. il stills NOSFERATU n6:50-55
        Apr 1991
FOLKLORE
        Russia (since 1992)
    Dumas, D. Alambic et vieilles querelles. AVANT-SCENE n437:85-87 Dec 1994
FONDA, JANE
    Atkinson, M. Jane Fonda in "Klute." still MOVIELINE 6:82 Apr 1995
FONER, NAOMI
    Taylor, E. Raising "Isaiah." port VILLAGE VOICE 40:64 Mar 28 1995
FONN, EGIL B.
    Fonn, E.B. Filmen i HHH 94 [Book Review]. F&K n1:39 1994
    Fonn, E.B. Ivo Caprino - portrett av askeladden i norsk film [Book Review].
        il F&K n1:19 1994
    Fonn, E.B. Minneord ved Terje Sjursens bare Troens kapell, Mollendal, 17.
        januar 1994. F&K n1:23 1994
    Fonn, E.B. Moskvafestivalens "grand old man" dod. obit F&K n1:23 1994
    Fonn, E.B. Regjeringen prioriterer kultur. il F&K n7:32-33 1993
FONS, JORGE See also CALLEJON DE LOS MILAGROS, EL
Fontane Effi Briest See EFFI BRIEST
FONTANE, THEODOR
    Gruber, E. Une reprise impossible? "Effi Briest" et la question de ses
        reecritures filmiques. CINEMAS 4:59-71 n1 1993
FONTANINI, CLAUDIO For film reviews see author under the following titles: IT
        COULD HAPPEN TO YOU; RICHIAMO, IL; SPEECHLESS; TERMINAL VELOCITY
FORCIER, ANDRE See also VENT DU WYOMING, LE
    Bonnevie, L. Entrevue avec Andre Forcier. filmog interv still SEQUENCES
        n174:10-13 Sep/Oct 1994
FORD, JEFFREY
    Ford, J. Classic corner: Maurice Jarre's "Is Paris Burning?" il F SCORE
        MONTHLY n36/37:31 Aug/Sep 1993
FORD, JOHN See also STAGECOACH
    Carlo Gaberscek: Il west di John Ford [Book Review]. IMMAGINE n28:30 Autumn
        1994
    Fornara, B. Carlo Gaberscek: Il west di John Ford [Book Review]. il C
        FORUM 34:91 Oct (n338) 1994
    John Ford. Par Lindsay Anderson [Book Review]. il GRAND ANGLE n176:40 Nov
        1994
    Livio, J. Il West di John Ford. Di Carlo Gaberscek [Book Review].
        GRIFFITHIANA n51/52:268 Oct 1994
    Nolley, K. John Ford and the Hollywood Indian. bibliog still F&HIST
        23:44-56 n1/4 1993
Foreign language film See DISTRIBUTION; IMPORT MARKET
Foreigners' employment See EMPLOYMENT, FOREIGNERS
Foreigners in film industry [Prior to V16, 1988 use FOREIGNERS IN FILM INDUSTRY]
        See EMPLOYMENT, FOREIGNERS
FORGACH, ANDRAS For film reviews see author under the following titles: PLAGUE,
        THE
FORGACS, PETER See also PRIVAT MAGYARORSZAG; [UNKNOWN WAR, AN]
    A tizenotezredik pillanat. interv stills F VILAG 38:18-23 n1 1995
FORGEAS, JACQUES
    Berthome, J.-P. Le "storyboard" en livres [Book Reviews]. POSITIF n407:90+
        [2p] Jan 1995
Forgetfulness See MEMORY
FORMALISM
        Union of Soviet Socialist Republics
    Sorensen, J. "Lef," Eisenstein, and the politics of form. bibliog F
        CRITICISM 19:55-74 n2 1994/95
FORMAN, MILOS
    Barson, M. Turnaround: a memoir. By Milos Forman and Jan Novak [Book
        Review]. DGA NEWS 19:32 n2 1994
FORNARA, BRUNO For film reviews see author under the following titles: ANNI
        RIBELLI; CLEAR AND PRESENT DANGER; DOROGA V RAI; DU FOND DU COEUR:
        GERMAINE ET BENJAMIN; JARDIN DEL EDEN, EL; STAIRS 1 GENEVA; WYATT EARP
    Fornara, B. Carlo Gaberscek: Il west di John Ford [Book Review]. il C
        FORUM 34:91 Oct (n338) 1994
    Fornara, B. Chimica inorganica. credits stills C FORUM 34:54-58 Nov (n339)
        1994
    Fornara, B. Critica della burocrazia... C FORUM 34:5+ [3p] Sep (n337) 1994
    Fornara, B. "True Lies." credits stills C FORUM 34:52-55 Sep (n337) 1994
    Poggi, E. Il critico al festival ovvero lo spettatore indiscreto. intervs
        SEGNO n71:19-33 Jan/Feb 1995
FORNARI, CARMINE See also AMICO ARABO, L'
FORREST GUMP f (d Zemeckis, Robert 1994 USA)
    Elrick, T. Gump becomes him. il interv port DGA NEWS 20:26-27+ [6p] n1
        1995
    Kehr, D. Who framed "Forrest Gump." il stills F COM 31:45-48+ [6p] Mar/Apr
        1995
    La Polla, F. "Forrest Gump." credits il stills C FORUM 34:60-67 Oct (n338)
        1994
    O'Neill, K. Gumption. il ports PREM 8:102-105+ [5p] Apr 1995
        Sound Track Reviews
    Pugliese, R. Segnodischi. stills SEGNO n71:71 Jan/Feb 1995
        Reviews
    Hamilton, A. "Forrest Gump." credits still FILM 4:21 n1 [1995]
    La Polla, F. "Forrest Gump." C FORUM 34:23 Sep (n337) 1994
    Larue, J. "Forrest Gump." credits stills SEQUENCES n174:42-43 Sep/Oct 1994
    Pearson, H., Jr. "Forrest Gump." FIR 45:60-61 Nov/Dec 1994
    Rousseau, Y. "Forrest Gump." still 24 IMAGES n75:75 Dec/Jan 1994/95
    Zetlin, M. "Forrest Gump." credits still C PAPERS n102:68-69 Dec 1994
FORS, MATS
    Fors, M. Johan Hagelback - piimaanimaation mestari. filmog il still PEILI
        17:14-15 n4 1993
FORSMAN, MICHAEL
    Forsman, M. Antropologi och rorliga bilder [Book Reviews]. F HAFTET
        22:60-62 n3 (n87) 1994
FORSYTH, SCOTT
    Forsyth, S. The failures of nationalism and documentary: "Grierson and

Gouzenko." CAN J F STUD 1:74-82 n1 1990
FORTIN, ERIC
  Fortin, E. Predal, Rene. Le cinema francais depuis 1945 [Book Review].
    CINEMAS 4:151-155 n1 1993
FORTINI, FRANCO
  Fortini, F. Cari amici non sempre chiari compagni. il C NUOVO 43:4-6
    Nov/Dec (n352) 1994
  Fortini, F. Cari amici non sempre chiari compagni. il C NUOVO 43:4-6
    Nov/Dec (n352) 1994
(Forty-eight) 48 Hours See WENT THE DAY WELL?
(FORTY-SECOND) 42ND STREET f (d Bacon, Lloyd 1933 USA)
  Ciment, M. BFI film classics [Book Reviews]. stills POSITIF n408:75-77 Feb
    1995
FOSTER, HAL
  Cantrill, A. Compulsive beauty. By Hal Foster [Book Review]. CANTRILL'S
    FMNTS n73/74:41 May 1994
FOSTER, NORMAN
  Foster, N. Hollywood by roller coaster. il ports stills F FAX n48:66-70+
    [6p] Jan/Feb 1995
  Foster, N. Hollywood by roller coaster. il ports stills F FAX n48:66-70+
    [6p] Jan/Feb 1995
FOTH, JOERG See also BIOLOGIE!; BLUMENLAND; DSCHUNGELZEIT; EISMEER RUFT, DAS;
    KNOTEN, DER; LETZTES AUS DER DADAER; PROZESS, DER; TUBA WA DUO
  Graef, J. Joerg Foth. biog filmog il F & FERNSEHEN 22:48-49 n6 1994
FOTHERGILL, ROBERT
  Fothergill, R. Canadian Film-makers' Distribution Centre: a founding memoir.
    CAN J F STUD 3:81-85 n2 1994
Found footage film See EXPERIMENTAL FILM
FOUR CORNERS OF NOWHERE, THE f (d Chbosky, Steve 1995 USA)
    Reviews
  McCarthy, T. "The Four Corners of Nowhere." credits still VARIETY 358:76
    Feb 6/12 1995
  Nagy, E. "The Four Corners of Nowhere." BOXOFFICE 131:bet p125 and 144
    [pR29] Apr 1995
FOUR ROOMS f (d Anders, Allison/Rockwell, Alexandre/Rodriguez,
    Robert/Tarantino, Quentin 1995 USA)
  Spines, C. Go to your room! il still PREM 8:31-32 Feb 1995
FOUR WEDDINGS AND A FUNERAL f (d Newell, Mike 1994 Gt Br)
    Distribution
  Roddick, N. "Four Weddings" and a final reckoning. il stat still table S&S
    5:12-15 Jan 1995
    Reviews
  Buccheri, V. "Quattro matrimoni e un funerale." credits stills SEGNO
    n71:51-53 Jan/Feb 1995
  Martini, E. "Quattro matrimoni e un funerale." credits still C FORUM 34:80
    Oct (n338) 1994
  Takacs, F. "Negy eskuvo es egy temetes." credits still F VILAG 38:57 n2
    1995
Four-wall exhibition See DISTRIBUTION
FOWLER, CATHY
  Fowler, C. and Kueppers, P. Creteil International Women's Film Festival,
    18-27 March 1994. SCREEN 35:394-397 n4 1994
FOX, DAVID
  Obituaries. obits VARIETY 358:54 Feb 13/19 1995
FOX, EYTAN See also SHIRAT HA'SIRENA
FOX, GEORGE S.
  Obituaries. biog obits VARIETY 357:83-84 Jan 2/8 1995
FOX, MICHAEL
  Fox, M. Looking for funds in some of the right places. il INDEP 18:40-41
    Apr 1995
FOX RECORDS
  Hirsch, D. (Twentieth) 20th Century Fox film scores: the first CDs! F SCORE
    MONTHLY n39:13 Nov 1993
FOXES f (d Lyne, Adrian 1980 USA)
  Margulies, E. To see just how riotously a young Hollywood movie can age,
    rent "Foxes." il MOVIELINE 6:78 Mar 1995
FRAME f (d Kobland, Ken 1977 USA)
  Kobland, K. Storyboards, plans and notes for "Frame" (1976) and "Flaubert
    Dreams of Travel" (1986). il MILLENNIUM n25:31-35 Summer 1991
France See as a subheading under individual subject headings
FRANCIS, FREDDIE See also SKULL, THE
FRANCIS OF ASSISI f (d Curtiz, Michael 1961 USA)
    Sound Track Reviews
  Deutsch, D.C. "Doctor Faustus"; "Francis of Assisi." il SCN 14:16-17 Mar
    1995
FRANCKE, LIZZIE For film reviews see author under the following titles: DALLAS
    DOLL; ONCE WERE WARRIORS; SHAWSHANK REDEMPTION, THE; YINSHI NAN NU
  Francke, L. All about Leigh. stills S&S 5:8-9 Feb 1995
  Francke, L. Introducing movie magic. il interv INTERV 25:106-107 Apr 1995
  Francke, L. What are you girls going to do? stills S&S 5:28-29 Apr 1995
  Slide, A. The Slide area film book notes [Book Reviews]. CLASSIC
    n237:42-44+ [4p] Mar 1995
  Swicord, R. Pioneer know-how [Book Review]. ports S&S 5:36-37 Feb 1995
FRANJU, GEORGES See also YEUX SANS VISAGE, LES
FRANKEL, DANIEL
  Lentz, H., III. Obituaries. biogs filmogs il obits ports CLASSIC
    n236:57-59 Feb 1995
FRANKEL, DAVID See also MIAMI RHAPSODY
FRANKEL, MARTHA
  Frankel, M. Labor daze. stills MOVIELINE 6:60-64+ [6p] Apr 1995
  Frankel, M. The young lion. il port stills MOVIELINE 6:42-46+ [8p] Mar
    1995
FRANKENSTEIN f (d Whale, James 1931 USA)
  Thomson, D. Really a part of me. stills F COM 31:17-18+ [8p] Jan/Feb 1995
FRANKENSTEIN FILM
  Freixas, R. and Bassa, J. Frankenstein: cadenas a la Creacion? il stills
    NOSFERATU n6:56-65 Apr 1991
  Kiraly, J. Frankenstein es Faust. credits filmog stills F VILAG 38:20-25
    n2 1995
  Kremski, P. Das Monster, das Mensch sein wollte. filmog il stills F BUL

36:36-39+ [9p] n6 (n197) 1994
    History
  Kiraly, J. Frankenstein es Orpheusz. stills F VILAG 38:18-23 n3 1995
FRANKENSTEIN MUST BE DESTROYED f (d Fisher, Terence 1969 Gt Br)
  Bernardo, J.M. "El cerebro de Frankenstein." credits stills NOSFERATU
    n6:98-99 Apr 1991
FRANKIE, JONNY UND DIE ANDEREN f (d Viet, Hans-Erich 1993 FR Ger)
    Reviews
  Gandini, L. "Frankie, Jonny und die anderen." still C FORUM 34:36 Sep
    (n337) 1994
FRANKOVICH, ALLAN See also MALTESE DOUBLE CROSS, THE
FRAPPIER, ROGER See also DERNIER GLACIER, LE
FRASER, FIL
  Fraser, F. The participation of Aboriginal and other cultural minorities in
    cultural development. bibliog CAN J COM 19:477-493 n3/4 1994
FREARS, STEPHEN See also HERO; MARY REILLY
FREE WILLY f (d Wincer, Simon 1993 USA)
    Sound Track Reviews
  Dursin, A. and others. Four by Basil Poledouris. F SCORE MONTHLY n36/37:32
    Aug/Sep 1993
    Reviews
  Tuominen, S. Valaalla opetetaan ymparistonsuojelua. credits il PEILI 18:32
    n1 1994
FREEDOM ON MY MIND f (d Field, Connie/Mulford, Marilyn 1994 USA)
  Lucia, C. Progress and misgivings in Mississippi. interv port stills
    CINEASTE 21:43-45 n1/2 1995
    Reviews
  Arthur, P. and Cutler, J. "Freedom on My Mind." credits still CINEASTE
    21:81-82 n1/2 1995
FREEMAN, DEREK
  Freeman, D. There's tricks i' th' world: an historical analysis of the
    Samoan researches of Margaret Mead. bibliog il map ports VISUAL ANTHRO R
    7:103-128 n1 1991
FREEMAN, MORGAN
  Webster, A. Filmographies. biogs filmogs stills PREM 8:104 Mar 1995
FREIXAS, RAMON
  Freixas, R. and Bassa, J. Frankenstein: cadenas a la Creacion? il stills
    NOSFERATU n6:56-65 Apr 1991
FRENCH, LAWRENCE
  French, L. "Tall Tale." il stills C FANTAS 26:8-9 n3 1995
FRENCH, PHILIP
  Axelsson, S. I filmralsta poeters sallskap [Book Review]. il CHAPLIN
    36:62 n6 (n255) 1994/95
FRENCH, TODD
  French, T. "Candyman 2." stills C FANTAS 26:40-41+ [3p] n3 1995
  French, T. "Candyman 2." stills C FANTAS 26:8-9 n2 1995
  French, T. Interview with the monster. stills C FANTAS 26:42 n3 1995
FREND, CHARLES See also CRUEL SEA, THE
FRESA Y CHOCOLATE f (Strawberry and Chocolate d Gutierrez Alea, Tomas/Tabio,
    Juan Carlos 1994 Cuba/Mex/Sp)
  Birringer, J. Homosexuality and the revolution. interv port CINEASTE
    21:21-22 n1/2 1995
  Carro, N. "Fresa y chocolate." interv stills DICINE n59:2-3 Nov/Dec 1994
  Hoberman, J. Cuban curios. port stills PREM 8:57+ [2p] Apr 1995
  West, D. "Strawberry and Chocolate," ice cream and tolerance. interv port
    stills CINEASTE 21:16-20 n1/2 1995
    Adaptations
  Toledo, T. "Fresa y chocolate." interv stills DICINE n59:4-6 Nov/Dec 1994
    Reviews
  Garcia Borrero, J.A. "Fresa y chocolate." credits stills DICINE n59:7-8
    Nov/Dec 1994
  Martelli, E. "Fragola e cioccolato." credits still C FORUM 34:83-84 Oct
    (n338) 1994
  Noh, D. "Strawberry and Chocolate." credits FJ 98:62-63 Mar 1995
  Oppenheimer, J. "Strawberry and Chocolate." still BOXOFFICE 131:bet p89
    and 96 [pR20] Mar 1995
  Travers, P. "Strawberry and Chocolate." still ROLLING STONE n701:63 Feb 9
    1995
FRESH f (d Yakin, Boaz 1994 Fr/USA)
  Kapetanovic, M. and Noel, J. "Fresh." bibliog credits stills GRAND ANGLE
    n178:11-12 Jan 1995
FRESH KILL f (d Cheang, Shu Lea 1994 USA)
    Reviews
  Marks, L.U. "Fresh Kill." stills C ACTION n36:31-33 1995
  Reynaud, B. "Fresh Kill." credits still CINEMAYA n25/26:85 Autumn/Winter
    1994/95
FRESNAY, PIERRE
  Pierre Fresnay. biog filmog il stills STARS n21:[25-28] Winter 1995
FREUDLOSE GASSE, DIE f (Joyless Street d Pabst, G.W. 1925 Ger)
    Restoration
  Volkmer, K. Vom Umgang mit Geschichte oder Die Augen der Asta Nielsen. il
    stills MEDIEN 38:344-347 n6 1994
FREY, MARTIN
  Frey, M. Film production [Book Review]. F KUNST n144:67-68 1994
  Frey, M. International guide to literature on film [Book Review]. F KUNST
    n144:70-71 1994
  Frey, M. Kulturstatistik 1992 [Book Review]. F KUNST n144:75-76 1994
  Frey, M. Oesterreichischer forschungsstaettenkatalog [Book Review]. F KUNST
    n144:76-77 1994
  Frey, M. Sound & vision/Oskar Fischinger [Book Review]. F KUNST n144:71-72
    1994
FREZZATO, ACHILLE
  Frezzato, A. Riga: lo "stato delle cose" nel cinema dell'ex URSS. stills C
    FORUM 34:10-12 Nov (n339) 1994
FRIEDBERG, ANNE
  Hastie, A. Window shopping: cinema and the postmodern. Anne Friedberg [Book
    Reviews]. DISCOURSE n17.2:171-176 Winter 1994/95
  McKinley, A. Anne Friedberg. Window shopping: cinema and the postmodern
    [Book Review]. ARACHNE 1:270-274 n2 1994
FRIEDGEN, BUD See also THAT'S ENTERTAINMENT! III

GARCIA BORRERO, JUAN ANTONIO For film reviews see author under the following
titles: FRESA Y CHOCOLATE
GARCIA, GILLES
    Aude, F. (Deux) 250 cineastes europeens d'aujourd'hui. Sous la direction de
    Gilles Garcia [Book Review]. POSITIF n409:73 Mar 1995
GARCIA LOPES, RODRIGO
    Higgins, G. and others. Grisled roots. interv ports MILLENNIUM n26:56-66
    Fall 1992
GARCIA, MARIA For film reviews see author under the following titles: BROWNING
VERSION, THE; I LIKE IT LIKE THAT
GARCIA, NICOLE See also FILS PREFERE, LE
    Aude, F. Entretien avec Nicole Garcia. il interv stills POSITIF n407:15-20
    Jan 1995
    Nicole Garcia. il still POSITIF n407:12 Jan 1995
GARCIA, ROGER
    Frank Tashlin, sous la direction de Roger Garcia e Bernard Eisenchitz [Book
    Review]. IMMAGINE n28:30-31 Autumn 1994
GARCIA TSAO, LEONARDO
    Garcia Tsao, L. Locarno 94. il stills DICINE n59:28-29 Nov/Dec 1994
GARCIADIEGO, PAZ ALICIA
    Lopez Aranda, S. Filmar el tiempo: Arturo Ripstein y Paz Alicia Garciadiego:
    segundo parte. il interv stills DICINE n59:9-13 Nov/Dec 1994
GARDIES, ANDRE
    Cleutat, M. L'espace au cinema. Par Andre Gardies [Book Reviews]. POSITIF
    n409:72 Mar 1995
    Gardies, A. Le genre co-operateur. CINEMAS 4:43-55 n3 1994
    Gardies, A. Narration et temporalite dans "Moderato cantabile." bibliog
    still CINEMAS 4:88-102 n1 1993
    Gregoire, P. Gardies, Andre. L'espace au cinema [Book Reviews]. CINEMAS
    5:229-232 n1/2 1994
GARDIES, RENE
    Gardies, R. Vers l'emotion documentaire. bibliog CINEMAS 4:49-60 n2 1994
GARDNER, R.H.
    Giuliano, M. R.H. Gardner. obit VARIETY 358:58 Mar 20/26 1995
GARDOS, PETER See also BROOKLYN TESTVER, A
    Snee, P. Honi kihivasok. il interv stills F VILAG 38:29-31 n1 1995
GARFIELD, DAVID
    Lentz, H., III. Obituaries. biogs filmogs obits ports CLASSIC n237:57-59
    Mar 1995
GARFIELD, JOHN
    Martin, A. Performing the city [Book Review]. Q REV F & VIDEO 15:71-76 n3
    1994
GARIAZZO, GIUSEPPE
    Gariazzo, G. Bogdanovich inedito. il C FORUM 34:88-90 Sep (n337) 1994
    Gariazzo, G. Cortocircuito mentale. FCR 45:298-300 Jun/Jul (n446/447) 1994
    Gariazzo, G. Quel raro equilibrio di sospensione. still C FORUM 34:78-79
    Nov (n339) 1994
GARMES, LEE See also HANNAH LEE
GARNIER, PHILIPPE
    Codelli, L. Fragments. Portraits from the inside. Par Andre De Toth [Book
    Reviews]. POSITIF n407:73 Jan 1995
GAROFALO, JANEANE
    Sorensen, H. Double feature. il interv PREM 8:42 Apr 1995
GAROFALO, MARCELLO For film reviews see author under the following titles: DARK
HALF, THE; MARY SHELLEY'S FRANKENSTEIN
    Garofalo, M. Estetica dello schifo. stills SEGNO n72:27-29 Mar/Apr 1995
    Garofalo, M. Peplum. filmog stills SEGNO n71:74-75 Jan/Feb 1995
    Garofalo, M. Scult movie. credits il still SEGNO n71:78-79 Jan/Feb 1995
    Garofalo, M. Scult movie. credits il stills SEGNO n72:74-75 Mar/Apr 1995
    Garofalo, M. Slapstick all'italiana. il interv stills SEGNO n72:3-9
    Mar/Apr 1995
GARREL, PHILIPPE
    Tributes
    Preziosi, A. Cerimonie segrete. stills SEGNO n71:61-64 Jan/Feb 1995
GARRIS, MICK
    Yonover, N.S. Mick Garris takes "The Stand." filmog il interv port DGA
    NEWS 19:26-28 n2 1994
GARRY, PATRICK M.
    Garry, P.M. A different voice. il COMMONWEAL 122:17-18 Mar 24 1995
GARSAULT, ALAIN For film reviews see author under the following titles: LION
KING, THE
    Garsault, A. John Carpenter. il still POSITIF n409:8-9 Mar 1995
GASHER, MIKE
    Gasher, M. Ted Magder. Canada's Hollywood: the Canadian state and feature
    films [Book Review]. CAN J F STUD 3:101-104 n2 1994
GASS, LARS HENRIK
    Gass, L.H. "Ich freue mich ja in dem Sterbenden zu sterben." C(SWITZ)
    40:135-152 1994
GASSER UND "GASSER" f (d Schumacher, Iwan 1994 Switz)
    Reviews
    Schaub, M. "Gasser und 'Gasser.'" credits still C(SWITZ) 40:224 1994
GASTON MIRON (LES OUTILS DU POETE) f (d Gladu, Andre 1994 Can)
    Reviews
    Landry, G. "Gaston Miron (Les outils du poete)." still 24 IMAGES n75:74-75
    Dec/Jan 1994/95
GATES, BILL
    Busch, A.M. and Weiner, R. Gates joins DreamWorks team. il VARIETY 358:15+
    [2p] Mar 27/Apr 2 1995
GATES, DAVID
    Gates, D. and Hall, C. Will Fry come in from the cold? port NEWSWK 125:69
    Mar 13 1995
GATTO A NOVE CODE, IL f (d Argento, Dario 1971 It)
    Sound Track Reviews
    Pugliese, R. Segnodischi. stills SEGNO n71:71 Jan/Feb 1995
GAUDREAULT, ANDRE
    Gaudreault, A. Filmographic analysis and early cinema. bibliog credits CAN
    J F STUD 1:57-73 n1 1990
    Gaudreault, A. and Lacasse, G. "Danse indienne": film Lumiere: no 1000: le
    premier film tourne au Quebec? stills 24 IMAGES n76:17-21 Spring 1995
    Gaudreault, A. and Lacasse, G. Fonctions et origines du bonimenteur du

cinema des premiers temps. bibliog il CINEMAS 4:132-147 n1 1993
    Gaudreault, A. and Marion, P. Dieu est l'auteur des documentaires...
    bibliog CINEMAS 4:11-26 n2 1994
    Jaubert, J.-C. Andre Gaudreault. Du litteraire au filmique, systeme du recit
    [Book Review]. CAN J F STUD 1:89-90 n1 1990
    Jaubert, J.-C. Sous la direction de J. Aumont, A. Gaudreault, M. Marie.
    Histoire du cinema, nouvelles approaches [Book Review]. CAN J F STUD
    1:91-92 n1 1990
GAUP, NILS See also HODET OVER VANNET
GAUTEUR, CLAUDE
    Gauteur, C. Un an de lecture. bibliog AVANT-SCENE n437:90-92 Dec 1994
GAVIRIA, VICTOR See also RODRIGO D. - NO FUTURO
GAYDOS, STEVEN For film reviews see author under the following titles: WILD
BUNCH, THE
    Gaydos, S. Karlovy Vary impacted by proposed rival fest. il VARIETY 357:24
    Jan 2/8 1995
    Gaydos, S. Oscar's prop. 187. still VARIETY 357:68+ [2p] Jan 9/15 1995
    Slide, A. The Slide area film book notes [Book Reviews]. CLASSIC
    n237:42-44+ [4p] Mar 1995
Gays in film See HOMOSEXUALS IN FILM
GAYTAN, FRANCISCO
    Gaytan, F. Mexico. J F PRES n49:28-29 Oct 1994
GAZE IN FILM
    McKinley, A. Anne Friedberg. Window shopping: cinema and the postmodern
    [Book Review]. ARACHNE 1:270-274 n2 1994
    United States
    Putnam, A. The bearer of the gaze in Ridley Scott's "Thelma and Louise."
    WESTERN AM LIT 27:291-302 n4 1993
    Feminist Analysis
    Hinton, L. A "woman's" view: the "Vertigo" frame-up. bibliog still F
    CRITICISM 19:2-22 n2 1994/95
GAZON MAUDIT f (d Balasko, Josiane 1995 Fr)
    Reviews
    Bruyn, O. de. "Gazon maudit." still POSITIF n409:43 Mar 1995
    Nesselson, L. "Bushwhacked" ("Gazon maudit"). credits VARIETY 358:48 Feb
    13/19 1995
GAZZO, MICHAEL
    Milestones. obits ports TIME 145:31 Mar 6 1995
    Obituaries. biogs obits VARIETY 358:74-75 Mar 6/12 1995
GEBER, NILS-HUGO
    Geber, N.-H. Krigarkulturen och popularfilmens etniska strategier. bibliog
    diag il stills F HAFTET 22:23-37 n3 (n87) 1994
GEBHARDT, LISA
    Allen, M. and others. Exposure to pornography and acceptance of rape myths.
    bibliog stat tables J COMM 45:5-26 n1 1995
GEFFEN, DAVID
    Corliss, R. Hey, let's put on a show! il ports TIME 145:54-60 Mar 27 1995
GEHEIMNIS, DAS f (d Thome, Rudolf 1994 FR Ger)
    "Das Geheimnis." biog credits filmog still KINO(BRD) n1:22-23 1995
GEHR, RICHARD For film reviews see author under the following titles: [NAKED
KILLER]; [RUMBLE IN THE BRONX]
GEISER, RUTH For film reviews see author under the following titles: ANDERE
GESCHICHTE, EINE
GEIST, KENNETH For film reviews see author under the following titles: ROAD TO
WELLVILLE, THE
GENDER ROLES
    Cantrill, A. Spectacular bodies: gender, genre and the action cinema. By
    Yvonne Tasker [Book Review]. CANTRILL'S FMNTS n73/74:43 May 1994
    Champagne, J. Psychoanalysis and cinema studies: a "queer" perspective.
    bibliog PS 14:33-44 n1/2 1994/95
    Horror Film
    Feminist Analysis
    Harris, J. Clover, Carol J. Men, women, and chain saws: gender in the modern
    horror film [Book Review]. MEDIA INFO AUSTRALIA n75:158-159 Feb 1995
    Canada
    Postcolonial Analysis
    Kaye, J. "Perfectly Normal," eh?: gender transformation and national
    identity in Canada. CAN J F STUD 3:63-80 n2 1994
    China (People's Republic, since 1949)
    Berry, C. A turn for the better? - genre and gender in "Girl From Hunan" and
    other recent mainland Chinese films. bibliog stills PS 14:81-103 n1/2
    1994/95
    Finland
    Pornography and Obscenity
    Nikunen, K. Lukottomat siveysvyot. il PEILI 18:6-7 n4 1994
    Hong Kong
    Cheung, T. and Gilson, M. Gender trouble in Hongkong cinema. bibliog glos
    stills CINEMAS 3:181-201 n2/3 1993
    United States
    Action Film
    Vahtera, H. Toimivatko toimintaleffojen roolimallit? still PEILI 18:26-27
    n4 1994
    Feminist Analysis
    Addison, E. Saving other women from other men: Disney's "Aladdin." stills
    CAM OBS n31:4-25 Jan/May 1993
    Psychoanalytic Analysis
    Bick, I.J. "Well, I guess I must make you nervous": woman and the space of
    "Alien3" bibliog stills PS 14:45-58 n1/2 1994/95
    Grieveson, L. Steven Cohan and Ina Rae Hark (eds). Screening the male:
    exploring masculinities in Hollywood cinema [Book Reviews]. SCREEN
    35:400-406 n4 1994
    McKee, A.L. Negotiating gender in post-World War II America [Book Reviews].
    Q REV F & VIDEO 15:47-56 n3 1994
    Self, R.T. Redressing the law in Kathryn Bigelow's "Blue Steel." bibliog
    stills UFAJ 46:31-43 n2 1994
    Western Film
    Dowell, P. The mythology of the western: Hollywood perspectives on race and
    gender in the nineties. stills CINEASTE 21:6-10 n1/2 1995

GENDRON, SYLVIE For film reviews see author under the following titles: FILLE DE D'ARTAGNAN, LA; GROSSE FATIGUE; SOURIRE, LE
  Gendron, S. Ed Wood. filmog il stills SEQUENCES n175:21-24 Nov/Dec 1994
  Gendron, S. John Turturro. filmog port still SEQUENCES n175:26-27 Nov/Dec 1994
  Gendron, S. Qu'est-ce que le cinema... canadien? stills SEQUENCES n174:13-16 Sep/Oct 1994
GENER, RANDY For film reviews see author under the following titles: SUM OF US, THE
GENIN, BERNARD
  Genin, B. En tournage. stills AVANT-SCENE n437:before p1-5 [6p] Dec 1994
GENINA, AUGUSTO See also TRE SENTIMENTALI, I
GENRE See also ACTION FILM; ADVENTURE FILM; ARCHETYPES; BIOGRAPHICAL FILM; COMEDY FILM; DETECTIVE FILM; EPIC FILM; FANTASY FILM; GANGSTER FILM; GOTHIC FILM; HORROR FILM; MUSICAL FILM; MYSTERY FILM; SCIENCE FICTION FILM; SNUFF FILM; SPECTACLE FILM; SPY FILM; STEREOTYPES; SUSPENSE FILM; WAR FILM; WESTERN FILM; WOMAN'S FILM
  Gardies, A. Le genre co-operateur. CINEMAS 4:43-55 n3 1994
GENS NORMAUX N'ONT RIEN D'EXCEPTIONNEL, LES f (d Ferreira Barbosa, Laurence 1993 Fr)
  Reviews
  Horguelin, T. Une folie sans frontieres. credits still 24 IMAGES n75:62 Dec/Jan 1994/95
GENTLY DOWN THE STREAM f (d Friedrich, Su 1983 USA)
  Homosexuals in Film
  Holmlund, C. Fractured fairytales and experimental identities: looking for lesbians in and around the films of Su Friedrich. bibliog stills DISCOURSE n17.1:16-46 Fall 1994
GENTRY, RIC
  Gentry, R. Writing with light. il interv stills FQ 48:2-9 n2 1994/95
GEORGE BALANCHINE'S THE NUTCRACKER f (d Ardolino, Emile 1993 USA)
  Reviews
  Johnston, T. "George Balanchine's the Nutcracker." credits S&S 5:44-45 Feb 1995
GEORGE WENDT SHOW, THE f (1995 USA)
  Reviews
  Carson, T. Foley squared. still VILLAGE VOICE 40:43 Mar 21 1995
GERALD, MARC
  Breen, J.L. Gerald, Marc, ed. Murder plus: true crime stories from the masters of detective fiction [Book Review]. ARMCHAIR DET 28:78 n1 1995
GERARD, JEREMY
  Gerard, J. George Abbott. obit VARIETY 358:84-85 Feb 6/12 1995
GERDA f (d Longfellow, Brenda 1992 Can)
  Baert, R. Skirting the issue. stills SCREEN 35:354-373 n4 1994
GERHARDT, KARL See also JAGD NACH DEM TODE, DIE
Germany (Democratic Republic, 1949-1990) See as a subheading under individual subject headings
Germany (Federal Republic, 1949-1990) See as a subheading under individual subject headings
Germany (Federal Republic, since 1990) See as a subheading under individual subject headings
  See DEUTSCHE FILM-AKTIEN-GESELLSCHAFT (DEFA)
Germany (until 1949) See as a subheading under individual subject headings
Germany Year 90 Nine Zero See ALLEMAGNE ANNEE 90 NEUF ZERO
GERMI, PIETRO
  Codelli, L. L'heritage de Germi. il stills POSITIF n406:70-71 Dec 1994
  Germi, P. Un cineaste "a l'americaine." il stills POSITIF n406:65-66 Dec 1994
  Gili, J.A. Filmographie de Pietro Germi. biog filmog il still POSITIF n406:72-73 Dec 1994
  Gili, J.A. Pietro Germi, moraliste contemporain. still POSITIF n406:64 Dec 1994
  Viviani, C. Pietruzzo le bon et Pietro le teigneux. il stills POSITIF n406:67-69 Dec 1994
GERMINAL f (d Berri, Claude 1993 Fr/Belg/It)
  Slodowski, J. "Germinal." biogs credits filmogs FSP 40:10 n4 (n758) 1994
GERONIMI, CLYDE See also (ONE HUNDRED AND ONE) 101 DALMATIANS
GERONIMO: AN AMERICAN LEGEND f (d Hill, Walter 1993 USA)
  Dowell, P. The mythology of the western: Hollywood perspectives on race and gender in the nineties. stills CINEASTE 21:6-10 n1/2 1995
GEROW, A.A.
  Gerow, A.A. Documentarists of Japan (second in a series). biog interv port stills DOC BOX 3:12-18 1993
  Makino, M. and Gerow, A.A. Prokino. biogs il interv port stills DOC BOX 5:6-14 1994
GERTRUD f (d Dreyer, Carl Theodor 1964 Denmk)
  Miguez, M. "Gertrud." credits stills NOSFERATU n5:70-71 Jan 1991
  Minguet Batllori, J.M. Carl Theodor Dreyer: clasicismo y cine. il port stills NOSFERATU n5:12-23 Jan 1991
  Torres, S. "Gertrud": un desafio amoroso. stills NOSFERATU n5:38-41 Jan 1991
  Religious Themes
  Miguez, M. La mirada Dreyer. il stills NOSFERATU n5:24-37 Jan 1991
GERVAI, ANDRAS
  Gervai, A. Marta Meszaros - fighting collective amnesia [Book Review]. il NEW HUNGARIAN Q 34:155-158 n132 1993
GETAWAY, THE f (d Donaldson, Roger 1994 USA)
  "Ucieczka gangstera." biogs credits filmogs FSP 40:11 n4 (n758) 1994
  Reviews
  Boyce, M. "The Getaway." FATAL VISIONS n17:7 1994
GETTYSBURG f (d Maxwell, Ronald F. 1993 USA)
  Reviews
  Bourget, J.-L. "Gettysburg, la derniere bataille." still POSITIF n408:57 Feb 1995
GEVER, MARTHA
  Bronski, M. Queer looks: perspectves on lesbian and gay film and video. Edited by Martha Gever, John Greyson and Pratibha Parmar [Book Reviews]. still CINEASTE 21:90-92 n1/2 1995
GEYRHOFER, FRIEDRICH
  Geyrhofer, F. and Pataki, H. Film in Oesterreich. BLIMP [n1]:60-64 Mar 1985

GEZEICHNETEN, DIE f (Love One Another d Dreyer, Carl Theodor 1921 Ger)
  Miguez, M. "Los marcados." credits stills NOSFERATU n5:50-51 Jan 1991
GEZEICHNETEN, DIE f (Search, The d Zinnemann, Fred 1948 Switz/USA)
  Zinnemann, F. Letter from Fred Zinnemann. F CRITICISM 19:86-88 n2 1994/95
GHEERBRANT, DENIS See also VIE EST IMMENSE ET PLEINE DE DANGERS, LA
GHULAM, LANCE ERICKSON
  Ghulam, L.E. Ann Blyth: Ann of a thousand smiles. biog il interv ports CLASSIC n236:18+ [4p] Feb 1995
GIACOVELLI, ENRICO For film reviews see author under the following titles: CARI FOTTUTISSIMI AMICI; MITICI - COLPO GOBBO A MILANO, I; NESTORE L'ULTIMA CORSA; REMAINS OF THE DAY, THE; SOUPER, LE; UNICO PAESE AL MONDO, L'
  Giacovelli, E. "Schindler's List": un nobile film che onora la memoria e la storia degli Ebrei contro la spietata crudelta' nazista. still C SUD 33:1-2 Jul/Aug/Sep (n113) 1994
GIANETTI, DAVID For film reviews see author under the following titles: CLERKS; VISITEURS, LES
GIANOPULOS, JIM
  Gianopulos, J. Asia's economic expansion creates big opportunities. FJ 98:92 Jan/Feb 1995
GIBSON, BRIAN See also POLTERGEIST II: THE OTHER SIDE
GIBSON, LEE
  Gibson, L. Geoffrey Hill. Illuminating shadows: the mythic power of film [Book Review]. PS 14:125-126 n1/2 1994/95
GIBSON, MEL
  Atkinson, M. Mel Gibson in "Gallipoli." still MOVIELINE 6:80 Mar 1995
GIBSON, WILLIAM
  Montesano, A.P. "Johnny Mnemonic." stills C FANTAS 26:44+ [2p] n3 1995
GIERY, MARY A.
  Allen, M. and others. Exposure to pornography and acceptance of rape myths. bibliog stat tables J COMM 45:5-26 n1 1995
GILBERT, BRIAN See also TOM & VIV
  Dawtrey, A. Gilbert, Samuelsons ink Miramax pic pact. il ports VARIETY 358:14+ [2p] Mar 20/26 1995
  Lachat, P. Das wueste Land. credits interv stills F BUL 36:49-50 n6 (n197) 1994
Gildersleeve, Throckmorton P. (fictional character) See THROCKMORTON P. GILDERSLEEVE (fictional character)
GILES, JANE
  Giles, J. Well-bound white sheets [Book Review]. S&S 5:35 Apr 1995
GILES, JEFF For film reviews see author under the following titles: BEFORE SUNRISE; BOYS ON THE SIDE; DUMB AND DUMBER; QUICK AND THE DEAD, THE
  Giles, J. Where the action is. biog port stills NEWSWK 125:64-65 Mar 27 1995
GILI, JEAN A. For film reviews see author under the following titles: AQUI NA TERRA; BARNABO DELLE MONTAGNE; CAIXA, A; CHA FORTE CON LIMAO; SIN COMPASION
  Gili, J.A. Entretien avec Gianni Amelio. il interv stills POSITIF n406:25-31 Dec 1994
  Gili, J.A. Filmographie de Pietro Germi. biog filmog il still POSITIF n406:72-73 Dec 1994
  Gili, J.A. Pietro Germi, moraliste contemporain. still POSITIF n406:64 Dec 1994
GILL, MARK
  Kuhn, E. Marketing executives. il ports table PREM 8:38 Mar 1995
GILL, MARK STUART
  Gill, M.S. Crisis management. il stills PREM 8:74-77+ [5p] Apr 1995
GILLEN, FRANK J.
  Long, C. Australia's first films: facts and fables, part eleven: Aborigines and actors. filmogs il map ports C PAPERS n102:52-57+ [8p] Dec 1994
GILLESPIE, DAVID
  Adamson, J. and others. Forgotten laughter. credits port stills GRIFFITHIANA n51/52:170-197 Oct 1994
  Adamson, J. and others. La fabbrica della risata. credits port stills GRIFFITHIANA n51/52:170-197 Oct 1994
GILLIAT, SIDNEY
  Gilliat, S. Le declin d'un empire. il still POSITIF n406:51-53 Dec 1994
GILLIES, ISABEL
  Fuller, G. Parker's party. ports INTERV 25:79-81 Feb 1995
GILLOOLY, JANE See also LEONA'S SISTER GERRI
GILMOUR, CLYDE
  Gilmour, C. Movies by Clyde Gilmour: the underground is here. CAN J F STUD 3:87-88 n2 1994
GILROY, PAUL
  Gilroy, P. Unwelcome. stills S&S 5:18-19 Feb 1995
GILSON, MICHAEL
  Cheung, T. and Gilson, M. Gender trouble in Hongkong cinema. bibliog glos stills CINEMAS 3:181-201 n2/3 1993
GILTZ, MICHAEL
  Giltz, M. Bruce Jay Friedman. il NEW YORK 28:94 Jan 30 1995
  Giltz, M. Hi-yaaaah! still NEW YORK 28:89 Jan 30 1995
  Giltz, M. John Waters on "Faster, Pussycat! Kill! Kill!" stills NEW YORK 28:66 Jan 16 1995
GINGRICH, NEWT
  Wharton, D. Gingrich vows to promote U.S. film interests. port VARIETY 358:20 Mar 20/26 1995
GIORDANA, MARCO TULLIO See also UNICO PAESE AL MONDO, L'
GIORGINO f (d Boutonnat, Laurent 1994 Fr)
  Reviews
  Kohn, O. "Giorgino." POSITIF n406:45-46 Dec 1994
GIOT LE HA LONG f (d Tran, Vu/Nguyen, Huu Phan 1995 Vietnam/Hong Kong)
  Reviews
  Elley, D. "The Teardrop Pearl of Ha Long" ("Giot le Ha Long"). credits VARIETY 358:84 Feb 20/26 1995
GIOVANNINI, CRISTINA For film reviews see author under the following titles: [KITCHEN, THE]; LITTLE WOMEN
GIOVANNINI, FABIO
  Comuzio, E. Fabio Giovannini: Serial killer. Guida ai grandi assassini nella storia del cinema [Book Review]. C FORUM 34:95 Nov (n339) 1994

GIRALDI, MASSIMO   For film reviews see author under the following titles: LISBON STORY
GIRARD, FRANCOIS   See also THIRTY TWO SHORT FILMS ABOUT GLENN GOULD
GIRARD, HELENE
   Jean, M. and Loiselle, M.-C.   A l'ombre du 7e art.   il interv stills   24 IMAGES n76:4-7+ [7p] Spring 1995
GIRARD, MARTIN   For film reviews see author under the following titles: MASK, THE; TRUE LIES; WES CRAVEN'S NEW NIGHTMARE
   Girard, M.   Les vampires et la critique.   still   SEQUENCES n175:47-48 Nov/Dec 1994
   Girard, M.   "Natural Born Killers" ou la controverse dans le sang.   stills   SEQUENCES n174:50-52 Sep/Oct 1994
   Girard, M.   Sur quelques exercices de style au FFM.   stills   SEQUENCES n174:16-18 Sep/Oct 1994
GIRITLIOGLU, TOMRIS   See also YAZ YAGMURU
   "Yaz yagmuru."   biog credits filmog il still   CINEMAYA n25/26:106 Autumn/Winter 1994/95
Girl From Hunan   See XIANG NU XIAO-XIAO
GIRL WITH THE HUNGRY EYES, THE   f (d Jacobs, Jon 1995 USA)
   Reviews
   Levy, E.   "The Girl With the Hungry Eyes."   credits   VARIETY 358:74 Feb 20/26 1995
GIROD, FRANCIS   See also CONTRE L'OUBLI
GIROUX, LACTANCE
   Montreal cinematographie en debut de siecle.   il port still   24 IMAGES n75:51-54 Dec/Jan 1994/95
GITAI, AMOS   See also AU PAYS DES ORANGES
   Hanet, K.   Willemen, Paul.   The films of Amos Gitai: a montage [Book Review].   MEDIA INFO AUSTRALIA n75:172 Feb 1995
GIUFFRIDA, SERGIO
   Giuffrida, S. and Angiari, L.   Sitges: al supermarket dell'orrore quotidiano.   stills   C FORUM 34:7-9 Nov (n339) 1994
GIULIANO, MIKE
   Giuliano, M.   R.H. Gardner.   obit   VARIETY 358:58 Mar 20/26 1995
GIZYCKI, MARCIN
   Gizycki, M.   Chcialem zatytulowac swoj film "Piotr Dumala."   interv port stills   KINO 27:36 Jul 1993
   Gizycki, M.   Pan uwalnia sie spod wladzy slugi.   il   KINO 27:35 Jul 1993
   Sobolewski, T.   Listy: odpowiedz Andrzejowi Wernerowi.   KINO 27:40 May 1993
   Werner, A.   Listy: szanowny panie redaktorze!   KINO 27:40 May 1993
GJELSVIK, ERLING T.
   Og alle var der...   ports   Z n4:36-38 (n46) 1993
GJESTLAND, ROLV
   Gjestland, R.   Maendene bag i biffen [Book Review].   still   F&K n1:35 1994
GLADU, ANDRE   See also GASTON MIRON (LES OUTILS DU POETE)
GLAESSNER, VERINA   For film reviews see author under the following titles: LITTLE RASCALS, THE; ONLY THE STRONG; SOLITAIRE FOR TWO
GLASNER, MATTHIAS   See also MEDIOCREN, DIE
GLASS SHIELD, THE   f (d Burnett, Charles 1994 USA)
   Taubin, A.   Burnett looks back.   still   VILLAGE VOICE 40:52 Jan 10 1995
GLAUZIUSZ, TAMAS   For film reviews see author under the following titles: MINA TANNENBAUM
GLIMCHER, ARNE   See also JUST CAUSE
GLINES, CAROLE   For film reviews see author under the following titles: MURIEL'S WEDDING; PICTURE BRIDE
GLOMDALSBRUDEN   f (Bride of Glomdal, The d Dreyer, Carl Theodor 1925 Norw)
   Miguez, M.   "La novia de Glomdal."   credits stills   NOSFERATU n5:58-59 Jan 1991
Glossaries   See TERMINOLOGY
GLOWACKI, JANUSZ
   Recollections
   Sendecka, M.   Nie mam nic wspolnego z filmem.   interv   REZYSER n18:8 1993
GNOAN, M'BALA ROGER   See also AU NOM DU CHRIST
GO FISH   f (d Troche, Rose 1994 USA)
   Chiacchiari, F.   "Go Fish."   credits stills   C FORUM 34:74-76 Oct (n338) 1994
   Reviews
   Adagio, C.   "Go Fish."   credits, still   C NUOVO 43:42-43 Nov/Dec (n352) 1994
   Menarini, R.   "Go Fish - segui il pesce."   credits stills   SEGNO n71:48-49 Jan/Feb 1995
GODARD, JEAN-LUC   See also ALLEMAGNE ANNEE 90 NEUF ZERO; CONTRE L'OUBLI; ENFANTS JOUENT A LA RUSSIE, LES; HELAS POUR MOI; JLG/JLG - AUTOPORTRAIT DE DECEMBRE; PASSION
   Brown, R.S.   Film music: the good, the bad, and the ugly.   stills   CINEASTE 21:62-64 n1/2 1995
   Bruno, E. and Roberti, B.   Il tempo della memoria.   FCR 45:274-275 Jun/Jul (n446/447) 1994
   Godard, J.-L.   Award-winning correspondence.   port   F COM 31:2 Mar/Apr 1995
   Hoberman, J.   Letter from Jean-Luc.   VILLAGE VOICE 40:49 Feb 14 1995
   Trenczak, H.   Passion Kino oder Die Haerte, alles zu registrieren.   credits il port BLIMP [n1]:4-13 Mar 1985
GODBOUT, JACQUES   See also AFFAIRE NORMAN WILLIAM, L'
GODZILLA (series of films)
   Thunqvist, D.   The king of destruction.   il stills   CHAPLIN 36:34-39 n6 (n255) 1994/95
[GODZILLA VS. SPACE GODZILLA]   f (1994 Japan)
   Thunqvist, D.   The king of destruction.   il stills   CHAPLIN 36:34-39 n6 (n255) 1994/95
GOFFETTE, CHRISTOPHE
   Noel, J.   Le petit livres des films-cultes. Par Christophe Goffette [Book Review].   il   GRAND ANGLE n177:50 Dec 1994
GOFFI, ANNA   For film reviews see author under the following titles: MAX ET JEREMIE
GOLDBERG, ERIC   See also POCAHONTAS
GOLDBERG, GARY   See also PLATES
   Goldberg, G.   "Plates."   il scenario still   MILLENNIUM n25:14-17 Summer 1991
GOLDBERG, GARY DAVID
   Lally, K.   "Bye Bye Love" sees funny side of divorce.   il still   FJ 98:16+ [2p] Mar 1995
GOLDBERG, PHILIP
   Goldberg, P.   You ain't lazy, you're incubating.   JOURNAL WGA 8:20 Dec/Jan

1995
GOLDBERG VARIACIOK   f (d Grunwalsky, Ferenc 1992 Hungary)
   Reviews
   Bikacsy, G.   Video eye and video weapon.   il   NEW HUNGARIAN Q 33:171-176 n128 1992
Golden Balls   See HUEVOS DE ORO
GOLDEN, EVE
   Golden, E.   Alla Nazimova: Mother Russia goes Hollywood.   biog ports still   CLASSIC n236:bet p32 and 33 [pC4+ (3p)] Feb 1995
   Golden, E.   Kay Kendall: too little, too late.   biog ports still   CLASSIC n237:26+ [2p] Mar 1995
Golden Globes   See AWARDS - United States - Hollywood Foreign Press Association
GOLDENEYE   f (d Campbell, Martin 1995 Gt Br/USA)
   Porter, B.   (Double 0) 007 invades aircraft hangar as "GoldenEye" action rolls.   port   FJ 98:24+ [2p] Mar 1995
GOLDMAN, ALAIN
   Williams, M.   Joffe gets French backing.   VARIETY 358:22 Feb 20/26 1995
GOLDMAN, CARL
   Goldman to receive ShoWest's Sturdivant Award.   port   FJ 98:94 Mar 1995
GOLDMAN, GARY   See also HANS CHRISTIAN ANDERSEN'S THUMBELINA
GOLDMAN, HARRY
   Goldman, H.   Mr. Electric.   il stills   F FAX n48:37-41 Jan/Feb 1995
GOLDMAN, WILLIAM
   Goldman, W.   Anything but "Gump."   stills   NEW YORK 28:32-33 Jan 30 1995
   Goldman, W.   What should win Best Picture?   il   PREM 8:96-97 Apr 1995
GOLDSMITH, GARY
   Clark, J.   A list is still a list [Book Review].   stills   PREM 8:93 Feb 1995
GOLDSMITH, JERRY
   Bond, J.   Concert report.   F SCORE MONTHLY n36/37:5 Aug/Sep 1993
   Handzo, S.   The golden age of film music.   il ports stills   CINEASTE 21:46-55 n1/2 1995
GOLDSTEIN, PATRICK
   Goldstein, P.   The japes of Roth.   il interv port   PREM 8:86-90 Apr 1995
GOLDSTEIN, ROBERT
   Codelli, L.   Robert Goldstein and the spirit of '76. A cura di Anthony Slide [Book Review].   GRIFFITHIANA n51/52:265 Oct 1994
GOLEBIEWSKA, MARIA
   Golebiewska, M.   Film pod presja.   filmog stills   KINO 27:27-29 Jul 1993
GOLFUS, BILLY   See also WHEN BILLY BROKE HIS HEAD... AND OTHER TALES OF WONDER
GOLOS TRAVY   f (d Motuzko, Natalia 1995 Ukraine)
   Reviews
   Stratton, D.   "The Voice of the Herbs" ("Golos travy").   credits   VARIETY 358:83 Feb 20/26 1995
GOMEZ, GABRIEL
   Gomez, G.   Homocolonialism: looking for Latinos in "Apartment Zero" and "Paris Is Burning."   bibliog stills   PS 14:117-124 n1/2 1994/95
GOMEZ MURIEL, EMILIO   See also REDES
GOMEZ, NICK   See also LAWS OF GRAVITY; NEW JERSEY DRIVE
   Mixon, V.   "New Jersey Drive."   il   INDEP 18:16+ [2p] Jan/Feb 1995
   Smith, G.   Teenage kicks.   il stills   F COM 31:74-77 Jan/Feb 1995
GONG, LI
   Elley, D. and Williams, M.   Going, going, gong?   il   VARIETY 358:9 Feb 27/Mar 5 1995
GONZALEZ LOPEZ, PALMIRA
   Livio, J.   Catalogo del cine espanol volumen F2: peliculas de ficcion 1921-1930. Di Palmira Gonzalez Lopez e Joaquin T. Canovas Belchi [Book Review].   GRIFFITHIANA n51/52:252 Oct 1994
GOODIS, DAVID
   Sallis, J.   David Goodis: life in black and white.   il   ARMCHAIR DET 26:16-22+ [12p] n2 1993
GOODMAN, JONATHAN
   McSherry, F.D., Jr.   Acts of murder. By Jonathan Goodman [Book Review].   ARMCHAIR DET 27:108-109 n1 1994
GOODRICH QUALITY THEATRES
   Oppenheimer, J.   A new take on the buying biz.   il port   BOXOFFICE 131:90+ [2p] Apr 1995
GOODWIN, RON
   Collector's corner.   discog   F SCORE MONTHLY n40:5 Dec 1993
GORBMAN, CLAUDIA
   Gorbman, C.   The state of film music criticism.   bibliog il   CINEASTE 21:72-75 n1/2 1995
   Rosenbaum, J.   Audio-vision: sound on screen. By Michael Chion. Edited and translated by Claudia Gorbman [Book Review].   CINEASTE 21:94-95 n1/2 1995
GORDON, STUART   See also ROBOTJOX
GORGON, THE   f (d Fisher, Terence 1964 Gt Br)
   Bernardo, J.M.   "La leyenda de Vandorf."   credits stills   NOSFERATU n6:92-93 Apr 1991
GOSSIP COLUMNISTS
   United States
   Lears, J.   Gutter populist [Book Review].   NEW REPUB 212:39-42 Jan 9/16 1995
GOSSIP COLUMNS
   United States
   Brodkey, H.   The last word on Winchell.   il   NEW YORKER 70:70-78 Jan 30 1995
GOTHAR, PETER   See also RESZLEG, A
   Gothar, P.   "Reszleg" - reszletek.   il interv stills   F VILAG 38:6-9 n2 1995
GOTHIC FILM
   Women in Film
   Psychological Analysis
   Berg, E.K.   "Rebecca."   bibliog stills   Z n1:26-29 (n47) 1994
GOTTARDI, MICHELE   For film reviews see author under the following titles: CON GLI OCCHI CHIUSI
   Gottardi, M.   Cinema arabo.   stills   SEGNO n63:88-89 Sep/Oct 1993
   Gottardi, M.   Dizionario dei cineasti albanesi.   il   SEGNO n72:67 Mar/Apr 1995
   Gottardi, M.   La prigione dell'anima.   il stills   SEGNO n63:14-16 Sep/Oct 1993
   Gottardi, M.   Vicina, lontana.   stills   SEGNO n72:66-68 Mar/Apr 1995
GOUDET, STEPHANE   For film reviews see author under the following titles: PERIL JEUNE, LE
   Ciment, M. and Goudet, S.   Entretien avec Abbas Kiarostami.   il interv stills

POSITIF n408:14-19 Feb 1995
Goudet, S. La reprise. il stills POSITIF n408:9-13 Feb 1995
GOUGH-YATES, KEVIN
   Codelli, L. Aufbruch ins Ungewisse. Oesterreichische Filmschaffende in der
      Emigration vor 1945. A cura di Christian Cargnelli, Michael Omasta [Book
      Reviews]. GRIFFITHIANA n51/52:251 Oct 1994
GOULD, HEYWOOD See also TRIAL BY JURY
GOUPIL, ROMAIN See also CONTRE L'OUBLI
GOVERNI, GIANCARLO
   Comuzio, E. Giancarlo Governi: Vittorio De Sica. Parlami d'amore Mariu [Book
      Review]. il C FORUM 34:93-94 Sep (n337) 1994
Government and politics See POLITICS AND GOVERNMENT
GOVERNMENT CONTROL
   Canada
      Loiselle, M.-C. La nef des fous. il 24 IMAGES n75:3 Dec/Jan 1994/95
   China (People's Republic, since 1949)
      Documentary Film
         Papineau, E. Le documentaire chinois de la "reforme": la Chine maquillee par
            l'etat. bibliog glos il CINEMAS 3:87-102 n2/3 1993
GOVERNMENT INVESTIGATION
   United States
      History
         Morlan, D.B. Slapstick contributions to WWII propaganda: The Three Stooges
            and Abbott and Costello. bibliog STUDIES POP CULT 17:29-43 n1 1994
GOVERNMENT REGULATION
   Europe, Western
      Audience, Youth
         Brudny, W. Jugendmedienschutz in Europa. table MEDIEN 38:376-377 n6 1994
      National Consciousness
         Attali, J. Hollywood vs. Europe: the next round. il JOURNAL WGA 7:26-27
            Feb 1994
GOVERNMENT SUPPORT
   Argentina
      Di Nubila, D. Argentine gov't OKs aid. stat VARIETY 358:54 Mar 27/Apr 2
         1995
   Australia
      Dutchak, P. Multimedia and the cultural statement. il stat stills C PAPERS
         n102:32-35 Dec 1994
      Woods, M. New S. Wales maps strategy to lure films. VARIETY 358:41 Mar
         27/Apr 2 1995
   Belgium
      Bilan 1994 de la Commission de Selection des Films du Ministere de la
         Communaute Francaise. stat tables MONITEUR n127:5-6 Jan 1995
      Qui s'occupe (encore) de la politique culturelle audiovisuelle en Communaute
         francaise? MONITEUR n126:11 Dec 1994
   Canada
      Acheson, K. and Maule, C.J. International regimes for trade, investment, and
         labour mobility in the cultural industries. bibliog CAN J COM 19:401-421
         n3/4 1994
      Dorland, M. The war machine: American culture, Canadian cultural sovereignty
         & film policy. CAN J F STUD 1:35-48 n2 1991
      Gasher, M. Ted Magder. Canada's Hollywood: the Canadian state and feature
         films [Book Review]. CAN J F STUD 3:101-104 n2 1994
      Straw, W. Canada's Hollywood: the Canadian state and feature films. By Ted
         Magder [Book Review]. CAN J COM 19:566-567 n3/4 1994
      Cultural Context
         Audley, P. Cultural industries policy: objectives, formulation, and
            evaluation. bibliog CAN J COM 19:317-352 n3/4 1994
   Europe, Western
      Bilan 1994 des films belges soutenus par les structures d'aides europeennes.
         MONITEUR n128:30-31 Feb 1995
      Ottmar, T.W. Fritt fram a soke ef-stotte. il interv port F&K n7:34-35 1993
      Williams, M. and Stern, A. EC wants to double financial support for film,
         TV. VARIETY 358:43-44 Feb 13/19 1995
   Germany (Federal Republic, 1949-1990)
      Trenczak, H. Gisela Hundertmark, Louis Saul (Hrsg.): "Foerderung essen Filme
         auf" [Book Review]. BLIMP [n1]:65 Mar 1985
   Germany (Federal Republic, since 1990)
      Blaney, M. Ein Gespraech mit Klaus Keil. port KINO(BRD) n1:6-7 1995
      Blaney, M. Interview with Klaus Keil. port KINO(BRD) n1:4-5 1995
   New Zealand
      Short Film
         Drinnan, J. Mates rates fade on shorts shoots. ONFILM 11:5 n11 1994/95
   Norway
      Exhibition
         Fonn, E.B. Regjeringen prioriterer kultur. il F&K n7:32-33 1993
   United States
      Bart, P. Newtering the arts. il VARIETY 358:6+ [2p] Feb 6/12 1995
      Nicholson, J. (Two) 2% solution. stat AFTERIMAGE 22:3 Dec 1994
      Media Arts
         Esbjornson, M. Media arts madness. il stills INDEP 18:6-7+ [3p] Jan/Feb
            1995
         Shapiro, M. Tough cookies. il ports INDEP 18:6-8 Mar 1995
GRADOWSKI, KRZYSZTOF
   Gradowski, K. Jutro Krakow. REZYSER n18:1 1993
   Gradowski, K. O zgromadzeniu europejskiej sekcji FISTAV, porozumieniu z
      Dunczykami i projekcie ustawy o kinematografii. REZYSER n15:5 1993
GRAEF, CHRISTEL
   Graef, C. Andreas Hoentsch. biog filmog il F & FERNSEHEN 22:28-29 n6 1994
   Graef, C. Der erste Film nach acht Jahren. port F & FERNSEHEN 22:98-99 n6
      1994
   Graef, C. Der erste Film nach elf Jahren. il F & FERNSEHEN 22:112-115 n6
      1994
   Graef, C. Der Weg zum ersten Spielfilm. il interv F & FERNSEHEN 22:54-69
      n6 1994
   Graef, C. Erfahrungen im Spielfilm-Studio. il F & FERNSEHEN 22:12-25 n6
      1994
   Graef, C. Erfahrungen im Spielfilm-Studio. il F & FERNSEHEN 22:36-41 n6
      1994
   Graef, C. "Erster Verlust." il F & FERNSEHEN 22:26-27 n6 1994

Graef, C. Hannes Schoenemann. biog filmog il F & FERNSEHEN 22:70-72 n6
   1994
Graef, C. Hochschulfilme. il F & FERNSEHEN 22:103-106 n6 1994
Graef, C. Hochschulfilme. il F & FERNSEHEN 22:30-35 n6 1994
Graef, C. Hochschulfilme. il F & FERNSEHEN 22:73-81 n6 1994
Graef, C. Hochschulfilme. il F & FERNSEHEN 22:8-11 n6 1994
Graef, C. Hochschulfilme. il interv F & FERNSEHEN 22:50-53 n6 1994
Graef, C. Joerg Foth. biog filmog il F & FERNSEHEN 22:48-49 n6 1994
Graef, C. Lehrzeit im Studio. il F & FERNSEHEN 22:102-103 n6 1994
Graef, C. Operativer Vorgang "Zweifler." il F & FERNSEHEN 22:92-97 n6 1994
Graef, C. Post Scriptum. il F & FERNSEHEN 22:116-119 n6 1994
Graef, C. Sibylle Schoenemann. biog filmog il F & FERNSEHEN 22:100-101 n6
   1994
Graef, C. Startversuche im Spielfilm-Studio. il interv F & FERNSEHEN
   22:107-111 n6 1994
Graef, C. Weitere Projekte. il F & FERNSEHEN 22:42-47 n6 1994
Graef, C. Weitere Versuche. F & FERNSEHEN 22:88-91 n6 1994
Graef, C. Zurueck im Spielfilm-Studio. il F & FERNSEHEN 22:82-87 n6 1994
GRAENICHER, DIETER See also TRANSIT URI
GRAF, DOMINIK See also SIEGER, DIE
GRAFE, FRIEDA
   Grafe, F. Eine Schweizer Erfindung. stills C(SWITZ) 40:37-50 1994
Grand Illusion See GRANDE ILLUSION, LA
GRANDE COCOMERO, IL f (d Archibugi, Francesca 1993 It/Fr)
   Reviews
      Beaulieu, J. "La grosse pasteque." SEQUENCES n174:48 Sep/Oct 1994
GRANDE ILLUSION, LA f (Grand Illusion d Renoir, Jean 1937 Fr)
   Jeancolas, J.-P. Geraniums [Book Reviews]. stills POSITIF n408:94-95 Feb
      1995
GRANGE, MARIE-FRANCOISE
   Grange, M.-F. Paysage resnaisien ou variations autour de la mise en espace
      du temps. bibliog still CINEMAS 5:135-146 n1/2 1994
GRANGE, PIERRE See also EN MAI...FAIS CE QU'IL TE PLAIT
GRANGER, DOROTHY
   Lentz, H., III. Obituaries. biogs filmogs obits ports CLASSIC n237:57-59
      Mar 1995
GRANIER-DEFERRE, PIERRE See also PETIT GARCON, LE
GRANT, EDMOND For film reviews see author under the following titles: COBB;
   SHALLOW GRAVE; SPEECHLESS
GRANUM, BJORN
   Dodsfall. biogs obits ports F&K n7:37 1993
GRASSO, MARY ANN
   Grasso, M.A. Coming together. il port BOXOFFICE 131:bet p82 and 83
      [pSW8-SW9] Apr 1995
GRAY, GARY
   Fitzgerald, M. Gary Gray: the former child star is heading for Memphis.
      biog credits filmog il ports stills CLASSIC n236:bet p32 and 33 [pC10-C11+
      (3p)] Feb 1995
GRAY, JAMES See also LITTLE ODESSA
   Aghed, J. Entretien avec James Gray. interv stills POSITIF n407:8-11 Jan
      1995
   Thomson, P. "Little Odessa." port INDEP 18:15-16 Apr 1995
GRAY, LOUISE For film reviews see author under the following titles: FAR FROM
   HOME: THE ADVENTURES OF YELLOW DOG
GRAY, TIM
   Gray, T. David Hodgin. obit VARIETY 358:58 Mar 20/26 1995
GRAZZINI, GIOVANNI
   Comuzio, E. Giovanni Grazzini: Cinema '93 [Book Review]. C FORUM 34:95 Oct
      (n338) 1994
GRBIC, BOGDAN
   Grbic, B. Hans-Michael Bock (Hrsg.): "Cinegraph" [Book Review]. BLIMP
      [n1]:65 Mar 1985
   Grbic, B. Meine persoenlichen Grenzueberschreitungen. BLIMP n30:68 Winter
      1994
   Grbic, B. Nicholas Ray=I'm a stranger here myself. filmog il BLIMP
      [n1]:26-33 Mar 1985
Great Britain See as a subheading under individual subject headings See
   BRITISH BOARD OF FILM CLASSIFICATION; BRITISH FILM INSTITUTE (London); BRITISH
   FILM INSTITUTE. NATIONAL FILM AND TELEVISION ARCHIVE (London)
GREAT DAY IN HARLEM, A f (d Bach, Jean 1995 USA)
   Comer, B. "A Great Day in Harlem" evokes the jazz age. AMCIN 76:83-84 Feb
      1995
   Reviews
      Beck, H.C. "A Great Day in Harlem." still VILLAGE VOICE 40:56 Feb 21 1995
      Kelleher, E. "A Great Day in Harlem." credits FJ 98:62 Mar 1995
GREAT OAKS ENTERTAINMENT
   Busch, A.M. Hughes and Mestres team in Disney-based Great Oaks Ent. port
      VARIETY 358:22 Feb 20/26 1995
GREAT SCIENCE FICTION
   These boots were made for hawkin': part IV - more rogue's gallery. il F
      SCORE MONTHLY n40:6 Dec 1993
GREED f (d Stroheim, Erich von 1925 USA)
   Ciment, M. BFI film classics [Book Reviews]. stills POSITIF n408:75-77 Feb
      1995
   Codelli, L. "Greed." Di Jonathan Rosenbaum [Book Reviews]. GRIFFITHIANA
      n51/52:260 Oct 1994
GREEEN, RAY For film reviews see author under the following titles: PRIEST
GREEN, JESSE
   Green, J. The bug. il PREM 8:20-21 Feb 1995
GREENAWAY, PETER See also DROWNING BY NUMBERS; STAIRS 1 GENEVA; ZED AND TWO
   NOUGHTS, A
   Caruso, G. Equoreo Greenaway. il interv still SEGNO n63:2-6 Sep/Oct 1993
GREENE, JAY
   Greene, J. Rights squabble begins over new media explosion. VARIETY 357:4+
      [2p] Jan 2/8 1995

GREENE, RAY For film reviews see author under the following titles: ADDICTION, THE; BASKETBALL DIARIES, THE; COLDBLOODED; CRUMB; HOMAGE; I JUST WASN'T MADE FOR THESE TIMES; KLA$H; RHYTHM THIEF; USUAL SUSPECTS, THE; WHEN BILLY BROKE HIS HEAD... AND OTHER TALES OF WONDER; YOUNG POISONER'S HANDBOOK, THE
Greene, R. Second sight: "Boxoffice" remembers 75 films from 75 years at the movies. il stills BOXOFFICE 131:36-38+ [28p] Mar 1995
Greene, R. The big picture. il BOXOFFICE 131:150 Apr 1995
GREENFIELD, AMY See also ANTIGONE/RITES FOR THE DEAD
Greenfield, A. "Tales of Hoffmann." il stills F COM 31:26-31 Mar/Apr 1995
Pipolo, T. Making "Antigone/Rites of Passion." interv stills MILLENNIUM n26:34-55 Fall 1992
GREENMAN, BEN For film reviews see author under the following titles: CIRCLE OF FRIENDS; LEGENDS OF THE FALL; SEX, DRUGS AND DEMOCRACY
Blank, I. Letters: flying Dutch. VILLAGE VOICE 40:4 Mar 7 1995
GREENSPAN, CHARLOTTE
Greenspan, C. Custen, George F. Bio/pics: how Hollywood constructed public history [Book Review]. stat UFAJ 46:47-49 n3 1994
GREENWALD, JOHN
Greenwald, J. Battle for remote control. il TIME 145:69-71 Spring 1995
GREENWALD, MAGGIE See also BALLAD OF LITTLE JO, THE
GREER, DABBS
Valley, R. Dabbs Greer. il interv port stills SCARLET STREET n17:43+ [6p] Winter 1995
GREGG, COLIN See also LAMB
GREGGORY, PASCAL
Millea, H. All the Queen's men. biogs il intervs ports still PREM 8:76-79 Feb 1995
GREGOIRE, PIERRE
Gregoire, P. Gardies, Andre. L'espace au cinema [Book Reviews]. CINEMAS 5:229-232 n1/2 1994
GREIMAS, ALGIRDAS JULIEN
Everaert-Desmedt, N. L'eternite au quotidien: la representation des temps dans "Les ailes du desir" de Wim Wenders. bibliog diag CINEMAS 5:105-122 n1/2 1994
GREMLINS f (d Dante, Joe 1984 USA)
   Sound Track Reviews
Dursin, A. "Gremlins." F SCORE MONTHLY n36/37:32 Aug/Sep 1993
GREYSON, JOHN See also MAKING OF "MONSTERS", THE; ZERO PATIENCE
Bronski, M. Queer looks: perspectves on lesbian and gay film and video. Edited by Martha Gever, John Greyson and Pratibha Parmar [Book Reviews]. still CINEASTE 21:90-92 n1/2 1995
GRIERSON AND GOUZENKO f (d Kinch, Martin 1986 Can)
   Marxist Analysis
Forsyth, S. The failures of nationalism and documentary: "Grierson and Gouzenko." CAN J F STUD 1:74-82 n1 1990
GRIERSON, JOHN
Grierson, J. Relations with the United States film industry. CAN J F STUD 1:83-88 n1 1990
GRIEVESON, LEE
Grieveson, L. Steven Cohan and Ina Rae Hark (eds). Screening the male: exploring masculinities in Hollywood cinema [Book Reviews]. SCREEN 35:400-406 n4 1994
GRIFFIN, NANCY
Griffin, N. New kid in town. il PREM 8:64-69 Feb 1995
GRIFFIN, SEAN
Griffin, S. The illusion of "identity": gender and racial representation in "Aladdin." ANIMATION J 3:64-73 n1 1994
Griffith, David Wark See GRIFFITH, D.W.
GRIFFITH, D.W. See also BIRTH OF A NATION, THE; INTOLERANCE
Cantrill, A. The films of D.W. Griffith. By Scott Simmon [Book Review]. CANTRILL'S FMNTS n73/74:19 May 1994
Cherchi Usai, P. The films of D.W. Griffith. By Scott Simmon [Book Reviews]. GRIFFITHIANA n51/52:259 Oct 1994
Cherchi Usai, P. The films of D.W. Griffith. By Scott Simmon [Book Reviews]. J F PRES n49:72-73 Oct 1994
Creekmur, C.K. Roberta Pearson. Eloquent gestures: the transformation of performance style in the Griffith Biograph films [Book Review]. ARACHNE 1:266-269 n2 1994
Daniel, F. Megszallott az utolso centig. il stills F VILAG 38:14-17 n3 1995
GRIFFITHS, KEITH
Griffiths, K. Anxious visions. il stills VERTIGO (UK) 1:47-52 n4 1994/95
GRILLO, VIRGIL
Movshovitz, H. Virgil Grillo. biog obit port INDEP 18:11-13 Jan/Feb 1995
GRINNAGE, JACK
Lilley, J. Jack Grinnage. il interv stills SCARLET STREET n17:59-61+ [4p] Winter 1995
GROB, NORBERT
Codelli, L. "Greed." Di Jonathan Rosenbaum [Book Reviews]. GRIFFITHIANA n51/52:260 Oct 1994
GROSOLI, FABRIZIO For film reviews see author under the following titles: DUNG CHE SAI DUK; ONLY THE BRAVE; VOILA
Grosoli, F. Locarno: seguendo la ricerca, senza scordare il pubblico. stills C FORUM 34:38-42 Sep (n337) 1994
Zappoli, G. Come e per chi? il port SEGNO n71:16-18 Jan/Feb 1995
GROSS, HOLGER
Prokop, T. Production design. il C FANTAS 26:52-53 n3 1995
GROSS, LARRY
Gross, L. Robust vanities [Book Review]. il S&S 5:38 Feb 1995
GROSSE FATIGUE f (d Blanc, Michel 1994 Fr)
   Reviews
Derrer, J.C. Doppeltes Spiel. credits stills F BUL 36:51-52 n6 (n197) 1994
Gendron, S. "Grosse fatigue." credits still SEQUENCES n174:36 Sep/Oct 1994
GROSSES
   International Aspects
Groves, D. "Gump" bows in Japan with $7.6 mil. stat VARIETY 358:8+ [2p] Mar 20/26 1995
Groves, D. Japan goes gaga over "The Mask." stat VARIETY 358:14+ [2p] Mar 6/12 1995

Groves, D. Japan, Oz high spots of overseas b.o. stat VARIETY 358:23-24 Mar 27/Apr 2 1995
Groves, D. O'seas b.o. year enters like "Lion." stat VARIETY 357:18+ [2p] Jan 9/15 1995
Groves, D. "Quiz" shows spotty b.o. overseas. stat VARIETY 358:18+ [2p] Feb 27/Mar 5 1995
Groves, D. "Star Trek" fever hits German b.o. stat VARIETY 358:12+ [2p] Feb 20/26 1995
Groves, D. Upscale pix draw big Euro crowds. stat VARIETY 358:12+ [2p] Mar 13/19 1995
Harris, M. "Lion" king over Euro holiday b.o. stat VARIETY 357:14 Jan 2/8 1995
Woods, M. O'seas b.o. is "Terminal." stat VARIETY 358:12+ [2p] Feb 13/19 1995
Woods, M. "Stargate" hits $30 mil o'seas cume. stat VARIETY 358:14+ [2p] Feb 6/12 1995
Worldwide rentals beat domestic take. stat table VARIETY 358:28 Feb 13/19 1995
      Belgium
         Brussels
L'annee 1994 a Bruxelles. stat tables MONITEUR n127:10-15 Jan 1995
      New Zealand
Wakefield, P. NZ b.o. continues to grow. stat ONFILM [12]:9 n2 1995
      United States
Barometer '95: 1994 in review. stat table BOXOFFICE 131:20-21 Mar 1995
Klady, L. Disney takes "Lion's" share of '94 boffo b.o. stat tables VARIETY 357:13+ [2p] Jan 9/15 1995
Klady, L. Pic pack uneven at record b.o. stat VARIETY 357:18 Jan 2/8 1995
Meisel, M. Are blockbuster releases devouring the industry? stat stills FJ 98:26+ [3p] Mar 1995
Thompson, A. Little giants. il stat F COM 31:56-60+ [6p] Mar/Apr 1995
Top 100 domestic grossers. stat table VARIETY 358:bet p88 and 173 [pA84] Feb 20/26 1995
         Independent Production
Top grossing independent films. stat table VARIETY 358:bet p88 and 173 [pA84] Feb 20/26 1995
GROSSESSE NERVEUSE f (d Rabaglia, Denis 1993 Fr/Switz)
   Reviews
Lachat, P. "Grossesse Nerveuse." credits C(SWITZ) 40:219 1994
GROSVENOR, CHARLES See also ONCE UPON A FOREST
GROULX, GILLES
Noel, C. Gilles Groulx et les medias. il obit port stills 24 IMAGES n75:20-25 Dec/Jan 1994/95
GROVES, DON
Groves, D. Aussie film scales walls of China. VARIETY 358:17 Mar 13/19 1995
Groves, D. Cox's plan for cable network Down Under hits roadblock. VARIETY 358:48 Mar 6/12 1995
Groves, D. "Gump" bows in Japan with $7.6 mil. stat VARIETY 358:8+ [2p] Mar 20/26 1995
Groves, D. It's bizzy down under. il stat stills VARIETY 358:61+ [2p] Feb 27/Mar 5 1995
Groves, D. Japan goes gaga over "The Mask." stat VARIETY 358:14+ [2p] Mar 6/12 1995
Groves, D. Japan, Oz high spots of overseas b.o. stat VARIETY 358:23-24 Mar 27/Apr 2 1995
Groves, D. Kiwi pix grab H'wood's eye. VARIETY 358:11+ [2p] Feb 6/12 1995
Groves, D. O'seas b.o. year enters like "Lion." stat VARIETY 357:18+ [2p] Jan 9/15 1995
Groves, D. "Quiz" shows spotty b.o. overseas. stat VARIETY 358:18+ [2p] Feb 27/Mar 5 1995
Groves, D. Ronin ankles Sydney arthouse exhibition. VARIETY 357:30 Jan 9/15 1995
Groves, D. "Star Trek" fever hits German b.o. stat VARIETY 358:12+ [2p] Feb 20/26 1995
Groves, D. UIP reups Williams-Jones. stat VARIETY 357:30 Jan 9/15 1995
Groves, D. Upscale pix draw big Euro crowds. stat VARIETY 358:12+ [2p] Mar 13/19 1995
GRUBER, EBERHARD
Gruber, E. Une reprise impossible? "Effi Briest" et la question de ses reecritures filmiques. CINEMAS 4:59-71 n1 1993
GRUENBERG, LEONARD S.
Obituaries. biogs obits VARIETY 358:74-75 Mar 6/12 1995
GRUENDGENS, GUSTAF See also SCHRITT VOM WEGE, DER
GRUGEAU, GERARD For film reviews see author under the following titles: AMOUREUX, LES; ANGE NOIR, L'; BOSNA!; SILENCES DU PALAIS, LES; VEILLEES D'ARMES: LE JOURNALISME EN TEMPS DE GUERRE
Grugeau, G. Images du monde arabe. 24 IMAGES n76:46 Spring 1995
GRUNDEN, CHRIS For film reviews see author under the following titles: BILLY MADISON; HEAVYWEIGHTS; HIDEAWAY; JERKY BOYS, THE; RICHIE RICH; STREET FIGHTER
GRUNDMANN, ROY
Grundmann, R. Black nationhood and the rest in the West. interv port CINEASTE 21:28-31 n1/2 1995
GRUNWALSKY, FERENC See also GOLDBERG VARIACIOK
GRUPPO FININVEST
Guider, E. Fininvest subsid Medusa opens L.A. office. VARIETY 358:176 Feb 20/26 1995
   Economic Aspects
Zecchinelli, C. Seven investors rumored eyeing Fininvest stake. stat VARIETY 358:41 Mar 27/Apr 2 1995
GSCHWANDTNER, MANFRED
Seiter, B. and Gschwandtner, M. (Acht und dreissigste) 38. Festival Internationale del Film Locarno. credits il BLIMP [n2]:54-55 Winter 1985
GUANGCHANG f (d Zhang, Yuan 1995 China)
   Reviews
Rooney, D. "The Square" ("Guangchang"). credits VARIETY 358:52 Feb 13/19 1995
GUARD, CANDY
Guard, C. Rough humour. still S&S 5:69 Jan 1995
GUEISSAZ-TEUFEL, DAGMAR See also PASSIFLORA

GUERIN, JOSE LUIS See also INNISFREE; MOTIVOS DE BERTA, LOS
  Angulo, J. and others. Entrevista: Garay, Guerin, Jorda y Portabella. il
    interv stills NOSFERATU n9:68-87 Jun 1992
  Torres, S. Los motivos de Guerin. biog il stills NOSFERATU n9:38-47 Jun
    1992
GUERRIERI, ROMOLO See also JOHNNY YUMA
GUERRINI, MINO See also DECAMERON NO. 2 - LE ALTRE NOVELLE DEL BOCCACCIO
GUGLIELMI, MASSIMO See also ESTATE DI BOBBY CHARLTON, L'
GUI TU f (d Leung, Ray 1995 Hong Kong)
    Reviews
  Elley, D. "Back to Roots" ("Gui tu"). credits VARIETY 358:76 Feb 27/Mar 5
    1995
GUIDA, FRED
  Guida, F. Merry Christmas from Charles Dickens... and Thomas Edison. il
    FIR 45:2-5 Nov/Dec 1994
GUIDER, ELIZABETH
  Guider, E. Fininvest subsid Medusa opens L.A. office. VARIETY 358:176 Feb
    20/26 1995
GUN THE MAN DOWN f (d McLaglen, Andrew V. 1956 USA)
  Anez, N. Westerns. stills FIR 45:18-27 Nov/Dec 1994
GUNNING, TOM
  Gunning, T. Obscure genealogies: Sitney's modernism of vision [Book Review].
    il MILLENNIUM n26:78-87 Fall 1992
GUNTHER, ALBERT C.
  Gunther, A. C. Overrating the X-rating: the third-person perception and
    support for censorship of pornography. bibliog stat tables J COMM 45:27-38
    n1 1995
GURUKU CANTIK SEKALI f (d Ida, Farida Indonesia)
  Sen, K. Women directors but whose films? il CINEMAYA n25/26:10-13
    Autumn/Winter 1994/95
GUSKIN, HAROLD
  Lahr, J. The great Guskin. il NEW YORKER 71:44-49 Mar 20 1995
GUSTAFSSON, ANDERS
  Nodfors, M. Tonsaker estet. port CHAPLIN 36:12-13 n6 (n255) 1994/95
GUSTAVE FLAUBERT DREAMS OF TRAVEL BUT THE ILLNESS OF HIS MOTHER PREVENTS IT f
  (d Kobland, Ken 1986 USA)
  Kobland, K. Storyboards, plans and notes for "Frame" (1976) and "Flaubert
    Dreams of Travel" (1986). il MILLENNIUM n25:31-35 Summer 1991
GUTIERREZ ALEA, TOMAS See also FRESA Y CHOCOLATE
  Carro, N. "Fresa y chocolate." interv stills DICINE n59:2-3 Nov/Dec 1994
  West, J. "Strawberry and Chocolate," ice cream and tolerance. interv port
    stills CINEASTE 21:16-20 n1/2 1995
GUTIERREZ ARAGON, MANUEL See also REY DEL RIO, EL
GYLLENHAAL, STEPHEN See also DANGEROUS WOMAN, A; LOSING ISAIAH
  Taylor, E. Raising "Isaiah." port VILLAGE VOICE 40:64 Mar 28 1995
GYORFFY, MIKLOS
  Gyorffy, M. Ha en filmlexikont szerkesztenek [Book Review]. F VILAG
    38:53-54 n4 1995
HACKETT, ALBERT
  Milestones. obit TIME 145:25 Mar 27 1995
HACKFORD, TAYLOR See also DOLORES CLAIBORNE
HADDAL, PER
  Fonn, E.B. Ivo Caprino - portrett av askeladden i norsk film [Book Review].
    il F&K n1:19 1994
  Iversen, G. Aerbodig biografi om norsk films askeladd [Book Review]. il Z
    n1:39 (n47) 1994
HADES f (d Achternbusch, Herbert 1995 FR Ger)
    Reviews
  Hansen, E. "Hades." credits VARIETY 358:66 Mar 6/12 1995
HADJIDAKIS, MANOS
  Hommages posthumes. biogs il obits port SEQUENCES n174:56-58 Sep/Oct 1994
HADJ-MOUSSA, RATIBA
  Hadj-Moussa, R. Le corps dansant au cinema. bibliog CINEMAS 3:205-221 n2/3
    1993
HAGELBACK, JOHAN
  Fors, M. Johan Hagelback - piimaanimaation mestari. filmog il still PEILI
    17:14-15 n4 1993
HAGOPIAN, KEVIN JACK
  Hagopian, K.J. Columbia Pictures: portrait of a studio. Edited by Bernard F.
    Dick [Book Review]. F CRITICISM 19:95-99 n2 1994/95
HAGYMAS, ISTVAN
  Komar, E. Casanova mas szemmel [Book Review]. F VILAG 38:43 n3 1995
HAHN, DON
  Alexander, M. The men behind the "King." ports VARIETY 357:10 Jan 9/15
    1995
HAILE, MICHAEL For film reviews see author under the following titles: STREET
  FIGHTER
  Haile, M. Reminting "Schindler's" gold. il stills BOXOFFICE 131:66+ [4p]
    Apr 1995
HAIM, MONICA
  Haim, M. Amerique autre et meme. stills 24 IMAGES n75:49-50 Dec/Jan
    1994/95
  Haim, M. Instinct de survie et determinisme social: quelques films d'Arturo
    Ripstein. stills 24 IMAGES n75:37-39 Dec/Jan 1994/95
HAINISCH, BERNHARD
  Hainisch, B. and Pilz, T. Werner Herzogs "Jeder fuer sich und Gott gegen
    alle" - ein Film. il stills BLIMP n30:16-22 Winter 1994
HAIZI WANG f (d Chen, Kaige 1988 China)
  Brochu, D. Marques d'un cinema moderne: "Le roi des enfants." bibliog glos
    still CINEMAS 3:8-22 n2/3 1993
HAJEK, PETER
  Winter, R. Interview mit Peter Hajek. il interv BLIMP [n1]:50-51 Mar 1985
HAKE, TED
  Slide, A. The Slide area film book notes [Book Reviews]. CLASSIC
    n237:42-44+ [4p] Mar 1995
HALACZINSKY, THOMAS
  Stern, A. Thomas Halaczinsky. port INDEP 18:20-21 Jan/Feb 1995
HALIMUN f (d Sofia, W.D. 1982 Indonesia)
  Sen, K. Women directors but whose films? il CINEMAYA n25/26:10-13
    Autumn/Winter 1994/95

HALL, CAROL
  Gates, D. and Hall, C. Will Fry come in from the cold? port NEWSWK 125:69
    Mar 13 1995
HALL, HOWARD See also INTO THE DEEP
HALLIGAN, FIONNUALA
  Halligan, F. Media Asia unveils pic slate. VARIETY 358:31 Mar 20/26 1995
HALPERIN, MICHAEL
  Halperin, M. A failure to communicate... il JOURNAL WGA 7:22-23 Feb 1994
HALTER, MAREK See also TZEDEK
HAMILL, MARK
  Weiner, R. Spaced out. port VARIETY 358:9 Feb 27/Mar 5 1995
HAMILTON, ALEX For film reviews see author under the following titles:
  ADVENTURES OF PRISCILLA, QUEEN OF THE DESERT, THE; FEAR OF A BLACK
  HAT; FORREST GUMP; LADYBIRD LADYBIRD; MINA TANNENBAUM; WAR OF THE
  BUTTONS
HAMLET f (d Coronado, Celestino 1976 Gt Br)
  Aldarondo, R. "Hamlet." credits NOSFERATU n8:71 Feb 1992
HAMLET f (d Zeffirelli, Franco 1990 USA)
  Latorre, J.M. Shakespeare segun Zeffirelli. il stills NOSFERATU n8:48-55
    Feb 1992
    Murders in Film
  Reeves, B. Murder most foul: the many uses of atropine. il ARMCHAIR DET
    27:82-84 n1 1994
HAMLET (fictional character)
  Kamp, D. The importance of being Hamlet. il stills VANITY FAIR 58:74+ [3p]
    Mar 1995
HAMMER FILM PRODUCTIONS, LTD.
  Angulo, J. Terence Fisher, revisitador de mitos. biog il stills NOSFERATU
    n6:22-43 Apr 1991
  Eriksen, F. Taste of fear. il stills Z n1:14-19 (n47) 1994
  Fuentes bibliograficas e iconograficas. bibliog NOSFERATU n6:102 Apr 1991
  Harrison, S. House of horror: the complete Hammer Films story. By Allen
    Eyles, Robert Adkinson & Nicholas Fry with additional revisions by Jack
    Hunter [Book Review]. il FATAL VISIONS n17:30 1994
  Ma Latorre, J. Terence Fisher: notas a la sombra de un estilo. il stills
    NOSFERATU n6:44-49 Apr 1991
  Molina Foix, J.A. Hammer Films: una herencia de miedo. il stills NOSFERATU
    n6:4-21 Apr 1991
  Schiller, R. Christopher Lee and Peter Cushing and horror cinema: a
    filmography of their 22 collaborations. By Mark A. Miller [Book Review]. F
    FAX n48:12+ [2p] Jan/Feb 1995
HAMMOND, STEFAN
  Hammond, S. Eyeball on Asia. il FATAL VISIONS n17:17-19 1994
HAMPSHIRE COLLEGE (Amherst, Massachusetts)
  Sherman, R.M. Letters: how about Hampshire? INDEP 18:5 Mar 1995
HAMRELL, HARALD
  (Sju) 7 debutanter. ports CHAPLIN 36:6-7 n6 (n255) 1994/95
HAMSUN, KNUT
  Jensen, J. This Knut's a hot media ticket in Scandinavia. VARIETY 358:47
    Mar 13/19 1995
HANCHARD, YVES See also PARTIE D'ECHECS, LA
HANCHE, OIVIND
  Hanche, O. Filmen og forste verdenskrig. still Z n4:34-35 (n46) 1993
  Hanche, O. "To liv." still Z n1:38 (n47) 1994
HAND, DAVID See also SNOW WHITE AND THE SEVEN DWARFS; SNOW WHITE AND THE SEVEN
  DWARFS
HANDELMAN, DAVID
  Handelman, D. The birth of the uncool. il stills PREM 8:84-88 Mar 1995
HANDS OF THE RIPPER f (d Sasdy, Peter 1971 Gt Br)
    Sound Track Reviews
  Larson, R.D. The vintage score: "Hands of the Ripper:" an exemplary horror
    score. il F SCORE MONTHLY n36/37:24 Aug/Sep 1993
HANDZO, STEPHEN
  Handzo, S. The golden age of film music. il ports stills CINEASTE 21:46-55
    n1/2 1995
HANEDA, SUMIKO
  Abe, M. N. Documentarists of Japan (first in a series). biog filmog port
    stills DOC BOX 1:9-13 1992
HANET, KARI
  Hanet, K. Orr, John. Cinema and modernity [Book Review]. MEDIA INFO
    AUSTRALIA n75:168 Feb 1995
  Hanet, K. Petrie, Duncan, ed. Cinema and the realms of enchantment:
    lectures, seminars and essays by Marina Warner and others [Book Review].
    MEDIA INFO AUSTRALIA n75:169 Feb 1995
  Hanet, K. Walker, John A. Art and artists on screen [Book Review]. MEDIA
    INFO AUSTRALIA n75:171 Feb 1995
  Hanet, K. Willemen, Paul. The films of Amos Gitai: a montage [Book Review].
    MEDIA INFO AUSTRALIA n75:172 Feb 1995
HANISCH, MICHAEL For film reviews see author under the following titles: SCHTONK
HANKE, KEN
  Breen, J.L. Hanke, Ken. Charlie Chan at the movies: history, filmography,
    and criticism [Book Review]. still ARMCHAIR DET 26:78 n3 1993
HANNAH, LANI For film reviews see author under the following titles: SPIDER &
  ROSE
HANNAH LEE f (d Ireland, John/Garmes, Lee 1953 USA)
  Anez, N. Westerns. stills FIR 45:18-27 Nov/Dec 1994
HANNAHAM, JAMES For film reviews see author under the following titles: MEET THE
  FEEBLES; SUPER 8 1/2
  Hannaham, J. A fellating Fellini. il VILLAGE VOICE 40:56 Mar 14 1995
HANNINEN, SAMPO
  Hanninen, S. and Auersalo, T. Animaatiota Italialaisittain. still PEILI
    17:39 n4 1993
HANNULA, MIKA For film reviews see author under the following titles:
  FLINTSTONES, THE
HANS CHRISTIAN ANDERSEN'S THUMBELINA f (d Bluth, Don/Goldman, Gary 1994
  USA/Ireland)
    Reviews
  Salakka, M. Usko rakkauteen niin kaikki jarjestyy. credit still PEILI
    18:31 n3 1994

HANS UND MARIE   f (d Hoentsch, Andreas unrealized project 1985 E Ger)
   Graef, C. Erfahrungen im Spielfilm-Studio. il F & FERNSEHEN 22:36-41 n6
      1994
HANSEN, ERIC   For film reviews see author under the following titles: BURNING
   LIFE; HADES; IN HASSLIEBE LOLA; NACHT DER REGISSEURE, DIE
   Hansen, E. German filmmaking takes commercial turn. VARIETY 358:50 Feb 6/12
      1995
HANSON, CURTIS   See also RIVER WILD, THE
HARA, KAZUO   See also YUKI YUKI TE SHINGUN; ZENSHIN SHOSETSUKA
   Gerow, A.A. Documentarists of Japan (second in a series). biog interv port
      stills DOC BOX 3:12-18 1993
HARATHER, PAUL   See also INDIEN
HARCOURT, PETER
   Harcourt, P. "Eclipse." stills C ACTION n36:17-19 1995
HARD TARGET   f (d Woo, John 1993 USA)
   Williams, T. To live and die in Hong Kong. bibliog stills C ACTION
      n36:42-52 1995
      Cinematography
   Scharres, B. The hard road to "Hard Target." il still AMCIN 74:62-64+
      [10p] Sep 1993
      Editing
   Scharres, B. "Hard Target's" first edit made easier by EMC2. AMCIN 74:68
      Sep 1993
Hard-boiled   See LATSAU SANTAM
HARDESTY, MARY
   Hardesty, M. Too PC or not too PC? DGA NEWS 19:28+ [5p] n6 1994/95
   Yonover, N.S. and others. Artists Rights Symposium: three days of
      discussion. DGA NEWS 19:26-27+ [3p] n3 1994
HAREL, PHILIPPE   See also HISTOIRE DU GARCON QUI VOULAIT QU'ON L'EMBRASSE, L'
HARK, INA RAE
   Grieveson, L. Steven Cohan and Ina Rae Hark (eds). Screening the male:
      exploring masculinities in Hollywood cinema [Book Reviews]. SCREEN
      35:400-406 n4 1994
HARLIN, RENNY   See also CUTTHROAT ISLAND; SAINT, THE
   Clark, J. Renny Harlin gets the girl. il port still PREM 8:56-64 Mar 1995
HARMAT, GYORGY   For film reviews see author under the following titles: MASK,
   THE; STAR TREK GENERATIONS
HARMON, JIM
   Breen, J.L. Harmon, Jim. Radio mystery and adventure and its appearances in
      film, television and other media [Book Review]. ARMCHAIR DET 26:78-79 n3
      1993
HARPER, ROBERT
   Laski, B. Harper back in saddle at Fox marketing. port VARIETY 357:36 Jan
      2/8 1995
HARRIS, DAMIAN   See also BAD COMPANY
HARRIS, ED
   Smith, D. FredandEd. il interv ports INTERV 25:116-123 Mar 1995
HARRIS, JAMES B.   See also BOILING POINT
   Harris, J.B. Radiographie de Woody Allen. il still POSITIF n408:33-35 Feb
      1995
HARRIS, JENNIFER
   Harris, J. Clover, Carol J. Men, women, and chain saws: gender in the modern
      horror film [Book Review]. MEDIA INFO AUSTRALIA n75:158-159 Feb 1995
HARRIS, JUDITH   For film reviews see author under the following titles: MARY
   SHELLEY'S FRANKENSTEIN; PUPPET MASTERS, THE; SCANNER COP
HARRIS, LESLEY ELLEN
   Harris, L.E. A roadmap for writers' rights on the information superhighway.
      il JOURNAL WGA 8:20-23 Feb 1995
HARRIS, MIKE
   Harris, M. "Lion" king over Euro holiday b.o. stat VARIETY 357:14 Jan 2/8
      1995
HARRISON, MATTHEW   See also RHYTHM THIEF
HARRISON, SHANE
   Harrison, S. House of horror: the complete Hammer Films story. By Allen
      Eyles, Robert Adkinson & Nicholas Fry with additional revisions by Jack
      Hunter [Book Review]. il FATAL VISIONS n17:30 1994
HARROW, KENNETH W.
   Harrow, K.W. Diawara, Manthia. African cinema: politics and culture [Book
      Review]. CINEMAS 4:183-185 n2 1994
HART, LLOYD
   Hart, L. Negotiation: "I hear what you say, but..." il C PAPERS n102:78-79
      Dec 1994
HARTLEY, HAL   See also AMATEUR; SIMPLE MEN
   Hearty, K.B. Cold as Hal. il PREM 8:46 Apr 1995
   Neff, R. Hartley's "Amateur" defies movie thriller conventions. il interv
      still FJ 98:18+ [2p] Mar 1995
HARVEY, DENNIS   For film reviews see author under the following titles: A.K.A.
   DON BONUS; ANATA GA SUKI DESU, DAI SUKI DES; CRIMINALS; LOVE IS BLIND;
   MAYA LIN: A STRONG CLEAR VISION; NEO-E-GE NARUL BONENDA
HASS, FRAUKE
   Hass, F. Der weibliche Blick - Der Blick aufs Weib. F KUNST n144:43-49 1994
HASTED, NICK   For film reviews see author under the following titles: CHASERS;
   TRAPPED IN PARADISE
HASTIE, AMELIE
   Hastie, A. Window shopping: cinema and the postmodern. Anne Friedberg [Book
      Reviews]. DISCOURSE n17.2:171-176 Winter 1994/95
HATCH, GEORGE
   Hatch, G. "Who Killed Teddy Bear?" il port stills SCARLET STREET
      n17:82-89+ [10p] Winter 1995
HATCH, JAMES V.   See also KKK BOUTIQUE AIN'T JUST REDNECKS, THE
HATTA, KAYO   See also PICTURE BRIDE
   Rony, F.T. "Picture Bride." il INDEP 18:15-16 Mar 1995
HAUN, HARRY   For film reviews see author under the following titles: JUST CAUSE;
   NOBODY'S FOOL
HAUNTING, THE   f (d Wise, Robert 1963 USA/Gt Br)
      Reviews
   Holt, W.G. "The Haunting." il stills F FAX n49:30+ [2p] Mar/Apr 1995
HAUPT, CLYDE V.
   Slide, A. The Slide area film book notes [Book Reviews]. CLASSIC n236:47-49
      Feb 1995

HAUSNER, THOMAS   See also ES LEBE UNSERE DDR
   "Es lebe unsere DDR." biog credits filmog still KINO(BRD) n1:20-21 1995
HAUT, WOODY   For film reviews see author under the following titles: TRIAL BY
   JURY
HAWKE, ETHAN
   Fuller, G. and Linklater, R. Truer than romance? il interv ports INTERV
      25:118-121 Feb 1995
   Mundy, C. Renaissance boy. biog ports stills ROLLING STONE n703:44-49+
      [7p] Mar 9 1995
HAWTHORNE, NIGEL
   Barber, L. Mad about Nigel. il VANITY FAIR 58:102-105 Jan 1995
HAYDON, JULIE
   Lentz, H., III. Obituaries. biogs filmogs il obits ports CLASSIC
      n236:57-59 Feb 1995
   Obituaries. obit VARIETY 357:80 Jan 9/15 1995
HAYWARD, SUSAN
   Cantrill, A. French national cinema. By Susan Hayward [Book Review].
      CANTRILL'S FMNTS n73/74:42-43 May 1994
HAZMAT   f (unrealized project 1989 USA)
   Clinch, C. Dancing on the truth. JOURNAL WGA 8:29 Mar 1995
HE, JIANJUN   See also YOUCHAI
HE, PING   See also PAODA SHUANG DENG
HEAD, GLENN   For film reviews see author under the following titles: CRUMB
HEALTH   See also AIDS
   United States
      Directors
   Elrick, T. Stamina on the set. DGA NEWS 19:10-11+ [3p] n3 1994
Heart in Winter, A   See COEUR EN HIVER, UN
HEARTY, KITTY BOWE
   Hearty, K.B. Bride & joy. il PREM 8:92-93 Apr 1995
   Hearty, K.B. Cold as Hal. il PREM 8:46 Apr 1995
   Hearty, K.B. "Drive" by shooting. il PREM 8:41 Mar 1995
   Hearty, K.B. Idol chatter. il interv PREM 8:48 Apr 1995
HEAVENLY CREATURES   f (d Jackson, Peter 1994 New Zealand/FR Ger)
   Jones, A. "Heavenly Creatures." il stills C FANTAS 26:42-43+ [3p] n2 1995
      Grosses
   "Divinely wicked" film wins New Yorkers. ONFILM 11:7 n11 1994/95
      Reviews
   Bruzzi, S. "Heavenly Creatures." credits S&S 5:45-46 Feb 1995
   Martini, E. "Heavenly Creatures." still C FORUM 34:11+ [2p] Sep (n337)
      1994
   Travers, P. "Heavenly Creatures." ROLLING STONE n694:104+ [2p] Nov 3 1994
HEAVY   f (d Mangold, James 1995 USA)
      Reviews
   McCarthy, T. "Heavy." credits still VARIETY 358:75 Feb 6/12 1995
HEAVYWEIGHTS   f (d Brill, Steven 1995 USA)
      Reviews
   Grunden, C. "Heavyweights." credits FJ 98:61 Mar 1995
   Klady, L. "Heavyweights." credits still VARIETY 358:74 Feb 20/26 1995
   Williamson, K. "Heavyweights." BOXOFFICE 131:bet p125 and 144 [pR31] Apr
      1995
HEBERT, PIERRE
   Jean, M. Des restes d'images non identifies. il interv stills 24 IMAGES
      n75:26-32+ [8p] Dec/Jan 1994/95
HECHT, ANN
   Codelli, L. Pre-cinema history: an encyclopedia and annotated bibliography
      of the moving image before 1896. Di Hermann Hecht, a cura di Ann Hecht [Book
      Reviews]. GRIFFITHIANA n51/52:263-264 Oct 1994
HECHT, HERMANN
   Codelli, L. Pre-cinema history: an encyclopedia and annotated bibliography
      of the moving image before 1896. Di Hermann Hecht, a cura di Ann Hecht [Book
      Reviews]. GRIFFITHIANA n51/52:263-264 Oct 1994
HEDLING, OLOF
   Hedling, O. Ekonomi och film [Book Review]. F HAFTET 22:62-63 n3 (n87) 1994
HEER, ROLF DE   See also BAD BOY BUBBY
HEFFERNAN, KEVIN
   Heffernan, K. A social poetics of pornography [Book Review]. Q REV F &
      VIDEO 15:77-83 n3 1994
HEGYI, GYULA   For film reviews see author under the following titles:
   TORVENYTELEN
HEILPERN, JOHN
   Heilpern, J. Roman's tortured holiday. il VANITY FAIR 58:88-91+ [5p] Jan
      1995
HEIMANS, FRANK   See also MARGARET MEAD AND SAMOA
Heimat II: Chronicle of a Generation   See ZWEITE HEIMAT, DIE
HEIN, BIRGIT   See also BABY I WILL MAKE YOU SWEAT
HEITALA, VEIJO
   Laine, K. Miksi perehtya elokuvateoriaan [Book Review]. PEILI 18:31 n2 1994
HELAS POUR MOI   f (d Godard, Jean-Luc 1993 Switz/Fr)
      Reviews
   Schaub, M. "Helas pour moi." credits still C(SWITZ) 40:208-209 1994
HELLMAN, LENA   See also KILLJAKTEN
HELLRAISER: BLOODLINE   f (d Smithee, Alan 1996 USA)
   Beeler, M. "Hellraiser IV: Bloodline." il stills C FANTAS 26:10-11+ [3p]
      n2 1995
   Beeler, M. "Hellraiser IV: Bloodline." il stills C FANTAS 26:32-33+ [4p]
      n3 1995
      Special Effects
   Beeler, M. Makeup effects. il still C FANTAS 26:39 n3 1995
HELM, BRIGITTE
   Livio, J. Brigitte Helm: from "Metropolis" to "Gold." Portrait of a goddess.
      Di Peter Herzog e Gene Vazzana [Book Review]. GRIFFITHIANA n51/52:251-252
      Oct 1994
HELMAN, ALICJA
   Helman, A. Kaleb potomek Kaina. il stills KINO 27:22-25 Jun 1993
   Helman, A. Swiat wedlug Hilla. still KINO 27:24-26 Jul 1993
HELMINEN, LIISA   See also MATKA ON PITKA
   Anttila, A.H. Dokumentteja vallattomista. port still PEILI 18:12-13 n3
      1994

HISPANIC-AMERICANS IN FILM
   (continued)
      AUSTRALIA n75:166-167 Feb 1995
         Festivals
   Preziosi, A. Americani, oggi. stills SEGNO n71:70 Jan/Feb 1995
HISPANIC-AMERICANS IN FILM INDUSTRY
   United States
   Moore, D.S. (Ninety-five) '95 a watershed for Latinos in H'wood. il
      VARIETY 358:43+ [3p] Mar 27/Apr 2 1995
HISTOIRE DU GARCON QUI VOULAIT QU'ON L'EMBRASSE, L' f (d Harel, Philippe 1994
Fr)
      Reviews
   Desjardins, D. "L'histoire du garcon qui voulait qu'on l'embrasse." credits
      still SEQUENCES n174:41-42 Sep/Oct 1994
HISTORICAL ANALYSIS
   Canada
   Lacasse, G. Cent temps de cinema ou le cinema dans les temps de l'histoire.
      bibliog CINEMAS 5:57-67 n1/2 1994
   Lagny, M. Le film et le temps braudelien. bibliog stills CINEMAS 5:15-39
      n1/2 1994
   Mariniello, S. Techniques audiovisuelles et reecriture de l'histoire. De la
      representation a la production du temps au cinema. bibliog still CINEMAS
      5:41-56 n1/2 1994
      AIDS
   Cagle, R.L. "Tell the story of my life...": the making of meaning,
      "Monsters," and music in John Greyson's "Zero Patience." il stills VEL LT
      TRAP n35:69-81 Spring 1995
      United States
   Nolley, K. John Ford and the Hollywood Indian. bibliog still F&HIST
      23:44-56 n1/4 1993
      Biographical Film
   Greenspan, C. Custen, George F. Bio/pics: how Hollywood constructed public
      history [Book Review]. stat UFAJ 46:47-49 n3 1994
HISTORICAL CONTEXT
   Germany (Federal Republic, since 1990)
   Linville, S.E. "Europa, Europa": a test case for German national cinema.
      stills WIDE ANGLE 16:38-51 n3 1995
      United States
   Manchel, F. Cultural confusion: a look back at Delmar Daves's "Broken
      Arrow." bibliog still F&HIST 23:58-69+ [13p] n1/4 1993
      Woman's Film
   McKee, A.L. "L'affaire praslin" and "All This, and Heaven Too": gender,
      genre, and history in the 1940s woman's film. VEL LT TRAP n35:33-51 Spring
      1995
      Venezuela
   Schwartzman, K. National cinema in translation: the politics of exhibition
      culture. il stills WIDE ANGLE 16:66-99 n3 1995
HISTORICAL FILM
   Bonnet, J.-C. Le XVIIIe siecle a l'ecran. bibliog still CINEMAS 4:48-58 n1
      1993
      Mexico
   Hershfield, J. Assimilation and identification in Nicholas Echeverria's
      "Cabeza de vaca." bibliog stills WIDE ANGLE 16:6-24 n3 1995
      United States
         Adventure Film
   Cantrill, A. The romance of adventure: the genre of historical adventure
      movies. By Brian Taves [Book Review]. CANTRILL'S FMNTS n73/74:42 May 1994
   Codelli, L. The romance of adventure: the genre of historical adventure
      movies. Di Brian Taves [Book Review]. GRIFFITHIANA n51/52:265 Oct 1994
HISTORIOGRAPHY
   Cherchi Usai, P. Cent'anni da riscrivere [Book Review]. still SEGNO n72:71
      Mar/Apr 1995
   Morris, P. Le passe trompeur. R CINEMATHEQUE n33:4-5 Mar/Apr 1995
      Canada
   Gaudreault, A. Filmographic analysis and early cinema. bibliog credits CAN
      J F STUD 1:57-73 n1 1990
   Jaubert, J.-C. Sous la direction de J. Aumont, A. Gaudreault, M. Marie.
      Histoire du cinema, nouvelles approches [Book Review]. CAN J F STUD
      1:91-92 n1 1990
      United States
   Muscio, G. The commerce of classicism [Book Review]. Q REV F & VIDEO
      15:57-69 n3 1994
HISTORY OF THE FILM
   Bitov, A. Szazeves a kattogo valami. il F VILAG 38:16-17 n1 1995
   Cherchi Usai, P. Cent'anni da riscrivere [Book Review]. still SEGNO n72:71
      Mar/Apr 1995
   Cherchi Usai, P. Film history: an introduction. By Kristin Thompson and
      David Bordwell [Book Review]. J F PRES n49:70-72 Oct 1994
   Cinema 1895-1995: un secolo di immagini. il ports stills FILM (ITALY) 3:bet
      p26 and 27 [8p] n13 1995
   Histoire du cinema. Abrege pedagogique par Rene Predal [Book Review]. il
      GRAND ANGLE n176:39-40 Nov 1994
   Livio, J. Film: an international history of the medium. Di Robert Sklar
      [Book Review]. GRIFFITHIANA n51/52:258 Oct 1994
   Melancon, A. Le cinema a cent ans... ou presque. il R CINEMATHEQUE n32:4-5
      Jan/Feb 1995
   Mikos, L. Film and Leben. filmog stills MEDIEN 38:333-339 n6 1994
   Rychcik, A. "Nie jestesmy juz mlodzi." still KINO 27:16-17 Jul 1993
   Schaar, E. (Hundert) 100 Jahre Kino. il MEDIEN 38:326 n6 1994
   Turconi, D. Film history: an introduction. Di Kristin Thompson e David
      Bordwell [Book Review]. GRIFFITHIANA n51/52:255-258 Oct 1994
      Conferences, Institutes, Workshops, etc.
   Orbanz, E. Domitor '94 - cinema turns 100. il J F PRES n49:56-63 Oct 1994
      Films Shown on Television/Video
         Film Lists
   The BBC 100. il stills S&S 5:16-23 Jan 1995
      Albania
   Gottardi, M. Dizionario dei cineasti albanesi. il SEGNO n72:67 Mar/Apr
      1995

Festivals
   Gottardi, M. Vicina, lontana. stills SEGNO n72:66-68 Mar/Apr 1995
      Asia
         Festivals
   Pattison, B. The 39th Asia-Pacific Film Festival. il stills C PAPERS
      n102:22-23 Dec 1994
      Europe
   Adagio, C. Per un sano e urgente rilancio del cinema europeo. stills C
      NUOVO 43:25-27 Nov/Dec (n352) 1994
      Europe, Western
   Hendrykowski, M. R jak Routledge [Book Reviews]. il KINO 27:41-42 Jul 1993
      France
   Fortin, E. Predal, Rene. Le cinema francais depuis 1945 [Book Review].
      CINEMAS 4:151-155 n1 1993
   Hendrykowska, M. Bole glowy Ludwika Lumiere [Book Review]. il KINO
      27:34-36 Jun 1993
   Mueller, J.E. Albersmeier, Franz-Josef. Theater, Film, Literatur in
      Frankreich. Medienwechsel und Intermedialitat [Book Review]. CINEMAS
      5:223-228 n1/2 1994
      Verviers
   Noel, J. Cinema de Verviers (1896-1993). Par Michel Bedeur et Paolo Zagaglia
      [Book Review]. il GRAND ANGLE n177:49-50 Dec 1994
      Germany (Democratic Republic, 1949-1990)
   Graef, C. Post Scriptum. il F & FERNSEHEN 22:116-119 n6 1994
      Germany (until 1949)
   Comuzio, C. Giovanni Spagnoletti (a cura di): Schermi Germanici [Book
      Review]. il C FORUM 34:93 Sep (n337) 1994
      Great Britain
   Routt, W.D. Dixon, Wheeler Winston, ed. Re-viewing British cinema,
      1900-1992: essays and interviews [Book Review]. MEDIA INFO AUSTRALIA
      n75:162 Feb 1995
      Hungary
   Baron, G. A kerdezo [Book Review]. il F VILAG 38:44-45 n3 1995
      Italy
   Comuzio, E. Aldo Bernardini (a cura di): Il cinema sonoro 1930-1969 [Book
      Reviews]. il C FORUM 34:95-96 Sep (n337) 1994
         Festivals
   Kohn, O. Annecy 1993. still POSITIF n406:61-62 Dec 1994
      Japan
   Neuwirth, G. Aufzeichnungen zum japanischen Film. BLIMP [n2]:4-5 Winter
      1985
   Oshima, N. Mes idees actuelles sur le cinema japonais. stills POSITIF
      n407:47-52 Jan 1995
   Yamane, S. Schon bald hundert Jahre Film. stills C(SWITZ) 40:163-174 1994
      Latin America
   Sinclair, J. King, John, Lopez, Ana M and Alvarado, Manuel, eds. Mediating
      two worlds: cinematic encounters in the Americas [Book Review]. MEDIA INFO
      AUSTRALIA n75:166-167 Feb 1995
      Philippines
   Sotto, A. Philippine independence and national cinema. stills CINEMAYA
      n24:8-21 Summer 1994
      Slovenia (since 1992)
   Codelli, L. Pregled razvoja kinematografije pri Slovencih (do 1918). Di
      Janko Traven, a cura di Lilijana Nedic, Stanko Simenc [Book Reviews].
      GRIFFITHIANA n51/52:264 Oct 1994
      Spain
         Catalonia
   Angulo, J. and others. Entrevista: Garay, Guerin, Jorda y Portabella. il
      interv stills NOSFERATU n9:68-87 Jun 1992
   Las peliculas del ciclo. credits il stills NOSFERATU n9:88-105 Jun 1992
   Riambau, E. Una cierta tendencia (vanguardista) del cine catalan. il stills
      NOSFERATU n9:16-25 Jun 1992
   Torreiro, M. De un tiempo y de un pais. stills NOSFERATU n9:4-15 Jun 1992
      Sweden
   Ahlund, J. Filmens historia ar Runes historia. il interv ports CHAPLIN
      36:42-45 n6 (n255) 1994/95
      Union of Soviet Socialist Republics
   Menashe, L. Requiem for Soviet cinema 1917-1991 [Book Reviews]. stills
      CINEASTE 21:23-27 n1/2 1995
      United States
   Greene, R. Second sight: "Boxoffice" remembers 75 films from 75 years at the
      movies. il stills BOXOFFICE 131:36-38+ [28p] Mar 1995
      Venezuela
         Festivals
   Schwartzman, K. National cinema in translation: the politics of exhibition
      culture. il stills WIDE ANGLE 16:66-99 n3 1995
      19th Century
   Codelli, L. Pre-cinema history: an encyclopedia and annotated bibliography
      of the moving image before 1896. Di Hermann Hecht, a cura di Ann Hecht [Book
      Reviews]. GRIFFITHIANA n51/52:263-264 Oct 1994
   Nagel, J. "Lebende Bilder" fuer die Oeffentlichkeit. stills MEDIEN
      38:340-343 n6 1994
      France
   Cherchi Usai, P. The cine goes to town: French cinema, 1896-1914. By Richard
      Abel [Book Review]. J F PRES n49:69 Oct 1994
   Codelli, L. The cine goes to town. French cinema, 1896-1914. Di Richard Abel
      [Book Review]. GRIFFITHIANA n51/52:252-253 Oct 1994
      United States
   Turconi, D. The American Film Institute catalog of motion pictures produced
      in the United States - film beginnings, 1893-1910 (edizione provvisoria). A
      cura di Elias Savada [Book Review]. GRIFFITHIANA n51/52:250-251 Oct 1994
      1900-29 (Silent Era)
   Gaudreault, A. Filmographic analysis and early cinema. bibliog credits CAN
      J F STUD 1:57-73 n1 1990
   Kasten, J. Fruehe Filmgeschichte [Book Review]. il F BUL 37:12-13 n1
      (n198) 1995
         Collections and Collecting
   Cherchi Usai, P. Film um 1910. Aus der Sammlung Joseph Joye (London). By
      Roland Cosandey [Book Review]. GRIFFITHIANA n51/52:258 Oct 1994
   Cherchi Usai, P. Film um 1910: Aus der Sammlung Joseph Joye (London). By

Roland Cosandey [Book Review]. J F PRES n49:73 Oct 1994
Cosandey, R. Le retour de l'Abbe Joye ou la cinematheque, l'historien et le cinema communal. il J F PRES n49:46-55 Oct 1994

Australia
Long, C. Australia's first films: facts and fables, part eleven: Aborigines and actors. filmogs il map ports C PAPERS n102:52-57+ [8p] Dec 1994

Canada. Quebec
Gaudreault, A. and Lacasse, G. Fonctions et origines du bonimenteur du cinema des premiers temps. bibliog il CINEMAS 4:132-147 n1 1993

France
Cherchi Usai, P. Catalogue Pathe des annees 1896 a 1914 [Book Review]. J F PRES n49:68-69 Oct 1994
Cherchi Usai, P. The cine goes to town: French cinema, 1896-1914. By Richard Abel [Book Review]. J F PRES n49:69 Oct 1994
Codelli, L. The cine goes to town. French cinema, 1896-1914. Di Richard Abel [Book Review]. GRIFFITHIANA n51/52:252-253 Oct 1994

Germany (until 1949)
Codelli, L. Der Film der Weimarer Republik: ein Handbuch der zeitgenoessischen Kritik 1929. A cura di Gero Gandert [Book Review]. GRIFFITHIANA n51/52:255 Oct 1994

Italy
Codella, L. and Scalzo, D. Una ipotesi di lavoro per il centenario del cinema. still C NUOVO 43:58-60 Nov/Dec (n352) 1994
Codelli, L. Il cinema muto italiano: i film degli anni d'oro, 1913, prima parte. Di Aldo Bernardini e Vittorio Martinelli [Book Review]. GRIFFITHIANA n51/52:253 Oct 1994
Montanaro, C. Il cinema italiano in Europa 1907-1929. A cura di Vittorio Martinelli [Book Review]. GRIFFITHIANA n51/52:253 Oct 1994
Montanaro, C. Storia del cinema italiano: il cinema muto 1895-1929, volume primo. Di Gian Piero Brunetta [Book Review]. GRIFFITHIANA n51/52:266 Oct 1994

Italy. Florence
Bovani, R. and Bovani, R. Le prime proiezioni in Italia: Firenze. il still IMMAGINE n28:20-23 Autumn 1994

Spain
Livio, J. Catalogo del cine espanol volumen F2: peliculas de ficcion 1921-1930. Di Palmira Gonzalez Lopez e Joaquin T. Canovas Belchi [Book Review]. GRIFFITHIANA n51/52:252 Oct 1994

United States
Livio, J. Reframing culture: the case of the Vitagraph Quality Films. Di William Uricchio e Roberta E. Pearson [Book Review]. GRIFFITHIANA n51/52:264-265 Oct 1994
Turconi, D. The American Film Institute catalog of motion pictures produced in the United States - film beginnings, 1893-1910 (edizione provvisoria). A cura di Elias Savada [Book Review]. GRIFFITHIANA n51/52:250-251 Oct 1994

United States. Festivals
Lodato, N. I quattro figli di Willy Wyler con le gemelle di Monta Bell. il stills C FORUM 34:10-12 Oct (n338) 1994

1930-39

France
Andrew, D. Appraising French images. WIDE ANGLE 16:53-65 n3 1995

1940-49

Festivals
Serravalli, L. "Dies irae" un revival dei film dell'anno 1943 nel catalogo curato da Francesco Bolzoni e Guido Fink per conto della Mostra del Cinema di Venezia (93) [Book Review]. C SUD 33:40-42 Jul/Aug/Sep (n113) 1994

1960-69

Czechoslovakia (1918-1990). Festivals
Diana, M. Prima del silenzio. stills SEGNO n71:62-64 Jan/Feb 1995

United States
Porton, R. Review of David James: allegories of cinema [Book Review]. il MILLENNIUM n25:114-120 Summer 1991
Slide, A. The Slide area film book notes [Book Reviews]. CLASSIC n236:47-49 Feb 1995

1970-79

United States
Slide, A. The Slide area film book notes [Book Reviews]. CLASSIC n236:47-49 Feb 1995

1980-89
The chronicle of cinema 1895-1995: 5, 1980-1994. graphs stat stills tables S&S 5:insert 23p Jan 1995

1990-96
The chronicle of cinema 1895-1995: 5, 1980-1994. graphs stat stills tables S&S 5:insert 23p Jan 1995

Asia
Elley, D. Buying search on for Chinese fare. VARIETY 358:60 Feb 6/12 1995

Australia
Stratton, D. Upbeat mood and quirky fare in land of Oz, Kiwis. VARIETY 358:60 Feb 6/12 1995

Belgium. Film Lists
Bilan 1994 de la production et de la coproduction belge. MONITEUR n126:12-21 Dec 1994

Canada
Gendron, S. Qu'est-ce que le cinema... canadien? stills SEQUENCES n174:13-16 Sep/Oct 1994

Canada. Festivals
Kelly, B. Canuck pix make a hefty contribution. still VARIETY 358:55 Feb 6/12 1995

Czech Republic (since 1993)
Battis, J. Czech film production rests on shaky ground. VARIETY 358:62 Feb 6/12 1995

Denmark
Castle, A. Ghosts in the kingdom. il stills BLIMP n30:4-11 Winter 1994

France
Sabouraud, F. Il cinema francese e i suoi fantasmi. FCR 45:359-363 Jun/Jul (n446/447) 1994

France. Festivals
Azzalin, C. L'amore di molti. stills SEGNO n71:65-66 Jan/Feb 1995
Beaulieu, J. Le nouveau cinema francais. stills SEQUENCES n174:22-24 Sep/Oct 1994

Crawley, T. Gallic films rely on proven star power. VARIETY 358:56 Feb 6/12 1995

Germany (Federal Republic, since 1990). Festivals
Hansen, E. German filmmaking takes commercial turn. VARIETY 358:50 Feb 6/12 1995

Great Britain. Festivals
Kemp, P. Count on solid British presence. VARIETY 358:55-56 Feb 6/12 1995

Hungary
Nadler, J. Cutbacks victimize filmmakers. VARIETY 358:52 Feb 6/12 1995

Hungary. Festivals
Bikacsy, G. Fragments. NEW HUNGARIAN Q 34:159-162 n130 1993

Italy
Rooney, D. Film quartet leads Italo product run. VARIETY 358:58 Feb 6/12 1995

Kazakhstan (since 1992)
Donmez Colin, G. Kazakh new wave: post perestroika, post Soviet Union. il stat stills table BLIMP n30:12-15 Winter 1994

Mexico
Paxman, A. Mexico leads way, but Latin pix have hard act to follow. VARIETY 358:60+ [2p] Feb 6/12 1995

New Zealand
Stratton, D. Upbeat mood and quirky fare in land of Oz, Kiwis. VARIETY 358:60 Feb 6/12 1995

Norway
Lochen, K. Jakten pa identitet. stills F&K n1:26-27 1994

Poland
(Dziewietnasty) XIX Festiwal Polskich Filmow Fabularnych. credits stills FSP 40:8-9 n10 (n764) 1994
Richardson, R. All's quiet on Polish movie front. VARIETY 358:58+ [2p] Feb 6/12 1995
Sobolewski, T. Sejmik filmowcow. KINO 27:2 Jul 1993

Scandinavia
Edmunds, M. (Nineteen ninety-five) 1995 could well be dandy for Scandi filmmakers. VARIETY 358:55 Feb 6/12 1995

Switzerland. Film Lists
Kritischer Index der Schweizer Produktion des Jahres 1994. credits stills C(SWITZ) 40:203-227 1994

United States
Barometer '95: 1994 in review. BOXOFFICE 131:16-19 Mar 1995
Moments out of time. stills F COM 31:54-59 Jan/Feb 1995
O'Neill, K. and Spines, C. "Premiere's" wrap party 1994. il port stat tables PREM 8:81-87 Feb 1995

HITCHCOCK, ALFRED See also BLACKMAIL; DIAL M FOR MURDER; REBECCA; VERTIGO
Bruno, M.W. Brian De Hitchcock. port stills SEGNO n63:9-13 Sep/Oct 1993
Redottee, H.W. Hitchcock-Glossarium. il stills F BUL 37:47-59 n1 (n198) 1995
Rieser, S.E. David Sterritt. The films of Alfred Hitchcock [Book Review]. BLIMP n30:74 Winter 1994
Roth-Lindberg, O. Varldens bedragliga sken. il stills CHAPLIN 36:18-25 n6 (n255) 1994/95
Turner, G. Soul in suspense: Hitchcock's fright and delight. By Neil P. Hurley [Book Review]. AMCIN 74:95-96 Sep 1993
Zaniello, T. Hitched or Lynched: who directed "Twin Peaks"? bibliog filmogs STUDIES POP CULT 17:55-64 n1 1994

HJORTOY, KIM
Kulas, G. and Hjortoy, K. Jost om Jost. interv port Z n4:6-8 (n46) 1993

HOAG, DAVID
Hoag, D. A match made in Hollywood. il JOURNAL WGA 7:14-20 Feb 1994

HOARE, STEPHANIE
Hoare, S. Romance du livre et du film: l'adaptation de la "Romance du livre et de l'epee" par Ann Hui. bibliog glos stills CINEMAS 3:141-155 n2/3 1993

HOBERMAN, J. For film reviews see author under the following titles: BEFORE THE RAIN; BOYS ON THE SIDE; EXOTICA; I.Q.; IA KUBA; ILE AU TRESOR, L'; KRAVA; MARTHA UND ICH; OKNO V PARIZH; OUTBREAK; PRIEST; QUICK AND THE DEAD, THE; RIGET; TSAHAL; ULTIMO TANGO A PARIGI; WU KUI
Alleva, R. Correspondence: the reviewer replies. COMMONWEAL 122:29 Mar 10 1995
Donohue, W.A. Correspondence: "Voice" vs. Alleva. COMMONWEAL 122:29 Mar 10 1995
Hoberman, J. Another new cult hero from HK. il still PREM 8:50-51 Mar 1995
Hoberman, J. Cuban curios. port stills PREM 8:57+ [2p] Apr 1995
Hoberman, J. Ghost story. still VILLAGE VOICE 40:49 Mar 7 1995
Hoberman, J. Letter from Jean-Luc. VILLAGE VOICE 40:49 Feb 14 1995
Hoberman, J. Mea Cuba II. il VILLAGE VOICE 40:49+ [2p] Mar 14 1995
Hoberman, J. Notes from the underground. il PREM 8:44-45 Feb 1995
Hoberman, J. Pulp dreams. stills VILLAGE VOICE 40:57+ [2p] Jan 3 1995
Hoberman, J. Victim victorious. stills VILLAGE VOICE 40:31-33 Mar 7 1995

HOBERMAN, JIM
Ciment, M. BFI film classics [Book Reviews]. stills POSITIF n408:75-77 Feb 1995

HODET OVER VANNET f (d Gaup, Nils 1993 Norw/Swed)
Lochen, K. En studie i panikk. stills F&K n7:12-13 1993
Lovlund, B.-F. Skjaersild i skjaergarden. credits still Z n4:16-17 (n46) 1993

Review Excerpts
Brochmann, K. "Hodet over vannet." credits still F&K n7:38-39 1993

HODGIN, DAVID
Gray, T. David Hodgin. obit VARIETY 358:58 Mar 20/26 1995

HODSON, JOEL
Hodson, J. Who wrote "Lawrence of Arabia"? il port stills JOURNAL WGA 8:16-20 Mar 1995

HOENTSCH, ANDREAS See also ALLE JAHRE WIEDER; ANDANTE CON MOTO; DON JUAN HEIMKEHR; HANS UND MARIE; KONTRAPUNKT; STRASS, DER
Graef, C. Andreas Hoentsch. biog filmog il F & FERNSEHEN 22:28-29 n6 1994
Graef, C. Weitere Projekte. il F & FERNSEHEN 22:42-47 n6 1994

HOFFMANN, DEBORAH See also COMPLAINTS OF A DUTIFUL DAUGHTER
Blackwell, E. "Complaints of a Dutiful Daughter." still INDEP 18:14-15 Mar 1995

HOGAN, DAVID J. For film reviews see author under the following titles: AELITA;
PIN-DOWN GIRL
Hogan, D.J. Races, chases & crashes. By Dave Mann and Ron Main [Book
Review]. il F FAX n48:12 Jan/Feb 1995
Hogan, D.J. Sam Fuller: film is a battleground. By Lee Server [Book Review].
il F FAX n49:12+ [2p] Mar/Apr 1995
HOGAN, ELEANOR
See, K.T. and others. Clara Law. filmog interv stills CINEMAYA
n25/26:50-54 Autumn/Winter 1994/95
HOGAN, P.J. See also MURIEL'S WEDDING
Kelleher, E. Miramax invites filmgoers to "Muriel's Wedding." il interv
still FJ 98:12+ [2p] Jan/Feb 1995
HOGUE, PETER
Hogue, P. At large in the century of Melies. F COM 31:16 Mar/Apr 1995
Hogue, P. Charley with a y. il stills F COM 31:76-81 Mar/Apr 1995
HOINEFF, NELSON
Hoineff, N. Brazilian prod'n gets real. il VARIETY 358:54+ [2p] Mar 27/Apr
2 1995
HOLLAND, AGNIESZKA See also EUROPA EUROPA; SECRET GARDEN, THE; TOTAL ECLIPSE
HOLLAND, JOSEPH
Obituaries. obits VARIETY 358:188-189 Feb 20/26 1995
HOLLOWAY, DOROTHEA For film reviews see author under the following titles:
BEWEGTE MANN, DER; EI IST EINE GESCHISSENE GOTTESGABE, DAS; SIEGER,
DIE
Holloway, D. "The Neverending Story III." still KINO(GF) n56:23 Nov 1994
Holloway, D. and Holloway, R. (Sieben und dreissigste) 37. DOKfilm Festival
Leipzig. KINO(GF) n56:3-4 Nov 1994
HOLLOWAY, GRAHAM See also CHASING THE DEER
HOLLOWAY, RONALD See also PARAJANOV For film reviews see author under the
following titles: BURNING LIFE; ICH GELOBE; KEINER LIEBT MICH; LABENDIG
Holloway, D. and Holloway, R. (Sieben und dreissigste) 37. DOKfilm Festival
Leipzig. KINO(GF) n56:3-4 Nov 1994
Holloway, R. Interview Dieter Kosslick. interv port KINO(GF) n56:5-6 Nov
1994
HOLLYWOOD IN LITERATURE
United States
Eaton, M. Casino trades [Book Review]. S&S 5:37 Feb 1995
Richards, S. The black mask murders. By William F. Nolan [Book Review].
ARMCHAIR DET 27:359 n3 1994
HOLLYWOOD KID EU SAENG-AE f (d Chung, Ji-young 1994 S Korea)
Reviews
Lyu, H.-m. "Hollywood kid eu saengae." credits still CINEMAYA n25/26:84
Autumn/Winter 1994/95
HOLLYWOOD KIDS
Hollywood Kids. Andrew Stevens: Q&A. interv port MOVIELINE 6:32 Mar 1995
Hollywood Kids. Mink Stole: Q&A. interv port MOVIELINE 6:34 Apr 1995
HOLLYWOOD KILLED ME f (d Janetzko, Christoph/Wenner, Dorothee 1988 USA)
Janetzko, C. and Wenner, D. Storyboards for "Hollywood Killed Me" (1990).
il still MILLENNIUM n25:18-23 Summer 1991
Hollywood Ten See HOUSE UNAMERICAN ACTIVITIES COMMITTEE. HEARINGS (United
States, 1947)
HOLMES, CECIL
Berryman, K. Cecil Holmes. biog il obit C PAPERS n102:19 Dec 1994
Holmes, Sherlock See SHERLOCK HOLMES (fictional character)
HOLMLUND, CHRIS
Holmlund, C. "CinemAction," no. 67 (1993), 200pp. "Vingt ans de theories
feministes sur le cinema." Eds Ginette Vincendeau and Berenice Reynaud [Book
Review]. SCREEN 35:407-410 n4 1994
Holmlund, C. Fractured fairytales and experimental identities: looking for
lesbians in and around the films of Su Friedrich. bibliog stills DISCOURSE
n17.1:16-46 Fall 1994
HOLST, JAN ERIK
Og alle var der... ports Z n4:36-38 (n46) 1993
HOLST, MARIUS See also TI KNIVER I HJERTET
HOLT, WESLEY G. For film reviews see author under the following titles:
HAUNTING, THE; INVADERS FROM MARS
Homage See REFERENCES TO FILMS IN FILM
HOMAGE f (d Marks, Ross Kagan 1995 USA)
Reviews
Greene, R. "Homage." BOXOFFICE 131:bet p125 and 144 [pR24] Apr 1995
Home movies See AMATEUR FILM AND FILMMAKING
HOMME DES CASERNES, L' f (d Veuve, Jacqueline 1994 Switz)
Reviews
Perret, J. "L'homme des casernes." credits C(SWITZ) 40:226-227 1994
HOMO FABER f (Voyager d Schloendorff, Volker 1991 FR Ger/Fr/Greece)
Reviews
Szymanska, A. Trudna sztuka optymizmu. still KINO 27:28-29 May 1993
Homocides in film See MURDERS IN FILM
Homosexual film See QUEER CINEMA
HOMOSEXUALITY See also BISEXUALITY; QUEER THEORY
Experimental Film
Festivals
Reid-Pharr, R. Mix-defying. il stills AFTERIMAGE 22:3-4 Jan 1995
Cuba
Birringer, J. Homosexuality and the revolution. interv port CINEASTE
21:21-22 n1/2 1995
Great Britain
Grundmann, R. Black nationhood and the rest in the West. interv port
CINEASTE 21:28-31 n1/2 1995
HOMOSEXUALS IN FILM
Bronski, M. Queer looks: perspectves on lesbian and gay film and video.
Edited by Martha Gever, John Greyson and Pratibha Parmar [Book Reviews].
still CINEASTE 21:90-92 n1/2 1995
Giles, J. Well-bound white sheets [Book Review]. S&S 5:35 Apr 1995
Kaltenecker, S. Richard Dyer: The matter of images. Essays on
representations [Book Review]. BLIMP n30:71 Winter 1994
United States
Russo, C.J. Images in the dark: an encyclopedia of gay and lesbian film and
video. Compiled by Raymond Murray [Book Review]. il AFTERIMAGE 22:16 Jan
1995

Women. Experimental Film
Holmlund, C. Fractured fairytales and experimental identities: looking for
lesbians in and around the films of Su Friedrich. bibliog stills DISCOURSE
n17.1:16-46 Fall 1994
HONDO, MED See also LUMIERE NOIRE
HONEGGER, ANDREAS See also AM ENDE DER SCHIENEN
HONES, LUKE
Hones, L. How to avoid a noise dive. il INDEP 18:42-43 Apr 1995
HONEY, I BLEW UP THE KID f (d Kleiser, Randal 1992 USA)
Reviews
Zappoli, G. "Tesoro, mi si e allargato il ragazzino." credits FILM (ITALY)
3:48 n13 1995
HONG GAOLIANG f (d Zhang, Yimou 1988 China)
Oedipal Narrative
Farquhar, M.A. Oedipality in "Red Sorghum" and "Judou." bibliog glos
scenario stills CINEMAS 3:60-86 n2/3 1993
Hong Kong See as a subheading under individual subject headings
HONG MEIGUI BAI MEIGUI f (d Kwan, Stanley 1995 Hong Kong/Taiwan)
Reviews
Elley, D. "Red Rose White Rose" ("Hong meigui bai meigui"). credits
VARIETY 358:76+ [2p] Feb 20/26 1995
HONGFEN f (d Li, Shaohong 1995 China/Hong Kong)
Reviews
Stratton, D. "Blush" ("Hongfen"). credits VARIETY 358:72 Feb 27/Mar 5 1995
HONIGMOND f (d Barylli, Gabriel 1995 FR Ger)
"Honigmond." credits port KINO(BRD) n1:8 1995
"Honigmond." credits port KINO(BRD) n1:8 1995
HOOGSTE TIJD f (d Weisz, Frans 1995 Neth)
Reviews
Rooney, D. "Last Call" ("Hoogste tijd"). credits VARIETY 358:84 Feb 20/26
1995
HOOKS, BELL
hooks, b. Dreams of conquest. still S&S 5:22-23 Apr 1995
HOOKS, KEVIN See also PASSENGER 57
HOOLBOOM, MIKE
Hoolboom, M. The place with many rooms is the body: the films of Fumiko
Kiyooka. il stills CANTRILL'S FMNTS n73/74:4-8 May 1994
Hoolboom, M. The queen of disaster. stills MILLENNIUM n26:26-32 Fall 1992
HOOP DREAMS f (d James, Steve 1994 USA)
Awards
Ansen, D. Why did Oscar drop the ball on "Hoop Dreams"? stills NEWSWK
125:71-72 Mar 27 1995
Corliss, R. How the winner lost. still TIME 145:66 Feb 27 1995
Cox, D. Fine Line has "Dreams" of best pic. VARIETY 357:16 Jan 2/8 1995
Spillane, M. Slam-dunked. NATION 260:333 Mar 13 1995
Contextual Analysis
hooks, b. Dreams of conquest. still S&S 5:22-23 Apr 1995
Reviews
Lipman, A. "Hoop Dreams." credits S&S 5:44-45 Apr 1995
Quart, L. "Hoop Dreams." CINEASTE 21:104 n1/2 1995
HOOPER, JOSEPH
Hooper, J. Dances with devils. port ESQUIRE 123:42-43 Mar 1995
Hooper, J. Playing the heavy. port ESQUIRE 123:36 Feb 1995
HOOPER, TOBE See also MANGLER, THE
HOPKINS, ANTHONY
Ciapara, E. Anthony Hopkins. filmog stills FSP 40:11-12 n6 (n760) 1994
Nangle, J. Anthony Hopkins, the unauthorized biography. By Michael Feeney
Callan [Book Review]. FIR 45:70-71 Nov/Dec 1994
HOPKINS, STEPHEN See also BLOWN AWAY
HOPPENSTAND, GARY
Hoppenstand, G. Dick Tracy and American culture: morality and mythology,
text and context. By Garyn G. Roberts [Book Review]. ARMCHAIR DET
27:236-237 n2 1994
Hoppenstand, G. Murder and other acts of high society. il port ARMCHAIR
DET 26:62-68 n4 1993
HOPPER, DENNIS See also CHASERS
HORGUELIN, THIERRY For film reviews see author under the following titles:
BATARD DE DIEU, LE; COLONEL CHABERT, LE; GENS NORMAUX N'ONT RIEN
D'EXCEPTIONNEL, LES; MACHINE, LA; PAS TRES CATHOLIQUE; PROFESSIONAL,
THE; SEPARATION, LA
HORNER, HARRY
Lentz, H., III. Obituaries. biogs filmogs il obits ports CLASSIC
n236:57-59 Feb 1995
HORNER, JAMES
Rixman, J. and Kendall, L. Horner corner. F SCORE MONTHLY n38:14 Oct 1993
HORNSBY, WENDY
Bakerman, J.S. Midnight baby. By Wendy Hornsby [Book Review]. il ARMCHAIR
DET 27:120 n1 1994
Horror Chamber of Dr. Faustus, The See YEUX SANS VISAGE, LES
HORROR FILM See also FRANKENSTEIN FILM; SNUFF FILM; VAMPIRE FILM
Cappabianca, A. L'enigma della bruttezza. il stills SEGNO n72:18-20
Mar/Apr 1995
Comuzio, C. Renato Venturelli: Horror in cento film [Book Reviews]. il C
FORUM 34:94-95 Nov (n339) 1994
Garofalo, M. Estetica dello schifo. stills SEGNO n72:27-29 Mar/Apr 1995
Pezzotta, A. Il brutto nel cinema. still SEGNO n72:17-18 Mar/Apr 1995
Festivals
Giuffrida, S. and Angiari, L. Sitges: al supermaket dell'orrore quotidiano.
stills C FORUM 34:7-9 Nov (n339) 1994
Martani, M. Fantafestival: l'orrore riciclato mortifica il fantastico.
stills C FORUM 34:24-26 Oct (n338) 1994
Gender Roles
Feminist Analysis
Harris, J. Clover, Carol J. Men, women, and chain saws: gender in the modern
horror film [Book Review]. MEDIA INFO AUSTRALIA n75:158-159 Feb 1995
Psychoanalytic Analysis
Peters, G. Barbara Creed. The monstrous-feminine: film, feminism,
psychoanalysis [Book Review]. bibliog CAN J F STUD 3:108-113 n2 1994
References to Literature in Film
Nangle, J. More things than are dreamt of: masterpieces of supernatural

horror - from Mary Shelley to Stephen King in literature and film. By Alain
Silver and James Ursini [Book Review]. FIR 45:71 Nov/Dec 1994
    Social Values
Kupiainen, R. "Kristityn liha kuusi denaaria naula." il PEILI 18:26-27 n1
    1994
        Women in Film
            Psychoanalytic Analysis
Cantrill, A. The monstrous-feminine: film, feminism, psychoanalysis. By
    Barbara Creed [Book Review]. CANTRILL'S FMNTS n73/74:42 May 1994
        Great Britain
            Directing. History
Ma Latorre, A. Terence Fisher: notas a la sombra de un estilo. il stills
    NOSFERATU n6:44-49 Apr 1991
            History
Angulo, J. Terence Fisher, revisitador de mitos. biog il stills NOSFERATU
    n6:22-43 Apr 1991
Molina Foix, J.A. Hammer Films: una herencia de miedo. il stills NOSFERATU
    n6:4-21 Apr 1991
Roper, J. Hammer and beyond: the British horror film. Peter Hutchings [Book
    Review]. il C PAPERS n102:73 Dec 1994
            History. Bibliographies
Fuentes bibliograficas e iconograficas. bibliog NOSFERATU n6:102 Apr 1991
        Italy
Della Casa, S. Tutti colpevoli. il stills SEGNO n72:31-32 Mar/Apr 1995
        Music
Larson, R.D. Goblin on CD from Cinevox/SLC. F SCORE MONTHLY n38:13 Oct 1993
        Japan
Japanese science fiction, fantasy and horror films. By Stuart Galbraith IV
    [Book Review]. FATAL VISIONS n17:32 1994
        United States
Baumgold, J. A graveyard smash. stills ESQUIRE 123:120+ [2p] Jan 1995
Bruno, M.W. Brian De Hitchcock. port stills SEGNO n63:9-13 Sep/Oct 1993
Lilley, J. How to make a monster movie. il interv stills SCARLET STREET
    n17:65-71+ [8p] Winter 1995
            Directors
Nangle, J. The fearmakers: the screen's directorial masters of suspense and
    terror. By John McCarty [Book Review]. FIR 45:69-70 Nov/Dec 1994
            Films Shown on Television/Video
Slide, A. The Slide area film book notes [Book Reviews]. CLASSIC
    n237:42-44+ [4p] Mar 1995
            Films Shown on Television/Video. Videocassettes
Slide, A. The Slide area film book notes [Book Reviews]. CLASSIC n236:47-49
    Feb 1995
            Psychoanalytic Analysis
kydd, E. Guess who else is coming to dinner: racial/sexual hysteria in
    "Candyman." stills C ACTION n36:63-72 1995
Horror of Dracula See DRACULA
HORTNAGL, ERICH
    (Sju) 7 debutanter. ports CHAPLIN 36:6-7 n6 (n255) 1994/95
HORTON, ANDREW
    Menashe, L. Requiem for Soviet cinema 1917-1991 [Book Reviews]. stills
        CINEASTE 21:23-27 n1/2 1995
HORTON, ROBERT
    Horton, R. Offhand enchantment. stills F COM 31:4-5+ [3p] Jan/Feb 1995
HOSKINS, COLIN
    Finn, A. and others. Marketing, management, and competitive strategy in the
        cultural industries. bibliog CAN J COM 19:523-550 n3/4 1994
    Hoskins, C. and others. The environment in which cultural industries operate
        and some implications. bibliog CAN J COM 19:353-376 n3/4 1994
HOSKYNS, BARNEY
    Noel, J. James Dean. De Barney Hoskyns [Book Review]. il GRAND ANGLE
        n177:49 Dec 1994
HOSSAIN, DILDAR
    Hossain, D. Problems and prospects of short-length film: a Bangladesh
        overview. biog port DOC BOX 2:2-4 1993
HOT SHOTS! PART DEUX f (d Abrahams, Jim 1993 USA)
        Sound Track Reviews
    Dursin, A. and others. Four by Basil Poledouris. F SCORE MONTHLY n36/37:32
        Aug/Sep 1993
HOTELS IN FILM
        Switzerland
    Grafe, F. Eine Schweizer Erfindung. stills C(SWITZ) 40:37-50 1994
HOU, HSIAO-HSIEN See also TONG NIEN WANG SHI
HOUND OF THE BASKERVILLES, THE f (d Fisher, Terence 1959 Gt Br)
    Bernardo, J.M. El perro de Baskerville. credits stills NOSFERATU n6:82-83
        Apr 1991
HOUSE OF DRACULA f (d Kenton, Erle C. 1945 USA)
    Scrivani, R. "House of Dracula." Edward T. Lowe; edited by Philip J. Riley
        [Book Review]. SCARLET STREET n17:99 Winter 1995
House of Fright See TWO FACES OF DR. JEKYLL, THE
HOUSE OF SCIENCE: A MUSEUM OF FALSE FACTS, THE f (d Sachs, Lynne 1991 USA)
    Sachs, L. Script pages, storyboards, and artwork from "The House of Science:
        a Museum of False Facts" (1991). il scenario MILLENNIUM n25:58-61 Summer
        1991
HOUSE OF THE SPIRITS, THE f (d August, Bille 1993 FR Ger/Denmk/Port)
    Christophersen, B.S. Latinske folelser med dansk aksent. stills F&K
        n7:8-10 1993
    Mazierska, E. "Dom duchow." credits FSP 40:11 n3 (n757) 1994
HOUSE UNAMERICAN ACTIVITIES COMMITTEE. HEARINGS (United States, 1947)
    Cohen, K. The importance of the FBI's "Walt Disney File" to animation
        scholars. ANIMATION J 3:67-77 n2 1995
HOUSEGUEST f (d Miller, Randall 1994 USA)
        Reviews
    Leydon, J. "Houseguest." credits still VARIETY 357:73 Jan 2/8 1995
    Noh, D. "Houseguest." credits FJ 98:53 Jan/Feb 1995
    Williamson, K. "Houseguest." BOXOFFICE 131:bet p89 and 96 [pR20] Mar 1995
HOUSTON, PENELOPE
    Ciment, M. BFI film classics [Book Reviews]. stills POSITIF n408:75-77 Feb
        1995
    Cosandey, R. Keepers of the frame: the film archives. Edited by Penelope

Houston [Book Review]. J F PRES n49:67-68 Oct 1994
    Hendrykowski, M. BFI Film Classics [Book Review]. il KINO 27:39-40 May
        1993
    Slide, A. The Slide area film book notes [Book Reviews]. CLASSIC n236:47-49
        Feb 1995
HOUX, PATRICE
    Houx, P. Concretiser le cinema. R CINEMATHEQUE n32:23 Jan/Feb 1995
HOVDENAKK, PER
    Og alle var der... ports Z n4:36-38 (n46) 1993
HOVIS, MICHAEL See also MAN WITH THE PERFECT SWING, THE
HOWARD, CRAIG
    Howard, C. Letters: get your act together. ONFILM 11:12 n11 1994/95
HOWARD, JOHN
    Obituaries. obits VARIETY 358:78 Feb 27/Mar 5 1995
HOWARD, TOM
    Tom Howard on mystery movies. By Tom Howard [Book Review]. FATAL VISIONS
        n17:32 1994
HOYERE ENN HIMMELEN f (d Nesheim, Berit 1993 Norw)
    Lovlund, B.-F. Variasjon over samme tema. credits still Z n1:24-25 (n47)
        1994
        Review Excerpts
    "Hoyere enn himmelen." still F&K n1:36 1994
HUANG, JIANXIN See also BEI KAO BEI, LIAN DUI LIAN; LUN HUI; WU KUI
HUANG, JUN
    Zhao, W. Huang Jun and his trilogy. il stills CHINA SCREEN n4:30-31 1994
HUANG, SHIXIAN
    Huang, S. The resurrection of Chinese art films. port CHINA SCREEN n4:33
        1994
HUANG, YU-SHAN See also [PEONY BIRDS]
    "Peony Birds." biog credits filmog still CINEMAYA n25/26:105 Autumn/Winter
        1994/95
HUBBARD, ROBERT
    Hubbard, R. Book reviews [Book Reviews]. F SCORE MONTHLY n40:9 Dec 1993
    Hubbard, R. Film score: the art and craft of movie music. Tony Thomas [Book
        Review]. F SCORE MONTHLY n36/37:22 Aug/Sep 1993
HUBERT, JEAN-LOUP See also A CAUSE D'ELLE; CONTRE L'OUBLI
HUBIN, ALLEN J.
    Breen, J.L. Hubin, Allen J. Crime fiction II: a comprehensive bibliography
        1749-1990 [Book Review]. ARMCHAIR DET 28:197 n2 1995
HUCKLEBERRY FINN (fictional character)
    Slide, A. The Slide area film book notes [Book Reviews]. CLASSIC n236:47-49
        Feb 1995
HUDSUCKER PROXY, THE f (d Coen, Joel 1994 USA)
    Arecco, S. L'ano solare dei Coen. still FCR 45:308-310 Jun/Jul (n446/447)
        1994
    Mazzotta, W. Tempo non indifferente. FCR 45:311-314 Jun/Jul (n446/447) 1994
        Reviews
    Asboth, E. "A nagy ugras." credits still F VILAG 38:57 n3 1995
HUERTA, RUDOLFO GUZMAN
    Rhodes, S. El Santo. biog filmog il stills F FAX n49:44-49 Mar/Apr 1995
HUET, ANDRE See also [UNKNOWN WAR, AN]
    Huet, A. On n'a pas tous les jours cent ans...: ou de l'interet du cinema
        amateur. il J F PRES n49:40-42 Oct 1994
HUEVOS DE ORO f (d Bigas Luna 1993 Sp)
        Reviews
    Castiel, E. "Macho." SEQUENCES n174:44 Sep/Oct 1994
HUFMANN, HELENA ENIZE
    Lentz, H., III. Obituaries. biogs filmogs il obits ports CLASSIC
        n236:57-59 Feb 1995
HUGHES, JOHN
    Busch, A.M. Hughes and Mestres team in Disney-based Great Oaks Ent. port
        VARIETY 358:22 Feb 20/26 1995
    Busch, A.M. and Laski, B. Hughes hightails it back to CAA. VARIETY 357:8
        Jan 9/15 1995
    Laski, B. Helmer Hughes moves to ICM. VARIETY 357:24 Jan 2/8 1995
HUGO, VICTOR
    Laster, A. Les miserables sur les ecrans de cinema et de television.
        credits filmog il stills AVANT-SCENE n438/439:81-91 Jan/Feb 1995
HUI, ANN See also KE TU CHIU HEN; NUIYAN, SEISAP; SHU JIAN EN CHOU LU
HUILLET, DANIELE
    Zach, P. Straub. filmog il interv BLIMP [n1]:14-25 Mar 1985
Human Monster, The See DARK EYES OF LONDON, THE
HUMAN RIGHTS See also CIVIL RIGHTS
        Festivals
    Cieutat, M. Strasbourg. stills POSITIF n409:67-68 Mar 1995
HUMANN, HELENA E.
    Obituaries. biog obits VARIETY 357:83-84 Jan 2/8 1995
HUMOR See also COMEDY; PARODY; SATIRE
        United States
    Sjogren, O. Kan en antilady sjunga blues? bibliog port stills F HAFTET
        22:38-47 n3 (n87) 1994
HUMOROUS ESSAYS
        United States
    Albrecht, R. Knights of the roundtable. il JOURNAL WGA 8:51 Dec/Jan 1995
    "Boxoffice's" eighth annual miscellaneous film awards! il BOXOFFICE 131:bet
        p82 and 83 [pSW32-SW37] Apr 1995
    Goldberg, P. You ain't lazy, you're incubating. JOURNAL WGA 8:20 Dec/Jan
        1995
    Moskowitz, A. Eating my words. JOURNAL WGA 7:29 Feb 1994
    Siegel, S. Writing is hell. JOURNAL WGA 7:39 Feb 1994
    Thonson, T. The happiness of an unhappy ending. JOURNAL WGA 8:46 Dec/Jan
        1995
HUMPHREYS, PADDY COSTELLO
    Catsos, G. J.M. Children of the corn. il intervs F FAX n48:64-65+ [3p]
        Jan/Feb 1995
HUNDERTMARK, GISELA
    Trenczak, H. Gisela Hundertmark, Louis Saul (Hrsg.): "Foerderung essen Filme
        auf" [Book Review]. BLIMP [n1]:65 Mar 1985

HUNG HEI-KUN   f (d Wong, Jing/Yuen, Kwai 1995 Hong Kong)
   Reviews
   Rooney, D. "The New Legend of Shaolin" ("Hung hei-kun"). credits VARIETY
      358:84 Feb 20/26 1995
Hungary   See as a subheading under individual subject headings
HUNGLER, TIMEA   For film reviews see author under the following titles: ONLY YOU
HUNT, MAURICE   See also PAGEMASTER, THE
HUNTED, THE   f (d Lawton, J.F. 1995 USA)
   Reviews
   Lowry, B. "The Hunted." credits still VARIETY 358:69 Feb 27/Mar 5 1995
HUNTER, JACK
   Harrison, S. House of horror: the complete Hammer Films story. By Allen
      Eyles, Robert Adkinson & Nicholas Fry with additional revisions by Jack
      Hunter [Book Review]. il FATAL VISIONS n17:30 1994
HUNTER, TIM   See also SAINT OF FORT WASHINGTON, THE
HUOT, MARIE CLAIRE
   Huot, M.C. Deux poles yang du nouveau cinema chinois: Chen Kaige et Zhang
      Yimou. bibliog glos stills CINEMAS 3:103-125 n2/3 1993
HUOZHE   f (To Live d Zhang, Yimou 1994 Hong Kong/China)
   Prayez, B. "Vivre!" bibliog credits still GRAND ANGLE n177:41-42 Dec 1994
   Reviews
   Koskinen, M. Det stora i det lilla. credits port stills CHAPLIN 36:65-66
      n6 (n255) 1994/95
   Lewis, K. "To Live." FIR 45:58-59 Nov/Dec 1994
   Teo, S. "Houzhe." credits stills CINEMAYA n24:38-41 Summer 1994
   Tessier, M. "Houzhe." credits stills CINEMAYA n24:38-41 Summer 1994
HURLEY, NEIL P.
   Turner, G. Soul in suspense: Hitchcock's fright and delight. By Neil P.
      Hurley [Book Review]. AMCIN 74:95-96 Sep 1993
HURST, MARGARET
   Lentz, H., III. Obituaries. biogs filmogs il obits ports CLASSIC
      n236:57-59 Feb 1995
HURT, JOHN
   Mazierska, E. "I kowbojki moga marzyc." biogs credits filmogs still FSP
      40:8 n5 (n759) 1994
HUSTER, FRANCIS
   Francis Huster. biog filmog port stills STARS n21:[29-30] Winter 1995
HUSTON, JOHN   See also AFRICAN QUEEN, THE; UNFORGIVEN, THE
   Brill, L. "The African Queen" and John Huston's filmmaking. CJ 34:3-21 n2
      1995
   Polan, D. Reflections in a male eye: John Huston and the American
      experience. Edited by Gaylyn Studlar and David Desser [Book Review]. F
      CRITICISM 19:103-108 n2 1994/95
HUSTON, PENELOPE
   Borger, L. Sisyphian struggles [Book Review]. S&S 5:37-38 Feb 1995
HUTCHINGS, PETER
   Roper, J. Hammer and beyond: the British horror film. Peter Hutchings [Book
      Review]. il C PAPERS n102:73 Dec 1994
HUTT, ROBIN
   Hutt, R. Gwyneth Walker. il FILM 4:14-15 n1 [1995]
HYAMS, PETER   See also CAPRICORN ONE; OUTLAND; TIMECOP
   Filmografie. biogs filmogs SEGNO n72:40 Mar/Apr 1995
HYTNER, NICHOLAS   See also MADNESS OF KING GEORGE, THE
IAD   See INSTITUT DES ARTS DE DIFFUSION (Brussels, Belgium)
ICM   See INTERNATIONAL CREATIVE MANAGEMENT, INC.
IMAX   See WIDE SCREEN
IP5: L'ILE AUX PACHYDERMS   f (d Beineix, Jean-Jacques 1992 Fr)
   Storyboards
   Berthome, J.-P. Le "storyboard" en livres [Book Reviews]. POSITIF n407:90+
      [2p] Jan 1995
I.Q.   f (d Schepisi, Fred 1994 USA)
   Reviews
   Denby, D. "Fool's gold. still NEW YORK 28:56-57 Jan 16 1995
   Hoberman, J. "I.Q." VILLAGE VOICE 40:72+ [2p] Jan 3 1995
   Kelleher, E. "I.Q." credits still FJ 98:51-52 Jan/Feb 1995
   Travers, P. Smart women, foolish choices. stills ROLLING STONE n700:66 Jan
      26 1995
I Am Cuba   See IA KUBA
I Don't Want to Talk About It   See DE ESO NO SE HABLA
I JUST WASN'T MADE FOR THESE TIMES   f (d Was, Don 1995 USA)
   Reviews
   Greene, R. "I Just Wasn't Made for These Times." still BOXOFFICE 131:bet
      p125 and 144 [pR24-R25] Apr 1995
I LIKE IT LIKE THAT   f (d Martin, Darnell 1994 USA)
   Dupagne, M.-F. "I Like It Like That." bibliog credits still GRAND ANGLE
      n178:15-16 Jan 1995
   Reviews
   Berthomieu, P. "Sleep With Me," "Clerks," "I Like It Like That." credits
      stills POSITIF n407:34-35 Jan 1995
   Cloutier, M. "I Like It Like That." SEQUENCES n175:43 Nov/Dec 1994
   Garcia, M. "I Like It Like That." FIR 45:59 Nov/Dec 1994
I LOVE A MAN IN UNIFORM   f (Man in Uniform, A d Wellington, David 1993 Can)
   Reviews
   Adagio, C. "L'uomo in uniforme." credits C NUOVO 43:51-52 Nov/Dec (n352)
      1994
   Paesano, A. "L'uomo in uniforme." credits still FILM (ITALY) 3:36-38 n13
      1995
I LOVE TROUBLE   f (d Shyer, Charles 1994 USA)
   Prayez, B. "Les complices." bibliog credits stills GRAND ANGLE n176:5-6
      Nov 1994
   Reviews
   Viviani, C. "Les complices." POSITIF n407:41 Jan 1995
I THANK A FOOL   f (d Stevens, Robert 1962 USA)
   Rebello, S. Fans of bad Susan Hayward films will thank the fools behind "I
      Thank a Fool." il MOVIELINE 6:80 Apr 1995
IA KUBA   f (I Am Cuba d Kalatozov, Mikhail 1964 USSR/Cuba)
   Hoberman, J. Cuban curios. port stills PREM 8:57+ [2p] Apr 1995
   Hoberman, J. Mea Cuba II. il VILLAGE VOICE 40:49+ [2p] Mar 14 1995
   Thomajan, D. Handheld heaven, agitprop purgatory. still F COM 31:87-88
      Mar/Apr 1995

   Reviews
   Hoberman, J. Cuba libre. still VILLAGE VOICE 40:49 Mar 14 1995
   Klawans, S. "I Am Cuba." NATION 260:394-397 Mar 20 1995
   Rafferty, T. The enemy within. il NEW YORKER 71:105-107 Mar 20 1995
IBSEN, TANCRED   See also TO MISTENKELIGE PERSONER
Iceland   See as a subheading under individual subject headings
ICH GELOBE   f (d Murnberger, Wolfgang 1994 Austria)
   Reviews
   Holloway, R. "Ich gelobe." credits KINO(GF) n56:9 Nov 1994
ICHASO, LEON   See also SUGAR HILL
ICHIKAWA, JUN   See also TOKYO KYODAI
ICHIKAWA, KON   See also SHIJUSHICHININ NO SHIKAKU
ICONOGRAPHY
   Italy
   Comuzio, E. Roberto Campari: Il fantasma del bello. Iconologia del cinema
      italiano [Book Review]. il C FORUM 34:93 Nov (n339) 1994
   United States
   Blaetz, R. Retelling the Joan of Arc story: women, war, and Hollywood's
      "Joan of Paris." bibliog still LIT/FQ 22:212-221 n4 1994
IDA, FARIDA   See also GURUKU CANTIK SEKALI
IDEI, NOBUYUKI
   Robinson, G. and Cox, D. Power shift at Sony Corp. port VARIETY 358:15+
      [2p] Mar 27/Apr 2 1995
IDEOLOGICAL ANALYSIS   See also POLITICAL ANALYSIS
   Programming
   Schwartzman, K. National cinema in translation: the politics of exhibition
      culture. il stills WIDE ANGLE 16:66-99 n3 1995
   Great Britain
   Marks, L.U. Ghosts of stories. stills C ACTION n36:53-62 1995
   Union of Soviet Socialist Republics
   Sorensen, J. "Lef," Eisenstein, and the politics of form. bibliog F
      CRITICISM 19:55-74 n2 1994/95
   United States
   Berry, C. A turn for the better? - genre and gender in "Girl From Hunan" and
      other recent mainland Chinese films. bibliog stills PS 14:81-103 n1/2
      1994/95
   Duckenfield, M. "Terminator 2": a call to economic arms? bibliog STUDIES
      POP CULT 17:1-16 n1 1994
   Layton, R. "Blue Velvet": a parable of male development. SCREEN 35:374-393
      n4 1994
   Sharma, S. Citizens of the empire: revisionist history and the social
      imaginary in "Gandhi." bibliog VEL LT TRAP n35:61-68 Spring 1995
   Sharma, S. Fassbinder's "Ali" and the politics of subject-formation.
      bibliog stills PS 14:104-116 n1/2 1994/95
   Torry, R. Awakening to the other: feminism and the ego-ideal in "Alien."
      bibliog WOMEN'S STUD 23:343-363 n4 1994
   Fetishism
   Mulvey, L. "Xala," Ousmane Sembene (1974): the carapace that failed. stills
      CAM OBS n31:48-71 Jan/May 1993
   United States - Civil War, 1861-1865
   McPherson, T. "Both kinds of arms": remembering the Civil War. bibliog il
      VEL LT TRAP n35:3-18 Spring 1995
IGNATZ & LOTTE   f (d King, Encke 1995 USA)
   Reviews
   Levy, E. "Ignatz & Lotte." credits VARIETY 358:52 Mar 13/19 1995
ILAYUM MULLUM   f (d Sasi, K.P. 1994 India)
   Reviews
   Fadda, M. "Ilayum mullum." still C FORUM 34:35 Sep (n337) 1994
ILE AU TRESOR, L'   f (Treasure Island d Ruiz, Raul 1991 prod 1985 Fr/USA)
   Reviews
   Hoberman, J. Ward play. still VILLAGE VOICE 40:45 Jan 10 1995
I'LL DO ANYTHING   f (d Brooks, James L. 1994 USA)
   Reviews
   Emiliani, S. "Una figlia in carriera." credits still FILM (ITALY) 3:31-32
      n13 1995
ILL MET BY MOONLIGHT   f (Night Ambush d Powell, Michael/Pressburger, Emeric 1957
Gt Br)
   Richards, P. "Ill Met by Moonlight." stills F COM 31:37-40 Mar/Apr 1995
ILLUSIONER   f (d Mullback, Lars 1994 Swed)
   Reviews
   Rehlin, G. "Illusions" ("Illusioner"). credits VARIETY 357:75 Jan 2/8 1995
Im, Kwon-taek   See IM, KWONTAIK
IM, KWONTAIK   See also TAEBAEK SANMAEK
IMAGE ANALYSIS
   Theory
   Cameron, E.W. Kant's station; the Lumieres' train: seeing things by means of
      film. CAN J F STUD 1:36-56 n1 1990
   Canada
   Gaudreault, A. Filmographic analysis and early cinema. bibliog credits CAN
      J F STUD 1:57-73 n1 1990
   Wees, W.C. From the rearview mirror to twenty minutes into the future: the
      video image in "Videodrome" and "Max Headroom." CAN J F STUD 1:29-35 n1
      1990
Image processing, computer controlled   See COMPUTER CONTROLLED IMAGE PROCESSING
Image processing equipment, computer controlled   See COMPUTER CONTROLLED IMAGE
PROCESSING EQUIPMENT
IMAGENES
   Lassacher, M. Spanische Schriften [Book Review]. il BLIMP n30:58-60 Winter
      1995
IMAGES   f (d Altman, Robert 1972 Gt Br)
   Music
   Brown, R.S. Film music: the good, the bad, and the ugly. stills CINEASTE
      21:62-67 n1/2 1995
IMAGINING INDIANS   f (d Masayesva, Victor, Jr. 1993 USA)
   Rony, F.T. Victor Masayesva, Jr., and the politics of "Imagining Indians."
      il stills FQ 48:20-33 n2 1994/95
IMBACH, THOMAS   See also WELL DONE
IMMIGRANT, THE   f (d Chaplin, Charlie 1917 USA)
   Woal, M. and Woal, L.K. Chaplin and the comedy of melodrama. bibliog stills
      UFAJ 46:3-15 n3 1994

INDIEN f (d Harather, Paul 1993 Austria)
    Reviews
    Kleber, R. "Indien." credits still MEDIEN 38:360-361 n6 1994
INDIEN DANS LA VILLE, UN f (d Palud, Herve 1995 Fr)
    Delval, D. "Un indien dans la ville." credits stills GRAND ANGLE
    n177:17-18 Dec 1994
    Dubbing
    Dawtrey, A. and Williams, M. To dub or not to dub. VARIETY 358:10 Mar
    27/Apr 2 1995
    Reviews
    Ciment, M. "Un indien dans la ville." POSITIF n408:60 Feb 1995
Indonesia See as a subheading under individual subject headings
INDUSTRIAL LIGHT AND MAGIC
    Kaplan, D.A. How to make a ghost. still NEWSWK 125:64 Feb 27 1995
    Magid, R. Perrier ad employs latest whistles and bells. stills AMCIN
    74:26-28+ [5p] Sep 1993
INDUSTRY See also names of corporations and studios; CONTRACTS; DISTRIBUTION;
EXPORT MARKET; FINANCING; HOLLYWOOD; IMPORT MARKET; NETWORKS AND NETWORKING;
STUDIO SYSTEM
    Africa
        History
    Harrow, K.W. Diawara, Manthia. African cinema: politics and culture [Book
    Review]. CINEMAS 4:183-185 n2 1994
    Argentina
    Di Nubila, D. Argentine gov't OKs aid. stat VARIETY 358:54 Mar 27/Apr 2
    1995
    Asia
    Riches, I.N. The dragon awakes: cinema growth in Asia. FJ 98:92 Jan/Feb
    1995
    Shugrue, J.E. On the verge of untold expansion. port FJ 98:88 Jan/Feb 1995
        Conferences, Institutes, Workshops, etc.
    Cheah, P. The NETPAC Asian Film Conference. il CINEMAYA n24:29 Summer 1994
    Australia
    Groves, D. It's bizzy down under. il stat stills VARIETY 358:61+ [2p] Feb
    27/Mar 5 1995
    Murray, S. Cathy Robinson. interv port C PAPERS n102:26-31+ [7p] Dec 1994
    Austria
    Geyrhofer, F. and Pataki, H. Film in Oesterreich. BLIMP [n1]:60-64 Mar 1985
    Winter, R. Interview mit Peter Hajek. il interv BLIMP [n1]:50-51 Mar 1985
    Canada
        History
    Grierson, J. Relations with the United States film industry. CAN J F STUD
    1:83-88 n1 1990
        Quebec
    Jean, M. and Loiselle, M.-C. A l'ombre du 7e art. il interv stills 24
    IMAGES n76:4-7+ [7p] Spring 1995
    China (People's Republic, since 1949)
    Zha, J. Killing chickens to show the monkey. il S&S 5:38-40 Jan 1995
    Czech Republic (since 1993)
    Turcsanyi, S. Sumava, a paradicsom. stills F VILAG 38:30-33 n3 1995
    Europe, Western
    Williams, M. and Dawtrey, A. Brits, Euros finally get the big picture.
    graph il stat VARIETY 357:1+ [2p] Jan 2/8 1995
    France
        History
    Turner, G. The cine goes to town. By Richard Abel [Book Review]. AMCIN
    76:85 Jan 1995
    Great Britain
    Deighton, L. Sand and sea. stills S&S 5:30-33 Jan 1995
    Routt, W.D. Petrie, Duncan, ed. New questions of British cinema [Book
    Review]. MEDIA INFO AUSTRALIA n75:169 Feb 1995
    Williams, M. and Dawtrey, A. Brits, Euros finally get the big picture.
    graph il stat VARIETY 357:1+ [2p] Jan 2/8 1995
    Hong Kong
    Scharres, B. The hard road to "Hard Target." il still AMCIN 74:62-64+
    [10p] Sep 1993
    India
    Nahta, K. Cinema industry in India faces heightened competition. FJ 98:91
    Jan/Feb 1995
    Ireland
    Garry, P.M. A different voice. il COMMONWEAL 122:17-18 Mar 24 1995
    Japan
    Knee, A. Cinema, censorship, and the state: the writings of Nagisa Oshima,
    1956-1978. Edited and with an introduction by Annette Michelson [Book
    Review]. UFAJ 46:66-68 n1 1994
    Latin America
    Latin America at a glance. stat VARIETY 358:70 Mar 27/Apr 2 1995
    Mexico
    Paxman, A. As peso drops, so does prod'n. il still VARIETY 358:50 Mar
    27/Apr 2 1995
    Paxman, A. Picture blurry for local prods. stat VARIETY 358:32-33 Feb 6/12
    1995
    New Zealand
    Groves, D. Kiwi pix grab H'wood's eye. VARIETY 358:11+ [2p] Feb 6/12 1995
    Poland
        Future
    Sobolewski, T. Smietnik historii? REZYSER n19:1-3 1993
    Russia (since 1992)
    Film, TV, video in Russia - 1994. Ed: Daniil Dondurei [Book Review]. il
    KINO(GF) n56:30 Nov 1994
    Singapore
    Choo, M. Cinemas will always have a place in Singapore! FJ 98:88+ [2p]
    Jan/Feb 1995
    United States
    Ankiewicz, D. Dziennik kalifornijski. port KINO 27:36-37 May 1993
    Evans, G. Showbiz is psyched for cybermalls. VARIETY 358:1+ [2p] Mar 27/Apr
    2 1995
    O'Neill, K. and Spines, C. "Premiere's" wrap party 1994. il port stat
    tables PREM 8:81-87 Feb 1995
    Schickel, R. What Oscar says about Hollywood. stills TIME 145:61-62 Mar 27

1995
    The studios in review, and film slate future for '95. il stat stills tables
    VARIETY 357:22+ [3p] Jan 9/15 1995
        Collaboration With Television/Video Industry
    O'Steen, K. Film, interactive marketeers uncoordinated. VARIETY 358:34 Feb
    27/Mar 5 1995
        Film Lists
    Blue sheets annual preview section. FJ 98:bet p24 and 43 [pB1-B18+ (36p)]
    Jan/Feb 1995
    Summer heat. stills BOXOFFICE 131:bet p82 and 83 [pSW24-SW26+ (7p)] Apr
    1995
        History
    Grierson, J. Relations with the United States film industry. CAN J F STUD
    1:83-88 n1 1990
    Muscio, G. The commerce of classicism [Book Review]. Q REV F & VIDEO
    15:57-69 n3 1994
        Personnel
    Bart, P. Suiting up. il VARIETY 358:4+ [2p] Mar 20/26 1995
        Vietnam (Socialist Republic, since 1975)
    Dang, N.M. Good cinema gasps for breath. CINEMAYA n24:55 Summer 1994
INFLUENCE OF FILM See also EFFECTS OF FILM
    Literature
    Savater, F. La palabra imaginaria (notas sobre cine y literatura). stills
    NOSFERATU n8:4-7 Feb 1992
        United States
            Young Adults' Film
    Hietala, V. Globaaliteinit arvotyhjiossa [Book Review]. PEILI 18:28 n4 1994
INFLUENCE ON FILM See also EFFECTS ON FILM
    Fairy Tales
    Hanet, K. Petrie, Duncan, ed. Cinema and the realms of enchantment:
    lectures, seminars and essays by Marina Warner and others [Book Review].
    MEDIA INFO AUSTRALIA n75:169 Feb 1995
    Literature
    Andersson, L.G. Ricoeur och film [Book Review]. F HAFTET 22:58 n3 (n87)
    1994
        Finland
            Computers
    Hintikka, K.A. Muokattu todellisuus arkipaivaistyy. stills PEILI 17:29-30
    n4 1993
        Japan
            Drama
    Vidal Estevez, M. William Akira Shakespeare Kurosawa. il stills NOSFERATU
    n8:40-47 Feb 1992
        New Zealand
            Networks and Networking
    Reynolds, P. The fast lane to the future. il ONFILM [12]:13 n1 1995
INFLUENCE ON TELEVISION/VIDEO
    United States
    Weiner, R. H'wood raids its past for interactive fodder. il VARIETY
    357:13+ [2p] Jan 9/15 1995
Information superhighway See NETWORKS AND NETWORKING
INNISFREE f (d Guerin, Jose Luis 1990 Sp)
    Marias, M. "Innisfree." credits il stills NOSFERATU n9:93-96 Jun 1992
    Torres, S. Los motivos de Guerin. biog il stills NOSFERATU n9:38-47 Jun
    1992
INNOCENCE
    Roth-Lindberg, O. Varldens bedragliga sken. il stills CHAPLIN 36:18-25 n6
    (n255) 1994/95
INNOCENT, THE f (d Schlesinger, John 1993 Gt Br/FR Ger)
    Ciapara, E. "Niewinni." biogs credits filmogs still FSP 40:6 n10 (n764)
    1994
    Noel, P. "The Innocent." bibliog credits stills GRAND ANGLE n177:19-20 Dec
    1994
INNOCENTE INTERDITE, L' f (d Maezelle, Guy 1995 Belg/Switz)
    "L'innocence interdite." credits still MONITEUR n127:18 Jan 1995
INSOMNIA f (d Stein, Carol 1995 USA)
    Reviews
    Leydon, J. "Insomnia." credits VARIETY 358:83 Feb 20/26 1995
INSTITUT DES ARTS DE DIFFUSION (Brussels, Belgium)
    Les promotions 1993 et 1994 de l'Institut des Arts de Diffusion (IAD).
    MONITEUR n127:28 Jan 1995
Institutes See CONFERENCES, INSTITUTES, WORKSHOPS, ETC.
INTEGRATION
    Minorities
    Medici, A. La follia come metafora del mar di vivere. stills C NUOVO
    43:16-19 Nov/Dec (n352) 1994
Intercultural analysis See CROSS-CULTURAL ANALYSIS
INTERNATIONAL ALLIANCE OF THEATRICAL STAGE EMPLOYEES & MOVING PICTURE MACHINE
OPERATORS OF THE U.S. AND CANADA
    Cox, D. IA boss won't sell West Coast Short. port stat VARIETY 357:1+ [3p]
    Jan 9/15 1995
International co-production See CO-PRODUCTION
INTERNATIONAL CREATIVE MANAGEMENT, INC.
    Busch, A.M. and Laski, B. Hughes hightails it back to CAA. VARIETY 357:8
    Jan 9/15 1995
    Laski, B. Helmer Hughes moves to ICM. VARIETY 357:24 Jan 2/8 1995
INTERNET (computer network)
    Heyman, K. The Internet: interactivity. il JOURNAL WGA 8:34-35 Mar 1995
    Heyman, K. The Internet: untimely tips. JOURNAL WGA 8:35 Dec/Jan 1995
    O'Steen, K. Oscar night hits the Internet. VARIETY 358:26 Feb 13/19 1995
    Warn, C. To live and die on the Internet. il DGA NEWS 20:14-15 n1 1995
INTERTEXTUAL ANALYSIS
    Canada
    Ropars-Wuilleumier, M.-C. L'oubli du texte. bibliog CINEMAS 4:11-22 n1
    1993
    Wees, W.C. From the rearview mirror to twenty minutes into the future: the
    video image in "Videodrome" and "Max Headroom." CAN J F STUD 1:29-35 n1
    1990
    Germany (Federal Republic, 1949-1990)
    Russell, C. The life and death of authorship in Wim Wenders' "The State of

Things." scenario CAN J F STUD 1:15-28 n1 1990
   United States
     Animation
Lindvall, T. and Melton, M. Toward a postmodern animated discourse: Bakhtin, intertextuality and the cartoon carnival. il stills ANIMATION J 3:44-63 n1 1994
INTERVIEW WITH THE VAMPIRE: THE VAMPIRE CHRONICLES f (d Jordan, Neil 1994 USA)
Conner, D.M. Correspondence: Alleva on "Vampire." COMMONWEAL [122]:22-23 Feb 10 1995
Girard, M. Les vampires et la critique. still SEQUENCES n175:47-48 Nov/Dec 1994
Murphy, K. Nativity scenes. stills F COM 31:12-16 Jan/Feb 1995
Prayez, B. "Entretien avec un vampire." credits stills GRAND ANGLE n177:13-14 Dec 1994
Taubin, A. Bloody tales. stills S&S 5:8-11 Jan 1995
Thomson, D. Really a part of me. stills F COM 31:17-18+ [8p] Jan/Feb 1995
     Cinematography
Pizzello, S. "Interview With the Vampire" taps new vein. il stills AMCIN 76:43-52 Jan 1995
     Sound Track Reviews
Pugliese, R. Segnodischi. filmog stills SEGNO n72:77 Mar/Apr 1995
     Special Effects
Magid, R. Digital domain arranges an "Interview With the Vampire." stills AMCIN 76:53-54+ [7p] Jan 1995
     Reviews
Bjorkman, S. Blodfattigt om vampyrer. credits stills CHAPLIN 36:67-68 n6 (n255) 1994/95
Cherchi Usai, P. "Intervista col vampiro" - "Cronache di vampiri." credits stills SEGNO n71:41-42 Jan/Feb 1995
Larue, J. "Interview With the Vampire." credits still SEQUENCES n175:41-42 Nov/Dec 1994
Newman, K. "Interview With the Vampire: the Vampire Chronicles." credits still S&S 5:46-47 Feb 1995
Paesano, A. "Intervista col vampiro - Cronache di vampiri." credits FILM (ITALY) 3:11-13 n13 1995
Rike, J.L. On fallen gods and guilt. CHR CENT 112:177+ [3p] Feb 15 1995
Rousseau, Y. "Interview With the Vampire." still 24 IMAGES n76:62 Spring 1995
Schubert, G. A ponyvahosok lazadasa. credits stills F VILAG 38:32-35 n4 1995
Travers, P. The dying game. il still ROLLING STONE n697:101-102+ [3p] Dec 15 1994
Viviani, C. "Frankenstein, d'apres Mary Shelley"; "Entretien avec un vampire." credits stills POSITIF n407:30-33 Jan 1995
INTO THE DEEP f (d Hall, Howard 1995 USA)
   Reviews
Albanese, A. "Into the Deep." BOXOFFICE 131:bet p125 and 144 [pR37] Apr 1995
INTOLERANCE f (d Griffith, D.W. 1916 USA)
Daniel, F. Megszallott az utolso centig. il stills F VILAG 38:14-17 n3 1995
INVADERS FROM MARS f (d Menzies, William Cameron 1953 USA)
   Reviews
Holt, W.G. "Invaders From Mars." il still F FAX n48:24+ [2p] Jan/Feb 1995
IOSELIANI, OTAR See also FAVORIS DE LA LUNE, LES
Brach, G. Gespraech mit Gerard Brach ueber Otar Iosseliani. biog filmog il still BLIMP [n2]:52-53 Winter 1985
IR JIS PASAKE JUMS SUDIE f (d Siusa, Anatolijus 1994 Lithuania)
   Reviews
Meils, C. "And He Bid You Farewell" ("Ir jis pasake jums sudie"). credits VARIETY 357:74 Jan 2/8 1995
Iran See as a subheading under individual subject headings
Ireland See as a subheading under individual subject headings
IRELAND, JOHN See also HANNAH LEE
Ireland, Northern, in film See NORTHERN IRELAND IN FILM
IRON CURTAIN, THE f (d Wellman, William A. 1948 USA)
   Political Analysis
Swann, P. International conspiracy in and around "The Iron Curtain." VEL LT TRAP n35:52-60 Spring 1995
IRON HORSEMEN f (d Charmant, Gilles 1994 Finl/Fr/It)
   Reviews
Nazzaro, G.A. "Iron Horsemen"/"Bad Trip." still C FORUM 34:35-36 Sep (n337) 1994
IRONY See also CYNICISM; SATIRE
Roth-Lindberg, O. Varldens bedragliga sken. il stills CHAPLIN 36:18-25 n6 (n255) 1994/95
   Television (broadcast)
Handelman, D. The birth of the uncool. il stills PREM 8:84-88 Mar 1995
IRVIN, JOHN See also WIDOWS' PEAK
IRVING, JOHN
Helman, A. Swiat wedlug Hilla. still KINO 27:24-26 Jul 1993
IS PARIS BURNING? f (d Clement, Rene 1966 USA/Fr)
   Sound Tracks
Ford, J. Classic corner: Maurice Jarre's "Is Paris Burning?" il F SCORE MONTHLY n36/37:31 Aug/Sep 1993
IS THAT ALL THERE IS? f (d Anderson, Lindsay 1993 Gt Br)
Anderton, J. Lindsay Anderson notes. il port VERTIGO (UK) 1:59-60 n4 1994/95
ISLAND OF TERROR f (d Fisher, Terence 1966 Gt Br)
Aguilar, C. "S.O.S., el mundo en peligro." credits stills NOSFERATU n6:96-97 Apr 1991
Israel See as a subheading under individual subject headings
ISRAEL, NEAL See also SURF NINJAS
Ciapara, E. "Surfujacy Ninja." credits filmogs still FSP 40:9 n4 (n758) 1994
ISSERMANN, ALINE See also OMBRE DU DOUTE, L'
ISTO, KAISU
Isto, K. Cartoon Forum 1993. il PEILI 17:36-37 n4 1993

IT COULD HAPPEN TO YOU f (d Bergman, Andrew 1994 USA)
Cicutat, M. "Milliardaire malgre lui." POSITIF n408:58 Feb 1995
Elia, M. "It Could Happen to You." SEQUENCES n174:46-47 Sep/Oct 1994
Fontanini, C. "Puo' succedere anche a te." credits still FILM (ITALY) 3:26-27 n13 1995
IT!: THE TERROR FROM BEYOND SPACE f (d Cahn, Edward L. 1958 USA)
Brunas, M. "It! The Terror From Beyond Space." il stills SCARLET STREET n17:56-58 Winter 1995
Italy See as a subheading under individual subject headings
ITO, DAISUKE See also CHUJI TABI NIKKI
IT'S A GIFT f (d McLeod, Norman Z. 1934 USA)
Ciment, M. BFI film classics [Book Reviews]. stills POSITIF n408:75-77 Feb 1995
IUSUPOVA, MAIRAM See also VREMIA ZHELTOI TRAVY
"Vremja jholtoi travy." biog credits filmog CINEMAYA n25/26:108 Autumn/Winter 1994/95
IVERSEN, GUNNAR
Iversen, G. Aerbodig biografi om norsk films askeladd [Book Review]. il Z n1:39 (n47) 1994
Iversen, G. Kjolig moralitet. stills F&K n7:14-15 1993
Iversen, G. Sa sprenger han verden. stills Z n1:30-35 (n47) 1994
IVERSEN, JON
Iversen, J. "Koloss." credits still Z n4:18-19 (n46) 1993
Iversen, J. Regissor eller ikke regissor? il interv Z n4:23-25 (n46) 1993
IVORY, JAMES See also JEFFERSON IN PARIS; REMAINS OF THE DAY, THE; ROOM WITH A VIEW, A
IWANAMI PRODUCTIONS
Abe, M.N. Documentarists of Japan (first in a series). biog filmog port stills DOC BOX 1:9-13 1992
JLG by JLG See JLG/JLG - AUTOPORTRAIT DE DECEMBRE
JLG/JLG - AUTOPORTRAIT DE DECEMBRE f (JLG by JLG d Godard, Jean-Luc 1994 Fr/Switz)
   Reviews
Rafferty, T. Double Godard. il NEW YORKER 70:92-95 Feb 6 1995
JABLONSKI, DAREK
Sendecka, M. Szkolenie w Burkina Faso. interv REZYSER n19:3-5 1993
JACK THE RIPPER
Bond, S.R. and Bond, S. Report form 221B Baker Street. il ARMCHAIR DET 26:70-71 n4 1993
JACKSON, DEVON For film reviews see author under the following titles: RUDYARD KIPLING'S THE JUNGLE BOOK
Jackson, D. Never do business with "Friends." il port PREM 8:36 Apr 1995
Jackson, D. Quentin Tarantino's Negro problem - and Hollywood's. il VILLAGE VOICE 40:39-40 Mar 28 1995
JACKSON, DIANNE See also SNOWMAN, THE
JACKSON, KATHY MERLOCK
Davidoff, S. Kathy Merlock Jackson, Walt Disney: a bio-bibliography [Book Review]. ANIMATION J 3:92 n1 1994
JACKSON, PETER See also HEAVENLY CREATURES; MEET THE FEEBLES
JACKSON, SAMUEL L.
Webster, A. Filmographies. biog filmogs stills PREM 8:160 Apr 1995
JACKSON, WENDY
Jackson, W. Cecile Starr: a pioneer's pioneer. biog port ANIMATION J 3:40-43 n2 1995
JACOBS, ALAN See also NINA TAKES A LOVER
JACOBS, JON See also GIRL WITH THE HUNGRY EYES, THE
JACOBS, KEN
Testa, B. The two religions of avant-garde film, or maybe three. CAN J F STUD 3:89-100 n2 1994
JACOBS, LEA
Jacobs, L. The woman's picture and the poetics of melodrama. il CAM OBS n31:120-147 Jan/May 1993
JACOBSEN, WOLFGANG
Codelli, L. "Greed." Di Jonathan Rosenbaum [Book Reviews]. GRIFFITHIANA n51/52:260 Oct 1994
JACQUINOT, GENEVIEVE
Jacquinot, G. Le documentaire, une fiction (pas) comme les autres. bibliog stills CINEMAS 4:61-81 n2 1994
JAEGGI, BRUNO
Jaeggi, B. and Knaebel, M. Look back in pain. filmog interv port stills CINEMAYA n24:44-47 Summer 1994
JAEHNE, KAREN For film reviews see author under the following titles: DE ESO NO SE HABLA
JAGD NACH DEM TODE, DIE f (serial d Gerhardt, Karl 1920-21 Ger)
   Restoration
Koerber, M. Reconstructing "Die Jagd nach dem Tode." il stills J F PRES n49:34-39 Oct 1994
JAILBIRD AND HOW HE FLEW, THE f (d Blackton, Stuart 1906 USA)
   Shot Description
Gaudreault, A. Filmographic analysis and early cinema. bibliog credits CAN J F STUD 1:57-73 n1 1990
JAMES, CHRISTINE For film reviews see author under the following titles: BEFORE SUNRISE; CIRCLE OF FRIENDS; EXOTICA; FILS DU REQUIN, LE; HIGHER LEARNING; JERKY BOYS, THE
James, C. Barbara Beam and the American dream. il port BOXOFFICE 131:74-77 Apr 1995
James, C. Driving passion. il BOXOFFICE 131:42+ [2p] Apr 1995
James, C. Ghost of a chance. il still BOXOFFICE 131:20-21 Apr 1995
JAMES, DAVID E.
Porton, R. Review of David James: allegories of cinema [Book Review]. il MILLENNIUM n25:114-120 Summer 1991
JAMES, HENRY
Birdsall, E. Interpreting Henry James: Bogdanovich's "Daisy Miller." bibliog still LIT/FQ 22:272-277 n4 1994
JAMES, NICK For film reviews see author under the following titles: BARCELONA; DEATH AND THE MAIDEN
JAMES, STEVE See also HOOP DREAMS
JAMESON, RICHARD T.
Jameson, R.T. Written, produced and directed by Michael Powell and Emeric

Pressburger. il stills F COM 31:18-19 Mar/Apr 1995
JANCSO, MIKLOS See also KOVEK UZENETE, A
JANE EYRE f (d Stevenson, Robert 1944 USA)
    Sound Track Reviews
  Raynes, D. "Jane Eyre." SCN 14:20 Mar 1995
JANEGA, ELEANOR
  Connors, R. and others. Letters: the king and us. MS 5:8 n4 1995
JANETZKO, CHRISTOPH See also HOLLYWOOD KILLED ME
  Janetzko, C. and Wenner, D. Storyboards for "Hollywood Killed Me" (1990).
    il still MILLENNIUM n25:18-23 Summer 1991
JANG, SUN-WOO See also NEO-E-GE NARUL BONENDA
JANISCH, ATTILA
  Janisch, A. "A fold se volt mas, mint egy folborult fazek." il interv
    stills F VILAG 38:14-17 n2 1995
JANKEL, ANNABEL See also SUPER MARIO BROS.
JANKO EN MARISKA f (d Zeman, Karel 1980 Czech)
    Reviews
  Niskanen, E. "Kertomus Jonista ja Mariasta." still PEILI 17:44 n4 1993
JANSER, ANDRES For film reviews see author under the following titles: KONGRESS
    DER PINGUINE, DER; ROBERT CREEP
Japan See as a subheading under individual subject headings
JARDIN DE PLANTES f (d Broca, Philippe de 1995 Fr/Hungary)
    Reviews
  Elley, D. "Tales From the Zoo" ("Jardin de plantes"). credits VARIETY
    358:87 Feb 20/26 1995
JARDIN DEL EDEN, EL f (d Novaro, Maria 1994 Mex/Can)
    Reviews
  Fornara, B. "El jardin del Eden." still C FORUM 34:21 Sep (n337) 1994
  Vasse, C. "Le Jardin de l'Eden." still POSITIF n409:44 Mar 1995
JARDINES COLGANTES f (d Llorca, Pablo 1993 Sp)
    Reviews
  Tamas, A. "Fuggokertek." credits still F VILAG 38:56 n2 1995
JARECKI, ANDREW R.
  Jarecki, A.R. Making it easier to go to the movies. il FJ 98:56+ [2p] Mar
    1995
JARL, STEFAN See also ANSTANDIGT LIV, ETT; DOM KALLAR OSS MODS; SOCIALA ARVET,
    DET
JARMAN, DEREK See also CARAVAGGIO
  Aasarod, P. Derek Jarman. il Z n4:26-27 (n46) 1993
JARRE, MAURICE
  Ford, J. Classic corner: Maurice Jarre's "Is Paris Burning?" il F SCORE
    MONTHLY n36/37:31 Aug/Sep 1993
JARVIE, IAN
  Paterson, R. Hollywood's overseas campaign: the North Atlantic movie trade,
    1920-1950. By Ian Jarvie [Book Review]. J COMM 45:171-173 n1 1995
JASON GOES TO HELL: THE FINAL FRIDAY f (d Marcus, Adam 1993 USA)
    Sound Track Reviews
  Hirsch, D. "Jason Goes to Hell: the Final Friday." F SCORE MONTHLY n38:12
    Oct 1993
JASON'S LYRIC f (d McHenry, Doug 1994 USA)
    Reviews
  Di Luzio, A. "Jason's Lyric." still C FORUM 34:22 Sep (n337) 1994
JAUBERT, JEAN-CLAUDE
  Jaubert, J.-C. Andre Gaudreault. Du litteraire au filmique, systeme du recit
    [Book Review]. CAN J F STUD 1:89-90 n1 1990
  Jaubert, J.-C. Sous la direction de J. Aumont, A. Gaudreault, M. Marie.
    Histoire du cinema, nouvelles approaches [Book Review]. CAN J F STUD
    1:91-92 n1 1990
JAWORSKI, ROBERT
  Jaworski, R. and Maniewski, M. Opowiesc Wandy Luczyckiej. still KINO
    27:26-27 Jun 1993
JAY, MARTIN
  Jay, M. The disenchantment of the eye: surrealism and the crisis of
    ocularcentrism. il stills VISUAL ANTHRO R 7:15-38 n1 1991
JEAN, MARCEL For film reviews see author under the following titles: CAIXA, A;
    ED WOOD; KABLOONAK; MASK, THE; RUDYARD KIPLING'S THE JUNGLE BOOK;
    TIMECOP
  Jean, M. Des restes d'images non identifies. il interv stills 24 IMAGES
    n75:26-32+ [8p] Dec/Jan 1994/95
  Jean, M. Entretien avec Real La Rochelle. il interv 24 IMAGES n75:32-33
    Dec/Jan 1994/95
  Jean, M. Esther Valiquette. obit port 24 IMAGES n75:36 Dec/Jan 1994/95
  Jean, M. Francois Delisle. il interv stills 24 IMAGES n76:24-26+ [4p]
    Spring 1995
  Jean, M. La force des films brefs. still 24 IMAGES n76:46 Spring 1995
  Jean, M. Voir rouge. stills 24 IMAGES n76:44-45 Spring 1995
  Jean, M. and Loiselle, M.-C. A l'ombre du 7e art. il interv stills 24
    IMAGES n76:4-7+ [7p] Spring 1995
JEANCOLAS, JEAN-PIERRE
  Jeancolas, J.-P. Geraniums [Book Reviews]. stills POSITIF n408:94-95 Feb
    1995
JEANNE LA PUCELLE f (d Rivette, Jacques 1994 Fr)
    Reviews
  Larue, J. "Jeanne La Pucelle." credits still SEQUENCES n174:34 Sep/Oct
    1994
  Loiselle, M.-C. La jeune fille et la mort. credits stills 24 IMAGES
    n75:64-65 Dec/Jan 1994/95
JEDER FUER SICH UND GOTT GEGEN ALLE f (Every Man for Himself and God Against
    All d Herzog, Werner 1974 W Ger)
  Hainisch, B. and Pilz, T. Werner Herzogs "Jeder fuer sich und Gott gegen
    alle" - ein Film. il stills BLIMP n30:16-22 Winter 1994
JEFFERIES, WILLIAM
  Brolley, M. Shallow graves. By William Jefferies [Book Reviews]. ARMCHAIR
    DET 26:104 n3 1993
JEFFERSON IN PARIS f (d Ivory, James 1995 USA)
  Francke, L. Introducing movie magic. il interv INTERV 25:106-107 Apr 1995
    Production
  Bagley, C. The pursuit of happiness. il PREM 8:64-67 Apr 1995
    Reviews
  McCarthy, T. "Jefferson in Paris." credits still VARIETY 358:74+ [2p] Mar

27/Apr 2 1995
JEFFREY, LISS
  Jeffrey, L. Rethinking audiences for cultural industries: implications for
    Canadian research. bibliog stat tables CAN J COM 19:495-522 n3/4 1994
JELES, ANDRAS See also PARHUZAMOS ELETRAJZOK
JENKINS, SUE
  Jenkins, S. Rugby & romance a winning team. il ONFILM 11:7 n11 1994/95
JENNINGS, KAREN
  McFarlane, B. Crofts, Stephen. Identification, gender and genre in film: the
    case of "Shame" [Book Reviews]. MEDIA INFO AUSTRALIA n75:159-160 Feb 1995
JENSEN, JORN
  Jensen, J. This Knut's a hot media ticket in Scandinavia. VARIETY 358:47
    Mar 13/19 1995
  Jensen, J.R. Nordisk film pa det naere marked. stat stills tables F&K
    n7:29-31 1993
JENSEN, PAUL M.
  Jensen, P.M. Inside "The Skull." il stills SCARLET STREET n17:26-28+ [6p]
    Winter 1994
JERKY BOYS, THE f (d Melkonian, James 1995 USA)
    Reviews
  Grunden, C. "The Jerky Boys." credits FJ 98:69 Mar 1995
  James, C. "Jerky Boys." still BOXOFFICE 131:bet p125 and 144 [pR35] Apr
    1995
  Leydon, J. "The Jerky Boys." credits still VARIETY 358:77 Feb 6/12 1995
  Salamon, J. "The Jerky Boys." VILLAGE VOICE 40:58 Feb 21 1995
JERRMAN, TONI
  Jerrman, T. Splatteria animaation keinoin. stills PEILI 17:17-19 n4 1993
JEUNE WERTHER, LE f (d Doillon, Jacques 1993 Fr)
    Reviews
  Vahtera, H. Rakkauden karsimykset. credits still PEILI 17:44 n4 1993
JEWISH DIRECTORS See also names of Jewish directors
    United States
  Dixon, W.W. American-Jewish filmmakers: traditions and trends. By David
    Desser and Lester D. Friedman [Book Review]. F CRITICISM 19:108-113 n2
    1994/95
JEWISON, NORMAN See also ONLY YOU
JEWS IN FILM
  Salamon, J. Beyond perestroika: Jews and history in the global village.
    VILLAGE VOICE 40:59 Jan 17 1995
JEZEBEL f (d Bomba, Enrico 1953? It)
  Chiti, R. Le tragicomiche disavventure del film "Jezebel" o "Muro
    d'asfalto." il stills IMMAGINE n28:24-27 Autumn 1994
JHABVALA, RUTH PRAWER
  Katz, S.B. "A conversation with... Ruth Prawer Jhabvala." filmog il interv
    JOURNAL WGA 8:38-41 Dec/Jan 1995
JIANG, SHAN
  Chen, R. Jiang Shan, a rising star in music and film. il ports CHINA
    SCREEN n4:36-37 1994
JIANG, WEN See also YANGGUANG CANLAN DE RIZI
JIN, YONG
  Hoare, S. Romance du livre et du film: l'adaptation de la "Romance du livre
    et de l'epee" par Ann Hui. bibliog glos stills CINEMAS 3:141-155 n2/3 1993
JIZDA f (d Sverak, Jan 1995 Czech R)
    Reviews
  Rooney, D. "The Ride" ("Jizda"). credits VARIETY 358:85 Feb 20/26 1995
Joan of Arc See JEANNE LA PUCELLE also
  Blaetz, R. Retelling the Joan of Arc story: women, war, and Hollywood's
    "Joan of Paris." bibliog still LIT/FQ 22:212-221 n4 1994
JOAN OF PARIS f (d Stevenson, Robert 1942 USA)
  Blaetz, R. Retelling the Joan of Arc story: women, war, and Hollywood's
    "Joan of Paris." bibliog still LIT/FQ 22:212-221 n4 1994
JOBIM, ANTONIO CARLOS
  Lentz, H., III. Obituaries. biogs filmogs il obits ports CLASSIC
    n236:57-59 Feb 1995
JODOROWSKI, ALEJANDRO
  Boswell, S. Neither Mozart nor Hendrix. il still S&S 5:37 Apr 1995
JODRELL, STEVE See also SHAME
JOE & MARIE f (d Stoecklin, Tania 1994 Switz/Fr/FR Ger)
    Reviews
  Lachat, P. "Joe & Marie." credits C(SWITZ) 40:225-226 1994
JOFFE, ROLAND
  Williams, M. Joffe gets French backing. VARIETY 358:22 Feb 20/26 1995
JOHNNY MNEMONIC f (d Longo, Robert 1995 Can)
  Montesano, A.P. "Johnny Mnemonic." port stills C FANTAS 26:14-15 n2 1995
  Pinchbeck, D. From artist to auteur. port ESQUIRE 123:17 Jan 1995
    Adaptations
  Montesano, A.P. "Johnny Mnemonic." stills C FANTAS 26:44+ [2p] n3 1995
    Production Design and Designers
  Montesano, A.P. "Mnemonic" design. il stills C FANTAS 26:46-47 n3 1995
JOHNNY YUMA f (d Guerrieri, Romolo 1966 It)
    Sound Track Reviews
  Deutsch, D.C. "Arizona Colt"; "Johnny Yuma." SCN 14:16 Mar 1995
JOHNSEN, FRANK
  Johnsen, F. Disneys nye flaggskip. stills F&K n7:4-6 1993
  Johnsen, F. Om joder og sjakk. interv port stills F&K n1:8-10 1994
JOHNSON, DON
  Jones, M. Don Johnson remembers Sal Mineo. still SCARLET STREET
    n17:106-107 Winter 1995
JOHNSON, LAMONT See also BROKEN CHAIN, THE
JOHNSON, MARTIN
  Williams, T. They married adventure: the wandering lives of Martin and Osa
    Johnson. By Pascal James Imperato and Eleanor M. Imperato [Book Review].
    WESTERN AM LIT 28:380-381 n4 1994
JOHNSON, OSA
  Williams, T. They married adventure: the wandering lives of Martin and Osa
    Johnson. By Pascal James Imperato and Eleanor M. Imperato [Book Review].
    WESTERN AM LIT 28:380-381 n4 1994
JOHNSON, PATRICK READ See also BABY'S DAY OUT
JOHNSON, TOM
  Eriksen, F. Leksikal Peter Cushing biografi [Book Review]. il Z n4:40

(n46) 1993

JOHNSTON, JOE See also PAGEMASTER, THE
JOHNSTON, TREVOR For film reviews see author under the following titles: GEORGE
  BALANCHINE'S THE NUTCRACKER; LITTLE BIG LEAGUE
JOHNSTONE, JYLL See also MARTHA & ETHEL
JOJOLA, TED
  Jojola, T. Absurd reality: Hollywood goes to the Indians... filmog F&HIST
    23:7-16 n1/4 1993
JONES, ALAN
  Jones, A. Dr. Jekyll & the maid. stills C FANTAS 26:12-13+ [3p] n3 1995
  Jones, A. "Heavenly Creatures." il stills C FANTAS 26:42-43+ [3p] n2 1995
  Jones, A. John Carpenter. il stills C FANTAS 26:44-45 n2 1995
JONES, CHUCK See also ONE FROGGY EVENING
JONES, MARVIN
  Jones, M. Don Johnson remembers Sal Mineo. still SCARLET STREET
    n17:106-107 Winter 1995
JONES, MICHAEL FORREST
  Jones, M.F. 'From where I sit...' il port BOXOFFICE 131:94-96 Apr 1995
JONES, TOMMY LEE
  Elia, M. Tommy Lee Jones. filmog port stills SEQUENCES n174:26-28 Sep/Oct
    1994
JORDA, JOAQUIN See also DANTE NO ES UNICAMENTE SEVERO; DIA DE LOS MUERTOS, EL;
  ENCARGO DEL CAZADOR, EL; NUMAX PRESENTA...; PORTOGALLO, PAESE TRANQUILLO
  Angulo, J. and others. Entrevista: Garay, Guerin, Jorda y Portabella. il
    interv stills NOSFERATU n9:68-87 Jun 1992
  Jorda, J. "Dante no es unicamente severo." credits stills NOSFERATU
    n9:97-99 Jun 1992
  Jorda, J. "El encargo del cazador." credits still NOSFERATU n9:100-102 Jun
    1992
  Jorda, J. Numax presenta... y otras cosas. still NOSFERATU n9:56-59 Jun
    1992
  Vidal, N. Joaquin Jorda: el circulo del perverso. biog il stills NOSFERATU
    n9:48-55 Jun 1992
JORDAN, LARRY See also BLACK OUD, THE
  Testa, B. The two religions of avant-garde film, or maybe three. CAN J F
    STUD 3:89-100 n2 1994
JORDAN, NEIL See also CRYING GAME, THE; INTERVIEW WITH THE VAMPIRE: THE VAMPIRE
  CHRONICLES
JORFALD, OIVIND S. See also FLYNDRA
JOST, FRANCOIS
  Jost, F. Direct, narration simultanee: frontieres de la temporalite.
    bibliog CINEMAS 5:81-90 n1/2 1994
  Jost, F. Le spectateur qui en savait trop. bibliog still CINEMAS 4:121-133
    n3 1994
JOST, JON See also SLOW MOVES; UNO A TE, UNO A ME, E UNO A RAFFAELE
  Jost, J. Notes for "Slow Moves." il MILLENNIUM n25:25-29 Summer 1991
  Kulas, G. and Hjortoy, K. Jost om Jost. interv port Z n4:6-8 (n46) 1993
  Piccardi, A. Qualche nota su un american filmaker. stills C FORUM 34:44-48
    Oct (n338) 1994
JOUBERT, BEVERLY
  Parker, H. "Wild at Heart." port MOVIELINE 6:18 Apr 1995
JOUEUR DE VIOLON, LE f (d Damme, Charlie van 1994 Belg/Fr/FR Ger)
  "Le joueur de violon." credits still MONITEUR n126:7-8 Dec 1994
JOUR DANS LA MORT DE SARAJEVO, UN f (d Ravalat, Thierry 1993 Fr)
  Sobolewski, T. Pamiec Bosni. il KINO 27:4-5 May 1993
JOUR DE FETE f (d Tati, Jacques 1949 Fr)
    Reviews
  Nesselson, L. "Jour de fete." credits VARIETY 357:72 Jan 9/15 1995
JOYE, JOSEPH
  Cherchi Usai, P. Film um 1910. Aus der Sammlung Joseph Joye (London). By
    Roland Cosandey [Book Review]. GRIFFITHIANA n51/52:258 Oct 1994
  Cherchi Usai, P. Film um 1910: Aus der Sammlung Joseph Joye (London). By
    Roland Cosandey [Book Review]. J F PRES n49:73 Oct 1994
  Cosandey, R. Le retour de l'Abbe Joye ou la cinematheque, l'historien et le
    cinema communal. il J F PRES n49:46-55 Oct 1994
Joyless Street See FREUDLOSE GASSE, DIE
JU DOU f (d Zhang, Yimou 1990 China/Japan)
  Muszynski, A. Marginesy melodramatu. stills KINO 27:18-19 Jul 1993
    Oedipal Narrative
  Farquhar, M.A. Oedipality in "Red Sorghum" and "Judou." bibliog glos
    scenario stills CINEMAS 3:60-86 n2/3 1993
JUDELL, BRANDON
  Judell, B. Letters: Kael! Kael! VILLAGE VOICE 40:4 Jan 31 1995
[JUDGE] f (d Negishi, Hiroshi 1994 Japan)
    Reviews
  Persons, D. "Judge." C FANTAS 26:59-60 n3 1995
JUDGE DREDD f (d Cannon, Danny 1995 USA)
  Changing lanes. interv port BOXOFFICE 131:12 Apr 1995
JUGERT, RUDOLF See also ROSEN IM HERBST
JUGOSLOVENSKA KINOTEKA (Belgrade, Yugoslavia)
  Kosanovic, D. Beograd. still J F PRES n49:23-25 Oct 1994
JUHASZ, ALEXANDRA
  Juhasz, A. So many alternatives. stills CINEASTE 21:37-39 n1/2 1995
Jules and Jim See JULES ET JIM
JULES ET JIM f (Jules and Jim d Truffaut, Francois 1962 Fr)
    Psychoanalytic Analysis
  DalMolin, E. A voice in the dark: feminine figuration in Truffaut's "Jules
    and Jim." bibliog still LIT/FQ 22:238-245 n4 1994
JULIA, RAUL
  Elia, M. Les bonnes (et parfois les dernieres) repliques de ceux qui nous
    ont quittes. biogs il obits port stills SEQUENCES n175:6 Nov/Dec 1994
JULICH, SOLVEIG
  Julich, S. Voxel-Man. diags F HAFTET 22:55-57 n3 (n87) 1994
JULIEN, ISAAC See also DARKER SIDE OF BLACK; LOOKING FOR LANGSTON
  Grundmann, R. Black nationhood and the rest in the West. interv port
    CINEASTE 21:28-31 n1/2 1995
  Nolan, A.M. Double dare. il still VILLAGE VOICE 40:50 Jan 10 1995
JUNG, ULI
  Jung, U. "Kintop" [Book Review]. il BLIMP n30:45-46 Winter 1994

JUNGEN, DIE f (d Schoenemann, Hannes 1988 W Ger)
  Graef, C. Der erste Film nach acht Jahren. port F & FERNSEHEN 22:98-99 n6
    1994
JUNIOR f (d Reitman, Ivan 1994 USA)
  Bjorkman, S. Arnold Schwarzenegger. filmog il interv stills CHAPLIN
    36:46-54 n6 (n255) 1994/95
  Thomson, D. Really a part of me. stills F COM 31:17-18+ [8p] Jan/Feb 1995
  Venchiarutti, M. "Junior." credits stills GRAND ANGLE n178:17-18 Jan 1995
    Reviews
  Asboth, E. "Junior." credits still F VILAG 38:58 n2 1995
  Ascione, G. "Junior." credits il stills SEGNO n71:44-45 Jan/Feb 1995
  Bruyn, O. de. "Junior." POSITIF n409:44 Mar 1995
  Feinstein, H. "Junior." credits still S&S 5:46-47 Jan 1995
  Travers, P. "Junior." still ROLLING STONE n697:104 Dec 15 1994
JURASSIC PARK f (d Spielberg, Steven 1993 USA)
    Ethics
  Warren, P. Pour une ethique cinematographique. bibliog CINEMAS 4:25-42 n3
    1994
    Sound Track Reviews
  Pugliese, R. Segnodischi. stills SEGNO n63:93 Sep/Oct 1993
    Reviews
  Karlsson, N. Liskojen yo. credits PEILI 17:30 n3 1993
  Norcen, L. "Jurassic Park." credits still SEGNO n63:97-98 Sep/Oct 1993
JURGENS, JO HJERTAKER
  Jurgens, J.H. Tegnefilmcompagniet. il Z n4:20-22 (n46) 1993
JUST CAUSE f (d Glimcher, Arne 1995 USA)
  Karmen, A. Letters: deathless prose. VILLAGE VOICE 40:6 Mar 14 1995
    Reviews
  Haun, H. "Just Cause." credits still FJ 98:61-62 Mar 1995
  Kramer, P. "Just Cause." still BOXOFFICE 131:bet p125 and 144 [pR30] Apr
    1995
  McCarthy, T. "Cause" unwinds in twists and turns. credits still VARIETY
    358:47+ [2p] Feb 13/19 1995
  Nolan, A.M. "Just Cause." still VILLAGE VOICE 40:76 Feb 28 1995
JUSTINIANO, GONZALO See also AMNESIA
JUURIKKALA, KAIJA See also ROSA WAS HERE
  Juurikkala, K. Lyhyt johdatus lyhytelokuvan sielunmaisemaan. stills PEILI
    17:4-5 n3 1993
KKK BOUTIQUE AIN'T JUST REDNECKS, THE f (d Billops, Camille/Hatch, James V.
  1994 USA)
    Reviews
  Camhi, L. "The KKK Boutique Ain't Just Rednecks." VILLAGE VOICE 40:61 Mar 7
    1995
KABAY, BARNA See also EUROPA MESSZE VAN
KABLOONAK f (d Massot, Claude 1994 Fr/Can)
  Benjamin, D. Sur le plateau de "Kabloonak." il still SEQUENCES n174:7-8
    Sep/Oct 1994
    Reviews
  Bourget, J.-L. "Kabloonak." POSITIF n409:44-45 Mar 1995
  Castiel, E. "Kabloonak." SEQUENCES n174:8 Sep/Oct 1994
  Jean, M. "Kabloonak." still 24 IMAGES n75:76 Dec/Jan 1994/95
KACHYNA, KAREL See also KRAVA
KACZMAREK, ROBERT
  Sendecka, M. Szkolenie w Burkina Faso. interv REZYSER n19:3-5 1993
KADISBELLAN f (Slingshot, The d Sandgren, Ake 1993 Swed)
  Romeo, A. "Colpo di fionda." credits still SEGNO n71:47-48 Jan/Feb 1995
KAEL, PAULINE
  Brown, G. Funny lady. il VILLAGE VOICE 40:47-48 Jan 17 1995
  Menand, L. Finding it at the movies [Book Review]. il NY R BKS 42:10-14+
    [7p] Mar 23 1995
KAEUTNER, HELMUT See also TEUFELS GENERAL, DES
KAGEMUSHA f (d Kurosawa, Akira 1980 Japan)
  Schruender, M. Gelobt sei der Alptraum bemerkungen zu Kurosawa Akiras
    "Kagemusha." credits stills BLIMP [n2]:21-24 Winter 1985
KALAGA, WOJCIECH
  Kalaga, W. Stam, Robert, Burgoyne, Robert, Flitterman-Lewis, Sandy. New
    vocabularies in film semiotics: structuralism, post-structuralism, and
    beyond [Book Review]. CINEMAS 4:167-175 n3 1994
KALATOZOV, MIKHAIL See also IA KUBA
KALIFORNIA f (d Sena, Dominic 1993 USA)
    Reviews
  Curry, J.-A. "Kalifornia." still FATAL VISIONS n17:8 1994
KALIN, TOM
  Juhasz, A. So many alternatives. stills CINEASTE 21:37-39 n1/2 1995
KALISH, KAREN
  Kalish, K. Preserving the funds that preserve the films. DGA NEWS 20:36-37
    n1 1995
  Kalish, K. Wake up and smell the vinegar. il DGA NEWS 20:24+ [6p] n1 1995
KALLINEN, SAMI
  Kallinen, S. Kissan kuolema. stills PEILI 18:14-15 n4 1994
  Kallinen, S. Pohjoismaista lastenelokuvaa suurin silmin [Book Review]. il
    PEILI 18:38 n4 1994
KALTENECKER, SIEGFRIED
  Kaltenecker, S. Richard Dyer: The matter of images. Essays on
    representations [Book Review]. BLIMP n30:71 Winter 1994
KALVERT, SCOTT See also BASKETBALL DIARIES, THE
  Neff, R. Kalvert shoots and scores in "Basketball Diaries" debut. il interv
    FJ 98:14+ [2p] Mar 1995
KAMINSKI, DIE f (d Schoenemann, Hannes 1980 E Ger)
  Graef, C. Hochschulfilme. il F & FERNSEHEN 22:73-81 n6 1994
KAMP, DAVID
  Kamp, D. The importance of being Hamlet. il stills VANITY FAIR 58:74+ [3p]
    Mar 1995
KANDEL, LINDA See also NAKED JANE
KANEVSKII, VITALII See also NOUS, LES ENFANTS DU XXEME SICLE
KANG, SOO-YEON
  Lyu, H.-M. Kang Soo Yeon. stills CINEMAYA n24:30-32 Summer 1994

KANG, WOO-SUK See also MANURA CHUGIGI
KANGASNIEMI, HANNA For film reviews see author under the following titles: LIFE
  WITH MIKEY
KANTOLA, MAIKKI
  Kantola, M. Oulun kansainvalinen lastenelokuvafestivaali. still PEILI
    17:40-41 n4 1993
KANYA YA MA KAN, BEYROUTH f (d Saab, Jocelyne 1995 Fr/Lebanon)
  "Kanya ya ma Kan, Beyrouth." biog credits filmog port still CINEMAYA
    n25/26:102 Autumn/Winter 1994/95
KAPETANOVIC, MICHEL
  Kapetanovic, M. "La machine." credits still GRAND ANGLE n177:25-26 Dec
    1994
  Kapetanovic, M. "La surprise." credits stills GRAND ANGLE n178:31-32 Jan
    1995
  Kapetanovic, M. "Miracle sur la 34e rue." credits stills GRAND ANGLE
    n177:29-30 Dec 1994
  Kapetanovic, M. "Mrs Parker et le cercle vicieux." bibliog credits stills
    GRAND ANGLE n178:19-20 Jan 1995
  Kapetanovic, M. "Sale sucre." bibliog credits stills GRAND ANGLE
    n177:37-38 Dec 1994
  Kapetanovic, M. "The Mask." bibliog credits stills GRAND ANGLE n177:27-28
    Dec 1994
  Kapetanovic, M. and Noel, J. "Fresh." bibliog credits stills GRAND ANGLE
    n178:11-12 Jan 1995
KAPLAN, DAVID A.
  Kaplan, D.A. How to make a ghost. still NEWSWK 125:64 Feb 27 1995
KAPLAN, E. ANN
  Kaplan, E.A. Disorderly disciplines. bibliog F CRITICISM 17:48-52 n2/3
    1992/93
KAPLAN, JONATHAN See also BAD GIRLS
  Calderale, M. Filmografie. biogs filmogs il SEGNO n71:40 Jan/Feb 1995
KAPLINSKA, ANNA
  Kaplinska, A. Edukacja filmowa. REZYSER n19:6 1993
  Kaplinska, A. Handlowiec i muzyk. il interv REZYSER n19:6-8 1993
  Kaplinska, A. Iluzjon czy iluzja? interv REZYSER n18:3-4 1993
  Kaplinska, A. Widziec muzyke. interv REZYSER n18:8 1993
KAPUR, SHEKHAR See also BANDIT QUEEN
  Prasad, U. Woman on the edge. stills S&S 5:14-17 Feb 1995
KARATSON, GABOR
  Karatson, G. Ozu eskuvoi. il stills F VILAG 38:24-29 n3 1995
KARBELNIKOFF, MICHAEL See also F.T.W.
KARLIN, FRED
  Redman, N. Competing composers [Book Reviews]. DGA NEWS 19:56-57 n6 1994/95
KARLSSON, NIKO For film reviews see author under the following titles: JURASSIC
  PARK
KARMEN, ANDREW
  Karmen, A. Letters: deathless prose. VILLAGE VOICE 40:6 Mar 14 1995
KARNEY, ROBYN
  Comuzio, E. Robyn Karney: Audrey Hepburn. La principessa di Tiffany [Book
    Review]. il C FORUM 34:94 Sep (n337) 1994
KARNICK, HANNES See also RADIO STAR - DIE AFN STORY
  "Radio Star - die AFN Story." biogs credits filmog still KINO(BRD) n1:38-39
    1995
KARTOZIAN, WILLIAM F.
  Kartozian, W.F. ShoWest achieves its majority. il port BOXOFFICE 131:bet
    p82 and 83 [pSW6] Apr 1995
KARUN, SHAJI N. See also SWAHAM
KASDAN, LAWRENCE See also WYATT EARP
KASDAN, MARGO
  Kasdan, M. and Tavernetti, S. The Hollywood Indian in "Little Big Man": a
    revisionist view. still F&HIST 23:70-80 n1/4 1993
KASPAR HAUSER f (d Sehr, Peter 1993 FR Ger)
    Reviews
  Derobert, E. "Kaspar Hauser." still POSITIF n408:58 Feb 1995
KASSAR, MARIO
  Brown, C. "Cutthroat Island's" high roller. il ports PREM 8:65-69 Mar 1995
KASTEN, JUERGEN
  Kasten, J. Fruehe Filmgeschichte [Book Review]. il F BUL 37:12-13 n1
    (n198) 1995
  Kasten, J. Slapstick, Indien, Wyler und die Garbo. il stills F BUL
    36:10-13 n6 (n197) 1994
KATCHMER, GEORGE
  Katchmer, G. Remembering the great silents. biogs filmogs port CLASSIC
    n236:50-53 Feb 1995
  Katchmer, G. Remembering the great silents. biogs filmogs port CLASSIC
    n237:35+ [3p] Mar 1995
KATIA ISMAILOVA f (d Todorovskii, Valerii 1994 Fr/Russia)
    Reviews
  Derobert, E. "Katia Ismailova." still POSITIF n406:46 Dec 1994
KATZ, ALYSSA
  Katz, A. Super Jackie. il VILLAGE VOICE 40:52 Jan 31 1995
KATZ, EPHRAIM
  Blomkvist, M. Mot filmhistorien - med sprang! port CHAPLIN 36:72 n6 (n255)
    1994/95
  Strick, P. Fresh slogans [Book Review]. still S&S 5:34-35 Apr 1995
KATZ, SUSAN BULLINGTON
  Katz, S.B. A conversation with... Frank Darabont. filmog interv port
    JOURNAL WGA 8:28-31 Feb 1995
  Katz, S.B. A conversation with... Richard Curtis. il interv JOURNAL WGA
    8:24-27 Mar 1995
  Katz, S.B. "A conversation with... Ruth Prawer Jhabvala." filmog il interv
    JOURNAL WGA 8:38-41 Dec/Jan 1995
KATZENBERG, JEFFREY
  Bart, P. The Roth regimen. il VARIETY 358:8+ [2p] Feb 27/Mar 5 1995
  Corliss, R. Hey, let's put on a show! il ports TIME 145:54-60 Mar 27 1995
KAUFFMANN, STANLEY For film reviews see author under the following titles:
  DISCLOSURE; LEGENDS OF THE FALL; MADNESS OF KING GEORGE, THE; MAN OF
  NO IMPORTANCE, A; NELL; NOBODY'S FOOL; SPEECHLESS; TOM & VIV
KAUFMAN, BEN L.
  Kaufman, B.L. Cincinnati's morality squad targets Pasolini. il INDEP

18:9-11 Jan/Feb 1995
KAUFMAN, J.B.
  Kaufman, J.B. Good mousekeeping: family-oriented publicity in Disney's
    golden age. il ANIMATION J 3:78-85 n2 1995
KAUFMAN, PATTI
  Evans, G. Confirmation of new N.Y. pic commish still pending. VARIETY
    358:36 Feb 27/Mar 5 1995
KAUFMAN, PHILIP See also RISING SUN
KAUFMANN, RAINER See also EINER MEINER AELTESTEN FREUNDE
  Einer meiner aeltesten Freunde. biog credits filmog still KINO(BRD)
    n1:18-19 1995
KAUPPILA, JEAN L.
  Slide, A. The Slide area film book notes [Book Reviews]. CLASSIC
    n237:42-44+ [4p] Mar 1995
KAURISMAKI, AKI See also PIDA HUIVISTA KIINNI, TATJANA; TOTAL BALALAIKA SHOW
KAVCIC, BOJAN
  Codelli, L. Pregled razvoja kinematografije pri Slovencih (do 1918). Di
    Janko Traven, a cura di Lilijana Nedic, Stanko Simenc [Book Reviews].
    GRIFFITHIANA n51/52:264 Oct 1994
KAVEL, PETER
  Kavel, P. The film exhibitor. il port CLASSIC n236:38-39 Feb 1995
KAWIN, BRUCE F.
  Kawin, B.F. Wild blueberry muffins. F CRITICISM 17:53-55 n2/3 1992/93
KAYE, JANICE
  Kaye, J. "Perfectly Normal," eh?: gender transformation and national
    identity in Canada. CAN J F STUD 3:63-80 n2 1994
Kazakhstan (since 1992) See as a subheading under individual subject headings
KAZAN, ELIA See also EAST OF EDEN; WILD RIVER
  Noel, J. Elia Kazan, une odyssee americaine. Par Michel Ciment [Book
    Review]. il GRAND ANGLE n177:50 Dec 1994
KAZIMI, ALI See also [NARMADA: A VALLEY RISES]
KAZUYUKI, YANO
  Kazuyuki, Y. From 1991 to 1993 - exploring new worlds at the Yamagata
    Documentary Film Festival. il still DOC BOX 1:1-3 1992
KE TU CHIU HEN f (Song of the Exile d Hui, Ann 1990 Hong Kong/Taiwan)
    Women in Film
  Rafman, C. Imagining a woman's world: roles for women in Chinese films.
    bibliog glos stills CINEMAS 3:126-140 n2/3 1993
KEATHLEY, CHRISTIAN
  Keathley, C. Robert Benton. il interv stills F COM 31:36-43+ [12p] Jan/Feb
    1995
KEATON, BUSTER
  Major, W. "Buster" forever. il BOXOFFICE 131:36+ [3p] Apr 1995
  Parshall, P.F. Buster Keaton and the space of farce: "Steamboat Bill, Jr."
    versus "The Cameraman." bibliog diag stills UFAJ 46:29-46 n3 1994
    Retrospectives
  Feingold, M. Crash course. still VILLAGE VOICE 40:60 Feb 14 1995
KEATON, DIANE
  Zaniello, T. Hitched or Lynched: who directed "Twin Peaks"? bibliog filmogs
    STUDIES POP CULT 17:55-64 n1 1994
KEATON, ELEANOR
  Major, W. "Buster" forever. il BOXOFFICE 131:36+ [3p] Apr 1995
KEENAN, RICHARD
  Keenan, R. Hail, Columbia! a studio odyssey [Book Review]. still LIT/FQ
    22:278-279 n4 1994
KEEP, CHRISTOPHER JAMES
  Fitzgerald, L. and Keep, C.J. "Barry Lyndon" demembre: la perte de
    l'histoire dans le film de Stanley Kubrick. bibliog still CINEMAS 4:23-33
    n1 1993
KEEPNEWS, PETER
  Keepnews, P. Letters: one froggy error. VILLAGE VOICE 40:6 Feb 21 1995
KEHR, DAVE
  Kehr, D. Who framed "Forrest Gump." il stills F COM 31:45-48+ [6p] Mar/Apr
    1995
KEIL, KLAUS
  Blaney, M. Ein Gespraech mit Klaus Keil. port KINO(BRD) n1:6-7 1995
  Blaney, M. Interview with Klaus Keil. port KINO(BRD) n1:4-5 1995
KEILL, SUSAN
  Connors, R. and others. Letters: the king and us. MS 5:8 n4 1995
KEILLER, PATRICK See also LONDON
KEINER LIEBT MICH f (d Doerrie, Doris 1995 FR Ger)
  "Keiner liebt mich." biog credits filmog still KINO(BRD) n1:32-33 1995
    Reviews
  Holloway, R. "Keiner liebt mich." credits KINO(GF) n56:10 Nov 1994
KELLEHER, ED For film reviews see author under the following titles: GREAT DAY
  IN HARLEM, A; I.Q.; MAN OF NO IMPORTANCE, A; MIAMI RHAPSODY; QUICK AND
  THE DEAD, THE; TOM & VIV
  Kelleher, E. Cinemark's Mitchell named 1995 ShoWester. port FJ 98:90 Mar
    1995
  Kelleher, E. Disney's "Roommates" explores generational ties. il FJ 98:12+
    [2p] Mar 1995
  Kelleher, E. Miramax invites filmgoers to "Muriel's Wedding." il interv
    still FJ 98:12+ [2p] Jan/Feb 1995
  Kelleher, E. Schroeder captures grim NYC in Fox's thriller, "Kiss of Death."
    il interv still FJ 98:8+ [2p] Mar 1995
KELLY, BRENDAN For film reviews see author under the following titles: ELDORADO
  Kelly, B. Canada pix thrive despite funding cuts. still VARIETY 358:bet
    p88 and 173 [pA16] Feb 20/26 1995
  Kelly, B. Canuck pix make a hefty contribution. still VARIETY 358:55 Feb
    6/12 1995
  Kelly, B. Competition between buyers gets tougher for Canucks. VARIETY
    358:bet p88 and 173 [pA16] Feb 20/26 1995
  Kelly, B. Phillip Borsos. obit VARIETY 358:85 Feb 6/12 1995
KELLY, CHRISTINA
  Kelly, C. No more tears. il ports PREM 8:78-84 Apr 1995
KELLY, GENE See also SINGIN' IN THE RAIN
KELLY, NANCY See also (ONE THOUSAND) 1000 PIECES OF GOLD
  Lentz, H., III. Obituaries. biogs filmogs obits ports CLASSIC n237:57-59
    Mar 1995
KELLY, RORY See also SLEEP WITH ME

KEMP, PHILIP For film reviews see author under the following titles: AMATEUR;
    AWFULLY BIG ADVENTURE, AN; BANDIT QUEEN; CLEAN, SHAVEN; PRINCESS
    CARABOO; SHALLOW GRAVE
    Kemp, P. Count on solid British presence. VARIETY 358:55-56 Feb 6/12 1995
    Kemp, P. Discworld [Book Review]. still S&S 5:34 Apr 1995
KEMPPINEN, PETRI
    Kemppinen, P. Saarivaltion kummajaiset. still PEILI 17:16 n4 1993
KENDALL, KAY
    Golden, E. Kay Kendall: too little, too late. biog ports still CLASSIC
        n237:26+ [2p] Mar 1995
KENDALL, LUKAS
    Dursin, A. and Kendall, L. Soundtrack watchdogs!: Andy and Lukas review lots
        of new CDs. il F SCORE MONTHLY n38:14-15 Oct 1993
    Dursin, A. and others. Four by Basil Poledouris. F SCORE MONTHLY n36/37:32
        Aug/Sep 1993
    Kendall, L. "Caboblanco." F SCORE MONTHLY n40:12 Dec 1993
    Kendall, L. John Beal. interv port F SCORE MONTHLY n36/37:18-19 Aug/Sep
        1993
    Kendall, L. Lukas reviews lots 'n' lots of new CDs. il F SCORE MONTHLY
        n40:13-15 Dec 1993
    Kendall, L. New CDs I'm supposed to review. F SCORE MONTHLY n36/37:34
        Aug/Sep 1993
    Kendall, L. "Outland"/"Capricorn One." F SCORE MONTHLY n39:12 Nov 1993
    Kendall, L. Richard Kraft & Nick Redman. il interv port F SCORE MONTHLY
        n36/37:27-30 Aug/Sep 1993
    Kendall, L. Richard Kraft & Nick Redman: part four. interv F SCORE MONTHLY
        n40:8-9 Dec 1993
    Kendall, L. Richard Kraft & Nick Redman: part three. il interv F SCORE
        MONTHLY n39:10-11 Nov 1993
    Kendall, L. Richard Kraft & Nick Redman: part two. il interv F SCORE
        MONTHLY n38:9-11 Oct 1993
    Kendall, L. "Robocop 3." F SCORE MONTHLY n40:12 Dec 1993
    Kendall, L. "Robotjox." F SCORE MONTHLY n36/37:33 Aug/Sep 1993
    Kendall, L. The re-making of Alex North's "2001": an interview with Robert
        Townson. interv F SCORE MONTHLY n36/37:26 Aug/Sep 1993
    Kendall, L. and Care, R. New from label "X": the Cinema Maestro series. F
        SCORE MONTHLY n38:13 Oct 1993
    Kendall, L. and others. The next great non-controversy: "The Nightmare
        Before Christmas." il F SCORE MONTHLY n39:14 Nov 1993
    Rixman, J. and Kendall, L. Horner corner. F SCORE MONTHLY n38:14 Oct 1993
KENNEDY, TOM
    Magid, R. Fine-tuning "Radioland Murders." il AMCIN 76:66-72 Mar 1995
KENT, MOHINI
    Kent, M. Gurinder Chadha. stills CINEMAYA n25/26:24-25 Autumn/Winter
        1994/95
KENTON, ERLE C. See also HOUSE OF DRACULA
KEREKES, DAVID
    Killing for culture: an illustrated history of death film from mondo to
        snuff. By David Kerekes & David Slater [Book Review]. il still FATAL
        VISIONS n17:29 1994
KERMADEC, LILIANE DE See also PISTE DU TELEGRAPHE, LA
KERMODE, MARK
    Kermode, M. Endnotes. still S&S 5:62 Feb 1995
    Kermode, M. Simon Boswell: filmography. filmog still S&S 5:62 Apr 1995
KERR, PHILIP
    Million dollar brain. S&S 5:3 Apr 1995
KERRIGAN, LODGE See also CLEAN, SHAVEN
KERSHAW, SARAH
    Kershaw, S. Against pornophobia. port NEW YORK 28:20+ [2p] Jan 16 1995
KERTES, TOM For film reviews see author under the following titles: HIDEAWAY
KESTER, GARY
    Kester, G. In memory of Roy Budd 1947-1993. biog obit F SCORE MONTHLY
        n36/37:25 Aug/Sep 1993
KEU SOME GAGO SIPTA f (d Park, Kwang-Su 1994 S Korea)
    Reviews
    Berry, C. "Keu-sum-e ga-go sip-de." credits still CINEMAYA n24:35-36
        Summer 1994
    Berthomieu, P. "L'ile etoilee." credits stills POSITIF n408:52-53 Feb 1995
KEWEZ, PETER
    Menashe, L. Requiem for Soviet cinema 1917-1991 [Book Reviews]. stills
        CINEASTE 21:23-27 n1/2 1994
KHODZHAEV, IURII
    Fonn, E.B. Moskvafestivalens "grand old man" dod. obit F&K n1:23 1994
KIAROSTAMI, ABBAS See also ZIRE DARAKHTAN ZEYTON
    Ciment, M. and Goudet, S. Entretien avec Abbas Kiarostami. il interv stills
        POSITIF n408:14-19 Feb 1995
    Euvrard, J. Retrouver l'enfance. interv stills 24 IMAGES n75:14-16 Dec/Jan
        1994/95
    Goudet, S. La reprise. il stills POSITIF n408:9-13 Feb 1995
    Hoberman, J. Another new cult hero from HK. il still PREM 8:50-51 Mar 1995
    Tanner, L. Accents and umlauts. FIR 45:38-39 Nov/Dec 1994
KID, THE f (d Chaplin, Charlie 1921 USA)
    Woal, M. and Woal, L.K. Chaplin and the comedy of melodrama. bibliog stills
        UFAJ 46:3-15 n3 1994
KIDAWA-BLONSKI, JAN See also PAMIETNIK ZNALEZIONY W GARBIE
KIDS f (d Clark, Larry 1995 USA)
    Evans, G. and McCarthy, T. Will "Kids" be too hot for Harvey? VARIETY
        358:1+ [2p] Feb 6/12 1995
    Ratings
    Controversy: "Kids" for adults. NEWSWK 125:69 Feb 20 1995
KIESLOWSKI, KRZYSZTOF See also BEZ KONCA; BLEU; DOUBLE VIE DE VERONIQUE, LA;
    KROTKI FILM O ZABIJANIU; ROUGE; TROIS COULEURS
    Amiel, V. "Vous ne savez pas, en France, ce qu il en coute de vivre dans un
        monde sans representation." filmog il stills POSITIF n409:58-60 Mar 1995
    Kieslowski, K. La dramaturgie du reel. il POSITIF n409:56-57 Mar 1995
    Lovell, G. Letters: KK kalls it kwits. F COM 31:2 Jan/Feb 1995
KIJOWSKI, JANUSZ
    Plazewski, J. Wspolprodukcje hydra, czy szansa? il interv ports KINO
        27:6-9 Jun 1993

KIKA f (d Almodovar, Pedro 1993 Sp)
    Reviews
    Falaschi, F. "Kika" - "Un corpo in prestito." credits stills SEGNO
        n72:45-46 Mar/Apr 1995
    Moresco, F. "Kika - un corpo in prestito." credits FILM (ITALY) 3:45-46
        n13 1995
KILAR, WOJCIECH
    Luzynska, J.A. Hollywoodzkie namaszczenie Wojciecha Kilara. il interv KINO
        27:34 Jul 1993
Killer, The See DIEXUE SHUANG XIONG
KILLING ZOE f (d Avary, Roger 1994 USA)
    Dupagne, M.-F. "Killing Zoe." bibliog credits stills GRAND ANGLE
        n177:21-22 Dec 1994
    Reviews
    Macnab, G. "Killing Zoe." credits still S&S 5:47-48 Jan 1995
KILLJAKTEN f (d Hellman, Lena 1992 Swed)
    Pimenoff, M. Kultainen nuoruus - armoton nuoruus. il PEILI 18:22-23 n3
        1994
KIMBALL, WARD
    Catsos, G.J.M. Disney's folly! il interv stills F FAX n48:49-53 Jan/Feb
        1995
    Lucanio, P. and Coville, G. Ward Kimball's wonderful world of motion. il
        port stills F FAX n48:54-55 Jan/Feb 1995
KIMMEL, ADAM
    Comer, B. "New Jersey Drive" puts Kimmel behind the wheel. still AMCIN
        76:83-84 Mar 1995
KIMMEL, DAN For film reviews see author under the following titles: KNUCKLEBALL;
    ONEAMIS NO TSUBASA
KINCAID, D.
    Breen, J.L. Kincaid, D., Pseudonym of Bert Fields. The lawyer's tale [Book
        Review]. ARMCHAIR DET 26:74-75 n3 1993
KINCH, MARTIN See also GRIERSON AND GOUZENKO
KINDER- UND JUGENDFILM KORRESPONDENZ
    "Kinder- und Jugendfilm Korrespondenz (KJK)" [Book Review]. il KINO(GF)
        n56:31 Nov 1994
KINDERKRIEGEN f (d Schoenemann, Sibylle 1976 E Ger)
    Graef, C. Hochschulfilme. il F & FERNSEHEN 22:103-106 n6 1994
KINEPOLIS (Brussels, Belgium)
    Economic Aspects
    Resultats 1994 de l'Imax a Kinepolis. stat table MONITEUR n128:9 Feb 1995
KING, BURTON See also MAN FROM BEYOND, THE
KING, ENCKE See also IGNATZ & LOTTE
KING, JOHN
    Sinclair, J. King, John, Lopez, Ana M and Alvarado, Manuel, eds. Mediating
        two worlds: cinematic encounters in the Americas [Book Review]. MEDIA INFO
        AUSTRALIA n75:166-167 Feb 1995
King Lear See KOROL' LIR
King of the Children See HAIZI WANG
KING, ROBERT LEE See also BOYS LIFE
KING, STEPHEN
    Vidal, J.-P. La Berlue et le mythe: S/K, ou de Stephen King a Stanley
        Kubrick. still CINEMAS 4:115-129 n1 1993
Kingdom, The See RIGET
KINGSLEY, SIDNEY
    Shields, S. Sidney Kingsley. biog obit VARIETY 358:86 Mar 27/Apr 2 1995
KINTOP
    Jung, U. "Kintop" [Book Review]. il BLIMP n30:45-46 Winter 1994
KIRALY, JENO
    Hirsch, T. Ha Bolyai, akkor nem-euklideszi [Book Review]. il still F VILAG
        38:42-44 n1 1995
    Kiraly, J. Frankenstein es Faust. credits filmog stills F VILAG 38:20-25
        n2 1995
    Kiraly, J. Frankenstein es Orpheusz. stills F VILAG 38:18-23 n3 1995
    Varadi, J. and Kovacs, A.B. A meseauto eselye. interv still F VILAG
        38:45-47 n1 1995
KIRBY, ROBERT
    Murdoch, B. Robert (Roc) Kirby. port FJ 98:84 Jan/Feb 1995
KIRBY, ROC
    Cineasia fetes Frumkes, Kirby. VARIETY 357:30 Jan 2/8 1995
KIRSH, ESTELLE F.
    Krasilovsky, A. Estelle F. Kirsh. interv port ANGLES 2:14-17 n4 1995
KIRSHNER, MIA
    Dargis, M. O solo Mia. port VILLAGE VOICE 40:58 Mar 14 1995
KISS, MARIANNA See also AM ENDE DER SCHIENEN
KISS OF DEATH f (d Schroeder, Barbet 1995 USA)
    Kelleher, E. Schroeder captures grim NYC in Fox's thriller, "Kiss of Death."
        il interv still FJ 98:8+ [2p] Mar 1995
    Reviews
    McCarthy, T. Lowlife realism fuels "Death." credits still VARIETY 358:74+
        [2p] Mar 27/Apr 2 1995
KISSAN KUOLEMA f (d Niemi, Raimo O. 1994 Finl)
    Kallinen, S. Kissan kuolema. stills PEILI 18:14-15 n4 1994
KISSIN, EVA H. For film reviews see author under the following titles: BARCELONA
KITANO, TAKESHI
    Stephens, C. Comedy plus massacre. il stills F COM 31:31-34 Jan/Feb 1995
[KITCHEN, THE] f (d Morita, Yoshimitsu 1991 Japan)
    Reviews
    Giovannini, C. "Kitchen." credits FILM (ITALY) 3:22 n13 1995
KITSCH
    Canova, G. L'unica igiene del cinema. still SEGNO n72:26 Mar/Apr 1995
KIYOOKA, FUMIKO
    Hoolboom, M. The place with many rooms is the body: the films of Fumiko
        Kiyooka. il stills CANTRILL'S FMNTS n73/74:4-8 May 1994
KLA$H f (d Parker, Bill 1995 USA?)
    Reviews
    Greene, R. "Kla$h." BOXOFFICE 131:bet p125 and 144 [pR25-R26] Apr 1995
    Klady, L. "Kla$h." credits VARIETY 358:76 Feb 6/12 1995

KLADY, LEONARD For film reviews see author under the following titles: BRADY
    BUNCH MOVIE, THE; BYE BYE, LOVE; CANDYMAN: FAREWELL TO THE FLESH;
    FAR FROM HOME: THE ADVENTURES OF YELLOW DOG; FLESH SUITCASE;
    HEAVYWEIGHTS; HIDEAWAY; IN THE MOUTH OF MADNESS; KLA$H; MAJOR PAYNE;
    NAKED JANE; SOUL SURVIVOR; TI KNIVER I HJERTET; VERSPRECHEN, DAS
    Klady, L. Buena Vista hits a billion. stat VARIETY 357:16 Jan 2/8 1995
    Klady, L. DGA fetes Ivory with Griffith. port VARIETY 358:18 Feb 6/12 1995
    Klady, L. Directors with seasoning. VARIETY 358:87 Feb 6/12 1995
    Klady, L. Disney takes "Lion's" share of '94 boffo b.o. stat tables
        VARIETY 357:13+ [2p] Jan 9/15 1995
    Klady, L. "Dreams" takes Chi crix nod. VARIETY 358:19 Mar 20/26 1995
    Klady, L. Earth to H'wood: you win. il stat VARIETY 358:1+ [2p] Feb 13/19
        1995
    Klady, L. Exhibs' expansion buoys distribs. VARIETY 358:7+ [2p] Mar 20/26
        1995
    Klady, L. Exhibs forecast bleak outlook for 1st-qtr. pix. il VARIETY
        357:11+ [2p] Jan 2/8 1995
    Klady, L. Foreign-language Oscar speaks tongue of its own. stat VARIETY
        358:11+ [2p] Feb 6/12 1995
    Klady, L. "Hoop Dreams" aside, dox remain low-profile. stat table VARIETY
        358:15-16 Mar 27/Apr 2 1995
    Klady, L. H'wood: land of the rising sum. stat VARIETY 358:14 Mar 13/19
        1995
    Klady, L. Indie prods targeted at Int'l Film Finance confab. VARIETY 357:30
        Jan 9/15 1995
    Klady, L. Oscar's gold standards. il VARIETY 358:11+ [2p] Feb 20/26 1995
    Klady, L. Pic pack uneven at record b.o. stat VARIETY 357:18 Jan 2/8 1995
    Klady, L. Small fish feed on big hope at AFM. il VARIETY 358:13-14 Feb
        27/Mar 5 1995
    Klady, L. Summer pix: swords and sequels. il still VARIETY 358:1+ [2p] Mar
        13/19 1995
    Klady, L. (Ten) $10 mil gets Moore to "Strip." VARIETY 358:22 Feb 20/26
        1995
    Klady, L. and Busch, A.M. Wintry b.o. chills ShoWest's sizzle. stat
        VARIETY 358:1+ [2p] Mar 6/12 1995
    Saperstein, P. and Klady, L. Fifteen seasons of sun & sums. il ports
        VARIETY 358:bet p88 and 173 [pA2+ (2p)] Feb 20/26 1995
KLAM, JULIE
    Klam, J. Parker Posey can't lose. port PREM 8:37 Mar 1995
KLANICZAY, GABOR
    A tizenotezredik pillanat. interv stills F VILAG 38:18-23 n1 1995
KLAPISCH, CEDRIC See also PERIL JEUNE, LE
KLATSCHMOHN - AUS DEM LEBEN MIT HEROIN f (d Laur, Stephan 1993 Switz)
    Reviews
    Sauter, M. "Klatschmohn - aus dem Leben mit Heroin." credits C(SWITZ)
        40:213 1994
KLAWANS, STUART For film reviews see author under the following titles: IA KUBA;
    TSAHAL
    Klawans, S. Illustrious Rosi. il stills F COM 31:60-63+ [5p] Jan/Feb 1995
    Klawans, S. Year-end celluloid wrap-up. NATION 260:106-108 Jan 23 1995
KLEBER, REINHARD For film reviews see author under the following titles: INDIEN
KLEIN, JAMES See also LETTER TO THE NEXT GENERATION
    Boruszkowski, L.A. An interview with documentary filmmaker Jim Klein.
        filmog interv port UFAJ 46:34-42 n1 1994
KLEIN, NORMAN
    Schaffer, W. Klein, Norman. Seven minutes: the life and death of the
        American animated cartoon [Book Review]. MEDIA INFO AUSTRALIA n75:167 Feb
        1995
KLEISER, RANDAL See also HONEY, I BLEW UP THE KID; WHITE FANG
KLIER, MICHAEL See also OUT OF AMERICA
    "Out of America." biog credits filmog still KINO(BRD) n1:36-37 1995
KLINE, JEFFERSON
    Lori, S. I films di Bernardo Bertolucci. Di Jefferson Kline [Book Review].
        C SUD 33:37 Jul/Aug/Sep (n113) 1994
KLINGENBERG KINO (Oslo, Norway)
    Lochen, K. Kinoen som verneverdig kulturhus. stat F&K n7:2 1993
KLOPFLER, TIBOR See also LAKATLAN EMBER, A
KLOVES, STEVE See also FLESH AND BONE
KLUTE f (d Pakula, Alan J. 1971 USA)
    Atkinson, M. Jane Fonda in "Klute." still MOVIELINE 6:82 Apr 1995
KNAEBEL, MARTIAL
    Jaeggi, B. and Knaebel, M. Look back in pain. filmog interv port stills
        CINEMAYA n24:44-47 Summer 1994
KNAGGS, SKELTON
    Seymour, B. Pentagram revues: Skelton Knaggs. stills CLASSIC n237:34 Mar
        1995
KNEE, ADAM
    Knee, A. Cinema, censorship, and the state: the writings of Nagisa Oshima,
        1956-1978. Edited and with an introduction by Annette Michelson [Book
        Review]. UFAJ 46:66-68 n1 1994
KNEUBUEHLER, THOMAS
    Kneubuehler, T. Ausstattungstag. il C(SWITZ) 40:105-111 1994
KNIGHT, GRAHAM
    Knight, G. The Beaver bites back? American popular culture in Canada. Edited
        by David H. Flaherty & Frank E. Manning [Book Review]. CAN J COM 19:560-561
        n3/4 1994
KNOTEN, DER f (d Foth, Joerg 1976 E Ger)
    Graef, C. Hochschulfilme. il interv F & FERNSEHEN 22:50-53 n6 1994
KNUCKLEBALL f (d MacNeil, John 1995 USA/Gt Br)
    Reviews
    Kimmel, D. "Knuckleball." credits VARIETY 358:70 Feb 27/Mar 5 1995
KOBLAND, KEN See also FRAME; GUSTAVE FLAUBERT DREAMS OF TRAVEL BUT THE ILLNESS
    OF HIS MOTHER PREVENTS IT
    Kobland, K. Storyboards, plans and notes for "Frame" (1976) and "Flaubert
        Dreams of Travel" (1986). il MILLENNIUM n25:31-35 Summer 1991
KOEHLER, MARGRET
    Koehler, M. (Fuenf) 5415 Minuten Kino. still MEDIEN 38:362-363 n6 1994
KOENIG, WALTER
    Uram, S. Chekov makes Captain. stills C FANTAS 26:32-33 n2 1995
KOENIG, WOLF See also CITY OF GOLD

KOEPP, DAVID
    Lantos, J. The sweet sting of success. il MOVIELINE 6:70-71 Mar 1995
KOERBER, MARTIN
    Koerber, M. Reconstructing "Die Jagd nach dem Tode." il stills J F PRES
        n49:34-39 Oct 1994
KOHLHIESELS TOECHTER f (d Lubitsch, Ernst 1920 Ger)
    Aldarondo, R. "Las hijas del cervecero"; "Romeo y Julia en la nieve."
        credits stills NOSFERATU n8:57-58 Feb 1992
KOHN, OLIVIER For film reviews see author under the following titles: GIORGINO;
    QUIZ SHOW; ROSINE; VA MOURIRE
    Berthome, J.-P. and Kohn, O. Entretien avec Jeff Balsmeyer. il interv still
        POSITIF n407:85-89 Jan 1995
    Kohn, O. Annecy 1993. still POSITIF n406:61-62 Dec 1994
    Kohn, O. Rennes 1994. POSITIF n407:57-58 Jan 1995
KOIVUSALO, TIMO See also PEKKO JA POIKA
KOKKINOS, ANA See also ONLY THE BRAVE
KOKKINOS, ANTONIS See also TELOS EPOCHUS
KOLLER, MICHAEL
    Koller, M. Films we love #3: "Waterfall." still C PAPERS n102:10-11 Dec
        1994
KOLODYNSKI, ANDRZEJ For film reviews see author under the following titles:
    CHUVSTVITEL'NYI MILITSIONER
KOLOSS f (d Leszczynski, Witold 1993 Norw/Poland)
    Iversen, G. Kjolig moralitet. stills F&K n7:14-15 1993
    Iversen, J. "Koloss." credits still Z n4:18-19 (n46) 1993
    Review Excerpts
    Brochmann, K. "Koloss." still F&K n7:38 1993
KOLSKI, JAN JAKUB See also CUDOWNE MIEJSCE
KOLTAI, ROBERT See also SOSE HALUNK MEG
KOMAR, ERZSEBET
    Komar, E. Casanova mas szemmel [Book Review]. F VILAG 38:43 n3 1995
KOMATSU, HIROSHI
    Komatsu, H. Questions regarding the genesis of nonfiction film. biog il
        stills DOC BOX 5:1-5 1994
KOMEDIA MALZENSKA f (d Zaluski, Roman 1994 Poland)
    "Komedia malzenska." biog credits filmog still FSP 40:12 n4 (n758) 1994
KOMORI, SHIZUO
    Makino, M. and Gerow, A.A. Prokino. biogs il interv port stills DOC BOX
        5:6-14 1994
    Makino, M. and Gerow, A.A. Prokino. biogs il interv port stills DOC BOX
        5:6-14 1994
KONCHALOVSKY, ANDREI See also MIKHALKOV-KONCHALOVSKII, ANDREI See also
    KUROCHKA RIABA
    Filmographie d'Andrei Konchalovsky. biog filmog il stills AVANT-SCENE
        n437:80-81 Dec 1994
    Menashe, L. Requiem for Soviet cinema 1917-1991 [Book Reviews]. stills
        CINEASTE 21:23-27 n1/2 1995
KONDRAT, MAREK
    Slodowski, J. Marek Kondrat. filmog still FSP 40:13 n11 (n765) 1994
KONGRESS DER PINGUINE, DER f (Congress of Penguins, The d Schlumpf, Hans-Ulrich
    1993 Switz)
    Reviews
    Brown, G. The birds (and a book). stills VILLAGE VOICE 40:48 Jan 10 1995
    Janser, A. "Der Kongress der Pinguine." credits still C(SWITZ) 40:223 1994
KONIECZNY, ZYGMUNT
    Recollections
    Kaplinska, A. Widziec muzyke. interv REZYSER n18:8 1993
KONINCK STUDIOS LTD.
    Griffiths, K. Anxious visions. il stills VERTIGO (UK) 1:47-52 n4 1994/95
KONLECHNER, PETER
    Konlechner, P. International Film Archive CD-ROM. J F PRES n49:15-17 Oct
        1994
KONTRAPUNKT f (d Hoentsch, Andreas 1982 E Ger)
    Graef, C. Hochschulfilme. il F & FERNSEHEN 22:30-35 n6 1994
KOPELSON, ARNOLD
    Gill, M.S. Crisis management. il stills PREM 8:74-77+ [5p] Apr 1995
KOPPLE, BARBARA See also AMERICAN DREAM
KOPPOLD, RUPERT
    Koppold, R. Das Genie und das Scheitern [Book Review]. MEDIEN 38:379-380 n6
        1994
Korea (Republic) See as a subheading under individual subject headings
KORKARLEN f (d Sjostrom, Victor 1921 Swed)
    Cremonini, G. Il carretto fantasma di Victor Sjostrom. credits stills C
        FORUM 34:18-23 Nov (n339) 1994
KORNGOLD, ERICH WOLFGANG
    Handzo, S. The golden age of film music. il ports stills CINEASTE 21:46-55
        n1/2 1995
KOROL' LIR f (King Lear d Kozintsev, Grigorii 1971 USSR)
    Angulo, J. "El rey Lear." credits NOSFERATU n8:66-67 Feb 1992
KORTE, HELMUT
    Korte, H. and Lowry, S. Heinz Ruehmann - ein Star der deutschen
        Filmgeschichte. stills MEDIEN 38:348-352+ [7p] n6 1994
KORTNER, JAN H.
    Kortner, J.H. Gammel modig kriger. still Z n1:20-22 (n47) 1994
KOSANOVIC, DEJAN
    Kosanovic, D. Beograd. still J F PRES n49:23-25 Oct 1994
KOSCINA, SYLVA
    Lentz, H., III. Obituaries. biogs filmogs il obits ports CLASSIC
        n236:57-59 Feb 1995
    Obituaries. biog obits VARIETY 357:83-84 Jan 2/8 1995
KOSKINEN, KIMMO
    Koskinen, K. Hannoverin Eurooppalaisfestari. PEILI 17:38-39 n4 1993
KOSKINEN, MAARET For film reviews see author under the following titles: HUOZHE
    Aberg, A. "Askadaren" vid glipan: Maaret Koskinen om Ingmar Bergman [Book
        Review]. F HAFTET 22:59-60 n3 (n87) 1994
KOSMORAMA
    Pill, M. "Kosmorama" [Book Review]. il BLIMP n30:46-47 Winter 1994
KOSSLICK, DIETER
    Holloway, R. Interview Dieter Kosslick. interv port KINO(GF) n56:5-6 Nov
        1994

KOSSOFF, ADAM
  Kossoff, A. A metaphysical mirror. il VERTIGO (UK) 1:45-46 n4 1994/95
KOSTER, HENRY See also ROBE, THE
KOSZARSKI, RICHARD
  Koszarski, R. The movies come home. il stills F COM 31:10-12+ [5p] Mar/Apr
    1995
KOU, HONGLIE
  Art director Kou Honglie. il port CHINA SCREEN n4:35 1994
KOVACS, ANDRAS
  Kovacs, A. Parbeszed a kozonseggel. F VILAG 38:10-11 n4 1995
  Kovacs, A.B. Az elfeledett nevetes. F VILAG 38:56-57 n1 1995
  Kovacs, A.B. Az eroszak lehasaga. credits stills F VILAG 38:26-31 n4 1995
  Kovacs, A.B. Krem torta nelkul. still F VILAG 38:4-5 n2 1995
KOVACS, ANDRAS BALINT
  Varadi, J. and Kovacs, A.B. A meseauto eselye. interv still F VILAG
    38:45-47 n1 1995
KOVALOV, IGOR
  Gizycki, M. Chcialem zatytulowac swoj film "Piotr Dumala." interv port
    stills KINO 27:36 Jul 1993
KOVEK UZENETE, A f (d Jancso, Miklos 1995 Hungary)
  Bona, L. Jakob oszlopa. stills F VILAG 38:18-19 n4 1995
KOZANECKA, ANNA
  Kaplinska, A. Iluzjon czy iluzja? interv REZYSER n18:3-4 1993
KOZIMNIN KARASY f (d Narimbetov, Satybaldy 1995 Kazakhstan)
    Reviews
  Nesselson, L. "The Biography of a Young Accordion Player" ("Kozimnin
    karasy"). credits VARIETY 358:53 Feb 13/19 1995
KOZINTSEV, GRIGORII See also KOROL' LIR
  Aldarondo, R. La tentacion de Shakespeare. stills NOSFERATU n8:20-27 Feb
    1992
KRACHER, JEANNE
  Lopez, C. and Kracher, J. Media activism. interv ANGLES 2:3+ [2p] n4 1995
KRAFT, RICHARD
  Kendall, L. Richard Kraft & Nick Redman. il interv port F SCORE MONTHLY
    n36/37:27-30 Aug/Sep 1993
  Kendall, L. Richard Kraft & Nick Redman: part four. interv F SCORE MONTHLY
    n40:8-9 Dec 1993
  Kendall, L. Richard Kraft & Nick Redman: part three. il interv F SCORE
    MONTHLY n39:10-11 Nov 1993
  Kendall, L. Richard Kraft & Nick Redman: part two. il interv F SCORE
    MONTHLY n38:9-11 Oct 1993
KRAJ SWIATA f (d Zmarz-Koczanowicz, Maria 1994 Poland)
  CD [author]. "Kraj swiata." biog credits filmog still FSP 40:13 n4 (n758)
    1994
  Sobolewski, T. Feliks Edmundowicz ze styropianu. il KINO 27:4-7 Jul 1993
KRAJEWSKI, PIOTR
  Krajewski, P. Kino sprute i zszyte na nowo. stills KINO 27:16-19 May 1993
KRAMER, PAT For film reviews see author under the following titles: IN THE MOUTH
  OF MADNESS; JUST CAUSE
KRAMER, REMI See also HIGH VELOCITY
KRAMER, ROBERT See also CONTRE L'OUBLI
KRANIAUSKAS, JOHN
  Kraniauskas, J. Notes from the underground. still S&S 5:41 Jan 1995
KRASILOVSKY, ALEXIS
  Krasilovsky, A. A sharper image. il port ANGLES 2:10-11 n4 1995
  Krasilovsky, A. Estelle F. Kirsh. interv port ANGLES 2:14-17 n4 1995
  Krasilovsky, A. Kelly Elder McGowen. interv ANGLES 2:11-13 n4 1995
KRAVA f (Cow, The d Kachyna, Karel 1994 Czech R)
    Reviews
  Hoberman, J. Deepest darkest Europe. still VILLAGE VOICE 40:63 Feb 28 1995
KREMSKI, PETER For film reviews see author under the following titles: THING
  CALLED LOVE, THE
  Kremski, P. Das Monster, das Mensch sein wollte. filmog il stills F BUL
    36:36-39+ [9p] n6 (n197) 1994
  Kremski, P. "Die Musik soll nicht das ausdruecken, was in der Szene zu sehen
    ist." credits il interv stills F BUL 37:33-38 n1 (n198) 1995
  Kremski, P. Film als Schule des Sehens. il interv stills F BUL 36:53-59 n6
    (n197) 1994
KREN, KURT
  Schmidt, E., Jr. Kurt Kren und der strukturalistische Film. biog filmog il
    BLIMP [n1]:42-49 Mar 1985
KRIM, ARTHUR
  Biskind, P. Beneficial life. obit port PREM 8:54-55 Mar 1995
  Lentz, H., III. Obituaries. biogs filmogs il obits ports CLASSIC
    n236:57-59 Feb 1995
KRIMA-KERIME: NOAH'S ARK f (d Curiel, Herbert 1995 Neth/FR Ger/Turkey)
    Reviews
  Rooney, D. "Krima-Kerime: Noah's Ark." credits VARIETY 358:85 Feb 20/26
    1995
KRISHNAMMA, SURI See also MAN OF NO IMPORTANCE, A
KROLIKOWSKA-AVIS, ELZBIETA
  Krolikowska-Avis, E. Alan Parker. il interv KINO 27:10-13 Jun 1993
  Krolikowska-Avis, E. Carlos Saura w Londynie. interv port KINO 27:40-41
    Jul 1993
KROLL, JACK For film reviews see author under the following titles: MADNESS OF
  KING GEORGE, THE; OUTBREAK
KRONISH, AMY
  The Nathan Axelrod collection, volume 1: Moledet Productions, 1927-1934,
    Carmel newsreels, series 1, 1935-1948. Ed: Amy Kronish, Edith Falk and Paula
    Weiman-Kelman [Book Review]. il KINO(GF) n56:31 Nov 1994
KROTKI FILM O ZABIJANIU f (d Kieslowski, Krzysztof 1988 Poland)
  Falkowska, J. "The political" in the films of Andrzej Wajda and Krzysztof
    Kieslowski. CJ 34:37-50 n2 1995
KROYER, BILL See also FERNGULLY... THE LAST RAINFOREST
KRUDY, GYULA
  Krudy, G. A feny hose. il still F VILAG 38:18-19 n2 1995
KRUMOV, KRASSIMIR See also ZABRANENIAT PLOD
KRUSCHKE, DOUG
  Brown, C. Gee, Officer Kruschke... il PREM 8:54-55+ [3p] Apr 1995
KUBALL, MICHAEL See also [UNKNOWN WAR, AN]

KUBO, CHRISTIAN
  Kubo, C. Institution Wanderkino. F KUNST n144:14-22 1994
KUBRICK, STANLEY See also BARRY LYNDON; LOLITA; SHINING, THE; (TWO THOUSAND AND
  ONE) 2001: A SPACE ODYSSEY
  Brown, R.S. Film music: the good, the bad, and the ugly. stills CINEASTE
    21:62-67 n1/2 1995
KUEHN, CHRISTOPH See also SOPHIE TAEUBER-ARP
KUEPPERS, PETRA
  Fowler, C. and Kueppers, P. Creteil International Women's Film Festival,
    18-27 March 1994. SCREEN 35:394-397 n4 1994
KUHN, ELEONORE
  Kuhn, E. Marketing executives. il ports table PREM 8:38 Mar 1995
  Kuhn, E. Production assistants. il table PREM 8:37 Feb 1995
KUHN, JOCHEN See also STIMME DES IGELS, DIE
  "Die Stimme des Igels." biog credits filmog still KINO(BRD) n1:44-45 1995
KULAS, GURI
  Kulas, G. and Hjortoy, K. Jost om Jost. interv port Z n4:6-8 (n46) 1993
KUMONOSUJO f (Throne of Blood d Kurosawa, Akira 1957 Japan)
  Mugiro, C. "El trono de sangre." credits still NOSFERATU n8:64-65 Feb 1992
  Vidal Estevez, M. William Akira Shakespeare Kurosawa. il stills NOSFERATU
    n8:40-47 Feb 1992
KUPIAINEN, REIJO For film reviews see author under the following titles: PEKKO
  JA POIKA
  Kupiainen, R. "Kristityn liha kuusi denaaria naula." il PEILI 18:26-27 n1
    1994
KUROCHKA RIABA f (d Konchalovsky, Andrei 1994 Russia/Fr)
    Folklore
  Dumas, D. Alambic et vieilles querelles. AVANT-SCENE n437:85-87 Dec 1994
    Review Excerpts
  La presse de Cannes. stills AVANT-SCENE n437:82-84 Dec 1994
    Screenplays
  "Riaba, ma poule": Andrei Konchalovsky: decoupage plan a plan et dialogues
    in-extenso. credits scenario stills AVANT-SCENE n437:6-79 Dec 1994
    Social Context
  Genin, B. En tournage. stills AVANT-SCENE n437:before p1-5 [6p] Dec 1994
    Reviews
  Derobert, E. "Riaba ma poule." credits stills POSITIF n408:50-51 Feb 1995
KUROSAWA, AKIRA See also KAGEMUSHA; KUMONOSUJO; RAN
  Kurosawa, A. Einige randbemerkungen zum Film. il stills BLIMP [n2]:16-20
    Winter 1985
  Vidal Estevez, M. William Akira Shakespeare Kurosawa. il stills NOSFERATU
    n8:40-47 Feb 1992
KURYS, DIANE See also A LA FOLIE
KUTZ, KAZIMIERZ See also ZAWROCONY
  Sendecka, M. Wazna jest dyscyplina. REZYSER n15:8 1993
KWAN, STANLEY See also HONG MEIGUI BAI MEIGUI; YANZHI KOU
KYDD, ELSPETH
  Kydd, E. Guess who else is coming to dinner: racial/sexual hysteria in
    "Candyman." stills C ACTION n36:63-72 1995
L.627 f (d Tavernier, Bertrand 1994 Fr)
  Sineux, M. and Vachaud, L. Entretien avec Bertrand Tavernier. il interv
    stills POSITIF n409:25-30 Mar 1995
LA BRUYERE, JEAN DE
  Vernet, M. Le voir-dire. CINEMAS 4:35-47 n1 1993
LA POLLA, FRANCO For film reviews see author under the following titles:
  FORREST GUMP
  La Polla, F. "Assassini nati." credits stills C FORUM 34:56-59 Sep (n337)
    1994
  La Polla, F. "Forrest Gump." credits il stills C FORUM 34:60-67 Oct (n338)
    1994
LA ROCHELLE, REAL For film reviews see author under the following titles: BUVOS
  VADASZ
  Jean, M. Entretien avec Real La Rochelle. il interv 24 IMAGES n75:32-33
    Dec/Jan 1994/95
  La Rochelle, R. Le combat du cineaste contre l'opera. discog filmog stills
    24 IMAGES n75:17-19 Dec/Jan 1994/95
  La Rochelle, R. Mythe du "That's Entertainment" ou creation d'un nouveau
    filmopera? filmog stills 24 IMAGES n76:50-52 Spring 1995
LA VEAUX, MICHEL
  Michel La Veaux. il interv 24 IMAGES n76:8 Spring 1995
LABENDIG f (d Schoenemann, Hannes 1994 FR Ger)
    Reviews
  Holloway, R. "L*a*b*e*n*d*i*g." KINO(GF) n56:26 Nov 1994
LABRUCE, BRUCE See also SUPER 8 1/2
  Hannaham, J. A fellating Fellini. il VILLAGE VOICE 40:56 Mar 14 1995
LACAN, JACQUES
  Walsh, M. Returns in the real: Lacan and the future of psychoanalysis in
    film studies. bibliog PS 14:22-32 n1/2 1994/95
LACASSE, ALAIN
  Lacasse, A. Considerations sur la portee ethique des propositions de
    Christian Metz pour une enonciation impersonnelle au cinema. bibliog
    CINEMAS 4:85-97 n3 1994
LACASSE, GERMAIN
  Gaudreault, A. and Lacasse, G. "Danse indienne": film Lumiere: no 1000: le
    premier film tourne au Quebec? stills 24 IMAGES n76:17-21 Spring 1995
  Gaudreault, A. and Lacasse, G. Fonctions et origines du bonimenteur du
    cinema des premiers temps. bibliog il CINEMAS 4:132-147 n1 1993
  Lacasse, G. Cent temps de cinema ou le cinema dans les temps de l'histoire.
    bibliog CINEMAS 5:57-67 n1/2 1994
LACHAT, PIERRE For film reviews see author under the following titles: AM ENDE
  DER SCHIENEN; GROSSESSE NERVEUSE; JOE & MARIE; LOU N'A PAS DIT NON;
  TOM & VIV
  Lachat, P. Das wueste Land. credits interv stills F BUL 36:49-50 n6 (n197)
    1994
  Lachat, P. "Die Hard" oder: "Vueu z'vueu Fueume!" il F BUL 37:18-23 n1
    (n198) 1995
  Lachat, P. Lodissea. credits stills F BUL 37:14-17 n1 (n198) 1995
LADY OF THE TROPICS f (d Conway, Jack 1939 USA)
  Marchetti, G. Pass och forforelse. bibliog stills F HAFTET 22:4-12 n3
    (n87) 1994

LADYBIRD LADYBIRD f (d Loach, Ken 1994 Gt Br)
     Reviews
  Corliss, R. When love isn't enough. still TIME 145:88 Jan 30 1995
  Hamilton, A. "Ladybird, Ladybird." credits still FILM 4:21 n1 [1995]
  Quart, L. "Ladybird, Ladybird." credits still CINEASTE 21:84-85 n1/2 1995
LAFOND, JEAN-DANIEL See also LIBERTE EN COLERE, LA
  Castiel, E. Jean-Daniel Lafond. interv still SEQUENCES n175:8 Nov/Dec 1994
LAGEIRA, JACINTO
  Rollet, S. Atom Egoyan. Par Carole Desbarats, Daniele Riviere et Jacinto
     Lageira; lettres-video de Paul Virilio et Atom Egoyan [Book Review]. il
     POSITIF n406:86 Dec 1994
LAGERFELD, KARL
     Lawsuits
  Molner, D. Designer suit blocks pic bow. still VARIETY 358:5 Mar 20/26
     1995
LAGNY, MICHELE
  Lagny, M. Le film et le temps braudelien. bibliog stills CINEMAS 5:15-39
     n1/2 1994
LAHR, JOHN
  Lahr, J. Bedazzled ports NEW YORKER 70:80-85 Jan 23 1995
  Lahr, J. The great Guskin. il NEW YORKER 71:44-49 Mar 20 1995
LAI, STAN See also FEIXIA AHDA
  Chiao, P. H.-P. Stan Lai: "illusions, lies and reality." interv stills
     CINEMAYA n24:48-54 Summer 1994
LAINE, KIMMO
  Laine, K. Miksi perehtya elokuvateoriaan [Book Review]. PEILI 18:31 n2 1994
  Laine, K. Vaapeli Kormy ja naiset. stills PEILI 18:16-17 n4 1994
LAKATLAN EMBER, A f (d Klopfler, Tibor 1991? Hungary)
     Reviews
  Bikacsy, B. Rough times for the cinema. il NEW HUNGARIAN Q 34:169-173 n129
     1993
LALLY, KEVIN For film reviews see author under the following titles: BOYS ON THE
     SIDE; LEGENDS OF THE FALL; MIXED NUTS; MURDER IN THE FIRST; MURIEL'S
     WEDDING
  Lally, K. Benton returns with tale of smalltown redemption. il still FJ
     98:10+ [2p] Jan/Feb 1995
  Lally, K. "Bye Bye Love" sees funny side of divorce. il still FJ 98:16+
     [2p] Mar 1995
  Lally, K. United Artists builds screens in Singapore and Malaysia. FJ 98:22
     Jan/Feb 1995
LAM, RINGO
  Pattison, B. On fire with Ringo Lam: part two. filmog il stills FATAL
     VISIONS n17:11-12 1994
LAMB f (d Gregg, Colin 1985 Gt Br)
     Reviews
  Stovall, N. "Lamb." VILLAGE VOICE 40:74 Feb 28 1995
LAMBERT, LOTHAR See also IN HASSLIEBE LOLA
LAMERICA f (d Amelio, Gianni 1994 It/Fr/Switz)
  Gili, J.A. Entretien avec Gianni Amelio. il interv stills POSITIF
     n406:25-31 Dec 1994
  Lachat, P. Lodissea. credits stills F BUL 37:14-17 n1 (n198) 1995
  Siciliani de Cumis, N. Ecce Lamelio alla scoperta della "Merica." C NUOVO
     43:2-3 Nov/Dec (n352) 1994
  Vasse, C. "Lamerica." credits il still POSITIF n406:23-24 Dec 1994
  Vecchi, P. "Lamerica." credits stills C FORUM 34:64-67 Sep (n337) 1994
     Sound Track Reviews
  Deutsch, D.C. "Lamerica." SCN 14:21 Mar 1995
     Reviews
  Bori, E. Eszak-deli atjaro. credits F VILAG 38:52-53 n3 1995
LAMONT, CHARLES See also ABBOTT AND COSTELLO GO TO MARS
LAMPELTO, RIITTA For film reviews see author under the following titles: DENNIS
     THE MENACE
LANCASTER, BURT
  Burt Lancaster. obit still AVANT-SCENE n437:93 Dec 1994
  Elia, M. Les bonnes (et parfois les dernieres) repliques de ceux qui nous
     ont quittes. biogs il obits port stills SEQUENCES n175:6 Nov/Dec 1994
  Legrand, G. Burt Lancaster. stills POSITIF n406:57-58 Dec 1994
  Molnar Gal, P. Lancester es Volonte. biogs obits stills F VILAG 38:2-3 n2
     1995
LANCTOT, MICHELINE See also VIE D'UN HEROS, LA
LANDRY, GABRIEL For film reviews see author under the following titles: AFFAIRE
     NORMAN WILLIAM, L'; ANNA 6-18; FILLE DE D'ARTAGNAN, LA; FILS DU
     REQUIN, LE; GASTON MIRON (LES OUTILS DU POETE); OCTOBRE; SOURIRE, LE
LANDSCAPE
     Theory
  Fry, K. Place/culture/representation. By James Duncan & David Ley (eds.)
     [Book Review]. bibliog J COMM 45:173-177 n1 1995
     Scandinavia
  Bono, F. Stillhet og landskap i nordisk film. stills F&K n7:24-28 1993
LANDSCAPE IN FILM
     Switzerland
  Wendt, U. Decor. stills C(SWITZ) 40:20-36 1994
Landscape in the Mist See TOPIO STIN OMIHLI
LANE, ANTHONY For film reviews see author under the following titles: BEFORE
     SUNRISE; BEFORE THE RAIN; DEATH AND THE MAIDEN; IN THE MOUTH OF
     MADNESS; MADNESS OF KING GEORGE, THE; PRIEST; QUICK AND THE DEAD, THE;
     SHALLOW GRAVE
LANE, DIANE
  Changing lanes. interv port BOXOFFICE 131:12 Apr 1995
LANG, FRITZ See also BIG HEAT, THE
  Bluemlinger, C. Bernard Eisenschitz & Paolo Bertetto (Hg.): Fritz Lang, La
     mise en scene [Book Review]. BLIMP n30:70 Winter 1994
LANG, JESSICA
  Webster, A. Filmographies. biog filmogs stills PREM 8:160 Apr 1995
LANG, ROBERT
  Cherchi Usai, P. The films of D.W. Griffith. By Scott Simmon [Book Reviews].
     GRIFFITHIANA n51/52:259 Oct 1994
  Cherchi Usai, P. The films of D.W. Griffith. By Scott Simmon [Book Reviews].
     J F PRES n49:72-73 Oct 1994

LANGE, JESSICA
  Sessums, K. Lange on life. ports VANITY FAIR 58:146-152+ [9p] Mar 1995
LANGER, MARC
  Langer, M. "Sight and Sound" [Book Review]. il BLIMP n30:54-56 Winter 1994
LANGMAN, LARRY
  Breen, J.L. Langman, Larry, and David Ebner. Encyclopedia of American spy
     films [Book Review]. ARMCHAIR DET 27:93-94 n1 1994
LANGUAGE
     Canada
        Phenomenology
  Roy, L. Langage cinematographique et faillibilite. bibliog CINEMAS
     4:99-118 n3 1994
     Italy
        Conferences, Institutes, Workshops, etc.
  Ferrante, E. Ad Agrigento si e tenuto il trentunesimo Convegno
     Internazionale sul linguaggio di Pirandello. C SUD 33:30 Jul/Aug/Sep (n113)
     1994
LANOT, MARRA P.L.
  Lanot, M. P.L. In a macho society gender makes a difference. il stills
     CINEMAYA n25/26:72-77 Autumn/Winter 1994/95
LANTOS, JEFFREY
  Lantos, J. The sweet sting of success. il MOVIELINE 6:70-71 Mar 1995
LANZMANN, CLAUDE See also SHOAH; TSAHAL
LAPINE, JAMES See also LIFE WITH MIKEY
LAPLANDERS IN FILM
     Finland
  Salmi, H. The Indian of the North: western traditions and Finnish Indians.
     still F&HIST 23:28-43+ [17p] n1/4 1993
LARA, FERNANDO
  Zappoli, G. Come e per chi? il port SEGNO n71:16-18 Jan/Feb 1995
LARSON, RANDALL D.
  Hubbard, R. Book reviews [Book Reviews]. F SCORE MONTHLY n40:9 Dec 1993
  Larson, R. D. The vintage score: "Hands of the Ripper:" an exemplary horror
     score. il F SCORE MONTHLY n36/37:24 Aug/Sep 1993
  Larson, R.D. ...And by "Bride" producer Soren Hyldgaard: "The Chaplin
     Puzzle." F SCORE MONTHLY n39:15 Nov 1993
  Larson, R.D. "Dial M for Murder." F SCORE MONTHLY n39:12 Nov 1993
  Larson, R.D. "Ed Wood." SCN 14:17 Mar 1995
  Larson, R.D. Franz Waxman (1907-1967): two unrecorded scores from 1936:
     "Fury" and "Devil Doll." F SCORE MONTHLY n39:15 Nov 1993
  Larson, R.D. Goblin on CD from Cinevox/SLC. F SCORE MONTHLY n38:13 Oct 1993
  Larson, R.D. "Maverick." il SCN 14:21 Mar 1995
  Larson, R.D. Music for Japanese animation: interview with Hiroshi Miyagawa.
     il interv port SCN 14:28-31 Mar 1995
  Larson, R.D. Review spotlight: "The Bride of Frankenstein" - at last! il F
     SCORE MONTHLY n39:15 Nov 1993
  Larson, R.D. Spotlight on: the Alhambra Morricone CDs. F SCORE MONTHLY
     n36/37:33 Aug/Sep 1993
  Larson, R.D. "Star Trek: Generations." il SCN 14:19-20 Mar 1995
  Larson, R.D. "Stargate." SCN 14:22-23 Mar 1995
  Larson, R.D. "The Santa Clause." SCN 14:21 Mar 1995
LARUE, JOHANNE For film reviews see author under the following titles: FORREST
     GUMP; INTERVIEW WITH THE VAMPIRE: THE VAMPIRE CHRONICLES; JEANNE LA
     PUCELLE; PRINCESS CARABOO; PULP FICTION; QUIZ SHOW; WINDIGO
  Larue, J. Erotique? stills SEQUENCES n174:18-19 Sep/Oct 1994
  Larue, J. L'autre cinema americain. stills SEQUENCES n174:20-22 Sep/Oct
     1994
Laserdiscs See Videodiscs as a subheading under individual subject headings
LASKI, BETH
  Busch, A.M. and Laski, B. Hughes hightails it back to CAA. VARIETY 357:8
     Jan 9/15 1995
  Laski, B. Fox's newborn Searchlight bows its first slate of 14 pix. VARIETY
     358:38 Feb 27/Mar 5 1995
  Laski, B. Harper back in saddle at Fox marketing. port VARIETY 357:36 Jan
     2/8 1995
  Laski, B. Helmer Hughes moves to ICM. VARIETY 357:24 Jan 2/8 1995
  Laski, B. Reeves, Davis ring up "Dead" cash. stat VARIETY 357:13+ [2p] Jan
     9/15 1995
LASKOWSKI, ADAM
  Kaplinska, A. Handlowiec i muzyk. il interv REZYSER n19:6-8 1993
LASSACHER, MARTINA
  Lassacher, M. Spanische Schriften [Book Review]. il BLIMP n30:58-60 Winter
     1994
LAST ACTION HERO f (d McTiernan, John 1993 USA)
     Reviews
  Meyers, R. The crime screen. il port stills ARMCHAIR DET 27:71-73 n1 1994
LAST GOOD TIME, THE f (d Balaban, Bob 1994 USA)
     Reviews
  Williams, E. "The Last Good Time." BOXOFFICE 131:bet p89 and 96 [pR19-R20]
     Mar 1995
LAST OF THE MOHICANS, THE f (d Mann, Michael 1992 USA)
  Dowell, P. The mythology of the western: Hollywood perspectives on race and
     gender in the nineties. stills CINEASTE 21:6-10 n1/2 1995
  Walker, J. Deconstructing an American myth: Hollywood and "The Last of the
     Mohicans." bibliog still F&HIST 23:104-116+ [14p] n1/4 1993
LAST PAGE, THE f (Manbait d Fisher, Terence 1952 Gt Br)
  Aldarondo, R. "Chantaje criminal." credits still NOSFERATU n6:77 Apr 1991
LAST SEDUCTION, THE f (d Dahl, John 1994 USA)
  Palminteri, C. The fire in Fiorentino. il interv port INTERV 25:88-91 Mar
     1995
     Reviews
  Ruppert, P. "The Last Seduction." CINEASTE 21:104 n1/2 1995
LAST SUPPER, THE f (d Roberts, Cynthia 1994 Can)
     Reviews
  Dubeau, A. "The Last Supper." SEQUENCES n174:14 Sep/Oct 1994
Last Tango in Paris See ULTIMO TANGO A PARIGI
LASTER, ARNAUD
  Laster, A. Les miserables sur les ecrans de cinema et de television.
     credits filmog il stills AVANT-SCENE n438/439:81-91 Jan/Feb 1995
Laterna Magica See AWARDS - Poland - Komitet Kinematografii

LEIGHT, WARREN See also NIGHT WE NEVER MET, THE
LEMHAGEN, ELLA
  (Sju) 7 debutanter. ports CHAPLIN 36:6-7 n6 (n255) 1994/95
LEMON, BRENDAN
  Lemon, B. Cinema Factory. port NEW YORKER 70:58-59 Jan 30 1995
LENI, PAUL See also WACHSFIGURENKABINETT, DAS
LENTZ, HARRIS, III
  Lentz, H., III. Obituaries. biogs filmogs il obits ports CLASSIC
    n236:57-59 Feb 1995
  Lentz, H., III. Obituaries. biogs filmogs obits ports CLASSIC n237:57-59
    Mar 1995
LEOLO f (d Lauzon, Jean-Claude 1992 Can/Fr)
    Reviews
  Vahtera, H. Lihan pauloissa." credits still PEILI 17:28 n3 1993
Leon See PROFESSIONAL, THE
LEONARD, BRETT See also HIDEAWAY
LEONA'S SISTER GERRI f (d Gillooly, Jane 1995 USA)
    Reviews
  Cheshire, G. "Leona's Sister Gerri." credits VARIETY 358:77 Mar 27/Apr 2
    1995
LEONE, SERGIO
  Burlingame, J. and Crowdus, G. Music at the service of the cinema. il
    interv port stills CINEASTE 21:76-80 n1/2 1995
LEPIEJ BYC PIEKNA I BOGATA f (d Bajon, Filip 1993 Poland/FR
  Ger/Hungary/Ukraine)
    Reviews
  Turcsanyi, S. "Jobb szepnek es gazdagnak lenni." credits still F VILAG
    38:54 n3 1995
Lesbians in film See HOMOSEXUALS IN FILM - Women
LESZCZYNSKI, WITOLD See also KOLOSS; ZYWOT MATEUSZA
LETTER FROM AN UNKNOWN WOMAN f (d Ophuls, Max 1948 USA)
    Intertextual Analysis
  Ropars-Wuilleumier, M.-C. L'oubli du texte. bibliog CINEMAS 4:11-22 n1
    1993
LETTER TO THE NEXT GENERATION f (d Klein, James 1990 USA)
  Boruszkowski, L.A. An interview with documentary filmmaker Jim Klein.
    filmog interv port UFAJ 46:34-42 n1 1994
LETTICH, SHELDON See also ONLY THE STRONG
LETTRES D'AMOUR EN SOMALIE f (d Mitterrand, Frederic 1982 Fr)
  Odin, R. Le documentaire interieur. Travail du JE et mise en phase dans
    "Lettres d'amour en Somalie." bibliog still CINEMAS 4:82-100 n2 1994
LETTRISM
    France
  Cantrill, A. Le cinema Lettriste (1951-1991). By Frederique Devaux [Book
    Review]. CANTRILL'S FMNTS n73/74:42 May 1994
LETZTES AUS DER DADAER f (d Foth, Joerg 1990 E Ger)
  Graef, C. Der Weg zum ersten Spielfilm. il interv F & FERNSEHEN 22:54-69
    n6 1994
LEUNG, CLARENCE See also [NAKED KILLER]
LEUNG, RAY See also GUI TU
LEUNG, SIU-HUNG (ALEX) See also CHUNGGAMSUK
LEUTRAT, JEAN-LOUIS
  Cremonini, G. AA vari (sotto la direzione di Jean-Louis Leutrat): L'amour a
    mort di A. Resnais [Book Review]. C FORUM 34:92-93 Oct (n338) 1994
  Gaberscek, C. Le carte del western: percorsi di un genere cinematografico.
    Di Jean-Louis Leutrat e Suzanne Liandrat-Guiges [Book Review]. GRIFFITHIANA
    n51/52:252 Oct 1994
  Jeancolas, J.-P. Geraniums [Book Reviews]. stills POSITIF n408:94-95 Feb
    1995
  Leutrat, J.-L. Ah! les salauds! bibliog CINEMAS 4:73-84 n3 1994
LEVANT, BRIAN See also FLINTSTONES, THE
LEVELEK PERZSIABOL f (d Lotfi, Rambod 1995 Hungary/Iran)
    Reviews
  Elley, D. "Letters From Persia" ("Levelek perzsiabol"). credits VARIETY
    358:88 Feb 20/26 1995
LEVEN, JEREMY See also DON JUAN DEMARCO
LEVIN, DAVID MICHAEL
  Stonehill, B. The debate over "ocularcentrism" [Book Reviews]. J COMM
    45:147-152 n1 1995
LEVINSON, BARRY See also DISCLOSURE
LEVY, BERNARD-HENRI See also BOSNA!
LEVY, DANI See also OHNE MICH; STILLE NACHT
LEVY, EMANUEL For film reviews see author under the following titles: BLACK
  IS... BLACK AIN'T; BOY CALLED HATE, A; CIRCLE OF FRIENDS; DEAR BABE;
  DENISE CALLS UP; DON JUAN DEMARCO; DOOM GENERATION, THE; DOROTHEA
  LANGE: A VISUAL LIFE; ECOLOGICAL DESIGN: INVENTING THE FUTURE; GIRL
  WITH THE HUNGRY EYES, THE; IGNATZ & LOTTE; INCREDIBLY TRUE ADVENTURE
  OF TWO GIRLS IN LOVE, THE; MANURA CHUGIGI; MUTE WITNESS; NO LOANS
  TODAY; STREET FIGHTER; TEEN DREAMS; TIE-DYED: ROCK 'N ROLL'S MOST
  DEADICATED FANS; WALKING DEAD, THE; WHEN BILLY BROKE HIS HEAD... AND
  OTHER TALES OF WONDER; WHEREVER YOU ARE; WIGSTOCK: THE MOVIE
  Levy, E. How to win the Oscar. still VARIETY 357:62+ [2p] Jan 2/8 1995
  Turner, G. George Cukor, master of elegance. By Emanuel Levy [Book Review].
    AMCIN 76:86 Jan 1995
LEVY, JEFERY See also S.F.W.
LEWIS, BRENT
  Lewis, B. Lee Tamahori's "Once Were Warriors." port stills C PAPERS
    n102:4-8 Dec 1994
LEWIS, JERRY
  Fuller, G. Thank you Jerry much. il interv port INTERV 25:92-93+ [3p] Apr
    1995
  Slide, A. The Slide area film book notes [Book Reviews]. CLASSIC
    n237:42-44+ [4p] Mar 1995
LEWIS, JON
  Hietala, V. Globaaliteinit arvotyhjiossa [Book Review]. PEILI 18:28 n4 1994
LEWIS, KEVIN For film reviews see author under the following titles: BULLETS
  OVER BROADWAY; HUOZHE
LEY, DAVID
  Fry, K. Place/culture/representation. By James Duncan & David Ley (eds.)
    [Book Review]. bibliog J COMM 45:173-177 n1 1995

LEYDON, JOE For film reviews see author under the following titles: CALLEJON DE
  LOS MILAGROS, EL; HOUSEGUEST; INSOMNIA; JERKY BOYS, THE; MAN WITH THE
  PERFECT SWING, THE; MORE PERFECT UNION, A; P'ESA DLIA PASSAZHIRA;
  RADIO STAR - DIE AFN STORY; RETURN OF THE TEXAS CHAINSAW MASSACRE,
  THE; RICHIE RICH; SCHATTEN DES SCHREIBERS, DER; SHIRAT HA'SIRENA; TALL
  TALE: THE UNBELIEVABLE ADVENTURES OF PECOS BILL; TELOS EPOCHUS;
  (THREE) 3 NINJAS KNUCKLE UP; TIAN WANG;
  Leydon, J. Soderbergh pic preems at Southwest arts confab. VARIETY 358:22
    Mar 13/19 1995
LEYENDECKER, FRANK
  Leyendecker, F. The "Boxoffice" story. il port BOXOFFICE 131:24-25 Mar
    1995
LI, ERWEI
  Li, E. Lu Wei, one of China's best scriptwriters. port stills CHINA SCREEN
    n4:10-11 1994
LI, JINSONG See also [LEGEND OF YANDI, THE]
LI, SHAOHONG See also HONGFEN; SISHI PUHUO; XUESE QINGCHEN
  Reynaud, B. Li Shaohong. port still CINEMAYA n25/26:8-9 Autumn/Winter
    1994/95
  "Sishi buho." biog credits filmog il still CINEMAYA n25/26:99 Autumn/Winter
    1994/95
LI, WEI
  Li, W. A pearl reveals its splendor. port stills CHINA SCREEN n4:24-25
    1994
LIANDRAT-GUIGES, SUZANNE
  Gaberscek, C. Le carte del western: percorsi di un genere cinematografico.
    Di Jean-Louis Leutrat e Suzanne Liandrat-Guiges [Book Review]. GRIFFITHIANA
    n51/52:252 Oct 1994
Liberators Take Liberties See BEFREIER UND BEFREITE
LIBERTE EN COLERE, LA f (d Lafond, Jean-Daniel 1995 Can)
  Castiel, E. Jean-Daniel Lafond. interv still SEQUENCES n175:8 Nov/Dec 1994
    Reviews
  Noel, C. "La liberte en colere." still 24 IMAGES n76:62-63 Spring 1995
LIBERTI, FABRIZIO
  Liberti, F. Michael Radford: Troisi, il cinema e l'Italia di oggi. credits
    interv stills C FORUM 34:46-50 Sep (n337) 1994
LIBRARY OF CONGRESS. MOTION PICTURE, BROADCASTING AND RECORDED SOUND DIVISION
  (Washington, D.C.)
  Loughney, P. Washington. stat J F PRES n49:33-34 Oct 1994
    Collections and Collecting
  Cherchi Usai, P. The Library of Congress video collection: rare silent films
    with piano scores composed and performed by Philip Carli. GRIFFITHIANA
    n51/52:262-263 Oct 1994
  Cherchi Usai, P. The Library of Congress video collection: rare silent films
    with piano scores composed and performed by Philip Carli. J F PRES
    n49:74-75 Oct 1994
LIBRARY OF CONGRESS. NATIONAL FILM PRESERVATION BOARD (Washington, D.C.)
  Kalish, K. Wake up and smell the vinegar. il DGA NEWS 20:24+ [6p] n1 1995
  Protecting film's heritage. AMCIN 76:96 Jan 1995
    Preservation
  The NFPB 150. DGA NEWS 20:34 n1 1995
Licensing, product See MERCHANDISING SPIN-OFFS; MERCHANDISING TIE-INS
LIE DOWN WITH DOGS f (d White, Wally 1995 USA)
    Reviews
  Stratton, D. "Lie Down With Dogs." credits VARIETY 358:80 Feb 20/26 1995
LIEBE LUEGEN f (d Schertenleib, Christof 1995 Switz/Austria)
    Production
  Derrer, J.C. "Liebe Luegen": Drehtag am Zuerichsee. il F BUL 37:9 n1
    (n198) 1995
LIEBERMAN, EVAN A.
  Lieberman, E.A. Charlie the trickster. bibliog stills UFAJ 46:16-28 n3
    1994
LIEBMAN, STUART
  Liebman, S. There should be no scissors in your mind. interv port stills
    CINEASTE 21:40-42 n1/2 1995
LIEBMANN-SMITH, RICHARD
  Liebmann-Smith, R. A studio of their own. il NEW YORKER 70:88 Jan 9 1995
LIER, MIRIAM VAN
  Lier, M. van. The European documentary: first of a three-part series.
    graphs stat DOC BOX 2:5-8 1993
Life and Extraordinary Adventures of Private Ivan Chonkin, The See ZIVOT A
  NEOBYCEJNA DOBRODRUZSTVI VOJAKA IVAN CONKINA
LIFE WITH MIKEY f (d Lapine, James 1993 USA)
    Reviews
  Kangasniemi, H. Tyttoroolion piristava poikkeus. credits still PEILI 18:32
    n1 1994
LIGHT, ALLIE See also DIALOGUES WITH MADWOMEN
  Milvy, E. Allie Light tells all. ANGLES 2:5 n4 1995
LIGHT SLEEPER f (d Schrader, Paul 1992 USA)
    Reviews
  Pezzotta, A. "Lo spacciatore." credits SEGNO n63:103 Sep/Oct 1993
LIGHTING
    Techniques
  Elrick, T. Matters of light & depth. By Ross Lowell [Book Review]. DGA NEWS
    20:43 n1 1995
    United States
      Technical Aspects
  O'Brien, K. Viera, John David, assisted by Maria Viera. Lighting for film
    and electronic cinematography [Book Review]. UFAJ 46:49-51 n3 1994
LIGHTNING OVER WATER f (d Ray, Nicholas/Wenders, Wim 1980 W Ger/Swed/USA)
  Morin, S. "Nick's Movie": le point de fuite. bibliog still CINEMAS
    4:101-117 n2 1994
LIGOURIS, NICOS See also HERZ AUS STEIN
  "Herz aus Stein." biog credits filmog still KINO(BRD) n1:26-27 1995
LILIENTHAL, PETER See also DAVID
LILJENBACK, SANI
  Liljenback, S. Isoja ja pienia asioita. biog filmog il stills PEILI
    17:26-28 n4 1993
LILLEY, JESSIE
  Lilley, J. How to make a monster movie. il interv stills SCARLET STREET

LOCCHI, PINO
  Lentz, H., III. Obituaries. biogs filmogs il obits ports CLASSIC
    n236:57-59 Feb 1995
LOCHEN, KALLE
  Lochen, K. Aggressiv satire. stills F&K n7:18-19 1993
  Lochen, K. Eksisterer det ufarlige? stat stills table F&K n1:28-30 1994
  Lochen, K. En spire til liv. stills F&K n1:4-5 1994
  Lochen, K. En studie i panikk. stills F&K n7:12-13 1993
  Lochen, K. Filmleksikon pa diskett [Book Review]. still F&K n7:41 1993
  Lochen, K. Gjenklang av entusiasme. il F&K n7:7 1993
  Lochen, K. Jakten pa identitet. stills F&K n1:26-27 1994
  Lochen, K. Kinoen som verneverdig kulturhus. stat F&K n7:2 1993
Locked-up Time See VERRIEGELTE ZEIT
LOCKERBIE, IAN
  Lockerbie, I. Le documentaire autoreflexif au Quebec. "L'emotion dissonante"
    et "Passiflora." still CINEMAS 4:118-132 n2 1994
LOCKWOOD, MICHAEL
  Lockwood, M. The many facets of Charles Laughton. FILM 4:6+ [2p] n1 [1995]
LODATO, NUCCIO
  Lodato, N. I quattro figli di Willy Wyler con le gemelle di Monta Bell. il
    stills C FORUM 34:10-12 Oct (n338) 1994
  Lodato, N. Pordenone: luci dell'Asia e fabbriche di risate. stills C FORUM
    34:8-10 Oct (n338) 1994
LODI, EDWARD
  Lodi, E. Dark of the night. By Richard Nehrbass [Book Review]. ARMCHAIR DET
    26:116 n3 1993
LOESCHE, CLAUS-DIETER
  Loesche, C.-D. Antonioni [Book Review]. F KUNST n144:73-75 1994
LOFFREDA, PIERPAOLO For film reviews see author under the following titles:
    AIQING WANSUI; AU PAYS DES ORANGES; BACKBEAT; DA QUALCHE PARTE IN
    CITTA; MARTHA; PASSE COMPOSE; S.F.W.
  Loffreda, P. Immagini, parole e suoni. credits stills C FORUM 34:57-58 Oct
    (n338) 1994
  Loffreda, P. Intervista a Enzo Monteleone. interv stills C FORUM 34:74-75
    Sep (n337) 1994
  Loffreda, P. Primi sguardi nella scuola: dalla descrizione al racconto. il
    stills C FORUM 34:3-7 Oct (n338) 1994
LOGAN'S RUN f (d Anderson, Michael 1976 USA)
    Adaptations
  Bradley, M.R. Nolan's "Run." biog il interv stills F FAX n48:42-48+ [8p]
    Jan/Feb 1995
LOISELLE, MARIE-CLAUDE For film reviews see author under the following titles:
    JEANNE LA PUCELLE; LOU N'A PAS DIT NON
  Jean, M. and Loiselle, M.-C. A l'ombre du 7e art. il interv stills 24
    IMAGES n76:4-7+ [7p] Spring 1995
  Loiselle, M.-C. La nef des fous. il 24 IMAGES n75:3 Dec/Jan 1994/95
  Racine, C. and Loiselle, M.-C. Partie de ping-pong. 24 IMAGES n76:2-3
    Spring 1995
LOKUDUWA f (d Peries, Sumitra 1994 Sri Lanka)
  "Loku duwa." biog credits il still CINEMAYA n25/26:104 Autumn/Winter
    1994/95
LOLA MONTES f (Sins of Lola Montes, The d Ophuels, Max 1955 Fr/W Ger)
    Intertextual Analysis
  Ropars-Wuilleumier, M.-C. L'oubli du texte. bibliog CINEMAS 4:11-22 n1
    1993
LOLITA f (d Kubrick, Stanley 1962 USA)
    Psychoanalytic Analysis
  Bick, I.J. "That hurts!": humor and sadomasochism in "Lolita." bibliog
    stills UFAJ 46:3-18 n2 1994
  Gabbard, K. The circulation of sadomasochistic desire in the "Lolita" texts.
    bibliog stills UFAJ 46:19-30 n2 1994
LOMBARDI, FRANCISCO JOSE See also SIN COMPASION
LOMBARDI, MARCO For film reviews see author under the following titles:
    POLIZIOTTI; SERIAL MOM; TIMECOP
LONDON f (d Keiller, Patrick 1994 Gt Br)
  Ballard, B. I sat glued to the screen. still VERTIGO (UK) 1:43 n4 1994/95
  Fisher, M. Why is it so hard to enjoy? VERTIGO (UK) 1:42-43 n4 1994/95
  Griffiths, K. Anxious visions. il stills VERTIGO (UK) 1:47-52 n4 1994/95
  Kossoff, A. A metaphysical mirror. il VERTIGO (UK) 1:45-46 n4 1994/95
  Mepham, J. The commonplace transfigured. VERTIGO (UK) 1:41-42 n4 1994/95
  Phillips, M. No time for contradiction. VERTIGO (UK) 1:44-45 n4 1994/95
  Raban, W. "London": the background. il VERTIGO (UK) 1:40 n4 1994/95
LONDON, JACK
  Nuernberg, S.M. Jack London - the movies, an historical survey. By Tony
    Williams [Book Review]. WESTERN AM LIT 28:173-174 n2 1993
LONG, CHRIS
  Long, C. Australia's first films: facts and fables, part eleven: Aborigines
    and actors. filmogs il map ports C PAPERS n102:52-57+ [8p] Dec 1994
LONG TAKE
  Cosandey, R. Wo ist die grosse Treppe hingekommen? il stills C(SWITZ)
    40:51-74 1994
LONG WALK HOME, THE f (d Pearce, Richard 1990 USA)
    Sound Track Reviews
  Pugliese, R. Segnodischi. stills SEGNO n63:93 Sep/Oct 1993
LONGFELLOW, BRENDA See also GERDA
  Longfellow, B. Gaylyn Studlar. In the realm of pleasure: Von Sternberg,
    Dietrich and the masochistic aesthetic [Book Review]. CAN J F STUD 1:83-89
    n2 1991
  Longfellow, B. "The Bandit Queen." stills C ACTION n36:10-16 1995
LONGO, ROBERT See also JOHNNY MNEMONIC
  Pinchbeck, D. From artist to auteur. port ESQUIRE 123:17 Jan 1995
LOOKING FOR LANGSTON f (d Julien, Isaac 1989 Gt Br)
  Grundmann, R. Black nationhood and the rest in the West. interv port
    CINEASTE 21:28-31 n1/2 1995
LOPEZ, ANA M.
  Sinclair, J. King, John, Lopez, Ana M and Alvarado, Manuel, eds. Mediating
    two worlds: cinematic encounters in the Americas [Book Review]. MEDIA INFO
    AUSTRALIA n75:166-167 Feb 1995
LOPEZ ARANDA, SUSANA
  Lopez Aranda, S. Filmar el tiempo: Arturo Ripstein y Paz Alicia Garciadiego:

  segundo parte. il interv stills DICINE n59:9-13 Nov/Dec 1994
LOPEZ, CYNTHIA
  Lopez, C. and Kracher, J. Media activism. interv ANGLES 2:3+ [2p] n4 1995
LOPPI, ALESSANDRO
  Loppi, A. L'enigma Sakamoto. filmog il stills C FORUM 34:36-38 Oct (n338)
    1994
LOQUASTO, SANTO
  Oppenheimer, J. "Team Woody" fires "Bullets Over Broadway." il stills
    AMCIN 76:66-70 Feb 1995
LORD OF ILLUSIONS f (d Barker, Clive 1995 USA)
  Beeler, M. Clive Barker's "Lord of Illusions." il stills C FANTAS 26:23-26
    n3 1995
  Beeler, M. "Lord of Illusions." il stills C FANTAS 26:6-7 n2 1995
  McDonagh, M. Barker works horrific magic with UA's "Lord of Illusions." il
    still FJ 98:14+ [2p] Jan/Feb 1995
LORD, PETER
  Sifianos, G. Aardman Animations. il interv stills POSITIF n407:25-28 Jan
    1995
LORI, SERGIO
  Lori, S. Ha conquistato anche il Nord l'ineffabile Enzo Cannavale. C SUD
    33:51-52 Jul/Aug/Sep (n113) 1994
  Lori, S. I films di Bernardo Bertolucci. Di Jefferson Kline [Book Review].
    C SUD 33:37 Jul/Aug/Sep (n113) 1994
  Lori, S. La sessantesima manifestazione del Mifed organizzata dalla Fiera di
    Milano. C SUD 33:31 Jul/Aug/Sep (n113) 1994
  Lori, S. Un sincero ricordo di Federico Fellini al Festival Cinematografico
    di Cannes 94. biog il C SUD 33:3-5 Jul/Aug/Sep (n113) 1994
LORIN, WILL
  Lorin, W. Game theory and the Guild: using management's weapons in our own
    self-interest. JOURNAL WGA 8:26-27 Feb 1995
LOS ANGELES CRITICS ASSOCIATION
  Slide, A. The Slide area film book notes [Book Reviews]. CLASSIC
    n237:42-44+ [4p] Mar 1995
LOSING ISAIAH f (d Gyllenhaal, Stephen 1995 USA)
  Taylor, E. Raising "Isaiah." port VILLAGE VOICE 40:64 Mar 28 1995
    Reviews
  Dauphin, G. "Losing Isaiah." VILLAGE VOICE 40:57 Mar 21 1995
  McCarthy, T. "Isaiah" tackles thorny issue. credits still VARIETY 358:47
    Mar 20/26 1995
[LOST PRINCE, THE] f (in production 1995- Hong Kong)
    Location Production
  Alexander, M. Kung-fu flick feels the heat. ONFILM [12]:5 n1 1995
LOTFI, RAMBOD See also LEVELEK PERZSIABOL
LOU N'A PAS DIT NON f (d Mieville, Anne-Marie 1994 Fr/Switz)
  Euvrard, J. Anne-Marie Mieville. il interv stills 24 IMAGES n76:12-14+
    [4p] Spring 1995
    Reviews
  Aude, F. "Lou n'a pas dit non." POSITIF n406:46-47 Dec 1994
  Lachat, P. "Lou n'as pas dit non." credits still C(SWITZ) 40:216-217 1994
  Loiselle, M.-C. "Lou n'a pas dit non." credits still 24 IMAGES n76:15
    Spring 1995
LOUDSPEAKERS
    United States
  Solman, G. Sound advice for editing, playback. il DGA NEWS 20:12-13 n1
    1995
LOUGHNEY, PATRICK
  Loughney, P. Washington. stat J F PRES n49:33-34 Oct 1994
LOUVISH, SIMON
  Ciment, M. BFI film classics [Book Reviews]. stills POSITIF n408:75-77 Feb
    1995
LOVE AFFAIR f (d Caron, Glenn Gordon 1994 USA)
  Brown, C. No love affair. ports PREM 8:46-47+ [3p] Feb 1995
    Reviews
  Cherchi Usai, P. "Love Affair" - "Un grande amore." credits still SEGNO
    n72:53-54 Mar/Apr 1995
  Travers, P. Misfires. stills ROLLING STONE n696:134 Dec 1 1994
LOVE AND DEATH f (d Allen, Woody 1975 USA)
    Narrative Analysis
  Deleyto, C. The narrator and the narrative: the evolution of Woody Allen's
    film comedies. bibliog F CRITICISM 19:40-54 n2 1994/95
LOVE AND HUMAN REMAINS f (d Arcand, Denys 1993 Can)
    Reviews
  Adagio, C. "Amateur"; "La natura ambigua dell'amore." credits still C
    NUOVO 43:47-48 Nov/Dec (n352) 1994
  Schwartzberg, S. "Love and Human Remains." BOXOFFICE 131:bet p89 and 96
    [pR18] Mar 1995
LOVE CHEAT & STEAL f (d Curran, William 1994 USA)
    Reviews
  Comino, J. "Love, Cheat & Steal." credits still S&S 5:48-49 Jan 1995
LOVE IN FILM
  Muszynski, A. Marginesy melodramatu. stills KINO 27:18-19 Jul 1993
    Italy
  Dusi, N. Il geloso a rotelle. bibliog stills SEGNO n71:3-7 Jan/Feb 1995
LOVE IS BLIND f (d Piel, Denis 1995 USA)
    Reviews
  Harvey, D. "Love Is Blind." credits VARIETY 358:76 Mar 27/Apr 2 1995
Love One Another See GEZEICHNETEN, DIE
LOVELL, GLENN
  Lovell, G. Letters: KK kalls it kwits. F COM 31:2 Jan/Feb 1995
LOVLUND, BJORN-FRODE
  Lovlund, B.-F. Guidet tur gjennom voldelig subkultur [Book Review]. il Z
    n4:41 (n46) 1993
  Lovlund, B.-F. Mord og vanvidd i London. stills Z n1:12-13 (n47) 1994
  Lovlund, B.-F. Skjaersild i skjaergarden. credits still Z n4:16-17 (n46)
    1993
  Lovlund, B.-F. Variasjon over samme tema. credits still Z n1:24-25 (n47)
    1994
LOW, COLIN See also CITY OF GOLD
LOW, STEPHEN See also TITANICA
  Sylvester, S. "Titanica" takes Imax into new waters. il stills AMCIN

76:32-34+ [5p] Jan 1995

LOWE, EDWARD T.
Scrivani, R. "House of Dracula." Edward T. Lowe; edited by Philip J. Riley
[Book Review]. SCARLET STREET n17:99 Winter 1995

LOWE, ROB
O'Neill, K. Idol chatter. interv port PREM 8:44 Mar 1995

LOWELL, ROSS
Elrick, T. Matters of light & depth. By Ross Lowell [Book Review]. DGA NEWS
20:43 n1 1995

LOWENSOHN, ELINA
Derryberry, J. Have you seen Elina? interv ports INTERV 25:32+ [2p] Apr
1995

LOWRY, BRIAN For film reviews see author under the following titles: BILLY
MADISON; DOLORES CLAIBORNE; HUNTED, THE; MAN OF THE HOUSE
Lowry, B. TV producer Carsey-Werner launches film unit. VARIETY 358:11 Feb
13/19 1995

LOWRY, STEPHEN
Korte, H. and Lowry, S. Heinz Ruehmann - ein Star der deutschen
Filmgeschichte. stills MEDIEN 38:348-352+ [7p] n6 1994

LOY, NANNI See also PACCO, DOPPIO PACCO E CONTROPACCOTTO

LOYEN, BENEDICTE
Benedicte Loyen. filmog port MONITEUR n128:26 Feb 1995

LU, TONGLIN
Lu, T. L'enfance, la maturite et la mort: la formation d'une identite
nationale problematisee. bibliog glos still CINEMAS 3:23-37 n2/3 1993

LU, WEI
Li, E. Lu Wei, one of China's best scriptwriters. port stills CHINA SCREEN
n4:10-11 1994

LUBASZENKO, OLAF
Slodowski, J. Olaf Lubaszenko. filmog port stills FSP 40:12-13 n7 (n761)
1994

LUBELSKI, TADEUSZ
Lubelski, T. Dziesiec lat spoznienia, czyli "Mala apokalipsa" ogladana we
Francji. KINO 27:8-9 May 1993
Lubelski, T. Seweryn. il interv KINO 27:10-15 Jul 1993

LUBIN, ARTHUR See also BUCK PRIVATES; PHANTOM OF THE OPERA

LUBITSCH, ERNST See also KOHLHIESELS TOECHTER; ROMEO UND JULIA IM SCHNEE
Aldarondo, R. La tentacion de Shakespeare. stills NOSFERATU n8:20-27 Feb
1992
Mitchell, L. Ernst Lubitsch: laughter in paradise. By Scott Eyman [Book
Review]. il DGA NEWS 19:32-33 n2 1994

LUC & MARIE: LE FILM f (d Boon, Philippe/Brandenbourger, Laurent 1995
Belg/Fr/Luxembourg)
"Luc et Marie le film." credits il MONITEUR n128:25 Feb 1995

LUCANIO, PATRICK
Lucanio, P. and Coville, G. Ward Kimball's wonderful world of motion. il
port stills F FAX n48:54-55 Jan/Feb 1995
Slide, A. The Slide area film book notes [Book Reviews]. CLASSIC
n237:42-44+ [4p] Mar 1995

LUCCHINI, DOMENICO
Zappoli, G. Come e per chi? il port SEGNO n71:16-18 Jan/Feb 1995

LUCHETTI, DANIELE See also UNICO PAESE AL MONDO, L'

LUCIA, CYNTHIA
Lucia, C. Montreal's feminist edge. stills CINEASTE 21:96-97 n1/2 1995
Lucia, C. Progress and misgivings in Mississippi. interv port stills
CINEASTE 21:43-45 n1/2 1995

LUCZYCKA, WANDA
Jaworski, R. and Maniewski, M. Opowiesc Wandy Luczyckiej. still KINO
27:26-27 Jun 1993

LUGOSI, BELA
Senn, B. Bela's dark triad. stills F FAX n48:71-75+ [7p] Jan/Feb 1995

LUKAS, KARL
Lentz, H., III. Obituaries. biogs filmogs obits ports CLASSIC n237:57-59
Mar 1995
Obituaries. obits VARIETY 358:58-59 Mar 20/26 1995

LULLI, FOLCO
Comuzio, E. Gino Lulli (a cura di): Folco Lulli attore solare [Book Review].
C FORUM 34:94 Sep (n337) 1994

LULLI, GINO
Comuzio, E. Gino Lulli (a cura di): Folco Lulli attore solare [Book Review].
C FORUM 34:94 Sep (n337) 1994

LUMET, SIDNEY
Dixon, W.W. American-Jewish filmmakers: traditions and trends. By David
Desser and Lester D. Friedman [Book Review]. F CRITICISM 19:108-113 n2
1994/95

LUMIERE, AUGUSTE
Bourget, J.-L. Correspondances 1890-1953. Par Auguste et Louis Lumiere [Book
Review]. POSITIF n409:72-73 Mar 1995
Cameron, E.W. Kant's station; the Lumieres' train: seeing things by means of
film. CAN J F STUD 1:36-56 n1 1990
Wyss, S. Korrekte Darstellung technischer Zusammenhaenge. F BUL 37:5 n1
(n198) 1995

LUMIERE DES ETOILES MORTES, LA f (d Matton, Charles 1993 Fr/FR Ger)
Noel, J. "La lumiere des etoiles mortes." bibliog credits stills GRAND
ANGLE n177:23-24 Dec 1994

LUMIERE, LOUIS
Bourget, J.-L. Correspondances 1890-1953. Par Auguste et Louis Lumiere [Book
Review]. POSITIF n409:72-73 Mar 1995
Cameron, E.W. Kant's station; the Lumieres' train: seeing things by means of
film. CAN J F STUD 1:36-56 n1 1990
Wyss, S. Korrekte Darstellung technischer Zusammenhaenge. F BUL 37:5 n1
(n198) 1995

LUMIERE NOIRE f (d Hondo, Med 1994 Fr/Gt Br/Mali)
Reviews
Thirard, P.L. "Lumiere noire." credits still POSITIF n406:43 Dec 1994

LUMIERE TEKERCSEK f (d Szirtes, Andras 1995 Hungary)
Berczes, L. Mozi van. still F VILAG 38:17 n4 1995

LUMIERE (United States)
These boots were made for hawkin': part IV - more rogue's gallery. il F
SCORE MONTHLY n40:6 Dec 1993

LUN HUI f (d Huang, Jianxin 1989 China)
Political Analysis
Berry, C. "Ce qui meritait le plus d'etre puni etait son penis":
postsocialisme, distopie et la mort du heros. bibliog glos still CINEMAS
3:38-59 n2/3 1993

LUNDKVIST, INGEMAR
Axelsson, S. I filmfralsta poeters sallskap [Book Review]. il CHAPLIN
36:62 n6 (n255) 1994/95

LUNES DE FIEL f (Bitter Moon d Polanski, Roman 1992 Fr/Gt Br)
Zienkiewicz, D. Listy: dwa moralitety. KINO 27:44-45 Jun 1993

LUO, JUN
Luo, J. A star in the world of science films. il CHINA SCREEN n4:26-27
1994

LUPO, MICHELE See also ARIZONA COLT

LURIE, ALISON
Lurie, A. She had it all. il still NY R BKS 42:3-5 Mar 2 1995

LUSKE, HAMILTON S. See also (ONE HUNDRED AND ONE) 101 DALMATIANS

LUYET, CLAUDE See also ROBERT CREEP

LUZYNSKA, JADWIGA ANNA
Luzynska, J.A. Hollywoodzkie namaszczenie Wojciecha Kilara. il interv KINO
27:34 Jul 1993

LVOFF, JOHN See also SALLE DE BAIN, LA

LVOVSKY, NOEMIE See also OUBLIEE-MOI
Aude, F. Entretien avec Noemie Lvovsky. il interv stills POSITIF
n408:39-42 Feb 1995

LYDON, PETER
Lydon, P. The goons and a bomb on Broadway. il S&S 5:39 Feb 1995

LYNCH, DAVID See also BLUE VELVET; TWIN PEAKS: FIRE WALK WITH ME
Zaniello, T. Hitched or Lynched: who directed "Twin Peaks"? bibliog filmogs
STUDIES POP CULT 17:55-64 n1 1994

LYNE, ADRIAN See also FOXES

LYONS, DONALD
Lyons, D. Family values. il stills F COM 31:78-81 Jan/Feb 1995

LYU, HYUN-MI For film reviews see author under the following titles: HOLLYWOOD
KID EU SAENG-AE
Lyu, H.-M. Kang Soo Yeon. stills CINEMAYA n24:30-32 Summer 1994

LZA KSIECIA CIEMNOSCI f (d Piestrak, Marek 1994 Poland/Estonia)
"Lza ksiecia ciemnosci." biog credits filmog still FSP 40:6 n7 (n761) 1994

MDP WORLDWIDE
Weiner, R. Alliance, MDP ink feature film joint venture. VARIETY 358:24 Mar
6/12 1995

MGM CINEMAS
Clarke, S. Carlton bids for MGM Cinemas. VARIETY 358:44 Mar 13/19 1995

MA LATORRE, JOSE
Aldarondo, R. and Ma Latorre, J. "Dracula." credits stills NOSFERATU
n6:78-80 Apr 1991
Ma Latorre, J. Retrato de Peter Cushing. il stills NOSFERATU n6:70-73 Apr
1991
Ma Latorre, J. Terence Fisher: notas a la sombra de un estilo. il stills
NOSFERATU n6:44-49 Apr 1991

MA SAISON PREFEREE f (d Techine, Andre 1993 Fr)
Pelka, B. "Moja ulubiona pora roku." biog credits filmog port still FSP
40:9 n6 (n760) 1994

MA SOEUR CHINOISE f (d Mazars, Alain 1994 Fr)
Reviews
Ramasse, F. "Ma soeur chinoise." credits still POSITIF n406:39-40 Dec 1994

MABABANGONG BANGUNGOT f (Perfumed Nightmare, The d Tahimik, Kidlat 1976 Phil)
Cantrill, A. and Cantrill, C. "Why Is Yellow the Middle of the Rainbow?" il
interv stills CANTRILL'S FMNTS n73/74:44-63 May 1994

MACAT, JULIO
Fisher, B. Creating another "Miracle on 34th Street." il stills AMCIN
76:50-52+ [6p] Mar 1995

MACBETH f (d Polanski, Roman 1971 Gt Br/USA)
Mugiro, C. "Macbeth." credits still NOSFERATU n8:62-63 Feb 1992

MACBETH f (d Welles, Orson 1948 USA)
Riambau, E. "Macbeth." credits still NOSFERATU n8:59-60 Feb 1992

MACDONALD, PETER See also UNENDLICHE GESCHICHTE III, DIE

MACEDO, ANTONIO DE See also CHA FORTE CON LIMAO

MACHINE, LA f (d Dupeyron, Francois 1994 Fr/FR Ger)
Kapetanovic, M. "La machine." credits still GRAND ANGLE n177:25-26 Dec
1994
Reviews
Derobert, E. "La machine." credits still POSITIF n406:44 Dec 1994
Horguelin, T. "La machine." 24 IMAGES n76:63 Spring 1995

MACINTOSH, JEANE
MacIntosh, J. Reaping your day job. il NEW YORK 28:29 Jan 30 1995

MACKENDRICK, ALEXANDER
Dodsfall. obits F&K n1:34 1994

MACKINNON, GILLIES See also SIMPLE TWIST OF FATE, A

MACLEAN, PAUL ANDREW
MacLean, P.A. Elmer Bernstein. il interv F SCORE MONTHLY n36/37:14-15
Aug/Sep 1993
MacLean, P.A. John Williams' swansong. F SCORE MONTHLY n39:4 Nov 1993
MacLean, P.A. The fantasy film music of Elmer Bernstein. il F SCORE
MONTHLY n36/37:15-17 Aug/Sep 1993

MACNAB, GEOFFREY For film reviews see author under the following titles: BLACK
BEAUTY; CHASING THE DEER; DROP ZONE; KILLING ZOE; MADNESS OF KING
GEORGE, THE; SECOND BEST

MACNEIL, JOHN See also KNUCKLEBALL

MACQUEEN, SCOTT
MacQueen, S. (Forty-three) '43 "Phantom" found new formula for classic tale.
credits il stills AMCIN 74:80-85 Sep 1993

MACWEENEY, INDIA COURT
MacWeeney, I.C. A forum for new work. ANGLES 2:7 n4 1995

MADNESS OF KING GEORGE, THE f (d Hytner, Nicholas 1994 USA/Gt Br)
Barber, L. Mad about Nigel. il VANITY FAIR 58:102-105 Jan 1995
Buruma, I. The great art of embarrassment. il still NY R BKS 42:15-18 Feb
16 1995
Coe, J. Power mad. stills S&S 5:30-31+ [3p] Apr 1995

MADNESS OF KING GEORGE, THE
(continued)
   Reviews
   Alleva, R. Royal treatment. il COMMONWEAL 122:15-16 Mar 10 1995
   Brown, G. "The Madness of King George." still VILLAGE VOICE 40:72 Jan 3
    1995
   Denby, D. It's a mad mad mad George. stills NEW YORK 28:66-67 Jan 2 1995
   Kauffmann, S. Madness in great ones. NEW REPUB 212:28-30 Jan 30 1995
   Kroll, J. King of the sleeper hits. still NEWSWK 125:68 Mar 6 1995
   Lane, A. Power mad. il NEW YORKER 70:86-88 Jan 16 1995
   Macnab, G. "The Madness of King George." credits still S&S 5:47 Apr 1995
   Neff, R. "The Madness of King George." credits FJ 98:44-45 Jan/Feb 1995
   Travers, P. "The Madness of King George." still ROLLING STONE n700:68 Jan
    26 1995
MAERINI, ORIANA For film reviews see author under the following titles:
  CAMERIERI
MAEZELLE, GUY See also INNOCENTE INTERDITE, L'
MAGDER, TED
   Gasher, M. Ted Magder. Canada's Hollywood: the Canadian state and feature
    films [Book Review]. CAN J F STUD 3:101-104 n2 1994
   Straw, W. Canada's Hollywood: the Canadian state and feature films. By Ted
    Magder [Book Review]. CAN J COM 19:566-567 n3/4 1994
MAGGENTI, MARIA See also INCREDIBLY TRUE ADVENTURE OF TWO GIRLS IN LOVE, THE
MAGHSOUDLOU, BAHMAN
   Comer, B. Behind the counter and the camera: Manhattan Video Center's owner
    produces feature film. AMCIN 76:83-84 Jan 1995
MAGID, RON
   Magid, R. Digital domain arranges an "Interview With the Vampire." stills
    AMCIN 76:53-54+ [7p] Jan 1995
   Magid, R. Fine-tuning "Radioland Murders." il AMCIN 76:66-72 Mar 1995
   Magid, R. Perrier ad employs latest whistles and bells. stills AMCIN
    74:26-28+ [5p] Mar 1993
MAILISI See also [LEGEND OF HEROES RETURNING EAST]
MAILLET, DOMINIQUE See also ROI DE PARIS, LE
MAIN, RON
   Hogan, D.J. Races, chases & crashes. By Dave Mann and Ron Main [Book
    Review]. il F FAX n48:12 Jan/Feb 1995
MAIN, STEWART See also DESPERATE REMEDIES
   Barlow, H. Pur ekstase. stills F&K n7:20-21 1993
MAINLINE PICTURES
   O'Steen, K. Settlement seen in "Boxing" case. VARIETY 358:20 Mar 13/19 1995
MAJESTIC FILMS & TELEVISION INTL.
   Dawtrey, A. Costner's Tig set for "Water" remake. VARIETY 358:175 Feb 20/26
    1995
MAJOIS, ISABELLE
   Majois, I. "Les faussaires." bibliog credits still GRAND ANGLE n178:7-8
    Jan 1995
MAJOR PAYNE f (d Castle, Nick 1995 USA)
   Reviews
   Klady, L. "Major Payne." credits still VARIETY 358:48-49 Mar 20/26 1995
MAJOR, WADE For film reviews see author under the following titles: OKNO V
  PARIZH; ROSEAUX SAUVAGES, LES
   Major, W. "Buster" forever. il BOXOFFICE 131:36+ [3p] Apr 1995
   Major, W. "Picture" perfect. port still BOXOFFICE 131:19 Apr 1995
MAKI-ISO, ERJA For film reviews see author under the following titles: MATKA ON
  PITKA
MAKING OF "MONSTERS", THE f (d Greyson, John 1991 Can)
   Queer Theory Analysis
   Brasell, R.B. Queer nationalism and the musical fag bashing of John
    Greyson's "The Making of 'Monsters'." il stills WIDE ANGLE 16:26-36 n3
    1995
MAKINO, MAMORU
   Makino, M. and Gerow, A.A. Prokino. biogs il interv port stills DOC BOX
    5:6-14 1994
MALAMUTH, NEIL
   namaste, k. Pornography (communication concepts 5). By Daniel Linz & Neil
    Malamuth [Book Reviews]. CAN J COM 20:120-122 n1 1995
MALATYNSKA, MARIA
   Malatynska, M. Koniec wieku. REZYSER n18:1-2 1993
MALICE f (d Becker, Harold 1993 USA)
   Reviews
   Meyers, R. The crime screen. port stills ARMCHAIR DET 27:207-209 n2 1994
MALKAMES, KARL
   Malkames, K. The non-obtrusive camera. port AMCIN 74:104 Sep 1993
MALLE, LOUIS See also SOUFFLE AU COEUR, LE; VANYA ON 42ND STREET; ZAZIE DANS LE
  METRO
MALLORY, MICHAEL
   Mallory, M. Beyond the crypt: on the set of "Demon Knight." il stills
    SCARLET STREET n17:22+ [3p] Winter 1995
MALONE, PETER
   Malone, P. (Cinquantoprimo) 51o Mostra internazionale d'arte cinematografica
    Venezia. stills C PAPERS n102:76-77+ [3p] Dec 1994
MALTESE DOUBLE CROSS, THE f (d Frankovich, Allan in production 1993- Gt Br)
   Chanan, M. "The Maltese Double Cross": Allan Francovich's film on Lockerbie
    and the CIA. il port VERTIGO (UK) 1:30-32 n4 1994/95
MAMET, DAVID See also OLEANNA
MAMIN, IURII See also DOZHDI V OKEANE; OKNO V PARIZH
MAMMA ROMA f (d Pasolini, Pier Paolo 1962 It)
   Chang, C. Disordinately absolute. stills F COM 31:8-10 Jan/Feb 1995
   Reviews
   Gagne, J. "Mamma Roma." credits FJ 98:58 Jan/Feb 1995
MAMOULIAN, ROUBEN
   Turner, G. Reinventing reality. By Mark Spergel [Book Review]. AMCIN
    76:85-86 Jan 1995
Man Bites Dog See C'EST ARRIVE PRES DE CHEZ VOUS
MAN FROM BEYOND, THE f (d King, Burton 1922 USA)
   Reviews
   DeBartolo, J. Video tape reviews. credits port stills CLASSIC n237:12+
    [3p] Mar 1995
Man From Nowhere, The See ARIZONA COLT

MAN, GLENN
   Slide, A. The Slide area film book notes [Book Reviews]. CLASSIC n236:47-49
    Feb 1995
Man in Uniform, A See I LOVE A MAN IN UNIFORM
MAN OF FLOWERS f (d Cox, Paul 1983 Australia)
   Muszynski, A. Marginesy melodramatu. stills KINO 27:18-19 Jul 1993
Man of Iron See CZLOWIEK Z ZELAZA
MAN OF NO IMPORTANCE, A f (d Krishnamma, Suri 1994 Gt Br/Ireland)
   Reviews
   Kauffmann, S. Early winter roundup. NEW REPUB 212:30-31 Jan 23 1995
   Kelleher, E. "A Man of No Importance." credits FJ 98:51 Jan/Feb 1995
MAN OF THE HOUSE f (d Orr, James 1995 USA)
   Reviews
   Lowry, B. "Man of the House." credits still VARIETY 358:63 Mar 6/12 1995
MAN WITH THE PERFECT SWING, THE f (d Hovis, Michael 1995 USA)
   Reviews
   Leydon, J. "The Man With the Perfect Swing." credits VARIETY 358:50 Mar
    20/26 1995
Managers See PERSONAL MANAGERS
Manbait See LAST PAGE, THE
MANCHEL, FRANK
   Manchel, F. Cultural confusion: a look back at Delmar Daves's "Broken
    Arrow." bibliog still F&HIST 23:58-69+ [13p] n1/4 1993
MANCHEVSKI, MILCHO See also BEFORE THE RAIN
   Woodward, R.B. Slav of New York. still VILLAGE VOICE 40:50 Feb 21 1995
MANCINI, HENRY
   Hommages posthumes. biogs il obits port SEQUENCES n174:56-58 Sep/Oct 1994
   So, M.G. Mancini jazzes things up in Central NY. F SCORE MONTHLY n40:4 Dec
    1993
MANCINO, ANTON GIULIO
   Mancino, A. G. Goffredo De Pascale: Fernando Birri, l'altramerica [Book
    Review]. C FORUM 34:93-94 Nov (n339) 1994
MANDERLEY f (d Garay, Jesus 1980 Sp)
   Casas, Q. Jesus Garay: la linea de sombra. biog il stills NOSFERATU
    n9:26-37 Jun 1992
   Garay, J. "Manderley." credits il NOSFERATU n9:89 Jun 1992
MANDOKI, LUIS See also WHEN A MAN LOVES A WOMAN
MANGLER, THE f (d Hooper, Tobe 1995 USA)
   Reviews
   Cheshire, G. "The Mangler." credits still VARIETY 358:66 Mar 6/12 1995
MANGOLD, JAMES See also HEAVY
   Alexander, M. The auteurist trap. port VARIETY 358:8 Feb 6/12 1995
MANHATTAN f (d Allen, Woody 1979 USA)
   Narrative Analysis
   Deleyto, C. The narrator and the narrative: the evolution of Woody Allen's
    film comedies. bibliog F CRITICISM 19:40-54 n2 1994/95
MANHATTAN BY NUMBERS f (d Naderi, Amir 1993 USA)
   Comer, B. Behind the counter and the camera: Manhattan Video Center's owner
    produces feature film. AMCIN 76:83-84 Jan 1995
MANIEWSKI, MACIEJ
   Jaworski, R. and Maniewski, M. Opowiesc Wandy Luczyckiej. still KINO
    27:26-27 Jun 1993
MANKIEWICZ, FRANCIS See also BEAUX SOUVENIRS, LES; BONS DEBARRAS, LES
MANKIEWICZ, JOSEPH L.
   Aldarondo, R. La tentacion de Shakespeare. stills NOSFERATU n8:20-27 Feb
    1992
   Plazewski, J. Joseph Leo Mankiewicz. biog il obit KINO 27:37 May 1993
MANN, DAVE
   Hogan, D.J. Races, chases & crashes. By Dave Mann and Ron Main [Book
    Review]. il F FAX n48:12 Jan/Feb 1995
MANN, MICHAEL See also LAST OF THE MOHICANS, THE
MANNEKEN PIS f (d Passel, Frank van 1995 Belg)
   "Manneken Pis." credits still MONITEUR n127:19 Jan 1995
MANNEN UTAN ANSIKTE f (d Torhonen, Lauri 1995 Finl/Swed)
   Reviews
   Stratton, D. "The Faceless Man" ("Mannen utan ansikte"). credits VARIETY
    358:83 Feb 20/26 1995
MANNING, FRANK E.
   Knight, G. The Beaver bites back? American popular culture in Canada. Edited
    by David H. Flaherty & Frank E. Manning [Book Review]. CAN J COM 19:560-561
    n3/4 1994
MANNONI, LAURENT
   Codelli, L. Pre-cinema history: an encyclopedia and annotated bibliography
    of the moving image before 1896. Di Hermann Hecht, a cura di Ann Hecht [Book
    Reviews]. GRIFFITHIANA n51/52:263-264 Oct 1994
MANSELL, JOHN
   Mansell, J. Francesco De Masi. il SCN 14:25-27 Mar 1995
MANSFIELD, JAYNE
   Slide, A. The Slide area film book notes [Book Reviews]. CLASSIC
    n237:42-44+ [4p] Mar 1995
MANSO, PETER
   Mitchell, L. Dueling Brandos [Book Reviews]. still DGA NEWS 19:55-56 n6
    1994/95
   Naremore, J. Brando: songs my mother taught me. By Marlon Brando, with
    Robert Lindsey [Book Reviews]. CINEASTE 21:92-94 n1/2 1995
MANTEGAZZA, ILARIA
   Mantegazza, I. L'unione fa i bei festival, o no? il stat SEGNO n71:34
    Jan/Feb 1995
MANUELLI, MASSIMO
   Manuelli, M. L'ANAC e lo stato delle cose. il still C NUOVO 43:30-31
    Nov/Dec (n352) 1994
   Manuelli, M. Lindsay Anderson anticonformismo e rabbia. still C NUOVO
    43:38-39 Nov/Dec (n352) 1994
MANULI, GUIDO See also EROE DEI DUE MONDI, L'
MANURA CHUGIGI f (d Kang, Woo-Suk 1995 S Korea)
   Reviews
   Levy, E. "How to Top My Wife" ("Manura chugigi"). credits VARIETY 358:74
    Feb 20/26 1995

MANUZZI, LUCIANO See also PAVONI, I
MARAJA, LIBICO
   Bendazzi, G. The first Italian animated feature film and its producer: "La
      Rosa di Bagdad" and Anton Gino Domeneghini. biogs il stat stills ANIMATION
      J 3:4-18 n2 1995
MARC, DAVID
   Marc, D. Scandal and the WASP. stills S&S 5:10-13 Feb 1995
MARCH OF TIME, THE f (series 1935-51 USA)
      Propaganda
   Leahy, J. Image, meaning, history... & the voice of God. stills VERTIGO
      (UK) 1:21-23 n4 1994/95
MARCHETTI, GINA
   Marchetti, G. Pass och forforelse. bibliog stills F HAFTET 22:4-12 n3
      (n87) 1994
MARCUS, ADAM See also JASON GOES TO HELL: THE FINAL FRIDAY
MARCUS, MITCH See also BOY CALLED HATE, A
MARELLO, HENRIETTE
   La cantiniere du cinema. Par Henriette Marello [Book Review]. il GRAND
      ANGLE n176:39 Nov 1994
MARGARET MEAD AND SAMOA f (d Heimans, Frank 1988 USA)
   Freeman, D. There's tricks i' th' world: an historical analysis of the
      Samoan researches of Margaret Mead. bibliog il map ports VISUAL ANTHRO R
      7:103-128 n1 1991
MARGULIES, EDWARD
   Campbell, V. and Margulies, E. More great moments in miscasting. stills
      MOVIELINE 6:62-66+ [8p] Mar 1995
   Margulies, E. It's just movies. il interv MOVIELINE 6:68-69 Mar 1995
   Margulies, E. To see just how riotously a young Hollywood movie can age,
      rent "Foxes." il MOVIELINE 6:78 Mar 1995
MARIACHI, EL f (d Rodriguez, Robert 1992 USA)
      Reviews
   Meyers, R. The crime screen. port still ARMCHAIR DET 27:430-431 n4 1994
MARIAS, MIGUEL
   Marias, M. "Innisfree." credits il stills NOSFERATU n9:93-96 Jun 1992
MARICA, PASQUALE
   Micalizzi, P. L'arte di "fare" un soggetto: 2. il still IMMAGINE n28:1-6
      Autumn 1994
MARIE, MICHEL
   Jaubert, J.-C. Sous la direction de J. Aumont, A. Gaudreault, M. Marie.
      Histoire du cinema, nouvelles approaches [Book Review]. CAN J F STUD
      1:91-92 n1 1990
MARIE-LOUISE OU LA PERMISSION f (d Fleche, Manuel 1995 Fr)
      Reviews
   Rooney, D. "Marie-Louise" ("Marie-Louise ou la permission"). credits
      VARIETY 358:86 Feb 20/26 1995
MARIN, RICK
   Marin, R. and Chang, Y. A wildly successful Bunch. stills NEWSWK 125:71
      Mar 6 1995
MARINIELLO, SILVESTRA
   Mariniello, S. Fellini: un humaniste anarchiste. il port R CINEMATHEQUE
      n32:6-7 Jan/Feb 1995
   Mariniello, S. Techniques audiovisuelles et reecriture de l'histoire. De la
      representation a la production du temps au cinema. bibliog still CINEMAS
      5:41-56 n1/2 1994
MARINO, CAMILLO
   Marino, C. A Cannes "Veillees d'Armes" di Marcel Ophuls girato sul
      sacrificio encomiabile e sulla generosa morte di tanti corrispondenti di
      guerra in Bosnia. C SUD 33:2 Jul/Aug/Sep (n113) 1994
MARION, FRANCES
   McCreadie, M. Pioneers. il ports FIR 45:40-53 Nov/Dec 1994
MARION, PHILIPPE
   Gaudreault, A. and Marion, P. Dieu est l'auteur des documentaires...
      bibliog CINEMAS 4:11-26 n2 1994
MARIOTTI, FRANCESCO
   Zappoli, G. Come e per chi? il port SEGNO n71:16-18 Jan/Feb 1995
Market See EXPORT MARKET; IMPORT MARKET
MARKETING
      Canada
         Economic Aspects
   Finn, A. and others. Marketing, management, and competitive strategy in the
      cultural industries. bibliog CAN J COM 19:523-550 n3/4 1994
      New Zealand
         Export Market
   Wakefield, P. AFM ushers in new NZFC era. ONFILM [12]:5 n2 1995
      United States
   Brodie, J. Distribs' marketing debate becomes tale of 3 cities. stat
      VARIETY 358:9+ [2p] Feb 13/19 1995
MARKETS [Prior to V17, 1989 use FESTIVALS] See also FESTIVALS
      Germany (Federal Republic, since 1990)
         Berlin 1995
   Molner, D. Invasion of buyers and sellers. VARIETY 358:49+ [2p] Feb 6/12
      1995
      Great Britain
         Inverness 1993
   Isto, K. Cartoon Forum 1993. il PEILI 17:36-37 n4 1993
         London 1994
   Shapiro, M. Stormy weather for Raindance. il stills INDEP 18:34-36 Mar
      1995
      United States
         California, Hollywood 1995
   Dawtrey, A. Miramax Intl. takes a world view. VARIETY 358:24 Mar 6/12 1995
         California, Los Angeles. History
   Saperstein, P. and Klady, L. Fifteen seasons of sun & sums. il ports
      VARIETY 358:bet p88 and 173 [pA2+ (2p)] Feb 20/26 1995
         California, Los Angeles. Directories
   What's for sale at the market. stills VARIETY 358:bet p88 and 173 [pA25+
      (26p)] Feb 20/26 1995
         California, Los Angeles 1995. Film Lists
   Market screenings. stills VARIETY 358:bet p88 and 173 [pA76+ (5p)] Feb
      20/26 1995

         California, Santa Monica 1995
   Dawtrey, A. AFM enjoys late rush. il VARIETY 358:13+ [3p] Mar 6/12 1995
   Dawtrey, A. and Cox, D. Days of "Dredd" at AFM. VARIETY 358:1+ [2p] Feb
      27/Mar 5 1995
   Klady, L. Small fish feed on big hope at AFM. il VARIETY 358:13-14 Feb
      27/Mar 5 1995
         California, Santa Monica 1995. Schedules
   AFM update. still VARIETY 358:43+ [2p] Feb 27/Mar 5 1995
MARKLE, PETER See also WAGONS EAST!
MARKOWITZ, RICHARD
   Lentz, H., III. Obituaries. biogs filmogs il obits ports CLASSIC
      n236:57-59 Feb 1995
MARKS, LAURA U. For film reviews see author under the following titles: FRESH
   KILL
   Marks, L.U. Ghosts of stories. stills C ACTION n36:53-62 1995
   Marks, L.U. Your fest of fests. stills INDEP 18:22-24 Jan/Feb 1995
MARKS, ROSS KAGAN See also HOMAGE
MAROCCO, PAOLO
   Marocco, P. Giocare il tempo. filmog port stills SEGNO n71:8-11 Jan/Feb
      1995
MARSHALL, GARRY See also PRETTY WOMAN
MARSHALL, GLORIA
   Lentz, H., III. Obituaries. biogs filmogs obits ports CLASSIC n237:57-59
      Mar 1995
MARSHALL, PENNY See also RENAISSANCE MAN
MARSHALL, TONIE See also PAS TRES CATHOLIQUE
MARSOLAIS, GILLES
   Marsolais, G. Festival du film de San Sebastian. still 24 IMAGES n75:35-36
      Dec/Jan 1994/95
   Marsolais, G. Les mots de la tribu. stills CINEMAS 4:133-150 n2 1994
MARTANI, MARCO
   Martani, M. Fantafestival: l'orrore riciclato mortifica il fantastico.
      stills C FORUM 34:24-26 Oct (n338) 1994
MARTELLI, ELENA For film reviews see author under the following titles: FRESA Y
   CHOCOLATE; LITTLE ODESSA
MARTHA f (d Fassbinder, Rainer Werner 1974 W Ger)
      Reviews
   Loffreda, P. "Martha." still C FORUM 34:18-19 Sep (n337) 1994
MARTHA & ETHEL f (d Johnstone, Jyll 1994 USA)
      Reviews
   Brown, G. Bringing up babies. stills VILLAGE VOICE 40:52 Feb 14 1995
   Mermelstein, D. "Martha & Ethel." still BOXOFFICE 131:bet p89 and 96
      [pR21] Mar 1995
   Neff, R. "Martha & Ethel." credits FJ 98:64-65 Mar 1995
   Travers, P. "Martha and Ethel." ROLLING STONE n702:81 Feb 23 1995
Martha and I See MARTHA UND ICH
MARTHA UND ICH f (Martha and I d Weiss, Jiri 1990 W Ger/Fr/Austria/It)
      Reviews
   Hoberman, J. Cardinal sins. still VILLAGE VOICE 40:55 Mar 28 1995
MARTIKAINEN, AINO
   Martikainen, A. Henkilokohtaisia vaikutuksia. filmog il stills PEILI
      17:6-7 n3 1993
MARTIN, ANDREW
   Martin, A. Performing the city [Book Review]. Q REV F & VIDEO 15:71-76 n3
      1994
MARTIN, CATHERINE
   J'irai come un cheval fou. filmogs il SEQUENCES n175:10-11 Nov/Dec 1994
   Martin, C. Le passage du temps. il SEQUENCES n175:12 Nov/Dec 1994
MARTIN, DARNELL See also I LIKE IT LIKE THAT
MARTIN, SOLANGE See also A CRAN
MARTIN, STEVEN M. See also THEREMIN: AN ELECTRONIC ODYSSEY
MARTIN-BARBERO, JESUS
   Richardson, D. Communication, culture and hegemony: from the media to
      mediations. By Jesus Martin-Barbero [Book Review]. CAN J COM 19:562-563
      n3/4 1994
MARTINELLI, VITTORIO
   Codelli, L. Il cinema muto italiano: i film degli anni d'oro, 1913, prima
      parte. Di Aldo Bernardini e Vittorio Martinelli [Book Review]. GRIFFITHIANA
      n51/52:253 Oct 1994
   Montanaro, C. Il cinema italiano in Europa 1907-1929. A cura di Vittorio
      Martinelli [Book Review]. GRIFFITHIANA n51/52:253 Oct 1994
MARTINI, EMANUELA For film reviews see author under the following titles:
   BULLETS OVER BROADWAY; CHASERS; CROW, THE; FOUR WEDDINGS AND A
   FUNERAL; HEAVENLY CREATURES; NIGHT AND THE MOMENT, THE; RIGET; ROMEO IS
   BLEEDING; SHADOWLANDS; TORO, IL
   Martini, E. Dolce e la vita? il stills C FORUM 34:45-52 Nov (n339) 1994
   Martini, E. Junk movie. il stills C FORUM 34:58-62 Nov (n339) 1994
   Martini, E. Una vecchia idea di cinema. stills tables C FORUM 34:4-10+
      [8p] Sep (n337) 1994
MARTINI, GIACOMO
   Martini, G. Nuovi scenari stessi protagonisti. il still C NUOVO 43:28-29
      Nov/Dec (n352) 1994
MARTONE, MARIO See also ANTONIO MASTRONUNZIO, PITTORE SANNITE; UNICO PAESE AL
   MONDO, L'
MARVEL, MARK
   Marvel, M. Claire Danes: start remembering her name - you're going to need
      to know it. interv ports INTERV 25:68-71 Jan 1995
MARX, GROUCHO
   Marx, G. Vie nocturne des dieux. still POSITIF n409:50-51 Mar 1995
MARX, KARL
   Casiraghi, U. Per Ejzenstein resto solo un sogno filmare il "capitale." il
      still C SUD 33:8-9 Jul/Aug/Sep (n113) 1994
MARXIST ANALYSIS
      Canada
         Documentary Film
   Forsyth, S. The failures of nationalism and documentary: "Grierson and
      Gouzenko." CAN J F STUD 1:74-82 n1 1990
MARY REILLY f (d Frears, Stephen 1996 USA)
   Jones, A. Dr. Jekyll & the maid. stills C FANTAS 26:12-13+ [3p] n3 1995

MARY SHELLEY'S FRANKENSTEIN f (d Branagh, Kenneth 1994 USA)
Dupagne, M.-F. "Frankenstein." bibliog credits stills GRAND ANGLE n178:9-10 Jan 1995
Kiraly, J. Frankenstein es Faust. credits filmog stills F VILAG 38:20-25 n2 1995
Kremski, P. Das Monster, das Mensch sein wollte. filmog il stills F BUL 36:36-39+ [9p] n6 (n197) 1994
Thomas, M.R. Mary Shelley's Frankenstein. Kenneth Branagh [Book Review]. il SCARLET STREET n17:97 Winter 1994
Thomson, D. Really a part of me. stills F COM 31:17-18+ [8p] Jan/Feb 1995
Sound Track Reviews
Lehti, S. J. and Theiss, K. "Mary Shelley's Frankenstein"; "The Specialist." il SCN 14:18-19 Mar 1995
Pugliese, R. Segnodischi. filmog stills SEGNO n72:77 Mar/Apr 1995
Reviews
Brownlie, T. "Mary Shelley's Frankenstein." credits still FILM 4:22 n1 [1995]
Caron, A. "Mary Shelley's Frankenstein." credits still SEQUENCES n175:34-35 Nov/Dec 1994
Garofalo, M. "Frankenstein di Mary Shelley." credits stills SEGNO n71:35-37 Jan/Feb 1995
Harris, J. "Mary Shelley's Frankenstein." still C FANTAS 26:59 n3 1995
Repetto, M. "Frankenstein di Mary Shelley." credits still FILM (ITALY) 3:4-5 n13 1995
Rike, J.L. On fallen gods and guilt. CHR CENT 112:177+ [3p] Feb 15 1995
Travers, P. You talking to me? il stills ROLLING STONE n696:131-132 Dec 1 1994
Viviani, C. "Frankenstein, d'apres Mary Shelley"; "Entretien avec un vampire." credits stills POSITIF n407:30-33 Jan 1995
MASALA, FABIO
Masala, F. Il ritorno di De Seta autore non "pacificato." interv stills C FORUM 34:63-66 Nov (n339) 1994
MASAYESVA, VICTOR, JR. See also IMAGINING INDIANS
Masayesva, V., Jr. Notes on the Native American Producers Alliance and the First Nations Film and Video World Alliance. biog il DOC BOX 4:4-7 1993
Rony, F.T. Victor Masayesva, Jr., and the politics of "Imagining Indians." il stills FQ 48:20-33 n2 1994/95
MASCULINITY [Prior to V24, 1996 use MEN IN FILM]
Zuberi, N. Running scared: masculinity and the representation of the male body. By Peter Lehman [Book Review]. VEL LT TRAP n35:82-84 Spring 1995
United States
Layton, L. "Blue Velvet": a parable of male development. SCREEN 35:374-393 n4 1994
MASK OF FU MANCHU, THE f (d Brabin, Charles J. 1932 USA)
Production
Turner, G.E. and Price, M.H. Behind "The Mask of Fu Manchu." credits il stills AMCIN 76:68-74 Jan 1995
MASK, THE f (d Russell, Charles 1994 USA)
Kapetanovic, M. "The Mask." bibliog credits stills GRAND ANGLE n177:27-28 Dec 1994
Reviews
Ascione, G. "The Mask." credits stills SEGNO n72:52-53 Mar/Apr 1995
Girard, M. "The Mask." still SEQUENCES n174:48 Sep/Oct 1994
Harmat, G. "A Maszk." credits still F VILAG 38:56-57 n4 1995
Jean, M. "The Mask." still 24 IMAGES n75:77-78 Dec/Jan 1994/95
Meyers, R. The crime screen. port stills ARMCHAIR DET 28:56-58 n1 1995
"The Mask." FATAL VISIONS n17:10 1994
MASOCHISM
United States
Woman's Film
White, S. I burn for him: female masochism and the iconography of melodrama in Stahl's "Back Street" (1932). bibliog stills PS 14:59-80 n1/2 1994/95
MASON, BERT
Montreal cinematographie en debut de siecle. il port still 24 IMAGES n75:51-54 Dec/Jan 1994/95
MASON, CLEMENT See also FLORODORA
Long, C. Australia's first films: facts and fables, part eleven: Aborigines and actors. filmogs il map ports C PAPERS n102:52-57+ [8p] Dec 1994
MASONI, TULLIO
Masoni, T. Carl Theodor Dreyer: l'assoluto e il dubbio. stills C FORUM 34:14-17 Nov (n339) 1994
Masoni, T. Latinos in USA. stills C FORUM 34:14-16 Oct (n338) 1994
Masoni, T. and Vecchi, P. "Il toro." credits stills C FORUM 34:68-71 Oct (n338) 1994
MASQUE OF THE RED DEATH, THE f (d Corman, Roger 1964 USA/Gt Br)
Loffreda, P. Primi sguardi nella scuola: dalla descrizione al racconto. il stills C FORUM 34:3-7 (n338) 1994
MASSON, ALAIN
Amiel, V. Liberte d'esprit [Book Review]. still POSITIF n407:59 Jan 1995
Amiel, V. and Masson, A. Entretien avec Marcel Ophuls. il interv POSITIF n406:15-21 Dec 1994
Masson, A. Au travers des oliviers. il stills POSITIF n408:6-8 Feb 1995
Masson, A. "Exotica." credits il stills POSITIF n406:76-77 Dec 1994
Masson, A. Le spectateur nocturne. Les ecrivains au cinema. Par Jerome Prieur [Book Review]. POSITIF n408:79 Feb 1995
Masson, A. Montpellier. still POSITIF n407:56-57 Jan 1995
MASSOT, CLAUDE See also KABLOONAK
Master of the House See DU SKAL AERE DIN HUSTRU
MATHAI, SHYAMA For film reviews see author under the following titles: SWAHAM
MATHEWS, TOM DEWE
Mathews, T.D. Strictly classified. il S&S 5:5 Jan 1995
MATHIS, JUNE
McCreadie, M. Pioneers. il ports FIR 45:40-53 Nov/Dec 1994
MATKA ON PITKA f (d Helminen, Liisa 1993 Finl)
Reviews
Maki-Iso, E. Jatkat ja pikku naiset koulussa. credits still PEILI 18:30 n3 1994
MATOKUNINGAS f (d Tuomainen, Hannu 1993 Finl)
Nummelin, P. Suuri matogangsterisota. il still PEILI 18:28-29 n1 1994

MATSUMOTO, JON For film reviews see author under the following titles: BEFORE THE RAIN
MATSUTANI, RAINER See also NUR UEBER MEINE LEICHE
MATTEI, JEAN-PIERRE
Mattei, J.-P. La Cinematheque de Corse. J F PRES n49:17-18 Oct 1994
MATTON, CHARLES See also LUMIERE DES ETOILES MORTES, LA
MATURE, VICTOR
Niderost, E. Victor Mature: the "Beefcake King" and underrated actor. port stills CLASSIC n237:16+ [4p] Mar 1995
MAUDENTE, FLORIANA
Maudente, F. Immagini e isolamento. il FCR 45:396-397 Sep (n448) 1994
Maudente, F. Paesaggio, uomini, animali, oggetti... interv still FCR 45:390-393 Sep (n448) 1994
Pastor, A. and Maudente, F. Cinema come memoria. interv stills FCR 45:339-348 Jun/Jul (n446/447) 1994
Pastor, A. and Maudente, F. Preservare le cose importanti... interv still FCR 45:329-338 Jun/Jul (n446/447) 1994
MAULE, CHRISTOPHER J.
Acheson, K. and Maule, C.J. Copyright and related rights: the international dimension. bibliog CAN J COM 19:423-446 n3/4 1994
Acheson, K. and Maule, C.J. International regimes for trade, investment, and labour mobility in the cultural industries. bibliog CAN J COM 19:401-421 n3/4 1994
MAURO, SANDRO For film reviews see author under the following titles: YINSHI NAN NU
MAVERICK f (d Donner, Richard 1994 USA)
Sound Track Reviews
Larson, R.D. "Maverick." il SCN 14:21 Mar 1995
Reviews
Della Casa, S. "Maverick." credits still C FORUM 34:82-83 Sep (n337) 1994
MAX f (d Coppens, Freddy 1995 Belg)
Degoudenne, L. "Max." credits stills GRAND ANGLE n176:15-16 Nov 1994
MAX ET JEREMIE f (d Devers, Claire 1992 Fr)
Reviews
Goffi, A. "Max & Jeremie devono morire." credits FILM (ITALY) 3:41-42 n13 1995
Max-Ophuels-Preis See FESTIVALS - Germany (Federal Republic) - Saarbruecken
MAXWELL, RONALD F. See also GETTYSBURG
MAY, SUE
May, S. Blue Sky breaks through. ONFILM 11:1+ [2p] n11 1994/95
May, S. Film & TV awards date confirmed. ONFILM [12]:20 n2 1995
May, S. Film & video: a new level of compatibility. ONFILM 11:6 n11 1994/95
MAYA LIN: A STRONG CLEAR VISION f (d Mock, Freida Lee 1995 USA)
Reviews
Harvey, D. "Maya Lin: a Strong Clear Vision." credits VARIETY 358:53 Mar 13/19 1995
MAYER, DAISY VON SCHERLER See also PARTY GIRL
MAYFIELD, LES See also MIRACLE ON 34TH STREET
MAYNE, JUDITH
Williams, L. Cinema and spectatorship. By Judith Mayne [Book Review]. FQ 48:56-57 n2 1994/95
MAYR, BRIGITTE
Codelli, L. Aufbruch ins Ungewisse. Oesterreichische Filmschaffende in der Emigration vor 1945. A cura di Christian Cargnelli, Michael Omasta [Book Reviews]. GRIFFITHIANA n51/52:251 Oct 1994
MAZARS, ALAIN See also MA SOEUR CHINOISE
MAZIERSKA, EWA
Mazierska, E. "Cienista dolina." biog credits filmog FSP 40:10 n3 (n757) 1994
Mazierska, E. "Dom duchow." credits FSP 40:11 n3 (n757) 1994
Mazierska, E. "I kowbojki moga marzyc." biogs credits filmogs still FSP 40:8 n5 (n759) 1994
Mazierska, E. "Total Balalajka Show." credits still FSP 40:8-9 n7 (n761) 1994
Mazierska, E. "Zycie Carlita." biog credits filmog FSP 40:8 n6 (n760) 1994
MAZURSKY, PAUL
Dixon, W.W. American-Jewish filmmakers: traditions and trends. By David Desser and Lester D. Friedman [Book Review]. F CRITICISM 19:108-113 n2 1994/95
MAZZACURATI, CARLO See also ALTRA VITA, UN'; TORO, IL; UNICO PAESE AL MONDO, L'
Vecchi, P. Un western mitteleuropeo. il interv still C FORUM 34:71-72 Oct (n338) 1994
MAZZANTI, NICOLA
Cherchi Usai, P. Il cinema ritrovato: teoria e metodologia del restauro cinematografico. Edited by Gian Luca Farinelli and Nicola Mazzanti [Book Review]. J F PRES n49:70 Oct 1994
Montanaro, C. Il cinema ritrovato: teoria e metodologia del restauro cinematografico. A cura di Gianluca Farinelli e Nicola Mazzanti [Book Review]. GRIFFITHIANA n51/52:254 Oct 1994
Montanaro, C. Il cinematografo al campo: l'arma nuova nel primo conflitto mondiale. A cura di Renzo Renzi con la collaborazione di Gianluca Farinelli e Nicola Mazzanti [Book Review]. GRIFFITHIANA n51/52:254 Oct 1994
MAZZOTTA, WALTER
Mazzotta, W. Tempo non indifferente. FCR 45:311-314 Jun/Jul (n446/447) 1994
MCARTHUR, COLIN
Ciment, M. BFI film classics [Book Reviews]. stills POSITIF n408:75-77 Feb 1995
Cremonini, G. Sam Rohdie: Rocco and his bothers (Rocco e i suoi fratelli) di L. Visconti [Book Reviews]. C FORUM 34:93 Sep (n337) 1994
MCBRIDE, JIM See also BREATHLESS
MCCAREY, LEO See also BELLE OF THE NINETIES
MCCARTHY, TODD For film reviews see author under the following titles: ADDICTION, THE; BASKETBALL DIARIES, THE; FOUR CORNERS OF NOWHERE, THE; HEAVY; HIGHER LEARNING; JEFFERSON IN PARIS; JUST CAUSE; KISS OF DEATH; LOSING ISAIAH; MY FAMILY; OUTBREAK; QUICK AND THE DEAD, THE; ROB ROY; ROOMMATES; SERP I MOLOT; TOUGHGUY; UNDERNEATH, THE
Evans, G. and McCarthy, T. Will "Kids" be too hot for Harvey? VARIETY 358:1+ [2p] Feb 6/12 1995
McCarthy, T. Nat'l Society crix fall for "Fiction." VARIETY 357:30 Jan 9/15 1995

MCCARTY, JOHN
  Nangle, J. The fearmakers: the screen's directorial masters of suspense and
    terror. By John McCarty [Book Review]. FIR 45:69-70 Nov/Dec 1994
MCCLATCHY, GREGORY
  Stalter, K. Explosive close-ups trigger "Blown Away." diag il AMCIN
    76:72-74 Feb 1995
MCCLURE, DOUG
  Lentz, H., III. Obituaries. biogs filmogs obits ports CLASSIC n237:57-59
    Mar 1995
  Obituaries. obits VARIETY 358:54 Feb 13/19 1995
MCCOY, TIM
  DeMarco, M. Colonel Tim McCoy. il CLASSIC n236:8 Feb 1995
MCCREADIE, MARSHA
  McCreadie, M. Pioneers. il ports FIR 45:40-53 Nov/Dec 1994
MCCUNN, RUTHANNE LUM
  Terry, P. A Chinese woman in the west: "Thousand Pieces of Gold" and the
    revision of the heroic frontier. bibliog still LIT/FQ 22:222-226 n4 1994
MCDANIEL, KEITH
  Shields, S. Keith McDaniel. biog obit VARIETY 358:56 Mar 13/19 1995
MCDONAGH, MAITLAND For film reviews see author under the following titles: BAD
  COMPANY; DISCLOSURE; DROP ZONE; HIGHER LEARNING; IN THE MOUTH OF
  MADNESS; S.F.W.
  McDonagh, M. Barker works horrific magic with UA's "Lord of Illusions." il
    still FJ 98:14+ [2p] Jan/Feb 1995
MCDONALD, T. LIAM
  McDonald, T.L. Kiss them goodbye. By Joseph Eastburn [Book Review].
    ARMCHAIR DET 27:107 n1 1994
MCDONNELL, FRANCIS
  McDonnell, F. Filmbank go West. stills FILM 4:28 n1 [1995]
MCDOWELL, MALCOLM
  Beeler, M. El-Aurian heavy. il still C FANTAS 26:23 n2 1995
  Hearty, K.B. Idol chatter. il interv PREM 8:48 Apr 1995
MCELWEE, ROSS See also SHERMAN'S MARCH
MCFADYEN, STUART
  Finn, A. and others. Marketing, management, and competitive strategy in the
    cultural industries. bibliog CAN J COM 19:523-550 n3/4 1994
  Hoskins, C. and others. The environment in which cultural industries operate
    and some implications. bibliog CAN J COM 19:353-376 n3/4 1994
MCFARLANE, BRIAN
  McFarlane, B. Crofts, Stephen. Identification, gender and genre in film: the
    case of "Shame" [Book Reviews]. MEDIA INFO AUSTRALIA n75:159-160 Feb 1995
  McFarlane, B. Lindsay Anderson. biog il obit C PAPERS n102:20-21 Dec 1994
MCGANN, NADINE L.
  McGann, N.L. True lives. stills AFTERIMAGE 22:4-5 Dec 1994
MCGEHEE, SCOTT See also SUTURE
  Romney, J. How did we get here? stills S&S 5:32-34 Feb 1995
MCGLYNN, DON See also CHAPLIN PUZZLE, THE
MCGOWEN, KELLY ELDER
  Krasilovsky, A. Kelly Elder McGowen. interv ANGLES 2:11-13 n4 1995
MCGUCKIAN, MARY See also WORDS UPON THE WINDOW PANE
MCGUINESS, PAUL
  Dawtrey, A. For McGuiness, film is a long way from rock 'n' roll. VARIETY
    358:36 Mar 6/12 1995
MCHENRY, DOUG See also JASON'S LYRIC
MCINTOSH, DAVID
  McIntosh, D. Porn, porosity and promiscuity. stills C ACTION n36:20-23
    1995
MCKEE, ALISON L.
  McKee, A.L. "L'affaire praslin" and "All This, and Heaven Too": gender,
    genre, and history in the 1940s woman's film. VEL LT TRAP n35:33-51 Spring
    1995
  McKee, A.L. Negotiating gender in post-World War II America [Book Reviews].
    Q REV F & VIDEO 15:47-56 n3 1994
MCKERNAN, LUKE
  Codelli, L. Walking shadows: Shakespeare in the National Film and Television
    Archive. A cura di Luke McKernan, Olwen Terris [Book Review]. GRIFFITHIANA
    n51/52:267 Oct 1994
  Pollock, N. McKernan, Luke and Terris, Olwen, eds. Walking shadows:
    Shakespeare in the National Film and Television Archive [Book Review].
    MEDIA INFO AUSTRALIA n75:168 Feb 1995
MCKINLEY, ANN
  McKinley, A. Anne Friedberg. Window shopping: cinema and the postmodern
    [Book Review]. ARACHNE 1:270-274 n2 1994
MCLAGLEN, ANDREW V. See also GUN THE MAN DOWN
MCLANE, BETSY A.
  McLane, B.A. Hollywood censored [Book Review]. DGA NEWS 19:58-59 n6 1994/95
MCLAREN, NORMAN
  Sifianos, G. and McLaren, N. The definition of animation: a letter from
    Norman McLaren. il ANIMATION J 3:62-66 n2 1995
  Starr, C. Conversations with Grant Munro and Ishu Patel: the influence of
    Norman McLaren and the National Film Board of Canada. ANIMATION J 3:44 n2
    1995
  Starr, C. Grant Munro. biog filmog il interv ANIMATION J 3:45-53 n2 1995
  Starr, C. Ishu Patel. biog filmog il interv stills ANIMATION J 3:54-61 n2
    1995
MCLEAN, JAMES
  McLean, J. Why Britain is best. F SCORE MONTHLY n36/37:17 Aug/Sep 1993
MCLEAN, STEVE See also POSTCARDS FROM AMERICA
MCLEOD, NORMAN Z. See also IT'S A GIFT
MCMILLAN, ROBERT
  McMillan, R. Ethnology and the N.F.B.: the Laura Boulton mysteries. CAN J F
    STUD 1:67-82 n2 1991
MCMILLAN, TERRY
  Parker, H. The waiting game. interv port MOVIELINE 6:66-67 Apr 1995
MCPHERSON, TARA
  McPherson, T. "Both kinds of arms": remembering the Civil War. bibliog il
    VEL LT TRAP n35:3-18 Spring 1995
MCSHERRY, FRANK D., JR.
  McSherry, F.D., Jr. Acts of murder. By Jonathan Goodman [Book Review].
    ARMCHAIR DET 27:108-109 n1 1994

MCTIERNAN, JOHN See also LAST ACTION HERO
MEADOW, HERB
  Obituaries. obits VARIETY 358:56 Mar 13/19 1995
MEDAK, PETER See also ROMEO IS BLEEDING
MEDHURST, ANDY For film reviews see author under the following titles: THAT'S
  ENTERTAINMENT! III
  Medhurst, A. Box of delights. stills S&S 5:23 Jan 1995
MEDIA ARTS
  United States
    Government Support
      Esbjornson, M. Media arts madness. il stills INDEP 18:6-7+ [3p] Jan/Feb
        1995
      Shapiro, M. Tough cookies. il ports INDEP 18:6-8 Mar 1995
MEDIA ASIA
  Projects
    Halligan, F. Media Asia unveils pic slate. VARIETY 358:31 Mar 20/26 1995
MEDIA STUDIES See also FILM STUDIES
  Australia
    Beale, A. Framing culture: criticism and policy in Australia. By Stuart
      Cunningham [Book Reviews]. CAN J COM 19:556-559 n3/4 1994
MEDIAMATIC
  Asselberghs, H. "Mediamatic" [Book Review]. il interv BLIMP n30:48-50
    Winter 1994
MEDICI, ANTONIO
  Medici, A. La follia come metafora del mar di vivere. stills C NUOVO
    43:16-19 Nov/Dec (n352) 1994
MEDIOCREN, DIE f (d Glasner, Matthias 1995 FR Ger)
  Reviews
    Elley, D. "Die Mediocren." credits VARIETY 358:82 Feb 20/26 1995
MEET THE FEEBLES f (d Jackson, Peter 1990 New Zealand)
  Reviews
    Hannaham, J. "Meet the Feebles." VILLAGE VOICE 40:74 Feb 28 1995
MEFFRE, POMME See also PECHE VENIEL... PECHE MORTEL...
Megaplexes See THEATERS
MEGINT TANU f (d Bacso, Peter 1995 Hungary/FR Ger/It)
  Reviews
    Almasi, M. Legenda csak egy van. credits still F VILAG 38:22-23 n4 1995
    Elley, D. "Witness Again" ("Megint tanu"). credits VARIETY 358:86-87 Feb
      20/26 1995
MEHRABI, MASSOUD For film reviews see author under the following titles: ZIRE
  DARAKHTAN ZEYTON
MEHTA, DEEPA See also CAMILLA
  Vasudev, A. Deepa Mehta. il interv still CINEMAYA n25/26:68-71
    Autumn/Winter 1994/95
MEHTA, KETAN See also OH! DARLING, YEH HAI INDIA
MEILS, CATHY For film reviews see author under the following titles: DWA
  KSIEZYCE; IR JIS PASAKE JUMS SUDIE; NA KRASNOM MODROM DUNAJI
MEISEL, MYRON For film reviews see author under the following titles: BEFORE THE
  RAIN; CENTURY; DEATH AND THE MAIDEN; FILS DU REQUIN, LE
  Meisel, M. Are blockbuster releases devouring the industry? stat stills FJ
    98:26+ [3p] Mar 1995
  Meisel, M. Baker leads MPA into new era of growth. port FJ 98:16+ [2p]
    Jan/Feb 1995
MEISSNER, GERHARD
  Meissner, G. Gunther Salje: Antonioni [Book Review]. BLIMP n30:72 Winter
    1994
MELANCON, ANDRE
  Melancon, A. Le cinema a cent ans... ou presque. il R CINEMATHEQUE n32:4-5
    Jan/Feb 1995
MELIES, GEORGES
  Ardai, Z. Babszinhaz tuzes szekeren. il port stills F VILAG 38:10-13 n3
    1995
  Hogue, P. At large in the century of Melies. F COM 31:16 Mar/Apr 1995
MELKONIAN, JAMES See also JERKY BOYS, THE
MELO f (d Resnais, Alain 1986 Fr)
  Canova, G. "Melo." filmog il stills SEGNO n72:72-73 Mar/Apr 1995
MELODRAMA
  United States
    White, S. I burn for him: female masochism and the iconography of melodrama
      in Stahl's "Back Street" (1932). bibliog stills PS 14:59-80 n1/2 1994/95
    Comedy Film
      Woal, M. and Woal, L.K. Chaplin and the comedy of melodrama. bibliog stills
        UFAJ 46:3-15 n3 1994
    Feminist Analysis
      McKee, A.L. Negotiating gender in post-World War II America [Book Reviews].
        Q REV F & VIDEO 15:47-56 n3 1994
    Woman's Film
      Jacobs, L. The woman's picture and the poetics of melodrama. il CAM OBS
        n31:120-147 Jan/May 1993
MELTON, MATTHEW
  Lindvall, T. and Melton, M. Toward a postmodern animated discourse: Bakhtin,
    intertextuality and the cartoon carnival. il stills ANIMATION J 3:44-63 n1
    1994
MELTZER, LEWIS
  Obituaries. biogs obits VARIETY 358:74-75 Mar 6/12 1995
MEMORY
  Perron, B. "La memoire, c'est ce qu'il me reste a defaut d'une vue."
    bibliog diag CINEMAS 5:91-103 n1/2 1994
  France
    Grange, M.-F. Paysage resnaisien ou variations autour de la mise en espace
      du temps. bibliog still CINEMAS 5:135-146 n1/2 1994
MEN IN FILM See also HEROES
  China (People's Republic, since 1949)
    Political Analysis
      Berry, C. "Ce qui meritait le plus d'etre puni etait son penis":
        postsocialisme, distopie et la mort du heros. bibliog glos still CINEMAS
        3:38-59 n2/3 1993
  United States
    Psychoanalytic Analysis
      Grieveson, L. Steven Cohan and Ina Rae Hark (eds). Screening the male:

MEN IN FILM
    United States
    (continued)
        exploring masculinities in Hollywood cinema [Book Reviews]. SCREEN
            35:400-406 n4 1994
        Social Attitudes
        Hoberman, J. Victim victorious. stills VILLAGE VOICE 40:31-33 Mar 7 1995
MENAND, LOUIS
    Menand, L. Finding it at the movies [Book Review]. il NY R BKS 42:10-14+
        [7p] Mar 23 1995
MENARD, ROBERT See also BEAUTE DES FEMMES, LA
MENARINI, ROY For film reviews see author under the following titles: BULLETS
    OVER BROADWAY; GO FISH; PRESTAZIONE STRAORDINARIA; STARGATE; TIMECOP
MENASHE, LOUIS
    Menashe, L. Requiem for Soviet cinema 1917-1991 [Book Reviews]. stills
        CINEASTE 21:23-27 n1/2 1995
MENGES, CHRIS See also SECOND BEST
MENZEL, JIRI See also ZIVOT A NEOBYCEJNA DOBRODRUZSTVI VOJAKA IVAN CONKINA
MENZIES, WILLIAM CAMERON See also INVADERS FROM MARS
MEPHAM, JOHN
    Mepham, J. The commonplace transfigured. VERTIGO (UK) 1:41-42 n4 1994/95
MERCHANDISING SPIN-OFFS
    Japan
        Animation
        Niskanen, E. Pienia pyoreakasvoisia tyttoja. il stills PEILI 17:20-21 n4
            1993
    United States
        Contracts
        O'Steen, K. Interactive rights give studios clause. VARIETY 358:18 Mar
            20/26 1995
MERCHANDISING TIE-INS
    United States
        Busch, A.M. Summer pix get a fast food fix. il VARIETY 358:1+ [2p] Feb
            20/26 1995
        Evans, G. Showbiz is psyched for cybermalls. VARIETY 358:1+ [2p] Mar 27/Apr
            2 1995
MERCOURI, MELINA
    Trentin, G. La ragazza del Pireo. obit C SUD 33:10 Jul/Aug/Sep (n113) 1994
MEREGHETTI, PAOLO
    Poggi, E. Il critico al festival ovvero lo spettatore indiscreto. intervs
        SEGNO n71:19-33 Jan/Feb 1995
    Thirard, P.L. Dizionario dei film. Sous la direction de Paolo Mereghetti
        [Book Review]. POSITIF n409:73 Mar 1995
MERENDINO, JAMES See also TOUGHHOUSE
MERLET, AGNES See also FILS DU REQUIN, LE
MERMELSTEIN, DAVID For film reviews see author under the following titles:
    MARTHA & ETHEL
MERRITT, RUSSELL
    Merritt, R. Pordenone Film Festival. CLASSIC n237:9 Mar 1995
    Merritt, R. Recharging "Alexander Nevsky." il musical scores stills FQ
        48:34-47 n2 1994/95
MES ENLLA DE LA PASSIO f (d Garay, Jesus 1986 Sp)
    Casas, Q. Jesus Garay: la linea de sombra. biog il stills NOSFERATU
        n9:26-37 Jun 1992
MESCHINI, ANGELA See also NICHT FUER DIE LIEBE GEBOREN?
MESTRES, RICARDO
    Busch, A.M. Hughes and Mestres team in Disney-based Great Oaks Ent. port
        VARIETY 358:22 Feb 20/26 1995
MESURES POUR ENCOURAGER LE DEVELOPPMENT DE L'INDUSTRIE DE PRODUCTION
    AUDIOVISUELLE (M.E.D.I.A.)
    Ottmar, T.W. Fritt fram a soke ef-stotte. il interv port F&K n7:34-35 1993
MESZAROS, MARTA
    Gervai, A. Marta Meszaros - fighting collective amnesia [Book Review]. il
        NEW HUNGARIAN Q 34:155-158 n132 1993
    Meszaros, M. Diary about myself. NEW HUNGARIAN Q 35:44-53 n133 1994
METAL SKIN f (d Wright, Geoffrey 1994 Australia)
    Reviews
    Di Luzio, A. "Metal Skin." still C FORUM 34:24 Sep (n337) 1994
METAPHOR
    Gruber, E. Une reprise impossible? "Effi Briest" et la question de ses
        reecritures filmiques. CINEMAS 4:59-71 n1 1993
    France
    Grange, M.-F. Paysage resnaisien ou variations autour de la mise en espace
        du temps. bibliog still CINEMAS 5:135-146 n1/2 1994
METRO-GOLDWYN-MAYER ENTERTAINMENT, INC.
    Retrospectives
    Morsiani, A. Il sogno americano. stills SEGNO n72:69-70 Mar/Apr 1995
METTER, ALAN See also POLICE ACADEMY: MISSION TO MOSCOW
METTLER, PETER See also PICTURE OF LIGHT
METZ, CHRISTIAN
    Chateauvert, J. Metz, Christian. L'enonciation impersonnelle ou le site du
        film [Book Review]. bibliog CINEMAS 3:241-246 n2/3 1993
    Lacasse, A. Considerations sur la portee ethique des propositions de
        Christian Metz pour une enonciation impersonnelle au cinema. bibliog
        CINEMAS 4:85-97 n3 1994
METZGER, ALAN See also NEW EDEN
MEUNIER, JEAN-PIERRE
    Meunier, J.-P. Image, cognition, centration, decentration. bibliog diags
        CINEMAS 4:27-47 n2 1994
Mexico See as a subheading under individual subject headings See UNIVERSIDAD
    NACIONAL AUTONOMA DE MEXICO. FILMOTECA (Mexico City)
MEYER, GUENTER See also SHERLOCK HOLMES UND DIE SIEBEN ZWERGE
    "Sherlock Holmes und die sieben Zwerge." biog credits filmog still
        KINO(BRD) n1:42-43 1995
MEYER, PAUL See also DEJA S'ENVOLE LA FLEUR MAIGRE
    Calderale, M. Filmografie. biogs filmogs il SEGNO n71:40 Jan/Feb 1995
    Fava, I. Intervista a Paul Meyer. interv stills C FORUM 34:81-83 Nov
        (n339) 1994

MEYER, RUSS See also FASTER, PUSSYCAT! KILL! KILL!
MEYERS, RIC For film reviews see author under the following titles: ACE VENTURA,
    PET DETECTIVE; ANOTHER STAKEOUT; BODY OF EVIDENCE; BOILING POINT;
    CLIENT, THE; CRYING GAME, THE; DEMOLITION MAN; DISCLOSURE; LAST ACTION
    HERO; MALICE; MARIACHI, EL; MASK, THE; NATURAL BORN KILLERS; PASSENGER
    57; PERFECT WORLD, A; PROFESSIONAL, THE; PULP FICTION; QUIZ SHOW; RED
    ROCK WEST; RESERVOIR DOGS; SHADOW, THE; SPEED; TRUE LIES; UNDER SIEGE
MEYERS, ROBERT
    Weiner, R. Meyers tapped prexy of new Village Roadshow int'l unit. VARIETY
        358:25 Feb 13/19 1995
MEZZOGIORNO, VITTORIO
    Bellocchio, M. and Petraglia, S. Due testimonianze di Marco Bellocchio e
        Sandro Petraglia su Vittorio Mezzogiorno strappato per un male inguaribile
        al cinema che aveva bisogno della sua preparazione artisticae severita
        morale. il C SUD 33:15-16 Jul/Aug/Sep (n113) 1994
Mi familia See MY FAMILY
MI, JIASHAN See also DIAGULUDE YAOLAN
MI VIDA LOCA f (d Anders, Allison 1993 USA)
    Rich, B.R. Slugging it out for survival. stills S&S 5:14-17 Apr 1995
    Reviews
    Dubeau, A. "Mi vida loca." SEQUENCES n175:44 Nov/Dec 1994
    Felperin, L. "Mi vida loca" ("My Crazy Life"). credits S&S 5:48 Apr 1995
MIAMI RHAPSODY f (d Frankel, David 1995 USA)
    Marketing
    Brodie, J. Distribs' marketing debate becomes tale of 3 cities. stat
        VARIETY 358:9+ [2p] Feb 13/19 1995
    Reviews
    Brown, G. Midsummer lite dreams. still VILLAGE VOICE 40:50 Jan 31 1995
    Kelleher, E. "Miami Rhapsody." credits FJ 98:64 Mar 1995
    Travers, P. New age funny girl. port still ROLLING STONE n701:61-62 Feb 9
        1995
    Williamson, K. "Miami Rhapsody." BOXOFFICE 131:bet p89 and 96 [pR16-R17]
        Mar 1995
MICALIZZI, PAOLO
    Micalizzi, P. L'arte di "fare" un soggetto: 2. il still IMMAGINE n28:1-6
        Autumn 1994
    Zappoli, G. Cosi vicino cosi lontano. il intervs SEGNO n71:24-27 Jan/Feb
        1995
MICELI, SERGIO
    Comuzio, E. Sergio Miceli: Morricone, la musica, il cinema [Book Review]. C
        FORUM 34:93-94 Oct (n338) 1994
Michael See MIKAEL
MICHALEK, BOLESLAW For film reviews see author under the following titles:
    PETITE APOCALYPSE, LA
MICHELSON, ANNETTE
    Cantrill, A. Cinema, censorship and the state: the writings of Nagisa
        Oshima, 1956-1978. Edited and with an introduction by Annette Michelson
        [Book Review]. CANTRILL'S FMNTS n73/74:41-42 May 1994
    Knee, A. Cinema, censorship, and the state: the writings of Nagisa Oshima,
        1956-1978. Edited and with an introduction by Annette Michelson [Book
        Review]. UFAJ 46:66-68 n1 1994
MICROSOFT CORPORATION
    Animation
    Weiner, R. Microsoft goes after animation mavens. stat VARIETY 357:87 Jan
        2/8 1995
MIDDING, GERHARD For film reviews see author under the following titles: QUIZ
    SHOW
    Midding, G. Bruchlose Verknuepfung von gebauten Dekors und Aussenszenen.
        stills F BUL 36:18-20 n6 (n197) 1994
    Midding, G. Lee Strasberg: Ein Traum der Leidenschaft [Book Review]. il F
        BUL 37:7 n1 (n198) 1995
    Midding, G. Richard Sylbert - production design als metapher. C(SWITZ)
        40:75-86 1994
Midnight movies See CULT FILM
Midsummer Night's Dream, A See SEN NOCI SVATOJANSKE
MIDSUMMER NIGHT'S DREAM, A f (d Reinhardt, Max/Dieterle, William 1935 USA)
    Angulo, J. "El sueno de una noche de verano." credits still NOSFERATU
        n8:63-64 Feb 1992
MIESO f (d Szulkin, Piotr 1993 Poland)
    CD [author]. "Mieso." biog credits filmog FSP 40:7 n6 (n760) 1994
MIEVILLE, ANNE-MARIE See also CONTRE L'OUBLI; LOU N'A PAS DIT NON
    Euvrard, J. Anne-Marie Mieville. il interv stills 24 IMAGES n76:12-14+
        [4p] Spring 1995
MIGUEZ, MARIO For film reviews see author under the following titles: ORDET;
    TVA MANNISKOR
    Miguez, M. Aproximacion bibliografica. il NOSFERATU n5:74-75 Jan 1991
    Miguez, M. Cortometrajes. stills NOSFERATU n5:72-73 Jan 1991
    Miguez, M. "El amo de la casa." credits stills NOSFERATU n5:56-57 Jan 1991
    Miguez, M. "Erase una vez." credits stills NOSFERATU n5:52-53 Jan 1991
    Miguez, M. "Gertrud." credits stills NOSFERATU n5:70-71 Jan 1991
    Miguez, M. La mirada Dreyer. il stills NOSFERATU n5:24-37 Jan 1991
    Miguez, M. "La mujer del parroco." credits stills NOSFERATU n5:48-49 Jan
        1991
    Miguez, M. "La novia de Glomdal." credits stills NOSFERATU n5:58-59 Jan
        1991
    Miguez, M. "Los marcados." credits stills NOSFERATU n5:50-51 Jan 1991
    Miguez, M. "Mikael." credits stills NOSFERATU n5:54-55 Jan 1991
    Miguez, M. No pongais vuestras sucias manos sobre Shakespeare! stills
        NOSFERATU n8:14-19 Feb 1992
MIKAEL f (Michael d Dreyer, Carl Theodor 1924 Ger)
    Miguez, M. "Mikael." credits stills NOSFERATU n5:54-55 Jan 1991
    Religious Themes
    Miguez, M. La mirada Dreyer. il stills NOSFERATU n5:24-37 Jan 1991
MIKHALKOV, NIKITA See also ANNA 6-18; UTOMLENNYE SOLNTSEM
MIKHALKOV-KONCHALOVSKII, ANDREI See also KONCHALOVSKY, ANDREI
    Mikhalkov-Konchalovskii, A. Lesz-e masodik evszazad? il F VILAG 38:15 n1
        1995
MIKOLA, GYONGYI
    Mikola, G. Napilapok zsellerei. stills F VILAG 38:4-6 n4 1995

MOLNAR GAL, PETER
Molnar Gal, P. Egy azsiai Parizsban. stills F VILAG 38:47-49 n4 1995
Molnar Gal, P. Lancester es Volonte. biogs obits stills F VILAG 38:2-3 n2 1995

MOLNER, DAVID
Molner, D. Berlin festival bows with record crowds. VARIETY 358:9+ [2p] Feb 13/19 1995
Molner, D. Designer suit blocks pic bow. still VARIETY 358:5 Mar 20/26 1995
Molner, D. Film exex keep confab dialogue under wraps. VARIETY 358:11 Feb 13/19 1995
Molner, D. Germans making a public appearance. VARIETY 358:31-32 Mar 20/26 1995
Molner, D. Invasion of buyers and sellers. VARIETY 358:49+ [2p] Feb 6/12 1995
Molner, D. "Kiss" seduces Berlin, stirring sluggish mood. stills VARIETY 358:11+ [2p] Feb 20/26 1995
Molner, D. October buys rights to Danish "Kingdom." VARIETY 358:27 Mar 13/19 1995
Molner, D. Zelnick looking to boost BMG's RCA label, pump up core business. port VARIETY 357:47-48 Jan 9/15 1995

MONDER, ERIC
Mitchell, L. George Sidney: a bio-bibliography. By Eric Monder [Book Review]. DGA NEWS 20:41-42 n1 1995
Monder, E. A Fuller view. il interv stills F FAX n49:73-76 Mar/Apr 1995
Monder, E. Six degrees of George Sidney. port DGA NEWS 20:52 n1 1995
The Slide area film book notes [Book Reviews]. CLASSIC n237:42-44+ [4p] Mar 1995

MONDO DI YOR, IL f (Yor, the Hunter From the Future d Dawson, Anthony M. 1983 It/Turkey)
    Sound Track Reviews
Kendall, L. and Care, R. New from label "X": the Cinema Maestro series. F SCORE MONTHLY n38:13 Oct 1993

MONETTE, PAUL
Obituaries. obits VARIETY 358:188-189 Feb 20/26 1995

MONGER, CHRISTOPHER See also ENGLISHMAN WHO WENT UP A HILL BUT CAME DOWN A MOUNTAIN, THE
Porter, B. How "The Englishman" dazzled a Welsh village. il FJ 98:20+ [2p] Mar 1995

MONICELLI, MARIO See also CARI FOTTUTISSIMI AMICI
Monster film See HORROR FILM; SCIENCE FICTION FILM
MONTAGE See also EDITING
    Union of Soviet Socialist Republics
        Theory
Sorensen, J. "Lef," Eisenstein, and the politics of form. bibliog F CRITICISM 19:55-74 n2 1994/95

MONTAGE/AV
Sallmann, B. "Montage/AV" [Book Review]. il BLIMP n30:52 Winter 1994

MONTANARO, CARL
Montanaro, C. Henri Storck: il litorale belga. A cura di Michele Canosa [Book Review]. GRIFFITHIANA n51/52:260 Oct 1994
Montanaro, C. Il cinema italiano in Europa 1907-1929. A cura di Vittorio Martinelli [Book Review]. GRIFFITHIANA n51/52:253 Oct 1994
Montanaro, C. Il cinema ritrovato: teoria e metodologia del restauro cinematografico. A cura di Gianluca Farinelli e Nicola Mazzanti [Book Review]. GRIFFITHIANA n51/52:254 Oct 1994
Montanaro, C. Il cinematografo al campo: l'arma nuova nel primo conflitto mondiale. A cura di Renzo Renzi con la collaborazione di Gianluca Farinelli e Nicola Mazzanti [Book Review]. GRIFFITHIANA n51/52:254 Oct 1994
Montanaro, C. Storia del cinema italiano: il cinema muto 1895-1929, volume primo. Di Gian Piero Brunetta [Book Review]. GRIFFITHIANA n51/52:266 Oct 1994

MONTELEONE, ENZO See also VERA VITA DI ANTONIO H., LA
Loffreda, P. Intervista a Enzo Monteleone. interv stills C FORUM 34:74-75 Sep (n337) 1994

MONTESANO, ANTHONY P.
Montesano, A.P. "Johnny Mnemonic." port stills C FANTAS 26:14-15 n2 1995
Montesano, A.P. "Johnny Mnemonic." stills C FANTAS 26:44+ [2p] n3 1995
Montesano, A.P. "Mnemonic" design. il stills C FANTAS 26:46-47 n3 1995
Montesano, A.P. "New Rose Hotel." il still C FANTAS 26:44-45 n3 1995

MONTGOMERY, FRANK See also SPIRIT OF '76, THE
MONTGOMERY, JENNIFER See also ART FOR TEACHERS OF CHILDREN
MONTOYA, EUSTASIO
Cherchi Usai, P. El rescate de un camarografo: las imagenes perdidas de Eustasio Montoya. By Fernando del Moral Gonzalez [Book Review]. J F PRES n49:75 Oct 1994
Cherchi Usai, P. El rescate de un camarografo: las imagenes perdidas de Eustasio Montoya. By Fernando del Moral Gonzalez [Book Review]. GRIFFITHIANA n51/52:265 Oct 1994

MONTY, IB
Monty, I. Symposium on legal rights, Bologna, 1994. J F PRES n49:10 Oct 1994
Monty, I. Vida y obras de Carl Theodor Dreyer. biog il port stills NOSFERATU n5:4-11 Jan 1991

MOON, SARAH See also CONTRE L'OUBLI
MOONEY, JOSHUA
Mooney, J. Visions of the apocalypse. il MOVIELINE 6:68-69 Apr 1995

MOORE, DANIEL S.
Moore, D.S. Foreign influence is felt at Oscars. still VARIETY 357:68-69 Jan 9/15 1995
Moore, D.S. (Ninety-five) '95 a watershed for Latinos in H'wood. il VARIETY 358:43+ [3p] Mar 27/Apr 2 1995
Moore, D.S. Oscars reflect, record history. still VARIETY 357:64 Jan 9/15 1995
Moore, D.S. Producers pick all-time faves. ports stills VARIETY 357:63+ [2p] Jan 9/15 1995

MOORE, DEMI
Udovitch, M. Demi Moore. interv ports ROLLING STONE n701:38-41+ [5p] Feb 9 1995

MOORE, MARY TYLER
Mary, Mary, slightly contrary. port NEW YORKER 70:32 Feb 13 1995

MOORE, MICHAEL See also ROGER & ME
MOORHOUSE, JOCELYN
Kelleher, E. Miramax invites filmgoers to "Muriel's Wedding." il interv still FJ 98:12+ [2p] Jan/Feb 1995
Moorhouse, J. Enduring. still S&S 5:61 Apr 1995

MORAES, SUSANA See also MIL E UMA
MORAHAN, ANDY See also HIGHLANDER III: THE SORCERER
MORAL ASPECTS
    Poland
Zienkiewicz, D. Listy: dwa moralitety. KINO 27:44-45 Jun 1993

MORAL GONZALEZ, FERNANDO DEL
Cherchi Usai, P. El rescate de un camarografo: las imagenes perdidas de Eustasio Montoya. By Fernando del Moral Gonzalez [Book Review]. J F PRES n49:75 Oct 1994
Cherchi Usai, P. El rescate de un camarografo: las imagenes perdidas de Eustasio Montoya. By Fernando del Moral Gonzalez [Book Review]. GRIFFITHIANA n51/52:265 Oct 1994

MORALES, ED
Morales, E. Cinema Novo's "Spirit of Light." still VILLAGE VOICE 40:62 Feb 7 1995

MORALITY See also CENSORSHIP; ETHICS; PORNOGRAPHY AND OBSCENITY
Muszynski, A. Marginesy melodramatu. stills KINO 27:18-19 Jul 1993
    Surrealism
Pauly, R. A revolution is not a dinner party: "The Discrete Charm" of Bunuel's "Bourgeoisie." bibliog LIT/FQ 22:232-237 n4 1994
    United States
        History
Barson, M. Hollywood censored: morality codes, Catholics and movies. By Gregory D. Black [Book Review]. DGA NEWS 19:59 n6 1994/95

MORE PERFECT UNION, A f (d Sheinkin, Stephen/Sheinkin, Ari 1995 USA)
    Reviews
Leydon, J. "A More Perfect Union." credits VARIETY 358:50 Mar 20/26 1995

MORESCO, FABRIZIO For film reviews see author under the following titles: CON GLI OCCHI CHIUSI; KIKA; ORSO DI PELUCHE, L'
MORETTI, NANNI See also BIANCA; CARO DIARIO; PALOMBELLA ROSSA; UNICO PAESE AL MONDO, L'
Faricciotti, C. Il diario di un regista "viaggiatore" e vincitore della "Palma d'Oro" per la regia a Cannes (94). C SUD 33:10-11 Jul/Aug/Sep (n113) 1994
Porton, R. and Ellickson, L. Comedy, communism, and pastry: an interview with Nanni Moretti. interv port stills CINEASTE 21:11-15 n1/2 1995

MORIN, ROBERT See also WINDIGO
Blois, M. de. Entretien avec Robert Morin. il interv stills 24 IMAGES n75:6-11 Dec/Jan 1994/95
Castiel, E. Robert Morin. filmog il interv SEQUENCES n175:13-16 Nov/Dec 1994

MORIN, STEPHANE
Morin, S. "Nick's Movie": le point de fuite. bibliog still CINEMAS 4:101-117 n2 1994

MORINI, ANDREA
Livio, J. La grande parata: il cinema di King Vidor. A cura di Sergio Toffetti e Andrea Morini [Book Review]. GRIFFITHIANA n51/52:260 Oct 1994

MORITA, YOSHIMITSU See also [KITCHEN, THE]
MORITSUGU, JON See also ELVIS, DER
Moritsugu, J. Plans for "Der Elvis" (1987). il MILLENNIUM n25:37-41 Summer 1991

MORLAN, DON B.
Morlan, D.B. Slapstick contributions to WWII propaganda: The Three Stooges and Abbott and Costello. bibliog STUDIES POP CULT 17:29-43 n1 1994

MORO, JOAQUIN
Moro, J. "Viridiana" [Book Review]. il BLIMP n30:64 Winter 1994

MORRICONE, ENNIO
Burlingame, J. and Crowdus, G. Music at the service of the cinema. il interv port stills CINEASTE 21:76-80 n1/2 1995
Comuzio, E. Sergio Miceli: Morricone, la musica, il cinema [Book Review]. C FORUM 34:93-94 Oct (n338) 1994
Deutsch, D.C. "I pugni in tasca"/"I basilischi"/"Gente di rispetto." SCN 14:20-21 Mar 1995
Larson, R.D. Spotlight on: the Alhambra Morricone CDs. F SCORE MONTHLY n36/37:33 Aug/Sep 1993

MORRIS, PETER
Morris, P. Le passe trompeur. R CINEMATHEQUE n33:4-5 Mar/Apr 1995

MORRISON, MICHAEL A.
Morrison, M.A. Mail bag - letters from readers: ...a couple of remarks on issues raised in "FSM" #34. F SCORE MONTHLY n36/37:38-39 Aug/Sep 1993

MORRISON, SUSAN
Morrison, S. John Woo, Wong Kar-wai, and me: an ethnographic mediation. stills C ACTION n36:37-41 1995

MORROW, DOUGLAS S.
Lentz, H., III. Obituaries. biogs filmogs il obits ports CLASSIC n236:57-59 Feb 1995

MORSE, SANDY
Oppenheimer, J. "Team Woody" fires "Bullets Over Broadway." il stills AMCIN 76:66-70 Feb 1995

MORSIANI, ALBERTO
Morsiani, A. Il sogno americano. stills SEGNO n72:69-70 Mar/Apr 1995

MORTON, ROCKY See also SUPER MARIO BROS.
MOSCA, UMBERTO For film reviews see author under the following titles: PATRIOTES, LES
MOSKALENKO, VITALII See also DOROGA V RAI
MOSKOWITZ, ALAN
Moskowitz, A. Eating my words. JOURNAL WGA 7:29 Feb 1994

MOSTRO, IL f (d Benigni, Roberto 1994 It/Fr)
Chiacchiari, F. "Il mostro." credits stills C FORUM 34:68-71 Nov (n339) 1994
    Reviews
Buccheri, V. "Il mostro." credits stills SEGNO n71:50-51+ [3p] Jan/Feb 1995

MOTION PICTURE ASSOCIATION (United States)
  Meisel, M. Baker leads MPA into new era of growth. port FJ 98:16+ [2p]
  Jan/Feb 1995
MOTION PICTURE EXPORT ASSOCIATION OF AMERICA
  Meisel, M. Baker leads MPA into new era of growth. port FJ 98:16+ [2p]
  Jan/Feb 1995
MOTIVOS DE BERTA, LOS f (d Guerin, Jose Luis 1985 Sp)
  Aldarondo, R. "Los motivos de Berta." credits still NOSFERATU n9:91-92 Jun
  1992
  Torres, S. Los motivos de Guerin. biog il stills NOSFERATU n9:38-47 Jun
  1992
MOTORCYCLING IN FILM
    United States
  Hogan, D.J. Races, chases & crashes. By Dave Mann and Ron Main [Book
  Review]. il F FAX n48:12 Jan/Feb 1995
MOTS PERDUS, LES f (d Simard, Marcel 1993 Can)
    Reviews
  Derobert, E. "Les mots perdus." still POSITIF n406:47 Dec 1994
MOTUZKO, NATALIA See also GOLOS TRAVY
MOUNTAIN CLIMBING IN FILM
    History
  Swiezynski, W. Gory. il stills KINO 27:24-27 May 1993
MOUNTAINS IN FILM
    Festivals
  Diciassette nazioni sono state ammesse dopo una scrupolosa selezione mirata.
  C SUD 33:32 Jul/Aug/Sep (n113) 1994
MOUVEMENTS DU DESIR f (d Pool, Lea 1994 Can/Switz)
    Reviews
  Braendli, S. "Mouvements du desir." credits still C(SWITZ) 40:218-219 1994
MOVIE MAKING MUSEUM (Riverstone, Australia)
  Movie Making Museum. il C PAPERS n102:65 Dec 1994
MOVING THE MOUNTAIN f (d Apted, Michael 1994 Gt Br)
    Reviews
  Causo, M. "Moving the Mountain." still C FORUM 34:37 Sep (n337) 1994
MOVSHOVITZ, HOWIE
  Movshovitz, H. Virgil Grillo. biog obit port INDEP 18:11-13 Jan/Feb 1995
MOWITT, JOHN
  Mowitt, J. Sembene Ousmane's "Xala": postcoloniality and foreign film
  languages. stills CAM OBS n31:72-95 Jan/May 1993
MOZHUKHIN, IVAN
  Molnar Gal, P. Egy azsiai Parizsban. stills F VILAG 38:47-49 n4 1995
MRS. DOUBTFIRE f (d Columbus, Chris 1993 USA)
  Finslo, Y. Klovnen og hans Janusmaske. stills F&K n1:14-15 1994
    Reviews
  Naranen, P. Ihanneisa mummoilee. credits PEILI 18:35 n2 1994
MRS. PARKER AND THE VICIOUS CIRCLE f (d Rudolph, Alan 1994 USA)
  Kapetanovic, M. "Mrs Parker et le cercle vicieux." bibliog credits stills
  GRAND ANGLE n178:19-20 Jan 1995
    Reviews
  Travers, P. "Mrs. Parker and the Vicious Circle." still ROLLING STONE
  n697:104 Dec 15 1994
MUELLER, JUERGEN E.
  Morin, S. "Nick's Movie": le point de fuite. bibliog still CINEMAS
  4:101-117 n2 1994
  Mueller, J.E. Albersmeier, Franz-Josef. Theater, Film, Literatur in
  Frankreich. Medienwechsel und Intermedialitat [Book Review]. CINEMAS
  5:223-228 n1/2 1994
  Mueller, J.E. "Top Hat" et l'intermedialite de la comedie musicale. bibliog
  CINEMAS 5:211-220 n1/2 1994
MUELLER, MARCO
  Zappoli, G. Come e per chi? il port SEGNO n71:16-18 Jan/Feb 1995
MUGGE, ROBERT
  Dollar, S. Music documentarian. il INDEP 18:18-19 Jan/Feb 1995
MUGIRO, CARLOS
  Mugiro, C. "El trono de sangre." credits still NOSFERATU n8:64-65 Feb 1992
  Mugiro, C. "Macbeth." credits still NOSFERATU n8:62-63 Feb 1992
MUI DU DU XANH f (Scent of the Green Papaya, The d Tran, Anh Hung 1993
  Fr/Vietnam)
  Cheng, S. Tran Anh Hung and the scents of Vietnam. stills CINEMAYA n24:4-7
  Summer 1994
  Lochen, K. En spire til liv. stills F&K n1:4-5 1994
    Reviews
  Dinh, T. "The Scent of Green Papaya": ambiguity of the Vietnamese essence.
  AMERASIA J 20:81-85 n3 1994
MULCAHY, RUSSELL See also RICOCHET; SHADOW, THE
MULFORD, MARILYN See also FREEDOM ON MY MIND
  Lucia, C. Progress and misgivings in Mississippi. interv port stills
  CINEASTE 21:43-45 n1/2 1995
MULHOLLAND FALLS f (d Tamahori, Lee 1996 USA)
  I'll be back, says Tamahori. ONFILM [12]:6 n1 1995
MULLBACK, LARS See also ILLUSIONER
MULTICULTURALISM
    Australia
  Wark, M. Berry, Chris. A bit on the side: East-West topographies of desire
  [Book Review]. MEDIA INFO AUSTRALIA n75:157 Feb 1995
  Multiplexes See THEATERS
MULVEY, LAURA
  Ciment, M. BFI film classics [Book Reviews]. stills POSITIF n408:75-77 Feb
  1995
  Mulvey, L. "Xala," Ousmane Sembene (1974): the carapace that failed. stills
  CAM OBS n31:48-71 Jan/May 1993
MUNDY, CHRIS
  Mundy, C. Renaissance boy. biog ports stills ROLLING STONE n703:44-49+
  [7p] Mar 9 1995
  Mundy, C. Slippin' around on the road with Brad Pitt. il ports stills
  ROLLING STONE n696:92-97+ [7p] Dec 1 1994
MUNE, IAN
  Mune, I. From handmade cameras to hand-morphed creatures. il stat ONFILM
  11:13 n11 1994/95

MUNOZ, JOXEAN
  Munoz, J. "Viaje a Melonia." NOSFERATU n8:68-70 Feb 1992
MUNRO, GRANT
  Starr, C. Grant Munro. biog filmog il interv ANIMATION J 3:45-53 n2 1995
MURAT, LUCIA See also QUE BOM TE VER VIVA
MURATOVA, KIRA See also CHUVSTVITEL'NYI MILITSIONER
MURDER BY TELEVISION f (d Sanforth, Clifford 1935 USA)
  Senn, B. Bela's dark triad. stills F FAX n48:71-75+ [7p] Jan/Feb 1995
MURDER IN THE FIRST f (d Rocco, Marc 1995 USA)
  Oliver, L. The Rocco horror picture show. il interv still INTERV 25:34 Jan
  1995
    Reviews
  Dauphin, G. "Murder in the First." still VILLAGE VOICE 40:52+ [2p] Jan 31
  1995
  Lally, K. "Murder in the First." credits FJ 98:66 Mar 1995
  Schultz, R. "Murder in the First." BOXOFFICE 131:bet p89 and 96 [pR17] Mar
  1995
  Travers, P. "Murder in the First." still ROLLING STONE n701:62-65 Feb 9
  1995
MURDERS IN FILM
    Psychological Analysis
  Sjogren, O. Murha (epa)miellyttavana taiteena. il stills PEILI 17:18-24 n3
  1993
    United States
  Bruno, M.W. Brian De Hitchcock. port stills SEGNO n63:9-13 Sep/Oct 1993
MURDOCH, BLAKE
  Murdoch, B. Australian cinemas in fast growth pattern. stat FJ 98:20+ [2p]
  Jan/Feb 1995
  Murdoch, B. Robert (Roc) Kirby. port FJ 98:84 Jan/Feb 1995
MURGIONDO, PELLO
  Murgiondo, P. "El fantasma de la Opera." credits stills NOSFERATU n6:88-89
  Apr 1991
  Murgiondo, P. "Paginas del libro de Satan." credits stills NOSFERATU
  n5:46-47 Jan 1991
MURIEL'S WEDDING f (d Hogan, P.J. 1994 Australia)
  Hearty, K.B. Bride & joy. il PREM 8:92-93 Apr 1995
  Kelleher, E. Miramax invites filmgoers to "Muriel's Wedding." il interv
  still FJ 98:12+ [2p] Jan/Feb 1995
    Reviews
  Brown, G. "Muriel's Wedding." VILLAGE VOICE 40:56-57 Mar 21 1995
  Derrer, J.C. Der Weg zu sich selbst. credits stills F BUL 37:45-46 n1
  (n198) 1995
  Glines, C. "Muriel's Wedding." BOXOFFICE 131:bet p89 and 96 [pR19] Mar 1995
  Lally, K. "Muriel's Wedding." credits still FJ 98:57 Mar 1995
  Travers, P. "Muriel's Wedding." still ROLLING STONE n704:128 Mar 23 1995
  Vallence, D. "Muriel's Wedding." credits still C PAPERS n102:69-70 Dec
  1994
  Yates, R. "Muriel's Wedding." credits S&S 5:49 Apr 1995
  Murmur of the Heart See SOUFFLE AU COEUR, LE
MURNAU, F.W. See also FAUST: EINE DEUTSCHE VOLKSSAGE; TARTUEFF
  Comuzio, E. Bruno Di Marino e Giovanni Spagnoletti (a cura di): Friedrich
  Wilhelm Murnau [Book Review]. il C FORUM 34:93 Nov (n339) 1994
MURNBERGER, WOLFGANG See also ICH GELOBE
MURPHY, KATHLEEN
  Murphy, K. Nativity scenes. stills F COM 31:12-16 Jan/Feb 1995
MURRAY, JAN
  Lilley, J. Jan Murray. il interv stills SCARLET STREET n17:90+ [4p] Winter
  1995
MURRAY, R. MIKE
  Murray, R.M. The adventures of recordman. il F SCORE MONTHLY n36/37:10-11
  Aug/Sep 1993
  Murray, R.M. The adventures of Recordman. il F SCORE MONTHLY n38:5-6 Oct
  1993
  Murray, R.M. The adventures of Recordman. il F SCORE MONTHLY n39:4-5 Nov
  1993
  Murray, R.M. The adventures of Recordman. il F SCORE MONTHLY n40:4-5 Dec
  1993
MURRAY, RAYMOND
  Giles, J. Well-bound white sheets [Book Review]. S&S 5:35 Apr 1995
  Russo, C.J. Images in the dark: an encyclopedia of gay and lesbian film and
  video. Compiled by Raymond Murray [Book Review]. il AFTERIMAGE 22:16 Jan
  1995
MURRAY, SCOTT
  Murray, S. Australian Film Commission. stat table C PAPERS n102:24-25 Dec
  1994
  Murray, S. Cathy Robinson. interv port C PAPERS n102:26-31+ [7p] Dec 1994
  Murray, S. Miramax and Australia - a distinct and bold vision. port C
  PAPERS n102:49-51 Dec 1994
  Murray, S. Songs my mother taught me. Marlon Brando, with Robert Lindsey
  [Book Review]. il C PAPERS n102:73-74 Dec 1994
  Murray, S. Tim Read. interv port stat C PAPERS n102:36-39+ [6p] Dec 1994
MURRAY, SUE
  Urban, A.L. Sue Murray. interv port C PAPERS n102:40-43 Dec 1994
MURRAY, TIMOTHY
  Cantrill, A. Like a film: ideological fantasy on screen, camera and canvas.
  By Timothy Murray [Book Review]. CANTRILL'S FMNTS n73/74:43 May 1994
MURTOSAARI, JUKKA
  Tuominen, S. Suomalaisten animaatioseikkailu paatyi ankkalinnaan. il PEILI
  17:24-25 n4 1993
MUSCIO, GIULIANA
  Muscio, G. The commerce of classicism [Book Review]. Q REV F & VIDEO
  15:57-69 n3 1994
MUSIC See also under film titles for Sound Track Reviews; COMPOSERS; COMPOSING;
  OPERA; RAP MUSIC; SCORES AND SCORING
  Boswell, S. Neither Mozart nor Hendrix. il still S&S 5:3/ Apr 1995
  Comuzio, E. Un musicista atipico: Gabriel Yared. biog filmog interv stills
  C FORUM 34:39-42 Oct (n338)
  Hubbard, R. Film score: the art and craft of movie music. Tony Thomas [Book
  Review]. F SCORE MONTHLY n36/37:22 Aug/Sep 1993
  Loppi, A. L'enigma Sakamoto. filmog il stills C FORUM 34:36-38 Oct (n338)

1994
MacLean, P.A. Elmer Bernstein. il interv F SCORE MONTHLY n36/37:14-15
  Aug/Sep 1993
Redman, N. Competing composers [Book Reviews]. DGA NEWS 19:56-57 n6 1994/95
    Appreciation
Fake, D. Listening to music without being a musician. il F SCORE MONTHLY
  n36/37:20 Aug/Sep 1993
    Criticism
Gorbman, C. The state of film music criticism. bibliog il CINEASTE
  21:72-75 n1/2 1995
    Silent Film
Comuzio, E. Nessuno nasce "imparato." interv still C FORUM 34:28-30 Nov
  (n339) 1994
Comuzio, E. Non sparate sul pianista dei film muti. stills C FORUM
  34:24-30 Nov (n339) 1994
    Sound Track Reviews
Dursin, A. Andy reviews more new CDs. F SCORE MONTHLY n40:12 Dec 1993
Dursin, A. and Kendall, L. Soundtrack watchdogs!: Andy and Lukas review lots
  of new CDs. il F SCORE MONTHLY n38:14-15 Oct 1993
Kendall, L. Lukas reviews lots 'n' lots of new CDs. il F SCORE MONTHLY
  n40:13-15 Dec 1993
Kendall, L. New CDs I'm supposed to review. F SCORE MONTHLY n36/37:34
  Aug/Sep 1993
Larson, R.D. Spotlight on: the Alhambra Morricone CDs. F SCORE MONTHLY
  n36/37:33 Aug/Sep 1993
Vallerand, F. Anthologies. il obit SEQUENCES n175:56-57 Nov/Dec 1994
    Sound Tracks
Kendall, L. Richard Kraft & Nick Redman: part four. interv F SCORE MONTHLY
  n40:8-9 Dec 1993
    France
        Sound Track Reviews
Upton, R. Truffaut and Delerue on the screen. F SCORE MONTHLY n39:12 Nov
  1993
    Great Britain
        Sound Recorders and Recording
McLean, J. Why Britain is best. F SCORE MONTHLY n36/37:17 Aug/Sep 1993
    Ireland
Pond, S. The Irish invasion. il MOVIELINE 6:30 Mar 1995
    Italy
Burlingame, J. and Crowdus, G. Music at the service of the cinema. il
  interv port stills CINEASTE 21:76-80 n1/2 1995
Comuzio, E. Omaggio a Carlo Rustichelli. C FORUM 34:96 Oct (n338) 1994
Comuzio, E. Sergio Miceli: Morricone, la musica, il cinema [Book Review]. C
  FORUM 34:93-94 Oct (n338) 1994
Mansell, J. Francesco De Masi. il SCN 14:25-27 Mar 1995
        Horror Film. Sound Track Reviews
Larson, R.D. Goblin on CD from Cinevox/SLC. F SCORE MONTHLY n38:13 Oct 1993
        Sound Track Reviews
Deutsch, D.C. Comedy, Italian style. SCN 14:20 Mar 1995
Deutsch, D.C. "I pugni in tasca"/"I basilischi"/"Gente di rispetto." SCN
  14:20-21 Mar 1995
        Sound Tracks
Carriou, A. and Radovich, G. The wonderful world of CAM. F SCORE MONTHLY
  n36/37:36-37 Aug/Sep 1993
        Western Film. Sound Track Reviews
Deutsch, D.C. Spaghetti Western encyclopedia. SCN 14:17-18 Mar 1995
    Japan
        Animation
Larson, R.D. Music for Japanese animation: interview with Hiroshi Miyagawa.
  il interv port SCN 14:28-31 Mar 1995
    Puerto Rico
Camunas, C.R. Film music in Puerto Rico. F SCORE MONTHLY n40:4 Dec 1993
    United States
Bond, J. Concert report. F SCORE MONTHLY n36/37:5 Aug/Sep 1993
Brown, R.S. Film music: the good, the bad, and the ugly. stills CINEASTE
  21:62-67 n1/2 1995
Buedinger, M. Returning to David Shire. interv ports SCN 14:4-7 Mar 1995
Hirsch, D. Ken Wannberg has no regrets. interv port SCN 14:8-10 Mar 1995
Hubbard, R. Book reviews [Book Reviews]. F SCORE MONTHLY n40:9 Dec 1993
Kendall, L. Richard Kraft & Nick Redman. il interv port F SCORE MONTHLY
  n36/37:27-30 Aug/Sep 1993
Whitaker, B. James Sedares. il F SCORE MONTHLY n40:10 Dec 1993
        Appreciation
Bowman, D.S. Mail bag: I wish to respond to several points raised by
  Douglass Fake. F SCORE MONTHLY n38:16 Oct 1993
        Awards
Pond, S. Paltry pleasures. il MOVIELINE 6:32 Apr 1995
        Fantasy Film
MacLean, P.A. The fantasy film music of Elmer Bernstein. il F SCORE
  MONTHLY n36/37:15-17 Aug/Sep 1993
        History
Handzo, S. The golden age of film music. il ports stills CINEASTE 21:46-55
  n1/2 1995
        Science Fiction Film
MacLean, P.A. The fantasy film music of Elmer Bernstein. il F SCORE
  MONTHLY n36/37:15-17 Aug/Sep 1993
        Sound Track Reviews
Care, R. Record rack. il stills SCARLET STREET n17:78-80 Winter 1995
Hirsch, D. Europe goes to Hollywood. F SCORE MONTHLY n40:11 Dec 1993
Hirsch, D. Hollywood's greatest hits vol. II. F SCORE MONTHLY n36/37:33
  Aug/Sep 1993
Hirsch, D. Miklos Rozsa: film music vol. 1. F SCORE MONTHLY n36/37:33
  Aug/Sep 1993
Hirsch, D. The film music of Don Davis: "Hyperspace." F SCORE MONTHLY
  n36/37:33 Aug/Sep 1993
Theiss, K. The film music of Allyn Ferguson, vol. 1. il SCN 14:18 Mar 1995
Upton, R. Mikis Theodorakis on the screen. F SCORE MONTHLY n39:12 Nov 1993
        Sound Tracks
Kendall, L. Richard Kraft & Nick Redman: part three. il interv F SCORE
  MONTHLY n39:10-11 Nov 1993

Kendall, L. Richard Kraft & Nick Redman: part two. il interv F SCORE
  MONTHLY n38:9-11 Oct 1993
Kermode, M. Endnotes. still S&S 5:62 Feb 1995
    Sound Tracks. Auctions
Murray, R.M. The adventures of Recordman. il F SCORE MONTHLY n38:5-6 Oct
  1993
    Sound Tracks. Collections and Collecting
Murray, R.M. The adventures of Recordman. il F SCORE MONTHLY n39:4-5 Nov
  1993
Murray, R.M. The adventures of Recordman. il F SCORE MONTHLY n40:4-5 Dec
  1993
    Sound Tracks. Compact Discs
Morrison, M.A. Mail bag - letters from readers: ...a couple of remarks on
  issues raised in "FSM" #34. F SCORE MONTHLY n36/37:38-39 Aug/Sep 1993
    Sound Tracks. Independent Production
Urban, H. Hip tunes perk pix. still VARIETY 358:bet p88 and 173 [pA8] Feb
  20/26 1995
    Theory
Creekmur, C.K. Strains of utopia: gender, nostalgia, and Hollywood music.
  Caryl Flinn [Book Review]. DISCOURSE n17.1:172-175 Fall 1994
    Vampire Film. Sound Track Reviews
Dursin, A. Vampire circus: the essential vampire theme collection. F SCORE
  MONTHLY n36/37:33 Aug/Sep 1993
MUSIC BOX f (d Costa-Gavras 1989 USA)
    Reviews
Stanislawska, O. Jedynie pozytywka. still KINO 27:29-30 May 1993
Musical comedy See MUSICAL FILM
MUSICAL FILM
    Union of Soviet Socialist Republics
De Santi, G. Soviet melodies. stills C FORUM 34:16-17 Oct (n338) 1994
        History. Festivals
Preziosi, A. Soviet melodies. il SEGNO n71:68-69 Jan/Feb 1995
    United States
Redman, N. The golden age of movie musicals and me. By Saul Chaplin [Book
  Review]. DGA NEWS 20:42 n1 1995
        History
La Rochelle, R. Mythe du "That's Entertainment" ou creation d'un nouveau
  filmopera? filmog stills 24 IMAGES n76:50-52 Spring 1995
MUSKER, JOHN See also ALADDIN
MUSTARD BATH f (d Wasyk, Darrell 1993 Can)
    Reviews
Castiel, E. "Mustard Bath." still SEQUENCES n175:43 Nov/Dec 1994
MUSTO, MICHAEL
Musto, M. Swifty: my life and good times. By Irving Lazar with Annette
  Tapert [Book Review]. VILLAGE VOICE 40:Literary Supplement n133:6-7 Mar 7
  1995
MUSUMECI, MARIO
Musumeci, M. Othello e i suoi doppi. il stills IMMAGINE n28:15-19 Autumn
  1994
MUSZYNSKI, ANDRZEJ
Muszynski, A. Marginesy melodramatu. stills KINO 27:18-19 Jul 1993
MUTE WITNESS f (d Waller, Anthony 1995 Gt Br/FR Ger/Russia)
    Reviews
Levy, E. "Mute Witness" credits VARIETY 358:50 Feb 13/19 1995
MUYL, PHILIPPE See also CONTRE L'OUBLI
MY COUNTRY f (d Plasto, Bob 1994 Australia)
    Reviews
Breen, M. "My Country." credits still C PAPERS n102:70-71 Dec 1994
My Crazy Life See MI VIDA LOCA
MY FAIR LADY f (d Cukor, George 1994 restored version, prod 1964 USA)
Sullivan, D. Still the fairest in the land. still SCARLET STREET n17:19
  Winter 1995
MY FAMILY f (d Nava, Gregory 1995 USA)
    Reviews
McCarthy, T. "My Family"/"Mi familia." credits VARIETY 358:74-75 Feb 6/12
  1995
MY LIFE f (d Rubin, Bruce Joel 1993 USA)
    Sound Track Reviews
Carrocino, J. "My Life." F SCORE MONTHLY n40:11 Dec 1993
MYSTERY FILM See also DETECTIVE FILM; SUSPENSE FILM
Tom Howard on mystery movies. By Tom Howard [Book Review]. FATAL VISIONS
  n17:32 1994
    Festivals
Bochicchio, G. Mostri. stills FCR 45:354-358 Jun/Jul (n446/447) 1994
Catelli, D. Il falso e i falsi. stills SEGNO n63:91-92 Sep/Oct 1993
Mystery of Kaspar Hauser, The See JEDER FUER SICH UND GOTT GEGEN ALLE
MYSTERY OF THE MARY CELESTE, THE f (Phantom Ship d Clift, Denison 1935 Gt Br)
Senn, B. Bela's dark triad. stills F FAX n48:71-75+ [7p] Jan/Feb 1995
MYTHIC ELEMENTS IN FILM
Gibson, L. Geoffrey Hill. Illuminating shadows: the mythic power of film
  [Book Review]. PS 14:125-126 n1/2 1994/95
Murphy, K. Nativity scenes. stills F COM 31:12-16 Jan/Feb 1995
    India
Chute, D. Gods walk the earth. il stills F COM 31:50-53 Jan/Feb 1995
Ganguly, S. No moksha: Arcadia lost in Satyajit Ray's "Days and Nights in
  the Forest." bibliog still F CRITICISM 19:75-85 n2 1994/95
    United States
Nolley, K. John Ford and the Hollywood Indian. bibliog still F&HIST
  23:44-56 n1/4 1993
Walker, J. Deconstructing an American myth: Hollywood and "The Last of the
  Mohicans." bibliog still F&HIST 23:104-116+ [14p] n1/4 1993
        Indians, American
Baird, R. "Going Indian" through "Dances With Wolves." bibliog still
  F&HIST 23:92-102+ [12p] n1/4 1993
Kasdan, M. and Tavernetti, S. The Hollywood Indian in "Little Big Man": a
  revisionist view. still F&HIST 23:70-80 n1/4 1993

NATIONAL FILM BOARD OF CANADA
(continued)
Animation
Starr, C. Conversations with Grant Munro and Ishu Patel: the influence of
Norman McLaren and the National Film Board of Canada. ANIMATION J 3:44 n2
1995
Starr, C. Grant Munro. biog filmog il interv ANIMATION J 3:45-53 n2 1995
Starr, C. Ishu Patel. biog filmog il interv stills ANIMATION J 3:54-61 n2
1995
National Film Preservation Board (United States) See LIBRARY OF CONGRESS.
NATIONAL FILM PRESERVATION BOARD (Washington, D.C.)
National identity See NATIONAL CONSCIOUSNESS
NATIONALISM See also MINORITIES; NATIONAL CONSCIOUSNESS
Asia
Sutton, G. Colonialism and nationalism in Asian cinema. Edited by Wimal
Dissanayake [Book Review]. il AFTERIMAGE 22:15 Jan 1995
Canada
Queer Theory Analysis
Brasell, R. B. Queer nationalism and the musical fag bashing of John
Greyson's "The Making of 'Monsters'." il stills WIDE ANGLE 16:26-36 n3
1995
Philippines
Sotto, A. Philippine independence and national cinema. stills CINEMAYA
n24:8-21 Summer 1994
NATIVE AMERICAN PRODUCER'S ALLIANCE (United States)
Masayesva, V., Jr. Notes on the Native American Producers Alliance and the
First Nations Film and Video World Alliance. biog il DOC BOX 4:4-7 1993
NATURAL BORN KILLERS f (d Stone, Oliver 1994 USA)
Girard, M. "Natural Born Killers" ou la controverse dans le sang. stills
SEQUENCES n174:50-52 Sep/Oct 1994
La Polla, F. "Assassini nati." credits stills C FORUM 34:56-59 Sep (n337)
1994
Schubert, G. A vernoszo angyal. credits stills F VILAG 38:32-36 n1 1995
Stone, O. Level a Cenzorhoz. F VILAG 38:34-35 n1 1995
Reviews
Caron, A. "Natural Born Killers." credits stills SEQUENCES n174:31-33
Sep/Oct 1994
Davidson, S. "Natural Born Killers." still FATAL VISIONS n17:10 1994
Meyers, R. The crime screen. port stills ARMCHAIR DET 28:56-58 n1 1995
Pawelczak, A. "Natural Born Killers." FIR 45:57-58 Nov/Dec 1994
Regosa, M. "Natural Born Killers." credits still C NUOVO 43:55-56 Nov/Dec
(n352) 1994
Rousseau, Y. La mort en direct. credits still 24 IMAGES n75:66-67 Dec/Jan
1994/95
Sharrett, C. "Natural Born Killers." credits still CINEASTE 21:83-84 n1/2
1995
NATURAL DISASTERS
United States
California. Theaters
Oppenheimer, J. The day the earth didn't stand still. il BOXOFFICE 131:30+
[2p] Apr 1995
Natural lighting See LIGHTING
NATURE IN FILM
Italy
Schenk, I. Natur und Anti-Natur in den Filmen von Michelangelo Antonioni.
C(SWITZ) 40:175-193 1994
NAUFRAGOS, LOS f (d Littin, Miguel 1994 Chile/Can/Fr)
Reviews
Beauchemin, E. "Les naufrages." still SEQUENCES n174:45 Sep/Oct 1994
NAVA, GREGORY See also MY FAMILY
NAZIMOVA, ALLA
Golden, E. Alla Nazimova: Mother Russia goes Hollywood. biog ports still
CLASSIC n236:bet p32 and 33 [pC4+ (3p)] Feb 1995
NAZZARO, GIONA A. For film reviews see author under the following titles:
EVERYNIGHT... EVERYNIGHT; IRON HORSEMEN; PAVONI, I; SHIJUSHICHININ NO
SHIKAKU; THAT EYE, THE SKY
Nazzaro, G.A. "La signora ammazzatutti." credits stills C FORUM 34:72-74
Nov (n339) 1994
NEAK SRE f (d Panh, Rithy 1994 Fr/Switz/FR Ger/Cambodia)
Bellion, C. "Les gens de la riziere." bibliog credits stills GRAND ANGLE
n176:13-14 Nov 1994
NEAL, TOM
Roberts, B. Tom Neal: unlucky in love. credits filmog port still CLASSIC
n237:14-15+ [6p] Mar 1995
NECKEBROECK, KJELL
Neckebroeck, K. Alan Silvestri's lego set. il SCN 14:14-15 Mar 1995
Neckebroeck, K. "High Velocity." SCN 14:19 Mar 1995
Neckebroeck, K. "Legends of the Fall." il SCN 14:23 Mar 1995
Neckebroeck, K. "The Pagemaster." SCN 14:22 Mar 1995
NEDIC, LILIJANA
Codelli, L. Pregled razvoja kinematografije pri Slovencih (do 1918). Di
Janko Traven, a cura di Lilijana Nedic, Stanko Simenc [Book Reviews].
GRIFFITHIANA n51/52:264 Oct 1994
NEEDFUL THINGS f (d Heston, Fraser C. 1993 USA)
Editing, Electronic
Heuring, D. Editing continues to evolve with "Needful Things." il AMCIN
74:55-56+ [5p] Sep 1993
Sound Track Reviews
Smith, T. "Needful Things." F SCORE MONTHLY n38:12 Oct 1993
NEELEY, TED
Sella, M. Is God Ted? port NEW YORK 28:46-47+ [3p] Jan 23 1995
NEFF, RENFREU For film reviews see author under the following titles: BROTHER
MINISTER: THE ASSASSINATION OF MALCOLM X; COLONEL CHABERT, LE;
MADNESS OF KING GEORGE, THE; MARTHA & ETHEL; SEX, DRUGS AND DEMOCRACY
Neff, R. Hartley's "Amateur" defies movie thriller conventions. il interv
still FJ 98:18+ [2p] Mar 1995
Neff, R. Kalvert shoots and scores in "Basketball Diaries" debut. il interv
FJ 98:14+ [2p] Mar 1995
NEGI, MANJULA
Negi, M. Mira Nair. il CINEMAYA n25/26:26-27 Autumn/Winter 1994/95

NEGISHI, HIROSHI See also [JUDGE]
NEGROPONTE, MICHEL
Edelman, R. "Jupiter's Wife." port INDEP 18:14-15 Jan/Feb 1995
NEHRBASS, RICHARD
Lodi, E. Dark of the night. By Richard Nehrbass [Book Review]. ARMCHAIR DET
26:116 n3 1993
NEIBAUR, JAMES L.
Slide, A. The Slide area film book notes [Book Reviews]. CLASSIC
n237:42-44+ [4p] Mar 1995
NEIHOUSE, JAMES See also DESTINY IN SPACE
NELL f (d Apted, Michael 1994 USA)
Reviews
Feld, B. "Nell." credits FJ 98:52 Jan/Feb 1995
Kauffmann, S. Early winter roundup. NEW REPUB 212:30-31 Jan 23 1995
Legrand, G. "Nell." still POSITIF n409:45-46 Mar 1995
Sanzone, D. "Nell." credits port FILM (ITALY) 3:3-4 n13 1995
NELSON, GARY See also ALLAN QUATERMAIN AND THE LOST CITY OF GOLD
NELSON, JESSIE See also CORRINA, CORRINA
NEMO f (d Garay, Jesus 1977 Sp)
Casas, Q. Jesus Garay: la linea de sombra. biog il stills NOSFERATU
n9:26-37 Jun 1992
NEO-E-GE NARUL BONENDA f (d Jang, Sun-woo 1995 S Korea)
Reviews
Harvey, D. "To You, From Me" ("Neo-e-ge narul bonenda"). credits VARIETY
358:52 Mar 13/19 1995
NEO-REALISM
Brescia, A. "Sotto il vecchio berso'." Di Giacomo D'Onofrio [Book Review].
biog C SUD 33:40 Jul/Aug/Sep (n113) 1994
NESHEIM, BERIT See also HOYERE ENN HIMMELEN
NESSELSON, LISA For film reviews see author under the following titles: ...A LA
CAMPAGNE; AINSI SOIENT-ELLES; APPAT, L'; CITIZEN LANGLOIS; DERNIER
STADE; ELISA; GAZON MAUDIT; JOUR DE FETE; KOZIMNIN KARASY; NOUVEAU
MONDE, LE; PISTE DU TELEGRAPHE, LA; VA MOURIRE; ZILETKY
NESTORE L'ULTIMA CORSA f (d Sordi, Alberto 1994 It/Fr)
Reviews
Giacovelli, E. "Nestore l'utima corsa." C SUD 33:22 Jul/Aug/Sep (n113) 1994
Netherlands See as a subheading under individual subject headings
NETWORKS AND NETWORKING See also names of networks
New Zealand
Influence on Film
Reynolds, P. The fast lane to the future. il ONFILM [12]:13 n1 1995
United States
Applications
Solman, G. New twists in video assists. il DGA NEWS 19:10-11+ [3p] n2 1994
Copyright
Harris, L.E. A roadmap for writers' rights on the information superhighway.
il JOURNAL WGA 8:20-23 Feb 1995
Effects on Film
Ehrlich, E. M. Virtual companies, walled cities, and the right-brained
economy: cinematographers on the information highway. AMCIN 76:96 Mar 1995
Neues Deutschland See OHNE MICH
NEUWIRTH, GOESTA
Neuwirth, G. Aufzeichnungen zum japanischen Film. BLIMP [n2]:4-5 Winter
1985
Neverending Story III, The See UNENDLICHE GESCHICHTE III, DIE
NEW EDEN f (d Metzger, Alan 1994 USA)
Reviews
Fischer, D. "New Eden." C FANTAS 26:59 n2 1995
NEW JACK CITY f (d Van Peebles, Mario 1991 USA)
Winokur, M. Marginal marginalia: the African-American voice in the nouvelle
gangster film. stills VEL LT TRAP n35:19-32 Spring 1995
NEW JERSEY DRIVE f (d Gomez, Nick 1995 USA)
Hearty, K.B. "Drive" by shooting. il PREM 8:41 Mar 1995
Mixon, V. "New Jersey Drive." il INDEP 18:16+ [2p] Jan/Feb 1995
Smith, G. Teenage kicks. il stills F COM 31:74-77 Jan/Feb 1995
Cinematography
Comer, B. "New Jersey Drive" puts Kimmel behind the wheel. still AMCIN
76:83-84 Mar 1995
Reviews
Dietmeier, P. "New Jersey Drive." still BOXOFFICE 131:bet p125 and 144
[pR29] Apr 1995
NEW LINE CINEMA CORP.
Cox, D. Fine Line ups profile in market battle. stat VARIETY 358:9+ [2p]
Feb 13/19 1995
NEW REGENCY
Busch, A.M. Oliver Stone, New Regency on the rocks? stat VARIETY 358:14+
[2p] Feb 20/26 1995
NEW ROSE HOTEL f (d Ferrara, Abel project 1988- USA)
Montesano, A.P. "New Rose Hotel." il still C FANTAS 26:44-45 n3 1995
NEW SHOES f (d Fleming, Ann Marie 1990 Can)
Hoolboom, M. The queen of disaster. stills MILLENNIUM n26:26-32 Fall 1992
NEW SOUTH WALES FILM AND TELEVISION OFFICE
Woods, M. New S. Wales maps strategy to lure films. VARIETY 358:41 Mar
27/Apr 2 1995
NEW YORK MAYOR'S OFFICE OF FILM, THEATRE, AND BROADCASTING (New York, New York)
Evans, G. Confirmation of new N.Y. pic commish still pending. VARIETY
358:36 Feb 27/Mar 5 1995
NEW YORK POLICE DEPARTMENT. MOTION PICTURE & TELEVISION UNIT (New York, New
York)
Evans, G. and Fleming, M. Location police's Gotham beat may die. VARIETY
358:36 Feb 27/Mar 5 1995
New Zealand See as a subheading under individual subject headings See
NEW ZEALAND FILM COMMISSION
NEW ZEALAND FILM & VIDEO TECHNICIANS' GUILD INC.
Bisset, B. Letters: Blue Book piece was half right. ONFILM 11:10-11 n11
1994/95
Drinnan, J. Letters: John Drinnan responds. ONFILM 11:11 n11 1994/95
Dryburgh, S. Letters: open letter from a film technician on the subject of
lunch. ONFILM 11:11 n11 1994/95
Howard, C. Letters: get your act together. ONFILM 11:12 n11 1994/95

NEW ZEALAND FILM COMMISSION
  NZFC performance is cause for concern. ONFILM [12]:12 n2 1995
    Distribution
  Wakefield, P. Comish eyes back catalogue selloff. ONFILM [12]:3 n2 1995
NEWBY, CHRIS See also ANCHORESS
NEWELL, MIKE See also AWFULLY BIG ADVENTURE, AN; FOUR WEDDINGS AND A FUNERAL
  Calderale, M. Filmografie. biogs filmogs il SEGNO n71:40 Jan/Feb 1995
NEWMAN, ALFRED
  Handzo, S. The golden age of film music. il ports stills CINEASTE 21:46-55
    n1/2 1995
NEWMAN, ATLANTIS JACK
  Alexander, P. "Vicar," "Space Case," "Killer" and "The Night City." filmogs
    il stills CANTRILL'S FMNTS n73/74:12-14 May 1994
NEWMAN, KIM For film reviews see author under the following titles: INTERVIEW
  WITH THE VAMPIRE: THE VAMPIRE CHRONICLES; NOSTRADAMUS; STARGATE;
  TIMECOP; WES CRAVEN'S NEW NIGHTMARE
NEWMAR, JULIE
  Greene, R. The big picture. il BOXOFFICE 131:150 Apr 1995
NEWS CORPORATION LTD.
  Woods, M. Studio plan mixed up in election. VARIETY 358:40 Mar 27/Apr 2
    1995
NEWSRADIO f (1995- USA)
    Reviews
  Carson, T. Foley squared. still VILLAGE VOICE 40:43 Mar 21 1995
NEWSREELS
  The Nathan Axelrod collection, volume 1: Moledet Productions, 1927-1934,
    Carmel newsreels, series 1, 1935-1948. Ed: Amy Kronish, Edith Falk and Paula
    Weiman-Kelman [Book Review]. il KINO(GF) n56:31 Nov 1994
NEWTON, MIKE
  Newton, M. White hats and black hats: what happened to Randolph Scott. il
    CLASSIC n237:10 Mar 1995
NEWTON, THANDIE
  Francke, L. Introducing movie magic. il interv INTERV 25:106-107 Apr 1995
N(f)ight Before Christmas, The See BOTTE DI NATALE
NGUYEN, HUU PHAN See also GIOT LE HA LONG
NI NA NEBU NI NA ZELMLJI f (d Radivojevic, Milos 1995 Yugo)
    Reviews
  Young, D. "Country Between Heaven and Earth" ("Ni na nebu ni na zelmiji").
    credits VARIETY 358:88 Feb 20/26 1995
NICCOLI, VIERI
  Niccoli, V. Fellini: i costumi e le mode. il C NUOVO 43:40-41 Nov/Dec
    (n352) 1994
NICHETTI, MAURIZIO See also STEFANO QUANTESTORIE
  Nichols, Leo See MORRICONE, ENNIO
NICHOLS, MIKE See also WOLF
NICHOLSON, JUDITH
  Nicholson, J. Facets African American video guide. Compiled by Patrick Ogle
    [Book Review]. il AFTERIMAGE 22:15 Jan 1995
  Nicholson, J. (Two) 2% solution. stat AFTERIMAGE 22:3 Dec 1994
NICHT FUER DIE LIEBE GEBOREN? f (d Meschini, Angela 1994 FR Ger)
    Reviews
  Schneider, A. "Nicht fuer die Liebe geboren?" credits still C(SWITZ)
    40:215 1994
NICKS, JOAN
  Nicks, J. Peter Steven. Brink of reality: new Canadian documentary film and
    video [Book Review]. CAN J F STUD 3:104-107 n2 1994
Nick's Movie See LIGHTNING OVER WATER
NIDEROST, ERIC
  Niderost, E. Victor Mature: the "Beefcake King" and underrated actor. port
    stills CLASSIC n237:16+ [4p] Mar 1995
NIEL, PHILIPPE
  Niel, P. Clermont-Ferrand. still POSITIF n408:73-74 Feb 1995
NIELSEN, ASTA
  Ostaijen, P. van. Asta Nielsen. ports F BUL 36:60 n6 (n197) 1994
NIELSEN, LESLIE
  Ciapara, E. "Surfujacy Ninja." credits filmogs still FSP 40:9 n4 (n758)
    1994
NIELSEN, RAY
  Nielsen, R. Ray's way: Ruth Warrick. il interv port CLASSIC n237:13 Mar
    1995
NIEMI, RAIMO O. See also KISSAN KUOLEMA
NIESSEN, SANDRA
  Niessen, S. Gaines, Jane, Herzog, Charlotte (eds). Fabrications: costume and
    the female body [Book Review]. CINEMAS 3:247-251 n2/3 1993
Night Ambush See ILL MET BY MOONLIGHT
NIGHT AND THE MOMENT, THE f (d Tato, Anna Maria 1994 Gt Br/Fr/It)
    Reviews
  Martini, E. "The Night and the Moment." still C FORUM 34:25-26 Sep (n337)
    1994
NIGHT OF THE HUNTER, THE f (d Laughton, Charles 1955 USA)
  Moorhouse, J. Enduring. still S&S 5:61 Apr 1995
NIGHT WE NEVER MET, THE f (d Leight, Warren 1993 USA)
  Prayez, B. "Chasse-croise." bibliog credits stills GRAND ANGLE n177:11-12
    Dec 1994
NIKUNEN, KAARINA
  Nikunen, K. Lukottomat siveysvyot. il PEILI 18:6-7 n4 1994
NIMOY, LEONARD
  Beeler, M. Spock speaks. il stills C FANTAS 26:20-21 n2 1995
NINA TAKES A LOVER f (d Jacobs, Alan 1994 USA)
    Reviews
  Williamson, K. "Nina Takes a Lover." still BOXOFFICE 131:bet p125 and 144
    [pR33-R34] Apr 1995
NIOGRET, HUBERT For film reviews see author under the following titles: RIVER
  WILD, THE
NIPPON-KOKU FURUYASHIKI-MURA f (d Ogawa, Shinsuke 1982? Japan)
  Ulwer, R. and Voser, S. Interview mit dem Filmemacher Ogawa Shinsuke. il
    interv stills BLIMP [n2]:10-15 Winter 1985
NISKANEN, EIJA For film reviews see author under the following titles: JANKO EN
  MARISKA; TALA! DET AR SA MORKT
  Niskanen, E. Elokuvakivalta yha pohdinnan alla. PEILI 17:36 n4 1993

Niskanen, E. Pienia pyoreakasvoisia tyttoja. il stills PEILI 17:20-21 n4
    1993
  Niskanen, E. Tallinnassa tehdaan taidokasta animaatiota. il still PEILI
    17:6-7 n4 1993
No End See BEZ KONCA
NO ESCAPE f (d Campbell, Martin 1994 USA)
  "Kolonia karna." biog credits filmog FSP 40:7 n7 (n761) 1994
    Reviews
  Della Casa, S. "Fuga da Absolom." credits still C FORUM 34:84 Sep (n337)
    1994
NO LOANS TODAY f (d Skyler, Lisanne 1995 USA)
    Reviews
  Levy, E. "No Loans Today." credits VARIETY 358:51 Feb 13/19 1995
NO SMOKING f (d Resnais, Alain 1993 Fr)
    Reviews
  Azzalin, C. "Smoking"; "No Smoking." credits stills SEGNO n72:38-39
    Mar/Apr 1995
NOBODY'S CHILDREN f (d Wheatley, David 1994 USA)
    Reviews
  Herpe, N. "Les enfants de la honte." POSITIF n409:42-43 Mar 1995
NOBODY'S FOOL f (d Benton, Robert 1994 USA)
  Lally, K. Benton returns with tale of smalltown redemption. il still FJ
    98:10+ [2p] Jan/Feb 1995
  Sarris, A. New places in the heart. F COM 31:44 Jan/Feb 1995
    Reviews
  Alleva, R. Paul Newman performs. il COMMONWEAL 122:54-55 Feb 24 1995
  Denby, D. "Fool's" gold. still NEW YORK 28:56-57 Jan 16 1995
  Haun, H. "Nobody's Fool." credits still FJ 98:43 Jan/Feb 1995
  Kauffmann, S. High gear and low. NEW REPUB 212:32-33 Jan 9/16 1995
  Schickel, R. Cool Hand Luke at 70. still TIME 145:72 Jan 16 1995
  Thompson, B. "Nobody's Fool." credits still S&S 5:49-50 Apr 1995
  Wall, J.M. Heights and depths. CHR CENT 112:259-260 Mar 8 1995
NOCAUT f (d Garcia Agraz, Jose Luis 1984 Mexico)
  Torres San Martin, P. El cine por sus creadores Jose Luis Garcia Agraz. il
    interv still DICINE n59:26-27 Nov/Dec 1994
NOCTURNO 29 f (d Portabella, Pere 1968 Sp)
  Riambau, E. "Nocturno 29." credits il NOSFERATU n9:102-103 Jun 1992
NODFORS, MAGNUS
  Nodfors, M. Tonsaker estet. port CHAPLIN 36:12-13 n6 (n255) 1994/95
NOEL, CHRISTINE For film reviews see author under the following titles: LIBERTE
  EN COLERE, LA
  Noel, C. Gilles Groulx et les medias. il obit port stills 24 IMAGES
    n75:20-25 Dec/Jan 1994/95
NOEL, JACQUES
  Broeck, C.V. and Noel, J. "Farinelli." bibliog credits stills GRAND ANGLE
    n177:15-16 Dec 1994
  Broeck, C.V. and Noel, J. "La separation." credits stills GRAND ANGLE
    n176:23-24 Nov 1994
  Broeck, C.V. and Noel, J. "L'ange noir." credits stills GRAND ANGLE
    n177:5-6 Dec 1994
  Broeck, C.V. and Noel, J. "Les nouvelles aventures de Croc Blanc - le mythe
    du loup." bibliog credits stills GRAND ANGLE n176:17-18 Nov 1994
  Delval, D. and Noel, J. "Only You." credits stills GRAND ANGLE n178:21-22
    Jan 1995
  Delval, D. and Noel, J. "Sirenes." bibliog credits stills GRAND ANGLE
    n178:25-26 Jan 1995
  Kapetanovic, M. and Noel, J. "Fresh." bibliog credits stills GRAND ANGLE
    n178:11-12 Jan 1995
  Lebouc, G. and Noel, J. "Stefano quantestorie." credits il still GRAND
    ANGLE n178:29-30 Jan 1995
  Noel, J. Cinema de Verviers (1896-1993). Par Michel Bedeur et Paolo Zagaglia
    [Book Review]. il GRAND ANGLE n177:49-50 Dec 1994
  Noel, J. Elia Kazan, une odyssee americaine. Par Michel Ciment [Book
    Review]. il GRAND ANGLE n177:50 Dec 1994
  Noel, J. James Dean. De Barney Hoskyns [Book Review]. il GRAND ANGLE
    n177:49 Dec 1994
  Noel, J. "La lumiere des etoiles mortes." bibliog credits stills GRAND
    ANGLE n177:23-24 Dec 1994
  Noel, J. le petit livres des films-cultes. Par Christophe Goffette [Book
    Review]. il GRAND ANGLE n177:50 Dec 1994
  Termont, D. and Noel, J. "Nostradamus." credits stills GRAND ANGLE
    n177:31-32 Dec 1994
  Termont, D. and Noel, J. "Suite 16." credits stills GRAND ANGLE n176:29-30
    Nov 1994
  Venchiarutti, M. and Noel, J. "Le roi lion." bibliog credits stills GRAND
    ANGLE n176:21-22 Nov 1994
  Venchiarutti, M. and Noel, J. "L'etrange Noel de Monsieur Jack." bibliog
    credits il still GRAND ANGLE n176:7-8 Nov 1994
  Venchiarutti, M. and Noel, J. "Timecop." credits stills GRAND ANGLE
    n176:31-32 Nov 1994
NOEL, PHILIPPE
  Noel, P. "Bebe part en vadrouille." bibliog credits stills GRAND ANGLE
    n176:3-4 Nov 1994
  Noel, P. "Les aventures de Priscilla, folle du desert." bibliog credits
    stills GRAND ANGLE n177:7-8 Dec 1994
  Noel, P. "The Innocent." bibliog credits stills GRAND ANGLE n177:19-20 Dec
    1994
NOH, DAVID For film reviews see author under the following titles: BOYS LIFE;
  BRADY BUNCH MOVIE, THE; FEDERAL HILL; FRESA Y CHOCOLATE; HOUSEGUEST;
  LITTLE WOMEN; READY TO WEAR (PRET-A-PORTER); REINE MARGOT, LA;
  RUDYARD KIPLING'S THE JUNGLE BOOK; SAFE PASSAGE; SECRET OF ROAN
  INISH, THE; WU KUI
NOLAN, ABBY MCGANNEY For film reviews see author under the following titles:
  JUST CAUSE; TWITCH AND SHOUT
  Karmen, A. Letters: deathless prose. VILLAGE VOICE 40:6 Mar 14 1995
  Nolan, A.M. Double dare. il still VILLAGE VOICE 40:50 Jan 10 1995
NOLAN, WILLIAM F.
  Bradley, M.R. Nolan's "Run." biog il interv stills F FAX n48:42-48+ [8p]
    Jan/Feb 1995
  Richards, S. The black mask murders. By William F. Nolan [Book Review].

ARMCHAIR DET 27:359 n3 1994
NOLLETTI, ARTHUR, JR.
Zinnemann, F. Letter from Fred Zinnemann. F CRITICISM 19:86-88 n2 1994/95
NOLLEY, KEN
Nolley, K. John Ford and the Hollywood Indian. bibliog still F&HIST 23:44-56 n1/4 1993
NON-FICTION FILM See also COMMISSIONED FILM; DOCUMENTARY FILM; PROPAGANDA FILM
History
Komatsu, H. Questions regarding the genesis of nonfiction film. biog il stills DOC BOX 5:1-5 1994
NORCEN, LUCA For film reviews see author under the following titles: JURASSIC PARK; WES CRAVEN'S NEW NIGHTMARE
Norcen, L. Dirigere la luce. il interv stills SEGNO n71:12-13 Jan/Feb 1995
Norcen, L. Le 7 vite del drago. stills SEGNO n63:7-8 Sep/Oct 1993
Norcen, L. "The Saint of Fort Washington" il sonno del cinema americano. C NUOVO 43:15 Nov/Dec (n352) 1994
NORIEGA, CHON A.
Castillo Durante, D. Noriega, Chon A. (ed). Chicanos and film. Representation and resistance [Book Review]. CINEMAS 4:177-181 n2 1994
NORRIS, BUD
Norris, B. Tom Mix scrapbook discovered. CLASSIC n236:9 Feb 1995
NORSK FILMKLUBBFORBUND
Og alle var der... ports Z n4:36-38 (n46) 1993
NORTH f (d Reiner, Rob 1994 USA)
Reviews
Beauchemin, E. "North." SEQUENCES n174:48 Sep/Oct 1994
NORTH, ALEX
Kendall, L. The re-making of Alex North's "2001": an interview with Robert Townson. interv F SCORE MONTHLY n36/37:26 Aug/Sep 1993
Northern Ireland See Great Britain
NORTHERN IRELAND IN FILM
Great Britain
Bennett, R. Telling the truth about Ireland. il stills VERTIGO (UK) n1:24-29 n4 1994/95
Norway See as a subheading under individual subject headings
NOSES IN FILM
De Marinis, G. Un nez qui voque. stills C FORUM 34:49-56 Oct (n338) 1994
NOSTALGIA
Hong Kong
Chow, R. Un souvenir d'amour. bibliog glos scenario still CINEMAS 3:156-180 n2/3 1993
NOSTRADAMUS f (d Christian, Roger 1994 Gt Br/FR Ger)
Termont, D. and Noel, J. "Nostradamus." credits stills GRAND ANGLE n177:31-32 Dec 1994
Reviews
Newman, K. "Nostradamus." credits S&S 5:51-52 Jan 1995
NOTARI, ELVIRA
Hastie, A. Window shopping: cinema and the postmodern. Anne Friedberg [Book Reviews]. DISCOURSE n17.2:171-176 Winter 1994/95
NOTO, SETSUO
Makino, M. and Gerow, A.A. Prokino. biogs il interv port stills DOC BOX 5:6-14 1994
NOUS, LES ENFANTS DU XXEME SICLE f (d Kanevskii, Vitalii 1994 Fr/Russia)
Reviews
Roy, A. "Nous, les enfants du XXe siecle." still 24 IMAGES n75:45-46 Dec/Jan 1994/95
NOUSSINOVA, NATALIA
Cantrill, A. Leonid Trauberg et l'excentrisme: les debuts de la fabrique de l'acteur excentrique (Leonid Trauberg and excentricism: the beginnings of the factory of the eccentric actor). By Natalia Noussinova [Book Review]. CANTRILL'S FMNTS n73/74:43 May 1994
NOUVEAU MONDE, LE f (d Corneau, Alain 1995 Fr)
Reviews
Herpe, N. "Le nouveau monde." still POSITIF n409:46 Mar 1995
Nesselson, L. "The New World" ("Le nouveau monde"). credits VARIETY 358:66 Mar 6/12 1995
NOVAK, JAN
Barson, M. Turnaround: a memoir. By Milos Forman and Jan Novak [Book Review]. DGA NEWS 19:32 n2 1994
NOVARO, MARIA See also JARDIN DEL EDEN, EL
Novels about film See FICTION ABOUT FILM
NOYCE, PHILLIP See also CLEAR AND PRESENT DANGER
Nuclear war See WAR
NUDITY See also CENSORSHIP; EXPLOITATION FILM; PORNOGRAPHY AND OBSCENITY
Thirard, P.L. Une encyclopedie du nu au cinema. Ouvrage reuni par Jacques Deniel et Patrick Leboutte, sur une idee d'Alain Bergala [Book Review]. still POSITIF n408:78-79 Feb 1995
NUERNBERG, SUSAN M.
Nuernberg, S.M. Jack London - the movies, an historical survey. By Tony Williams [Book Review]. WESTERN AM LIT 28:173-174 n2 1993
NUITS FAUVES, LES f (Savage Nights d Collard, Cyril 1992 Fr/It)
Reviews
"Savage Nights." still FATAL VISIONS n17:7-8 1994
Wroblewski, J. Nowa "nowa fala." credits still KINO 27:33-34 Jul 1993
NUIYAN, SEISAP f (d Hui, Ann 1995 Hong Kong)
Reviews
Elley, D. "Summer Snow" ("Nuiyan, seisap"). credits VARIETY 358:75-76 Feb 27/Mar 5 1995
NUKANEN, ERNEST
Obituaries. obits VARIETY 358:56 Mar 13/19 1995
NUMAX PRESENTA... f (d Jorda, Joaquin 1980 Sp)
Jorda, J. Numax presenta... y otras cosas. still NOSFERATU n9:56-59 Jun 1992
NUMMELIN, PEKKA
Nummelin, P. Suuri matogangsterisota. il still PEILI 18:28-29 n1 1994
NUR UEBER MEINE LEICHE f (d Matsutani, Rainer 1995 FR Ger)
"Nur ueber meine Leiche." credits still KINO(BRD) n1:9 1995
"Nur ueber meine Leiche." credits still KINO(BRD) n1:9 1995
NUREN HUA f (d Wang, Jin 1995 China)
"Withering Flowers." credits stills CHINA SCREEN n4:16-17 1994

Reviews
Elley, D. "Women Flowers" ("Nuren hua"). credits VARIETY 358:64 Mar 6/12 1995
NUTI, FRANCESCO See also OCCHIOPINOCCHIO
NY, SOKLY See also A.K.A. DON BONUS
NYGREN, ANNELI For film reviews see author under the following titles: AIDIN TYTTO
O'BARR, JAMES
Adamek, P. "The Crow." il interv stills FATAL VISIONS n17:33-34 1994
Obituaries See names of individuals
O'BRIEN, KEVIN
O'Brien, K. Viera, John David, assisted by Maria Viera. Lighting for film and electronic cinematography [Book Review]. UFAJ 46:49-51 n3 1994
O'BRIEN, MARGARET
Ellenberger, A.R. Journey for Margaret's Oscar. il ports stills CLASSIC n237:bet p32 and 33 [pC12-C13] Mar 1995
Obscenity See PORNOGRAPHY AND OBSCENITY
OCCHIOPINOCCHIO f (d Nuti, Francesco 1994 It)
Reviews
Buccheri, V. "OcchioPinocchio." credits stills SEGNO n72:51-53 Mar/Apr 1995
Poggi, E. "Occhiopinocchio." credits FILM (ITALY) 3:40-41 n13 1995
Rooney, D. "Occhiopinocchio." credits VARIETY 357:73 Jan 9/15 1995
O'CONNELL, RAOUL See also BOYS LIFE
O'CONNOR, JOHN E.
O'Connor, J.E. The white man's Indian. bibliog F&HIST 23:17-26 n1/4 1993
O'CONNOR, PAT See also CIRCLE OF FRIENDS
October See OKTIABR'
OCTOBER FILMS
Molner, D. October buys rights to Danish "Kingdom." VARIETY 358:27 Mar 13/19 1995
OCTOBRE f (d Falardeau, Pierre 1994 Can)
Reviews
Beaulieu, J. "Octobre." credits still SEQUENCES n174:30-31 Sep/Oct 1994
Landry, G. FLQ intra-muros. credits stills 24 IMAGES n75:56-57 Dec/Jan 1994/95
Odeur de la papaye verte, L' See MUI DU DU XANH
ODIN, ROGER
Morin, S. "Nick's Movie": le point de fuite. bibliog still CINEMAS 4:101-117 n2 1994
Odin, R. Le documentaire interieur. Travail du JE et mise en phase dans "Lettres d'amour en Somalie." bibliog still CINEMAS 4:82-100 n2 1994
Odin, R. Narrative comprehended [Book Review]. Q REV F & VIDEO 15:35-46 n3 1994
ODYSSEY ENTERTAINMENT GROUP
Weiner, R. Recounting Odyssey's long fall. il VARIETY 358:11+ [2p] Feb 6/12 1995
OEDIPAL NARRATIVE
China (People's Republic, since 1949)
Farquhar, M.A. Oedipality in "Red Sorghum" and "Judou." bibliog glos scenario stills CINEMAS 3:60-86 n2/3 1993
United States
Layton, L. "Blue Velvet": a parable of male development. SCREEN 35:374-393 n4 1994
Office national du film du Canada See NATIONAL FILM BOARD OF CANADA
OFFRET f (Sacrifice, The d Tarkovsky, Andrei 1986 Swed/Fr)
Paquette, J.-M. Tarkovski, cineaste cynique. bibliog CINEMAS 4:15-23 n3 1994
OGAWA, SHINSUKE See also NIPPON-KOKU FURUYASHIKI-MURA
Kazuyuki, Y. From 1991 to 1993 - exploring new worlds at the Yamagata Documentary Film Festival. il still DOC BOX 1:1-3 1992
Ulwer, R. and Voser, S. Interview mit dem Filmemacher Ogawa Shinsuke. il interv stills BLIMP [n2]:10-15 Winter 1985
OH! DARLING, YEH HAI INDIA f (d Mehta, Ketan 1994 India)
Gangar, A. On location with Ketan Mehta. CINEMAYA n24:42-43 Summer 1994
OHMER, SUSAN
Ohmer, S. Index to "Cineaste," vol. XX. CINEASTE 21:89+ [2p] n1/2 1995
OHNE MICH f (d Levy, Dani 1993 FR Ger)
Reviews
Wendt, U. "Ohne mich." credits C(SWITZ) 40:214 1994
OKI, HIROYUKI See also ANATA GA SUKI DESU, DAI SUKI DES
OKNO V PARIZH f (Window to Paris d Mamin, Iurii 1993 Russia/Fr)
Reviews
Bartholomew, D. "Window to Paris." credits FJ 98:69-70 Mar 1995
Hoberman, J. The natives are westless. stills VILLAGE VOICE 40:47 Feb 21 1995
Major, W. "Window to Paris." BOXOFFICE 131:bet p125 and 144 [pR32] Apr 1995
Pioppo, M. "Insalata russa." credits still C FORUM 34:81-82 Oct (n338) 1994
OKTIABR' f (October d Eisenstein, Sergei Mikhailovich/Aleksandrov, Grigorii 1928 USSR)
Sorensen, J. "Lef," Eisenstein, and the politics of form. bibliog F CRITICISM 19:55-74 n2 1994/95
OKUBO, KEN'ICHI
Okubo, K. Islands in the mist. port stills CINEMAYA n25/26:30-32 Autumn/Winter 1994/95
OKUDA, TED
The Slide area film book notes [Book Reviews]. CLASSIC n237:42-44+ [4p] Mar 1995
OKUN, JEFFREY
Prokop, T. "Stargate." il stills C FANTAS 26:48-49+ [4p] n3 1995
OLDANI, MARIA TERESA
Oldani, M.T. Incontro con Mickey Rourke. interv still FCR 45:364-368 Jun/Jul (n446/447) 1994
Oldani, M.T. Kazakhstan: la nuova ondata. still FCR 45:386-389 Sep (n448) 1994
Oldani, M.T. Taormina. still CINEMAYA n25/26:90-91 Autumn/Winter 1994/95
OLEANNA f (d Mamet, David 1994 USA/Gt Br)
Reviews
Travers, P. "David Mamet's Oleanna." still ROLLING STONE n696:132+ [2p]

1995
O'Steen, K. Managers on the march. il VARIETY 357:11+ [2p] Jan 2/8 1995
O'Steen, K. Oscar night hits the Internet. VARIETY 358:26 Feb 13/19 1995
O'Steen, K. Second strings play sans sweet security of studios. VARIETY 358:86 Feb 27/Mar 5 1995
O'Steen, K. Settlement seen in "Boxing" case. VARIETY 358:20 Mar 13/19 1995
O'Steen, K. The sound and the jury. VARIETY 358:13+ [2p] Mar 6/12 1995
O'Steen, K. Videodisc format focus of CES talk. VARIETY 357:36 Jan 9/15 1995
O'Steen, K. and Brodie, J. Acad rebounds after "Hoop" airball. il VARIETY 358:11+ [2p] Feb 20/26 1995
OSTEN, SUZANNE See also TALAI DET AR SA MORKT
OSTERHOLM, J. ROGER
Slide, A. The Slide area film book notes [Book Reviews]. CLASSIC n236:47-49 Feb 1995
OTHELLO f (d Buchowetzki, Dimitri 1922 Ger)
Angulo, J. "Otelo." credits NOSFERATU n8:65-66 Feb 1992
OTHELLO f (d Welles, Orson 1951 Morocco)
Musumeci, M. Othello e i suoi doppi. il stills IMMAGINE n28:15-19 Autumn 1994
Riambau, E. "Otelo." credits still NOSFERATU n8:60-61 Feb 1992
Riambau, E. Shakespeare y Welles. stills NOSFERATU n8:32-39 Feb 1992
OTT, THOMAS See also ROBERT CREEP
OTTMAR, TOM W.
Ottmar, T.W. Fritt fram a soke ef-stotte. il interv port F&K n7:34-35 1993
OUBLIE-MOI f (d Lvovsky, Noemie 1994 Fr)
Aude, F. Entretien avec Noemie Lvovsky. il interv stills POSITIF n408:39-42 Feb 1995
Vasse, C. "Oublie-moi." credits il stills POSITIF n408:37-38 Feb 1995
    Reviews
Di Luzio, A. "Oublie-moi." still C FORUM 34:30 Sep (n337) 1994
OUEDRAOGO, IDRISSA See also AFRIQUE, MON AFRIQUE...; CRI DU COEUR, LE
OUELLETTE, LAURIE
Ouellette, L. Reel women. stills INDEP 18:28-34 Apr 1995
OUIMET, LEO ERNEST
Montreal cinematographie en debut de siecle. il port still 24 IMAGES n75:51-54 Dec/Jan 1994/95
OUT OF AMERICA f (d Klier, Michael 1994 FR Ger)
"Out of America." biog credits filmog still KINO(BRD) n1:36-37 1995
OUTBREAK f (d Petersen, Wolfgang 1995 USA)
Gill, M.S. Crisis management. il stills PREM 8:74-77+ [5p] Apr 1995
    Reviews
Corliss, R. This virus isn't catching. still TIME 145:71 Mar 20 1995
Hoberman, J. Life's fitful fever. still VILLAGE VOICE 40:47 Mar 21 1995
Kroll, J. Getting the bugs out. still NEWSWK 125:65 Mar 20 1995
McCarthy, T. "Outbreak" looks like b.o. wildfire. credits still VARIETY 358:49+ [2p] Mar 13/19 1995
Rafferty, T. The enemy within. il NEW YORKER 71:105-107 Mar 20 1995
OUTLAND f (d Hyams, Peter 1981 USA)
    Sound Track Reviews
Kendall, L. "Outland"/"Capricorn One." F SCORE MONTHLY n39:12 Nov 1993
Outlaw Territory See HANNAH LEE
OWEN, ALUN
Lentz, H., III. Obituaries. biogs filmogs il obits ports CLASSIC n236:57-59 Feb 1995
OWEN, RENA
Millea, H. Surviving the game. port PREM 8:39 Feb 1995
Patterson, A. Warrior woman. il VILLAGE VOICE 40:72 Feb 28 1995
OZKAN, YAVUZ See also BIR SONBAHAR HIKAYESI
OZU, YASUJIRO
Karatson, G. Ozu eskuvoi. il stills F VILAG 38:24-29 n3 1995
Sato, T. Das Verhalten des Auges in den Filmen von Ozu und Naruse. il stills BLIMP [n2]:6-10 Winter 1985
POO RECORDS
These boots were made for hawkin': part II - POO Records. il F SCORE MONTHLY n38:6-7 Oct 1993
PAAKKANEN, HEIKKI
Liljenback, S. Isoja ja pienia asioita. biog filmog il stills PEILI 17:26-28 n4 1993
PABST, G.W. See also FREUDLOSE GASSE, DIE
PACCIARELLI, DOROTA
Sobolewski, T. Zycie na moscie. interv port KINO 27:20-21+ [3p] Jun 1993
PACCO, DOPPIO PACCO E CONTROPACCOTTO f (d Loy, Nanni 1993 It)
Lori, S. Ha conquistato anche il Nord l'ineffabile Enzo Cannavale. C SUD 33:51-52 Jul/Aug/Sep (n113) 1994
PACIFIC DATA IMAGES
Weiner, R. Effects houses enter cutthroat competition. il VARIETY 358:7+ [2p] Mar 13/19 1995
PACIFIC INTERNATIONAL ENTERPRISES, INC.
Wasser, F. Four walling exhibition: regional resistance to the Hollywood film industry. CJ 34:51-65 n2 1995
PACSKOVSZKY, JOZSEF See also ESTI KORNEL CSODALATOS UTAZASA
Bakacs, T. S. Es a vonat megy... interv port stills F VILAG 38:14-16 n4 1995
PADGAONKAR, LATIKA For film reviews see author under the following titles: BANDIT QUEEN
PAESANO, ALESSANDRO For film reviews see author under the following titles: I LOVE A MAN IN UNIFORM; INTERVIEW WITH THE VAMPIRE: THE VAMPIRE CHRONICLES; PARFUM D'YVONNE, LE; RAPA NUI; THIRTY TWO SHORT FILMS ABOUT GLENN GOULD
PAGE, JAKE
Miller, R.C. The knotted strings. By Jake Page [Book Review]. ARMCHAIR DET 28:98 n1 1995
PAGEMASTER, THE f (d Hunt, Maurice/Johnston, Joe 1994 USA)
    Sound Track Reviews
Neckebroeck, K. "The Pagemaster." SCN 14:22 Mar 1995
    Reviews
Felperin, L. "The Pagemaster." credits still S&S 5:49-50 Feb 1995
PAGLIANO, JEAN-PIERRE
Pagliano, J.-P. Entretien avec Sylvia Bataille. il interv still POSITIF

n408:90-93 Feb 1995
PAIETTA, ANN C.
Slide, A. The Slide area film book notes [Book Reviews]. CLASSIC n237:42-44+ [4p] Mar 1995
Painters and painting See ART AND ARTISTS
PAJER, ROBERT See also ORDOG VIGYE
PAKULA, ALAN J. See also KLUTE
PALETZ, DAVID L.
Paletz, G.M. and Paletz, D.L. Mike Leigh's "Naked" truth. bibliog stills F CRITICISM 19:23-39 n2 1994/95
PALETZ, GABRIEL M.
Paletz, G.M. and Paletz, D.L. Mike Leigh's "Naked" truth. bibliog stills F CRITICISM 19:23-39 n2 1994/95
PALJAKKA, KARI See also AIDIN TYTTO
PALLY, MARCIA
De Grazia, E. Sex de jure [Book Reviews]. NATION 260:242-249 Feb 20 1995
Palme d'or See FESTIVALS - France - Cannes
PALMER, CHRISTOPHER
Elley, D. Christopher Palmer. biog obit VARIETY 358:59 Mar 20/26 1995
PALMINTERI, CHAZZ
Palminteri, C. The fire in Fiorentino. il interv port INTERV 25:88-91 Mar 1995
PALOMBELLA ROSSA f (d Moretti, Nanni 1989 It/Fr)
Porton, R. and Ellickson, L. Comedy, communism, and pastry: an interview with Nanni Moretti. interv port stills CINEASTE 21:11-15 n1/2 1995
PALUD, HERVE See also INDIEN DANS LA VILLE, UN
PALUMBO, DENNIS
Palumbo, D. Jealousy. JOURNAL WGA 8:32 Mar 1995
Palumbo, D. The pitch. JOURNAL WGA 8:37 Feb 1995
Palumbo, D. Writer's block is good news! JOURNAL WGA 8:49 Dec/Jan 1995
PALUMBO, RON
Palumbo, R. and Furmanek, B. This island mirth. il stills F FAX n48:56-63 Jan/Feb 1995
PAMIETNIK ZNALEZIONY W GARBIE f (d Kidawa-Blonski, Jan 1993 Poland/Can)
    Reviews
Boutroy, P. "Le journal d'un bossu." SEQUENCES n174:45 Sep/Oct 1994
Panavision See WIDE SCREEN
PANH, RITHY See also NEAK SRE
Jaeggi, B. and Knaebel, M. Look back in pain. filmog interv port stills CINEMAYA n24:44-47 Summer 1994
PANNE DE SENS f (d Chibane, Malik in production 1995- Algeria)
Ditmars, H. The Algerian connection. il S&S 5:5 Feb 1995
Panrama [Prior to V16, 1988 use also PANRAMA] See WIDE SCREEN
PAODA SHUANG DENG f (Red Firecracker, Green Firecracker d He, Ping 1994 Hong Kong/China)
    Reviews
Bartholomew, D. "Red Firecracker, Green Firecracker." credits FJ 98:63 Mar 1995
PAPINEAU, ELISABETH
Papineau, E. Le documentaire chinois de la "reforme": la Chine maquillee par l'etat. bibliog glos il CINEMAS 3:87-102 n2/3 1993
PAQUETTE, JEAN-MARCEL
Paquette, J.-M. Tarkovski, cineaste cynique. bibliog CINEMAS 4:15-23 n3 1994
PARADZHANOV, SERGEI See also ASHIK-KERIB
"Asik-Kerib." Ed: Gianroberto Scarcia [Book Review]. il KINO(GF) n56:29 Nov 1994
Michele Picchi. Sergei Paradzanov [Book Review]. il KINO(GF) n56:29 Nov 1994
Patrick Cazals: Serguei Paradjanov [Book Review]. il KINO(GF) n56:29 Nov 1994
PARAJANOV f (d Holloway, Ronald 1994 FR Ger)
    Reviews
Rauzi, P. "Paradzanov - a Requiem." C FORUM 34:31 Sep (n337) 1994
PARFUM D'YVONNE, LE f (d Leconte, Patrice 1994 Fr)
    Reviews
De Bernardinis, F. "Il profumo di Yvonne." credits still SEGNO n72:48-49 Mar/Apr 1995
Elia, M. "Le parfum d'Yvonne." credits still SEQUENCES n175:39-40 Nov/Dec 1994
Paesano, A. "Il profumo di Yvonne." credits still FILM (ITALY) 3:38-39 n13 1995
PARHUZAMOS ELETRAJZOK f (d Jeles, Andras 1993 Hungary)
    Reviews
Bikacsy, G. Spectacle and stammer. NEW HUNGARIAN Q 34:166-168 n132 1993
PARIS IS BURNING f (d Livingston, Jennie 1988 USA)
    Queer Theory Analysis
Gomez, G. Homocolonialism: looking for Latinos in "Apartment Zero" and "Paris Is Burning." bibliog stills PS 14:117-124 n1/2 1994/95
PARK, KWANG-SU See also KEU SOME GAGO SIPTA
PARKE, HENRY C.
Parke, H.C. Delmar Watson. il interv ports stills F FAX n49:77-82 Mar/Apr 1995
PARKER, ALAN See also ROAD TO WELLVILLE, THE
Krolikowska-Avis, E. Alan Parker. il interv KINO 27:10-13 Jun 1993
PARKER, BILL See also KLA$H
PARKER, HEIDI
Parker, H. The waiting game. interv port MOVIELINE 6:66-67 Apr 1995
Parker, H. "Wild at Heart." port MOVIELINE 6:18 Apr 1995
PARKERSON, MICHELLE See also LITANY FOR SURVIVAL: THE LIFE AND WORK OF AUDRE LORDE, A
PARMAR, PRATIBHA
Bronski, M. Queer looks: perspectves on lesbian and gay film and video. Edited by Martha Gever, John Greyson and Pratibha Parmar [Book Reviews]. still CINEASTE 21:90-92 n1/2 1994/95
PARODY [Prior to V17, 1989 use also PARODIES] See also COMEDY; HUMOR; SATIRE
    United States
Deleyto, C. The narrator and the narrative: the evolution of Woody Allen's film comedies. bibliog F CRITICISM 19:40-54 n2 1994/95

PARSHALL, PETER F.
  Parshall, P.F. Buster Keaton and the space of farce: "Steamboat Bill, Jr." versus "The Cameraman." bibliog diag stills UFAJ 46:29-46 n3 1994
PARTIE DE CAMPAGNE, UNE f (Day in the Country, A d Renoir, Jean 1946 prod 1936 Fr)
  Berthome, J.-P. Voir un peu d'herbe avant de mourir... il POSITIF n408:84-89 Feb 1995
  Curchod, O. Autour de "Partie de campagne." il still POSITIF n408:82-83 Feb 1995
  Pagliano, J.-P. Entretien avec Sylvia Bataille. il interv still POSITIF n408:90-93 Feb 1995
PARTIE D'ECHECS, LA f (d Hanchard, Yves 1994 Belg/Fr/Switz)
    Reviews
  Bruyn, O. de. "La partie d'echecs." POSITIF n406:48 Dec 1994
PARTRIDGE, MEG See also DOROTHEA LANGE: A VISUAL LIFE
PARTY GIRL f (d Mayer, Daisy von Scherler 1995 USA)
    Reviews
  Oppenheimer, J. "Party Girl." BOXOFFICE 131:bet p89 and 96 [pR21] Mar 1995
  Travers, P. "Party Girl." still ROLLING STONE n704:128 Mar 23 1995
PAS TRES CATHOLIQUE f (d Marshall, Tonie 1994 Fr)
    Reviews
  Horguelin, T. Allegro vivace. credits stills 24 IMAGES n75:58-59 Dec/Jan 1994/95
PASIKOWSKI, WLADYSLAW See also PSY
PASOLINI, PIER PAOLO See also MAMMA ROMA; SALO O LE CENTOVENTI GIORNATE DI SODOMA
  Mariniello, S. Techniques audiovisuelles et reecriture de l'histoire. De la representation a la production du temps au cinema. bibliog still CINEMAS 5:41-56 n1/2 1994
  Orr, C. A certain realism: making use of Pasolini's theory and practice. By Maurizio Viano [Book Review]. F CRITICISM 19:99-103 n2 1994/95
Pasolini's 120 Days of Sodom See SALO O LE CENTOVENTI GIORNATE DI SODOMA
PASQUIN, JOHN See also SANTA CLAUSE, THE
PASSE COMPOSE f (d Romand, Francoise 1994 Fr)
    Reviews
  Loffreda, P. "Passe compose." C FORUM 34:37 Sep (n337) 1994
PASSEL, FRANK VAN See also MANNEKEN PIS
PASSENGER 57 f (d Hooks, Kevin 1992 USA)
    Reviews
  Meyers, R. The crime screen. port stills ARMCHAIR DET 26:69-71 n2 1993
PASSIFLORA f (d Belanger, Fernand/Gueissaz-Teufel, Dagmar 1986 Can)
  Lockerbie, I. Le documentaire autoreflexif au Quebec. "L'emotion dissonante" et "Passiflora." still CINEMAS 4:118-132 n2 1994
PASSION f (d Godard, Jean-Luc 1982 Fr/Switz)
  Trenczak, H. Passion Kino oder Die Haerte, alles zu registrieren. credits il port BLIMP [n1]:4-13 Mar 1985
PASSION DE JEANNE D'ARC, LA f (Passion of Joan of Arc, The d Dreyer, Carl Theodor 1928 Fr)
  Angulo, J. "La pasion de Juana de Arco." credits stills NOSFERATU n5:60-61 Jan 1991
  Masoni, T. Carl Theodor Dreyer: l'assoluto e il dubbio. stills C FORUM 34:14-17 Nov (n339) 1994
  Minguet Batllori, J.M. Carl Theodor Dreyer: clasicismo y cine. il port stills NOSFERATU n5:12-23 Jan 1991
    Religious Themes
  Miguez, M. La mirada Dreyer. il stills NOSFERATU n5:24-37 Jan 1991
Passion of Joan of Arc, The See PASSION DE JEANNE D'ARC, LA
PASTOR, ANDREA
  Pastor, A. Accadde, a maggio. stills FCR 45:286-291 Jun/Jul (n446/447) 1994
  Pastor, A. and Maudente, F. Cinema come memoria. interv stills FCR 45:339-348 Jun/Jul (n446/447) 1994
  Pastor, A. and Maudente, F. Preservare le cose importanti... interv still FCR 45:329-338 Jun/Jul (n446/447) 1994
PATAKI, HEIDI
  Geyrhofer, F. and Pataki, H. Film in Oesterreich. BLIMP [n1]:60-64 Mar 1985
PATAKI, KALMAN
  Pataki, K. The trouble with Oscar. interv NEW HUNGARIAN Q 34:172-175 n131 1993
PATEL, ISHU
  Starr, C. Ishu Patel. biog filmog il interv stills ANIMATION J 3:54-61 n2 1995
PATERSON, RICHARD
  Paterson, R. Hollywood's overseas campaign: the North Atlantic movie trade, 1920-1950. By Ian Jarvie [Book Review]. J COMM 45:171-173 n1 1995
PATHE-FRERES
  Thoraval, Y. Pathe, empire centenaire du cinema. AVANT-SCENE n437:88 Dec 1994
    Film Lists
  Cherchi Usai, P. Catalogue Pathe des annees 1896 a 1914 [Book Review]. J F PRES n49:68-69 Oct 1994
PATRIOTES, LES f (d Rochant, Eric 1994 Fr)
    Reviews
  Mosca, U. "Storie di spie." credits still C FORUM 34:84 Nov (n339) 1994
PATTERSON, ALEX For film reviews see author under the following titles: SAFE PASSAGE
  Patterson, A. Warrior woman. il VILLAGE VOICE 40:72 Feb 28 1995
PATTERSON, SHIRLEY See also SMITH, SHAWN
  Wiseman, T. Shirley Patterson a.k.a. Shawn Smith. il interv ports stills F FAX n49:56-61 Mar/Apr 1995
PATTISON, BARRIE
  Pattison, B. On fire with Ringo Lam: part two. filmog il stills FATAL VISIONS n17:11-12 1994
  Pattison, B. The 39th Asia-Pacific Film Festival. il stills C PAPERS n102:22-23 Dec 1994
PATWARDHAN, ANAND See also PITRA, PUTRA AUR DHARAMYUDDHA
PAUL BOWLES - HALBMOND f (d Schlaich, Frieder/Alberti, Irene von 1995 FR Ger)
  "Paul Bowles - Halbmond." biogs credits still KINO(BRD) n1:24-25 1995

PAULUS, WOLFRAM See also DU BRINGST MICH NOCH UM
PAULY, REBECCA
  Pauly, R. A revolution is not a dinner party: "The Discrete Charm" of Bunuel's "Bourgeoisie." bibliog LIT/FQ 22:232-237 n4 1994
PAVICEVIC, GORAN
  Norcen, L. Dirigere la luce. il interv stills SEGNO n71:12-13 Jan/Feb 1995
PAVONI, I f (d Manuzzi, Luciano 1994 It)
    Reviews
  Nazzaro, G.A. "I pavoni." still C FORUM 34:22 Sep (n337) 1994
PAWELCZAK, ANDY For film reviews see author under the following titles: NATURAL BORN KILLERS; QUIZ SHOW; SHAWSHANK REDEMPTION, THE
PAXMAN, ANDREW For film reviews see author under the following titles: BIENVENIDO; EN EL AIRE
  Paxman, A. A latin screen play. stat VARIETY 358:59-60 Feb 27/Mar 5 1995
  Paxman, A. As peso drops, so does prod'n. il still VARIETY 358:50 Mar 27/Apr 2 1995
  Paxman, A. Del Toro latest H'wood recruit. il VARIETY 358:54+ [2p] Mar 27/Apr 2 1995
  Paxman, A. Mexico leads way, but latin pix have hard act to follow. VARIETY 358:60+ [2p] Feb 6/12 1995
  Paxman, A. Picture blurry for local prods. stat VARIETY 358:32-33 Feb 6/12 1995
PAZ, SENEL
  Toledo, T. "Fresa y chocolate." interv stills DICINE n59:4-6 Nov/Dec 1994
PEARCE, RICHARD See also LONG WALK HOME, THE
PEARSON, HARRY, JR. For film reviews see author under the following titles: ADVENTURES OF PRISCILLA, QUEEN OF THE DESERT, THE; FORREST GUMP
PEARSON, ROBERTA E.
  Creekmur, C.K. Roberta Pearson. Eloquent gestures: the transformation of performance style in the Griffith Biograph films [Book Review]. ARACHNE 1:266-269 n2 1994
  Livio, J. Reframing culture: the case of the Vitagraph Quality Films. Di William Uricchio e Roberta E. Pearson [Book Review]. GRIFFITHIANA n51/52:264-265 Oct 1994
PEARY, DANNY
  Peary, D. What's the catch? il MOVIELINE 6:72-73 Mar 1995
PEARY, HAROLD
  Bowman, D.K. The great Gildersleeve. il port stills F FAX n49:69-72 Mar/Apr 1995
PECHE VENIEL... PECHE MORTEL... f (d Meffre, Pomme 1994 Fr)
    Reviews
  Derobert, E. "Peche veniel... peche mortel..." POSITIF n409:47 Mar 1995
PECKINPAH, SAM See also STRAW DOGS; WILD BUNCH, THE; WILD BUNCH, THE
  Redman, N. A Siegel film: an autobiography. By Don Siegel [Book Reviews]. il DGA NEWS 19:33-34 n2 1994
  Redman, N. Peckinpah and Sidney reconsidered [Book Reviews]. il DGA NEWS 20:40-41 n1 1995
  Strauss, U. von. Play it again, Sam! il CHAPLIN 36:40-41 n6 (n255) 1994/95
  Williams, T. Justified lives: morality and narrative in the films of Sam Peckinpah. By Michael Bliss [Book Review]. il FQ 48:62-63 n2 1994/95
    Retrospectives
  Brown, G. Once were westerns. still VILLAGE VOICE 40:54 Mar 7 1995
PEDERSEN, MONA
  Pedersen, M. Om "Mildred Pierce" som filmkunst og industriprodukt. credits still Z n4:10-14 (n46) 1993
PEDLER, GARTH
  Pedler, G. Garth's vintage viewing: Julien Duvivier's "Revelation." biogs il stills CLASSIC n237:30+ [3p] Mar 1995
PEEPING TOM f (d Powell, Michael 1960 Gt Br)
    Psychological Analysis
  Bronfen, E. Bilder, die toeten - Tod im Bild. bibliog il stills C(SWITZ) 40:112-134 1994
PEERS, MARTIN
  Busch, A.M. and Peers, M. Troika has its eyes on $1 bil prize. stat VARIETY 358:13 Feb 27/Mar 5 1995
  Peers, M. Cinemark, Cineplex merge ops. VARIETY 358:22 Mar 6/12 1995
  Peers, M. Disney hits Street looking for cash. stat VARIETY 357:11+ [2p] Jan 2/8 1995
  Peers, M. Is Milken mulling moguldom? VARIETY 358:1+ [2p] Mar 13/19 1995
  Peers, M. Risk-ridden H'wood is casting for cash. il VARIETY 357:1+ [2p] Jan 9/15 1995
  Peers, M. Skouras nixes public offering. VARIETY 358:9 Feb 27/Mar 5 1995
PEIRCE, CHARLES S.
  Everaert-Desmedt, N. L'eternite au quotidien: la representation des temps dans "Les ailes du desir" de Wim Wenders. bibliog diag CINEMAS 5:105-122 n1/2 1994
PEKKO JA POIKA f (d Koivusalo, Timo 1994 Finl)
    Reviews
  Kupiainen, R. Pahat joutuvat brysseliin. credits still PEILI 18:30 n4 1994
PELECANOS, GEORGE
  Pelecanos, G. Hollywood nocturnes. By James Ellroy [Book Review]. ARMCHAIR DET 27:361 n3 1994
PELKA, BARBARA
  Pelka, B. "Lato milosci." credits stills FSP 40:8-9 n11 (n765) 1994
  Pelka, B. Marzena Trybala. filmog stills FSP 40:12-13 n10 (n764) 1994
  Pelka, B. "Moja ulubiona pora roku." biog credits filmog port still FSP 40:9 n6 (n760) 1994
  Pelka, B. Stanislawa Celinska. filmog still FSP 40:10 n11 (n765) 1994
PENG, XIAO LIAN See also SAN GE NU: REN
PENN, ARTHUR See also ALICE'S RESTAURANT; LITTLE BIG MAN
PENNY SERENADE f (d Stevens, George 1941 USA)
    Music
  Creekmur, C.K. Strains of utopia: gender, nostalgia, and Hollywood music. Caryl Flinn [Book Review]. DISCOURSE n17.1:172-175 Fall 1994
PENSIONAT OSKAR f (d Bier, Susanne 1995 Swed)
    Reviews
  Rehlin, G. "Like It Never Was Before" ("Pensionat Oskar"). credits VARIETY 358:51 Mar 20/26 1995
[PEONY BIRDS] f (d Huang, Yu-Shan 1993 Taiwan)
  "Peony Birds." biog credits filmog still CINEMAYA n25/26:105 Autumn/Winter

1994/95
PERCEPTION
Kremski, P. Film als Schule des Sehens. il interv stills F BUL 36:53-59 n6 (n197) 1994
Theory
Simon, J.A. Neuro-cineasm. il BLIMP n30:39-43 Winter 1994
Stonehill, B. The debate over "ocularcentrism" [Book Reviews]. J COMM 45:147-152 n1 1995
Pereira dos Santos, Nelson See SANTOS, NELSON PEREIRA DOS
PERETIE, OLIVIER
Peretie, O. Kell-e gyilkossaggal vadolnunk Hollywoodot? stills F VILAG 38:37-39 n1 1995
PEREZ FAMILY, THE f (d Nair, Mira 1995 USA)
Carreon, J. "The Perez Family" embraces a diverse cast and crew. still FJ 98:22+ [2p] Mar 1995
PEREZ, VINCENT
Millea, H. All the Queen's men. biogs il intervs ports still PREM 8:76-79 Feb 1995
PERFECT WORLD, A f (d Eastwood, Clint 1993 USA)
Reviews
Meyers, R. The crime screen. port stills ARMCHAIR DET 27:207-209 n2 1994
PERFECTLY NORMAL f (d Simoneau, Yves 1990 Can/Gt Br)
Postcolonial Analysis
Kaye, J. "Perfectly Normal," eh?: gender transformation and national identity in Canada. CAN J F STUD 3:63-80 n2 1994
Perfumed Nightmare, The See MABABANGONG BANGUNGOT
PERIES, SUMITRA See also LOKUDUWA
"Loku duwa." biog credits il still CINEMAYA n25/26:104 Autumn/Winter 1994/95
Ratnavibhushana, A. Sumitra Peries. filmog port stills CINEMAYA n25/26:78-80 Autumn/Winter 1994/95
PERIL JEUNE, LE f (d Klapisch, Cedric 1994 Fr)
Reviews
Goudet, S. "Peril jeune." POSITIF n407:43-44 Jan 1995
PERILLI, IVO
Lentz, H., III. Obituaries. biogs filmogs il obits ports CLASSIC n236:57-59 Feb 1995
PERIODICALS See also titles of periodicals
Indexing
Konlechner, P. International Film Archive CD-ROM. J F PRES n49:15-17 Oct 1994
Music
Gorbman, C. The state of film music criticism. bibliog il CINEASTE 21:72-75 n1/2 1995
Europe, Western
Zielinski, S. Mediale Grenzueberschreitungen: Audiovisionen einer Zeitschriftenlandschaft. BLIMP n30:66-67 Winter 1994
Conferences, Institutes, Workshops, etc.
Grbic, B. Meine persoenlichen Grenzueberschreitungen. BLIMP n30:68 Winter 1994
Perlita See SEQUEYRO, ADELA
PERRAULT, PIERRE
Elia, M. Le Prix Albert-Tessier a Pierre Perrault. port SEQUENCES n175:5 Nov/Dec 1994
PERRET, JEAN For film reviews see author under the following titles: CORPS ET AMES; ERNESTO "CHE" GUEVARA: DAS BOLIVIANISCHE TAGEBUCH; FAITS DIVERS; HOMME DES CASERNES, L'; REGARDE-MOI
PERRON, BERNARD
Perron, B. "La memoire, c'est ce qu'il me reste a defaut d'une vue." bibliog diag CINEMAS 5:91-103 n1/2 1994
Persistence of vision See PERCEPTION
PERSONAL MANAGERS
United States
Brodie, J. Managers pounding at the studio gates. VARIETY 358:15-16 Mar 27/Apr 2 1995
Brodie, J. and O'Steen, K. Antsy agents make mutant managers. il VARIETY 358:1+ [3p] Mar 20/26 1995
O'Steen, K. Managers on the march. il VARIETY 357:11+ [2p] Jan 2/8 1995
PERSONAL PAIN f (d Unruh, Evan 1995 USA)
Reviews
Rooney, D. "Personal Pain." credits VARIETY 358:84 Feb 20/26 1995
PERSONNE NE M'AIME f (d Vernoux, Marion 1994 Fr/Switz)
Reviews
Boutroy, P. "Personne ne m'aime." SEQUENCES n174:45 Sep/Oct 1994
PERSONS, DAN For film reviews see author under the following titles: ED WOOD; [JUDGE]; SWAN PRINCESS, THE
Persons, D. Svankmajer. still C FANTAS 26:56 n3 1995
PERSPECTIVE
History
Berger, C. Das Panorama - Paradigma eines Perspektivenwechsels. F KUNST n144:4-13 1994
Japan
Burch, N. Flaeche und Tiefe. BLIMP [n2]:24-27 Winter 1985
PERUGORRIA, JORGE
Birringer, J. Homosexuality and the revolution. interv port CINEASTE 21:21-22 n1/2 1995
P'ESA DLIA PASSAZHIRA f (d Abdrashitov, Vadim 1995 Russia)
Reviews
Leydon, J. "The Play for a Passenger" ("Pjesa dlja passahira"). credits VARIETY 358:65 Mar 6/12 1995
PESCE, ALBERTO
Pesce, A. "Al Cinematografo," insieme appassionatamente. port IMMAGINE n28:28-29 Autumn 1994
PETENYI, KATALIN See also EUROPA MESSZE VAN
PETERCHENS MONDFAHRT f (d Urchs, Wolfgang 1990 W Ger)
Bellion, C. "Petit Pierre au pays des reves." credits stills GRAND ANGLE n177:33-34 Dec 1994
PETERNAK, MIKLOS
Peternak, M. A kovetkezo szaz ev. il stills F VILAG 38:10-14 n1 1995

PETERS, GARY
Peters, G. Barbara Creed. The monstrous-feminine: film, feminism, psychoanalysis [Book Review]. bibliog CAN J F STUD 3:108-113 n2 1994
PETERS, HOUSE
Katchmer, G. Remembering the great silents. biogs filmogs port CLASSIC n236:50-53 Feb 1995
PETERS, MICHAEL
Lentz, H., III. Obituaries. biogs filmogs il obits ports CLASSIC n236:57-59 Feb 1995
PETERSEN, WOLFGANG See also IN THE LINE OF FIRE; OUTBREAK
PETERSON, SIDNEY See also LEAD SHOES, THE
PETICCA, SANDRO See also ALTRA ESTATE, UN'
PETIT GARCON, LE f (d Granier-Deferre, Pierre 1995 Fr)
Reviews
Vachaud, L. "Le petit garcon." POSITIF n409:47 Mar 1995
PETITE APOCALYPSE, LA f (d Costa-Gavras 1993 Fr/It/Poland)
Lubelski, T. Dziesiec lat spoznienia, czyli "Mala apokalipsa" ogladana we Francji. KINO 27:8-9 May 1993
Sobolewski, T. "Nie bedziemy umie rac za Sarajewo." il KINO 27:6-8 May 1993
Reviews
Michalek, B. Szkoda tematu. still KINO 27:30-31 May 1993
Plazewski, J. "Apokalipsa" z inspiracji. credits stills KINO 27:10-11 May 1993
PETITS ARRANGEMENTS AVEC LES MORTS f (d Ferran, Pascale 1994 Fr)
Bellion, C. "Petits arrangements avec la mort." bibliog credits still GRAND ANGLE n178:23-24 Jan 1995
Reviews
Roy, A. "Petits arrangements avec les morts." still 24 IMAGES n75:41-42 Dec/Jan 1994/95
PETLEY, JULIAN
Petley, J. Henri Storck - documentarist, surrealist, anarchist. port VERTIGO (UK) 1:33 n4 1994/95
Petley, J. and Chanan, M. Henri Storck interviewed for "Vertigo." interv stills VERTIGO (UK) 1:34-36 n4 1994/95
PETRAGLIA, SANDRO
Bellocchio, M. and Petraglia, S. Due testimonianze di Marco Bellocchio e Sandro Petraglia su Vittorio Mezzogiorno strappato per un male inguaribile al cinema che aveva bisogno della sua preparazione artisticae severita morale. il C SUD 33:15-16 Jul/Aug/Sep (n113) 1994
PETRIE, DANIEL, JR.
Petrie, D., Jr. The long and winding road. port JOURNAL WGA 8:2 Mar 1995
PETRIE, DONALD See also RICHIE RICH
Pette, Graham See PETTIE, GRAHAM
PETTIE, GRAHAM
Katchmer, G. Remembering the great silents. biogs filmogs port CLASSIC n236:50-53 Feb 1995
PETTY, LORI
Fuller, G. T'anks to Petty... il interv ports still INTERV 25:110-113 Mar 1995
PETZALL, JILL
Petzall, J. Want to see more work by independents? still ANGLES 2:6-7 n4 1995
PEYSER, MARC
Peyser, M. No experience necessary: can celebrities save Broadway? graph ports NEWSWK 125:66 Mar 6 1995
PEYTON, LAWRENCE
Katchmer, G. Remembering the great silents. biogs filmogs port CLASSIC n236:50-53 Feb 1995
PEZZOTTA, ALBERTO For film reviews see author under the following titles: LIGHT SLEEPER; PULP FICTION
Fittante, A. and Pezzotta, A. "Rivelazioni." credits stills SEGNO n72:63-64 Mar/Apr 1995
Pezzotta, A. Il brutto nel cinema. still SEGNO n72:17-18 Mar/Apr 1995
Pezzotta, A. Imitation of life. stills SEGNO n63:23-24 Sep/Oct 1993
Pezzotta, A. La fragilita del brutto. il stills SEGNO n72:24-26 Mar/Apr 1995
PFAUNDLER, CASPAR
Pfaundler, C. Am Meer - im Film. F KUNST n144:56-64 1994
PHANTOM OF THE OPERA f (d Fisher, Terence 1962 Gt Br)
Murgiondo, P. "El fantasma de la Opera." credits stills NOSFERATU n6:88-89 Apr 1991
PHANTOM OF THE OPERA f (d Lubin, Arthur 1943 USA)
Production
MacQueen, S. (Forty-three) '43 "Phantom" found new formula for classic tale. credits il stills AMCIN 74:80-85 Sep 1993
Phantom Ship See MYSTERY OF THE MARY CELESTE, THE
PHENOMENOLOGY
Sobchack, V. Vivian Sobchack responds. UFAJ 46:64-66 n1 1994
Stadler, H. Sobchack, Vivian. The address of the eye: a phenomenology of film experience [Book Review]. UFAJ 46:61-64 n1 1994
Canada
Roy, L. L'infatigable image ou les horizons du temps au cinema. bibliog CINEMAS 5:147-166 n1/2 1994
Documentary Film
Meunier, J.-P. Image, cognition, centration, decentration. bibliog diags CINEMAS 4:27-47 n2 1994
Language
Roy, L. Langage cinematographique et faillibilite. bibliog CINEMAS 4:99-118 n3 1994
PHILADELPHIA f (d Demme, Jonathan 1993 USA)
Sound
Weis, E. Sync tanks. il CINEASTE 21:56-61 n1/2 1995
Philippines See as a subheading under individual subject headings
PHILLIPS, DAVID
Brownlie, T. David Phillips BFFS Chair. il ports FILM 4:16-18 n1 [1995]
PHILLIPS, MIKE
Phillips, M. No time for contradiction. VERTIGO (UK) 1:44-45 n4 1994/95
PHILOSOPHY See also AESTHETICS; CYNICISM
Puntigam, R. Mark C. Taylor, Esa Saarinen. Imagologies [Book Review]. BLIMP

n30:72 Winter 1994
PHOENIX, RIVER
  Dodsfall. biogs obits ports F&K n7:37 1993
PHOTOGRAPHY
    United States
      Actors and Actresses
  Nangle, J. Heavies/drag/lovers/weddings. Edited by J.C. Suares [Book
    Review]. FIR 45:69 Nov/Dec 1994
Photonics See PHOTOGRAPHY
PICASSO WOULD HAVE MADE A GLORIOUS WAITER f (d Schell, Jonathan 1995 USA)
  MacIntosh, J. Reaping your day job. il NEW YORK 28:29 Jan 30 1995
PICCARDI, ADRIANO
  Piccardi, A. "Anime fiammeggianti." credits stills C FORUM 34:68-71 Sep
    (n337) 1994
  Piccardi, A. "Bleak Moments." credits filmog stills C FORUM 34:41-44 Nov
    (n339) 1994
  Piccardi, A. Qualche nota su un american filmaker. stills C FORUM 34:44-48
    Oct (n338) 1994
PICCHI, MICHELE For film reviews see author under the following titles: BRANCO,
  IL
  Michele Picchi. Sergei Paradzanov [Book Review]. il KINO(GF) n56:29 Nov
    1994
  Picchi, M. "Critica della ragion pura" e "puttana santa." C NUOVO 43:53-54
    Nov/Dec (n352) 1994
  Picchi, M. Futuro con lotteria nel sogno fatto di spot. stills C NUOVO
    43:11-15 Nov/Dec (n352) 1994
PICCOLO GRANDE AMORE f (d Vanzina, Carlo 1993 It)
    Reviews
  Poggi, E. "Piccolo grande amore." credits FILM (ITALY) 3:43-44 n13 1995
PICTURE BRIDE f (d Hatta, Kayo 1994 USA)
  Major, W. "Picture" perfect. port still BOXOFFICE 131:19 Apr 1995
  Rony, F.T. "Picture Bride." il INDEP 18:15-16 Mar 1995
    Reviews
  Glines, C. "Picture Bride." BOXOFFICE 131:bet p125 and 144 [pR31] Apr 1995
PICTURE OF LIGHT f (d Mettler, Peter 1994 Can/Switz)
    Reviews
  Wendt, U. "Picture of Light." credits still C(SWITZ) 40:215-216 1994
PIDA HUIVISTA KIINNI, TATJANA f (d Kaurismaki, Aki 1994 Finl/FR Ger)
  Fabry, S. Zug a Volga. credits still F VILAG 38:52-53 n2 1995
PIEL, DENIS See also LOVE IS BLIND
PIERPONT, PHILIPPE DE
  Berthome, J.-P. Le "storyboard" en livres [Book Reviews]. POSITIF n407:90+
    [2p] Jan 1995
PIERSANTI, UMBERTO See also ALTRA ESTATE, UN'; RITORNO D'AUTUNNO
PIERSON, FRANK
  Pierson, F. President's memorandum. JOURNAL WGA 8:21 Mar 1995
PIERSON, LEO
  Katchmer, G. Remembering the great silents. biogs filmogs port CLASSIC
    n236:50-53 Feb 1995
PIESKE, MANFRED
  Graef, C. Erfahrungen im Spielfilm-Studio. il F & FERNSEHEN 22:12-25 n6
    1994
PIESTRAK, MAREK See also LZA KSIECIA CIEMNOSCI
  "Lza ksiecia ciemnosci." biog credits filmog still FSP 40:6 n7 (n761) 1994
PIGALLE f (d Dridi, Karim 1994 Fr/Switz)
    Reviews
  Bozza, G. "Pigalle." still C FORUM 34:17 Sep (n337) 1994
PIIL, MORTEN
  Piil, M. "Kosmorama" [Book Review]. il BLIMP n30:46-47 Winter 1994
PILLING, JAYNE
  Pilling, J. The greatest art condensed [Book Review]. still FILM 4:25 n1
    [1995]
PILON, BENOIT
  J'irai come un cheval fou. filmogs il SEQUENCES n175:10-11 Nov/Dec 1994
PILZ, THOMAS
  Hainisch, B. and Pilz, T. Werner Herzogs "Jeder fuer sich und Gott gegen
    alle" - ein Film. il stills BLIMP n30:16-22 Winter 1994
PIMENOFF, MARINA
  Pimenoff, M. Kultainen nuoruus - armoton nuoruus. il PEILI 18:22-23 n3
    1994
  Pimenoff, M. Kuvapinnan syvyysaukot. il still PEILI 17:15-17 n3 1993
  Pimenoff, M. Laulavat lantiot ja suositut salat. il still PEILI 17:31-33
    n4 1993
PINCHBECK, DANIEL
  Pinchbeck, D. From artist to auteur. port ESQUIRE 123:17 Jan 1995
PIN-DOWN GIRL f (d Derteno, Robert C. 1950 USA)
    Reviews
  Hogan, D. J. "Pin Down Girl." il F FAX n48:18+ [2p] Jan/Feb 1995
PINELLI, TULLIO
  Fellini, F. and Pinelli, T. "Utazas Tulunba." il F VILAG 38:44-51 n2 1995
PINTILIE, LUCIAN See also ETE INOUBLIABLE, UN
  Faber, A. Mozarttol keletre. il interv still F VILAG 38:50-52 n4 1995
PIONEERS OF X-RAY TECHNOLOGY f (d Fleming, Ann Marie 1991 Can)
  Hoolboom, M. The queen of disaster. stills MILLENNIUM n26:26-32 Fall 1992
PIOPPO, MARIACHIARA For film reviews see author under the following titles:
  OKNO V PARIZH
  Pioppo, M. Rimini: cronache e storie di mondi separati. stills C FORUM
    34:13-14 Oct (n338) 1994
Piovani, Nicola See MORRICONE, ENNIO
PIPOLO, TONY
  Pipolo, T. Making "Antigone/Rites of Passion." interv stills MILLENNIUM
    n26:34-55 Fall 1992
PIRANDELLO, LUIGI
  Ferrante, E. Ad Agrigento si e tenuto il trentunesimo Convegno
    Internazionale sul linguaggio di Pirandello. C SUD 33:30 Jul/Aug/Sep (n113)
    1994
PIROLINI, ALESSANDRO
  Pirolini, A. Delitti e segreti di Stephen Soderbergh. C SUD 33:29
    Jul/Aug/Sep (n113) 1994

PISTE DU TELEGRAPHE, LA f (d Kermadec, Liliane de 1994 Fr)
    Reviews
  Aude, F. "La piste du telegraphe." POSITIF n408:58-59 Feb 1995
  Nesselson, L. "The Telegraph Route" ("La piste du telegraphe"). credits
    VARIETY 357:75 Jan 2/8 1995
PITRA, PUTRA AUR DHARAMYUDDHA f (d Patwardhan, Anand 1995 India)
    Reviews
  Stratton, D. "Father, Son and Holy War" ("Pitra, putra aur dharamyuddha").
    credits VARIETY 358:80 Feb 20/26 1995
  Waugh, T. "Father Son and Holy War." still C ACTION n36:34-36 1995
PITT, BRAD
  Mundy, C. Slippin' around on the road with Brad Pitt. il ports stills
    ROLLING STONE n696:92-97+ [7p] Dec 1 1994
  Schneller, J. Brad attitude. il VANITY FAIR 58:70-79+ [12p] Feb 1995
PIWNICA POD BARANAMI (Cracow, Poland)
  Sendecka, M. Szalona noc w Krakowie. REZYSER n18:7 1993
PIZZELLO, CHRIS
  Fisher, B. and Pizzello, C. "In the Line of Fire": an action film for
    existentialists. il stills AMCIN 74:36-40+ [7p] Sep 1993
  Pizzello, C. Digital time machine transports Clint to Dealey Plaza. AMCIN
    74:44+ [2p] Sep 1993
PIZZELLO, STEPHEN
  Pizzello, S. "Interview With the Vampire" taps new vein. il stills AMCIN
    76:43-52 Jan 1995
  Pizzello, S. "Legends of the Fall" exploits scenic locale. il stills AMCIN
    76:30-38 Mar 1995
PLACIDO, MICHELE See also EROE BORGHESE, UN
PLAGUE, THE f (d Puenzo, Luis 1992 Fr/Gt Br/Arg)
    Reviews
  Forgach, A. Kamu. credits still F VILAG 38:54-55 n2 1995
PLASTO, BOB See also MY COUNTRY
PLATER, EDWARD M.V.
  Plater, E. M.V. Helmut Kaeutner's film adaptation of "Des Teufels General."
    bibliog LIT/FQ 22:253-264 n4 1994
PLATES f (d Goldberg, Gary 1990 USA)
  Goldberg, G. "Plates." il scenario still MILLENNIUM n25:14-17 Summer 1991
PLATT, POLLY
  Lowry, B. TV producer Carsey-Werner launches film unit. VARIETY 358:11 Feb
    13/19 1995
PLATTNER, PATRICIA See also LIVRE DE CRISTAL, LE
PLAZEWSKI, JERZY For film reviews see author under the following titles: HERO;
  PETITE APOCALYPSE, LA; SHADOWS AND FOG
  Hendrykowska, M. Bole glowy Ludwika Lumiere [Book Review]. il KINO
    27:34-36 Jun 1993
  Plazewski, J. Joseph Leo Mankiewicz. biog il obit KINO 27:37 May 1993
  Plazewski, J. Kryzys w branzy biografow. stills KINO 27:28-29 Jun 1993
  Plazewski, J. Wspolprodukcje hydra, czy szansa? il interv ports KINO
    27:6-9 Jun 1993
PLEASENCE, DONALD
  Elley, D. Donald Pleasence. obit VARIETY 358:85 Feb 6/12 1995
  Lentz, H., III. Obituaries. biogs filmogs obits ports CLASSIC n237:57-59
    Mar 1995
  Milestones. obit still TIME 145:23 Feb 13 1995
PLENIZIO, GIANFRANCO
  Comuzio, E. "Il Faust" di Murnau con la musica di Gianfranco Plenizio -
    registrazione live del reparto fonico dell'istituto Cine TV "Roberto
    Rossellini." C FORUM 34:96 Nov (n339) 1994
Po Dezju See BEFORE THE RAIN
POCAHONTAS f (d Gabriel, Mike/Goldberg, Eric 1995 USA)
    Premieres
  Evans, G. "Pocahontas" bows in the park. VARIETY 358:21 Feb 6/12 1995
PODALYDES, BRUNO See also VOILA
PODESWA, JEREMY See also ECLIPSE
POELVOORDE, BENOIT See also C'EST ARRIVE PRES DE CHEZ VOUS
Poe's Tales of Terror See TALES OF TERROR
POETRY
  Axelsson, S. I filmfralsta poeters sallskap [Book Review]. il CHAPLIN
    36:62 n6 (n255) 1994/95
  Ostaijen, P. van. Asta Nielsen. ports F BUL 36:60 n6 (n197) 1994
POGGI, EVELINA For film reviews see author under the following titles:
  OCCHIOPINOCCHIO; PICCOLO GRANDE AMORE
  Poggi, E. Il critico al festival ovvero lo spettatore indiscreto. intervs
    SEGNO n71:19-33 Jan/Feb 1995
POINT OF NO RETURN f (d Badham, John 1993 USA)
    Reviews
  Vahtera, H. Naistappajan rakkaudet. credits still PEILI 17:29 n3 1993
POINT OF VIEW
    France
  Odin, R. Le documentaire interieur. Travail du JE et mise en phase dans
    "Lettres d'amour en Somalie." bibliog still CINEMAS 4:82-100 n2 1994
POIRE, JEAN-MARIE See also VISITEURS, LES
  Calderale, M. Filmografie. biogs filmogs il SEGNO n71:40 Jan/Feb 1995
POIRET, JEAN See also ZEBRE, LE
  "Jak uwiesc wlasna zone." credits filmog FSP 40:7 n3 (n757) 1994
POIRIER, MANUEL See also ...A LA CAMPAGNE
POLAN, DANA
  Ciment, M. BFI film classics [Book Reviews]. stills POSITIF n408:75-77 Feb
    1995
  Polan, D. Reflections in a male eye: John Huston and the American
    experience. Edited by Gaylyn Studlar and David Desser [Book Review]. F
    CRITICISM 19:103-108 n2 1994/95
Poland See as a subheading under individual subject headings
POLANSKI, ROMAN See also DEATH AND THE MAIDEN; LUNES DE FIEL; MACBETH;
  ROSEMARY'S BABY
  Carroll, T. From "Knife" to "Death" with Roman Polanski. filmog il interv
    DGA NEWS 19:38-39+ [5p] n6 1994/95
  Heilpern, J. Roman's tortured holiday. il VANITY FAIR 58:88-91+ [5p] Jan
    1995
  Thompson, D. I make films for adults. biog filmog interv port stills S&S
    5:6-11 Apr 1995

POLAR PRODUCTIONS
Dawtrey, A. Chrysalis deal leads to U.K. pic ventures. VARIETY 358:14 Mar 13/19 1995
POLEDOURIS, BASIL
Dursin, A. and others. Four by Basil Poledouris. F SCORE MONTHLY n36/37:32 Aug/Sep 1993
POLIAKOFF, STEPHEN See also CENTURY
POLICE ACADEMY: MISSION TO MOSCOW f (d Metter, Alan 1994 USA)
Location Production
Hill, C. Lights, camera, revolution! il DGA NEWS 19:17+ [2p] n2 1994
POLITICAL ANALYSIS See also MARXIST ANALYSIS; POSTCOLONIAL ANALYSIS
Brazil
Spectatorship
Sippl, D. Terrorist acts and "legitimate" torture in Brazil: "How Nice to See You Alive." bibliog il stills DISCOURSE n17.1:77-92 Fall 1994
Canada
Berry, C. "Ce qui meritait le plus d'etre puni etait son penis": postsocialisme, distopie et la mort du heros. bibliog glos still CINEMAS 3:38-59 n2/3 1993
Great Britain
Rap Music
Grundmann, R. Black nationhood and the rest in the West. interv port CINEASTE 21:28-31 n1/2 1995
Italy
Porton, R. and Ellickson, L. Comedy, communism, and pastry: an interview with Nanni Moretti. interv port stills CINEASTE 21:11-15 n1/2 1995
United States
Falkowska, J. "The political" in the films of Andrzej Wajda and Krzysztof Kieslowski. CJ 34:37-50 n2 1995
Linville, S.E. "Europa, Europa": a test case for German national cinema. stills WIDE ANGLE 16:38-51 n3 1995
Morlan, D.B. Slapstick contributions to WWII propaganda: The Three Stooges and Abbott and Costello. bibliog STUDIES POP CULT 17:29-43 n1 1994
Documentary Film
Orvell, M. Documentary film and the power of interrogation. il stills FQ 48:10-18 n2 1994/95
Export Market
Swann, P. International conspiracy in and around "The Iron Curtain." VEL LT TRAP n35:52-60 Spring 1995
POLITICAL ASPECTS
Japan
Documentary Film
Makino, M. and Gerow, A.A. Prokino. biogs il interv port stills DOC BOX 5:6-14 1994
Union of Soviet Socialist Republics
Christie, I. Really the most important art. stills F COM 31:41-44 Mar/Apr 1995
United States
Public Attitudes
Vowe, K.W. Political Correctness und Hollywood. still MEDIEN 38:356-359 n6 1994
POLITICAL CONTEXT
France
History
Cantrill, A. French national cinema. By Susan Hayward [Book Review]. CANTRILL'S FMNTS n73/74:42-43 May 1994
Germany (Federal Republic, 1949-1990)
History
Plater, E. M.V. Helmut Kaeutner's film adaptation of "Des Teufels General." bibliog LIT/FQ 22:253-264 n4 1994
United States
Hardesty, M. Too PC or not too PC? DGA NEWS 19:28+ [5p] n6 1994/95
POLITICAL FILM
Poland
Falkowska, J. "The political" in the films of Andrzej Wajda and Krzysztof Kieslowski. CJ 34:37-50 n2 1995
POLITICAL THEMES
United States
Piccardi, A. Qualche nota su un american filmaker. stills C FORUM 34:44-48 Oct (n338) 1994
POLITICS AND GOVERNMENT See also ANTI-COMMUNISM; CENSORSHIP; COLONIALISM; COMMUNISM; FILM COMMISSIONS; GOVERNMENT CONTROL; GOVERNMENT REGULATION; GOVERNMENT SUPPORT; LAWS AND LEGISLATION; PROPAGANDA FILM; RATING SYSTEMS; TAXES; WAR
Cherchi Usai, P. La mediocrita al potere. il still SEGNO n72:33-34 Mar/Apr 1995
Egypt
Warg, P. Fiery sermons-on-tape imperil Arab entertainers. VARIETY 357:57 Jan 2/8 1995
Poland
Prendowska, K. Artist as politician: an interview with Polish director Andrzej Wajda. interv port LIT/FQ 22:246-252 n4 1994
Sobolewski, T. Dziennik serio. il KINO 27:7-9 Jul 1993
United States
Sutton, G. Stript-o-caucus neA. AFTERIMAGE 22:3 Jan 1995
Export Market
Wharton, D. Gingrich vows to promote U.S. film interests. port VARIETY 358:20 Mar 20/26 1995
POLIZIOTTI f (d Base, Giulio 1995 It/Fr)
Reviews
Lombardi, M. "Poliziotti." credits il FILM (ITALY) 3:13-14 n13 1995
Young, D. "Policemen" ("Poliziotti"). credits VARIETY 358:78 Feb 20/26 1995
POLIZZI, ROSALIA See also ANNI RIBELLI
POLLOCK, NEIL
Pollock, N. McKernan, Luke and Terris, Olwen, eds. Walking shadows: Shakespeare in the National Film and Television Archive [Book Review]. MEDIA INFO AUSTRALIA n75:168 Feb 1995

POLLS AND SURVEYS See also AWARDS; COMMENDATIONS
Archives
Exhibition
Survey and other activities of the Commission for Programming and Access. stat J F PRES n49:11-14 Oct 1994
United States
Moore, D.S. Producers pick all-time faves. ports stills VARIETY 357:63+ [2p] Jan 9/15 1995
Boxoffice
Blue ribbon awards. BOXOFFICE 131:34-35 Apr 1995
POLO, EDDIE
Katchmer, G. Remembering the great silents. biogs filmogs port CLASSIC n236:50-53 Feb 1995
POLONI, PAOLO See also ASMARA
POLONSKY, ABRAHAM See also TELL THEM WILLIE BOY IS HERE
POLSKI INSTYTUT KULTURALNY (Berlin, Germany)
Sobolewski, T. Zycie na moscie. interv port KINO 27:20-21+ [3p] Jun 1993
POLTERGEIST II: THE OTHER SIDE f (d Gibson, Brian 1986 USA)
Sound Track Reviews
Shapiro, L. "Poltergeist II." F SCORE MONTHLY n38:12 Oct 1993
POMPEII IN FILM
Livio, J. Gli ultimi giorni di Pompei. A cura di Riccardo Redi e Pier Luigi Raffaelli [Book Review]. GRIFFITHIANA n51/52:267 Oct 1994
POMPUCCI, LEONE See also CAMERIERI
Filmografie. biogs filmogs SEGNO n72:40 Mar/Apr 1995
PONCE, VICENTE
Ponce, V. Pere Portabella... y algunas marcas de su soledad filmica. il stills NOSFERATU n9:60-67 Jun 1992
Ponce, V. "Puente de Varsovia." credits il port stills NOSFERATU n9:103-105 Jun 1992
POND, STEVE
Pond, S. Paltry pleasures. il MOVIELINE 6:32 Apr 1995
Pond, S. Putting it together. il PREM 8:109+ [24p] Apr 1995
Pond, S. The Irish invasion. il MOVIELINE 6:30 Mar 1995
PONT DE VARSOVIA f (d Portabella, Pere 1990 Sp)
Ponce, V. "Puente de Varsovia." credits il port stills NOSFERATU n9:103-105 Jun 1992
PONTECORVO, GILLO
La terza Mostra "firmata Pontecorvo" punta sempre piu sull'equilibrio tra cinema di qualita e grandi eventi. port C SUD 33:6 Jul/Aug/Sep (n113) 1994
POOL, LEA See also MOUVEMENTS DU DESIR
POPE, ANGELA See also CAPTIVES
POPPER, KARL
Picchi, M. "Critica della ragion pura" e "puttana santa." C NUOVO 43:53-54 Nov/Dec (n352) 1994
POPULAR CULTURE See also AUDIENCE; PUBLIC ATTITUDES
Hirsch, T. Ha Bolyai, akkor nem-euklideszi [Book Review]. il still F VILAG 38:42-44 n1 1995
Varadi, J. and Kovacs, A.B. A meseauto eselye. interv still F VILAG 38:45-47 n1 1995
Brazil
Stam, R. Sao Nelson. stills F COM 31:82-86+ [6p] Jan/Feb 1995
Canada
Cultural Context
Knight, G. The Beaver bites back? American popular culture in Canada. Edited by David H. Flaherty & Frank E. Manning [Book Review]. CAN J COM 19:560-561 n3/4 1994
United States
Queer Theory Analysis
Bronski, M. Queer looks: perspectves on lesbian and gay film and video. Edited by Martha Gever, John Greyson and Pratibha Parmar [Book Reviews]. still CINEASTE 21:90-92 n1/2 1995
PORNOGRAPHY AND OBSCENITY See also CENSORSHIP; EXPLOITATION FILM; MORALITY
namaste, k. Pornography (communication concepts 5). By Daniel Linz & Neil Malamuth [Book Reviews]. CAN J COM 20:120-122 n1 1995
Canada
McIntosh, D. Porn, porosity and promiscuity. stills C ACTION n36:20-23 1995
Finland
Gender Roles
Nikunen, K. Lukottomat siveysvyot. il PEILI 18:6-7 n4 1994
United States
De Grazia, E. Sex de jure [Book Reviews]. NATION 260:242-249 Feb 20 1995
Effects of Film. Audience Research
Allen, M. and others. Exposure to pornography and acceptance of rape myths. bibliog stat tables J COMM 45:5-26 n1 1995
Gunther, A.C. Overrating the X-rating: the third-person perception and support for censorship of pornography. bibliog stat tables J COMM 45:27-38 n1 1995
Feminism
Kershaw, S. Against pornophobia. port NEW YORK 28:20+ [2p] Jan 16 1995
Feminist Analysis
Heffernan, K. A social poetics of pornography [Book Review]. Q REV F & VIDEO 15:77-83 n3 1994
Political Aspects
Sunstein, C.R. Porn on the Fourth of July [Book Review]. NEW REPUB 212:42-45 Jan 9/16 1995
PORTABELLA, PERE See also NOCTURNO 29; PONT DE VARSOVIA
Angulo, J. and others. Entrevista: Garay, Guerin, Jorda y Portabella. il interv stills NOSFERATU n9:68-87 Jun 1992
Ponce, V. Pere Portabella... y algunas marcas de su soledad filmica. il stills NOSFERATU n9:60-67 Jun 1992
PORTAMI VIA f (d Tavarelli, Gianluca Maria 1994 It)
Reviews
Fittante, A. "Portami via." credits still SEGNO n71:43-44 Jan/Feb 1995
Gandini, L. "Portami via." still C FORUM 34:26 Sep (n337) 1994
PORTER, BETH For film reviews see author under the following titles: CAMILLA
Porter, B. (Double 0) 007 invades aircraft hangar as "GoldenEye" action rolls. port FJ 98:24+ [2p] Mar 1995
Porter, B. How "The Englishman" dazzled a Welsh village. il FJ 98:20+ [2p]

Mar 1995
Porter, B. Wide-ranging London festival has its eye on box office. FJ 98:18 Jan/Feb 1995

PORTILLO, LOURDES See also DIABLO NUNCA DUERME, EL
Thompson, A. "The Devil Never Sleeps." il INDEP 18:20-22 Apr 1995

PORTMAN ENTERTAINMENT
Woods, M. Co-prods high on the Aussie agenda. VARIETY 358:62 Feb 27/Mar 5 1995

PORTMAN, NATALIE
Sischy, I. Natalie: a star/friend is born. il interv ports INTERV 25:112-113+ [3p] Feb 1995

PORTOGALLO, PAESE TRANQUILLO f (d Jorda, Joaquin 1969 Sp)
Jorda, J. Numax presenta... y otras cosas. still NOSFERATU n9:56-59 Jun 1992

PORTON, RICHARD For film reviews see author under the following titles: DEATH AND THE MAIDEN
Porton, R. Review of David James: allegories of cinema [Book Review]. il MILLENNIUM n25:114-120 Summer 1991
Porton, R. and Ellickson, L. Comedy, communism, and pastry: an interview with Nanni Moretti. interv port stills CINEASTE 21:11-15 n1/2 1995

Portugal See CINEMATECA PORTUGUESA (Lisbon, Portugal)

PORTUGUES, CATHERINE
Gervai, A. Marta Meszaros - fighting collective amnesia [Book Review]. il NEW HUNGARIAN Q 34:155-158 n132 1993

POSEY, PARKER
Fuller, G. Parker's party. ports INTERV 25:79-81 Feb 1995
Klam, J. Parker Posey can't lose. port PREM 8:37 Mar 1995

POSSE f (d Van Peebles, Mario 1993 USA)
Dowell, P. The mythology of the western: Hollywood perspectives on race and gender in the nineties. stills CINEASTE 21:6-10 n1/2 1995

POST, TED
Post, T. Age doesn't matter, unless you're cheese. port DGA NEWS 19:68 n6 1994/95

POSTCARDS FROM AMERICA f (d McLean, Steve 1994 USA/Gt Br)
Reviews
Burston, P. "Postcards From America." credits S&S 5:51-52 Apr 1995

POSTCOLONIAL ANALYSIS
Australia
Wark, M. Berry, Chris. A bit on the side: East-West topographies of desire [Book Review]. MEDIA INFO AUSTRALIA n75:157 Feb 1995
Canada
National Consciousness
Kaye, J. "Perfectly Normal," eh?: gender transformation and national identity in Canada. CAN J F STUD 3:63-80 n2 1994
France
Faulkner, C. Affective identities: French national cinema and the 1930s. CAN J F STUD 3:3-23 n2 1994
Great Britain
Sharma, S. Citizens of the empire: revisionist history and the social imaginary in "Gandhi." bibliog VEL LT TRAP n35:61-68 Spring 1995
India
Ganguly, S. No moksha: Arcadia lost in Satyajit Ray's "Days and Nights in the Forest." bibliog still F CRITICISM 19:75-85 n2 1994/95
Longfellow, B. "The Bandit Queen." stills C ACTION n36:10-16 1995
Senegal
Semiotic Analysis
Mowitt, J. Sembene Ousmane's "Xala": postcoloniality and foreign film languages. stills CAM OBS n31:72-95 Jan/May 1993

POSTERS
History
Codelli, L. L'invitation au cinematographe: les affiches des origines, 1895-1914. A cura di Jean-Louis Capitaine [Book Review]. GRIFFITHIANA n51/52:262 Oct 1994
United States
Auctions
Vintage items sold at auction. stat CLASSIC n237:12 Mar 1995

POSTINO, IL f (d Radford, Michael 1994 It/Fr/Belg)
Liberti, F. Michael Radford: Troisi, il cinema e l'Italia di oggi. credits interv stills C FORUM 34:46-50 Sep (n337) 1994
Sound Track Reviews
Deutsch, D.C. "Anni rebelli"; "Il postino." SCN 14:22 Mar 1995
Reviews
Adagio, C. "Il postino." credits still C NUOVO 43:48-50 Nov/Dec (n352) 1994
Desio, G. "Il postino." credits FILM (ITALY) 3:14-15 n13 1995

Postman, The See POSTINO, IL

POSTMODERNISM
Hanet, K. Orr, John. Cinema and modernity [Book Review]. MEDIA INFO AUSTRALIA n75:168 Feb 1995
McKinley, A. Anne Friedberg. Window shopping: cinema and the postmodern [Book Review]. ARACHNE 1:270-274 n2 1994
Sobolewski, T. Listy: odpowiedz Andrzejowi Wernerowi. KINO 27:40 May 1993
Werner, A. Listy: szanowny panie redaktorze! KINO 27:40 May 1993
Italy
Bruno, M.W. Il punto di non ritorno. stills SEGNO n63:19-20 Sep/Oct 1993
United States
Bruno, M.W. Brian De Hitchcock. port stills SEGNO n63:9-13 Sep/Oct 1993
Animation
Lindvall, T. and Melton, M. Toward a postmodern animated discourse: Bakhtin, intertextuality and the cartoon carnival. il stills ANIMATION J 3:44-63 n1 1994

POST-PRODUCTION
United States
Sound
Weis, E. Sync tanks. il CINEASTE 21:56-61 n1/2 1995

POST-PRODUCTION EQUIPMENT
New Zealand
Digital
Digipost turns up the heat. ONFILM [12]:13 n2 1995

Potemkin See BRONENOSETS POTEMKIN

POTTER, MAXIMILLIAN
Potter, M. Burn victim. il PREM 8:38 Apr 1995

POWELL, ELEANOR
The Slide area film book notes [Book Reviews]. CLASSIC n237:42-44+ [4p] Mar 1995

POWELL, MICHAEL See also BATTLE OF THE RIVER PLATE, THE; CANTERBURY TALE, A; ILL MET BY MOONLIGHT; PEEPING TOM; TALES OF HOFFMAN, THE
Combs, R. "Battle of the River Plate." il stills F COM 31:20-22+ [4p] Mar/Apr 1995
Jameson, R.T. Written, produced and directed by Michael Powell and Emeric Pressburger. il stills F COM 31:18-19 Mar/Apr 1995
Retrospectives
Stein, E. Sure shots. still VILLAGE VOICE 40:53-54 Mar 21 1995

POYRAZ, SEMA
Donmez Colin, G. Sema Poyraz: contending with an alien land. il CINEMAYA n25/26:60-61 Autumn/Winter 1994/95

POZZI, MOANA
Picchi, M. "Critica della ragion pura" e "puttana santa." C NUOVO 43:53-54 Nov/Dec (n352) 1994

PRAESIDENTEN f (President, The d Dreyer, Carl Theodor 1919 Denmk)
Aldarondo, R. "El presidente." credits stills NOSFERATU n5:44-45 Jan 1991

PRASAD, UDAYAN
Prasad, U. Woman on the edge. stills S&S 5:14-17 Feb 1995

PRASTANKEN f (d Dreyer, Carl Theodor 1920 Swed)
Miguez, M. "La mujer del parroco." credits stills NOSFERATU n5:48-49 Jan 1991

PRAYEZ, BENEDICTE
Prayez, B. "Chasse-croise." bibliog credits stills GRAND ANGLE n177:11-12 Dec 1994
Prayez, B. "Descente a paradise." credits stills GRAND ANGLE n178:5-6 Jan 1995
Prayez, B. "Entretien avec un vampire." credits stills GRAND ANGLE n177:13-14 Dec 1994
Prayez, B. "Les complices." bibliog credits stills GRAND ANGLE n176:5-6 Nov 1994
Prayez, B. "Pour l'amour d'une femme." bibliog credits stills GRAND ANGLE n176:19-20 Nov 1994
Prayez, B. "Sleep With Me." bibliog credits stills GRAND ANGLE n178:27-28 Jan 1995
Prayez, B. "Vivre!" bibliog credits still GRAND ANGLE n177:41-42 Dec 1994

PRECHT, ANDREW
Obituaries. obits VARIETY 358:58-59 Mar 20/26 1995

PREDAL, RENE
Fortin, E. Predal, Rene. Le cinema francais depuis 1945 [Book Review]. CINEMAS 4:151-155 n1 1993
Histoire du cinema. Abrege pedagogique par Rene Predal [Book Review]. il GRAND ANGLE n176:39-40 Nov 1994

PRENDOWSKA, KRYSTYNA
Prendowska, K. Artist as politician: an interview with Polish director Andrzej Wajda. interv port LIT/FQ 22:246-252 n4 1994

PRESERVATION See also RESTORATION
Great Britain
Slide, A. The Slide area film book notes [Book Reviews]. CLASSIC n236:47-49 Feb 1995
United States
Kalish, K. Wake up and smell the vinegar. il DGA NEWS 20:24+ [6p] n1 1995
Protecting film's heritage. AMCIN 76:96 Jan 1995
Stebinger, J. Preservation '95. CLASSIC n236:5 Feb 1995
Economic Aspects
Kalish, K. Preserving the funds that preserve the films. DGA NEWS 20:36-37 n1 1995
Film Lists
The NFPB 150. DGA NEWS 20:34 n1 1995
Uruguay
A committee for film protection has been created in Uruguay. J F PRES n49:29-30 Oct 1994

President, The See PRAESIDENTEN

PRESLE, MICHELINE
Micheline Presle: l'arriere-memoire. Par Serge Toubiana [Book Review]. il GRAND ANGLE n176:39 Nov 1994

PRESLEY, ELVIS
Baumgold, J. Midnight in the garden of good and Elvis. il ports ESQUIRE 123:92-102 Mar 1995
The King and I. il port INTERV 25:36-37 Jan 1995

Press agents See AGENTS

PRESSBURGER, EMERIC See also CANTERBURY TALE, A; ILL MET BY MOONLIGHT; TALES OF HOFFMAN, THE
Combs, R. "Battle of the River Plate." il stills F COM 31:20-22+ [4p] Mar/Apr 1995
Jameson, R.T. Written, produced and directed by Michael Powell and Emeric Pressburger. il stills F COM 31:18-19 Mar/Apr 1995
Retrospectives
Stein, E. Sure shots. still VILLAGE VOICE 40:53-54 Mar 21 1995

PRESTAZIONE STRAORDINARIA f (d Rubini, Sergio 1994 It)
Reviews
De Marinis, G. "Prestazione straordinaria." credits still C FORUM 34:86 Nov (n339) 1994
Menarini, R. "Prestazione straordinaria." credits stills SEGNO n71:55 Jan/Feb 1995

PRETTY WOMAN f (d Marshall, Garry 1990 USA)
Effects of Film
Pimenoff, M. Laulavat lantiot ja suositut salat. il still PEILI 17:31-33 n4 1993

PREVERT, JACQUES
Berthome, J.-P. Voir un peu d'herbe avant de mourir... il POSITIF n408:84-89 Feb 1995

PREZIOSI, ADELINA For film reviews see author under the following titles: ONCE WERE WARRIORS; SERIAL MOM; UTOMLENNYE SOLNTSEM
Preziosi, A. Americani, oggi. stills SEGNO n71:70 Jan/Feb 1995
Preziosi, A. Cerimonie segrete. stills SEGNO n71:61-64 Jan/Feb 1995

Preziosi, A. Finestre sul mondo. stills SEGNO n71:67-69 Jan/Feb 1995
Preziosi, A. Soviet melodies. il SEGNO n71:68-69 Jan/Feb 1995
PRICE, DAVID F. See also (DOCTOR) DR. JEKYLL & MS. HYDE
Scapperotti, D. "Dr. Jekyll & Ms. Hyde." il stills C FANTAS 26:10-11 n3 1995
PRICE, MICHAEL H.
Turner, G.E. and Price, M.H. Behind "The Mask of Fu Manchu." credits il stills AMCIN 76:68-74 Jan 1995
PRICE, STEPHEN
Zinnemann, F. Letter from Fred Zinnemann. F CRITICISM 19:86-88 n2 1994/95
PRICE, VINCENT
Dodsfall. biogs obits ports F&K n7:37 1993
PRIEST f (d Bird, Antonia 1994 Gt Br)
Shacter, S. Sundance: Antonia Bird & Danny Boyle. intervs port stills BOMB n51:36-41 Spring 1995
    Exhibition
Evans, G. Miramax shifts "Priest's" date. VARIETY 358:25-26 Mar 27/Apr 2 1995
    Reviews
Ansen, D. A priest at war with himself. still NEWSWK 125:72 Mar 27 1995
Greeen, R. "Priest." BOXOFFICE 131:bet p125 and 144 [pR26] Apr 1995
Hoberman, J. Cardinal sins. still VILLAGE VOICE 40:55 Mar 28 1995
Lane, A. The sins of the fathers. il NEW YORKER 71:107-109 Mar 27 1995
PRIEUR, JEROME
Masson, A. Le spectateur nocturne. Les ecrivains au cinema. Par Jerome Prieur [Book Review]. POSITIF n408:79 Feb 1995
PRINCE, STEPHEN
Prince, S. Stephen Prince replies. F CRITICISM 19:89 n2 1994/95
PRINCESS CARABOO f (d Austin, Michael 1994 USA)
    Cultural Context
Russett, M. The "Caraboo" hoax: romantic woman as mirror and mirage. bibliog il DISCOURSE n17.2:26-47 Winter 1994/95
    Reviews
Kemp, P. "Princess Caraboo." credits still S&S 5:53 Jan 1995
Larue, J. "Princess Caraboo." still SEQUENCES n174:46 Sep/Oct 1994
PRINCIPIO Y FIN f (d Ripstein, Arturo 1994 Mex)
Lopez Aranda, S. Filmar el tiempo: Arturo Ripstein y Paz Alicia Garciadiego: segundo parte. il interv stills DICINE n59:9-13 Nov/Dec 1994
PRIVAT MAGYARORSZAG f (Private Hungary d Forgacs, Peter 1990 Hungary)
A tizenotezredik pillanat. interv stills F VILAG 38:18-23 n1 1995
Bori, E. Itt lapatol a kommunista part! still F VILAG 38:24-25 n1 1995
Private Hungary See PRIVAT MAGYARORSZAG
Private-eye film See DETECTIVE FILM
PRIVILEGE f (d Rainer, Yvonne 1990 USA)
Rainer, Y. Script pages and production notes for "Privilege" (1990). il scenario MILLENNIUM n25:50-55 Summer 1991
Prix Albert-Tessier See AWARDS - Canada - Quebec. Prix Albert-Tessier
Prix du Cinema Europeen See AWARDS - Europe - European Film Academy
Prizes See AWARDS
PRODUCERS See also names of producers
    United States
        Contracts
Cox, D. and Busch, A.M. Producers draw battle lines over credit order. ports VARIETY 358:28+ [2p] Feb 20/26 1995
        Credit Disputes
Cox, D. and Busch, A.M. Producers piqued. VARIETY 358:8-9 Feb 27/Mar 5 1995
        Polls and Surveys
Moore, O.S. Producers pick all-time faves. ports stills VARIETY 357:63+ [2p] Jan 9/15 1995
PRODUCERS, THE f (d Brooks, Mel 1967 USA)
Lydon, P. The goons and a bomb on Broadway. il S&S 5:39 Feb 1995
PRODUCING
    Poland
Sendecka, M. Szkolenie w Burkina Faso. interv REZYSER n19:3-5 1993
    United States
Bach, S. "Legend to leper" [Book Review]. port F COM 31:82-83+ [3p] Mar/Apr 1995
Ernrooth, A. Filmproducenter gor det tillbakalutade [Book Review]. still CHAPLIN 36:60 n6 (n255) 1994/95
Lilley, J. How to make a monster movie. il interv stills SCARLET STREET n17:65-71+ [8p] Winter 1995
Product licensing See MERCHANDISING TIE-INS
Product placement See MERCHANDISING TIE-INS
PRODUCTION [Prior to V16, 1988 use also FILMMAKING] See also LOCATION PRODUCTION; POST-PRODUCTION
    Techniques
Frey, M. Film production [Book Review]. F KUNST n144:67-68 1994
    China (Republic, since 1949)
Comer, B. "Eat Drink Man Woman": a feast for the eyes. il still AMCIN 76:62-67 Jan 1995
    New Zealand
        History
Mune, I. From handmade cameras to hand-morphed creatures. il stat ONFILM 11:13 n11 1994/95
    Union of Soviet Socialist Republics
Tsymbal, E. Zonen. il stills CHAPLIN 36:26-30 n6 (n255) 1994/95
    United States
Bart, P. H'wood's slow shooters. il VARIETY 358:9+ [2p] Feb 13/19 1995
        History
Catsos, G. J.M. Disney's folly! il interv stills F FAX n48:49-53 Jan/Feb 1995
Galbraith, S., IV. Long long ago before "Jurassic Park." il stills F FAX n48:32-36 Jan/Feb 1995
MacQueen, S. (Forty-three) '43 "Phantom" found new formula for classic tale. credits il stills AMCIN 74:80-85 Sep 1993
Palumbo, R. and Furmanek, B. This island mirth. il stills F FAX n48:56-63 Jan/Feb 1995
Turner, G.E. and Price, M.H. Behind "The Mask of Fu Manchu." credits il stills AMCIN 76:68-74 Jan 1995

    Wide Screen
Sylvester, S. "Titanica" takes Imax into new waters. il stills AMCIN 76:32-34+ [5p] Jan 1995
PRODUCTION ASSISTANTS See also names of production assistants
    United States
Kuhn, E. Production assistants. il table PREM 8:37 Feb 1995
PRODUCTION DESIGN AND DESIGNERS See also names of production designers; SOUND DESIGN AND DESIGNERS
    Switzerland
Baur, P.J. Ich tue, also bin ich! il C(SWITZ) 40:97-104 1994
    United States
Midding, G. Richard Sylbert - production design als metapher. C(SWITZ) 40:75-86 1994
Products See EQUIPMENT
PROFESSIONAL EDUCATION See also STUDY AND TEACHING
    New Zealand
May, S. Blue Sky breaks through. ONFILM 11:1+ [2p] n11 1994/95
    Poland
        Directories
Kaplinska, A. Edukacja filmowa. REZYSER n19:6 1993
PROFESSIONAL, THE f (d Besson, Luc 1994 Fr)
Sischy, I. Natalie: a star/friend is born. il interv ports INTERV 25:112-113+ [3p] Feb 1995
    Reviews
Avondola, C. "Leon." credits still SEGNO n72:54-55 Mar/Apr 1995
Caron, A. "The Professional." credits still SEQUENCES n175:38-39 Nov/Dec 1994
Horguelin, T. "Leon." still 24 IMAGES n75:77 Dec/Jan 1994/95
Lipman, A. "Leon." credits S&S 5:47-48 Feb 1995
Meyers, R. The crime screen. port stills ARMCHAIR DET 28:173-174 n2 1995
Travers, P. "The Professional." still ROLLING STONE n694:106 Nov 3 1994
PROFESSIONNELS DE LA CREATION ET DE LA PRODUCTION AUDIOVISUELLES, LES (PRO SPERE, Belgium)
Qui s'occupe (encore) de la politique culturelle audiovisuelle en Communaute francaise? MONITEUR n126:11 Dec 1994
PROGRAMMING
    Ideological Analysis
Schwartzman, K. National cinema in translation: the politics of exhibition culture. il stills WIDE ANGLE 16:66-99 n3 1995
PROJECTORS AND PROJECTION
    United States
        History
Guida, F. Merry Christmas from Charles Dickens... and Thomas Edison. il FIR 45:2-5 Nov/Dec 1994
PROJECTS
    New Zealand
Wakefield, P. Boom year ahead. stat ONFILM [12]:1+ [2p] n1 1995
Prokino See PROLETARIAN FILM LEAGUE OF JAPAN
PROKOFIEV, SERGEI
Merritt, R. Recharging "Alexander Nevsky." il musical scores stills FQ 48:34-47 n2 1994/95
PROKOP, TIM
Prokop, T. CGI effects. il stills C FANTAS 26:50 n3 1995
Prokop, T. Production design. il C FANTAS 26:52-53 n3 1995
Prokop, T. "Stargate." il stills C FANTAS 26:48-49+ [4p] n3 1995
PROLETARIAN FILM LEAGUE OF JAPAN
Makino, M. and Gerow, A.A. Prokino. biogs il interv port stills DOC BOX 5:6-14 1994
Promise, The See VERSPRECHEN, DAS
Promotional film See COMMISSIONED FILM
PROPAGANDA
    World War I, 1914-1918
Thirard, P.L. Il cinematografo al campo - l'arma nuova nel primo conflitto mondiale. Sous la direction de Renzo Renzi [Book Review]. POSITIF n409:73 Mar 1995
    United States
        World War II, 1939-1945
Morlan, D.B. Slapstick contributions to WWII propaganda: The Three Stooges and Abbott and Costello. bibliog STUDIES POP CULT 17:29-43 n1 1994
PROPAGANDA FILM
    United States
        World War II, 1939-1945
Slide, A. The Slide area film book notes [Book Reviews]. CLASSIC n237:42-44+ [4p] Mar 1995
PROPAGANDA FILMS (corporate body)
Weiner, R. Co-founder ankles Propaganda. VARIETY 357:26 Jan 2/8 1995
    Properties, Literary
Fleming, M. Propaganda buys "Sleepers." VARIETY 358:4 Feb 20/26 1995
PROPERTIES [Prior to V17, 1989 use SET DESIGN AND DESIGNERS]
    Theory
Christen, T. Die Praesenz der Dinge und die Absenz der Protagonisten. bibliog C(SWITZ) 40:9-19 1994
    Switzerland
        Theory
Wendt, U. Decor. stills C(SWITZ) 40:20-36 1994
PROPERTIES, LITERARY
    Great Britain
Million dollar brain. S&S 5:3 Apr 1995
    United States
        Copyright
Evans, G. Random act opens can of bookworms. il VARIETY 358:1+ [3p] Mar 6/12 1995
Props See PROPERTIES
PROTAZANOV, IAKOV See also AELITA
PROYAS, ALEX See also CROW, THE
PROZESS, DER f (d Foth, Joerg 1977 E Ger)
Graef, C. Hochschulfilme. il interv F & FERNSEHEN 22:50-53 n6 1994
PRUDENTE, ROSY
Prudente, R. Diario di un vizio. il SEGNO n71:31-33 Jan/Feb 1995
Prudente, R. Le ragazze Gainsborough. stills C NUOVO 43:23-24 Nov/Dec

QUEER THEORY ANALYSIS
(continued)
  Canada
    Nationalism
Brasell, R.B. Queer nationalism and the musical fag bashing of John
  Greyson's "The Making of 'Monsters'." il stills WIDE ANGLE 16:26-36 n3
  1995
  United States
Gomez, G. Homocolonialism: looking for Latinos in "Apartment Zero" and
  "Paris Is Burning." bibliog stills PS 14:117-124 n1/2 1994/95
    Popular Culture
Bronski, M. Queer looks: perspectves on lesbian and gay film and video.
  Edited by Martha Gever, John Greyson and Pratibha Parmar [Book Reviews].
  still CINEASTE 21:90-92 n1/2 1995
QUENEAU, RAYMOND
Benard, J. Un cinema zazique? bibliog still CINEMAS 4:135-154 n3 1994
QUICK AND THE DEAD, THE f (d Raimi, Sam 1995 USA)
Clark, J. Some of Sam. il stills PREM 8:74-78 Mar 1995
    Reviews
Giles, J. and Schoemer, K. Hear me roar. stills NEWSWK 125:72 Feb 20 1995
Hoberman, J. The natives are westless. stills VILLAGE VOICE 40:47 Feb 21
  1995
Kelleher, E. "The Quick and the Dead." credits FJ 98:58-59 Mar 1995
Lane, A. Balkan homecoming. il NEW YORKER 71:109-111 Mar 13 1995
McCarthy, T. "The Quick and the Dead." credits still VARIETY 358:47+ [2p]
  Feb 13/19 1995
O'Neill, S. "The Quick and the Dead." still BOXOFFICE 131:bet p125 and 144
  [pR31] Apr 1995
Travers, P. Sharon and the wild bunch. il stills ROLLING STONE n703:69-70
  Mar 9 1995
QUIET DAYS IN HOLLYWOOD f (d Rusnak, Josef in production 1994- FR Ger)
"Quiet Days in Hollywood." credits il KINO(BRD) n1:10 1995
"Quiet Days in Hollywood." credits il KINO(BRD) n1:10 1995
QUIGLEY, MARTIN S.
Turner, G. The first century of film. By Martin S. Quigley [Book Review].
  AMCIN 76:85-86 Mar 1995
Quince Tree Sun, The See SOL DEL MEMBRILLO, EL
QUIZ SHOW f (d Redford, Robert 1994 USA)
Marc, D. Scandal and the WASP. stills S&S 5:10-13 Feb 1995
    Reviews
De Bernardinis, F. "Quiz Show." credits stills SEGNO n72:58-59+ [3p]
  Mar/Apr 1995
Doherty, T. "Quiz Show." credits still CINEASTE 21:85-87 n1/2 1995
Emiliani, S. "Quiz Show." credits still FILM (ITALY) 3:22-24 n13 1995
Kohn, O. "Quiz Show." credits still POSITIF n408:48-49 Feb 1995
Larue, J. "Quiz Show." credits still SEQUENCES n175:40-41 Nov/Dec 1994
Meyers, R. The crime screen. port stills ARMCHAIR DET 28:173-174 n2 1995
Midding, G. Konsequenzen des Erfolgdrucks. credits still F BUL 37:41+
  [2p] n1 (n198) 1995
Nagy, G. "Kviz Show." credits still F VILAG 38:55 n3 1995
Pawelczak, A. "Quiz Show." FIR 45:56-57 Nov/Dec 1994
Rousseau, Y. "Quiz Show." still 24 IMAGES n75:78 Dec/Jan 1994/95
QUIZZES
    New Zealand
"Onfilm's" annual Christmas quiz. ONFILM 11:28 n11 1994/95
RCA VICTOR LIVING STEREO
Collector's corner. F SCORE MONTHLY n39:5 Nov 1993
RABAGLIA, DENIS See also GROSSESSE NERVEUSE
RABAN, WILLIAM
Raban, W. "London": the background. il VERTIGO (UK) 1:40 n4 1994/95
RACE See also MINORITIES
Cantrill, A. Spectacular bodies: gender, genre and the action cinema. By
  Yvonne Tasker [Book Review]. CANTRILL'S FMNTS n73/74:43 May 1994
    Great Britain
Grundmann, R. Black nationhood and the rest in the West. interv port
  CINEASTE 21:28-31 n1/2 1995
Marks, L.U. Ghosts of stories. stills C ACTION n36:53-62 1995
    United States
Dyer, R. Varldens ljus. bibliog il ports stills F HAFTET 22:13-22 n3 (n87)
  1994
Lucia, C. Progress and misgivings in Mississippi. interv port stills
  CINEASTE 21:43-45 n1/2 1995
      Gangster Film
Winokur, M. Marginal marginalia: the African-American voice in the nouvelle
  gangster film. stills VEL LT TRAP n35:19-32 Spring 1995
      Psychoanalytic Analysis
kydd, E. Guess who else is coming to dinner: racial/sexual hysteria in
  "Candyman." stills C ACTION n36:63-72 1995
      Western Film
Dowell, P. The mythology of the western: Hollywood perspectives on race and
  gender in the nineties. stills CINEASTE 21:6-10 n1/2 1995
RACINE, CLAUDE
Racine, C. and Loiselle, M.-C. Partie de ping-pong. 24 IMAGES n76:2-3
  Spring 1995
RACISM
Fuehrer, P. Strovtag mot fornimmelsens nollpunkt. bibliog stills F HAFTET
  22:48-54 n3 (n87) 1994
    United States
      Arabs in Film
Addison, E. Saving other women from other men: Disney's "Aladdin." stills
  CAM OBS n31:4-25 Jan/May 1993
RADFORD, MICHAEL See also POSTINO, IL
Liberti, F. Michael Radford: Troisi, il cinema e l'Italia di oggi. credits
  interv stills C FORUM 34:46-50 Sep (n337) 1994
RADI f (d Dessau, Maxim 1979 E Ger)
Graef, C. Hochschulfilme. il F & FERNSEHEN 22:8-11 n6 1994
RADIO
    United States
      Adaptations
Breen, J.L. Harmon, Jim. Radio mystery and adventure and its appearances in

film, television and other media [Book Review]. ARMCHAIR DET 26:78-79 n3
  1993
RADIO STAR - DIE AFN STORY f (d Karnick, Hannes/Richter, Wolfgang 1994 FR Ger)
"Radio Star - die AFN Story." biogs credits filmog still KINO(BRD) n1:38-39
  1995
    Reviews
Leydon, J. "Radio Star - the AFN Story." credits VARIETY 358:55 Mar 13/19
  1995
RADIOLAND MURDERS f (d Smith, Mel 1994 USA)
    Special Effects
Magid, R. Fine-tuning "Radioland Murders." il AMCIN 76:66-72 Mar 1995
    Reviews
Travers, P. Misfires. stills ROLLING STONE n696:134 Dec 1 1994
RADIVOJEVIC, MILOS See also NI NA NEBU NI NA ZELMLJI
RADNOTI, SANDOR For film reviews see author under the following titles:
  RESZLEG, A
RADOVICH, GARY
Carriou, A. and Radovich, G. The wonderful world of CAM. F SCORE MONTHLY
  n36/37:36-37 Aug/Sep 1993
Dursin, A. and others. Four by Basil Poledouris. F SCORE MONTHLY n36/37:32
  Aug/Sep 1993
Radovich, G. "In the Line of Fire." F SCORE MONTHLY n36/37:32 Aug/Sep 1993
RAFFAELLI, PIER LUIGI
Livio, G. Gli ultimi giorni di Pompei. A cura di Riccardo Redi e Pier Luigi
  Raffaelli [Book Review]. GRIFFITHIANA n51/52:267 Oct 1994
RAFFERTY, TERRENCE For film reviews see author under the following titles:
  ALLEMAGNE ANNEE 90 NEUF ZERO; IA KUBA; JLG - AUTOPORTRAIT DE
  DECEMBRE; LEGENDS OF THE FALL; LITTLE WOMEN; OUTBREAK; WILD BUNCH, THE
  Mitchell, L. The thing happens: ten years of writing about the movies. By
  Terrence Rafferty [Book Review]. DGA NEWS 19:30 n3 1994
RAFMAN, CAROLYNN
Rafman, C. Imagining a woman's world: roles for women in Chinese films.
  bibliog glos stills CINEMAS 3:126-140 n2/3 1993
RAGGHIANTI, CARLO L.
Comuzio, E. AA. VV. (Auditorium du Louvre): Histoire de l'art et cinema. Les
  critofilms de C.L. Ragghianti [Book Review]. C FORUM 34:92 Oct (n338) 1994
RAGING BULL f (d Scorsese, Martin 1980 USA)
Borden, L. Blood and redemption. still S&S 5:61 Feb 1995
RAIMI, SAM See also QUICK AND THE DEAD, THE
Clark, J. Some of Sam. il stills PREM 8:74-78 Mar 1995
RAINER, YVONNE See also PRIVILEGE
Rainer, Y. Script pages and production notes for "Privilege" (1990). il
  scenario MILLENNIUM n25:50-55 Summer 1991
RAIZMAN, IULII
Birchenough, T. Yuli Raizman. biog obit VARIETY 357:83 Jan 2/8 1995
RAMASSE, FRANCOIS For film reviews see author under the following titles: MA
  SOEUR CHINOISE
RAMONA f (d Schoenemann, Sibylle 1979 E Ger)
Graef, C. Hochschulfilme. il F & FERNSEHEN 22:103-106 n6 1994
RAMOS, DANTE
Ramos, D. Jane's addiction. port NEW REPUB 212:23+ [2p] Jan 9/16 1995
RAMSAY, JEAN-PIERRE
Williams, M. Poetic pic raises flap in France. port VARIETY 358:5-6 Mar
  20/26 1995
RAN f (d Kurosawa, Akira 1985 Japan/Fr)
Vidal Estevez, M. William Akira Shakespeare Kurosawa. il stills NOSFERATU
  n8:40-47 May 1992
RANDISI, STEVE
Randisi, S. Lifetime contract. il port stills F FAX n48:76-81+ [8p]
  Jan/Feb 1995
RANDOM HOUSE
Evans, G. Random act opens can of bookworms. il VARIETY 358:1+ [3p] Mar
  6/12 1995
RANIN, MATTI
Salakka, M. Puhumme Suomea. il port still PEILI 18:6-7 n1 1994
RAP MUSIC
    Great Britain
      Political Analysis
Grundmann, R. Black nationhood and the rest in the West. interv port
  CINEASTE 21:28-31 n1/2 1995
RAPA NUI f (d Reynolds, Kevin 1994 USA)
    Reviews
Berry, J. "Rapa Nui." credits still S&S 5:54 Jan 1995
Paesano, A. "Rapa Nui." credits still FILM (ITALY) 3:46-48 n13 1995
Rape See SEXUAL ASSAULT
RASSAM, JULIEN
Millea, H. All the Queen's men. biogs il intervs ports still PREM 8:76-79
  Feb 1995
RATHBONE, BASIL
Seymour, B. Pentagram revues: Basil Rathbone. il ports stills CLASSIC
  n236:bet p32 and 33 [pC20+ (4p)] Feb 1995
RATHBONE, TINA
Zaniello, T. Hitched or Lynched: who directed "Twin Peaks"? bibliog filmogs
  STUDIES POP CULT 17:55-64 n1 1994
RATHNAM, MANI
Chute, D. Gods walk the earth. il stills F COM 31:50-53 Jan/Feb 1995
RATING SYSTEMS
    Finland
Lehtonen, V.-P. "K" niin kuin kielletty. PEILI 18:25 n1 1994
RATNAVIBHUSHANA, ASHLEY
Ratnavibhushana, A. Sumitra Peries. filmog port stills CINEMAYA
  n25/26:78-80 Autumn/Winter 1994/95
RAUZI, PIERGIORGIO For film reviews see author under the following titles: CRI
  DU COEUR, LE; DU BRINGST MICH NOCH UM; ENASTROS THOLOS; MIL E UMA;
  PARAJANOV
RAVALAT, THIERRY See also JOUR DANS LA MORT DE SARAJEVO, UN
RAVEN, THE f (d Brabin, Charles J. 1915 USA)
    Reviews
DeBartolo, J. Video tape reviews. credits port stills CLASSIC n237:12+
  [3p] Mar 1995

Raw Meat   See DEATH LINE
RAY, NICHOLAS   See also IN A LONELY PLACE; LIGHTNING OVER WATER; REBEL WITHOUT A
   CAUSE
   Grbic, B. Nicholas Ray=I'm a stranger here myself. filmog il BLIMP
     [n1]:26-33 Mar 1985
RAY, ROBERT B.
   Ray, R.B. Film studies/crisis/experimentation. bibliog F CRITICISM
     17:56-78 n2/3 1992/93
RAY, SATYAJIT   See also ARANYER DIN RAATRI
RAYNES, DOUG
   Raynes, D. "Jane Eyre." SCN 14:20 Mar 1995
RAYNS, TONY   For film reviews see author under the following titles: TOTALLY
   F***ED UP
   Rayns, T. A few sparks of flair. il S&S 5:5 Apr 1995
   Rayns, T. Here and now. biog stills S&S 5:18-20 Apr 1995
READ, TIM
   Murray, S. Tim Read. interv port stat C PAPERS n102:36-39+ [6p] Dec 1994
READY TO WEAR (PRET-A-PORTER) f (d Altman, Robert 1994 USA)
   Fuller, G. Tracey Ullman: a comic chameleon who never acts the same way
     twice. interv port INTERV 25:32-33 Jan 1995
       Fashion in Film
   Miles, M.R. Fashioning the self. CHR CENT 112:273-275 Mar 8 1995
       Lawsuits
   Molner, D. Designer suit blocks pic bow. still VARIETY 358:5 Mar 20/26
     1995
       Reviews
   Ansen, D. Dressed up with nowhere to go. still NEWSWK 125:58 Jan 9 1995
   Cherchi Usai, P. "Pret a porter." credits stills SEGNO n72:35-37 Mar/Apr
     1995
   Denby, D. It's a mad mad mad George. stills NEW YORK 28:66-67 Jan 2 1995
   Noh, D. "Ready to Wear (Pret-a-porter)." credits FJ 98:49 Jan/Feb 1995
   Rousseau, Y. Un Americain a Paris. credits il 24 IMAGES n76:58 Spring 1995
REALISM   See also MIMESIS
   Bottiroli, G. Il bello del brutto. stills SEGNO n72:21-23 Mar/Apr 1995
       France
   Cremonini, G. Il fascino discreto dell'intelligenza. stills C FORUM
     34:28-35 Oct (n338) 1994
       Italy
         Theory
   Orr, C. A certain realism: making use of Pasolini's theory and practice. By
     Maurizio Viano [Book Review]. F CRITICISM 19:99-103 n2 1994/95
REALITY
       Documentary Film
   Morin, S. "Nick's Movie": le point de fuite. bibliog still CINEMAS
     4:101-117 n2 1994
         Canada
           Documentary Film
   Jacquinot, G. Le documentaire, une fiction (pas) comme les autres. bibliog
     stills CINEMAS 4:61-81 n2 1994
         United States
           Crime in Film
   Breen, J.L. Gerald, Marc, ed. Murder plus: true crime stories from the
     masters of detective fiction [Book Review]. ARMCHAIR DET 28:78 n1 1995
REBECCA f (d Hitchcock, Alfred 1940 USA)
       Psychological Analysis
   Berg, E.K. "Rebecca." bibliog stills Z n1:26-29 (n47) 1994
REBEL WITHOUT A CAUSE f (d Ray, Nicholas 1955 USA)
   Lilley, J. Jack Grinnage. il interv stills SCARLET STREET n17:59-61+ [4p]
     Winter 1995
REBELLO, STEPHEN
   Rebello, S. Fans of bad Susan Hayward films will thank the fools behind "I
     Thank a Fool." il MOVIELINE 6:80 Apr 1995
   Rebello, S. Halle terror. ports MOVIELINE 6:52-56+ [7p] Apr 1995
   Rebello, S. The crown princess of young Hollywood. ports MOVIELINE
     6:48-52+ [7p] Mar 1995
   Rebello, S. The star next door. il ports MOVIELINE 6:44-47+ [7p] Apr 1995
RECKLESS MOMENT, THE f (d Ophuls, Max 1949 USA)
   Lyons, D. Family values. il stills F COM 31:78-81 Jan/Feb 1995
Red Desert   See DESERTO ROSSO
Red Firecracker, Green Firecracker   See PAODA SHUANG DENG
RED ROCK WEST f (d Dahl, John 1993 USA)
       Reviews
   Meyers, R. The crime screen. port still ARMCHAIR DET 27:430-431 n4 1994
Red Sorghum   See HONG GAOLIANG
REDES f (Wave, The d Zinnemann, Fred/Gomez Muriel, Emilio 1935 Mex)
   Zinnemann, F. Letter from Fred Zinnemann. F CRITICISM 19:86-88 n2 1994/95
REDFORD, ROBERT   See also QUIZ SHOW
REDI, RICCARDO
   Livio, J. Gli ultimi giorni di Pompei. A cura di Riccardo Redi e Pier Luigi
     Raffaelli [Book Review]. GRIFFITHIANA n51/52:267 Oct 1994
   Redi, R. King Vidor a Venezia. credits filmog stills IMMAGINE n28:7-14
     Autumn 1994
REDMAN, NICK
   Kendall, L. Richard Kraft & Nick Redman. il interv port F SCORE MONTHLY
     n36/37:27-30 Aug/Sep 1993
   Kendall, L. Richard Kraft & Nick Redman: part four. interv F SCORE MONTHLY
     n40:8-9 Dec 1993
   Kendall, L. Richard Kraft & Nick Redman: part three. il interv F SCORE
     MONTHLY n39:10-11 Nov 1993
   Kendall, L. Richard Kraft & Nick Redman: part two. il interv F SCORE
     MONTHLY n38:9-11 Oct 1993
   Redman, N. A Siegel film: an autobiography. By Don Siegel [Book Reviews].
     il DGA NEWS 19:33-34 n2 1994
   Redman, N. Competing composers [Book Reviews]. DGA NEWS 19:56-57 n6 1994/95
   Redman, N. Peckinpah and Sidney reconsidered [Book Reviews]. il DGA NEWS
     20:40-41 n1 1995
   Redman, N. The golden age of movie musicals and me. By Saul Chaplin [Book
     Review]. DGA NEWS 20:42 n1 1995
REDOTTEE, HARTMUT W.
   Kremski, P. Film als Schule des Sehens. il interv stills F BUL 36:53-59 n6

(n197) 1994
   Redottee, H.W. Hitchcock-Glossarium. il stills F BUL 37:47-59 n1 (n198)
     1995
REDSTONE, SHARI
   Schwartzberg, S. National Amusements: the next generation. port BOXOFFICE
     131:54+ [2p] Apr 1995
["REDUNDANT" HUSBAND] f (d Chen, Guoxing 1994 China)
   "'Redundant' Husband." credits stills CHINA SCREEN n4:28-29 1994
REED, TOBY   For film reviews see author under the following titles: DAZED AND
   CONFUSED
REES, ROBERT R.
   Rees, R.R. Vampira remembers Jimmy. il interv SCARLET STREET n17:40 Winter
     1995
REEVES, BILL
   Reeves, B. Murder most foul: the many uses of atropine. il ARMCHAIR DET
     27:82-84 n1 1994
REFERENCE WORKS [Prior to V24, 1996 use REFERENCE BOOKS] See also DICTIONARIES
   AND ENCYCLOPEDIAS; DIRECTORIES; INDEXES; YEARBOOKS
     Germany (Federal Republic, 1949-1990)
   Grbic, B. Hans-Michael Bock (Hrsg.): "Cinegraph" [Book Review]. BLIMP
     [n1]:65 Mar 1985
     United States
   Clark, J. A list is still a list [Book Review]. stills PREM 8:93 Feb 1995
REFERENCES TO FILMS IN FILM [Prior to V20, 1992 use also ALLUSION]
     France
   Sabouraud, F. Il cinema francese e i suoi fantasmi. FCR 45:359-363 Jun/Jul
     (n446/447) 1994
REFERENCES TO LITERATURE IN FILM [Prior to V20, 1992 use ALLUSION]
     Horror Film
   Nangle, J. More things than are dreamt of: masterpieces of supernatural
     horror - from Mary Shelley to Stephen King in literature and film. By Alain
     Silver and James Ursini [Book Review]. FIR 45:71 Nov/Dec 1994
REFLEXIVITY
   Fuehrer, P. Strovtag mot fornimmelsens nollpunkt. bibliog stills F HAFTET
     22:48-54 n3 (n87) 1994
     Canada
       Quebec. Documentary Film
   Lockerbie, I. Le documentaire autoreflexif au Quebec. "L'emotion dissonante"
     et "Passiflora." still CINEMAS 4:118-132 n2 1994
     France
   Benard, J. Un cinema zazique? bibliog still CINEMAS 4:135-154 n3 1994
   Lacasse, A. Considerations sur la portee ethique des propositions de
     Christian Metz pour une enonciation impersonnelle au cinema. bibliog
     CINEMAS 4:85-97 n3 1994
     United States
       Animation
   Lindvall, T. and Melton, M. Toward a postmodern animated discourse: Bakhtin,
     intertextuality and the cartoon carnival. il stills ANIMATION J 3:44-63 n1
     1994
REFN, PETER
   Stratton, D. Peter Refn. biog obit VARIETY 358:59 Mar 20/26 1995
REGARDE-MOI f (d Aubert, Elisabeth 1993 Fr/Switz)
       Reviews
   Perret, J. "Regarde-moi." credits C(SWITZ) 40:204 1994
REGENT, BENOIT
   Elia, M. Les bonnes (et parfois les dernieres) repliques de ceux qui nous
     ont quittes. biogs il obits port stills SEQUENCES n175:6 Nov/Dec 1994
REGLE DU JEU, LA f (Rules of the Game, The d Renoir, Jean 1939 Fr)
   Smith, G. A man of excess. interv port stills S&S 5:24-29 Jan 1995
REGOSA, MAURIZIO   For film reviews see author under the following titles:
   NATURAL BORN KILLERS; TRUE LIES
Regulation   See GOVERNMENT REGULATION
REHLIN, GUNNAR   For film reviews see author under the following titles:
   ILLUSIONER; PENSIONAT OSKAR
REICHERT, HOLGER
   Reichert, H. Film und Kino. Die Maschinerie des Sehens. F KUNST n144:23-34
     1994
REID, FIONA CUNNINGHAM   See also THIN ICE
REID-PHARR, ROBERT
   Reid-Pharr, R. Mix-defying. il stills AFTERIMAGE 22:3-4 Jan 1995
REIJNDERS, GUSTA
   Reijnders, G. How to have a vision. JOURNAL WGA 8:38 Mar 1995
   Reijnders, G. What is a "European" story? JOURNAL WGA 7:35 Feb 1994
   Reijnders, G. Who's afraid of the European screenwriter. JOURNAL WGA 8:45
     Dec/Jan 1995
REINA DE LA NOCHE, LA f (d Ripstein, Arturo 1994 Mex/USA/Fr)
   Lopez Aranda, S. Filmar el tiempo: Arturo Ripstein y Paz Alicia Garciadiego:
     segundo parte. il interv stills DICINE n59:9-13 Nov/Dec 1994
REINE MARGOT, LA f (Queen Margot d Chereau, Patrice 1994 Fr/FR Ger/It)
       Reviews
   Darke, C. "La Reine Margot." credits still S&S 5:55 Jan 1995
   Noh, D. "Queen Margot." credits FJ 98:52-53 Jan/Feb 1995
   Travers, P. Smart women, foolish choices. stills ROLLING STONE n700:66 Jan
     26 1995
REINER, ROB   See also FEW GOOD MEN, A; NORTH
REINHARDT, MAX   See also MIDSUMMER NIGHT'S DREAM, A
REISMAN, DAVID
   Reisman, D. Delphine Seyrig 1932-1990. biog obit port MILLENNIUM n25:76
     Summer 1991
REISNER, CHARLES F.   See also STEAMBOAT BILL, JR.
REITHERMAN, WOLFGANG   See also (ONE HUNDRED AND ONE) 101 DALMATIANS
REITMAN, IVAN   See also JUNIOR
REITZ, EDGAR   See also NACHT DER REGISSEURE, DIE; ZWEITE HEIMAT, DIE
   Gottardi, M. La prigione dell'anima. il stills SEGNO n63:14-16 Sep/Oct
     1993
RELIGIOUS ASPECTS
     United States
   Dyer, R. Varldens ljus. bibliog il ports stills F HAFTET 22:13-22 n3 (n87)
     1994

RELIGIOUS THEMES
  Denmark
  Miguez, M. La mirada Dreyer. il stills NOSFERATU n5:24-37 Jan 1991
    United States
  Wall, J.M. No sense of the sacred. CHR CENT 112:283-284 Mar 15 1995
    Independent Film
  Testa, B. The two religions of avant-garde film, or maybe three. CAN J F
    STUD 3:89-100 n2 1994
REMAINS OF THE DAY, THE f (d Ivory, James 1993 Gt Br/USA)
  Alnaes, K. Pliktens blinde oyne. stills F&K n1:6-7 1994
    Screenplays
  Chambers, L. Fade in. il scenario JOURNAL WGA 8:43 Dec/Jan 1995
    Reviews
  Giacovelli, E. "Quel che resta del giorno." C SUD 33:22-23 Jul/Aug/Sep
    (n113) 1994
REMEN, ODD
  Dodsfall. obits F&K n1:34 1994
REMENYI, JOZSEF TAMAS
  Remenyi, J.T. Cseresznyeskert, 1936. credits stills F VILAG 38:29-30 n2
    1994
RENAISSANCE MAN f (d Marshall, Penny 1994 USA)
    Reviews
  Barotanyi, Z. "Reneszansz ember." credits still F VILAG 38:56 n3 1995
RENOIR, JEAN See also BOUDU SAUVE DES EAUX; CHIENNE, LA; CRIME DE MONSIEUR
  LANGE, LE; GRANDE ILLUSION, LA; PARTIE DE CAMPAGNE, UNE; REGLE DU JEU, LA; VIE
  EST A NOUS, LA
  Bonneville, L. Jean Renoir. Par Celia Bertin [Book Review]. il SEQUENCES
    n174:59 Sep/Oct 1994
  Smith, G. A man of excess. interv port stills S&S 5:24-29 Jan 1995
RENOV, MICHAEL
  Cantrill, A. Theorizing documentary. Edited by Michael Renov [Book Review].
    CANTRILL'S FMNTS n73/74:43 May 1994
Rental See DISTRIBUTION
RENZI, RENZO
  Comuzio, E. Renzo Renzi: L'ombra di Fellini. Quarant'anni di rapporti con il
    grande regista e uno Stupidario degli anni Ottanta [Book Review]. il C
    FORUM 34:94-95 Sep (n337) 1994
  Montanaro, C. Il cinematografo al campo: l'arma nuova nel primo conflitto
    mondiale. A cura di Renzo Renzi con la collaborazione di Gianluca Farinelli
    e Nicola Mazzanti [Book Review]. GRIFFITHIANA n51/52:254 Oct 1994
  Thirard, P.L. Il cinematografo al campo - l'arma nuova nel primo conflitto
    mondiale. Sous la direction de Renzo Renzi [Book Review]. POSITIF n409:73
    Mar 1995
REPETTO, MONICA For film reviews see author under the following titles: MARY
  SHELLEY'S FRANKENSTEIN
  Repetto, M. Tutti in gara. il SEGNO n71:28-30 Jan/Feb 1995
REPRESENTATION
  Kaltenecker, S. Richard Dyer: The matter of images. Essays on
    representations [Book Review]. BLIMP n30:71 Winter 1994
    Canada
  Lacasse, G. Cent temps de cinema ou le cinema dans les temps de l'histoire.
    bibliog CINEMAS 5:57-67 n1/2 1994
    France
  Calle-Gruber, M. La chimere du modele. bibliog still CINEMAS 4:72-87 n1
    1993
RESAN TILL MELONIA f (d Ahlin, Per 1989 Swed)
  Munoz, J. "Viaje a Melonia." NOSFERATU n8:68-70 Feb 1992
RESEARCH See also AUDIENCE RESEARCH
    Australia
  Research in progress. bibliog MEDIA INFO AUSTRALIA n75:173-182 Feb 1995
RESERVOIR DOGS f (d Tarantino, Quentin 1992 USA)
    Reviews
  Meyers, R. The crime screen. port stills ARMCHAIR DET 26:69-71 n2 1993
RESNAIS, ALAIN See also AMOUR A MORT, L'; CONTRE L'OUBLI; HIROSHIMA MON AMOUR;
  MELO; NO SMOKING; SMOKING; STAVISKY
  Filmografie. biogs filmogs SEGNO n72:40 Mar/Apr 1995
  Saulnier, J. "Man muss in unserem Metier flexibel sein." biog filmog il
    interv stills F BUL 36:21-35 n6 (n197) 1994
Respectable Life, A See ANSTANDIGT LIV, ETT
RESTORATION [Prior to V18, 1990 use PRESERVATION] See also PRESERVATION
    Festivals
  Bori, E. Elet a dobozban. still F VILAG 38:58-59 n1 1995
    Theory
      Conferences, Institutes, Workshops, etc.
  Cherchi Usai, P. Il cinema ritrovato: teoria e metodologia del restauro
    cinematografico. Edited by Gian Luca Farinelli and Nicola Mazzanti [Book
    Review]. J F PRES n49:70 Oct 1994
  Montanaro, C. Il cinema ritrovato: teoria e metodologia del restauro
    cinematografico. A cura di Gianluca Farinelli e Nicola Mazzanti [Book
    Review]. GRIFFITHIANA n51/52:254 Oct 1994
    United States
      Digital, Technical Aspects
  Fisher, B. Off to work we go: the digital restoration of "Snow White." il
    stills AMCIN 74:48-50+ [6p] Sep 1993
RESZLEG, A f (d Gothar, Peter 1995 Hungary)
  Gothar, P. "Reszleg" - reszletek. il interv stills F VILAG 38:6-9 n2 1995
    Reviews
  Radnoti, S. Weisz Gizella. credits still F VILAG 38:20-21 n4 1995
  Stratton, D. "The Outpost" ("A reszleg"). credits VARIETY 358:86 Feb 20/26
    1995
RETES, GABRIEL See also BIENVENIDO
RETIREMENT
    United States
  Post, T. Age doesn't matter, unless you're cheese. port DGA NEWS 19:68 n6
    1994/95
RETURN OF THE TEXAS CHAINSAW MASSACRE, THE f (d Henkel, Ken 1995 USA)
    Reviews
  Leydon, J. "The Return of the Texas Chainsaw Massacre." credits VARIETY
    358:49 Mar 20/26 1995

RETZER, OTTO W. See also TIERAERZTIN CHRISTINE II
  "Tieraerztin Christine II." biog credits filmog still KINO(BRD) n1:48-49
    1995
REVE AVEUGLE f (d Beaudry, Diane 1994 Can)
    Reviews
  Beaulieu, J. "Reve aveugle." still SEQUENCES n175:43 Nov/Dec 1994
Revelation See AGONIE DE JERUSALEM, L'
Reviews See titles of films
REY DEL RIO, EL f (d Gutierrez Aragon, Manuel 1995 Sp/Port/Gt Br)
    Reviews
  Stratton, D. "King of the River" ("El rey del rio"). credits VARIETY
    358:65 Mar 6/12 1995
REYNAUD, BERENICE For film reviews see author under the following titles: FRESH
  KILL
  Holmlund, C. "CinemAction," no. 67 (1993), 200pp. "Vingt ans de theories
    feministes sur le cinema." Eds Ginette Vincendeau and Berenice Reynaud [Book
    Review]. SCREEN 35:407-410 n4 1994
  Reynaud, B. HongKong. still CINEMAYA n24:57-59 Summer 1994
  Reynaud, B. Li Shaohong. port still CINEMAYA n25/26:8-9 Autumn/Winter
    1994/95
  Reynaud, B. Trinh T. Minh-Ha. il stills CINEMAYA n25/26:28-29
    Autumn/Winter 1994/95
  Reynaud, B. Vancouver. CINEMAYA n25/26:95-96 Autumn/Winter 1994/95
REYNOLDS, GENE
  Reynolds, G. Credits where they're due. port DGA NEWS 19:5 n6 1994/95
  Reynolds, G. Directors, writers need cooperation not competition. port DGA
    NEWS 19:3 n3 1994
REYNOLDS, KEVIN See also RAPA NUI; WATERWORLD
REYNOLDS, PAUL
  Reynolds, P. The fast lane to the future. il ONFILM [12]:13 n1 1995
REYNOLDS, WILLIAM
  Gallagher, B. It's a print!: detective fiction from page to screen. Edited
    by William Reynolds and Elizabeth A. Trembley [Book Review]. MICHIGAN
    ACADEMICIAN 27:229-231 n2 1995
RHEA, MARJI
  Rhea, M. Around the world's film commissions. il AMCIN 76:14+ [6p] Feb
    1995
  Rhea, M. The rise of stock footage companies. AMCIN 76:14+ [3p] Jan 1995
RHETORICAL ANALYSIS
    United States
      Documentary Film
  Orvell, M. Documentary film and the power of interrogation. il stills FQ
    48:10-18 n2 1994/95
RHINO RECORDS
  Sandler, A. Rhino tunes in to Oscar song winners. VARIETY 357:28 Jan 2/8
    1995
RHODES, SCOTT
  Rhodes, S. El Santo. biog filmog il stills F FAX n49:44-49 Mar/Apr 1995
RHYTHM THIEF f (d Harrison, Matthew 1994 USA)
    Reviews
  Greene, R. "Rhythm Thief." still BOXOFFICE 131:bet p125 and 144 [pR26] Apr
    1995
RIAMBAU, ESTEVE
  Riambau, E. "Campanadas a medianoche." credits still NOSFERATU n8:61-62
    Feb 1992
  Riambau, E. "Macbeth." credits still NOSFERATU n8:59-60 Feb 1992
  Riambau, E. "Nocturno 29." credits il NOSFERATU n9:102-103 Jun 1992
  Riambau, E. "Otelo." credits still NOSFERATU n8:60-61 Feb 1992
  Riambau, E. Shakespeare y Welles. stills NOSFERATU n8:32-39 Feb 1992
  Riambau, E. Una cierta tendencia (vanguardista) del cine catalan. il stills
    NOSFERATU n9:16-25 Jun 1992
RIAZANOV, EL'DAR
  Birchenough, T. Director to head anti-piracy org. VARIETY 358:59 Feb 27/Mar
    5 1995
RICCI, CHRISTINA
  James, C. Ghost of a chance. il still BOXOFFICE 131:20-21 Apr 1995
RICCI, GIUSEPPE
  Comuzio, E. Gianfranco Miro Gori e Giuseppe Ricci (a cura di): Io F.F. il re
    del cine [Book Review]. C FORUM 34:96 Sep (n337) 1994
Rice People See NEAK SRE
RICH, B. RUBY For film reviews see author under the following titles: FASTER,
  PUSSYCAT! KILL! KILL!
  Rich, B.R. Mark Finch, 1961-1995. obit VILLAGE VOICE 40:62 Feb 7 1995
  Rich, B.R. Slugging it out for survival. stills S&S 5:14-17 Apr 1995
RICH, RICHARD See also SWAN PRINCESS, THE
RICHARDS, PETER
  Richards, P. "Ill Met by Moonlight." stills F COM 31:37-40 Mar/Apr 1995
RICHARDS, SALLY
  Richards, S. The black mask murders. By William F. Nolan [Book Review].
    ARMCHAIR DET 27:359 n3 1994
RICHARDSON, DON
  Richardson, D. Communication, culture and hegemony: from the media to
    mediations. By Jesus Martin-Barbero [Book Review]. CAN J COM 19:562-563
    n3/4 1994
RICHARDSON, MIRANDA
  Biskind, P. Viv a little. il port PREM 8:80-82 Mar 1995
  Fuller, G. and Dafoe, W. Two chums who see eye to eye. il INTERV 25:38+
    [2p] Feb 1995
  Webster, A. Filmographies. biogs filmogs stills PREM 8:104 Mar 1995
RICHARDSON, RICK
  Richardson, R. All's quiet on Polish movie front. VARIETY 358:58+ [2p] Feb
    6/12 1995
RICHES, IAN N.
  Riches, I.N. The dragon awakes: cinema growth in Asia. FJ 98:92 Jan/Feb
    1995
RICHIAMO, IL f (d Bondi, Claudio 1995 It)
    Reviews
  Fontanini, C. "Il richiamo." credits FILM (ITALY) 3:33-34 n13 1995
RICHIE, DONALD
  Richie, D. Fukuoka. CINEMAYA n25/26:88-89 Autumn/Winter 1994/95

ROGERS, RAY
Rogers, R. Box office Le Gros. il interv port INTERV 25:96-99 Mar 1995

ROHDIE, SAM
Ciment, M. BFI film classics [Book Reviews]. stills POSITIF n408:75-77 Feb 1995
Cremonini, G. Sam Rohdie: Rocco and his bothers (Rocco e i suoi fratelli) di L. Visconti [Book Reviews]. C FORUM 34:93 Sep (n337) 1994

ROHMER, ERIC See also ARBRE, LE MAIRE ET LA MEDIATHEQUE OU LES SEPT HASARDS, L'
ROI DE PARIS, LE f (d Maillet, Dominique 1994 Fr)
Reviews
Herpe, N. "Le roi de Paris." POSITIF n409:47 Mar 1995

ROLAND, FRITZ
Roland, F. Embracing the concept of color correction. AMCIN 76:22+ [3p] Jan 1995

ROLICK, JEFFREY M.
Rolick, J.M. Viola Dana: one of the silent screen's shining stars. il port CLASSIC n236:28+ [2p] Feb 1995

ROLLET, SYLVIE
Rollet, S. Atom Egoyan. Par Carole Desbarats, Daniele Riviere et Jacinto Lageira; lettres-video de Paul Virilio et Atom Egoyan [Book Review]. il POSITIF n406:86 Dec 1994
Rollet, S. Le cinema d'Atom Egoyan. stills POSITIF n406:84-87 Dec 1994

ROLLINS, PETER C.
Rollins, P.C. The Hollywood Indian: still on a scholarly frontier? F&HIST 23:1-6 n1/4 1993

ROMANCE
United States
Blaetz, R. Retelling the Joan of Arc story: women, war, and Hollywood's "Joan of Paris." bibliog still LIT/FQ 22:212-221 n4 1994

ROMAND, FRANCOISE See also PASSE COMPOSE
Romantic comedy See COMEDY FILM
ROMEO AND JULIET f (d Zeffirelli, Franco 1968 Gt Br/It)
Angulo, J. "Romeo y Julieta." credits still NOSFERATU n8:70-71 Feb 1992
Latorre, J.M. Shakespeare segun Zeffirelli. il stills NOSFERATU n8:48-55 Feb 1992

ROMEO, ANDREA For film reviews see author under the following titles:
KADISBELLAN

ROMEO IS BLEEDING f (d Medak, Peter 1993 USA)
Reviews
Martini, E. "Triplo gioco." credits still C FORUM 34:81 Sep (n337) 1994

ROMEO UND JULIA IM SCHNEE f (d Lubitsch, Ernst 1920 Ger)
Aldarondo, R. "Las hijas del cervecero"; "Romeo y Julia en la nieve." credits stills NOSFERATU n8:57-58 Feb 1992

ROMERO, GEORGE A. See also DARK HALF, THE

ROMMETVEIT, INGRID
Rommetveit, I. "Thelma & Louise." stills Z n1:6-10 (n47) 1994

ROMNEY, JONATHAN
Romney, J. How did we get here? stills S&S 5:32-34 Feb 1995

RONCSFILM f (d Szomjas, Gyorgy 1992 Hungary)
Reviews
Bikacsy, G. Rough times for the cinema. il NEW HUNGARIAN Q 34:169-173 n129 1993

RONIN FILMS
Groves, D. Ronin ankles Sydney arthouse exhibition. VARIETY 357:30 Jan 9/15 1995

RONNBERG, MARGARETA
Naranen, P. Reunamerkintoja Ronnbergin lapsikuvasta. bibliog il PEILI 18:14-15 n2 1994

RONY, FATIMAH TOBING
Rony, F.T. "Picture Bride." il INDEP 18:15-16 Mar 1995
Rony, F.T. Victor Masayesva, Jr., and the politics of "Imagining Indians." il stills FQ 48:20-33 n2 1994/95

ROOM WITH A VIEW, A f (d Ivory, James 1986 Gt Br)
Screenplays
Chambers, L. Fade in. il scenario JOURNAL WGA 8:43 Dec/Jan 1995

ROOMMATES f (d Yates, Peter 1995 USA)
Kelleher, E. Disney's "Roommates" explores generational ties. il FJ 98:12+ [2p] Mar 1995
Reviews
McCarthy, T. Falk holds key for "Roommates." credits still VARIETY 358:63 Mar 6/12 1995

ROONEY, DAVID For film reviews see author under the following titles: BELLE AL BAR; CAMERIERI; COLPO DI LUNA; CON GLI OCCHI CHIUSI; DOUSI CHINGYUN; DOZHDI V OKEANE; EROE BORGHESE, UN; GUANGCHANG; HOOGSTE TIJD; HUNG HEI-KUN; JIZDA; KRIMA-KERIME: NOAH'S ARK; LISBON STORY; MARIE-LOUISE OU LA PERMISSION; OCCHIOPINOCCHIO; PERSONAL PAIN; SCHADUWLOPERS, DE; SKIN DEEP; THALASSA, THALASSA. RUCKKEHR ZUM MEER; UOMINI UOMINI UOMINI; YOUCHAI
Rooney, D. Angelopoulos' odyssey. VARIETY 358:12 Mar 27/Apr 2 1995
Rooney, D. Chinese indie "Postman" delivers win in Rotterdam. stat VARIETY 358:27 Feb 13/19 1995
Rooney, D. Eye on the future. port VARIETY 358:47 Mar 6/12 1995
Rooney, D. Ferruccio Tagliavini. obit VARIETY 358:87 Mar 27/Apr 2 1995
Rooney, D. Film quartet leads Italo product run. VARIETY 358:58 Feb 6/12 1995
Rooney, D. Italo helmers try novel ideas. il VARIETY 358:7+ [2p] Mar 20/26 1995
Rooney, D. Moris Ergas. biog obit VARIETY 358:74-75 Mar 6/12 1995
Rooney, D. Moris Ergas. obit VARIETY 358:56 Mar 13/19 1995

ROPARS-WUILLEUMIER, MARIE-CLAIRE
Ropars-Wuilleumier, M.-C. L'oubli du texte. bibliog CINEMAS 4:11-22 n1 1993

ROPER, JONATHAN
Roper, J. Hammer and beyond: the British horror film. Peter Hutchings [Book Review]. il C PAPERS n102:73 Dec 1994

ROSA DI BAGDAD, LA f (d Domeneghini, Anton Gino 1949 It)
Bendazzi, G. The first Italian animated feature film and its producer: "La Rosa di Bagdad" and Anton Gino Domeneghini. biogs il stat stills ANIMATION J 3:4-18 n2 1995

ROSA, PAOLO See also DOV'E YANKEL?

ROSA WAS HERE f (d Juurikkala, Kaija 1993 Finl)
Reviews
Vahtera, H. Aikuiset puuttuvat Rosan maailmasta. credits still PEILI 18:33 n1 1994

ROSE, BERNARD See also CANDYMAN; IMMORTAL BELOVED
ROSEAUX SAUVAGES, LES f (d Techine, Andre 1994 Fr)
Reviews
Elia, M. "Les roseaux sauvages." credits still SEQUENCES n175:31 Nov/Dec 1994
Farber, S. Teen tales. still MOVIELINE 6:42-43 Apr 1995
Major, W. "The Wild Reeds." BOXOFFICE 131:bet p125 and 144 [pR36] Apr 1995

ROSEMARY'S BABY f (d Polanski, Roman 1968 USA)
Diski, J. Sitting inside. stills S&S 5:12-13 Apr 1995

ROSEN IM HERBST f (d Jugert, Rudolf 1955 W Ger)
Gruber, A. Une reprise impossible? "Effi Briest" et la question de ses reecritures filmiques. CINEMAS 4:59-71 n1 1993

ROSENBAUM, JONATHAN
Ciment, M. BFI film classics [Book Reviews]. stills POSITIF n408:75-77 Feb 1995
Codelli, L. "Greed." Di Jonathan Rosenbaum [Book Reviews]. GRIFFITHIANA n51/52:260 Oct 1994
Rosenbaum, J. Audio-vision: sound on screen. By Michael Chion. Edited and translated by Claudia Gorbman [Book Review]. CINEASTE 21:94-95 n1/2 1995

ROSENBERG, ROBERT
Silet, C. L.P. The cutting room. By Robert Rosenberg [Book Review]. ARMCHAIR DET 26:117 n3 1993

ROSENBURG, JACK
Rosenburg, J. Motion picture guide on CD-ROM. CLASSIC n237:bet p32 and 33 [pC15] Mar 1995

ROSENDAHL, CARL
Weiner, R. Effects houses enter cutthroat competition. il VARIETY 358:7+ [2p] Mar 13/19 1995

ROSI, FRANCESCO
Feinstein, H. Francesco Rosi. il interv F COM 31:64 Jan/Feb 1995
Klawans, S. Illustrious Rosi. il stills F COM 31:60-63+ [5p] Jan/Feb 1995

ROSINE f (d Carriere, Christine 1994 Fr)
Reviews
Kohn, O. "Rosine." POSITIF n408:59 Feb 1995

ROSS, BENJAMIN See also YOUNG POISONER'S HANDBOOK, THE
Ross, Edward See BRAZZI, ROSSANO
ROSS, HERBERT See also BOYS ON THE SIDE
ROSS, NAT See also APRIL FOOL

ROSSELINI, ISABELLA
Ciapara, E. "Niewinni." biogs credits filmogs still FSP 40:6 n10 (n764) 1994

ROSSI, UMBERTO
Rossi, U. Venice. CINEMAYA n25/26:96 Autumn/Winter 1994/95

ROTH, JOE
Bart, P. The Roth regimen. il VARIETY 358:8+ [2p] Feb 27/Mar 5 1995

ROTH, TIM
Goldstein, P. The japes of Roth. il interv port PREM 8:86-90 Apr 1995

ROTH-LINDBERG, ORJAN
Roth-Lindberg, O. Varldens bedragliga sken. il stills CHAPLIN 36:18-25 n6 (n255) 1994/95

ROTHSCHILD, WAYNE
Rothschild, W. Branigan, Edward. Narrative comprehension and film [Book Review]. CINEMAS 4:177-182 n3 1994

ROTWANG MUSS WEG! f (d Blumenberg, Hans-Christoph 1994 FR Ger)
"Rotwang muss weg!" biog credits filmog still KINO(BRD) n1:40-41 1995

ROUCH, JEAN
Taylor, L. A conversation with Jean Rouch. biog interv port VISUAL ANTHRO R 7:92-102 n1 1991

ROUFFIO, JACQUES See also V'LA L'CINEMA OU LE ROMAN DE CHARLES PATHE
Rouge See YANZHI KOU
ROUGE f (d Kieslowski, Krzysztof 1994 Fr/Switz/Poland)
Evans, G. Miramax to urge Acad to see "Red" as Swiss. VARIETY 357:20 Jan 9/15 1995
Awards
Travers, P. Controversy in three colors. stills ROLLING STONE n702:80 Feb 23 1995
Reviews
Bentley, M. "Red." CINEASTE 21:104 n1/2 1995
Elia, M. "Trois couleurs - Rouge." credits still SEQUENCES n174:37-38 Sep/Oct 1994

ROUGH DIAMONDS f (d Crombie, Donald 1994 Australia)
Reviews
Felperin, L. "Rough Diamonds." credits still S&S 5:51 Feb 1995

ROURKE, MICKEY
Baumgold, J. Tough guys don't wear underwear. ports ESQUIRE 123:83-87 Feb 1995
Oldani, M.T. Incontro con Mickey Rourke. interv still FCR 45:364-368 Jun/Jul (n446/447) 1994

ROUSSEAU, YVES For film reviews see author under the following titles: A LA BELLE ETOILE; DEATH AND THE MAIDEN; FORREST GUMP; INTERVIEW WITH THE VAMPIRE: THE VAMPIRE CHRONICLES; NATURAL BORN KILLERS; QUIZ SHOW; READY TO WEAR (PRET-A-PORTER)

ROUSSELOT, PHILIPPE
Pizzello, S. "Interview With the Vampire" taps new vein. il stills AMCIN 76:43-52 Jan 1995

ROUTT, WILLIAM D.
Routt, W.D. Dixon, Wheeler Winston, ed. Re-viewing British cinema, 1900-1992: essays and interviews [Book Review]. MEDIA INFO AUSTRALIA n75:162 Feb 1995
Routt, W.D. Petrie, Duncan, ed. New questions of British cinema [Book Review]. MEDIA INFO AUSTRALIA n75:169 Feb 1995

ROUYER, PHILIPPE For film reviews see author under the following titles: ELISA; ONLY YOU
Ciment, M. and Rouyer, P. Entretien avec Atom Egoyan. il interv stills POSITIF n406:79-83 Dec 1994
Rouyer, P. "Calendar." credits stills POSITIF n406:91-92 Dec 1994

Rouyer, P. "L'antre de la folie." credits stills POSITIF n409:6-7 Mar 1995
ROY, ANDRE For film reviews see author under the following titles: NOUS, LES
ENFANTS DU XXEME SICLE; PETITS ARRANGEMENTS AVEC LES MORTS; VIE D'UN
HEROS, LA
    Roy, A. Festival des films du monde. stills 24 IMAGES n75:40-48 Dec/Jan
        1994/95
ROY, LUCIE
    Roy, L. Langage cinematographique et faillibilite. bibliog CINEMAS
        4:99-118 n3 1994
    Roy, L. L'infatigable image ou les horizons du temps au cinema. bibliog
        CINEMAS 5:147-166 n1/2 1994
    Roy, L. Presentation. bibliog CINEMAS 4:7-14 n3 1994
    Roy, L. Presentation. bibliog CINEMAS 5:7-13 n1/2 1994
ROY, TULA See also ANDERE GESCHICHTE, EINE
ROZEMA, PATRICIA See also WHEN NIGHT IS FALLING
ROZSA, MIKLOS
    Handzo, S. The golden age of film music. il ports stills CINEASTE 21:46-55
        n1/2 1995
    Hirsch, D. Miklos Rozsa: film music vol. 1. F SCORE MONTHLY n36/37:33
        Aug/Sep 1993
RUANE, JOHN See also THAT EYE, THE SKY
RUBIN, BRUCE JOEL See also MY LIFE
RUBIN, SAM
    Rubin, S. Sam Rubin's classic clinic: the Hollywood West has changed, but it
        ain't real! il CLASSIC n237:47-48 Mar 1995
RUBINI, SERGIO See also PRESTAZIONE STRAORDINARIA
    Calderale, M. Filmografie. biogs filmogs il SEGNO n71:40 Jan/Feb 1995
RUBINSTEIN, AMNON See also AHARE HAHAGIM
RUDAVSKY, ONDREJ
    Rudavsky, O. Ideas for "The Wall or The Bridge" (work in progress, 1991).
        il MILLENNIUM n25:56-57 Summer 1991
RUDOLPH, ALAN See also MRS. PARKER AND THE VICIOUS CIRCLE
RUDYARD KIPLING'S THE JUNGLE BOOK f (d Sommers, Stephen 1994 USA)
    Reviews
    Ansen, D. A wild child revisited. still NEWSWK 125:66 Jan 16 1995
    Jackson, D. "The Jungle Book." VILLAGE VOICE 40:74 Jan 3 1995
    Jean, M. "The Jungle Book." 24 IMAGES n76:62 Spring 1995
    Noh, D. "Rudyard Kipling's the Jungle Book." credits still FJ 98:47
        Jan/Feb 1995
RUEHMANN, HEINZ
    Korte, H. and Lowry, S. Heinz Ruehmann - ein Star der deutschen
        Filmgeschichte. stills MEDIEN 38:348-352+ [7p] n6 1994
RUGGLE, WALTER
    Ruggle, W. In den bittersuessen Gruenden der Liebe. stills F BUL 36:14-17
        n6 (n197) 1994
    Trenczak, H. Walter Ruggle. Theo Angelopoulos: Filmische Landschaft [Book
        Review]. BLIMP n30:74 Winter 1994
RUIZ, RAUL See also ILE AU TRESOR, L'
Rules of the Game, The See REGLE DU JEU, LA
RULLI, STEFANO See also UNICO PAESE AL MONDO, L'
Rumania See Romania
[RUMBLE IN THE BRONX] f (d Chan, Jackie 1994 Hong Kong)
    Reviews
    Gehr, R. "Rumble in the Bronx." VILLAGE VOICE 40:74+ [2p] Feb 28 1995
RUNNING TARGET f (d Weinstein, Marvin 1956 USA)
    Anez, N. Westerns. stills FIR 45:18-27 Nov/Dec 1994
RUPPERT, PETER For film reviews see author under the following titles: LAST
SEDUCTION, THE
RUSH, RICHARD See also COLOR OF NIGHT
RUSHDIE, SALMAN
    Ciment, M. BFI film classics [Book Reviews]. stills POSITIF n408:75-77 Feb
        1995
    Hendrykowski, M. BFI Film Classics [Book Review]. il KINO 27:39-40 May
        1993
RUSNAK, JOSEF See also QUIET DAYS IN HOLLYWOOD
RUSSELL, CATHERINE
    Russell, C. Mourning the woman's film: the dislocated spectator of "The
        Company of Strangers." stills CAN J F STUD 3:25-40 n2 1994
    Russell, C. The life and death of authorship in Wim Wenders' "The State of
        Things." scenario CAN J F STUD 1:15-28 n1 1990
RUSSELL, CHARLES See also MASK, THE
    Filmografie. biogs filmogs SEGNO n72:40 Mar/Apr 1995
RUSSETT, MARGARET
    Russett, M. The "Caraboo" hoax: romantic woman as mirror and mirage.
        bibliog il DISCOURSE n17.2:26-47 Winter 1994/95
Russia (since 1992) See as a subheading under individual subject headings
RUSSO, CHRISTINE J.
    Russo, C.J. Images in the dark: an encyclopedia of gay and lesbian film and
        video. Compiled by Raymond Murray [Book Review]. il AFTERIMAGE 22:16 Jan
        1995
RUSSO, RENE
    Giles, J. Where the action is. biog port stills NEWSWK 125:64-65 Mar 27
        1995
RUSSO, TOM
    Russo, T. Unsung Oscars. il ports still PREM 8:108 Apr 1995
RUST, ROLAND
    Rust, R. (Fuenfte) V. Filmfestival Potsdam. KINO(GF) n56:24 Nov 1994
RUSTICHELLI, CARLO
    Comuzio, E. Omaggio a Carlo Rustichelli. C FORUM 34:96 Oct (n338) 1994
RUTH f (d Delisle, Francois 1995 Can)
    Jean, M. Francois Delisle. il interv stills 24 IMAGES n76:24-26+ [4p]
        Spring 1995
    Reviews
    Blois, M. de. "Ruth." credits still 24 IMAGES n76:26-27 Spring 1995
RUTTMANN, WALTER
    Comuzio, C. Leonardo Quaresima (a cura di) - Walter Ruttmann - Cinema,
        pittura, ars acustica [Book Review]. il C FORUM 34:91 Oct (n338) 1994
    Livio, J. Walter Ruttmann: cinema, pittura, ars acustica. A cura di Leonardo
        Quaresima [Book Review]. GRIFFITHIANA n51/52:268 Oct 1994

RYALL, TOM
    Ciment, M. BFI film classics [Book Reviews]. stills POSITIF n408:75-77 Feb
        1995
    Cremonini, G. Sam Rohdie: Rocco and his bothers (Rocco e i suoi fratelli) di
        L. Visconti [Book Reviews]. C FORUM 34:93 Sep (n337) 1994
RYAN, JAMES
    Ryan, J. Screenwriters, unite! il INDEP 18:33 Mar 1995
RYCHCIK, ANDRZEJ
    Rychcik, A. "Nie jestesmy juz mlodzi." still KINO 27:16-17 Jul 1993
RYDER, WINONA
    Corliss, R. Take a bow, Winona. il ports still TIME 145:64-66 Jan 9 1995
RYDZEWSKI, STEVE
    Adamson, J. and others. Forgotten laughter. credits port stills
        GRIFFITHIANA n51/52:170-197 Oct 1994
    Adamson, J. and others. La fabbrica della risata. credits port stills
        GRIFFITHIANA n51/52:170-197 Oct 1994
RYSHER ENTERTAINMENT
    Brodie, J. Rysher sets to make splash into pic pool. stat VARIETY 358:13+
        [2p] Mar 6/12 1995
S.F.W. f (d Levy, Jefery 1994 USA)
    Reviews
    Loffreda, P. "S.F.W." still C FORUM 34:29 Sep (n337) 1994
    McDonagh, M. "S.F.W." credits FJ 98:72 Mar 1995
SAAB, JOCELYNE See also KANYA YA MA KAN, BEYROUTH
    "Kanya ya ma Kan, Beyrouth." biog credits filmog port still CINEMAYA
        n25/26:102 Autumn/Winter 1994/95
    Thoraval, Y. Jocelyne Saab's Beirut. stills CINEMAYA n25/26:14-16
        Autumn/Winter 1994/95
SAARINEN, ESA
    Puntigam, R. Mark C. Taylor, Esa Saarinen. Imagologies [Book Review]. BLIMP
        n30:72 Winter 1994
SABAN ENTERTAINMENT, INC.
    Lawsuits
    Sandler, A. Ousted licensing VP sues Saban for $2 mil. VARIETY 358:16 Feb
        13/19 1995
SABOURAUD, FREDERIC
    Sabouraud, F. Il cinema francese e i suoi fantasmi. FCR 45:359-363 Jun/Jul
        (n446/447) 1994
SACHS, LYNNE See also HOUSE OF SCIENCE: A MUSEUM OF FALSE FACTS, THE
    Sachs, L. Script pages, storyboards, and artwork from "The House of Science:
        a Museum of False Facts" (1991). il scenario MILLENNIUM n25:58-61 Summer
        1991
Sacrifice, The See OFFRET
SADOFF, MARTY
    James, C. Driving passion. il BOXOFFICE 131:42+ [2p] Apr 1995
SADOMASOCHISM See also MASOCHISM
    United States
    Bick, I.J. "That hurts!": humor and sadomasochism in "Lolita." bibliog
        stills UFAJ 46:3-18 n2 1994
    Gabbard, K. The circulation of sadomasochistic desire in the "Lolita" texts.
        bibliog still UFAJ 46:19-30 n2 1994
SAE SANG BAKURO f (d Yeo, Kyun-dong 1994 S Korea)
    Reviews
    Stratton, D. "Out in the World" ("Sesang bakkuro"). credits VARIETY 358:75
        Feb 27/Mar 5 1995
SAETHER, YNGVE
    Saether, Y. Filmen vi ikke far se. stills F&K n1:20-22 1994
SAFE PASSAGE f (d Ackerman, Robert Allan 1994 USA)
    Reviews
    Noh, D. "Safe Passage." credits FJ 98:71-72 Mar 1995
    Patterson, A. "Safe Passage." VILLAGE VOICE 40:54 Jan 10 1995
    Travers, P. Smart women, foolish choices. stills ROLLING STONE n700:66 Jan
        26 1995
SAFETY
    Egypt
    Warg, P. Fiery sermons-on-tape imperil Arab entertainers. VARIETY 357:57
        Jan 2/8 1995
    New Zealand
    Chisnall, K. Get reel, Thornten. ONFILM [12]:15 n1 1995
SAFFORD, TONY
    Murray, S. Miramax and Australia - a distinct and bold vision. port C
        PAPERS n102:49-51 Dec 1994
SAIFU See also [LEGEND OF HEROES RETURNING EAST]
SAIJA, PAULIINA
    Saija, P. Adolf Born on kuuluisimpia animaation tekijoita Tsekinmaassa.
        port still PEILI 18:17-18 n3 1994
SAINT OF FORT WASHINGTON, THE f (d Hunter, Tim 1993 USA)
    Norcen, L. "The Saint of Fort Washington" il sonno del cinema americano. C
        NUOVO 43:15 Nov/Dec (n352) 1994
SAINT, THE f (d Harlin, Renny project 1991- USA)
    Breen, J.L. Barer, Burl. The Saint: a complete history in print, radio, film
        and television of Leslie Charteris' Robin Hood of crime, Simon Templar,
        1928-1992 [Book Review]. ARMCHAIR DET 27:222-223 n2 1994
SAKAMOTO, RYUICHI
    Loppi, A. L'enigma Sakamoto. filmog il stills C FORUM 34:36-38 Oct (n338)
        1994
SALAJEV, AJAS See also YARASA
SALAKKA, MATTI For film reviews see author under the following titles: ALADDIN;
FERNGULLY... THE LAST RAINFOREST; HANS CHRISTIAN ANDERSEN'S
THUMBELINA
    Salakka, M. Puhumme Suomea. il port still PEILI 18:6-7 n1 1994
SALAMON, JEFF For film reviews see author under the following titles: JERKY
BOYS, THE
    Salamon, J. Beyond perestroika: Jews and history in the global village.
        VILLAGE VOICE 40:59 Jan 17 1995
Salaries See WAGES AND SALARIES
SALJE, GUNTHER
    Loesche, C.-D. Antonioni [Book Review]. F KUNST n144:73-75 1994
    Meissner, G. Gunther Salje: Antonioni [Book Review]. BLIMP n30:72 Winter
        1994

SALLE, DAVID   See also SEARCH AND DESTROY
SALLE DE BAIN, LA   f (d Lvoff, John 1989 Fr)
   Sommier, J.-C. "La salle de bain": l'immobilite cinetique. bibliog CINEMAS
      4:103-114 n1 1993
SALLI, OLLI-PEKKA
   Salli, O.-P. Festivaalivieraan paivakirjasta. il PEILI 17:25-26 n3 1993
SALLIS, JAMES
   Sallis, J. David Goodis: life in black and white. il ARMCHAIR DET
      26:16-22+ [12p] n2 1993
SALLMANN, BERNHARD
   Sallmann, B. Karl Sierek. Ophuels: Bachtin. Versuch mit Film zu reden [Book
      Review]. BLIMP n30:73 Winter 1994
   Sallmann, B. "Montage/AV" [Book Review]. il BLIMP n30:52 Winter 1994
SALMI, HANNU
   Salmi, H. The Indian of the North: western traditions and Finnish Indians.
      still F&HIST 23:28-43+ [17p] n1/4 1993
Salo, 120 Days of Sodom   See SALO O LE CENTOVENTI GIORNATE DI SODOMA
SALO O LE CENTOVENTI GIORNATE DI SODOMA   f (Salo, 120 Days of Sodom d Pasolini,
Pier Paolo 1975 It/Fr)
      Censorship
   Kaufman, B.L. Cincinnati's morality squad targets Pasolini. il INDEP
      18:9-11 Jan/Feb 1995
      Reviews
   Bikacsy, G. Rokapofak es szarformancia. credits stills F VILAG 38:49-51 n3
      1995
SALOME, JEAN-PAUL   See also BRAQUEUSES, LES
SALT, BARRY
   Cantrill, A. Film style and technology: history and analysis. By Barry Salt
      [Book Review]. CANTRILL'S FMNTS n73/74:19 May 1994
SALTER, HANS J.
   Vallerand, F. Anthologies. il obit SEQUENCES n175:56-57 Nov/Dec 1994
SALTO AL VACIO   f (d Calparsoro, Daniel 1995 Sp/Fr)
      Reviews
   Stratton, D. "Jump Into the Void" ("Salto al vacio"). credits VARIETY
      358:71 Feb 27/Mar 5 1995
SALVADORI, PIERRE   See also CIBLE EMOUVANTE
   Slodowski, J. "Czuly cel." biogs credits filmogs stills FSP 40:7 n10
      (n764) 1994
SALVATORES, GABRIELE
   Rooney, D. Eye on the future. port VARIETY 358:47 Mar 6/12 1995
   Santucci, E. Obiettivo festival. il SEGNO n71:19-23 Jan/Feb 1995
SALVI, DEMETRIO
   Salvi, D. Un bel sacco di Verdone. il C FORUM 34:86 Oct (n338) 1994
SALWEN, HAL   See also DENISE CALLS UP
SAMFILM
   Edmunds, M. Blazing trails in exhib biz. port still VARIETY 358:38 Mar
      20/26 1995
   Edmunds, M. Distribber freezes out its competish. still VARIETY 358:40+
      [2p] Mar 20/26 1995
   Edmunds, M. Island's exhibition arena proves cutthroat. il VARIETY 358:42+
      [2p] Mar 20/26 1995
   Edmunds, M. Leading the pack. il still VARIETY 358:37 Mar 20/26 1995
      History
   Sam Film chronology. VARIETY 358:38 Mar 20/26 1995
SAMPLES, KEITH
   Brodie, J. Rysher sets to make splash into pic pool. stat VARIETY 358:13+
      [2p] Mar 6/12 1995
SAMSON AND DELILAH   f (d DeMille, Cecil B. 1949 USA)
   Niderost, E. Victor Mature: the "Beefcake King" and underrated actor. port
      stills CLASSIC n237:16+ [4p] Mar 1995
SAMUELSON, MARC
   Dawtrey, A. Gilbert, Samuelsons ink Miramax pic pact. il ports VARIETY
      358:14+ [2p] Mar 20/26 1995
SAMUELSON, PETER
   Dawtrey, A. Gilbert, Samuelsons ink Miramax pic pact. il ports VARIETY
      358:14+ [2p] Mar 20/26 1995
SAMUELSSON, ARNI
   Edmunds, M. Blazing trails in exhib biz. port still VARIETY 358:38 Mar
      20/26 1995
   Edmunds, M. Leading the pack. il still VARIETY 358:37 Mar 20/26 1995
SAN GE NU: REN   f (Women's Story d Peng, Xiao Lian 1990 China)
      Women in Film
   Rafman, C. Imagining a woman's world: roles for women in Chinese films.
      bibliog glos stills CINEMAS 3:126-140 n2/3 1993
SANDER, HELKE   See also BEFREIER UND BEFREITE
   Liebman, S. There should be no scissors in your mind. interv port stills
      CINEASTE 21:40-42 n1/2 1995
SANDGREN, AKE   See also KADISBELLAN
   Calderale, M. Filmografie. biogs filmogs il SEGNO n71:40 Jan/Feb 1995
SANDLER, ADAM
   Sandler, A. Ousted licensing VP sues Saban for $2 mil. VARIETY 358:16 Feb
      13/19 1995
   Sandler, A. Rhino tunes in to Oscar song winners. VARIETY 357:28 Jan 2/8
      1995
SANDOS, JAMES A.
   Sandos, J.A. and Burgess, L.E. Film as mirror, film as mask: the Hollywood
      Indian versus Native Americans in "Tell Them Willie Boy Is Here." still
      F&HIST 23:82-91+ [10p] n1/4 1993
SANDREW FILM & TEATER AB
   Hedling, O. Ekonomi och film [Book Review]. F HAFTET 22:62-63 n3 (n87) 1994
SANDRICH, MARK   See also TOP HAT
SANDS, RICK
   Evans, G. Sands shifts to Miramax Int'l prexy. port VARIETY 358:26 Feb
      13/19 1995
SANDUSKY, SHARON
   Sandusky, S. The archaeology of redemption: toward archival film. port
      stills MILLENNIUM n26:2-25 Fall 1992

SANFORTH, CLIFFORD   See also MURDER BY TELEVISION
SANG, LI KIN   See also [CRYSTAL FORTUNE RUN]
SANJEK, DAVID
   Sanjek, D. Home alone: the phenomenon of direct-to-video. stills CINEASTE
      21:98-100 n1/2 1995
Sans pitie   See SIN COMPASION
SANTA CLAUS: THE MOVIE   f (d Szwarc, Jeannot 1985 Gt Br/USA)
   Garofalo, M. Scult movie. credits il stills SEGNO n72:74-75 Mar/Apr 1995
SANTA CLAUSE, THE   f (d Pasquin, John 1994 USA)
      Sound Track Reviews
   Larson, R.D. "The Santa Clause." SCN 14:21 Mar 1995
SANTA CRUZ, ABEL
   Di Nubila, D. Abel Santa Cruz. obit VARIETY 358:54 Feb 13/19 1995
SANTILLI, CHRIS
   Santilli, C. Keeping ahead of the pack. il BOXOFFICE 131:118-120 Apr 1995
SANTOS, NELSON PEREIRA DOS
   Stam, R. Sao Nelson. stills F COM 31:82-86+ [6p] Jan/Feb 1995
      Retrospectives
   Morales, E. Cinema Novo's "Spirit of Light." still VILLAGE VOICE 40:62 Feb
      7 1995
SANTUCCI, EMMA   For film reviews see author under the following titles: WIDOWS'
PEAK
   Santucci, E. Obiettivo festival. il SEGNO n71:19-23 Jan/Feb 1995
SANZONE, DANIELA   For film reviews see author under the following titles: AIQING
WANSUI; NELL; UOMINI UOMINI UOMINI; UTOMLENNYE SOLNTSEM
SAPERSTEIN, PATRICIA
   Saperstein, P. A market where U.S. indies love to sell. still VARIETY
      358:50+ [2p] Feb 6/12 1995
   Saperstein, P. and Klady, L. Fifteen seasons of sun & sums. il ports
      VARIETY 358:bet p88 and 173 [pA2+ (2p)] Feb 20/26 1995
SARAFIAN, DERAN   See also TERMINAL VELOCITY
SARRIS, ANDREW
   Judell, B. Letters: Kael! Kael! VILLAGE VOICE 40:4 Jan 31 1995
   Sarris, A. New places in the heart. F COM 31:44 Jan/Feb 1995
SASDY, PETER   See also HANDS OF THE RIPPER
SASI, K.P.   See also ILAYUM MULLUM
SATANTANGO   f (d Tarr, Bela 1994 Hungary/FR Ger/Austria)
   Maudente, F. Paesaggio, uomini, animali, oggetti... interv still FCR
      45:390-393 Sep (n448) 1994
      Reviews
   Bikacsy, G. Satan's festival? il NEW HUNGARIAN Q 35:161-164 n134 1994
SATIRE   See also COMEDY; HUMOR; IRONY; PARODY
      United States
   Kehr, D. Who framed "Forrest Gump." il stills F COM 31:45-48+ [6p] Mar/Apr
      1995
SATO, TADAO
   Sato, T. Das Verhalten des Auges in den Filmen von Ozu und Naruse. il
      stills BLIMP [n2]:6-10 Winter 1985
SAUCER OF WATER FOR THE BIRDS, A   f (d Shenfield, Ann 1993 Australia)
   Shenfield, A. "A Saucer of Water for the Birds." il CANTRILL'S FMNTS
      n73/74:66-71 May 1994
SAUL, LOUIS
   Trenczak, H. Gisela Hundertmark, Louis Saul (Hrsg.): "Foerderung essen Filme
      auf" [Book Review]. BLIMP [n1]:65 Mar 1985
SAULNIER, JACQUES
   Midding, G. Bruchlose Verknuepfung von gebauten Dekors und Aussenszenen.
      stills F BUL 36:18-20 n6 (n197) 1994
   Saulnier, J. "Man muss in unserem Metier flexibel sein." biog filmog il
      interv stills F BUL 36:21-35 n6 (n197) 1994
   Saulnier, J. "Man muss in unserem Metier flexibel sein." biog filmog il
      interv stills F BUL 36:21-35 n6 (n197) 1994
SAUNDERS, WAL
   Dutchak, P. Wal Saunders. port stat C PAPERS n102:44+ [2p] Dec 1994
SAURA, CARLOS
   Krolikowska-Avis, E. Carlos Saura w Londynie. interv port KINO 27:40-41
      Jul 1993
SAURER, KARL   See also TRAUM VOM GROSSEN BLAUEN WASSER, DER
SAUTER, MARIANNE   For film reviews see author under the following titles:
KLATSCHMOHN - AUS DEM LEBEN MIT HEROIN; TRAUM VOM GROSSEN BLAUEN
WASSER, DER
SAUTET, CLAUDE   See also COEUR EN HIVER, UN
   Slodowski, J. "Serce jak lod." biog credits filmog port still FSP 40:7 n11
      (n765) 1994
SAUVAGET, DANIEL   For film reviews see author under the following titles: ASMARA
SAVADA, ELIAS
   Turconi, D. The American Film Institute catalog of motion pictures produced
      in the United States - film beginnings, 1893-1910 (edizione provvisoria). A
      cura di Elias Savada [Book Review]. GRIFFITHIANA n51/52:250-251 Oct 1994
Savage Nights   See NUITS FAUVES, LES
SAVAGE PLAY   f (d Lindsay, Alan in production 1995- Gt Br/New Zealand)
   Jenkins, S. Rugby & romance a winning team. il ONFILM 11:7 n11 1994/95
SAVALAS, TELLY
   Telly Savalas. biog filmog il stills STARS n21:[35-38] Winter 1995
SAVATER, FERNANDO
   Savater, F. Escalofriantemente suyo, Christopher Lee. ports stills
      NOSFERATU n6:66-69 Apr 1991
   Savater, F. La palabra imaginaria (notas sobre cine y literatura). stills
      NOSFERATU n8:4-7 Feb 1992
SAYLES, JOHN   See also SECRET OF ROAN INISH, THE
   Heuring, D. "The Secret of Roan Inish" revealed. il interv stills AMCIN
      76:34-42 Feb 1995
SCACE, NORMAN
   Obituaries. biogs filmogs il obits ports CLASSIC n236:57-59 Feb 1995
SCALERA, BUDDY
   Scalera, B. Over my dead body. Lee Server [Book Review]. SCARLET STREET
      n17:99 Winter 1995
SCALZO, DOMENICO
   Codella, L. and Scalzo, D. Una ipotesi di lavoro per il centenario del
      cinema. still C NUOVO 43:58-60 Nov/Dec (n352) 1994

SCANNER COP f (d David, Pierre 1994 USA)
    Reviews
    Harris, J. "Scanner Cop." C FANTAS 26:59 n2 1995
SCAPPEROTTI, DAN
    Scapperotti, D. "Dr. Jekyll & Ms. Hyde." il stills C FANTAS 26:10-11 n3
    1995
    Scapperotti, D. "Highlander III: the Magician." stills C FANTAS 26:54-55+
    [3p] n2 1995
Scenarios See SCREENPLAYS
Scenery See SET DESIGN AND DESIGNERS
SCENT OF A WOMAN f (d Brest, Martin 1992 USA)
    Reviews
    Uminska, B. Pulkownik i Kordeliusz. credits still KINO 27:31-32 Jun 1993
Scent of the Green Papaya, The See MUI DU DU XANH
SCHAAR, ERWIN
    Schaar, E. (Hundert) 100 Jahre Kino. il MEDIEN 38:326 n6 1994
    Schaar, E. Kommunikation und Leben. MEDIEN 38:321 n6 1994
SCHADUWLOPERS, DE f (d Dop, Peter 1995 Neth)
    Reviews
    Rooney, D. "The Shadow Walkers" ("Die Schaduwlopers"). credits VARIETY
    358:85 Feb 20/26 1995
SCHAFFER, WILLIAM
    Schaffer, W. Klein, Norman. Seven minutes: the life and death of the
    American animated cartoon [Book Review]. MEDIA INFO AUSTRALIA n75:167 Feb
    1995
SCHARRES, BARBARA
    Scharres, B. "Hard Target's" first edit made easier by EMC2. AMCIN 74:68
    Sep 1993
    Scharres, B. The hard road to "Hard Target." il still AMCIN 74:62-64+
    [10p] Sep 1993
SCHATTEN DES SCHREIBERS, DER f (d List, Niki 1995 Austria)
    Reviews
    Leydon, J. "The Poet's Princess" ("Der Schatten des Schreibers"). credits
    VARIETY 358:74 Feb 27/Mar 5 1995
SCHAUB, MARTIN For film reviews see author under the following titles: ECRIVAIN
    PUBLIC, L'; GASSER UND "GASSER"; HELAS POUR MOI
SCHEINMAN, ANDREW See also LITTLE BIG LEAGUE
SCHELL, JONATHAN See also PICASSO WOULD HAVE MADE A GLORIOUS WAITER
SCHENK, IRMBERT
    Schenk, I. Natur und Anti-Natur in den Filmen von Michelangelo Antonioni.
    C(SWITZ) 40:175-193 1994
SCHENK, RALF
    Das zweite Leben der Filmstadt Babelsberg DEFA-Spielfilme 1946-1992 [Book
    Review]. il KINO(GF) n56:28 Nov 1994
SCHEPISI, FRED See also I.Q.
SCHERTENLEIB, CHRISTOF See also LIEBE LUEGEN
SCHICKEL, RICHARD For film reviews see author under the following titles:
    BEFORE THE RAIN; BRADY BUNCH MOVIE, THE; CIRCLE OF FRIENDS; DOLORES
    CLAIBORNE; DUMB AND DUMBER; HIGHER LEARNING; LEGENDS OF THE FALL;
    NOBODY'S FOOL
    Ciment, M. BFI film classics [Book Reviews]. stills POSITIF n408:75-77 Feb
    1995
    Cremonini, G. Sam Rohdie: Rocco and his bothers (Rocco e i suoi fratelli) di
    L. Visconti [Book Reviews]. C FORUM 34:93 Sep (n337) 1994
    Hendrykowski, M. BFI Film Classics [Book Review]. il KINO 27:39-40 May
    1993
    Schickel, R. What Oscar says about Hollywood. stills TIME 145:61-62 Mar 27
    1995
SCHIFF, MICHAEL J.
    Kendall, L. and others. The next great non-controversy: "The Nightmare
    Before Christmas." il F SCORE MONTHLY n39:14 Nov 1993
SCHILLER, RALPH
    Schiller, R. Christopher Lee and Peter Cushing and horror cinema: a
    filmography of their 22 collaborations. By Mark A. Miller [Book Review]. F
    FAX n48:12+ [2p] Jan/Feb 1995
SCHINDLER'S LIST f (d Spielberg, Steven 1993 USA)
    Giacovelli, E. "Schindler's List": un nobile film che onora la memoria e la
    storia degli Ebrei contro la spietata crudelta' nazista. still C SUD
    33:1-2 Jul/Aug/Sep (n113) 1994
    Svendsen, T.O. Spielbergs versjon av Shoa. stills F&K n1:10-12 1994
SCHLAEPFER, CYRILL See also UR-MUSIG
SCHLAICH, FRIEDER See also PAUL BOWLES - HALBMOND
    "Paul Bowles - Halbmond." biogs credits still KINO(BRD) n1:24-25 1995
SCHLESINGER, JOHN See also INNOCENT, THE
    Ciapara, E. "Niewinni." biogs credits filmogs still FSP 40:6 n10 (n764)
    1994
SCHLOENDORFF, VOLKER See also HOMO FABER
    Wertenstein, W. Schloendorff z Babelsbergu. il interv KINO 27:32-33 May
    1993
SCHLOZMAN, MORRIS
    Recollections
    Williamson, K. Our man Morrie. ports BOXOFFICE 131:26+ [2p] Mar 1995
SCHLUMPF, HANS-ULRICH See also KONGRESS DER PINGUINE, DER
SCHMID, DANIEL
    Daniel Schmid Retrospektive. biog credits filmog il port BLIMP [n2]:56-59
    Winter 1985
SCHMIDT, ERNST, JR.
    Schmidt, E., Jr. Der besessene Chronist einer Welt von Godjstaplern und
    armen Kreaturen: in Wien und anderswo. biog filmog stills BLIMP [n2]:30-47
    Winter 1985
    Schmidt, E., Jr. Kurt Kren und der strukturalistische Film. biog filmog il
    BLIMP [n1]:42-49 Mar 1985
SCHNAUZER f (d Dessau, Maxim unfinished film 1984 E Ger)
    Graef, C. Erfahrungen im Spielfilm-Studio. il F & FERNSEHEN 22:12-25 n6
    1994
SCHNEIDER, ALEXANDRA For film reviews see author under the following titles:
    NICHT FUER DIE LIEBE GEBOREN?
SCHNELLER, JOHANNA
    Schneller, J. Brad attitude. il VANITY FAIR 58:70-79+ [12p] Feb 1995

SCHOEMER, KAREN
    Giles, J. and Schoemer, K. Hear me roar. stills NEWSWK 125:72 Feb 20 1995
SCHOENEMANN, HANNES See also ANNE SCHULZ; DOESCHERS; JUNGEN, DIE; KAMINSKI,
    DIE; LABENDIG; OSTBAHNHOF; SONNABEND, SONNTAG UND MONTAG FRUEH; UNTERBRECHUNG,
    DIE; UNTERWEGS; WAS AUS UNS GEWORDEN IST
    Graef, C. Hannes Schoenemann. biog filmog il F & FERNSEHEN 22:70-72 n6
    1994
    Graef, C. Operativer Vorgang "Zweifler." il F & FERNSEHEN 22:92-97 n6 1994
    Graef, C. Weitere Versuche. F & FERNSEHEN 22:88-91 n6 1994
SCHOENEMANN, SIBYLLE See also DREI ROSEN UND EIN LUFTBALLON; KINDERKRIEGEN;
    RAMONA; SKIZZE UEBER EINEN CLOWN; VERRIEGELTE ZEIT
    Graef, C. Lehrzeit im Studio. il F & FERNSEHEN 22:102-103 n6 1994
    Graef, C. Sibylle Schoenemann. biog filmog il F & FERNSEHEN 22:100-101 n6
    1994
    Graef, C. Startversuche im Spielfilm-Studio. il interv F & FERNSEHEN
    22:107-111 n6 1994
SCHOOLS IN FILM
    Italy
    Alighiero Manacorda, M. La scuola nel cinema, il cinema nella scuola. il
    still C NUOVO 43:7-10 Nov/Dec (n352) 1994
SCHRADER, PAUL See also LIGHT SLEEPER
    Smith, G. A man of excess. interv port stills S&S 5:24-29 Jan 1995
Schrei aus stein See SCREAM OF STONE
SCHRITT VOM WEGE, DER f (d Gruendgens, Gustaf 1939 Ger)
    Gruber, E. Une reprise impossible? "Effi Briest" et la question de ses
    reecritures filmiques. CINEMAS 4:59-71 n1 1993
SCHROBSDORFF, INGALISA
    Shapiro, M. and Schrobsdorff, I. It's showtime! stills INDEP 18:7+ [3p]
    Apr 1995
SCHROEDER, BARBET See also KISS OF DEATH
    Kelleher, E. Schroeder captures grim NYC in Fox's thriller, "Kiss of Death."
    il interv still FJ 98:8+ [2p] Mar 1995
    Smith, G. Barbet Schroeder. il interv stills F COM 31:64-75 Mar/Apr 1995
SCHRUENDER, MICHAEL
    Schruender, M. Gelobt sei der Alptraum bemerkungen zu Kurosawa Akiras
    "Kagemusha." credits stills BLIMP [n2]:21-24 Winter 1985
SCHRUERS, FRED
    Schruers, F. Tristan the night away. il stills PREM 8:60-63 Feb 1995
SCHTONK f (d Dietl, Helmut 1992 FR Ger)
    Reviews
    Hanisch, M. Fuehrer jest niepalny - wyjatek, ktory potwierdza regule.
    credits still KINO 27:33-34 Jun 1993
SCHUBERT, GUSZTAV For film reviews see author under the following titles:
    INTERVIEW WITH THE VAMPIRE: THE VAMPIRE CHRONICLES; RIVER WILD, THE
    Schubert, G. A vernoszo angyal. credits stills F VILAG 38:32-36 n1 1995
SCHULTZ, MARGIE
    The Slide area film book notes [Book Reviews]. CLASSIC n237:42-44+ [4p] Mar
    1995
SCHULTZ, RICK For film reviews see author under the following titles: MURDER IN
    THE FIRST
SCHUMACHER, IWAN See also GASSER UND "GASSER"
SCHUMACHER, JOEL See also CLIENT, THE
SCHUMAN, JOSEPH
    Schuman, J. "Ich kann nicht arbeiten, wenn schlechte Laune herrscht."
    filmog il interv stills F BUL 37:24-31 n1 (n198) 1995
SCHWARTZ, SHERWOOD
    Bellafante, G. The inventor of bad TV. ports TIME 145:111 Mar 13 1995
SCHWARTZBERG, SHLOMO For film reviews see author under the following titles:
    HIGHLANDER III: THE SORCERER; LOVE AND HUMAN REMAINS
    Schwartzberg, S. National Amusements opens newest showcase cinemas in East
    Windsor, Conn. il BOXOFFICE 131:58 Apr 1995
    Schwartzberg, S. National Amusements: the next generation. port BOXOFFICE
    131:54+ [2p] Apr 1995
    Schwartzberg, S. Touching the future. il BOXOFFICE 131:98+ [2p] Apr 1995
SCHWARTZMAN, KAREN
    Schwartzman, K. National cinema in translation: the politics of exhibition
    culture. il stills WIDE ANGLE 16:66-99 n3 1995
SCHWARZENEGGER, ARNOLD
    Arnold Schwarzenegger. biog filmog il stills STARS n21:[39-40] Winter 1995
    Bjorkman, S. Arnold Schwarzenegger. filmog il interv stills CHAPLIN
    36:46-54 n6 (n255) 1994/95
SCHYGULLA, HANNA
    Trenczak, H. Passion Kino oder Die Haerte, alles zu registrieren. credits
    il port BLIMP [n1]:4-13 Mar 1985
SCIENCE FICTION FILM
    Festivals
    Martani, M. Fantafestival: l'orrore riciclato mortifica il fantastico.
    stills C FORUM 34:24-26 Oct (n338) 1994
    Silent Film
    Miller, R. Silent space. il stills F FAX n49:35-43+ [11p] Mar/Apr 1995
    Japan
    Japanese science fiction, fantasy and horror films. By Stuart Galbraith IV
    [Book Review]. FATAL VISIONS n17:32 1994
    United States
    Music
    MacLean, P.A. The fantasy film music of Elmer Bernstein. il F SCORE
    MONTHLY n36/37:15-17 Aug/Sep 1993
SCOCO, DAVID R.
    Scoco, D.R. Off the street and into the lobby. port BOXOFFICE 131:bet p82
    and 83 [pSW12] Apr 1995
SCORES AND SCORING [Prior to V16, 1988 use MUSIC]
    United States
    Trailers
    Kendall, L. John Beal. interv port F SCORE MONTHLY n36/37:18-19 Aug/Sep
    1993
SCORSESE, MARTIN See also AGE OF INNOCENCE, THE; RAGING BULL
    Wharton, D. Scorsese plugs for artists' rights on Hill. port VARIETY
    358:20 Mar 20/26 1995
SCOTT, CHRIS
    Newton, M. White hats and black hats: what happened to Randolph Scott. il

MEDIA INFO AUSTRALIA n75:168 Feb 1995
Riambau, E. Shakespeare y Welles. stills NOSFERATU n8:32-39 Feb 1992
Vidal Estevez, M. William Akira Shakespeare Kurosawa. il stills NOSFERATU n8:40-47 Feb 1992

SHALLOW GRAVE f (d Boyle, Danny 1994 Gt Br)
Bennett, R. Lean mean and cruel. interv stills S&S 5:34-36 Jan 1995
Shacter, S. Sundance: Antonia Bird & Danny Boyle. intervs port stills BOMB n51:36-41 Spring 1995
  Reviews
Brown, G. Bringing up babies. stills VILLAGE VOICE 40:52 Feb 14 1995
Farber, S. Two good, violent films. still MOVIELINE 6:40-41 Mar 1995
Grant, E. "Shallow Grave." credits still FJ 98:59-60 Mar 1995
Kemp, P. "Shallow Grave." credits still S&S 5:57-58 Jan 1995
Lane, A. Scare tactics. il NEW YORKER 70:92-94 Feb 13 1995
Travers, P. "Shallow Grave." still ROLLING STONE n702:81 Feb 23 1995

SHAME f (d Jodrell, Steve 1988 Australia)
McFarlane, B. Crofts, Stephen. Identification, gender and genre in film: the case of "Shame" [Book Reviews]. MEDIA INFO AUSTRALIA n75:159-160 Feb 1995

SHANGHAI f (d Flood, James 1935 USA)
Marchetti, G. Pass och forforelse. bibliog stills F HAFTET 22:4-12 n3 (n87) 1994

SHAPIRO, LUCY
Shapiro, L. "Poltergeist II." F SCORE MONTHLY n38:12 Oct 1993

SHAPIRO, MICHELE
Shapiro, M. Stormy weather for Raindance. il stills INDEP 18:34-36 Mar 1995
Shapiro, M. Tough cookies. il ports INDEP 18:6-8 Mar 1995
Shapiro, M. and Schrobsdorff, I. It's showtime! stills INDEP 18:7+ [3p] Apr 1995

SHAPIRO, MIKE
Kendall, L. and others. The next great non-controversy: "The Nightmare Before Christmas." il F SCORE MONTHLY n39:14 Nov 1993

SHARAKU f (d Shinoda, Masahiro 1995 Japan)
Tessier, M. On locatin with Masahiro Shinoda. CINEMAYA n24:43 Summer 1994

SHARMA, SHAILJA
Sharma, S. Citizens of the empire: revisionist history and the social imaginary in "Gandhi." bibliog VEL LT TRAP n35:61-68 Spring 1995
Sharma, S. Fassbinder's "Ali" and the politics of subject-formation. bibliog stills PS 14:104-116 n1/2 1994/95

SHARMAN, LESLIE FELPERIN
Sharman, L.F. International Animation Festival, Cardiff, 16-22 May 1994. SCREEN 35:397-399 n4 1994

SHARRETT, CHRISTOPHER For film reviews see author under the following titles: NATURAL BORN KILLERS

SHATNER, WILLIAM
Beeler, M. Two captains. il still C FANTAS 26:18 n2 1995

SHAW, JOHN
Shaw, J. Ticketpro staff applies theatre experience. FJ 98:86+ [2p] Mar 1995

SHAW, SAM
Weber, B. A buddy. il INTERV 25:106-111 Feb 1995

SHAW, SEBASTIAN
Lentz, H., III. Obituaries. biogs filmogs obits ports CLASSIC n237:57-59 Mar 1995

SHAWSHANK REDEMPTION, THE f (d Darabont, Frank 1994 USA)
  Reviews
Catelli, D. "Le ali della liberta." credits still SEGNO n72:43-44 Mar/Apr 1995
Elia, M. "The Shawshank Redemption." still SEQUENCES n175:43-44 Nov/Dec 1994
Francke, L. "The Shawshank Redemption." credits still S&S 5:52 Feb 1995
Pawelczak, A. "The Shawshank Redemption." FIR 45:55 Nov/Dec 1994

SHEEN, SIMON S. See also (THREE) 3 NINJAS KNUCKLE UP
SHEINKIN, ARI See also MORE PERFECT UNION, A
SHEINKIN, STEPHEN See also MORE PERFECT UNION, A
SHELLEY, MARY
Kremski, P. Das Monster, das Mensch sein wollte. filmog il stills F BUL 36:36-39+ [9p] n6 (n197) 1994

SHELTERING SKY, THE f (d Bertolucci, Bernardo 1990 Gt Br/It/USA)
Fuehrer, P. Strovtag mot fornimmelsens nollpunkt. bibliog stills F HAFTET 22:48-54 n3 (n87) 1994

SHELTON, RON See also COBB; WHITE MEN CAN'T JUMP
SHENFIELD, ANN See also SAUCER OF WATER FOR THE BIRDS, A
Shenfield, A. "A Saucer of Water for the Birds." il CANTRILL'S FMNTS n73/74:66-71 May 1994

SHERIDAN, MICHAEL J. See also THAT'S ENTERTAINMENT! III
Sherlock Holmes and the Deadly Necklace See SHERLOCK HOLMES UND DAS HALSBAND DES TODES

SHERLOCK HOLMES (fictional character)
Bond, S.R. and Bond, S. Report form 221B Baker Street. il ARMCHAIR DET 26:70-71 n4 1993

SHERLOCK HOLMES UND DAS HALSBAND DES TODES f (Sherlock Holmes and the Deadly Necklace d Fisher, Terence/Winterstein, Frank 1962 W Ger/Fr/It)
Bernardo, J.M. "El collar de la muerte." credits il NOSFERATU n6:90-91 Apr 1991

SHERLOCK HOLMES UND DIE SIEBEN ZWERGE f (d Meyer, Guenter 1994 FR Ger)
"Sherlock Holmes und die sieben Zwerge." biog credits filmog still KINO(BRD) n1:42-43 1995

SHERMAN, GARY See also DEATH LINE
SHERMAN, ROGER M.
Sherman, R.M. Letters: how about Hampshire? INDEP 18:5 Mar 1995

SHERMAN'S MARCH f (d McElwee, Ross 1986 USA)
  Ideological Analysis
McPherson, T. "Both kinds of arms": remembering the Civil War. bibliog il VEL LT TRAP n35:3-18 Spring 1995

SHIELDS, SUSAN
Cox, D. and Shields, S. Calder Willingham. obit VARIETY 358:78 Feb 27/Mar 5 1995
Shields, S. David Wayne. biog obit VARIETY 358:188 Feb 20/26 1995
Shields, S. Earl Blackwell. biog obit VARIETY 358:75 Mar 6/12 1995

Shields, S. Keith McDaniel. biog obit VARIETY 358:56 Mar 13/19 1995
Shields, S. Sidney Kingsley. biog obit VARIETY 358:86 Mar 27/Apr 2 1995

SHIJUSHICHININ NO SHIKAKU f (d Ichikawa, Kon 1994 Japan)
  Reviews
Nazzaro, G.A. "Shijushichinin no shikaku." still C FORUM 34:25 Sep (n337) 1994

SHILS, BARRY See also WIGSTOCK: THE MOVIE
SHINING, THE f (d Kubrick, Stanley 1980 Gt Br)
  Adaptations
Vidal, J.-P. La Berlue et le mythe: S/K, ou de Stephen King a Stanley Kubrick. still CINEMAS 4:115-129 n1 1993

SHINODA, MASAHIRO See also SHARAKU
SHIPMAN, BARRY
Shipman, B. Where are the good guys? il JOURNAL WGA 7:33 Feb 1994

SHIRAT HA'SIRENA f (d Fox, Eytan 1995 Israel)
  Reviews
Leydon, J. "Song of the Siren" ("Shirat ha'sirena"). credits VARIETY 358:74 Feb 27/Mar 5 1995

SHIRE, DAVID
Buedinger, M. Returning to David Shire. interv ports SCN 14:4-7 Mar 1995

SHLAPENTOKH, DMITRY
Menashe, L. Requiem for Soviet cinema 1917-1991 [Book Reviews]. stills CINEASTE 21:23-27 n1/2 1995

SHLAPENTOKH, VLADIMIR
Menashe, L. Requiem for Soviet cinema 1917-1991 [Book Reviews]. stills CINEASTE 21:23-27 n1/2 1995

SHLYEN, BEN
Leyendecker, F. The "Boxoffice" story. il port BOXOFFICE 131:24-25 Mar 1995

SHLYEN, JESSE
Shlyen, S. Jesse's song. il ports BOXOFFICE 131:30-31 Mar 1995

SHLYEN, STEVE
Shlyen, S. Jesse's song. il ports BOXOFFICE 131:30-31 Mar 1995

SHOAH f (d Lanzmann, Claude 1985 Fr/Switz)
Roy, I. L'infatigable image ou les horizons du temps au cinema. bibliog CINEMAS 5:147-166 n1/2 1994

SHOOTER FILM PRODUCTIONS
Howard, C. Letters: get your act together. ONFILM 11:12 n11 1994/95

SHORT FILM
  Festivals
Di Luzio, A. Montecatini: il cinema "corto" va riscoprendo il racconto. stills C FORUM 34:18-20 Oct (n338) 1994
Koskinen, K. Hannoverin Eurooppalaisfestari. PEILI 17:38-39 n4 1993
Niel, P. Clermont-Ferrand. still POSITIF n408:73-74 Feb 1995
  Bangladesh
Hossain, D. Problems and prospects of short-length film: a Bangladesh overview. biog port DOC BOX 2:2-4 1993
  Finland
    Children's Film
Juurikkala, K. Lyhyt johdatus lyhytelokuvan sielunmaisemaan. stills PEILI 17:4-5 n3 1993
    Study and Teaching. Youth
Martikainen, A. Henkilokohtaisia vaikutuksia. filmog il stills PEILI 17:6-7 n3 1993
  New Zealand
    Government Support
Drinnan, J. Mates rates fade on shorts shoots. ONFILM 11:5 n11 1994/95
  Poland
Dabrowski, W. Krakow '93. REZYSER n18:1 1993
Dumala, P. Indianin. KINO 27:34 May 1993
Gradowski, K. Jutro Krakow. REZYSER n18:1 1993
  Scandinavia
    Festivals
Uggeldahl, K. Suomalaiselokuva jyllasi Nordisk Panoramassa. stills PEILI 17:26-28 n3 1993
Short Film About Killing, A See KROTKI FILM O ZABIJANIU

SHORT, THOMAS C.
Cox, D. IA boss won't sell West Coast Short. port stat VARIETY 357:1+ [3p] Jan 9/15 1995

SHOWCASE CINEMAS (East Windsor, Connecticut)
Schwartzberg, S. National Amusements opens newest showcase cinemas in East Windsor, Conn. il BOXOFFICE 131:58 Apr 1995

SHU JIAN EN CHOU LU f (d Hui, Ann 1987 Hong Kong)
Hoare, J. Romance du livre et du film: l'adaptation de la "Romance du livre et de l'epee" par Ann Hui. bibliog glos stills CINEMAS 3:141-155 n2/3 1993

SHUGRUE, J. EDWARD
Shugrue, J.E. On the verge of untold expansion. port FJ 98:88 Jan/Feb 1995

SHYER, CHARLES See also I LOVE TROUBLE
SICILIANI DE CUMIS, NICOLA
Alighiero Manacorda, M. La scuola nel cinema, il cinema nella scuola. il still C NUOVO 43:7-10 Nov/Dec (n352) 1994
Siciliani de Cumis, N. Ecce Lamelio alla scoperta della "Merica." C NUOVO 43:2-3 Nov/Dec (n352) 1994

SIDNEY, GEORGE
Mitchell, L. George Sidney: a bio-bibliography. By Eric Monder [Book Review]. DGA NEWS 20:41-42 n1 1995
Monder, E. Six degrees of George Sidney. port DGA NEWS 20:52 n1 1995
The Slide area film book notes [Book Reviews]. CLASSIC n237:42-44+ [4p] Mar 1995

SIEGEL, DAVID See also SUTURE
Romney, J. How did we get here? stills S&S 5:32-34 Feb 1995

SIEGEL, DONALD
Redman, N. A Siegel film: an autobiography. By Don Siegel [Book Reviews]. il DGA NEWS 19:33-34 n2 1994

SIEGEL, SANDY
Siegel, S. Writing is hell. JOURNAL WGA 7:39 Feb 1994

SIEGER, DIE f (d Graf, Dominik 1994 FR Ger)
  Reviews
Holloway, D. "Die Sieger." credits still KINO(GF) n56:11-12 Nov 1994

22:38-47 n3 (n87) 1994
Sjogren, O. Murha (epa)miellyttavana taiteena. il stills PEILI 17:18-24 n3 1993
SJOSTROM, VICTOR See also KORKARLEN
SJUNDE INSEGLET, DET f (Seventh Seal, The d Bergman, Ingmar 1957 Swed)
Ciment, M. BFI film classics [Book Reviews]. stills POSITIF n408:75-77 Feb 1995
Cremonini, G. Sam Rohdie: Rocco and his bothers (Rocco e i suoi fratelli) di L. Visconti [Book Reviews]. C FORUM 34:93 Sep (n337) 1994
SJURSEN, TERJE
Fonn, E.B. Minneord ved Terje Sjursens bare Troens kapell, Mollendal, 17. januar 1994. F&K n1:23 1994
Solstad, O. Terje Sjursen dod. obit port F&K n1:23 1994
SKALA, LILIA
Obituaries. biog obits VARIETY 357:83-84 Jan 2/8 1995
Obituaries. biogs filmogs il obits ports CLASSIC n236:57-59 Feb 1995
SKIFT, PER
Per Skift. obit F&K n1:23 1994
SKIN DEEP f (d Onodera, Midi 1995 Can)
    Reviews
Rooney, D. "Skin Deep." credits VARIETY 358:85-86 Feb 20/26 1995
SKIZZE UEBER EINEN CLOWN f (d Schoenemann, Sibylle 1978 E Ger)
Graef, C. Hochschulfilme. il F & FERNSEHEN 22:103-106 n6 1994
SKLAR, ROBERT
Livio, J. Film: an international history of the medium. Di Robert Sklar [Book Review]. GRIFFITHIANA n51/52:258 Oct 1994
Martin, A. Performing the city [Book Review]. Q REV F & VIDEO 15:71-76 n3 1994
SKORUPSKA, KATARZYNA For film reviews see author under the following titles: TWIN PEAKS: FIRE WALK WITH ME
SKOURAS PICTURES
    Economic Aspects
Peers, M. Skouras nixes public offering. VARIETY 358:9 Feb 27/Mar 5 1995
SKOW, JOHN
Skow, J. Hippo critical [Book Review]. il TIME 145:79 Feb 20 1995
SKRIEN
Bernink, M. "Skrien" [Book Review]. il BLIMP n30:57-58 Winter 1994
SKULL, THE f (d Francis, Freddie 1965 Gt Br)
    Adaptations
Jensen, P.M. Inside "The Skull." il stills SCARLET STREET n17:26-28+ [6p] Winter 1995
SKWARA, ANITA For film reviews see author under the following titles: FEW GOOD MEN, A
SKY TELEVISION
Dawtrey, A. Sky moves into movies. stat VARIETY 358:9 Mar 27/Apr 2 1995
SKYLER, LISANNE See also NO LOANS TODAY
SLAPSTICK
    United States
        History
Morlan, D.B. Slapstick contributions to WWII propaganda: The Three Stooges and Abbott and Costello. bibliog STUDIES POP CULT 17:29-43 n1 1994
SLATER, DAVID
Killing for culture: an illustrated history of death film from mondo to snuff. By David Kerekes & David Slater [Book Review]. il still FATAL VISIONS n17:29 1994
SLEEP WITH ME f (d Kelly, Rory 1994 USA)
Prayez, B. "Sleep With Me." bibliog credits stills GRAND ANGLE n178:27-28 Jan 1995
    Reviews
Berthomieu, P. "Sleep With Me," "Clerks," "I Like It Like That." credits stills POSITIF n407:34-35 Jan 1995
SLIDE, ANTHONY
Codelli, L. Robert Goldstein and the spirit of '76. A cura di Anthony Slide [Book Review]. GRIFFITHIANA n51/52:265 Oct 1994
Slide, A. The Slide area film book notes [Book Reviews]. CLASSIC n236:47-49 Feb 1995
Slide, A. The Slide area film book notes [Book Reviews]. CLASSIC n237:42-44+ [4p] Mar 1995
Slingshot, The See KADISBELLAN
SLOAN, BRIAN See also BOYS LIFE
SLODOWSKI, JAN
Slodowski, J. Adrianna Biedrzynska. filmog stills FSP 40:12-13 n3 (n757) 1994
Slodowski, J. Anna Dymna. filmog still FSP 40:11 n11 (n765) 1994
Slodowski, J. Beata Tyszkiewicz. filmog stills FSP 40:10-11 n5 (n759) 1994
Slodowski, J. "Czuly cel." biogs credits filmogs stills FSP 40:7 n10 (n764) 1994
Slodowski, J. "Germinal." biogs credits filmogs FSP 40:10 n4 (n758) 1994
Slodowski, J. Janusz Gajos. filmog port still FSP 40:14-15 n4 (n758) 1994
Slodowski, J. Marek Kondrat. filmog still FSP 40:13 n11 (n765) 1994
Slodowski, J. Mariusz Benoit. filmog still FSP 40:12 n11 (n765) 1994
Slodowski, J. "Obcy w Berlinie." biog credits filmog FSP 40:9 n5 (n759) 1994
Slodowski, J. Olaf Lubaszenko. filmog port stills FSP 40:12-13 n7 (n761) 1994
Slodowski, J. "Serce jak lod." biog credits filmog port still FSP 40:7 n11 (n765) 1994
Slodowski, J. "Swiatloczula historia." biog credits filmog FSP 40:6 n11 (n765) 1994
SLONIM, JEFFREY
Slonim, J. (Happy birthday) to David Caruso, an actor who's a law unto himself. il INTERV 25:22 Jan 1995
Slovenia (since 1992) See as a subheading under individual subject headings
SLOW MOVES f (d Jost, Jon 1984 USA)
Jost, J. Notes for "Slow Moves." il MILLENNIUM n25:25-29 Summer 1991
SMITH, BROOKE
Smith, B. FredandEd. il interv ports INTERV 25:116-123 Mar 1995
SMITH, GAVIN
Smith, G. A man of excess. interv port stills S&S 5:24-29 Jan 1995
Smith, G. Barbet Schroeder. il interv stills F COM 31:64-75 Mar/Apr 1995

Smith, G. Sundance kids. still F COM 31:8-9 Mar/Apr 1995
Smith, G. Teenage kicks. il stills F COM 31:74-77 Jan/Feb 1995
SMITH, JOHN
Lentz, H., III. Obituaries. biogs filmogs obits ports CLASSIC n237:57-59 Mar 1995
Obituaries. obits VARIETY 358:188-189 Feb 20/26 1995
SMITH, JOHN N. See also BOYS OF ST. VINCENT, THE
SMITH, KEVIN See also CLERKS
Peary, D. What's the catch? il MOVIELINE 6:72-73 Mar 1995
SMITH, MARGARET
Ueda, C. and Smith, M. "Eat Drink Man Woman." credits still C PAPERS n102:67-68 Dec 1994
SMITH, MEL See also RADIOLAND MURDERS
SMITH, PAUL
Grieveson, L. Steven Cohan and Ina Rae Hark (eds). Screening the male: exploring masculinities in Hollywood cinema [Book Reviews]. SCREEN 35:400-406 n4 1994
SMITH, SHAWN See also PATTERSON, SHIRLEY
Wiseman, T. Shirley Patterson a.k.a. Shawn Smith. il interv ports stills F FAX n49:56-61 Mar/Apr 1995
SMITH, THORNE
Hoppenstand, G. Murder and other acts of high society. il port ARMCHAIR DET 26:62-68 n4 1993
SMITH, TODD
Smith, T. "Needful Things." F SCORE MONTHLY n38:12 Oct 1993
Smith, T. "The Fugitive." F SCORE MONTHLY n38:12 Oct 1993
SMITHEE, ALAN See also HELLRAISER: BLOODLINE
SMITHER, ROGER
The Slide area film book notes [Book Reviews]. CLASSIC n237:42-44+ [4p] Mar 1995
SMOKE f (d Wang, Wayne 1995 USA)
    Reviews
Stratton, D. "Smoke." credits still VARIETY 358:76 Feb 20/26 1995
SMOKING f (d Resnais, Alain 1993 Fr)
    Reviews
Azzalin, C. "Smoking"; "No Smoking." credits stills SEGNO n72:38-39 Mar/Apr 1995
SMOKTUNOVSKII, INNOKENTII
Daniel, F. Dosztojevszkij-mutatvany. stills F VILAG 38:31-33 n2 1995
SNEE, PETER For film reviews see author under the following titles: DROP ZONE
Snee, P. Honi kihivasok. il interv stills F VILAG 38:29-31 n1 1995
SNIPER f (d Llosa, Luis 1993 USA)
    Reviews
Nanay, B. "Lopakodok." credits F VILAG 38:55 n3 1995
SNOW WHITE AND THE SEVEN DWARFS f (d Hand, David 1937 USA)
    Production
Catsos, G. J.M. Disney's folly! il interv stills F FAX n48:49-53 Jan/Feb 1995
SNOW WHITE AND THE SEVEN DWARFS f (d Hand, David 1993 restored version, prod 1937 USA)
    Restoration
Fisher, B. Off to work we go: the digital restoration of "Snow White." il stills AMCIN 74:48-50+ [6p] Sep 1993
SNOWMAN, THE f (d Jackson, Dianne 1982 Gt Br)
Termont, D. "Le bonhomme de neige." bibliog credits stills GRAND ANGLE n177:9-10 Dec 1994
SNUFF FILM
Killing for culture: an illustrated history of death film from mondo to snuff. By David Kerekes & David Slater [Book Review]. il still FATAL VISIONS n17:29 1994
SO LONG AT THE FAIR f (d Fisher, Terence/Darnborough, Antony 1950 Gt Br)
Aldarondo, R. "Extrano suceso." credits still NOSFERATU n6:76 Apr 1991
SO, MARK G.
So, M.G. Mancini jazzes things up in Central NY. F SCORE MONTHLY n40:4 Dec 1993
SO WHERE'S MY PRINCE, ALREADY? f (d Lister, Ardele 1976 Gt Br)
Baert, R. Skirting the issue. stills SCREEN 35:354-373 n4 1994
SOAVI, MICHELE See also DELLAMORTE DELLAMORE
SOBCHACK, VIVIAN
Sobchack, V. Vivian Sobchack responds. UFAJ 46:64-66 n1 1994
Stadler, H. Sobchack, Vivian. The address of the eye: a phenomenology of film experience [Book Review]. UFAJ 46:61-64 n1 1994
SOBOLEWSKI, TADEUSZ
Sobolewski, T. Dziennik serio. il KINO 27:7-9 Jul 1993
Sobolewski, T. Feliks Edmundowicz ze styropianu. il KINO 27:4-7 Jul 1993
Sobolewski, T. Krysia is the best. interv ports still KINO 27:20-23+ [5p] May 1993
Sobolewski, T. Listy: odpowiedz Andrzejowi Wernerowi. KINO 27:40 May 1993
Sobolewski, T. "Nie bedziemy umie rac za Sarajewo." il KINO 27:6-8 May 1993
Sobolewski, T. Pamiec Bosni. il KINO 27:4-5 May 1993
Sobolewski, T. Sejmik filmowcow. KINO 27:2 Jul 1993
Sobolewski, T. Smietnik historii? REZYSER n19:1-3 1993
Sobolewski, T. Zycie na moscie. interv port KINO 27:20-21+ [3p] Jun 1993
SOCAL CINEMAS
Santilli, C. Keeping ahead of the pack. il BOXOFFICE 131:118-120 Apr 1995
SOCIAL ATTITUDES See also PUBLIC ATTITUDES
    United States
        Men in Film
Hoberman, J. Victim victorious. stills VILLAGE VOICE 40:31-33 Mar 7 1995
SOCIAL CONTEXT
    India
Stern, J. Sara Dickey. Cinema and the urban poor in South India [Book Review]. STUDIES POP CULT 17:102 n1 1994
    United States
Kehr, D. Who framed "Forrest Gump." il stills F COM 31:45-48+ [6p] Mar/Apr 1995
Sandos, J.A. and Burgess, L.E. Film as mirror, film as mask: the Hollywood Indian versus Native Americans in "Tell Them Willie Boy Is Here." still F&HIST 23:82-91+ [10p] n1/4 1993

SOCIAL INFLUENCE   See also INFLUENCE OF FILM
   United States
      Technology
    White, J. Sympathy for the devil: Elia Kazan looks at the dark side of
     technological progress in "Wild River." bibliog still LIT/FQ 22:227-231 n4
     1994
SOCIAL ISSUES
   Union of Soviet Socialist Republics
    Christie, I. Really the most important art. stills F COM 31:41-44 Mar/Apr
     1995
Social problem film See SOCIAL ISSUES
SOCIAL VALUES   See also CRIME IN FILM; MORALITY; POPULAR CULTURE
   Horror Film
    Kupiainen, R. "Kristityn liha kuusi denaaria naula." il PEILI 18:26-27 n1
     1994
SOCIALA ARVET, DET f (d Jarl, Stefan 1993 Swed)
   Vahtera, H. Kapinallisten perinto. still PEILI 18:31 n4 1994
SOCIALIST REALISM
   Europe
    Adagio, C. Per un sano e urgente rilancio del cinema europeo. stills C
     NUOVO 43:25-27 Nov/Dec (n352) 1994
    Europe, Eastern
     Animation
     Lawrence, A. Masculinity in Eastern European animation. stills ANIMATION J
      3:32-43 n1 1994
SOCIOLOGICAL ANALYSIS
   Kaltenecker, S. Richard Dyer: The matter of images. Essays on
    representations [Book Review]. BLIMP n30:71 Winter 1994
    Canada
     Documentary Film
     Meunier, J.-P. Image, cognition, centration, decentration. bibliog diags
      CINEMAS 4:27-47 n2 1994
    Sweden
     Geber, N.-H. Krigarkulturen och popularfilmens etniska strategier. bibliog
     diag il stills F HAFTET 22:23-37 n3 (n87) 1994
SODERBERGH, STEVEN See also UNDERNEATH, THE
   Pirolini, A. Delitti e segreti di Stephen Soderbergh. C SUD 33:29
    Jul/Aug/Sep (n113) 1994
SOFIA, W.D. See also HALIMUN
SOFIE f (d Ullmann, Liv 1992 Denmk/Norw/Swed)
   Reviews
    Viviani, C. "Sofie." still POSITIF n408:59-60 Feb 1995
SOFTLEY, IAIN See also BACKBEAT
Software See COMPUTER SOFTWARE
SOGNO DELLA FARFALLA, IL f (d Bellocchio, Marco 1994 It/Switz/Fr)
   Roberti, B. Ascoltare il mondo. stills FCR 45:315-318 Jun/Jul (n446/447)
    1994
   Roberti, B. and others. Lavorare sulla bellezza del "niente." interv stills
    FCR 45:322-328 Jun/Jul (n446/447) 1994
   Turco, D. Una ricerca sul vuoto. still FCR 45:319-321 Jun/Jul (n446/447)
    1994
SOL DEL MEMBRILLO, EL f (d Erice, Victor 1992 Sp)
   Ehrlich, L.C. Interior gardens: Victor Erice's "Dream of Light" and the
    Bodegon tradition. il stills CJ 34:22-36 n2 1995
SOLDINI, SILVIO See also D'ESTATE
SOLITAIRE FOR TWO f (d Sinyor, Gary 1995 Gt Br)
   Reviews
    Elley, D. "Solitaire for 2." credits VARIETY 358:70-71 Feb 27/Mar 5 1995
    Glaessner, V. "Solitaire for Two." credits still S&S 5:53 Feb 1995
SOLMAN, GREGORY
   Solman, G. Hollywood's high-fiber diet. il DGA NEWS 19:18 n6 1994/95
   Solman, G. New twists in video assists. il DGA NEWS 19:10-11+ [3p] n2 1994
   Solman, G. Sound advice for editing, playback. il DGA NEWS 20:12-13 n1
    1995
SOLSTAD, ODDBJORN
   Solstad, O. Terje Sjursen dod. obit port F&K n1:23 1994
SOMBRA YA PRONTO SERAS, UNA f (d Olivera, Hector 1994 Arg)
   Reviews
    Comuzio, E. "Una sombra ya pronto seras." still C FORUM 34:16 Sep (n337)
    1994
SOMEBODY TO LOVE f (d Rockwell, Alexandre 1994 USA)
   Reviews
    Adagio, C. "Qualcuno da amare." credits still C NUOVO 43:42-43 Nov/Dec
    (n352) 1994
SOMES, MICHAEL
   Obituaries. biogs filmogs il obits ports CLASSIC n236:57-59 Feb 1995
SOMMERS, STEPHEN See also RUDYARD KIPLING'S THE JUNGLE BOOK
SOMMIER, JEAN-CLAUDE
   Sommier, J.-C. "La salle de bain": l'immobilite cinetique. bibliog CINEMAS
    4:103-114 n1 1993
Son of the Shark See FILS DU REQUIN, LE
SONDER, CARSTEN See also ELSKER, ELSKER IKKE
Song of the Exile See KE TU CHIU HEN
SONNABEND, SONNTAG UND MONTAG FRUEH f (d Schoenemann, Hannes 1979 E Ger)
   Graef, C. Hochschulfilme. il F & FERNSEHEN 22:73-81 n6 1994
SONY CORPORATION
   Evans, G. Sony spreads its "Wings." stat VARIETY 358:7+ [2p] Mar 13/19
    1995
   Robinson, G. and Cox, D. Power shift at Sony Corp. port VARIETY 358:15+
    [2p] Mar 27/Apr 2 1995
SONY LINCOLN SQUARE THEATRE (New York, New York)
   Sony Lincoln Square Theatre provides view of the future. il FJ 98:34+ [2p]
    Mar 1995
SONY PICTURES CLASSICS
   Evans, G. Sony Classics finds place for "Sun." VARIETY 358:28 Feb 13/19
    1995
SONY PICTURES ENTERTAINMENT
   Cox, D. New day dawns at Sony. il stat VARIETY 358:11+ [2p] Feb 6/12 1995
SONY THEATRES LINCOLN SQUARE (New York, New York)
   Albanese, A. The shape of things to come? il BOXOFFICE 131:bet p82 and 83

[pSW16-SW18] Apr 1995
SOPHIE TAEUBER-ARP f (d Kuehn, Christoph 1993 Switz)
   Reviews
    Weilenmann, C. "Sophie Taeuber-Arp." credits still C(SWITZ) 40:212-213
    1994
SOPSITS, ARPAD See also VIDEO BLUES
SORDI, ALBERTO See also NESTORE L'ULTIMA CORSA
SORDILLO, MICHELE See also DA QUALCHE PARTE IN CITTA
SORENSEN, HOLLY
   Sorensen, H. Double feature. il interv PREM 8:42 Apr 1995
   Sorensen, H. Kevin Bacon wants to be the guy. il ports stills PREM 8:70-73
    Mar 1995
SORENSEN, JANET
   Sorensen, J. "Lef," Eisenstein, and the politics of form. bibliog F
    CRITICISM 19:55-74 n2 1994/95
SORENSON, ELISABETH
   Sorenson, E. Bjud upp till dans! port CHAPLIN 36:69 n6 (n255) 1994/95
SOSE HALUNK MEG f (d Koltai, Robert 1993 Hungary)
   Reviews
    Bikacsy, G. A clowning success. NEW HUNGARIAN Q 35:172-173 n133 1994
SOTRA, ZDRAVKO See also DNEVNIK UVREDA 1993
SOTTO, AUGUSTIN
   Sotto, A. Philippine independence and national cinema. stills CINEMAYA
    n24:8-21 Summer 1994
SOUFFLE AU COEUR, LE f (Murmur of the Heart d Malle, Louis 1971 Fr)
   Sexuality in Film
    Varto, J. Lapsen seksuaalisuus elokuvassa ja sen ulkopuolella. stills
    PEILI 18:18-20 n2 1994
SOUL SURVIVOR f (d Williams, Stephen 1995 Can)
   Reviews
    Klady, L. "Soul Survivor." credits VARIETY 358:51 Feb 13/19 1995
SOUND
   Techniques
    Chateauvert, J. Altman, Rick (direction). Sound theory. Sound practice [Book
    Review]. CINEMAS 4:157-166 n3 1994
   Theory
    Chateauvert, J. Altman, Rick (direction). Sound theory. Sound practice [Book
    Review]. CINEMAS 4:157-166 n3 1994
    Rosenbaum, J. Audio-vision: sound on screen. By Michael Chion. Edited and
    translated by Claudia Gorbman [Book Review]. CINEASTE 21:94-95 n1/2 1995
   France
    History
    Cremonini, G. Il fascino discreto dell'intelligenza. stills C FORUM
     34:28-35 Oct (n338) 1994
   United States
    Awards
    O'Steen, K. The sound and the jury. VARIETY 358:13+ [2p] Mar 6/12 1995
    Post-production
    Weis, E. Sync tanks. il CINEASTE 21:56-61 n1/2 1995
SOUND DESIGN AND DESIGNERS
   United States
    Altman, R. Deep-focus sound: "Citizen Kane" and the radio aesthetic. diag
    scenario Q REV F & VIDEO 15:1-34 n3 1994
SOUND EQUIPMENT   See also LOUDSPEAKERS; SOUND RECORDERS AND RECORDING
   United States
    Theater Equipment
    Altman, R. The sound of sound. diags il CINEASTE 21:68-71 n1/2 1995
SOUND RECORDERS AND RECORDING
   United States
    Techniques
    Hones, L. How to avoid a noise dive. il INDEP 18:42-43 Apr 1995
SOUND/STAGE RECORDINGS
   These boots were made for hawkin': part III - rogue's gallery. il F SCORE
    MONTHLY n39:6 Nov 1993
SOUPER, LE f (d Molinaro, Edouard 1993 Fr)
   Reviews
    Giacovelli, E. "A cena col diavolo." C SUD 33:22 Jul/Aug/Sep (n113) 1994
SOURIRE, LE f (d Miller, Claude 1994 Fr)
   Reviews
    Gendron, S. "Le sourire." credits still SEQUENCES n174:40-41 Sep/Oct 1994
    Landry, G. Jump for Odile. credits stills 24 IMAGES n75:63 Dec/Jan 1994/95
SOUTH SEAS ADVENTURE f (1958 USA)
   Sound Track Reviews
    Kendall, L. and Care, R. New from label "X": the Cinema Maestro series. F
    SCORE MONTHLY n38:13 Oct 1993
South, The See SUR, EL
Soy Cuba See IA KUBA
SPACE
   Cosandey, R. Wo ist die grosse Treppe hingekommen? il stills C(SWITZ)
    40:51-74 1994
   Theory
    Gregoire, P. Gardies, Andre. L'espace au cinema [Book Reviews]. CINEMAS
    5:229-232 n1/2 1994
   France
    Grange, M.-F. Paysage resnaisien ou variations autour de la mise en espace
    du temps. bibliog still CINEMAS 5:135-146 n1/2 1994
   United States
    Marocco, P. Giocare il tempo. filmog port stills SEGNO n71:8-11 Jan/Feb
    1995
    Theory
    Parshall, P.F. Buster Keaton and the space of farce: "Steamboat Bill, Jr."
    versus "The Cameraman." bibliog diag stills UFAJ 46:29-46 n3 1994
SPACESHIPS IN FILM
   United States
    Stein, M. The dream machines: an illustrated history of the spaceship in
    art, science and literature. By Ron Miller [Book Review]. il F FAX n49:12
    Mar/Apr 1995
SPADOLA, DON
   Obituary. obit FJ 98:80 Mar 1995
Spaghetti westerns See WESTERN FILM

SPAGNOLETTI, GIOVANNI
  Comuzio, C. Giovanni Spagnoletti (a cura di): Schermi Germanici [Book
    Review]. il C FORUM 34:93 Sep (n337) 1994
  Comuzio, E. Bruno Di Marino e Giovanni Spagnoletti (a cura di): Friedrich
    Wilhelm Murnau [Book Review]. il C FORUM 34:93 Nov (n339) 1994
Spain See as a subheading under individual subject headings
Sparrow See STORIA DI UNA CAPINERA
Speakers See LOUDSPEAKERS
SPEAKING PARTS f (d Egoyan, Atom 1989 Can)
  Egoyan, A. Tension en surface. il still POSITIF n406:88-90 Dec 1994
SPECIAL EFFECTS See also PROPERTIES
    France
        Commercials
  Magid, R. Perrier ad employs latest whistles and bells. stills AMCIN
    74:26-28+ [5p] Sep 1993
    United States
  Magid, R. Fine-tuning "Radioland Murders." il AMCIN 76:66-72 Mar 1995
  Prokop, T. "Stargate." il stills C FANTAS 26:48-49+ [4p] n3 1995
        Computer Applications. Digital
  Alomorszagba belep a szamitogep. il stills F VILAG 38:6-9 n3 1995
        Effects on Film
  Weiner, R. Helmers hear effective siren song. VARIETY 358:10 Mar 13/19 1995
        History
  Goldman, H. Mr. Electric. il stills F FAX n48:37-41 Jan/Feb 1995
        Industry
  Weiner, R. Effects houses enter cutthroat competition. il VARIETY 358:7+
    [2p] Mar 13/19 1995
        Technical Aspects
  Magid, R. Digital domain arranges an "Interview With the Vampire." stills
    AMCIN 76:53-54+ [7p] Jan 1995
SPECIALE, ALESSANDRA
  Speciale, A. La speranza e tutta nella donna. still SEGNO n63:90 Sep/Oct
    1993
SPECIALIST, THE f (d Llosa, Luis 1994 USA)
  Venchiarutti, M. "L'expert." credits stills GRAND ANGLE n176:11-12 Nov
    1994
    Sound Track Reviews
  Lehti, S.J. and Theiss, K. "Mary Shelley's Frankenstein": "The Specialist."
    il SCN 14:18-19 Mar 1995
  Pugliese, R. Segnodischi. filmog stills SEGNO n72:77 Mar/Apr 1995
    Reviews
  Atkinson, M. "The Specialist." credits still S&S 5:58-59 Jan 1995
  Biro, P. "A specialista." credits still F VILAG 38:63 n1 1995
  Cieutat, M. "L'expert." POSITIF n407:41 Jan 1995
SPECIALTY FILM IMPORT LIMITED
  Montreal cinematographie en debut de siecle. il port still 24 IMAGES
    n75:51-54 Dec/Jan 1994/95
SPECOGNA, HEIDI See also DECKNAME: ROSA
SPECTACLE FILM
    Italy
        History
  Slide, A. The Slide area film book notes [Book Reviews]. CLASSIC
    n237:42-44+ [4p] Mar 1995
SPECTATORSHIP
  McKinley, A. Anne Friedberg. Window shopping: cinema and the postmodern
    [Book Review]. ARACHNE 1:270-274 n2 1994
    Documentary Film
  Morin, S. "Nick's Movie": le point de fuite. bibliog still CINEMAS
    4:101-117 n2 1994
    Australia
  McFarlane, B. Crofts, Stephen. Identification, gender and genre in film: the
    case of "Shame" [Book Reviews]. MEDIA INFO AUSTRALIA n75:159-160 Feb 1995
    Brazil
        Political Analysis
  Sippl, D. Terrorist acts and "legitimate" torture in Brazil: "How Nice to
    See You Alive." bibliog il stills DISCOURSE n17.1:77-92 Fall 1994
    Canada
  Gardies, R. Vers l'emotion documentaire. bibliog CINEMAS 4:49-60 n2 1994
  Jost, F. Le spectateur qui en savait trop. bibliog still CINEMAS 4:121-133
    n3 1994
  Roy, L. L'infatigable image ou les horizons du temps au cinema. bibliog
    CINEMAS 5:147-166 n1/2 1994
        Feminist Analysis
  Russell, C. Mourning the woman's film: the dislocated spectator of "The
    Company of Strangers." stills CAN J F STUD 3:25-40 n2 1994
    Quebec. Documentary Film
  Marsolais, G. Les mots de la tribu. stills CINEMAS 4:133-150 n2 1994
    Great Britain
        Feminist Analysis
  Stacey, J. Hollywood memories. SCREEN 35:317-335 n4 1994
    Hungary
  Kovacs, A. Parbeszed a kozonseggel. F VILAG 38:10-11 n4 1995
    Italy
  Bruno, M.W. Il punto di non ritorno. stills SEGNO n63:19-20 Sep/Oct 1993
    United States
  Williams, L. Cinema and spectatorship. By Judith Mayne [Book Review]. FQ
    48:56-57 n2 1994/95
        Feminist Analysis
  Hastie, A. Window shopping: cinema and the postmodern. Anne Friedberg [Book
    Reviews]. DISCOURSE n17.2:171-176 Winter 1994/95
SPEECHLESS f (d Underwood, Ron 1994 USA)
    Reviews
  Fontanini, C. "Ciao Julia sono Kevin." credits still FILM (ITALY) 3:19-20
    n13 1995
  Grant, E. "Speechless." credits FJ 98:54 Jan/Feb 1995
  Kauffmann, S. Early winter roundup. NEW REPUB 212:30-31 Jan 23 1995
  Travers, P. Smart women, foolish choices. stills ROLLING STONE n700:66 Jan
    26 1995

SPEED f (d De Bont, Jan 1994 USA)
    Sound Track Reviews
  Pugliese, R. Segnodischi. filmog stills SEGNO n72:77 Mar/Apr 1995
    Reviews
  De Marinis, G. "Speed." credit still C FORUM 34:80-81 Oct (n338) 1994
  Meyers, R. The crime screen. port still ARMCHAIR DET 27:430-431 n4 1994
SPENCE, PETE
  Spence, P. Visual poem no. 10. il CANTRILL'S FMNTS n73/74:65 May 1994
SPENCER, W. BALDWIN
  Long, C. Australia's first films: facts and fables, part eleven: Aborigines
    and actors. filmogs il map ports C PAPERS n102:52-57+ [8p] Dec 1994
SPERGEL, MARK
  Turner, G. Reinventing reality. By Mark Spergel [Book Review]. AMCIN
    76:85-86 Jan 1995
SPHEERIS, PENELOPE See also LITTLE RASCALS, THE
SPIDER & ROSE f (d Bennett, Bill 1994 Australia)
    Reviews
  Hannah, L. "Spider & Rose." credits still C PAPERS n102:71-72 Dec 1994
SPIELBERG, STEVEN See also JURASSIC PARK; SCHINDLER'S LIST
  Corliss, R. Hey, let's put on a show! il ports TIME 145:54-60 Mar 27 1995
  Haile, M. Reminting "Schindler's" gold. il stills BOXOFFICE 131:66+ [4p]
    Apr 1995
SPIKE OF LOVE f (d DiMarco, Steve 1995 Can)
    Reviews
  Elley, D. "Spike of Love." credits VARIETY 358:75 Feb 27/Mar 5 1995
SPILLANE, MARGARET
  Spillane, M. Slam-dunked. NATION 260:333 Mar 13 1995
SPINES, CHRISTINE
  O'Neill, K. and Spines, C. "Premiere's" wrap party 1994. il port stat
    tables PREM 8:81-87 Feb 1995
  Spines, C. Go to your room! il still PREM 8:31-32 Feb 1995
  Spines, C. This boy's film. il PREM 8:33-34 Apr 1995
SPIRIT OF '76, THE f (d Montgomery, Frank 1917 USA)
  Codelli, L. Robert Goldstein and the spirit of '76. A cura di Anthony Slide
    [Book Review]. GRIFFITHIANA n51/52:265 Oct 1994
Spirit of the Beehive, The See ESPIRITU DE LA COLMENA, EL
SPIRITUALITY
  Paquette, J.-M. Tarkovski, cineaste cynique. bibliog CINEMAS 4:15-23 n3
    1994
SPLATTING IMAGE
  Riepe, M. "Splatting Image" [Book Review]. il BLIMP n30:60-61 Winter 1994
SPOLIN, VIOLA
  Obituaries. biogs filmogs il obits ports CLASSIC n236:57-59 Feb 1995
Sponsored film See COMMISSIONED FILM
SPOTTISWOODE, ROGER See also AND THE BAND PLAYED ON
SPRINGER, JOHN
  Springer, J. The films of Sylvia Sydney. il stills FIR 45:31-34 Nov/Dec
    1994
SPY FILM
    United States
        History
  Breen, J.L. Langman, Larry, and David Ebner. Encyclopedia of American spy
    films [Book Review]. ARMCHAIR DET 27:93-94 n1 1994
STACEY, JACKIE
  Stacey, J. Hollywood memories. SCREEN 35:317-335 n4 1994
STADLER, HARALD
  Sobchack, V. Vivian Sobchack responds. UFAJ 46:64-66 n1 1994
  Stadler, H. Sobchack, Vivian. The address of the eye: a phenomenology of
    film experience [Book Review]. UFAJ 46:61-64 n1 1994
Stag film See PORNOGRAPHY AND OBSCENITY
STAGECOACH f (d Ford, John 1939 USA)
  Ciment, M. BFI film classics [Book Reviews]. stills POSITIF n408:75-77 Feb
    1995
  Cremonini, G. Sam Rohdie: Rocco and his bothers (Rocco e i suoi fratelli) di
    L. Visconti [Book Reviews]. C FORUM 34:93 Sep (n337) 1994
  Hendrykowski, M. BFI Film Classics [Book Review]. il KINO 27:39-40 May
    1993
STAHL, JOHN M. See also BACK STREET
STAIRS 1 GENEVA f (d Greenaway, Peter 1994 Gt Br)
    Reviews
  Fornara, B. "Stairs 1 Geneva." still C FORUM 34:28 Sep (n337) 1994
STALKER f (d Tarkovskii, Andrei 1979 USSR)
    Production
  Tsymbal, E. Zonen. il stills CHAPLIN 36:26-30 n6 (n255) 1994/95
STALLONE, SYLVESTER
  Williamson, K. On the Sly. port BOXOFFICE 131:10-12 Apr 1995
STALTER, KATHERINE
  Stalter, K. Explosive close-ups trigger "Blown Away." diag il AMCIN
    76:72-74 Feb 1995
STAM, ROBERT
  Kalaga, W. Stam, Robert, Burgoyne, Robert, Flitterman-Lewis, Sandy. New
    vocabularies in film semiotics: structuralism, post-structuralism, and
    beyond [Book Review]. CINEMAS 4:167-175 n3 1994
  Stam, R. Sao Nelson. stills F COM 31:82-86+ [6p] Jan/Feb 1995
STANBURY, PATRICK
  Adamson, J. and others. Forgotten laughter. credits port stills
    GRIFFITHIANA n51/52:170-197 Oct 1994
  Adamson, J. and others. La fabbrica della risata. credits port stills
    GRIFFITHIANA n51/52:170-197 Oct 1994
STAND DER DINGE, DER f (State of Things, The d Wenders, Wim 1982 USA/W
  Ger/Port)
  Russell, C. The life and death of authorship in Wim Wenders' "The State of
    Things." scenario CAN J F STUD 1:15-28 n1 1990
STANDARDS AND RECOMMENDED PRACTICES
    Europe, Eastern
        Conferences, Institutes, Workshops, etc.
  Gradowski, K. O zgromadzeniu europejskiej sekcji FISTAV, porozumieniu z
    Dunczykami i projekcie ustawy o kinematografii. REZYSER n15:5 1993
    New Zealand
  Missing in action - the Production Code of Practice. il ONFILM [12]:14 n2

Stone, O. Level a Cenzorhoz. F VILAG 38:34-35 n1 1995

STONE, SHARON
Zehme, B. Is Sharon Stone scaring you yet? ports ESQUIRE 123:84-91 Mar 1995

STONEHILL, BRIAN
Stonehill, B. The debate over "ocularcentrism" [Book Reviews]. J COMM 45:147-152 n1 1995

STORA, BERNARD See also CONSENTEMENT MUTUEL

STORAGE OF FILM
United States
Weiner, R. Healthy film libraries prove indie treasure trove. VARIETY 358:bet p88 and 173 [pA5+ (2p)] Feb 20/26 1995

STORARO, VITTORIO
Gentry, R. Writing with light. il interv stills FQ 48:2-9 n2 1994/95
Storaro, V. The right to sign ourselves as "authors of cinematography." AMCIN 76:96 Feb 1995

STORCK, HENRI
Montanaro, C. Henri Storck: il litorale belga. A cura di Michele Canosa [Book Review]. GRIFFITHIANA n51/52:260 Oct 1994
Petley, J. Henri Storck - documentarist, surrealist, anarchist. port VERTIGO (UK) 1:33 n4 1994/95
Petley, J. and Chanan, M. Henri Storck interviewed for "Vertigo." interv stills VERTIGO (UK) 1:34-36 n4 1994/95
Storck, H. Why the documentary cinema? VERTIGO (UK) 1:34-36 n4 1994/95

STORIA DI UNA CAPINERA f (Sparrow d Zeffirelli, Franco 1993 It)
Sound Track Reviews
Comuzio, E. Claudio Capponi e Alessio Vlad: "Storia di una capinera. C FORUM 34:96 Sep (n337) 1994
Reviews
Tamas, A. "Egy apaca szerelme." credits still F VILAG 38:58 n4 1995

STORYBOARDS
Berthome, J.-P. Le "storyboard." il POSITIF n407:76-84 Jan 1995
France
Exhibitions
Berthome, J.-P. "Storyboard" et bande dessinee. il POSITIF n407:90-91 Jan 1995
United States
Berthome, J.-P. and Kohn, O. Entretien avec Jeff Balsmeyer. il interv still POSITIF n407:85-89 Jan 1995

STOVALL, NATASHA For film reviews see author under the following titles: LAMB

STOWARZYSZENIA NIEZALEZNYCH PRODUCENTOW FILMOWYCH (Poland)
Sendecka, M. Szkolenie w Burkina Faso. interv REZYSER n19:3-5 1993

STOWE, MADELEINE
Ciapara, E. "Blink." biog credits filmogs still FSP 40:8 n4 (n758) 1994

STRANE STORIE - RACCONTI DI FINE SECOLO f (d Baldoni, Sandro 1994 It)
Reviews
Coco, A. "Strane storie." credits il still SEGNO n72:49-50 Mar/Apr 1995
Fadda, M. "Strane storie." still C FORUM 34:31-32 Sep (n337) 1994

Strangers in Good Company See COMPANY OF STRANGERS, THE

STRASBERG, LEE
Midding, G. Lee Strasberg: Ein Traum der Leidenschaft [Book Review]. il F BUL 37:7 n1 (n198) 1995

STRASS, DER f (d Hoentsch, Andreas 1991 FR Ger)
Graef, C. Weitere Projekte. il F & FERNSEHEN 22:42-47 n6 1994

STRASSER, TODD
Lehtonen, V.-P. "Super-Mario" - kirja tuli, elokuvaa el. credits il still PEILI 17:46 n4 1993

STRATTON, DAVID For film reviews see author under the following titles: A CAUSA SECRETA; AFRIQUE, MON AFRIQUE...; AHARE HAHAGIM; AMEERIKA MAED; BABY I WILL MAKE YOU SWEAT; BLUE IN THE FACE; BROOKLYN TESTVER, A; CARMEN & BABYFACE; DUPE OD MRAMORA; EBREDES; ESTATE DI BOBBY CHARLTON, L'; FILS DE GASCOGNE, LE; GOLOS TRAVY; HONGFEN; LAZOS; LIE DOWN WITH DOGS; MANNEN UTAN ANSIKTE; PITRA, PUTRA AUR DHARAMYUDDHA; RESZLEG, A; REY DEL RIO, EL; SAE SANG BAKURO; SALTO AL VACIO; SMOKE; SUITE 16; TAEBAEK SANMAEK; TOKYO KYODAI; TORVENYTELEN; VOROS COLIBRI; VUELCOS DEL CORAZON, LOS; YARASA; ZAWROCONY; ZENSHIN SHOSETSUKA
Elley, D. and Stratton, D. "Bait" lures Berlin's top bear. VARIETY 358:30 Feb 27/Mar 5 1995
Stratton, D. Peter Refn. biog obit VARIETY 358:59 Mar 20/26 1995
Stratton, D. Upbeat mood and quirky fare in land of Oz, Kiwis. VARIETY 358:60 Feb 6/12 1995

STRAUB, JEAN-MARIE
Zach, P. Straub. filmog il interv BLIMP [n1]:14-25 Mar 1985

STRAUSS, ULF VON
Strauss, U. von. Play it again, Sam! il CHAPLIN 36:40-41 n6 (n255) 1994/95

STRAW DOGS f (d Peckinpah, Sam 1971 Gt Br/USA)
Feminist Analysis
Williams, L.R. Women can only misbehave. still S&S 5:26-27 Feb 1995
Production
Weddle, D. "Straw Dogs": they want to see brains flying out? il stills S&S 5:20-25 Feb 1995

STRAW, WILL
Straw, W. Canada's Hollywood: the Canadian state and feature films. By Ted Magder [Book Review]. CAN J COM 19:566-567 n3/4 1994

Strawberry and Chocolate See FRESA Y CHOCOLATE

STRAZEWSKI, RYSZARD
Plazewski, J. Wspolprodukcje hydra, czy szansa? il interv ports KINO 27:6-9 Jun 1993

STREET FIGHTER f (d De Souza, Steven E. 1994 USA)
Brandt, J.B. "Street Fighter." il stills C FANTAS 26:56-57 n2 1995
Reviews
Grunden, C. "Street Fighter." credits FJ 98:55 Jan/Feb 1995
Haile, M. "Street Fighter." BOXOFFICE 131:bet p89 and 96 [pR20] Mar 1995
Levy, E. Van Damme plays F/X-laden "Fighter." credits still VARIETY 357:72+ [2p] Jan 2/8 1995

STRICK, JOSEPH See also CRIMINALS

STRICK, PHILIP For film reviews see author under the following titles: MIRACLE ON 34TH STREET; VANYA ON 42ND STREET
Strick, P. Fresh slogans [Book Review]. still S&S 5:34-35 Apr 1995

STRICKFADEN, KENNETH
Goldman, H. Mr. Electric. il stills F FAX n48:37-41 Jan/Feb 1995

STRIKES
France
Williams, M. Unions suspend dubbing strike. VARIETY 357:49 Jan 9/15 1995
United States
Actors and Actresses
Cox, D. Studios running scared. VARIETY 358:6 Mar 13/19 1995

STRINGER, HOWARD
Zoglin, R. Kicked while it's down. graph port still TIME 145:71 Mar 6 1995

STRIPTEASE f (d Bergman, Andrew 1996 USA)
Klady, L. (Ten) $10 mil gets Moore to "Strip." VARIETY 358:22 Feb 20/26 1995

STRODE, WOODY
Milestones. obit still TIME 145:22 Jan 16 1995
Obituaries. biogs filmogs il obits ports CLASSIC n236:57-59 Feb 1995

STROHEIM, ERICH VON See also GREED
Codelli, L. "Greed." Di Jonathan Rosenbaum [Book Reviews]. GRIFFITHIANA n51/52:260 Oct 1994
Schmidt, E., Jr. Der besessene Chronist einer Welt von Godjstaplern und armen Kreaturen: in Wien und anderswo. biog filmog stills BLIMP [n2]:30-47 Winter 1985

STROSSEN, NADINE
De Grazia, E. Sex de jure [Book Reviews]. NATION 260:242-249 Feb 20 1995
Kershaw, S. Against pornophobia. port NEW YORK 28:20+ [2p] Jan 16 1995
Sunstein, C.R. Porn on the Fourth of July [Book Review]. NEW REPUB 212:42-45 Jan 9/16 1995

STRUCTURAL ANALYSIS See also DECONSTRUCTIVE ANALYSIS
France
Chateauvert, J. Metz, Christian. L'enonciation impersonnelle ou le site du film [Book Review]. bibliog CINEMAS 3:241-246 n2/3 1993

STRUCTURALIST FILM
Austria
Schmidt, E., Jr. Kurt Kren und der strukturalistische Film. biog filmog il BLIMP [n1]:42-49 Mar 1985

STRUCTURE See also ENDINGS; SCENE; SPACE; TIME
United States
Mueller, J.E. "Top Hat" et l'intermedialite de la comedie musicale. bibliog CINEMAS 5:211-220 n1/2 1994

STUART, ANDREA
Stuart, A. Looking at Josephine Baker. WOMEN 5:137-143 n2 1994

STUART, BRUCE
Barson, M. Hollywood's first choices: how the greatest casting decisions were made. By Jeff Burkhart & Bruce Stuart [Book Review]. DGA NEWS 20:42-43 n1 1995

STUDIO DRIVE-IN (Culver City, California)
James, C. Driving passion. il BOXOFFICE 131:42+ [2p] Apr 1995

STUDIO SYSTEM See also STAR SYSTEM
United States
History
Muscio, G. The commerce of classicism [Book Review]. Q REV F & VIDEO 15:57-69 n3 1994

Studios See names of studios (e.g. WARNER BROS. INC.)

STUDLAR, GAYLYN
Longfellow, B. Gaylyn Studlar. In the realm of pleasure: Von Sternberg, Dietrich and the masochistic aesthetic [Book Review]. CAN J F STUD 1:83-89 n2 1991
Polan, D. Reflections in a male eye: John Huston and the American experience. Edited by Gaylyn Studlar and David Desser [Book Review]. F CRITICISM 19:103-108 n2 1994/95
Studlar, G. Seduced and abandoned? Feminist film theory and psychoanalysis in the 1990s. bibliog PS 14:5-13 n1/2 1994/95

STUDY AND TEACHING See also APPRECIATION; FILM STUDIES; MEDIA STUDIES; PROFESSIONAL EDUCATION
Finland
Animation
Lehtonen, V.-p. Nimekkaat opettajat ja kova innostus. il PEILI 17:4-5 n4 1993
Short Film. Youth
Martikainen, A. Henkilokohtaisia vaikutuksia. filmog il stills PEILI 17:6-7 n3 1993
Italy
Alighiero Manacorda, M. La scuola nel cinema, il cinema nella scuola. il still C NUOVO 43:7-10 Nov/Dec (n352) 1994
Loffreda, P. Primi sguardi nella scuola: dalla descrizione al racconto. il stills C FORUM 34:3-7 Oct (n338) 1994

Stunt cinematography See SPECIAL EFFECTS

STYLE
Cantrill, A. Film style and technology: history and analysis. By Barry Salt [Book Review]. CANTRILL'S FMNTS n73/74:19 May 1994
Malkames, K. The non-obtrusive camera. port AMCIN 74:104 Sep 1993
Spain
Ehrlich, L.C. Interior gardens: Victor Erice's "Dream of Light" and the Bodegon tradition. il stills CJ 34:22-36 n2 1995
United States
Williams, T. Justified lives: morality and narrative in the films of Sam Peckinpah. By Michael Bliss [Book Review]. il FQ 48:62-63 n2 1994/95

STYPULKOWSKA, KRYSTYNA
Sobolewski, T. Krysia is the best. interv ports still KINO 27:20-23+ [5p] May 1993

SUARES, J.C.
Nangle, J. Heavies/drag/lovers/weddings. Edited by J.C. Suares [Book Review]. FIR 45:69 Nov/Dec 1994

SUBJECTIVITY
France
Lacasse, A. Considerations sur la portee ethique des propositions de Christian Metz pour une enonciation impersonnelle au cinema. bibliog CINEMAS 4:85-97 n3 1994

Subsidies See GOVERNMENT SUPPORT
SUDBURY, LAWRENCE M.F.
  Sudbury, L. M.F. Per favore, mordimi sul collo. il stills SEGNO n72:10-14
    Mar/Apr 1995
SUGAR HILL f (d Ichaso, Leon 1993 USA)
  Dewasse, G. "Sugar Hill." bibliog credits stills GRAND ANGLE n176:27-28
    Nov 1994
SUITE 16 f (d Deruddere, Dominique 1994 Belg/Neth/Gt Br)
  Termont, D. and Noel, J. "Suite 16." credits stills GRAND ANGLE n176:29-30
    Nov 1994
      Reviews
  Stratton, D. "Suite 16." credits VARIETY 358:76 Feb 27/Mar 5 1995
SULEIMAN, SUSAN RUBIN
  Suleiman, S.R. Between the street and the salon: the dilemma of surrealist
    politics in the 1930's. il stills VISUAL ANTHRO R 7:39-50 n1 1991
SULLIVAN, DREW
  Sullivan, D. Still the fairest in the land. still SCARLET STREET n17:19
    Winter 1995
  Sullivan, D. The mysteries of James Dean. il still SCARLET STREET
    n17:37-41+ [6p] Winter 1995
SULLIVAN, JEFFREY
  Sullivan, J. Story development software. il table JOURNAL WGA 8:24-28
    Dec/Jan 1995
SUM OF US, THE f (d Dowling, Kevin/Burton, Geoff 1994 Australia)
      Reviews
  Gener, R. "The Sum of Us." VILLAGE VOICE 40:61 Mar 14 1995
  Hess, P. "The Sum of Us." still BOXOFFICE 131:bet p125 and 144 [pR32] Apr
    1995
SUMMERS, WALTER See also DARK EYES OF LONDON, THE
SUNN CLASSIC PICTURES, INC.
  Wasser, F. Four walling exhibition: regional resistance to the Hollywood
    film industry. CJ 34:51-65 n2 1995
SUNSTEIN, CASS R.
  Sunstein, C.R. Porn on the Fourth of July [Book Review]. NEW REPUB
    212:42-45 Jan 9/16 1995
SUPER 8 1/2 f (d LaBruce, Bruce 1994 Can)
  Hannaham, J. A fellating Fellini. il VILLAGE VOICE 40:56 Mar 14 1995
  McIntosh, D. Porn, porosity and promiscuity. stills C ACTION n36:20-23
    1995
      Reviews
  Hannaham, J. "Super 8 1/2." still VILLAGE VOICE 40:60 Mar 7 1995
SUPER MARIO BROS. f (d Morton, Rocky/Jankel, Annabel 1993 USA)
      Book Trade
  Lehtonen, V.-P. "Super-Mario" - kirja tuli, elokuvaa el. credits il still
    PEILI 17:46 n4 1993
SUPER-EIGHT MM FILM
      Australia
  Alexander, P. "Vicar," "Space Case," "Killer" and "The Night City." filmogs
    il stills CANTRILL'S FMNTS n73/74:12-14 May 1994
      Experimental Film
  Bridges, J. Cinematic interruptus. il stills CANTRILL'S FMNTS n73/74:20-31
    May 1994
SUPPORTING ROLES
      United States
  O'Steen, K. Second strings play sans sweet security of studios. VARIETY
    358:86 Feb 27/Mar 5 1995
      Wages and Salaries
  O'Steen, K. Best buds, bad guys feel player pay pinch. il stat VARIETY
    358:1+ [2p] Feb 27/Mar 5 1995
SUR, EL f (d Erice, Victor 1983 Sp/Fr)
  Ehrlich, L.C. Interior gardens: Victor Erice's "Dream of Light" and the
    Bodegon tradition. il stills CJ 34:22-36 n2 1995
SURF NINJAS f (d Israel, Neal 1993 USA)
  Ciapara, E. "Surfujacy Ninja." credits filmogs still FSP 40:9 n4 (n758)
    1994
SURIANO, FRANCESCO
  Roberti, B. and others. La lingua interiore degli spazi. interv FCR
    45:425-428 Sep (n448) 1994
  Roberti, B. and others. Lavorare sulla bellezza del "niente." interv stills
    FCR 45:322-328 Jun/Jul (n446/447) 1994
  Roberti, B. and Suriano, F. La Biennale, la Mostra e l'archivio. interv
    still FCR 45:371-381 Sep (n448) 1994
  Suriano, F. I contaminati. stills FCR 45:417-420 Sep (n448) 1994
SURREALISM
  Cantrill, A. Compulsive beauty. By Hal Foster [Book Review]. CANTRILL'S
    FMNTS n73/74:41 May 1994
  Jay, M. The disenchantment of the eye: surrealism and the crisis of
    ocularcentrism. il stills VISUAL ANTHRO R 7:15-38 n1 1991
      History
  Suleiman, S.R. Between the street and the salon: the dilemma of surrealist
    politics in the 1930's. il stills VISUAL ANTHRO R 7:39-50 n1 1991
      Morality
  Pauly, R. A revolution is not a dinner party: "The Discrete Charm" of
    Bunuel's "Bourgeoisie." bibliog LIT/FQ 22:232-237 n4 1994
      Belgium
        History
  Petley, J. Henri Storck - documentarist, surrealist, anarchist. port
    VERTIGO (UK) 1:33 n4 1994/95
Surveys See POLLS AND SURVEYS
SURVIVORS OF THE SHOAH VISUAL HISTORY FOUNDATION (Los Angeles, California)
  Haile, M. Reminting "Schindler's" gold. il stills BOXOFFICE 131:66+ [4p]
    Apr 1995
SUSPENSE FILM See also DETECTIVE FILM; MYSTERY FILM
      Festivals
  Zagari, P. Dracula e serial-killer per "cinetalpe" incallite. still C
    NUOVO 43:20-21 Nov/Dec (n352) 1994
SUTTON, GLORIA
  Sutton, G. Colonialism and nationalism in Asian cinema. Edited by Wimal
    Dissanayake [Book Review]. il AFTERIMAGE 22:15 Jan 1995
  Sutton, G. Script-o-caucus neA. AFTERIMAGE 22:3 Jan 1995

SUTURE f (d McGehee, Scott/Siegel, David 1993 USA)
  Degoudenne, L. "Suture." bibliog credits stills GRAND ANGLE n178:33-34 Jan
    1995
  Romney, J. How did we get here? stills S&S 5:32-34 Feb 1995
  Darke, C. "Suture." credits still S&S 5:54-55 Feb 1995
SUZUKI, SHIROYASU
  Abe, M.N. Documentarists of Japan (second in a series). biog il interv
    stills DOC BOX 2:9-16 1993
SVANKMAJER, JAN See also FAUST
  Clarke, J. Jan Svankmajer: puppetry's dark poet. il stills C FANTAS
    26:54-57 n3 1995
  Griffiths, K. Anxious visions. il stills VERTIGO (UK) 1:47-52 n4 1994/95
  Lawrence, A. Masculinity in Eastern European animation. stills ANIMATION J
    3:32-43 n1 1994
  Persons, D. Svankmajer. still C FANTAS 26:56 n3 1995
SVENDSEN, TROND OLAV
  Svendsen, T.O. Spielbergs versjon av Shoa. stills F&K n1:10-12 1994
SVENSK FILMINDUSTRI AB
  Hedling, O. Ekonomi och film [Book Review]. F HAFTET 22:62-63 n3 (n87) 1994
SVERAK, JAN See also AKUMULATOR 1; JIZDA
SWACKHAMER, E.W.
  Obituaries. biogs filmogs il obits ports CLASSIC n236:57-59 Feb 1995
SWAHAM f (d Karun, Shaji N. 1994 India)
      Reviews
  Mathai, S. "Swaham." credits still CINEMAYA n24:34-35 Summer 1994
SWAN PRINCESS, THE f (d Rich, Richard 1994 USA)
      Reviews
  Persons, D. "The Swan Princess." C FANTAS 26:60 n3 1995
SWANN, PAUL
  Swann, P. International conspiracy in and around "The Iron Curtain." VEL LT
    TRAP n35:52-60 Spring 1995
Swashbucklers See ADVENTURE FILM
Sweden See as a subheading under individual subject headings
SWICORD, ROBIN
  Campbell, V. Open secret. port MOVIELINE 6:70-71 Apr 1995
  Dargis, M. Reworking "Women." port still VILLAGE VOICE 40:70-71 Jan 3 1995
  Swicord, R. Pioneer know-how [Book Review]. ports S&S 5:36-37 Feb 1995
SWIEZYNSKI, WACLAW
  Swiezynski, W. Gory. il stills KINO 27:24-27 May 1993
Switzerland See as a subheading under individual subject headings
SYDNEY SHOWGROUNDS
  Woods, M. Studio plan mixed up in election. VARIETY 358:40 Mar 27/Apr 2
    1995
SYDNEY, SYLVIA
  Springer, J. The films of Sylvia Sydney. il stills FIR 45:31-34 Nov/Dec
    1994
SYLBERT, RICHARD
  Midding, G. Richard Sylbert - production design als metapher. C(SWITZ)
    40:75-86 1994
SYLVESTER, SHAUNE
  Sylvester, S. "Titanica" takes Imax into new waters. il stills AMCIN
    76:32-34+ [5p] Jan 1995
Symposia See CONFERENCES, INSTITUTES, WORKSHOPS, ETC.
SZABO, ISTVAN
  Schuman, J. "Ich kann nicht arbeiten, wenn schlechte Laune herrscht."
    filmog il interv stills F BUL 37:24-31 n1 (n198) 1995
SZASZ, JANOS See also WOYZECK
  Janisch, A. "A fold se volt mas, mint egy folborult fazek." il interv
    stills F VILAG 38:14-17 n2 1995
SZEKELY, GABRIELLA
  Szekely, G. Berend Ivan gyemantjai. interv stills F VILAG 38:12-13 n4 1995
SZILAGYI, AKOS
  A tizenotezredik pillanat. interv stills F VILAG 38:18-23 n1 1995
SZIRTES, ANDRAS See also LUMIERE TEKERCSEK
SZODA, JAREK
  Szoda, J. Panavision (czesc trzecia). il REZYSER n15:6-7 1993
SZOMJAS, GYORGY See also CSOKKAL ES KOROMMEL; RONCSFILM
SZULKIN, PIOTR See also MIESO
  CD [author]. "Mieso." biog credits filmog FSP 40:7 n6 (n760) 1994
  Szulkin, P. "Psy" wieszane non stop. il still KINO 27:12-13 May 1993
SZWARC, JEANNOT See also SANTA CLAUS: THE MOVIE
SZYMANSKA, ADRIANA For film reviews see author under the following titles: HOMO
    FABER
TABIO, JUAN CARLOS See also FRESA Y CHOCOLATE
  Carro, N. "Fresa y chocolate." interv stills DICINE n59:2-3 Nov/Dec 1994
  West, D. An interview with Juan Carlos Tabio. interv port CINEASTE 21:20
    n1/2 1995
TABULA RASA
  "Tabula Rasa" [Book Review]. FATAL VISIONS n17:31 1994
TACCHELLA, JEAN-CHARLES See also SEVEN SUNDAYS
TAEBAEK SANMAEK f (d Im, Kwontaik 1995 S Korea)
      Reviews
  Stratton, D. "The Taebaek Mountains" (Taebaek sanmaek"). credits VARIETY
    358:80 Feb 20/26 1995
TAGGI, PAOLO For film reviews see author under the following titles: BEFORE THE
    RAIN
TAGLIAVINI, FERRUCCIO
  Rooney, D. Ferruccio Tagliavini. obit VARIETY 358:87 Mar 27/Apr 2 1995
TAHIMIK, KIDLAT See also MABABANGONG BANGUNGOT; TURUMBA; WHY IS YELLOW THE
    MIDDLE OF THE RAINBOW?
  Cantrill, A. and Cantrill, C. "Why Is Yellow the Middle of the Rainbow?" il
    interv stills CANTRILL'S FMNTS n73/74:44-63 May 1994
  Tahimik, K. Diary entries of a never-ending docu (seizing the shots of
    shooting). biog il DOC BOX 4:1-3 1993
TAJIMA, RENE See also WHO KILLED VINCENT CHIN?
  Tajima, R. To be Asian American. filmog CINEMAYA n25/26:44-45
    Autumn/Winter 1994/95
TAKACS, FERENC For film reviews see author under the following titles: BRONX
    TALE, A; FOUR WEDDINGS AND A FUNERAL

Take Care of Your Scarf, Tatjana See PIDA HUIVISTA KIINNI, TATJANA
TALA! DET AR SA MORKT f (d Osten, Suzanne 1993 Swed)
    Reviews
    Niskanen, E. "Puhu! On niin pimeaa." credits still PEILI 17:30 n3 1993
TALALAY, RACHEL See also TANK GIRL
    Mooney, J. Visions of the apocalypse. il MOVIELINE 6:68-69 Apr 1995
Talent agents See AGENTS
TALES FROM THE CRYPT PRESENTS DEMON KNIGHT f (d Dickerson, Ernest 1995 USA)
    Eby, D. "Demon Knight." stills C FANTAS 26:12-13 n2 1995
    Mallory, M. Beyond the crypt: on the set of "Demon Knight." il stills
        SCARLET STREET n17:22+ [3p] Winter 1995
    Reviews
    Dauphin, G. "Tales From the Crypt: Demon Knight." VILLAGE VOICE 40:54-55
        Jan 31 1995
    Williamson, K. "Demon Knight." still BOXOFFICE 131:bet p89 and 96 [pR18]
        Mar 1995
TALES OF HOFFMAN, THE f (d Powell, Michael/Pressburger, Emeric 1951 Gt Br)
    Greenfield, A. "Tales of Hoffmann." il stills F COM 31:26-31 Mar/Apr 1995
TALES OF TERROR f (d Corman, Roger 1962 USA)
    Loffreda, P. Primi sguardi nella scuola: dalla descrizione al racconto. il
        stills C FORUM 34:3-7 Oct (n338) 1994
TALL TALE: THE UNBELIEVABLE ADVENTURES OF PECOS BILL f (d Chechik, Jeremiah
        1995 USA)
    French, L. "Tall Tale." il stills C FANTAS 26:8-9 n3 1995
    Reviews
    Leydon, J. "Tall Tale: the Unbelievable Adventures of Pecos Bill." credits
        still VARIETY 358:48 Mar 20/26 1995
TALLINNFIL'M
    Niskanen, E. Tallinnassa tehdaan taidokasta animaatiota. il still PEILI
        17:6-7 n4 1993
TAMAHORI, LEE See also MULHOLLAND FALLS; ONCE WERE WARRIORS
    I'll be back, says Tamahori. ONFILM [12]:6 n1 1995
    Lewis, B. Lee Tamahori's "Once Were Warriors." port stills C PAPERS
        n102:4-8 Dec 1994
TAMAS, AMARYLLIS For film reviews see author under the following titles:
        JARDINES COLGANTES; SHADOW, THE; STORIA DI UNA CAPINERA
TAMATTORI, LEE
    Filmografie. biogs filmogs SEGNO n72:40 Mar/Apr 1995
TAMEN ZHENG NIANQING f (d Zhou, Xiaowen 1987 China)
    Reviews
    Elley, D. "In Their Prime" ("Tamen zheng nianqing"). credits VARIETY
        358:77 Feb 6/12 1995
TAMING OF THE SHREW, THE f (d Taylor, Sam 1929 USA)
    Aldarondo, R. "La Fierecilla domada." credits still NOSFERATU n8:72 Feb
        1992
TAMING OF THE SHREW, THE f (d Zeffirelli, Franco 1967 USA/It)
    Latorre, J.M. Shakespeare segun Zeffirelli. il stills NOSFERATU n8:48-55
        Feb 1992
TAN, KENNETH
    Tan, K. Singapore. CINEMAYA n24:62-63 Summer 1994
TANAKA, KINUYO
    Tessier, M. Tanaka's tales of love and history. stills CINEMAYA
        n25/26:33-35 Autumn/Winter 1994/95
TANDY, JESSICA
    Elia, M. Les bonnes (et parfois les dernieres) repliques de ceux qui nous
        ont quittes. biogs il obits port stills SEQUENCES n175:6 Nov/Dec 1994
TANK GIRL f (d Talalay, Rachel 1995 USA)
    Fuller, G. T'anks to Petty... il interv ports still INTERV 25:110-113 Mar
        1995
    Mooney, J. Visions of the apocalypse. il MOVIELINE 6:68-69 Apr 1995
TANNER, ALAIN
    Wendt, U. Decor. stills C(SWITZ) 40:20-36 1994
TANNER, LOUISE
    Tanner, L. Accents and umlauts. FIR 45:38-39 Nov/Dec 1994
TANU, A f (d Bacso, Peter 1979 prod 1968 Hungary)
    Zsugan, I. Pelikan ladikjan. il interv stills F VILAG 38:26-28 n1 1995
TANZ DER BLAUEN VOEGEL f (d Faessler, Lisa 1993 Switz)
    Reviews
    Senn, D. "Tanz der blauen Voegel." credits still C(SWITZ) 40:206-207 1994
TANZI-MIRA, FEDERICO
    Tanzi-Mira, F. L'immagine virale di David Cronenberg. C SUD 33:18-19
        Jul/Aug/Sep (n113) 1994
TARANTINO, QUENTIN See also FOUR ROOMS; PULP FICTION; RESERVOIR DOGS
    Asboth, E. Quentin es John ma este balba mennek. il interv stills F VILAG
        38:28-29 n4 1995
    Jackson, D. Quentin Tarantino's Negro problem - and Hollywood's. il
        VILLAGE VOICE 40:39-40 Mar 28 1995
    Kermode, M. Endnotes. still S&S 5:62 Feb 1995
    Wild, D. Quentin Tarantino. biog ports ROLLING STONE n694:76-78+ [6p] Nov
        3 1994
TARD, JEAN-BAPTISTE
    Jean, M. and Loiselle, M.-C. A l'ombre du 7e art. il interv stills 24
        IMAGES n76:4-7+ [7p] Spring 1995
TARKOVSKII, ANDREI See also TARKOVSKY, ANDREI See also STALKER
TARKOVSKY, ANDREI See also TARKOVSKII, ANDREI See also OFFRET
    Paquette, J.-M. Tarkovski, cineaste cynique. bibliog CINEMAS 4:15-23 n3
        1994
TARLOV, MARK
    Dawtrey, A. Chrysalis deal leads to U.K. pic ventures. VARIETY 358:14 Mar
        13/19 1995
TARR, BELA See also SATANTANGO
    Maudente, F. Paesaggio, uomini, animali, oggetti... interv still FCR
        45:390-393 Sep (n448) 1994
TARTAGLIA, JERRY See also FIN DE SIECLE
    Tartaglia, J. The making of "Fin de Siecle" (1989): a film journal. diag
        still table MILLENNIUM n25:66-71 Summer 1991
TARTUEFF f (d Murnau, F.W. 1926 Ger)
    Vernet, M. Le voir-dire. CINEMAS 4:35-47 n1 1993
TASHLIN, FRANK
    Frank Tashlin, sous la direction de Roger Garcia e Bernard Eisenchitz [Book

Review]. IMMAGINE n28:30-31 Autumn 1994
    Retrospectives
    Buffa, M. Pop models and Tashlin's art. still FCR 45:398-399 Sep (n448)
        1994
TASKER, ANNE
    Elley, D. Anne Tasker. obit VARIETY 358:87 Mar 27/Apr 2 1995
TASKER, YVONNE
    Cantrill, A. Spectacular bodies: gender, genre and the action cinema. By
        Yvonne Tasker [Book Review]. CANTRILL'S FMNTS n73/74:43 May 1994
    Grieveson, L. Steven Cohan and Ina Rae Hark (eds). Screening the male:
        exploring masculinities in Hollywood cinema [Book Reviews]. SCREEN
        35:400-406 n4 1994
TATE, GREG
    Tate, G. "Higher Learning's" lessons. stills VILLAGE VOICE 40:33 Feb 21
        1995
TATI, JACQUES See also JOUR DE FETE
TATO, ANNA MARIA See also NIGHT AND THE MOMENT, THE
TAUBIN, AMY For film reviews see author under the following titles: MINA
        TANNENBAUM
    Taubin, A. A sense of place. il VILLAGE VOICE 40:56-57 Feb 7 1995
    Taubin, A. Berlin's bear market. ports VILLAGE VOICE 40:54 Mar 14 1995
    Taubin, A. Bloody tales. stills S&S 5:8-11 Jan 1995
    Taubin, A. Bringing in the new. still VILLAGE VOICE 40:52 Mar 21 1995
    Taubin, A. Burnett looks back. still VILLAGE VOICE 40:52 Jun 10 1995
    Taubin, A. "Cahiers du Cinema" selects. still VILLAGE VOICE 40:74 Feb 28
        1995
    Taubin, A. Sundance kids. il VILLAGE VOICE 40:58 Feb 14 1995
    Taubin, A. The nouvelle femmes. still VILLAGE VOICE 40:58-59 Mar 7 1995
    Taubin, A. The outside edge. still VILLAGE VOICE 40:60 Mar 28 1995
    Taubin, A. The ten best films of 1994. il stills VILLAGE VOICE 40:62-63
        Jan 3 1995
TAVARELLI, GIANLUCA MARIA See also PORTAMI VIA
    Calderale, M. Filmografie. biogs filmogs il SEGNO n71:40 Jan/Feb 1995
TAVERNETTI, SUSAN
    Kasdan, M. and Tavernetti, S. The Hollywood Indian in "Little Big Man": a
        revisionist view. still F&HIST 23:70-80 n1/4 1993
TAVERNIER, BERTRAND See also APPAT, L'; CONTRE L'OUBLI; FILLE DE D'ARTAGNAN,
        LA; L.627
    Sineux, M. and Vachaud, L. Entretien avec Bertrand Tavernier. il interv
        stills POSITIF n409:25-30 Mar 1995
    Tavernier, B. Andre De Toth: eblouissement et zones d'ombre. il stills
        POSITIF n407:64-67 Jan 1995
TAVES, BRIAN
    Cantrill, A. The romance of adventure: the genre of historical adventure
        movies. By Brian Taves [Book Review]. CANTRILL'S FMNTS n73/74:42 May 1994
    Codelli, L. The romance of adventure: the genre of historical adventure
        movies. Di Brian Taves [Book Review]. GRIFFITHIANA n51/52:265 Oct 1994
TAVIANI, PAOLO See also FIORILE
TAVIANI, VITTORIO See also FIORILE
TAXANDRIA f (d Servais, Raoul 1994 Belg/FR Ger/Fr)
    "Taxandria." credits still MONITEUR n126:9 Dec 1994
TAXES See also ECONOMIC ASPECTS
    Egypt
    Warg, P. Egyptian film woes a taxing situation. VARIETY 358:46 Mar 13/19
        1995
    United States
    Ellison, J. A taxing encounter. JOURNAL WGA 8:30 Mar 1995
TAYLOR, ELIZABETH
    Elizabeth Taylor. biog filmog il stills STARS n21:[41-44] Winter 1995
TAYLOR, ELLA
    Taylor, E. Raising "Isaiah." port VILLAGE VOICE 40:64 Mar 28 1995
TAYLOR, GREGORY
    Taylor, G. Beyond interpretation "The Lead Shoes" as an abstract film. il
        still tables MILLENNIUM n25:78-99 Summer 1991
TAYLOR, LUCIEN
    Taylor, L. A conversation with Jean Rouch. biog interv port VISUAL ANTHRO
        R 7:92-102 n1 1991
TAYLOR, MARK C.
    Puntigam, R. Mark C. Taylor, Esa Saarinen. Imagologies [Book Review]. BLIMP
        n30:72 Winter 1994
TAYLOR, SAM See also TAMING OF THE SHREW, THE
Teaching See STUDY AND TEACHING
TEAS, WILLIAM ELLIS
    Obituaries. biogs filmogs il obits ports CLASSIC n236:57-59 Feb 1995
TECHINE, ANDRE See also MA SAISON PREFEREE; ROSEAUX SAUVAGES, LES
    Pelka, B. "Moja ulubiona pora roku." biog credits filmog port still FSP
        40:9 n6 (n760) 1994
TECHNICOLOR ENTERTAINMENT SERVICES
    Airborne/Technicolor system tracks prints. FJ 98:94 Jan/Feb 1995
TECHNOLOGY
    Cantrill, A. Film style and technology: history and analysis. By Barry Salt
        [Book Review]. CANTRILL'S FMNTS n73/74:19 May 1994
    Digital
        Conferences, Institutes, Workshops, etc.
    Beacham, F. Digital artists: reinventing electronic media. il AMCIN
        76:59-60+ [3p] Mar 1995
    United States
        Social Influence
    White, J. Sympathy for the devil: Elia Kazan looks at the dark side of
        technological progress in "Wild River." bibliog still LIT/FQ 22:227-231 n4
        1994
TEEN DREAMS f (d Ziv, Ilan 1995 USA)
    Reviews
    Levy, E. "Teen Dreams." credits VARIETY 358:88 Feb 20/26 1995
Teenagers in film See YOUTH IN FILM
TEGNEFILMCOMPAGNIET
    Jurgens, J.H. Tegnefilmcompagniet. il Z n4:20-22 (n46) 1993
TELECINE
    New Zealand
    Healthy competition in telecine chains. ONFILM 11:20 n11 1994/95

TELL THEM WILLIE BOY IS HERE f (d Polonsky, Abraham 1969 USA)
  Sandos, J.A. and Burgess, L.E. Film as mirror, film as mask: the Hollywood
    Indian versus Native Americans in "Tell Them Willie Boy Is Here." still
    F&HIST 23:82-91+ [10p] n1/4 1993
TELOS EPOCHUS f (d Kokkinos, Antonis 1995 Greece)
    Reviews
  Leydon, J. "End of an Era" ("Telos epochus"). credits VARIETY 358:74 Feb
    27/Mar 5 1995
Ten-best lists See COMMENDATIONS
TENG, JINXIAN
  Teng, J. A new light on Chinese film. il CHINA SCREEN n4:32 1994
TENNANT, BARBARA
  Katchmer, G. Remembering the great silents. biogs filmogs port CLASSIC
    n236:50-53 Feb 1995
TEO, STEPHEN For film reviews see author under the following titles: HUOZHE;
    TRAPS
  Teo, S. Melbourne. CINEMAYA n24:60-61 Summer 1994
  Teo, S. The silken screen. stills CINEMAYA n25/26:46-49 Autumn/Winter
    1994/95
  Teo, S. Wenyi Madonna. CINEMAYA n25/26:7 Autumn/Winter 1994/95
TERAZZAN, STEFANIA
  Terazzan, S. Il festival ritrovato: l'undicesima edizione del Festival del
    Cinema Giovani. C SUD 33:27-28 Jul/Aug/Sep (n113) 1994
TERMINAL VELOCITY f (d Sarafian, Deran 1994 USA)
  Termont, D. "Terminal Velocity." credits still GRAND ANGLE n178:35-36 Jan
    1995
    Reviews
  Fontanini, C. "Terminal Velocity." credits still FILM (ITALY) 3:16-17 n13
    1995
  Nagy, G. "Vegsebesseg." credits still F VILAG 38:57 n2 1995
  Thirard, P.L. "Terminal Velocity." POSITIF n409:48 Mar 1995
TERMINATOR 2: JUDGMENT DAY f (d Cameron, James 1991 USA)
    Ideological Analysis
  Duckenfield, M. "Terminator 2": a call to economic arms? bibliog STUDIES
    POP CULT 17:1-16 n1 1994
    Study and Teaching
  Pimenoff, M. Kuvapinnan syvyysaukot. il still PEILI 17:15-17 n3 1993
TERMINOLOGY See also DICTIONARIES AND ENCYCLOPEDIAS
  Slide, A. The Slide area film book notes [Book Reviews]. CLASSIC n236:47-49
    Feb 1995
    Canada
      Quebec. Documentary Film
  Marsolais, G. Les mots de la tribu. stills CINEMAS 4:133-150 n2 1994
    United States
      Semiotic Analysis
  Kalaga, W. Stam, Robert, Burgoyne, Robert, Flitterman-Lewis, Sandy. New
    vocabularies in film semiotics: structuralism, post-structuralism, and
    beyond [Book Review]. CINEMAS 4:167-175 n3 1994
TERMONT, DANIEL
  Termont, D. "Exotica." bibliog credits stills GRAND ANGLE n176:9-10 Nov
    1994
  Termont, D. "Le bonhomme de neige." bibliog credits stills GRAND ANGLE
    n177:9-10 Dec 1994
  Termont, D. "Terminal Velocity." credits still GRAND ANGLE n178:35-36 Jan
    1995
  Termont, D. "The Shadow." bibliog credits still GRAND ANGLE n177:39-40 Dec
    1994
  Termont, D. "Wildgroi." credits stills GRAND ANGLE n176:33-34 Nov 1994
  Termont, D. and Noel, J. "Nostradamus." credits stills GRAND ANGLE
    n177:31-32 Dec 1994
  Termont, D. and Noel, J. "Suite 16." credits stills GRAND ANGLE n176:29-30
    Nov 1994
TERRIS, OLWEN
  Codelli, L. Walking shadows: Shakespeare in the National Film and Television
    Archive. A cura di Luke McKernan, Olwen Terris [Book Review]. GRIFFITHIANA
    n51/52:267 Oct 1994
  Pollock, N. McKernan, Luke and Terris, Olwen, eds. Walking shadows:
    Shakespeare in the National Film and Television Archive [Book Review].
    MEDIA INFO AUSTRALIA n75:168 Feb 1995
TERRY, PATRICIA
  Terry, P. A Chinese woman in the west: "Thousand Pieces of Gold" and the
    revision of the heroic frontier. bibliog still LIT/FQ 22:222-226 n4 1994
TESSIER, MAX For film reviews see author under the following titles: HUOZHE
  Tessier, M. Cannes. CINEMAYA n24:56-57 Summer 1994
  Tessier, M. La Rochelle. CINEMAYA n24:59-60 Summer 1994
  Tessier, M. Montreal. still CINEMAYA n25/26:89-90 Autumn/Winter 1994/95
  Tessier, M. On locatin with Masahiro Shinoda. CINEMAYA n24:43 Summer 1994
  Tessier, M. San Sebastian. CINEMAYA n25/26:96 Autumn/Winter 1994/95
  Tessier, M. Tanaka's tales of love and history. stills CINEMAYA
    n25/26:33-35 Autumn/Winter 1994/95
Test film See STOCK
TESTA, BART
  Testa, B. Out of theory [Book Reviews]. CAN J F STUD 1:49-65 n2 1991
  Testa, B. The two religions of avant-garde film, or maybe three. CAN J F
    STUD 3:89-100 n2 1994
TETA I LA LLUNA, LA f (d Bigas Luna 1994 Sp/Fr)
    Reviews
  Causo, M. "La teta i la lluna." still C FORUM 34:16-17 Sep (n337) 1994
TETON, CHARLES See also DARK SUMMER
  Teton, C. Don't let the bastards grind you down! VERTIGO (UK) 1:60-61 n4
    1994/95
TEUFELS GENERAL, DES f (d Kaeutner, Helmut 1955 W Ger)
  Plater, E.M.V. Helmut Kaeutner's film adaptation of "Des Teufels General."
    bibliog LIT/FQ 22:253-264 n4 1994
TEXASVILLE f (d Bogdanovich, Peter 1990 USA)
    Reviews
  Viviani, C. "Texasville." POSITIF n406:49 Dec 1994
TEXTUAL ANALYSIS See also CONTEXTUAL ANALYSIS; INTERTEXTUAL ANALYSIS
    Australia
  McFarlane, B. Crofts, Stephen. Identification, gender and genre in film: the

case of "Shame" [Book Reviews]. MEDIA INFO AUSTRALIA n75:159-160 Feb 1995
    Canada
  Vidal, J.-P. La Berlue et le mythe: S/K, ou de Stephen King a Stanley
    Kubrick. still CINEMAS 4:115-129 n1 1993
THAL, ORTWIN
  Thal, O. Cinemania '94 - der interaktive Kinofuehrer. MEDIEN 38:369-373 n6
    1994
THALASSA, THALASSA. RUCKKEHR ZUM MEER f (d Dumitrescu, Bogdan 1995 FR
    Ger/Romania)
  "Thalassa, Thalassa - Rueckkehr zum Meer." biog credits filmog still
    KINO(BRD) n1:46-47 1995
    Reviews
  Rooney, D. "Thalassa, Thalassa. Return to the Sea" ("Thalassa, Thalassa.
    Ruckkehr zum meer"). credits VARIETY 358:52 Feb 13/19 1995
THAT EYE, THE SKY f (d Ruane, John 1994 Australia)
    Reviews
  Nazzaro, G.A. "That Eye, the Sky." still C FORUM 34:35 Sep (n337) 1994
THAT'S ENTERTAINMENT! III f (d Friedgen, Bud/Sheridan, Michael J. 1994 USA)
    Reviews
  Medhurst, A. "That's Entertainment! III." credits still S&S 5:64-65 Jan
    1995
  Tobin, Y. "That's Entertainment III." credits stills POSITIF n406:36-38
    Dec 1994
THEATER EQUIPMENT
    Canada
      Cinetouch
  Schwartzberg, S. Touching the future. il BOXOFFICE 131:98+ [2p] Apr 1995
    United States
      Computer Applications
  CCS has varied menu of selling systems. FJ 98:86+ [2p] Mar 1995
      Sound Equipment
  Altman, R. The sound of sound. diags il CINEASTE 21:68-71 n1/2 1995
      Trade Fairs
  The NATO/ShoWest new products buying guide. il BOXOFFICE 131:106-113 Apr
    1995
THEATER MANAGEMENT
    United States
  Widem, A.M. "From where I sit..." port BOXOFFICE 131:32-33 Mar 1995
      Computer Applications
  Jarecki, A.R. Making it easier to go to the movies. il FJ 98:56+ [2p] Mar
    1995
      Computer Software
  Litzman, T. Automation paints a total picture. FJ 98:88 Mar 1995
      Contracts
  Battersby, M.E. Buying the competition. il BOXOFFICE 131:60+ [3p] Apr 1995
THEATERS See also names of theaters
    Asia
  Lally, K. United Artists builds screens in Singapore and Malaysia. FJ 98:22
    Jan/Feb 1995
  The same old story. FJ 98:3 Jan/Feb 1995
    Australia
  Murdoch, B. Australian cinemas in fast growth pattern. stat FJ 98:20+ [2p]
    Jan/Feb 1995
    Europe, Western
  Dawtrey, A. Euros go on screen-building spree. graph VARIETY 358:1+ [2p]
    Feb 6/12 1995
    Germany (Federal Republic, since 1990)
  Brinkmoeller-Becker, H. Kino und die Wahrnehmung von Filmen. il MEDIEN
    38:327-332 n6 1994
    Germany (until 1949)
  Schriftsteller im Kino. il F BUL 37:60 n1 (n198) 1995
    Japan
  Robinson, G. 'Plexes proliferate amid downward box office trend. stat
    VARIETY 358:49 Mar 6/12 1995
    New Zealand
      Wellington
  Hot competition boosts Capital screen numbers. ONFILM [12]:6 n2 1995
    Norway
      History
  Gjestland, R. Maendene bag i biffen [Book Review]. still F&K n1:35 1994
      Lillehammer
  Lochen, K. Gjenklang av entusiasme. il F&K n7:7 1993
    United States
  Evans, G. Showbiz is psyched for cybermalls. VARIETY 358:1+ [2p] Mar 27/Apr
    2 1995
      Awards
  Jones, M.F. "From where I sit..." il port BOXOFFICE 131:94-96 Apr 1995
      California. Natural Disasters
  Oppenheimer, J. The day the earth didn't stand still. il BOXOFFICE 131:30+
    [2p] Apr 1995
      Nevada, Las Vegas
  Brill, L.M. Las Vegas: mega-movie mecca. il table BOXOFFICE 131:24-25+
    [3p] Apr 1995
THEATRE EQUIPMENT ASSOCIATION (United States)
  Allen, I. Winds of change. il port BOXOFFICE 131:bet p82 and 83 [pSW14]
    Apr 1995
THEISS, KORY
  Lehti, S.J. and Theiss, K. "Mary Shelley's Frankenstein"; "The Specialist."
    il SCN 14:18-19 Mar 1995
  Theiss, K. The film music of Allyn Ferguson, vol. 1. il SCN 14:18 Mar 1995
THELMA & LOUISE f (d Scott, Ridley 1991 USA)
  Rommetveit, I. "Thelma & Louise." stills Z n1:6-10 (n47) 1994
    Gaze in Film
  Putnam, A. The bearer of the gaze in Ridley Scott's "Thelma and Louise."
    WESTERN AM LIT 27:291-302 n4 1993
THEMATIC ANALYSIS
    Canada
  Beard, W. Cronenberg, flyness, and the other-self. bibliog still CINEMAS
    4:153-173 n2 1994
  Gendron, S. Qu'est-ce que le cinema... canadien? stills SEQUENCES

THEMATIC ANALYSIS
(continued)
   n174:13-16 Sep/Oct 1994
   China (People's Republic, since 1949)
   Huot, M.C. Deux poles yang du nouveau cinema chinois: Chen Kaige et Zhang
      Yimou. bibliog glos stills CINEMAS 3:103-125 n2/3 1993
   Norway
   Lochen, K. Jakten pa identitet. stills F&K n1:26-27 1994
   Russia (since 1992)
   Troshin, A. Ki hulyult meg? stills F VILAG 38:26-28 n2 1995
   Spain
      Catalonia
      Ponce, V. Pere Portabella... y algunas marcas de su soledad filmica. il
         stills NOSFERATU n9:60-67 Jun 1992
   Sweden
   Roth-Lindberg, O. Varldens bedragliga sken. il stills CHAPLIN 36:18-25 n6
      (n255) 1994/95
   Switzerland
   Redottee, H.W. Hitchcock-Glossarium. il stills F BUL 37:47-59 n1 (n198)
      1995
   United States
   Kehr, D. Who framed "Forrest Gump." il stills F COM 31:45-48+ [6p] Mar/Apr
      1995
   Rieser, S.E. Love was in the air, and so was Agent Orange. il stills BLIMP
      n30:23-27 Winter 1994
   Williams, T. Justified lives: morality and narrative in the films of Sam
      Peckinpah. By Michael Bliss [Book Review]. il FQ 48:62-63 n2 1994/95
THEODORAKIS, MIKIS
   Upton, R. Mikis Theodorakis on the screen. F SCORE MONTHLY n39:12 Nov 1993
THEORY See also types of analysis (e.g. MARXIST ANALYSIS); AESTHETICS; AUTEUR
   THEORY; AUTHORSHIP THEORY; CRITICISM; FORMALISM; PHENOMENOLOGY; QUEER THEORY;
   SEMIOLOGY
   Lehman, P. Safeguarding the real advances: psychoanalysis and the history of
      film theory. bibliog PS 14:14-21 n1/2 1994/95
   Testa, B. Out of theory [Book Reviews]. CAN J F STUD 1:49-65 n2 1991
   Vaughan, D. The broken trust of the image. stills VERTIGO (UK) 1:16-20 n4
      1994/95
   Documentary Film
   Cantrill, A. Theorizing documentary. Edited by Michael Renov [Book Review].
      CANTRILL'S FMNTS n73/74:43 May 1994
   Gaudreault, A. and Marion, P. Dieu est l'auteur des documentaires...
      bibliog CINEMAS 4:11-26 n2 1994
   Odin, R. Le documentaire interieur. Travail du JE et mise en phase dans
      "Lettres d'amour en Somalie." bibliog still CINEMAS 4:82-100 n2 1994
   Image Analysis
   Cameron, E.W. Kant's station; the Lumieres' train: seeing things by means of
      film. CAN J F STUD 1:36-56 n1 1990
   Landscape
   Fry, K. Place/culture/representation. By James Duncan & David Ley (eds.)
      [Book Review]. bibliog J COMM 45:173-177 n1 1995
   Melodrama
   Jacobs, L. The woman's picture and the poetics of melodrama. il CAM OBS
      n31:120-147 Jan/May 1993
   Narrative
   Odin, R. Narrative comprehended [Book Review]. Q REV F & VIDEO 15:35-46 n3
      1994
   Perception
   Stonehill, B. The debate over "ocularcentrism" [Book Reviews]. J COMM
      45:147-152 n1 1995
   Restoration
      Conferences, Institutes, Workshops, etc.
   Cherchi Usai, P. Il cinema ritrovato: teoria e metodologia del restauro
      cinematografico. Edited by Gian Luca Farinelli and Nicola Mazzanti [Book
      Review]. J F PRES n49:70 Oct 1994
   Montanaro, C. Il cinema ritrovato: teoria e metodologia del restauro
      cinematografico. A cura di Gianluca Farinelli e Nicola Mazzanti [Book
      Review]. GRIFFITHIANA n51/52:254 Oct 1994
   Sound
   Chateauvert, J. Altman, Rick (direction). Sound theory. Sound practice [Book
      Review]. CINEMAS 4:157-166 n3 1994
   Rosenbaum, J. Audio-vision: sound on screen. By Michael Chion. Edited and
      translated by Claudia Gorbman [Book Review]. CINEASTE 21:94-95 n1/2 1995
   Time
   Roy, L. Presentation. bibliog CINEMAS 5:7-13 n1/2 1994
   Canada
      Documentary Film
   Jacquinot, G. Le documentaire, une fiction (pas) comme les autres. bibliog
      stills CINEMAS 4:61-81 n2 1994
      Time
   Roy, L. L'infatigable image ou les horizons du temps au cinema. bibliog
      CINEMAS 5:147-166 n1/2 1994
   Quebec. Documentary Film
   Marsolais, G. Les mots de la tribu. stills CINEMAS 4:133-150 n2 1994
   China (People's Republic, since 1949)
   Yang, M.-Y. Film in contemporary China: critical debates, 1979-1989. Edited
      by George S. Semsel, Chen Xihe, and Xia Hong [Book Review]. FQ 48:61-62 n2
      1994/95
   Finland
   Laine, K. Miksi perehtya elokuvateoriaan [Book Review]. PEILI 18:31 n2 1994
   France
      History
   Cantrill, A. French film theory and criticism, volume 1: 1907-1929; volume
      2: 1929-1939. By Richard Abel [Book Reviews]. CANTRILL'S FMNTS n73/74:41
      May 1994
      Space
   Gregoire, P. Gardies, Andre. L'espace au cinema [Book Reviews]. CINEMAS
      5:229-232 n1/2 1994
      Time
   Bensmaia, R. De l'"automate spirituel" ou le temps dans le cinema moderne
      selon Gilles Deleuze. bibliog CINEMAS 5:167-186 n1/2 1994

Great Britain
   Hendrykowski, M. R jak Routledge [Book Reviews]. il KINO 27:41-42 Jul 1993
   Audience Research
   Stacey, J. Hollywood memories. SCREEN 35:317-335 n4 1994
   Italy
      Realism
   Orr, C. A certain realism: making use of Pasolini's theory and practice. By
      Maurizio Viano [Book Review]. F CRITICISM 19:99-103 n2 1994/95
   Poland
   Kieslowski, K. La dramaturgie du reel. il POSITIF n409:56-57 Mar 1995
   United States
   Buscombe, E. Classical Hollywood narrative: the paradigm wars. Edited by
      Jane Gaines [Book Review]. FQ 48:60-61 n2 1994/95
   Kawin, B.F. Wild blueberry muffins. F CRITICISM 17:53-55 n2/3 1992/93
   Documentary Film
   Bernstein, M. "Roger and Me": documentaphobia and mixed modes. bibliog
      stills UFAJ 46:3-20 n1 1994
   Music
   Creekmur, C.K. Strains of utopia: gender, nostalgia, and Hollywood music.
      Caryl Flinn [Book Review]. DISCOURSE n17.1:172-175 Fall 1994
THEREMIN: AN ELECTRONIC ODYSSEY f (d Martin, Steven M. 1994 USA)
   Hoberman, J. Notes from the underground. il PREM 8:44-45 Feb 1995
THIEF OF ALWAYS, THE f (in production 1995- USA)
   Beeler, M. "The Thief of Always." il C FANTAS 26:20-21 n3 1995
THIN ICE f (d Reid, Fiona Cunningham 1994 Gt Br)
   Reviews
   Elley, D. "Thin Ice." credits still VARIETY 358:50 Feb 13/19 1995
THING CALLED LOVE, THE f (d Bogdanovich, Peter 1993 USA)
   Kremski, P. "Die Musik soll nicht das ausdruecken, was in der Szene zu sehen
      ist." credits il interv stills F BUL 37:33-38 n1 (n198) 1995
   Reviews
   Kremski, P. Die erste Vorstellung. stills F BUL 37:32-33 n1 (n198) 1995
THIRARD, PAUL LOUIS For film reviews see author under the following titles:
   AU NOM DU CHRIST; FAUSSAIRES, LES; LUMIERE NOIRE; TERMINAL VELOCITY;
   TIMECOP
   Thirard, P.L. Dizionario dei film. Sous la direction de Paolo Mereghetti
      [Book Review]. POSITIF n409:73 Mar 1995
   Thirard, P.L. Il cinematografo al campo - l'arma nuova nel primo conflitto
      mondiale. Sous la direction de Renzo Renzi [Book Review]. POSITIF n409:73
      Mar 1995
   Thirard, P.L. Une encyclopedie du nu au cinema. Ouvrage reuni par Jacques
      Deniel et Patrick Leboutte, sur une idee d'Alain Bergala [Book Review].
      still POSITIF n408:78-79 Feb 1995
THIRTY TWO SHORT FILMS ABOUT GLENN GOULD f (d Girard, Francois 1993 Can)
   Reviews
   Paesano, A. "Trentadue piccoli film su Glenn Gould." credits FILM (ITALY)
      3:34-36 n13 1993
   Sineux, M. "32 Short Films About Glenn Gould." credits still POSITIF
      n407:36-37 Jan 1995
THOMAJAN, DALE
   Thomajan, D. Handheld heaven, agitprop purgatory. still F COM 31:87-88
      Mar/Apr 1995
THOMAS, BETTY See also BRADY BUNCH MOVIE, THE
THOMAS, BOB
   Thomas, B. All about evil. il stills MOVIELINE 6:72-77 Apr 1995
THOMAS, HENRY
   Webster, A. Filmographies. biogs filmogs stills PREM 8:100 Feb 1995
THOMAS, JEANMARIE
   Thomas, J. La Videotheque de Paris. J F PRES n49:19-20 Oct 1994
THOMAS, MICHAEL R.
   Thomas, M.R. Mary Shelley's Frankenstein. Kenneth Branagh [Book Review]. il
      SCARLET STREET n17:97 Winter 1995
THOMAS, RACHEL
   Obituaries. obits VARIETY 358:58-59 Mar 20/26 1995
THOMAS, TONY
   Hubbard, R. Film score: the art and craft of movie music. Tony Thomas [Book
      Review]. F SCORE MONTHLY n36/37:22 Aug/Sep 1993
THOME, RUDOLF See also GEHEIMNIS, DAS
   "Das Geheimnis." biog credits filmog still KINO(BRD) n1:22-23 1995
THOMPSON, ANDREW
   Thompson, A. "The Devil Never Sleeps." il INDEP 18:20-22 Apr 1995
THOMPSON, ANNE
   Thompson, A. Little giants. il stat F COM 31:56-60+ [6p] Mar/Apr 1995
THOMPSON, BEN For film reviews see author under the following titles: EVEN
   COWGIRLS GET THE BLUES; NOBODY'S FOOL
THOMPSON, CAROLINE See also BLACK BEAUTY
THOMPSON, DAVID
   Thompson, D. I make films for adults. biog filmog interv port stills S&S
      5:6-11 Apr 1995
THOMPSON, J. LEE See also CABO BLANCO
THOMPSON, KRISTIN
   Cherchi Usai, P. Cent'anni da riscrivere [Book Review]. still SEGNO n72:71
      Mar/Apr 1995
   Cherchi Usai, P. Film history: an introduction. By Kristin Thompson and
      David Bordwell [Book Review]. J F PRES n49:70-72 Oct 1994
   Turconi, D. Film history: an introduction. Di Kristin Thompson e David
      Bordwell [Book Review]. GRIFFITHIANA n51/52:255-258 Oct 1994
THOMSON, DAVID
   Brown, G. The birds (and a book) [Book Review]. stills VILLAGE VOICE 40:48
      Jan 10 1995
   Cabrera Infante, G. Cinema paradiso [Book Review]. NEW REPUB 212:40-42 Jan
      23 1995
   Strick, P. Fresh slogans [Book Review]. still S&S 5:34-35 Apr 1995
   Thomson, D. Really a part of me. stills F COM 31:17-18+ [8p] Jan/Feb 1995
THOMSON, FRED
   Wyatt, E. Thomson defied desert heat, rattlesnakes in motorcycle dash. il
      map CLASSIC n237:22+ [2p] Mar 1995
THOMSON, PATRICIA
   Thomson, P. It's a wrap. il stills INDEP 18:36-39 Apr 1995
   Thomson, P. "Little Odessa." port INDEP 18:15-16 Apr 1995

TREOLE, VICTORIA
  Murray, S. Miramax and Australia - a distinct and bold vision. port C
    PAPERS n102:49-51 Dec 1994
TRES IRMAOS f (d Villaverde, Teresa 1994 Port/Fr/FR Ger)
    Reviews
  Comuzio, E. "Tres irmaos." still C FORUM 34:14-15 Sep (n337) 1994
TRES PALMEIRAS f (d Botelho, Joao 1994 Port)
  Pastor, A. and Maudente, F. Preservare le cose importanti... interv still
    FCR 45:329-338 Jun/Jul (n446/447) 1994
TRESOR DE BARBE ROUGE, LE f (d Frydman, Gerald 1995 Belg)
  "Le tresor de Barbe Rouge." credits MONITEUR n127:16 Jan 1995
TREVI, GLORIA
  Weiner, R. Don't call Trevi "Mexican Madonna." il VARIETY 358:56 Mar
    27/Apr 2 1995
TRIAL BY JURY f (d Gould, Heywood 1994 USA)
    Reviews
  Candeloro, L. "Il verdetto della paura." credits still FILM (ITALY)
    3:32-33 n13 1995
  Haut, W. "Trial by Jury." credits S&S 5:60 Jan 1995
TRIER, LARS VON See also EUROPA; RIGET
TRILOGY, A f (d Sternberg, Barbara 1985 Can)
  Sternberg, B. Editing and script notes for "A Trilogy" (1985) and "The
    Waters Are the Beginning and End of All Things" (1981). il MILLENNIUM
    n25:63-65 Summer 1991
TRINH, T. MINH-HA
  Reynaud, B. Trinh T. Minh-Ha. il stills CINEMAYA n25/26:28-29
    Autumn/Winter 1994/95
TRINTIGNANT, NADINE See also CONTRE L'OUBLI
TRNKA, JIRI See also SEN NOCI SVATOJANSKE
TROCHE, ROSE See also GO FISH
  Calderale, M. Filmografie. biogs filmogs il SEGNO n71:40 Jan/Feb 1995
TROIS COULEURS f (d Kieslowski, Krzysztof 1993-94 Fr/Switz/Poland)
  Jean, M. Voir rouge. stills 24 IMAGES n76:44-45 Spring 1995
Trois couleurs bleu See BLEU
Trois couleurs rouge See ROUGE
TROISI, MASSIMO
  Liberti, F. Michael Radford: Troisi, il cinema e l'Italia di oggi. credits
    interv stills C FORUM 34:46-50 Sep (n337) 1994
TROSHIN, ALEKSANDR
  Troshin, A. Ki hulyult meg? stills F VILAG 38:26-28 n2 1995
TROTTA, MARGARETHE VON See also VERSPRECHEN, DAS
  Golebiewska, M. Film pod presja. filmog stills KINO 27:27-29 Jul 1993
Troubles We've Seen, The See VEILLEES D'ARMES: LE JOURNALISME EN TEMPS DE GUERRE
TRUE LIES f (d Cameron, James 1994 USA)
  Fornara, B. "True Lies." credits stills C FORUM 34:52-55 Sep (n337) 1994
    Reviews
  Girard, M. "True Lies." still SEQUENCES n174:47 Sep/Oct 1994
  Meyers, R. The crime screen. port stills ARMCHAIR DET 28:56-58 n1 1995
  Naranen, P. Pussillinen tehosteita. still PEILI 18:30 n4 1994
  Regosa, M. "True Lies." credits still C NUOVO 43:56 Nov/Dec (n352) 1994
TRUFFAUT, FRANCOIS See also JULES ET JIM
TRUMBULL, BRAD
  Obituaries. biogs filmogs il obits ports CLASSIC n236:57-59 Feb 1995
TRYBALA, MARZENA
  Pelka, B. Marzena Trybala. filmog stills FSP 40:12-13 n10 (n764) 1994
TRYSTER, HILLEL
  Tryster, H. Due belle scoperte. il ports stills SEGNO n71:72-73 Jan/Feb
    1995
TSAHAL f (d Lanzmann, Claude 1994 Israel/Fr)
    Reviews
  Hoberman, J. Never again. stills VILLAGE VOICE 40:45+ [2p] Jan 31 1995
  Klawans, S. "Tsahal." NATION 260:179-180 Feb 6 1995
TSAI, MING-LIANG See also AIQING WANSUI
  Calderale, M. Filmografie. biogs filmogs il SEGNO n71:40 Jan/Feb 1995
  Roberti, B. and others. La lingua interiore degli spazi. interv FCR
    45:425-428 Sep (n448) 1994
TSERENDOLGOR, YONDONBALIN See also TOOROG
  "Toorog." biog credits stills CINEMAYA n25/26:103 Autumn/Winter 1994/95
TSILIMIDOS, ALKINOS See also EVERYNIGHT... EVERYNIGHT
TSYMBAL, EVGENII
  Tsymbal, E. Zonen. il stills CHAPLIN 36:26-30 n6 (n255) 1994/95
TUBA WA DUO f (d Foth, Joerg 1988 E Ger)
  Graef, C. Der Weg zum ersten Spielfilm. il interv F & FERNSEHEN 22:54-69
    n6 1993
TUNNEY, ROBIN
  Fuller, G. Parker's party. ports INTERV 25:79-81 Feb 1995
TUNNEY, TOM For film reviews see author under the following titles: D2: THE
    MIGHTY DUCKS; WAGONS EAST!
TUOMAINEN, HANNU See also MATOKUNINGAS
TUOMINEN, SAMI For film reviews see author under the following titles: FREE
    WILLY
  Tuominen, S. Huoli eurooppalaisesta elokuvasta Berliinissa. il stills
    PEILI 18:22-23 n1 1994
  Tuominen, S. Suomalaisten animaatioseikkailu paatyi ankkalinnaan. il PEILI
    17:24-25 n4 1993
TURCO, DANIELA
  Roberti, B. and others. La lingua interiore degli spazi. interv FCR
    45:425-428 Sep (n448) 1994
  Roberti, B. and others. Lavorare sulla bellezza del "niente." interv stills
    FCR 45:322-328 Jun/Jul (n446/447) 1994
  Turco, D. Una ricerca sul vuoto. still FCR 45:319-321 Jun/Jul (n446/447)
    1994
TURCONI, DAVIDE
  Turconi, D. Film history: an introduction. Di Kristin Thompson e David
    Bordwell [Book Review]. GRIFFITHIANA n51/52:255-258 Oct 1994
  Turconi, D. The American Film Institute catalog of motion pictures produced
    in the United States - film beginnings, 1893-1910 (edizione provvisoria). A
    cura di Elias Savada [Book Review]. GRIFFITHIANA n51/52:250-251 Oct 1994

TURCSANYI, SANDOR For film reviews see author under the following titles:
    LEPIEJ BYC PIEKNA I BOGATA; ROAD TO WELLVILLE, THE; VOROS COLIBRI
  Turcsanyi, S. Sumava, a paradicsom. stills F VILAG 38:30-33 n3 1995
Turkey See as a subheading under individual subject headings
TURNER, ANN See also DALLAS DOLL
TURNER, D.J.
  Adamson, J. and others. Forgotten laughter. credits port stills
    GRIFFITHIANA n51/52:170-197 Oct 1994
  Adamson, J. and others. La fabbrica della risata. credits port stills
    GRIFFITHIANA n51/52:170-197 Oct 1994
TURNER, GEORGE
  Turner, G. George Cukor, master of elegance. By Emanuel Levy [Book Review].
    AMCIN 76:86 Jan 1995
  Turner, G. Hollywood censored. By Gregory D. Black [Book Review]. AMCIN
    76:85 Mar 1995
  Turner, G. Lon Chaney: the man behind the thousand faces. By Michael F.
    Blake [Book Review]. AMCIN 74:96 Sep 1993
  Turner, G. Memo from Darryl F. Zanuck. By Rudy Behlmer [Book Review]. AMCIN
    74:95 Sep 1993
  Turner, G. Projections of war. By Thomas Doherty [Book Review]. AMCIN 76:85
    Feb 1995
  Turner, G. Reinventing reality. By Mark Spergel [Book Review]. AMCIN
    76:85-86 Jan 1995
  Turner, G. Soul in suspense: Hitchcock's fright and delight. By Neil P.
    Hurley [Book Review]. AMCIN 74:95-96 Sep 1993
  Turner, G. Strangers in Hollywood. By Hans J. Wollstein [Book Review].
    AMCIN 76:86 Feb 1995
  Turner, G. The cine goes to town. By Richard Abel [Book Review]. AMCIN
    76:85 Jan 1995
  Turner, G. The first century of film. By Martin S. Quigley [Book Review].
    AMCIN 76:85-86 Mar 1995
  Turner, G. Walter Wanger, Hollywood independent. By Matthew Bernstein [Book
    Review]. AMCIN 76:85 Feb 1995
  Turner, G.E. and Price, M.H. Behind "The Mask of Fu Manchu." credits il
    stills AMCIN 76:68-74 Jan 1995
TURNER, GRAEME
  Beale, A. Framing culture: criticism and policy in Australia. By Stuart
    Cunningham [Book Reviews]. CAN J COM 19:556-559 n3/4 1994
TURNER, LANA
  Lana Turner. biog filmog il ports stills STARS n21:[45-48] Winter 1995
TURPIN, ANDRE
  J'irai come un cheval fou. filmogs il SEQUENCES n175:10-11 Nov/Dec 1994
TURTON, DAVID
  Forsman, M. Antropologi och rorliga bilder [Book Reviews]. F HAFTET
    22:60-62 n3 (n87) 1994
TURTURRO, JOHN
  Gendron, S. John Turturro. filmog port still SEQUENCES n175:26-27 Nov/Dec
    1994
TURUMBA f (d Tahimik, Kidlat 1983 Phil)
  Cantrill, A. and Cantrill, C. "Why Is Yellow the Middle of the Rainbow?" il
    interv stills CANTRILL'S FMNTS n73/74:44-63 May 1994
TUTEN, FREDERIC
  Tuten, F. David Salle's "Search and Destroy" mission. il interv stills
    INTERV 25:104-109 Mar 1995
TVA MANNISKOR f (Two People d Dreyer, Carl Theodor 1945 Swed)
    Reviews
  Miguez, M. "Dos seres." credits stills NOSFERATU n5:66-67 Jan 1991
TWAIN, MARK
  Slide, A. The Slide area film book notes [Book Reviews]. CLASSIC n236:47-49
    Feb 1995
TWAMLEY, MACK
  Twamley, M. Mail bag - letters from readers: "the P word and other musings."
    F SCORE MONTHLY n36/37:39 Aug/Sep 1993
TWENTIETH CENTURY-FOX FILM CORPORATION
  Dawtrey, A. Fox's Elstree plan dealt setback. VARIETY 358:43 Feb 13/19 1995
  Laski, B. Harper back in saddle at Fox marketing. port VARIETY 357:36 Jan
    2/8 1995
    History
  Turner, G. Memo from Darryl F. Zanuck. By Rudy Behlmer [Book Review]. AMCIN
    74:95 Sep 1993
TWIN PEAKS: FIRE WALK WITH ME f (d Lynch, David 1992 USA)
    Reviews
  Skorupska, K. Mistyczna zagadka kryminalna. credits still KINO 27:30 Jul
    1993
TWITCH AND SHOUT f (d Chiten, Laurel 1995 USA)
    Reviews
  Nolan, A.M. "Twitch and Shout." VILLAGE VOICE 40:54 Jan 10 1995
TWO FACES OF DR. JEKYLL, THE f (House of Fright d Fisher, Terence 1960 Gt Br)
  Bernardo, J.M. "Las dos caras del Doctor Jekyll." credits still NOSFERATU
    n6:84-85 Apr 1991
Two People See TVA MANNISKOR
(TWO THOUSAND AND ONE) 2001: A SPACE ODYSSEY f (d Kubrick, Stanley 1968 Gt Br)
    Music
  Brown, R.S. Film music: the good, the bad, and the ugly. stills CINEASTE
    21:62-67 n1/2 1995
  Kendall, L. The re-making of Alex North's "2001": an interview with Robert
    Townson. interv F SCORE MONTHLY n36/37:26 Aug/Sep 1993
TYC, ZDENEK See also ZILETKY
TYKWER, TOM See also TOEDLICHE MARIA, DIE
TYLER, LIV
  Cohen, R. Liv in the fast lane. biog ports ROLLING STONE n694:62-66 Nov 3
    1994
TYNAN, KATHLEEN
  Obituaries. biogs filmogs obits ports CLASSIC n237:57-59 Mar 1995
TYSZKIEWICZ, BEATA
  Slodowski, J. Beata Tyszkiewicz. filmog stills FSP 40:10-11 n5 (n759) 1994
TYTLA, VLADIMIR
  Canemaker, J. Vladimir Tytla - master animator. biog il ANIMATION J 3:4-30
    n1 1994

TZEDEK f (d Halter, Marek 1994 Fr/Switz)
    Reviews
    Amiel, V. "Les justes." still POSITIF n407:43 Jan 1995
UFA See UNIVERSUM FILM A.G. (UFA)
UFO's in film See UNIDENTIFIED FLYING OBJECTS IN FILM
UDOVITCH, MIM
    Udovitch, M. Demi Moore. interv ports ROLLING STONE n701:38-41+ [5p] Feb 9
    1995
UEDA, CAROLYN For film reviews see author under the following titles: YINSHI NAN
NU
UGGELDAHL, KRISTER
    Uggeldahl, K. Sandnesin Kinossa elokuvissa. stills PEILI 18:36-37 n3 1994
    Uggeldahl, K. Suomalaiselokuva jyllasi Nordisk Panoramassa. stills PEILI
    17:26-28 n3 1993
UGLINESS IN FILM
    Avondola, C. Una faccia splatter. stills SEGNO n72:30-31 Mar/Apr 1995
    Bottiroli, G. Il bello del brutto. stills SEGNO n72:21-23 Mar/Apr 1995
    Cappabianca, A. L'enigma della bruttezza. il stills SEGNO n72:18-20
    Mar/Apr 1995
    Cherchi Usai, P. La mediocrita al potere. il still SEGNO n72:33-34 Mar/Apr
    1995
    Garofalo, M. Estetica dello schifo. stills SEGNO n72:27-29 Mar/Apr 1995
    Pezzotta, A. Il brutto nel cinema. still SEGNO n72:17-18 Mar/Apr 1995
    Pezzotta, A. La fragilita del brutto. il stills SEGNO n72:24-26 Mar/Apr
    1995
    Italy
    Della Casa, S. Tutti colpevoli. il stills SEGNO n72:31-32 Mar/Apr 1995
ULICKA, DANUTA
    Ulicka, D. Post mortem postmoderny [Book Review]. il KINO 27:38 May 1993
ULLMAN, TRACEY
    Fuller, G. Tracey Ullman: a comic chameleon who never acts the same way
    twice. interv port INTERV 25:32-33 Jan 1995
ULLMANN, LIV See also SOFIE
ULMER, EDGAR G. See also DETOUR
ULTIMO TANGO A PARIGI f (Last Tango in Paris d Bertolucci, Bernardo 1972 It/Fr)
    Reviews
    Hoberman, J. Life's fitful fever. still VILLAGE VOICE 40:47 Mar 21 1995
ULTRA VIOLET
    Ulicka, D. Post mortem postmoderny [Book Review]. il KINO 27:38 May 1993
ULWER, REGINA
    Ulwer, R. and Voser, S. Interview mit dem Filmemacher Ogawa Shinsuke. il
    interv stills BLIMP [n2]:10-15 Winter 1985
Ulysses' Gaze See VLEMMA TOU ODYSSEA, TO
UMINSKA, BOZENA For film reviews see author under the following titles: SCENT OF
A WOMAN
UNDER SIEGE f (d Davis, Andrew 1992 USA)
    Reviews
    Meyers, R. The crime screen. port stills ARMCHAIR DET 26:69-71 n2 1993
Underground film See INDEPENDENT FILM
UNDERNEATH, THE f (d Soderbergh, Steven 1995 USA)
    Reviews
    McCarthy, T. "The Underneath." credits still VARIETY 358:47+ [2p] Mar
    20/26 1995
UNDERWOOD, RON See also SPEECHLESS
UNENDLICHE GESCHICHTE III, DIE f (d MacDonald, Peter 1994 FR Ger)
    Holloway, D. "The Neverending Story III." still KINO(GF) n56:23 Nov 1994
    Reviews
    Felperin, L. "The Neverending Story III." credits still S&S 5:50-51 Jan
    1995
Unforgettable Summer, An See ETE INOUBLIABLE, UN
UNFORGIVEN f (d Eastwood, Clint 1992 USA)
    Beard, W. "Unforgiven" and the uncertainties of the heroic. CAN J F STUD
    3:41-62 n2 1994
UNFORGIVEN, THE f (d Huston, John 1960 USA)
    Music
    Brown, R.S. Film music: the good, the bad, and the ugly. stills CINEASTE
    21:62-67 n1/2 1995
UNGRIA, ALPHONSO See also LAZOS
UNGVARY, RUDOLF
    A tizenotezredik pillanat. interv stills F VILAG 38:18-23 n1 1995
UNICO PAESE AL MONDO, L' f (d Luchetti, Daniele/Rulli, Stefano/Mazzacurati,
    Carlo/Martone, Mario/Giordana, Marco Tullio/Archibugi, Francesca/Risi,
    Marco/Capuano, Antonio/Moretti, Nanni 1994 It)
    Reviews
    Giacovelli, E. "L'unico paese al mondo." C SUD 33:23 Jul/Aug/Sep (n113)
    1994
UNIDENTIFIED FLYING OBJECTS IN FILM
    United States
    Stein, M. The dream machines: an illustrated history of the spaceship in
    art, science and literature. By Ron Miller [Book Review]. il F FAX n49:12
    Mar/Apr 1995
Union of Soviet Socialist Republics See as a subheading under individual
    subject headings
UNITED ARTISTS CORPORATION
    Biskind, P. Beneficial life. obit port PREM 8:54-55 Mar 1995
UNITED ARTISTS THEATRE CIRCUIT, INC.
    Cunha, U. da. UA Theaters to build in India. VARIETY 358:14 Feb 20/26 1995
    Lally, K. United Artists builds screens in Singapore and Malaysia. FJ 98:22
    Jan/Feb 1995
UNITED INTERNATIONAL PICTURES
    Groves, D. UIP reups Williams-Jones. stat VARIETY 357:30 Jan 9/15 1995
United States See as a subheading under individual subject headings See
    EXPORT-IMPORT BANK OF THE UNITED STATES; FEDERAL BUREAU OF INVESTIGATION
    (United States); LIBRARY OF CONGRESS. NATIONAL FILM PRESERVATION BOARD
    (Washington, D.C.); NATIONAL ENDOWMENT FOR THE ARTS (United States)
UNITED STATES - CIVIL WAR, 1861-1865
    United States
    Ideological Analysis
    McPherson, T. "Both kinds of arms": remembering the Civil War. bibliog il
    VEL LT TRAP n35:3-18 Spring 1995

UNITED STATES, WESTERN, IN FILM
    United States
    Livio, J. Il West di John Ford. Di Carlo Gaberscek [Book Review].
    GRIFFITHIANA n51/52:268 Oct 1994
    Terry, P. A Chinese woman in the west: "Thousand Pieces of Gold" and the
    revision of the heroic frontier. bibliog still LIT/FQ 22:222-226 n4 1994
UNITED TALENT AGENCY
    Brown, C. Gee, Officer Kruschke... il PREM 8:54-55+ [3p] Apr 1995
UNIVERSAL PICTURES CORPORATION
    History
    Herman, J. William Wyler. bibliog biog il stills GRIFFITHIANA n51/52:213+
    [19p] Oct 1994
    Herman, J. William Wyler. biog il stills GRIFFITHIANA n51/52:212+ [19p]
    Oct 1994
UNIVERSIDAD NACIONAL AUTONOMA DE MEXICO. FILMOTECA (Mexico City)
    Gaytan, F. Mexico. J F PRES n49:28-29 Oct 1994
UNIVERSUM FILM A.G. (UFA)
    Codelli, L. Das Ufa-Buch. A cura di Hans-Michael Bock e Michael Toeteberg
    [Book Review]. GRIFFITHIANA n51/52:267 Oct 1994
[UNKNOWN WAR, AN] f (d Behrens, Alfred/Kuball, Michael/Forgacs, Peter/Heyden,
    Goodeliede van der/Huet, Andre 1994 Austria/Hungary/Czech R/Poland/Neth)
    A tizenotezredik pillanat. interv stills F VILAG 38:18-23 n1 1995
    Bori, E. Itt lapatol a kommunista part! still F VILAG 38:24-25 n1 1995
UNO A TE, UNO A ME, E UNO A RAFFAELE f (d Jost, Jon 1994 It)
    Reviews
    Causo, M. "Uno a me, uno a te, uno a Raffaele." C FORUM 34:32 Sep (n337)
    1994
UNREALIZED FILM PROJECTS
    Germany (Democratic Republic, 1949-1990)
    Graef, C. Startversuche im Spielfilm-Studio. il interv F & FERNSEHEN
    22:107-111 n6 1994
UNRUH, EVAN See also PERSONAL PAIN
UNTAMED HEART f (d Bill, Tony 1993 USA)
    Sound Track Reviews
    Pugliese, R. Segnodischi. stills SEGNO n63:93 Sep/Oct 1993
UNTERBRECHUNG, DIE f (d Schoenemann, Hannes unrealized project 1982 E Ger)
    Graef, C. Zurueck im Spielfilm-Studio. il F & FERNSEHEN 22:82-87 n6 1994
UNTERWEGS f (d Schoenemann, Hannes 1978 E Ger)
    Graef, C. Hochschulfilme. il F & FERNSEHEN 22:73-81 n6 1994
UOMINI UOMINI UOMINI f (d De Sica, Christian 1995 It)
    Reviews
    Rooney, D. "Men, Men, Men" ("Uomini, uomini, uomini"). credits VARIETY
    358:51 Mar 20/26 1995
    Sanzone, D. "Uomini uomini uomini." credits il FILM (ITALY) 3:6-7 n13 1995
UPTON, RICH
    Upton, R. Mikis Theodorakis on the screen. F SCORE MONTHLY n39:12 Nov 1993
    Upton, R. Truffaut and Delerue on the screen. F SCORE MONTHLY n39:12 Nov
    1993
URAM, SUE
    Uram, S. Chekov makes Captain. stills C FANTAS 26:32-33 n2 1995
URBAN, ANDREW L.
    Urban, A.L. Michael Robertson's "Back of Beyond." il stills C PAPERS
    n102:12-18 Dec 1994
    Urban, A.L. Sue Murray. interv port C PAPERS n102:40-43 Dec 1994
URBAN, HOPE
    Urban, H. Hip tunes perk pix. still VARIETY 358:bet p88 and 173 [pA8] Feb
    20/26 1995
URCHS, WOLFGANG See also PETERCHENS MONDFAHRT
URICCHIO, WILLIAM
    Livio, J. Reframing culture: the case of the Vitagraph Quality Films. Di
    William Uricchio e Roberta E. Pearson [Book Review]. GRIFFITHIANA
    n51/52:264-265 Oct 1994
UR-MUSIG f (d Schlaepfer, Cyrill 1993 Switz)
    Reviews
    Senn, D. "Ur-Musig." credits still C(SWITZ) 40:222-223 1994
URSINI, JAMES
    Nangle, J. More things than are dreamt of: masterpieces of supernatural
    horror - from Mary Shelley to Stephen King in literature and film. By Alain
    Silver and James Ursini [Book Review]. FIR 45:71 Nov/Dec 1994
Uruguay See as a subheading under individual subject headings
Usai, Paolo Cherchi See CHERCHI USAI, PAOLO
USUAL SUSPECTS, THE f (d Singer, Bryan 1995 USA)
    Reviews
    Greene, R. "The Usual Suspects." still BOXOFFICE 131:bet p125 and 144
    [pR26-R27] Apr 1995
Utilization See PROGRAMMING
UTOMLENNYE SOLNTSEM f (Burnt by the Sun d Mikhalkov, Nikita 1994 Russia/Fr)
    Dupagne, M.-F. "Soleil trompeur." bibliog credits il still GRAND ANGLE
    n176:25-26 Nov 1994
    Remenyi, J.T. Cseresznyeskert, 1936. credits stills F VILAG 38:29-30 n2
    1995
    Ruggle, W. In den bittersuessen Gruenden der Liebe. stills F BUL 36:14-17
    n6 (n197) 1994
    Distribution
    Evans, G. Sony Classics finds place for "Sun." VARIETY 358:28 Feb 13/19
    1995
    Reviews
    Elia, M. "Soleil trompeur." credits still SEQUENCES n174:35 Sep/Oct 1994
    Preziosi, A. "Sole ingannatore." credits stills SEGNO n72:42-43+ [3p]
    Mar/Apr 1995
    Sanzone, D. "Sole ingannatore." credits still FILM (ITALY) 3:21 n13 1995
VT4
    Edmunds, M. Belgium may back VT4. VARIETY 358:176 Feb 20/26 1995
VA MOURIRE f (d Boukhrief, Nicolas 1995 Fr/Can)
    Reviews
    Kohn, O. "Va mourire." POSITIF n409:48 Mar 1995
    Nesselson, L. "Up Yours" ("Va mourire"). credits VARIETY 358:77 Feb 6/12
    1995

1995

VIAN, WALT R.   For film reviews see author under the following titles: BULLETS
OVER BROADWAY
VIANO, MAURIZIO
Orr, C. A certain realism: making use of Pasolini's theory and practice. By
Maurizio Viano [Book Review]. F CRITICISM 19:99-103 n2 1994/95
VIBE-MULLER, TITUS   See also TO LIV
VIDAL ESTEVEZ, M.
Vidal Estevez, M. William Akira Shakespeare Kurosawa. il stills NOSFERATU
n8:40-47 Feb 1992
VIDAL, JEAN-PIERRE
Vidal, J.-P. La Berlue et le mythe: S/K, ou de Stephen King a Stanley
Kubrick. still CINEMAS 4:115-129 n1 1993
VIDAL, NURIA
Vidal, N. Joaquin Jorda: el circulo del perverso. biog il stills NOSFERATU
n9:48-55 Jun 1992
VIDEO BLUES f (d Sopsits, Arpad 1992 Hungary/Fr)
Reviews
Bikacsy, G. Video eye and video weapon. il NEW HUNGARIAN Q 33:171-176 n128
1992
VIDEODROME f (d Cronenberg, David 1983 Can)
Wees, W. C. From the rearview mirror to twenty minutes into the future: the
video image in "Videodrome" and "Max Headroom." CAN J F STUD 1:29-35 n1
1990
VIDEOTHEQUE DE PARIS (France)
Thomas, J. La Videotheque de Paris. J F PRES n49:19-20 Oct 1994
VIDOR, KING
Livio, J. La grande parata: il cinema di King Vidor. A cura di Sergio
Toffetti e Andrea Morini [Book Review]. GRIFFITHIANA n51/52:260 Oct 1994
Retrospectives
Cappabianca, A. Destini di un sognatore. FCR 45:421-424 Sep (n448) 1994
Redi, R. King Vidor a Venezia. credits filmog stills IMMAGINE n28:7-14
Autumn 1994
VIE D'UN HEROS, LA f (d Lanctot, Micheline 1994 Can)
Reviews
Cloutier, M. "La vie d'un heros." stills SEQUENCES n174:9 Sep/Oct 1994
Roy, A. "La vie d'un heros." still 24 IMAGES n75:79 Dec/Jan 1994/95
VIE EST A NOUS, LA f (d Renoir, Jean/Le Chanois, Jean-Paul/Becker,
Jacques/Zwoboda, Andre 1969 prod 1936 Fr)
Leahy, J. Image, meaning, history... & the voice of God. stills VERTIGO
(UK) 1:21-23 n4 1994/95
VIE EST IMMENSE ET PLEINE DE DANGERS, LA f (d Gheerbrant, Denis 1995 Fr)
Reviews
Vasse, J. "La vie est immense et pleine de dangers." credits POSITIF
n409:38 Mar 1995
VIERA, JOHN DAVID
O'Brien, K. Viera, John David, assisted by Maria Viera. Lighting for film
and electronic cinematography [Book Review]. UFAJ 46:49-51 n3 1994
VIERA, MARIA
O'Brien, K. Viera, John David, assisted by Maria Viera. Lighting for film
and electronic cinematography [Book Review]. UFAJ 46:49-51 n3 1994
VIET, HANS-ERICH   See also FRANKIE, JONNY UND DIE ANDEREN
Vietnam (Socialist Republic, since 1975) See as a subheading under individual
subject headings
VIETNAMESE CONFLICT, 1961-1975
United States
Beltz, J. von. The neverending story. JOURNAL WGA 7:37 Feb 1994
Slide, A. The Slide area film book notes [Book Reviews]. CLASSIC n236:47-49
Feb 1995
Stewart, M. Receptions of war: Vietnam in American Culture. By Andrew Martin
[Book Review]. WAR LIT & ARTS 6:83-86 n2 1994
VIGANO, ALDO
Comuzio, C. Renato Venturelli: Horror in cento film [Book Reviews]. il C
FORUM 34:94-95 Nov (n339) 1994
VIGO, JEAN   See also ATALANTE, L'
VILLAGE ROADSHOW CORPORATION LIMITED
Murdoch, B. Robert (Roc) Kirby. port FJ 98:84 Jan/Feb 1995
Personnel
Weiner, R. Meyers tapped prexy of new Village Roadshow int'l unit. VARIETY
358:25 Feb 13/19 1995
VILLAINS IN FILM
United States
Women
Thomas, B. All about evil. il stills MOVIELINE 6:72-77 Apr 1995
VILLARONGA, AGUSTIN   See also TRAS EL CRISTAL
VILLAVERDE, TERESA   See also TRES IRMAOS
VILLENEUVE, DENIS
Comte, J. Denis Villeneuve: portrait surrealiste d'un cerveaunaute en vol.
biog SEQUENCES n175:11 Nov/Dec 1994
VINCENDEAU, GINETTE
Hendrykowski, M. R jak Routledge [Book Reviews]. il KINO 27:41-42 Jul 1993
Holmlund, C. "CinemAction," no. 67 (1993), 200pp. "Vingt ans de theories
feministes sur le cinema." Eds Ginette Vincendeau and Berenice Reynaud [Book
Review]. SCREEN 35:407-410 n4 1994
VINCENT, CHRISTIAN   See also SEPARATION, LA
VINCZ, JASON   For film reviews see author under the following titles: WALKING
DEAD, THE
VIOLENCE IN FILM
Fitzgerald, L. and Keep, C.J. "Barry Lyndon" demembre: la perte de
l'histoire dans le film de Stanley Kubrick. bibliog still CINEMAS 4:23-33
n1 1993
Warren, P. Pour une ethique cinematographique. bibliog CINEMAS 4:25-42 n3
1994
Effects of Film
Lochen, K. Eksisterer det ufarlige? stat stills table F&K n1:28-30 1994
Audience, Youth
Peretie, O. Kell-e gyilkossaggal vadolnunk Hollywoodot? stills F VILAG
38:37-39 n1 1995
Sociological Analysis
Geber, N.-H. Krigarkulturen och popularfilmens etniska strategier. bibliog

diag il stills F HAFTET 22:23-37 n3 (n87) 1994
Finland
Conferences, Institutes, Workshops, etc.
Niskanen, E. Elokuvakivalta yha pohdinnan alla. PEILI 17:36 n4 1993
United States
Bailey, J. Bangbangbangbang, ad nauseum. il DGA NEWS 19:12+ [3p] n6
1994/95
VIRIDIANA (periodical)
Moro, J. "Viridiana" [Book Review]. il BLIMP n30:64 Winter 1994
VIRILIO, PAUL
Rollet, S. Atom Egoyan. Par Carole Desbarats, Daniele Riviere et Jacinto
Lageira; lettres-video de Paul Virilio et Atom Egoyan [Book Review]. il
POSITIF n406:86 Dec 1994
VIRTUAL REALITY IN FILM
Julich, S. Voxel-Man. diags F HAFTET 22:55-57 n3 (n87) 1994
VIRZI, PAOLO   See also BELLA VITA, LA
VISCONTI, LUCHINO   See also ROCCO E I SUOI FRATELLI
VISIONS IN MEDITATION #1 f (d Brakhage, Stan 1989 USA)
Brakhage, S. Gertrude Stein: meditative literature and film. il MILLENNIUM
n25:100-107 Summer 1991
VISITEURS, LES f (d Poire, Jean-Marie 1993 Fr)
Reviews
De Marinis, G. "I visitatori." credits still C FORUM 34:85-86 Nov (n339)
1994
Gianetti, D. "I visitatori." credits still SEGNO n71:38-39 Jan/Feb 1995
Vistavision See WIDE SCREEN
Visual perception See PERCEPTION
VISWANATHAN, JACQUELINE
Viswanathan, J. L'un(e) dort, l'autre pas: la scene de la veille dans les
scenarios et quelques romans de Rejean Ducharme. bibliog scenario still
table CINEMAS 5:189-209 n1/2 1994
VITAGRAPH COMPANY OF AMERICA
Livio, J. Reframing culture: the case of the Vitagraph Quality Films. Di
William Uricchio e Roberta E. Pearson [Book Review]. GRIFFITHIANA
n51/52:264-265 Oct 1994
VIVIANI, CHRISTIAN   For film reviews see author under the following titles: I
LOVE TROUBLE; INTERVIEW WITH THE VAMPIRE: THE VAMPIRE CHRONICLES;
MARY SHELLEY'S FRANKENSTEIN; MIRACLE ON 34TH STREET; NAKED IN NEW
YORK; SOFIE; TEXASVILLE
Viviani, C. Coups de feu sur Broadway. credits il stills POSITIF
n408:21-23 Feb 1995
Viviani, C. Pietruzzo le bon et Pietro le teigneux. il stills POSITIF
n406:67-69 Dec 1994
V'LA L'CINEMA OU LE ROMAN DE CHARLES PATHE f (d Rouffio, Jacques 1994
Fr/Belg/Can)
"V'la l'cinema ou le roman de Charles Pathe." credits still MONITEUR
n128:24 Feb 1995
VLEMMA TOU ODYSSEA, TO f (d Angelopoulos, Theodoros 1995 Greece/Fr/It)
Rooney, D. Angelopoulos' odyssey. VARIETY 358:12 Mar 27/Apr 2 1995
VLIEGENDE HOLLANDER, DE f (d Stelling, Jos 1995 Neth/Belg/FR Ger)
"Le hollandais volant." credits still MONITEUR n126:10 Dec 1994
Voice-over narration See NARRATION
VOILA f (d Podalydes, Bruno 1994 Fr)
Reviews
Grosoli, F. "Voila." C FORUM 34:33 Sep (n337) 1994
VOLKMER, KLAUS
Volkmer, K. Vom Umgang mit Geschichte oder Die Augen der Asta Nielsen. il
stills MEDIEN 38:344-347 n6 1994
VOLONTE, GIAN MARIA
Legrand, G. Gian Maria Volonte (1933-1994). biog il obit stills POSITIF
n409:61-62 Mar 1995
Molnar Gal, P. Lancester es Volonte. biogs obits stills F VILAG 38:2-3 n2
1995
Obituaries. biogs filmogs il obits ports CLASSIC n236:57-59 Feb 1995
VOLPI, GIANNI
Fofi, G. and Volpi, G. Entretien avec Federico Fellini. il interv stills
POSITIF n409:76-92 Mar 1995
Von Sternberg, Josef See STERNBERG, JOSEF VON
Von Stroheim, Erich See STROHEIM, ERICH VON
VOORHEES, BARBARA JASPERSEN
Voorhees, B.J. The endless loop of the human continuum: Dominic Angerame's
"Deconstruction Sight." stills MILLENNIUM n25:108-113 Summer 1991
VOROS COLIBRI f (d Boszormenyi, Zsuzsa 1995 Hungary/It)
Bakacs, T.S. Csaladi vallalkozas. interv still F VILAG 38:46-47 n3 1995
Reviews
Stratton, D. "Red Colibri" ("Voros Colibri"). credits VARIETY 358:87 Feb
20/26 1995
Turcsanyi, S. Nyolcadik utas: a taxisofor. credits F VILAG 38:48 n3 1995
VOSER, SILVIA
Ulwer, R. and Voser, S. Interview mit dem Filmemacher Ogawa Shinsuke. il
interv stills BLIMP [n2]:10-15 Winter 1985
VOWE, KLAUS W.
Vowe, K.W. Political Correctness und Hollywood. still MEDIEN 38:356-359 n6
1994
Voyager See HOMO FABER
VOYEURISM
United States
Bruno, M.W. Brian De Hitchcock. port stills SEGNO n63:9-13 Sep/Oct 1993
VRDLOVEC, ZDENKO
Codelli, L. Pregled razvoja kinematografije pri Slovencih (do 1918). Di
Janko Traven, a cura di Lilijana Nedic, Stanko Simenc [Book Reviews].
GRIFFITHIANA n51/52:264 Oct 1994
VREDENS DAG f (Day of Wrath d Dreyer, Carl Theodor 1943 Denmk)
Aparicio, J. "Dies Irae." credits stills NOSFERATU n5:64-65 Jan 1991
Masoni, T. Carl Theodor Dreyer: l'assoluto e il dubbio. stills C FORUM
34:14-17 Nov (n339) 1994
VREMIA ZHELTOI TRAVY f (d Iusupova, Mairam 1991 USSR)
"Vremya jholtoi travy." biog credits filmog CINEMAYA n25/26:108
Autumn/Winter 1994/95

VUELCOS DEL CORAZON, LOS f (d Valdez, Mitl 1995 Mex)
   Reviews
   Stratton, D. "Jolts to the Heart" ("Los vuelcos del corazon"). credits
     VARIETY 358:75 Feb 27/Mar 5 1995
WACHSFIGURENKABINETT, DAS f (d Leni, Paul 1924 Ger)
   Screenplays
   "Das Wachsfigurenkabinett." Drehbuch von Henrik Galeen zu Paul Lenis film von
     1923/Waxworks: screenplay by Henrik Galeen for Paul Leni's film in 1923
     [Book Review]. il KINO(GF) n56:31 Nov 1994
WADLEIGH, MICHAEL See also WOODSTOCK: 3 DAYS OF PEACE AND MUSIC: THE DIRECTOR'S
CUT
WAGENKNECHT, EDWARD
   Wagenknecht, E. "Strangers in Hollywood: the history of Scandinavian actors
     in American films from 1910 to World War II." By Hans J. Wollstein [Book
     Review]. CLASSIC n236:49 Feb 1995
WAGES AND SALARIES
   United States
     Actors and Actresses
   Brodie, J. Stars' double standards. il stat VARIETY 358:13-14 Feb 27/Mar 5
     1995
     Supporting Roles
   O'Steen, K. Best buds, bad guys feel player pay pinch. il stat VARIETY
     358:1+ [2p] Feb 27/Mar 5 1995
WAGNER, CHRISTIAN See also TRANSATLANTIS
WAGNER, DAGMAR See also EI IST EINE GESCHIESSENE GOTTESGABE, DAS
WAGNER, SOKHI
   Wagner, S. Film photographs. il MILLENNIUM n25:72-75 Summer 1991
WAGONS EAST! f (d Markle, Peter 1994 USA)
   Reviews
   Tunney, T. "Wagons East!" credits still S&S 5:53-54 Apr 1995
WAITING TO EXHALE f (d Whitaker, Forest 1995 USA)
   Adaptations
   Parker, H. The waiting game. interv port MOVIELINE 6:66-67 Apr 1995
WAJDA, ANDRZEJ See also CZLOWIEK Z ZELAZA
   Prendowska, K. Artist as politician: an interview with Polish director
     Andrzej Wajda. interv port LIT/FQ 22:246-252 n4 1994
WAKEFIELD, PHILIP
   Wakefield, P. AFM ushers in new NZFC era. ONFILM [12]:5 n2 1995
   Wakefield, P. Boom year ahead. stat ONFILM [12]:1+ [2p] n1 1995
   Wakefield, P. Censor's new broom cleans up "Warriors." ONFILM [12]:9 n1
     1995
   Wakefield, P. Comish eyes back catalogue selloff. ONFILM [12]:3 n2 1995
   Wakefield, P. Film NZ in 1st location. ONFILM [12]:1 n2 1995
   Wakefield, P. Hungry Yanks stalk our films. ONFILM 11:8 n11 1994/95
   Wakefield, P. NZ b.o. continues to grow. stat ONFILM [12]:9 n2 1995
WALDEKRANZ, RUNE
   Ahlund, J. Filmens historia ar Runes historia. il interv ports CHAPLIN
     36:42-45 n6 (n255) 1994/95
WALKEN, CHRISTOPHER
   Walken on the wild side. port NEW YORKER 70:23 Jan 9 1995
WALKER, GWYNETH
   Hutt, R. Gwyneth Walker. il FILM 4:14-15 n1 [1995]
WALKER, JANET
   Bean, J.M. Couching resistance: women, film and psychoanalytic psychiatry.
     By Janet Walker [Book Review]. VEL LT TRAP n35:85-87 Spring 1995
   McKee, A.L. Negotiating gender in post-World War II America [Book Reviews].
     Q REV F & VIDEO 15:47-56 n3 1994
WALKER, JEFFREY
   Walker, J. Deconstructing an American myth: Hollywood and "The Last of the
     Mohicans." bibliog still F&HIST 23:104-116+ [14p] n1/4 1993
WALKER, JOHN A.
   Hanet, K. Walker, John A. Art and artists on screen [Book Review]. MEDIA
     INFO AUSTRALIA n75:171 Feb 1995
WALKER, MARK
   Farrell, S. Ghostmasters. Mark Walker [Book Review]. il SCARLET STREET
     n17:98-99 Winter 1995
WALKING DEAD, THE f (d Whitmore, Preston A., II 1995 USA)
   Reviews
   Levy, E. "Dead" walks into untrendy territory. credits still VARIETY
     358:69 Feb 27/Mar 5 1995
   Vincz, J. "The Walking Dead." VILLAGE VOICE 40:59+ [2p] Mar 14 1995
WALL, JAMES M. For film reviews see author under the following titles: NOBODY'S
FOOL; TRANSATLANTIS
   Wall, J.M. No sense of the sacred. CHR CENT 112:283-284 Mar 15 1995
WALLACE, TOM
   Wallace, T. "Once Upon a Forest." F SCORE MONTHLY n36/37:32 Aug/Sep 1993
WALLER, ANTHONY See also MUTE WITNESS
WALLNER, MARTHA
   Wallner, M. Chicago mediamakers get organized. INDEP 18:58 Apr 1995
WALSER, ROBERT
   Echte, B. Dieses grazioese Vorueberhuschen der Bedeutungen. C(SWITZ)
     40:153-162 1994
WALSH, MICHAEL
   Walsh, M. Returns in the real: Lacan and the future of psychoanalysis in
     film studies. bibliog PS 14:22-32 n1/2 1994/95
WALTON, BRIAN
   Walton, B. Let's make a deal: Brian Walton on the state of the Guild. il
     JOURNAL WGA 8:10-13 Mar 1995
WANG, JIN See also NUREN HUA
WANG, WAYNE See also BLUE IN THE FACE; SMOKE
WANG, ZHIWEN
   Chu, H. Wang Zhiwen, a new star bursts onto the scene. il ports CHINA
     SCREEN n4:14-15 1994
WANGER, WALTER
   Turner, G. Walter Wanger, Hollywood independent. By Matthew Bernstein [Book
     Review]. AMCIN 76:85 Feb 1995
WANNBERG, KEN
   Hirsch, D. Ken Wannberg has no regrets. interv port SCN 14:8-10 Mar 1995

WAR See also MILITARY; POLITICS AND GOVERNMENT; UNITED STATES - CIVIL WAR,
1861-1865; VIETNAMESE CONFLICT, 1961-1975; WORLD WAR I, 1914-1918; WORLD WAR
II, 1939-1945
   Sociological Analysis
   Geber, N.-H. Krigarkulturen och popularfilmens etniska strategier. bibliog
     diag il stills F HAFTET 22:23-37 n3 (n87) 1994
WAR FILM
   United States
     History
   Turner, G. Projections of war. By Thomas Doherty [Book Review]. AMCIN 76:85
     Feb 1995
WAR OF THE BUTTONS f (d Roberts, John 1994 Gt Br/Fr)
   Reviews
   Hamilton, A. "War of the Buttons." credits still FILM 4:23 n1 [1995]
WAR PAINT f (d Selander, Lesley 1953 USA)
   Anez, N. Westerns. stills FIR 45:18-27 Nov/Dec 1994
WAR, THE f (d Avnet, Jon 1994 USA)
   Reviews
   Delisle, M. "The War." SEQUENCES n175:44 Nov/Dec 1994
   Travers, P. "The War." still ROLLING STONE n696:134 Dec 1 1994
WARD, FRED
   Smith, B. FredandEd. il interv ports INTERV 25:116-123 Mar 1995
WARG, PETER
   Warg, P. Egyptian film woes a taxing situation. VARIETY 358:46 Mar 13/19
     1995
   Warg, P. Fiery sermons-on-tape imperil Arab entertainers. VARIETY 357:57
     Jan 2/8 1995
   Warg, P. Prophet pic nets profit before ban. VARIETY 357:48-49 Jan 9/15
     1995
WARHOL, ANDY
   Ulicka, D. Post mortem postmoderny [Book Review]. il KINO 27:38 May 1993
   Retrospectives
   Lemon, B. Cinema Factory. port NEW YORKER 70:58-59 Jan 30 1995
WARK, MCKENZIE
   Wark, M. Berry, Chris. A bit on the side: East-West topographies of desire
     [Book Review]. MEDIA INFO AUSTRALIA n75:157 Feb 1995
WARN, CHUCK
   Warn, C. To live and die on the Internet. il DGA NEWS 20:14-15 n1 1995
WARNER BROS. INC.
   Edward Frumkes. port FJ 98:82 Jan/Feb 1995
WARNER, MARINA
   Ciment, M. BFI film classics [Book Reviews]. stills POSITIF n408:75-77 Feb
     1995
WARNER, TIM
   Warner, T. A magical journey. il port BOXOFFICE 131:bet p82 and 83 [pSW4]
     Apr 1995
WARNOW, CATHERINE See also COMPLETE OUTSIDER, THE
WARREN, PAUL
   Warren, P. Pour une ethique cinematographique. bibliog CINEMAS 4:25-42 n3
     1994
WARREN, SUZANNE For film reviews see author under the following titles:
DIALOGUES WITH MADWOMEN
WARRICK, RUTH
   Nielsen, R. Ray's way: Ruth Warrick. il interv port CLASSIC n237:13 Mar
     1995
WARTH, EVA-MARIA
   Warth, E.-M. "Millennium Film Journal" [Book Review]. il BLIMP n30:51
     Winter 1994
WAS AUS UNS GEWORDEN IST f (d Schoenemann, Hannes 1975 E Ger)
   Graef, C. Hochschulfilme. il F & FERNSEHEN 22:73-81 n6 1994
WAS, DON See also I JUST WASN'T MADE FOR THESE TIMES
WASHINGTON, DENZEL
   Denzel Washington. biog filmog stills FSP 40:16-17 n10 (n764) 1994
WASILEWSKI, PIOTR
   Sendecka, M. Swieto reklamy. interv REZYSER n18:4-5 1993
WASKIN, LAURA
   Waskin, L. Buddy Rogers honored at Palm Springs Film Festival. still
     CLASSIC n237:9 Mar 1995
WASSER, FREDERICK
   Wasser, F. Four walling exhibition: regional resistance to the Hollywood
     film industry. CJ 34:51-65 n2 1995
WASYK, DARRELL See also MUSTARD BATH
WATABE, MINORU
   Watabe, M. Japanese documentary films of recent years. stills DOC BOX
     1:5-8 1992
WATER AND POWER f (d O'Neill, Pat 1989 USA)
   O'Neill, P. Notes for "Water and Power" (1989). il still MILLENNIUM
     n25:42-49 Summer 1991
WATERFALL f (d Cantrill, Arthur/Cantrill, Corinne 1984 Australia)
   Koller, M. Films we love #3: "Waterfall." still C PAPERS n102:10-11 Dec
     1994
WATERS ARE THE BEGINNING AND END OF ALL THINGS, THE f (d Sternberg, Barbara
1981 Can)
   Sternberg, B. Editing and script notes for "A Trilogy" (1985) and "The
     Waters Are the Beginning and End of All Things" (1981). il MILLENNIUM
     n25:63-65 Summer 1991
WATERS, JOHN See also SERIAL MOM
   Calderale, M. Filmografie. biogs filmogs il SEGNO n71:40 Jan/Feb 1995
   Giltz, M. John Waters on "Faster, Pussycat! Kill! Kill!" stills NEW YORK
     28:66 Jan 16 1995
   John Waters, teorico del cattivo gusto. filmog still C FORUM 34:74-75 Nov
     (n339) 1994
   Waters, J. Botrany! filmog il port still F VILAG 38:36-43 n4 1995
WATERWORLD f (d Reynolds, Kevin 1995 USA)
   Production
   Corliss, R. That sinking feeling. stills table TIME 145:70-72 Feb 20 1995
WATSON, DELMAR
   Parke, H.C. Delmar Watson. il interv ports stills F FAX n49:77-82 Mar/Apr
     1995

WATZ, EDWARD
  Slide, A. The Slide area film book notes [Book Reviews]. CLASSIC n236:47-49
    Feb 1995
WAUGH, THOMAS For film reviews see author under the following titles: PITRA,
  PUTRA AUR DHARAMYUDDHA
Wave, The See REDES
WAVING f (d Fleming, Ann Marie 1987 Can)
  Hoolboom, M. The queen of disaster. stills MILLENNIUM n26:26-32 Fall 1992
WAX, MO
  Obituaries. obits VARIETY 358:188-189 Feb 20/26 1995
WAXMAN, FRANZ
  Handzo, S. The golden age of film music. il ports stills CINEASTE 21:46-55
    n1/2 1995
  Larson, R.D. Franz Waxman (1907-1967): two unrecorded scores from 1936:
    "Fury" and "Devil Doll." F SCORE MONTHLY n39:15 Nov 1993
Waxworks See WACHSFIGURENKABINETT, DAS
WAYNE, DAVID
  Shields, S. David Wayne. biog obit VARIETY 358:188 Feb 20/26 1995
We Don't Want to Talk About It See DE ESO NO SE HABLA
WEBER, BRUCE
  Weber, B. A buddy. il INTERV 25:106-111 Feb 1995
WEBSTER, ANDY
  Webster, A. Filmographies. biog filmogs stills PREM 8:160 Apr 1995
  Webster, A. Filmographies. biogs filmogs stills PREM 8:100 Feb 1995
  Webster, A. Filmographies. biogs filmogs stills PREM 8:104 Mar 1995
WEBSTER, EMMA
  Webster, E. The motion picture guide [Book Review]. il VARIETY 358:42-43
    Mar 13/19 1995
WEDDINGS IN FILM
  Karatson, G. Ozu eskuvoi. il stills F VILAG 38:24-29 n3 1995
WEDDLE, DAVID
  Redman, N. Peckinpah and Sidney reconsidered [Book Reviews]. il DGA NEWS
    20:40-41 n1 1995
  Weddle, D. "Straw Dogs": they want to see brains flying out? il stills S&S
    5:20-25 Feb 1995
WEES, WILLIAM C.
  Wees, W.C. From the rearview mirror to twenty minutes into the future: the
    video image in "Videodrome" and "Max Headroom." CAN J F STUD 1:29-35 n1
    1990
WEHRBEIN, JEANENE
  Wehrbein, J. A special movie fan. il BOXOFFICE 131:102+ [2p] Apr 1995
WEILENMANN, CLAUDIA For film reviews see author under the following titles:
  SOPHIE TAEUBER-ARP; WELL DONE
WEIMAN-KELMAN, PAULA
  The Nathan Axelrod collection, volume 1: Moledet Productions, 1927-1934,
    Carmel newsreels, series 1, 1935-1948. Ed: Amy Kronish, Edith Falk and Paula
    Weiman-Kelman [Book Review]. il KINO(GF) n56:31 Nov 1994
WEINER, REX
  Busch, A.M. and Weiner, R. Gates joins DreamWorks team. il VARIETY 358:15+
    [2p] Mar 27/Apr 2 1995
  Weiner, R. Alliance, MDP ink feature film joint venture. VARIETY 358:24 Mar
    6/12 1995
  Weiner, R. Behind the illusion. VARIETY 358:6-7 Feb 13/19 1995
  Weiner, R. Co-founder ankles Propaganda. VARIETY 357:26 Jan 2/8 1995
  Weiner, R. Dillman takes Giants step. port VARIETY 357:4 Jan 2/8 1995
  Weiner, R. Don't call Trevi "Mexican Madonna." il VARIETY 358:56 Mar
    27/Apr 2 1995
  Weiner, R. Effects houses enter cutthroat competition. il VARIETY 358:7+
    [2p] Mar 13/19 1995
  Weiner, R. F/X Oscar pits rookie vs. veteran. VARIETY 358:14 Feb 20/26 1995
  Weiner, R. Healthy film libraries prove indie treasure trove. VARIETY
    358:bet p88 and 173 [pA5+ (2p)] Feb 20/26 1995
  Weiner, R. Helmers hear effective siren song. VARIETY 358:10 Mar 13/19 1995
  Weiner, R. H'wood raids its past for interactive fodder. il VARIETY
    357:13+ [2p] Jan 9/15 1995
  Weiner, R. L.A. indies set stage for first film fest. VARIETY 358:22 Feb
    27/Mar 5 1995
  Weiner, R. Market & post/LA seminars. il still VARIETY 358:bet p88 and 173
    [pA20] Feb 20/26 1995
  Weiner, R. Meyers tapped prexy of new Village Roadshow int'l unit. VARIETY
    358:25 Feb 13/19 1995
  Weiner, R. Microsoft goes after animation mavens. stat VARIETY 357:87 Jan
    2/8 1995
  Weiner, R. Partner at the periphery. port VARIETY 358:5 Mar 20/26 1995
  Weiner, R. Pirates up, profits are down in '94. graph stat VARIETY 358:bet
    p88 and 173 [pA2+ (2p)] Feb 20/26 1995
  Weiner, R. Recounting Odyssey's long fall. il VARIETY 358:11+ [2p] Feb
    6/12 1995
  Weiner, R. Spaced out. port VARIETY 358:9 Feb 27/Mar 5 1995
  Weiner, R. Vidgames won't play by Hollywood's rules. VARIETY 358:1+ [2p]
    Mar 20/26 1995
  Weiner, R. Visual F/X morphs its own Acad wing. VARIETY 358:22 Feb 13/19
    1995
WEINRICH, REGINA See also COMPLETE OUTSIDER, THE
WEINSTEIN, MARVIN See also RUNNING TARGET
WEINSTEIN, WENDY For film reviews see author under the following titles: BEFORE
  SUNRISE
WEIR, PETER See also GALLIPOLI
WEIS, ELISABETH
  Weis, E. Sync tanks. il CINEASTE 21:56-61 n1/2 1995
WEISMAN, SAM See also BYE BYE, LOVE; D2: THE MIGHTY DUCKS
WEISS, ANDREA
  Bronski, M. Queer looks: perspectves on lesbian and gay film and video.
    Edited by Martha Gever, John Greyson and Pratibha Parmar [Book Reviews].
    still CINEASTE 21:90-92 n1/2 1995
WEISS, CARL
  Jackson, D. Never do business with "Friends." il port PREM 8:36 Apr 1995
WEISS, JIRI See also MARTHA UND ICH
WEISS, ROB See also AMONGST FRIENDS
WEISZ, FRANS See also HOOGSTE TIJD

WELCOME II THE TERRORDOME f (d Onwurah, Ngozi 1995 Gt Br)
  Gilroy, P. Unwelcome. stills S&S 5:18-19 Feb 1995
    Reviews
  Elley, D. "Welcome II the Terrordome." credits VARIETY 358:48+ [2p] Feb
    13/19 1995
  Yates, R. "Welcome II the Terrordome." credits S&S 5:56-57 Feb 1995
WELL DONE f (d Imbach, Thomas 1994 Switz)
    Reviews
  Weilenmann, C. "Well Done." credits still C(SWITZ) 40:211-212 1994
WELLES, ORSON See also CAMPANADAS A MEDIANOCHE; CITIZEN KANE; CRADLE WILL ROCK,
  THE; MACBETH; OTHELLO
  Comuzio, E. Davide Ferrario: Dissolvenza al nero [Book Review]. il C FORUM
    34:91-92 Oct (n338) 1994
  Gross, L. Robust vanities [Book Review]. il S&S 5:38 Feb 1995
  Koppold, R. Das Genie und das Scheitern [Book Review]. MEDIEN 38:379-380 n6
    1994
  Riambau, E. Shakespeare y Welles. stills NOSFERATU n8:32-39 Feb 1992
WELLINGTON, DAVID See also I LOVE A MAN IN UNIFORM
WELLMAN, WILLIAM A. See also IRON CURTAIN, THE
WELLS, PETER See also DESPERATE REMEDIES
  Barlow, H. Pur ekstase. stills F&K n7:20-21 1993
WELSH, PATRICIA
  Obituaries. obits VARIETY 358:58-59 Mar 20/26 1995
WELTWUNDER DER KINEMATOGRAPHIE
  "Weltwunder der Kinematographie" - Beitraege zu einer Kulturgeschichte der
    Filmtechnik [Book Review]. il KINO(GF) n56:30 Nov 1994
WELZ, PETER See also BURNING LIFE
  "Burning Life." biog credits filmog still KINO(BRD) n1:14-15 1995
WENDERS, WIM See also ARISHA, DER BAR UND DER STEINERNE RING; HIMMEL UEBER
  BERLIN, DER; LIGHTNING OVER WATER; LISBON STORY; STAND DER DINGE, DER
  "Lisbon Story." biog credits filmog still KINO(BRD) n1:34-35 1995
  Najman, M. Europa-Ameryka. interv port KINO 27:4-5 Jun 1993
  Russell, C. The life and death of authorship in Wim Wenders' "The State of
    Things." scenario CAN J F STUD 1:15-28 n1 1990
  Wenders, W. Egyszer. il stills F VILAG 38:34-43 n2 1995
WENDT, ULRICH For film reviews see author under the following titles: DECKNAME:
  ROSA; OHNE MICH; PICTURE OF LIGHT
  Wendt, U. Decor. stills C(SWITZ) 40:20-36 1994
WENNER, DOROTHEE See also HOLLYWOOD KILLED ME
  Janetzko, C. and Wenner, D. Storyboards for "Hollywood Killed Me" (1990).
    il still MILLENNIUM n25:18-23 Summer 1991
WENT THE DAY WELL? f ((Forty-eight) 48 Hours d Cavalcanti, Alberto 1942 Gt Br)
  Ciment, M. BFI film classics [Book Reviews]. stills POSITIF n408:75-77 Feb
    1995
  Hendrykowski, M. BFI Film Classics [Book Review]. il KINO 27:39-40 May
    1993
WENTZY, JAMES
  Juhasz, A. So many alternatives. stills CINEASTE 21:37-39 n1/2 1995
WERKER, ALFRED See also THREE HOURS TO KILL
WERNER, ANDRZEJ
  Sobolewski, T. Listy: odpowiedz Andrzejowi Wernerowi. KINO 27:40 May 1993
  Werner, A. Listy: szanowny panie redaktorze! KINO 27:40 May 1993
WERTENSTEIN, WANDA
  Plazewski, J. Wspolprodukcje hydra, czy szansa? il interv ports KINO
    27:6-9 Jun 1993
  Wertenstein, W. Schloendorff z Babelsbergu. il interv KINO 27:32-33 May
    1993
WES CRAVEN'S NEW NIGHTMARE f (d Craven, Wes 1994 USA)
    Sound Track Reviews
  Feigelson, R. "Wes Craven's New Nightmare." SCN 14:17 Mar 1995
    Reviews
  Blois, M. de. Freddy Krueger persiste et signe. credits still 24 IMAGES
    n75:68 Dec/Jan 1994/95
  Girard, M. "Wes Craven's New Nightmare." SEQUENCES n175:46 Nov/Dec 1994
  Newman, K. "Wes Craven's New Nightmare." credits still S&S 5:62-63 Jan
    1995
  Norcen, L. "Nightmare - Nuovo incubo." credits stills SEGNO n72:56-57
    Mar/Apr 1995
WEST, DENNIS
  West, D. An interview with Juan Carlos Tabio. interv port CINEASTE 21:20
    n1/2 1995
  West, D. "Strawberry and Chocolate," ice cream and tolerance. interv port
    stills CINEASTE 21:16-20 n1/2 1995
WEST, KIT
  Prokop, T. "Stargate." il stills C FANTAS 26:48-49+ [4p] n3 1995
WEST, MAE
  Sjogren, O. Kan en antilady sjunga blues? bibliog port stills F HAFTET
    22:38-47 n3 (n87) 1994
WEST, STEPHEN
  West, S. Panel probes Byzantine art of Euro financing. VARIETY 358:11+ [2p]
    Feb 20/26 1995
WESTERN FILM
  Comuzio, C. Renato Venturelli: Horror in cento film [Book Reviews]. il C
    FORUM 34:94-95 Nov (n339) 1994
  Gaberscek, C. Le carte del western: percorsi di un genere cinematografico.
    Di Jean-Louis Leutrat e Suzanne Liandrat-Guiges [Book Review]. GRIFFITHIANA
    n51/52:252 Oct 1994
    Finland
  Salmi, H. The Indian of the North: western traditions and Finnish Indians.
    still F&HIST 23:28-43+ [17p] n1/4 1993
    Italy
  Vecchi, P. Un western mitteleuropeo. il interv still C FORUM 34:71-72 Oct
    (n338) 1994
    Music
  Deutsch, D.C. Spaghetti Western encyclopedia. SCN 14:17-18 Mar 1995
    United States
  Beard, W. "Unforgiven" and the uncertainties of the heroic. CAN J F STUD
    3:41-62 n2 1994
  Fornara, B. Carlo Gaberscek: Il west di John Ford [Book Review]. il C
    FORUM 34:91 Oct (n338) 1994

Rollins, P.C. The Hollywood Indian: still on a scholarly frontier? F&HIST
  23:1-6 n1/4 1993
    B Movie
Anez, N. Westerns. stills FIR 45:18-27 Nov/Dec 1994
    History
Rubin, S. Sam Rubin's classic clinic: the Hollywood West has changed, but it
  ain't real! il CLASSIC n237:47-48 Mar 1995
    Race
Dowell, P. The mythology of the western: Hollywood perspectives on race and
  gender in the nineties. stills CINEASTE 21:6-10 n1/2 1995
Western United States in film See UNITED STATES, WESTERN, IN FILM
WEXLER, HASKELL
  Heuring, D. "The Secret of Roan Inish" revealed. il interv stills AMCIN
  76:34-42 Feb 1995
WHALE, JAMES See also BRIDE OF FRANKENSTEIN; FRANKENSTEIN
WHARTON, DENNIS
  Wharton, D. Copyright extension on the House table. port VARIETY 358:18
  Feb 6/12 1995
  Wharton, D. Gingrich vows to promote U.S. film interests. port VARIETY
  358:20 Mar 20/26 1995
  Wharton, D. House bills aim to add 20 years to copyrights. port VARIETY
  358:30 Feb 20/26 1995
  Wharton, D. Intellectual property no. 2 in export sales. stat VARIETY
  358:30 Feb 20/26 1995
  Wharton, D. Scorsese plugs for artists' rights on Hill. port VARIETY
  358:20 Mar 20/26 1995
WHEATLEY, DAVID See also NOBODY'S CHILDREN
WHEELER, BERT
  Slide, A. The Slide area film book notes [Book Reviews]. CLASSIC n236:47-49
  Feb 1995
WHEN A MAN LOVES A WOMAN f (d Mandoki, Luis 1994 USA)
  Prayez, B. "Pour l'amour d'une femme." bibliog credits stills GRAND ANGLE
  n176:19-20 Nov 1994
WHEN BILLY BROKE HIS HEAD... AND OTHER TALES OF WONDER f (d Simpson, David
  E./Golfus, Billy 1995 USA)
    Reviews
Greene, R. "When Billy Broke His Head... and Other Tales of Wonder." still
  BOXOFFICE 131:bet p125 and 144 [pR27] Apr 1995
Levy, E. "When Billy Broke His Head... and Other Tales of Wonder." credits
  VARIETY 358:75 Feb 6/12 1995
WHEN NIGHT IS FALLING f (d Rozema, Patricia 1995 Can)
    Reviews
Elley, D. "When Night Is Falling." credits VARIETY 358:82 Feb 20/26 1995
WHEREVER YOU ARE f (d Siguion-Reyna, Carlos 1994 Phil)
    Reviews
Levy, E. "Wherever You Are." credits VARIETY 357:75 Jan 2/8 1995
WHITAKER, BILL
  Whitaker, B. James Sedares. il F SCORE MONTHLY n40:10 Dec 1993
WHITAKER, FOREST See also WAITING TO EXHALE
WHITE FANG f (d Kleiser, Randal 1991 USA)
    Thematic Analysis
Sihvonen, J. Villi koira vai kesy susi? bibliog credits still PEILI
  18:22-23 n2 1994
WHITE FANG 2: MYTH OF THE WHITE WOLF f (d Olin, Ken 1994 USA)
  Broeck, C.V. and Noel, J. "Les nouvelles aventures de Croc Blanc - le mythe
  du loup." bibliog credits stills GRAND ANGLE n176:17-18 Nov 1994
WHITE, JERRY
  White, J. Telluride. il CINEMAYA n25/26:91-92 Autumn/Winter 1994/95
WHITE, JUDY
  White, J. Sympathy for the devil: Elia Kazan looks at the dark side of
  technological progress in "Wild River." bibliog still LIT/FQ 22:227-231 n4
  1994
WHITE, JULES See also YOU NAZTY SPY
WHITE MEN CAN'T JUMP f (d Shelton, Ron 1992 USA)
    Reviews
Cherchi Usai, P. "Chi non salta bianco e." credits still SEGNO n63:100-101
  Sep/Oct 1993
WHITE, SUSAN
  White, S. I burn for him: female masochism and the iconography of melodrama
  in Stahl's "Back Street" (1932). bibliog stills PS 14:59-80 n1/2 1994/95
WHITE, WALLY See also LIE DOWN WITH DOGS
WHITEHEAD, OLIVER
  Martikainen, A. Henkilokohtaisia vaikutuksia. filmog il stills PEILI
  17:6-7 n3 1993
WHITMAN, WALT
  Murphy, K. Nativity scenes. stills F COM 31:12-16 Jan/Feb 1995
WHITMORE, PRESTON A., II See also WALKING DEAD, THE
WHO KILLED TEDDY BEAR? f (d Cates, Joseph 1965 USA)
  Hatch, G. "Who Killed Teddy Bear?" il port stills SCARLET STREET
  n17:82-89+ [10p] Winter 1995
WHO KILLED VINCENT CHIN? f (d Choy, Christine/Tajima, Rene 1988 USA)
  Bernstein, M. "Roger and Me": documentaphobia and mixed modes. bibliog
  stills UFAJ 46:3-20 n1 1994
WHO NEEDS A HEART? f (d Akomfrah, John 1991 Gt Br)
  Marks, L.U. Ghosts of stories. stills C ACTION n36:53-62 1995
WHY IS YELLOW THE MIDDLE OF THE RAINBOW? f (d Tahimik, Kidlat 1993? Phil)
  Cantrill, A. and Cantrill, C. "Why Is Yellow the Middle of the Rainbow?" il
  interv stills CANTRILL'S FMNTS n73/74:44-63 May 1994
WIDE SCREEN [Prior to V16, 1988 use also CINERAMA; OMNIMAX PROJECTION SYSTEM;
  PANRAMA]
  O'Neill, K. Assume crash position. il PREM 8:45 Apr 1995
    History
Cherchi Usai, P. Widescreen cinema. By John Belton [Book Review]. J F PRES
  n49:75 Oct 1994
Cherchi Usai, P. Widescreen cinema. By John Belton [Book Review].
  GRIFFITHIANA n51/52:266-267 Oct 1994
    Poland
      Panavision
Szoda, J. Panavision (czesc trzecia). il REZYSER n15:6-7 1993

WIDEM, ALLEN M.
  Widem, A.M. "From where I sit..." port BOXOFFICE 131:32-33 Mar 1995
WIDOWS' PEAK f (d Irvin, John 1994 Gt Br)
    Reviews
Cleutat, M. "Parfum de scandale." POSITIF n406:47-48 Dec 1994
Santucci, E. "Tre vedove e un delitto." credits FILM (ITALY) 3:28 n13 1995
WIECZYNSKI, RAFAL
  Sendecka, M. Szkolenie w Burkina Faso. interv REZYSER n19:3-5 1993
WIEDERKEHR f (d Abbrescia-Rath, Silvana 1994 FR Ger)
    Reviews
Besas, P. "Return" ("Wiederkehr"). credits VARIETY 357:75 Jan 2/8 1995
WIENER LUST f (d Rischert, Christian 1994 FR Ger)
  "Wiener Lust." biog credits filmog still KINO(BRD) n1:52-53 1995
WIESE, INGRID
  Wiese, I. Evas dotre. il ports Z n4:28-33 (n46) 1993
WIGSTOCK: THE MOVIE f (d Shils, Barry 1995 USA)
    Reviews
Levy, E. "Wigstock: the Movie." credits VARIETY 358:50-51 Feb 13/19 1995
WILD BUNCH, THE f (d Peckinpah, Sam 1969 USA)
  Redman, N. Peckinpah and Sidney reconsidered [Book Reviews]. il DGA NEWS
  20:40-41 n1 1995
WILD BUNCH, THE f (d Peckinpah, Sam 1994 restored version, prod 1969 USA)
  Ansen, D. The return of a bloody great classic. still NEWSWK 125:70-71 Mar
  13 1995
    Reviews
Brown, G. Once were westerns. still VILLAGE VOICE 40:54 Mar 7 1995
Gaydos, S. Peckinpah's "Wild" vision restored after 26 years. still
  VARIETY 358:70+ [2p] Feb 27/Mar 5 1995
Rafferty, T. Artist of death. il NEW YORKER 71:127-129 Mar 6 1995
Travers, P. "The Wild Bunch." still ROLLING STONE n703:70+ [2p] Mar 9 1995
WILD, DAVID
  Wild, D. Quentin Tarantino. biog ports ROLLING STONE n694:76-78+ [6p] Nov
  3 1994
WILD RIVER f (d Kazan, Elia 1960 USA)
  White, J. Sympathy for the devil: Elia Kazan looks at the dark side of
  technological progress in "Wild River." bibliog still LIT/FQ 22:227-231 n4
  1994
Wild Target See CIBLE EMOUVANTE
WILDER, BILLY See also DOUBLE INDEMNITY
  Wilder, B. Senki sem lehet tokeletes. il stills F VILAG 38:48-55 n1 1995
WILDERNESS FILM
    United States
Wasser, F. Four walling exhibition: regional resistance to the Hollywood
  film industry. CJ 34:51-65 n2 1995
WILDGROEI f (d Fokkema, Frouke 1994 Neth)
  Termont, D. "Wildgroi." credits stills GRAND ANGLE n176:33-34 Nov 1994
WILDLIFE FILM
    United States
      Narrative Analysis
Bouse, D. True life fantasies: storytelling traditions in animated features
  and wildlife films. stat ANIMATION J 3:19-39 n2 1995
WILLEMEN, PAUL
  Hanet, K. Willemen, Paul. The films of Amos Gitai: a montage [Book Review].
  MEDIA INFO AUSTRALIA n75:172 Feb 1995
WILLIAMS, ERIC For film reviews see author under the following titles: BAD
  COMPANY; LAST GOOD TIME, THE
WILLIAMS, FRANCES E.
  Obituaries. biogs filmogs obits ports CLASSIC n237:57-59 Mar 1995
WILLIAMS, JOHN
  Brown, R.S. Film music: the good, the bad, and the ugly. stills CINEASTE
  21:62-67 n1/2 1995
  MacLean, P.A. John Williams' swansong. F SCORE MONTHLY n39:4 Nov 1993
WILLIAMS, LINDA
  Heffernan, K. A social poetics of pornography [Book Review]. Q REV F &
  VIDEO 15:77-83 n3 1994
  Williams, L. Cinema and spectatorship. By Judith Mayne [Book Review]. FQ
  48:56-57 n2 1994/95
WILLIAMS, LINDA RUTH
  Williams, L.R. Women can only misbehave. still S&S 5:26-27 Feb 1995
WILLIAMS, MICHAEL
  Dawtrey, A. and Williams, M. To dub or not to dub. VARIETY 358:10 Mar
  27/Apr 2 1995
  Elley, D. and Williams, M. Going, going, gong? il VARIETY 358:9 Feb 27/Mar
  5 1995
  Williams, M. Credit Lyonnais ankles the biz. VARIETY 358:4 Mar 20/26 1995
  Williams, M. Czech fests fight for A list. VARIETY 357:36 Mar 9/15 1995
  Williams, M. French prime minister Balladur lambastes state-backed bank CL.
  VARIETY 358:33 Mar 20/26 1995
  Williams, M. Joffe gets French backing. VARIETY 358:22 Feb 20/26 1995
  Williams, M. Pic biz sees French resistance: helmers eschew H'wood way. il
  VARIETY 358:44-45 Mar 13/19 1995
  Williams, M. Pic biz sees French resistance: U.S. slices bigger share in
  France. stat VARIETY 358:44 Mar 13/19 1995
  Williams, M. Poetic pic raises flap in France. port VARIETY 358:5-6 Mar
  20/26 1995
  Williams, M. "Sauvages" snatches the Cesar top pic title. VARIETY 358:34
  Mar 6/12 1995
  Williams, M. Unions suspend dubbing strike. VARIETY 357:49 Jan 9/15 1995
  Williams, M. and Dawtrey, A. Brits, Euros finally get the big picture.
  graph il stat VARIETY 357:1+ [2p] Jan 2/8 1995
  Williams, M. and Stern, A. EC wants to double financial support for film,
  TV. VARIETY 358:43-44 Feb 13/19 1995
WILLIAMS, STEPHEN See also SOUL SURVIVOR
WILLIAMS, TONY
  Nuernberg, S.M. Jack London - the movies, an historical survey. By Tony
  Williams [Book Review]. WESTERN AM LIT 28:173-174 n2 1993
  Williams, T. Justified lives: morality and narrative in the films of Sam
  Peckinpah. By Michael Bliss [Book Review]. il FQ 48:62-63 n2 1994/95
  Williams, T. They married adventure: the wandering lives of Martin and Osa
  Johnson. By Pascal James Imperato and Eleanor M. Imperato [Book Review].

WESTERN AM LIT 28:380-381 n4 1994
Williams, T. To live and die in Hong Kong. bibliog stills C ACTION
n36:42-52 1995
WILLIAMS-JONES, MICHAEL
Groves, D. UIP reups Williams-Jones. stat VARIETY 357:30 Jan 9/15 1995
WILLIAMSON, KIM For film reviews see author under the following titles: BOYS ON
THE SIDE; DESTINY IN SPACE; FAR FROM HOME: THE ADVENTURES OF YELLOW
DOG; HEAVYWEIGHTS; HOUSEGUEST; LITTLE ODESSA; MIAMI RHAPSODY; NINA TAKES
A LOVER; RICHIE RICH; TALES FROM THE CRYPT PRESENTS DEMON KNIGHT;
TOM & VIV; ZIRE DARAKHTAN ZEYTON
Williamson, K. On the Sly. port BOXOFFICE 131:10-12 Apr 1995
Williamson, K. Our man Morrie. ports BOXOFFICE 131:26+ [2p] Mar 1995
WILLINGHAM, CALDER
Cox, D. and Shields, S. Calder Willingham. obit VARIETY 358:78 Feb 27/Mar
5 1995
WILLIS, GORDON
Heuring, D. Gordon Willis to receive ASC Lifetime Achievement Award. filmog
interv port AMCIN 76:44-46+ [5p] Feb 1995
WILLS, DAVID
Cantrill, A. Deconstruction and the visual arts: art, media, architecture.
Edited by Peter Brunette and David Wills [Book Review]. CANTRILL'S FMNTS
n73/74:40-41 May 1994
WILSON, MICHAEL
Hodson, J. Who wrote "Lawrence of Arabia"? il port stills JOURNAL WGA
8:16-20 Mar 1995
WINCER, SIMON See also FREE WILLY
WINCHELL, WALTER
Brodkey, H. The last word on Winchell. il NEW YORKER 70:70-78 Jan 30 1995
Lears, J. Gutter populist [Book Review]. NEW REPUB 212:39-42 Jan 9/16 1995
WIND f (d Ballard, Carroll 1992 USA)
Sound Track Reviews
Dursin, A. and others. Four by Basil Poledouris. F SCORE MONTHLY n36/37:32
Aug/Sep 1993
WINDIGO f (d Morin, Robert 1994 Can)
Castiel, E. Robert Morin. filmog il interv SEQUENCES n175:13-16 Nov/Dec
1994
Reviews
Blois, M. de. Apocalypse now. credits il still 24 IMAGES n75:4-5 Dec/Jan
1994/95
Larue, J. "Windigo." still SEQUENCES n175:14-16 Nov/Dec 1994
Window to Paris See OKNO V PARIZH
[WINDS OF GOD] f (d Narahashi, Yoko 1993 Japan)
"Winds of God." biog credits il still CINEMAYA n25/26:101 Autumn/Winter
1994/95
WINGER, DEBRA
Ciapara, E. "Niebezpieczna kobieta." biog credits filmog FSP 40:14 n3
(n757) 1994
WINGS OF COURAGE f (d Annaud, Jean-Jacques 1995 USA)
Evans, G. Sony spreads its "Wings." stat VARIETY 358:7+ [2p] Mar 13/19
1995
O'Neill, K. Assume crash position. il PREM 8:45 Apr 1995
Wings of Desire See HIMMEL UEBER BERLIN, DER
Wings of Honneamise: Royal Space Force See ONEAMIS NO TSUBASA
Wings of Honneamise, The See ONEAMIS NO TSUBASA
WINIKOFF, KENNETH
Winikoff, K. "Hideaway." il stills C FANTAS 26:14-15+ [3p] n3 1995
WINOKUR, MARK
Winokur, M. Marginal marginalia: the African-American voice in the nouvelle
gangster film. stills VEL LT TRAP n35:19-32 Spring 1995
WINTER, RIKI
Winter, R. Interview mit Peter Hajek. il interv BLIMP [n1]:50-51 Mar 1985
WINTERBOTTOM, MICHAEL See also BUTTERFLY KISS
WINTERS, LAURA
Winters, L. Atom Egoyan is watching us. il interv stills INTERV 25:58+
[2p] Mar 1995
WINTERSTEIN, FRANK See also SHERLOCK HOLMES UND DAS HALSBAND DES TODES
WISE, ROBERT See also HAUNTING, THE
Bradley, M.R. "The Haunting" and other Wise tales... il interv port stills
F FAX n49:50-55+ [9p] Mar/Apr 1995
WISEMAN, FREDERICK See also BALLET
WISEMAN, THOMAS
Wiseman, T. Shirley Patterson a.k.a. Shawn Smith. il interv ports stills F
FAX n49:56-61 Mar/Apr 1995
WISHART, DAVID
Morrison, M.A. Mail bag - letters from readers: ...a couple of remarks on
issues raised in "FSM" #34. F SCORE MONTHLY n36/37:38-39 Aug/Sep 1993
Wit and humor See HUMOR
WITHOUT AIR f (d Abramson, Neil 1995 USA)
Reviews
Elley, D. "Without Air." credits VARIETY 358:64 Mar 6/12 1995
Witness, The See TANU, A
WIZARD OF OZ, THE f (d Fleming, Victor 1939 USA)
Ciment, M. BFI film classics [Book Reviews]. stills POSITIF n408:75-77 Feb
1995
Hendrykowski, M. BFI Film Classics [Book Review]. il KINO 27:39-40 May
1993
WLASCHIN, KEN
Axelsson, S. I filmfralsta poeters sallskap [Book Review]. il CHAPLIN
36:62 n6 (n255) 1994/95
WOAL, LINDA KOWALL
Woal, M. and Woal, L.K. Chaplin and the comedy of melodrama. bibliog stills
UFAJ 46:3-15 n3 1994
WOAL, MICHAEL
Woal, M. and Woal, L.K. Chaplin and the comedy of melodrama. bibliog stills
UFAJ 46:3-15 n3 1994
WODITSCH, PETER See also HEY STRANGER
"Hey Stranger." biog credits still KINO(BRD) n1:28-29 1995
WOLF f (d Nichols, Mike 1994 USA)
Reviews
Adagio, C. "Wolf - la belva e fuori." credits still C NUOVO 43:50-51

Nov/Dec (n352) 1994
Comuzio, E. "Wolf: la belva e fuori." credits still C FORUM 34:80-81 Sep
(n337) 1994
WOLLEN, PETER
Ciment, M. BFI film classics [Book Reviews]. stills POSITIF n408:75-77 Feb
1995
WOLLSTEIN, HANS J.
Turner, G. Strangers in Hollywood. By Hans J. Wollstein [Book Review].
AMCIN 76:86 Feb 1995
Wagenknecht, E. "Strangers in Hollywood: the history of Scandinavian actors
in American films from 1910 to World War II." By Hans J. Wollstein [Book
Review]. CLASSIC n236:49 Feb 1995
WOLODARSKY, M. WALLACE See also COLDBLOODED
WOMAN'S FILM [Prior to V21, 1993 use WOMEN IN FILM]
Canada
Feminist Analysis
Russell, C. Mourning the woman's film: the dislocated spectator of "The
Company of Strangers." stills CAN J F STUD 3:25-40 n2 1994
China (People's Republic, since 1949)
Teo, S. Wenyi Madonna. CINEMAYA n25/26:7 Autumn/Winter 1994/95
Indonesia
Sen, K. Women directors but whose films? il CINEMAYA n25/26:10-13
Autumn/Winter 1994/95
Philippines
Lanot, M. P.L. In a macho society gender makes a difference. il stills
CINEMAYA n25/26:72-77 Autumn/Winter 1994/95
United States
Feminist Analysis
McKee, A.L. "L'affaire praslin" and "All This, and Heaven Too": gender,
genre, and history in the 1940s woman's film. VEL LT TRAP n35:33-51 Spring
1995
Masochism
White, S. I burn for him: female masochism and the iconography of melodrama
in Stahl's "Back Street" (1932). bibliog stills PS 14:59-80 n1/2 1994/95
Melodrama
Jacobs, L. The woman's picture and the poetics of melodrama. il CAM OBS
n31:120-147 Jan/May 1993
WOMEN CINEMATOGRAPHERS See also names of women cinematographers
United States
Abbe, E. Michelle Crenshaw. il interv ANGLES 2:12-16 n4 1995
Krasilovsky, A. A sharper image. il port ANGLES 2:10-11 n4 1995
Krasilovsky, A. Estelle F. Kirsh. interv port ANGLES 2:14-17 n4 1995
Krasilovsky, A. Kelly Elder McGowen. interv ANGLES 2:11-13 n4 1995
WOMEN DIRECTORS See also names of women directors
Festivals
Aude, F. Creteil. still POSITIF n409:64 Mar 1995
Fowler, C. and Kueppers, P. Creteil International Women's Film Festival,
18-27 March 1994. SCREEN 35:394-397 n4 1994
Australia
De Santi, G. Cinema e donne: la grande barriera corallina. stills C FORUM
34:21-23 Oct (n338) 1994
China (People's Republic, since 1949)
Clark, P. Chronicles of Chinese life. port stills CINEMAYA n25/26:4-6+
[4p] Autumn/Winter 1994/95
Hong Kong
Teo, S. The silken screen. stills CINEMAYA n25/26:46-49 Autumn/Winter
1994/95
India
Bose, S. The contemporaries. il port stills CINEMAYA n25/26:20-23
Autumn/Winter 1994/95
History
Chatterjee, P. Over the years. il still CINEMAYA n25/26:18-19
Autumn/Winter 1994/95
Iran
Amiri, N. Daughters of the revolution. filmog il port stills CINEMAYA
n25/26:36-41 Autumn/Winter 1994/95
Japan
Okubo, K. Islands in the mist. port stills CINEMAYA n25/26:30-32
Autumn/Winter 1994/95
Philippines
Lanot, M. P.L. In a macho society gender makes a difference. il stills
CINEMAYA n25/26:72-77 Autumn/Winter 1994/95
Turkey
Dorsay, A. Before tomorrow after yesterday. stills CINEMAYA n25/26:56-58
Autumn/Winter 1994/95
United States
Independent Production. Feminist Analysis
Ouellette, L. Reel women. stills INDEP 18:28-34 Apr 1995
WOMEN IN FILM
Ankiewicz, D. Kobiety w kinie. port KINO 27:39-40 Jul 1993
Feminist Analysis
Baert, R. Skirting the issue. stills SCREEN 35:354-373 n4 1994
Niessen, S. Gaines, Jane, Herzog, Charlotte (eds). Fabrications: costume and
the female body [Book Review]. CINEMAS 3:247-251 n2/3 1993
Festivals
Speciale, A. La speranza e tutta nella donna. still SEGNO n63:90 Sep/Oct
1993
Wiese, I. Evas dotre. il ports Z n4:28-33 (n46) 1993
Gothic Film
Psychological Analysis
Berg, E.K. "Rebecca." bibliog stills Z n1:26-29 (n47) 1994
Horror Film
Psychoanalytic Analysis
Cantrill, A. The monstrous-feminine: film, feminism, psychoanalysis. By
Barbara Creed [Book Review]. CANTRILL'S FMNTS n73/74:42 May 1994
Austria
History
Auderlitzky, C. Vom netten Mariandl zur schamlosen Annabella. F KUNST
n144:50-55 1994

XIAO, LANG See also [YE JIANYING TAKES XIANGZHOU]
Xich lo See CYCLO
XIE, FEI See also BEN MING NIAN; XIANG NU XIAO-XIAO
XUESE QINGCHEN f (d Li, Shaohong 1991 China)
Reynaud, B. Li Shaohong. port still CINEMAYA n25/26:8-9 Autumn/Winter 1994/95
YAGHER, KEVIN
Beeler, M. Kevin Yagher, director. il C FANTAS 26:34 n3 1995
YAKIN, BOAZ See also FRESH
YAMAGA, HIROYUKI See also ONEAMIS NO TSUBASA
YAMANE, SADAO
Yamane, S. Schon bald hundert Jahre Film. stills C(SWITZ) 40:163-174 1994
YAN, XUESHU See also [STEPPING INTO GLORY]
YANAGIMACHI, MITSUO
Richie, D. Mitsuo Yanagimachi. bibliog credits filmog il interv stills CINEMAYA n24:22-28 Summer 1994
YANAGISAWA, HISAO
Abe, M.N. Documentarists of Japan (fourth in a series). biog interv port stills DOC BOX 4:8-12 1993
Yang, Dechang See YANG, EDWARD
YANG, EDWARD See also DULI SHIDAI
YANG, MING-YU
Yang, M.-Y. Film in contemporary China: critical debates, 1979-1989. Edited by George S. Semsel, Chen Xihe, and Xia Hong [Book Review]. FQ 48:61-62 n2 1994/95
YANGGUANG CANLAN DE RIZI f (d Jiang, Wen 1994 Hong Kong/Taiwan/China)
Reviews
Bozza, G. "Yangguang can lan de rizi." still C FORUM 34:16 Sep (n337) 1994
YANZHI KOU f (d Kwan, Stanley 1988 Hong Kong)
Chow, R. Un souvenir d'amour. bibliog glos scenario still CINEMAS 3:156-180 n2/3 1993
YARASA f (d Salajev, Ajas 1995 Azerbaijan)
Reviews
Stratton, D. "The Bat" ("Yarasa"). credits VARIETY 358:82 Feb 20/26 1995
YARED, GABRIEL
Comuzio, E. Un musicista atipico: Gabriel Yared. biog filmog interv stills C FORUM 34:39-42 Oct (n338) 1994
YATES, PETER See also ROOMMATES
Kelleher, E. Disney's "Roommates" explores generational ties. il FJ 98:12+ [2p] Mar 1995
YATES, ROBERT For film reviews see author under the following titles: DARK SUMMER; MURIEL'S WEDDING; ROAD TO WELLVILLE, THE; WELCOME II THE TERRORDOME
YAZ YAGMURU f (d Giritlioglu, Tomris 1994 Turkey)
"Yaz yagmuru." biog credits filmog il still CINEMAYA n25/26:106 Autumn/Winter 1994/95
[YE JIANYING TAKES XIANGZHOU] f (d Xiao, Lang/Qiu, Lili 1994 China)
"Ye Jianying Takes Xiangzhou." credits stills CHINA SCREEN n4:20-21 1994
YEARBOOKS
Italy
Comuzio, E. Giovanni Grazzini: Cinema '93 [Book Review]. C FORUM 34:95 Oct (n338) 1994
YEO, KYUN-DONG See also SAE SANG BAKURO
YEUX SANS VISAGE, LES f (Horror Chamber of Dr. Faustus, The d Franju, Georges 1960 Fr/It)
Sinclair, I. Homeopathic horror. stills S&S 5:24-27 Apr 1995
YILMAZ, ATIF See also BERDEL
YINGXIONG BENSE f (Better Tomorrow, A d Woo, John 1986 Hong Kong)
Williams, T. To live and die in Hong Kong. bibliog stills C ACTION n36:42-52 1995
YINGXIONG BENSE II f (Better Tomorrow II, A d Woo, John 1987 Hong Kong)
Williams, T. To live and die in Hong Kong. bibliog stills C ACTION n36:42-52 1995
YINSHI NAN NU f (Eat Drink Man Woman d Lee, Ang 1994 Taiwan)
Kapetanovic, M. "Sale sucre." bibliog credits stills GRAND ANGLE n177:37-38 Dec 1994
Production
Comer, B. "Eat Drink Man Woman": a feast for the eyes. il still AMCIN 76:62-67 Jan 1995
Reviews
Delisle, M. "Sale sucre." SEQUENCES n175:46 Nov/Dec 1994
Francke, L. "Yinshi nan nu" ("Eat Drink Man Woman"). credits still S&S 5:63-64 Jan 1995
Mauro, S. "Mangiare bere uomo donna." credits stills SEGNO n72:46-47+ [3p] Mar/Apr 1995
Ueda, C. and Smith, M. "Eat Drink Man Woman." credits still C PAPERS n102:67-68 Dec 1994
YONOVER, NEAL S.
Yonover, N.S. Mick Garris takes "The Stand." filmog il interv port DGA NEWS 19:26-28 n2 1994
Yonover, N.S. and others. Artists Rights Symposium: three days of discussion. DGA NEWS 19:26-27+ [3p] n3 1994
Yor, the Hunter From the Future See MONDO DI YOR, IL
YORK, DEREK
Elley, D. Derek York. biog obit VARIETY 358:87 Mar 27/Apr 2 1995
YOU NAZTY SPY f (d White, Jules 1940 USA)
Morlan, D.B. Slapstick contributions to WWII propaganda: The Three Stooges and Abbott and Costello. bibliog STUDIES POP CULT 17:29-43 n1 1994
YOU TAKE CARE NOW f (d Fleming, Ann Marie 1989 Can)
Fleming, A.M. "You Take Care Now." scenario MILLENNIUM n25:10-13 Summer 1991
Hoolboom, M. The queen of disaster. stills MILLENNIUM n26:26-32 Fall 1992
YOUCHAI f (d He, Jianjun 1995 China)
Reviews
Rooney, D. "The Postman" ("Youchai"). credits VARIETY 358:52 Feb 13/19 1995
YOUNG ADULTS' FILM
Festivals
Uggeldahl, K. Sandnesin Kinossa elokuvissa. stills PEILI 18:36-37 n3 1994

Scandinavia
History
Kallinen, S. Pohjoismaista lastenelokuvaa suurin silmin [Book Review]. il PEILI 18:38 n3 1994
United States
Influence of Film
Hietala, V. Globaaliteinit arvotyhjiossa [Book Review]. PEILI 18:28 n4 1994
YOUNG AT HEARTS f (d Campbell, Don 1995 USA)
Reviews
Elley, D. "Young at Hearts." credits still VARIETY 358:55 Mar 13/19 1995
YOUNG, DEBORAH For film reviews see author under the following titles: AMICO IMMAGINARIO, L'; CRONACA DI UN AMORE VIOLATO; DNEVNIK UVREDA 1993; EL-BAHR BI-YEDHAK LEY; NI NA NEBU NI NA ZELMLJI; POLIZIOTTI; SEGRETO DI STATO; TITO PO DRUGI PUT MEDU SRBIMA
Young, D. Belgrade unspools despite war. VARIETY 358:61 Feb 6/12 1995
Young, D. Finnish fest comes up shorts. VARIETY 358:19 Mar 20/26 1995
YOUNG, DEBRA
Lawsuits
Sandler, A. Ousted licensing VP sues Saban for $2 mil. VARIETY 358:16 Feb 13/19 1995
YOUNG, PAUL F.
Young, P.F. Gaga gaga for additional capital. VARIETY 358:90 Mar 27/Apr 2 1995
Young, P.F. Wooden perf pays off. port VARIETY 358:6 Mar 13/19 1995
Young, P.F. Writing tip. VARIETY 358:10 Mar 27/Apr 2 1995
YOUNG POISONER'S HANDBOOK, THE f (d Ross, Benjamin 1995 Gt Br)
Reviews
Greene, R. "The Young Poisoner's Handbook." BOXOFFICE 131:bet p125 and 144 [pR27-R28] Apr 1995
YOUNGBLOOD, DENISE J.
Menashe, L. Requiem for Soviet cinema 1917-1991 [Book Reviews]. stills CINEASTE 21:23-27 n1/2 1995
Youth See as a subheading under individual subject headings [Prior to V17, 1989 use as a subject heading]
Youth audience See AUDIENCE, YOUTH
YOUTH IN FILM
Festivals
Azzalin, C. Storie adolescenti. stills SEGNO n71:60-61 Jan/Feb 1995
Catelli, D. Un diluvio di film. stills SEGNO n71:58-59 Jan/Feb 1995
Terazzan, S. Il festival ritrovato: l'undicesima edizione dei Festival del Cinema Giovani. C SUD 33:27-28 Jul/Aug/Sep (n113) 1994
YU, QIAN
Yu, Q. An escape from desperation. il CHINA SCREEN n4:33 1994
YUEN, KWAI See also HUNG HEI-KUN
Yugoslavia See JUGOSLOVENSKA KINOTEKA (Belgrade, Yugoslavia)
YUKI YUKI TE SHINGUN f (Emperor's Naked Army Marches On, The d Hara, Kazuo 1987 Japan)
Gerow, A.A. Documentarists of Japan (second in a series). biog interv port stills DOC BOX 3:12-18 1993
YUTANI, KIMBERLY
Yutani, K. Gregg Araki and the queer new wave. il AMERASIA J 20:84-91 n1 1994
ZAALBERG, JAN
Adamson, J. and others. Forgotten laughter. credits port stills GRIFFITHIANA n51/52:170-197 Oct 1994
Adamson, J. and others. La fabbrica della risata. credits port stills GRIFFITHIANA n51/52:170-197 Oct 1994
ZABRANENIAT PLOD f (d Krumov, Krassimir 1995 Bulg)
Reviews
Elley, D. "The Forbidden Fruit" ("Zabraneniyat plod"). credits VARIETY 358:65 Mar 6/12 1995
ZABRISKIE POINT f (d Antonioni, Michelangelo 1970 USA)
Schenk, I. Natur und Anti-Natur in den Filmen von Michelangelo Antonioni. C(SWITZ) 40:175-193 1994
ZACH, PETER
Zach, P. (Sieben) 7 1/2 beziehungen und bestimmungen zu den Guenstlingen des mondes. credits il stills BLIMP [n2]:48-51 Winter 1985
Zach, P. Straub. filmog il interv BLIMP [n1]:14-25 Mar 1985
ZAGAGLIA, PAOLO
Noel, J. Cinema de Verviers (1896-1993). Par Michel Bedeur et Paolo Zagaglia [Book Review]. il GRAND ANGLE n177:49-50 Dec 1994
ZAGARI, PAOLO
Zagari, P. Dracula e serial-killer per "cinetalpe" incallite. still C NUOVO 43:20-21 Nov/Dec (n352) 1994
ZAILLIAN, STEVE
Johnsen, F. Om joder og sjakk. interv port stills F&K n1:8-10 1994
ZALAN, VINCE
Zalan, V. Keleti szel. stills F VILAG 38:34-35 n3 1995
ZALUSKI, ROMAN See also KOMEDIA MALZENSKA
"Komedia malzenska." biog credits filmog still FSP 40:12 n4 (n758) 1994
ZAMBETTI, SANDRO
Zambetti, S. Venezia '94: come si traghetta da una Repubblica all'altra. il C FORUM 34:3-4 Sep (n337) 1994
ZANGARDI, TONINO See also ALLULLO DROM
ZANIELLO, TOM
Zaniello, T. Hitched or Lynched: who directed "Twin Peaks"? bibliog filmogs STUDIES POP CULT 17:55-64 n1 1994
ZANOLIN, DANIELA
Zanolin, D. Indici di "Segnocinema" 1994 (nn. 65-70). SEGNO n72:bet p40 and 41 [8p] Mar/Apr 1995
ZANUCK, DARRYL F.
Turner, G. Memo from Darryl F. Zanuck. By Rudy Behlmer [Book Review]. AMCIN 74:95 Sep 1993
ZANUSSI, KRZYSZTOF
Plazewski, J. Wspolprodukcje hydra, czy szansa? il interv ports KINO 27:6-9 Jun 1993
ZAPPOLI, GIANCARLO For film reviews see author under the following titles: EROE DEI DUE MONDI, L'; HONEY, I BLEW UP THE KID; STARGATE
Zappoli, G. Come e per chi? il port SEGNO n71:16-18 Jan/Feb 1995
Zappoli, G. Cosi vicino cosi lontano. il intervs SEGNO n71:24-27 Jan/Feb

Section Two: Television/Video

GENERAL POLICIES

USE OF TERMS *TELEVISION* and *VIDEO*

The terms *TELEVISION* and *VIDEO* are not used before main subject headings if they can be inferred from the subject headings (They appear separately as qualifiers).

Examples
TELEVISION INDUSTRY entered under:
INDUSTRY
  Television (broadcast)

TELEVISION/VIDEO ECONOMIC ASPECTS entered under:
ECONOMIC ASPECTS
  Television (broadcast)/Video (non-broadcast)

VIDEO DIRECTORS entered under:
DIRECTORS
  Video (non-broadcast)

TITLES OF TELEVISION/VIDEO PROGRAMS

Articles which discuss television/video programs appear under the original language titles with the following information, if available, in parentheses: American release title for foreign language programs, director's name, date of first public showing and country of production. A *v* is found directly after the title of television/video programs to denote television/video titles and a d is used to indicate director.

Example
CRISTOFORO COLOMBO v (Christopher Columbus d Lattuada, Alberto 1985 It/USA/Fr/W Ger)

Cross references appear from the American release titles and directors to their respective television/video titles.

Examples
Christopher Columbus See CRISTOFORO COLOMBO
LATTUADA, ALBERTO See also CRISTOFORO COLOMBO

REVIEWS OF TELEVISION/VIDEO PROGRAMS

All television/video reviews appear together under the titles of television/video programs with the subheading Reviews.

FESTIVALS

Festivals appear under the general subject heading *FESTIVALS* arranged by country, state or province, city, and date.

Example
FESTIVALS
  Television (broadcast)
    Canada. Alberta, Banff 1988

GEOGRAPHIC NAMES

Geographic names appear as subheadings under specific subject headings following all other subheadings.

Example
INDUSTRY
  Video (non-broadcast)
    Laws and Legislation
    France

ABBREVIATIONS

Arg	Argentina	bet	between
Belg	Belgium	bibliog	bibliography
Bulg	Bulgaria	biog	biography
Can	Canada	credits	credits
China	China (People's Republic)	d	director
CIS	Commonwealth of Independent States	diag(s)	diagram(s)
Czech	Czech and Slovak Federative Republic	discog(s)	discography(s)
Denmk	Denmark	filmog(s)	filmography(s)
E Ger	Germany (Democratic Republic)	glos	glossary
Finl	Finland	graph(s)	graph(s)
Fr	France	il	illustrations
FR Ger	Germany (Federal Republic)	interv(s)	interview(s)
Ger	Germany (before 1949)	map(s)	map(s)
Gt Br	Great Britain	n	number
It	Italy	obit	obituary
Mex	Mexico	p	page(s)
Neth	Netherlands	port(s)	portrait(s)
N Korea	Korea (Democratic People's Republic)	prod	produced/producer
N Vietnam	Vietnam (Democratic Republic)	pt	part
Norw	Norway	scenario	scenario(s)/scenario excerpt(s)
Phil	Philippines	score	musical score(s)
Port	Portugal	sec	section
S Afr	South Africa	specs	specifications
S Korea	Korea (Republic)	stat	statistics
S Vietnam	Vietnam (Republic)	sup	supplement
Sp	Spain	table(s)	table(s)
Swed	Sweden	v	video
Switz	Switzerland		
Taiwan	China (Republic)		
Thai	Thailand		
USA	United States		
USSR	Union of Soviet Socialist Republics		
W Ger	Germany (Federal Republic) [1949-1990]		
Yugo	Yugoslavia		

SUBHEADINGS

The following terms appear only as subheadings.

Adults	Men	Schedules
Applications	Nineteen mm	SECAM
Beta	Nonprofessional Activities	Social Aspects
Cable	NTSC	Sociological Aspects
Children	One Inch	Sound Track Reviews
Comparison With Film	One-quarter Inch	Super-VHS
Digital	PAL	Super-VHSC
D-MAC	PAL-Plus	Technical Aspects
D2-MAC	Personal Lives	Techniques
Eight mm	Personnel	Testing and Measurement
Four mm	Product Guides	Three-quarter Inch
Half-inch	Professional Activities	Tributes
HD-MAC	Public	Two Inch
Hi-8	Quad-C	VHS
International Aspects	Recollections	VHS-C
M-II	Rental	Women
Maintenance	Retrospectives	Youth
Membership Lists	Review Excerpts	

In addition, most subject headings also appear as subheadings.

STANDARDS AND RECOMMENDED PRACTICES [Prior to V15, 1987 use BROADCASTING
  STANDARDS AND PRACTICES]
    Television (broadcast) and Video (non-bro   **FORMER SUBJECT HEADINGS**
  Ridder, F. Audio technology: on board the ESb
    1988
  Clusser, D.E. Keynote address. il SMPTE J 97:81-89 Jan 1988
  Streeter, R.G. Engineering report: what is a standard? il SMPTE J 97:79-80
    Jan 1988
      Associations
  Streeter, R.G. Engineering report. port SMPTE J 97:263-267 Apr Part I 1988
    Television (broadcast)
  Baldwin, J.L. Enhancing television - an evolving scene. diags il SMPTE J
    97:374-377 May 1988
STARDUST THEATER
  Beermann, F. Stardust film service to debut for home dishers come July 4.
    VARIETY 331:56 Jun 15 1988
STARSHIP HOME v (in production 1988 Australia)
  "Starship Home" stall was costly for South Australian Film Corp. VARIETY
    331:240 Apr 27 1988
STEIN, MICHAEL ◄————   **AUTHOR ENTRIES**
  Stein, M. A candid conversation wi   il interv ports
    stills F FAX n10:68-71+ [6p] Apr/May 1988
Stellas See AWARDS - Television - Great Britain. British Academy of Film
  and Television Arts
STENO
  Obituaries. VARIETY 330:108-110 Mar 16 1988
STEREOPHONIC SOUND [Prior to V16, 1988 use SOUND, STEREOPHONIC]
    Television (broadcast)
      Great Britain. Digital. Technical Aspects
  Moffat, 9. Television engineering research in the BBC, today and tomorrow.
    diags il stills SMPTE J 97:17-24 Jan 1988
    Video (non-broadcast)
      United States. Music Video
  Media stereotypes of women also found in music videos. MEDIA RPT 16:8
    Mar/Apr 1988
STEREOPHONIC SOUND EQUIPMENT [Prior to V16, 1988 use EQUIPMENT, SOUND,
  STEREOPHONIC]
    Video (non-broadcast)
      United States. Videorecorders and Videorecording
  Brewin, B. Video guide: the sound and the fury. il PREM 1:97+ [2p] Feb 1988
    Television (broadcast) ◄——   **TELEVISION/VIDEO QUALIFIERS**
STEREOSCOPE
      Technical Aspects
  Kost, B. Konstruktion von Zwischenansichten fuer
    Multi-Viewpoint-3DTV-Systeme. diags il FKT 42:67-73 Feb 1988
    Video (non-broadcast)
      United States. Graphics
  Birkmaier, C. The user interface: rendering an opinion on 3D. port
    VIDEOGRAPHY 13:72-73 May 1988
STEREOTYPES
    Television (broadcast) and Video (non-broadcast)
      Theory
  McManon, B. Stories and stereotypes. diag il METRO n72:40-45 Summer/Autumn
    1987
    Television (broadcast)
      Programming for the Physically Handicapped
  Karpf, A. TV charity: "give us a break, not a begging bowl." NEW STATESM
    115:13 May 27 1988
      United States. Women in Television/Video
  Professional women on TV are now less stereotyped, more complex, study
    concludes. MEDIA RPT 16:4-5 Mar/Apr 1988
STEVENS, DAVID See also ALWAYS AFTERNOON
  A director's progress. port INTERVIEW 18:17-18 Dec 1989
STEVENS, ROSS   **TELEVISION/VIDEO PROGRAM CROSS REFERENCES**
  Stevens, R. Irate Hudson
    VARIETY 331:62 Jun 8 1988
STILES, BILL
  Besas, P. Hallmark pulls new Latin net to NY. VARIETY 330:1+ [2p] Mar 23
    1988
STOCK FOOTAGE ◄————   **SUBJECT HEADING ENTRIES**
    Video (non-broadcast)
      United States. Technical Aspects
  Slide, A. Stock footage: a vital link. il AMCIN 69:83-88 Feb 1988
STOCKLER, BRUCE
  Stockler, B. The mind readers. il ports stills MILLIMETER 16:90-94+ [12p]
    Apr 1988
STODDARD, BRANDON
  Boyer, P.J. A show on the 60's helps a network in the 80's. port still NY
    TIMES 137:C18 Apr 11 1988
STORAGE OF VIDEOTAPE
    Television (broadcast) and Video (non-broadcast)
      Sweden
  Haney, F.J. Television: networks: studio concept in the TV center - Sweden.
    il SMPTE J 97:288-289 Apr Part I 1988
STORER CABLE
  Several interested buyers said to be looking at SCI holdings. VARIETY
    330:67+ [2p] Mar 16 1988
STORER COMMUNICATIONS INC. ◄——   **CORPORATE BODY ENTRIES**
  Fabrikant, G. (Two) 2 cable TV companie
    Apr 25 1988
Storyteller, The See LUCK CHILD, THE
STRAND, KURT
  Strand, K. TV a la Tivi. il port LB 4:30-33 Apr 1988
STRANITSY SOVETSKOGO ISKUSSTVA LITERATURA I TEATR
  Nilin, A. Na robkuiu pamiat'. ISKUS K n10:77-82 1987
STRAUSS, BOB
  Strauss, B. Cameos: actor Ray Liotta. port PREM 1:28 Mar 1988

STRAUSS, FREDERIC
  Strauss, F. Des aventures solitaires. still CAHIERS n401:Journal n77:X Nov
    1987
STREET, THE v (1988 USA) ◄————   **TELEVISION/VIDEO PROGRAM ENTRIES**
  Bennetts, L. "The Street" is miles
    137:39+ [2p] sec 2 Apr 10 1988
  Heuring, D. "The Street" - shooting video with eye for film. il stills
    AMCIN 69:73-74+ [6p] Jun 1988
  No sunny side for MCA's "Street," syndie show off to rocky start. stat
    VARIETY 330:106+ [2p] Apr 20 1988
    Reviews   **TELEVISION/VIDEO PROGRAM REVIEW ENTRIES**
  O'Connor, J.J. Review/te
    NY TIMES 137:C18 Apr 12 1988
STREETER, RICHARD G.
  Streeter, R.G. Engineering report. port SMPTE J 97:263-267 Apr Part I 1988
  Streeter, R.G. Engineering report: what is a standard? il SMPTE J 97:79-80
    Jan 1988
STRESSED TO KILL v (1988 USA)
    Reviews
  Kaufman, D. "Stressed to Kill." credits VARIETY 331:536 May 4 1988
STRIKES
    Television (broadcast)   **SUBHEADING ENTRIES**
      Actors and Actresses ◄————
  Robb, D. Blurb producer may hire foreign actors after all. VARIETY 331:33+
    [2p] Apr 27 1988
      United States ◄————   **GEOGRAPHIC SUBHEADING ENTRIES**
  Jensen, E. It's no Summer Olym
    1988
      United States. Actors and Actresses
  Ballots sent to end union strike. VARIETY 331:524 May 4 1988
  Tentative agreement in actors' strike. VARIETY 330:50 Apr 13 1988
      United States. Actors and Actresses. Commercials
  Tentative settlement in commercials strike. il SCREEN ACTOR HOLLYWOOD 9:1-2
    n1 1988
      United States. Commercials
  Robb, D. Blurb thesps suspend strike; back at work. VARIETY 330:107+ [2p]
    Apr 20 1988
      United States. Economic Aspects
  Harmetz, A. Strike costs assayed. stat NY TIMES 137:C38 Apr 22 1988
      United States. Effects on Television/Video
  Blau, E. TV notes: substitute scriptwriters filling a creative void. port
    NY TIMES 137:C29 Apr 21 1988
  Harmetz, A. Abrupt end for TV dramas' seasons. still NY TIMES 137:C22 Apr
    18 1988
      United States. Writers
  Boyer, P.J. NBC plans a "writerproof" schedule. port NY TIMES 137:C22 Jun
    30 1988
  Hourlong resids hushhush focus of WGA talks. VARIETY 331:69 Jun 1 1988
  Kaufman, D. Just when CBS thought it was safe to start its fall season early,
    the WGA strike lingers. VARIETY 331:531 May 4 1988
  Negotiators nix AMPTP proposal but leave strike in WGA hands. VARIETY 331:60
    Jun 22 1988
  SAG supports Writers Guild strike effort. SCREEN ACTOR HOLLYWOOD 9:1 n1 1988
  Strike takes toll. stat VARIETY 331:5 Apr 27 1988
  WGA soap rebellion exaggerated. VARIETY 331:542 May 4 1988
  Writers picket in strike's 3d week. VARIETY 330:7 Mar 23 1988
STRINGER v (1988 Australia)
    Reviews
  Harris, M. "Stringer." credits VARIETY 330:126 Apr 20 1988
STRITCH, ELAINE
  Chanko, K.M. Elaine Stritch. il FIR 39:211-212 Apr 1988
STRUCTURAL ANALYSIS
    Television (broadcast) and Video (non-broadcast)
      Music Video
  Kungel, R. Das Musik-Video und seine gestaltung? diag filmog graph table
    F&TV KAM 37:44+ [7p] Feb 1988
STUART, MEL See WITH PETER BEARD IN AFRICA
STUDENT PRODUCTION
    Video (non-broadcast)   **SEE REFERENCES**
      Canada. Festivals
  Ontario grads honoured. C CAN n143:46 Jul/Aug 1987
Studios See names of studios (e.g. LORIMAR-TELEPICTURES CORPORATION)
Studios, production [Prior to V16, 1988 use STUDIOS, PRODUCTION] See PRODUCTION
  STUDIOS
STUDY AND TEACHING See also PROFESSIONAL EDUCATION ◄——   **SEE ALSO REFERENCES**
    Television (broadcast) and Video (non-broadcast)
      Scandinavia
  Iversen, G. Danske TV-analyser. F HAFTET n4/n1:95-96 Jan 1988
SUEURS FROIDES v (1988 Fr)
  Belie, B.de "Sueurs froides." stills C REVUE n5:26-27 Feb 4 1988
SUGARMAN, BURT
  Jones, A.S. The press: Media General fight raises questions of vulnerability.
    il NY TIMES 137:D10 May 16 1988
SUNDBY, SISSEL For film reviews see author under the following titles: DARLING
  DOWNS; NOBODY   **TELEVISION/VIDEO PROGRAM REVIEWER ENTRIES**
SUPER CHANNEL
      Economic Aspects
  After year's debts, Super Channel gets future refinancing. VARIETY 331:525+
    [2p] May 4 1988
SUPERCARRIER v (1988 USA)
    Reviews
  Scott, T. "Supercarrier."   **COUNTRY SEE REFERENCES**
SUSSKIND, DAVID
  Obituaries. ports CLASSIC n142:60 Apr 1987
Sweden See as a subheading under individual subject headings
SYLVIA PLATH v (d Pitkethly, Lawrence 1988 USA)
    Reviews
  O'Connor, J.J. Review/television: Sylvia Plath in painful retrospect. port
    NY TIMES 137:C32 Apr 21 1988

BEBAN, BREDA
Darke, C. Everything is connected. stills S&S 5:28-31 Feb 1995
BECKETTT, SAMUEL
Kalb, J. Screenings. port VILLAGE VOICE 40:76 Jan 31 1995
BEDFORD, BRIAN
Giltz, M. Oh, lucky guy. port NEW YORK 28:72 Jan 23 1995
BEDTIME STORY v (d Romanek, Mark 1995 USA)
Aletti, V. Dream on. still VILLAGE VOICE 40:68 Mar 21 1995
BEELER, MICHAEL
Beeler, M. Feature vs. series. il still C FANTAS 26:24-25 n2 1995
Beeler, M. Keep on trekkin'. stills C FANTAS 26:41 n2 1995
Beeler, M. Kevin Yagher, director. il C FANTAS 26:34 n3 1995
Beeler, M. The Star Trek curse. stills C FANTAS 26:26 n2 1995
Beeler, M. Two captains. il still C FANTAS 26:18 n2 1995
BEHIND THE LENS (United States)
Krasilovsky, A. A sharper image. il port ANGLES 2:10-11 n4 1995
BEHLMER, RUDY
Behlmer, R. Directors' paper trails. table DGA NEWS 19:50+ [3p] n6 1994/95
BEHREND, JEAN
Behrend, J. ADs, UPMs, directors explain it all at Expo. il DGA NEWS 20:22 n1 1995
Behrend, J. DGA goes indie at IFFM. il DGA NEWS 19:24-25 n6 1994/95
Behrend, J. News, serials, commercials. il DGA NEWS 19:8-9 n3 1994
Behrend, J. "Sometimes you took off, sometimes you crashed and burned." il DGA NEWS 19:12-13 n2 1994
Belgium See as a subheading under individual subject headings
BELL, PHILIP
Bell, P. Jakubowicz, Andrew, Goodall, Heather, Martin, Jeannie, Mitchell, Tony, Randall, Lois and Seneviratne, Kalinga. Racism, ethnicity and the media [Book Review]. MEDIA INFO AUSTRALIA n75:165-166 Feb 1995
BELLAFANTE, GINIA For film reviews see author under the following titles: SERVING IN SILENCE: THE MARGARETHE CAMMERMEYER STORY
Bellafante, G. Playing "get the guest." il stills TIME 145:77 Mar 27 1995
Bellafante, G. The inventor of bad TV. ports TIME 145:111 Mar 13 1995
Bellafante, G. The network that Newt built. il TIME 145:30 Jan 9 1995
BENNETT, ALAN
Corliss, R. Bard of embarrassment. biog il port still TIME 145:65-66 Feb 27 1995
BENNETT, RONAN
Bennett, R. Telling the truth about Ireland. il stills VERTIGO (UK) 1:24-29 n4 1994/95
BENOIT, MARIUSZ
Slodowski, J. Mariusz Benoit. filmog still FSP 40:12 n11 (n765) 1994
BENSON, JIM
Benson, J. Carolco sells "Soldier" rights to Skyvision. VARIETY 358:25+ [2p] Feb 6/12 1995
Benson, J. Hours lose power in syndie market. port stat VARIETY 357:39+ [2p] Jan 9/15 1995
Benson, J. New World closes on Cannell. VARIETY 358:35 Mar 27/Apr 2 1995
Benson, J. O.J. coverage tries syndie rates. VARIETY 358:40 Mar 6/12 1995
Benson, J. "Simpsons" tops syndie race. stat VARIETY 358:29 Feb 6/12 1995
Benson, J. Syndicated hours shine thanks to Simpson trial, Clinton talk. stat VARIETY 358:41 Feb 13/19 1995
Benson, J. Syndie shows slow out of gate. stat VARIETY 358:195 Feb 20/26 1995
Benson, J. Syndie talk off, mags up post-sweeps. stat VARIETY 358:34 Mar 27/Apr 2 1995
Benson, J. Syndies slip despite sweeps boost. stat VARIETY 358:43 Mar 6/12 1995
Benson, J. Talkshows rate murder case an ethical dilemma. il port VARIETY 358:23+ [2p] Mar 20/26 1995
Benson, J. Trial coverage crimps syndies. stat VARIETY 358:53-54 Feb 27/Mar 5 1995
Benson, J. Trial's tribulations dog field of syndies. stat VARIETY 358:27-28 Mar 20/26 1995
Benson, J. Trying to gain access. stat VARIETY 357:88 Jan 2/8 1995
Benson, J. Worldvision takes "Stand" on big ticket. port VARIETY 358:193+ [2p] Feb 20/26 1995
Benson, J. and Flint, J. Disney hunts for Telco topper. VARIETY 358:6 Mar 20/26 1995
Benson, J. and Walsh, T. "Home" enters original syndie to duel "Seinfeld." stills VARIETY 358:29+ [2p] Mar 27/Apr 2 1995
Flint, J. and Benson, J. WB, Par weblets square off. il stat VARIETY 357:37+ [2p] Jan 2/8 1995
BENSON, JOHN
Benson, J. Thyme of death. By Susan Wittig Albert [Book Review]. ARMCHAIR DET 26:109 n2 1993
BERGESEN, ALBERT
Hoover, S. M. Media and the moral order in postpositivist approaches to media studies [Book Reviews]. bibliog J COMM 45:136-146 n1 1995
BERLUSCONI, SILVIO
Bachrach, J. Arrivederci, Berlusconi? il VANITY FAIR 58:106-115+ [15p] Jan 1995
Rooney, D. Back to business for Berlusconi? stat VARIETY 357:56+ [2p] Jan 2/8 1995
BERNSTEIN, STEVEN
Frey, M. Film production [Book Review]. F KUNST n144:67-68 1994
BERRY, GORDON L.
Lewis, R.F. Children and television: images in a changing sociocultural world. Edited by Gordon L. Berry & Joy K. Asamen [Book Review]. CAN J COM 19:555-556 n3/4 1994
BERTELSMANN MUSIC GROUP (BMG)
Molner, D. Zelnick looking to boost BMG's RCA label, pump up core business. port VARIETY 357:47-48 Jan 9/15 1995
Beta See as a subheading under individual subject headings
BEZANSON, RANDALL P.
Trager, R. Entangled values: the First Amendment in the 1990s [Book Reviews]. bibliog J COMM 45:163-170 n1 1995
BIEDERMAN, CHRISTINE
Biederman, C. The OJ papers. il VILLAGE VOICE 40:29-30 Feb 28 1995

BIEDRZYNSKA, ADRIANNA
Slodowski, J. Adrianna Biedrzynska. filmog stills FSP 40:12-13 n3 (n757) 1994
BIETE NIERE - SUCHE HERZ v (1992 FR Ger)
Reviews
Koehler, M. "Biete Niere - suche Herz." MEDIEN 38:364 n6 1994
BIGELOW, KATHRYN See also WILD PALMS
BINAME, CHARLES
Beaulieu, J. Entrevue avec Charles Biname. il interv SEQUENCES n174:15 Sep/Oct 1994
BIONDI, FRANK
Auletta, K. Redstone's secret weapon. il NEW YORKER 70:46-52+ [17p] Jan 16 1995
BIRCHENOUGH, TOM
Birchenough, T. Director to head anti-piracy org. VARIETY 358:59 Feb 27/Mar 5 1995
Birchenough, T. Fate of Russian TV up in air. VARIETY 358:39 Mar 27/Apr 2 1995
Birchenough, T. It's Veltsin Democrats vs. hard-liners for Ch. 5. VARIETY 357:49 Jan 9/15 1995
Birchenough, T. Newsman's murder jolts Moscow. VARIETY 358:47 Mar 6/12 1995
Birchenough, T. Ostankino takes a leap forward with tapping of new CEO. stat VARIETY 358:176 Feb 20/26 1995
Birchenough, T. State TV's ad ban worries other webs. stat VARIETY 358:59 Feb 27/Mar 5 1995
Birchenough, T. TV has role in Chechnya war. VARIETY 358:59-60 Feb 27/Mar 5 1995
Birchenough, T. Vladislav Listyev. biog obit VARIETY 358:74 Mar 6/12 1995
BISHKO, LESLIE
Bishko, L. Expressive technology: the tool as metaphor of aesthetic sensibility. il stills ANIMATION J 3:74-91 n1 1994
BISSET, BRUCE
Bisset, B. Letters: Blue Book piece was half right. ONFILM 11:10-11 n11 1994/95
Drinnan, J. Letters: John Drinnan responds. ONFILM 11:11 n11 1994/95
BLACKS IN TELEVISION/VIDEO [Prior to V21, 1993 use AFRO-AMERICANS IN TELEVISION/VIDEO]
Television (broadcast)
United States
Schone, M. Black hour at black rock. VILLAGE VOICE 40:51-52 Mar 28 1995
United States. Ideological Analysis
Zook, K.B. Test patterns [Book Reviews]. il VILLAGE VOICE 40:64 Jan 10 1995
Video (non-broadcast)
United States
Nicholson, J. Facets African American video guide. Compiled by Patrick Ogle [Book Review]. il AFTERIMAGE 22:15 Jan 1995
BLACKS IN TELEVISION/VIDEO INDUSTRY [Prior to V21, 1993 use AFRO-AMERICANS IN TELEVISION/VIDEO INDUSTRY]
Television (broadcast)
United States
Zook, K.B. Warner bruthas. il VILLAGE VOICE 40:36-37 Jan 17 1995
BLACKWELL, EARL
Shields, S. Earl Blackwell. biog obit VARIETY 358:75 Mar 6/12 1995
BLACKWELL, ERIN
Blackwell, E. "Complaints of a Dutiful Daughter." still INDEP 18:14-15 Mar 1995
BLAIN, NEIL
Blain, N. Garry Whannel, Fields in vision [Book Review]. MEDIA CUL & SOC 17:169-172 n1 1995
BLAIR, DAVID See also WAX, OR THE DISCOVERY OF TELEVISION AMONG THE BEES
BLAIR, FRANK
Transition. obit NEWSWK 125:55 Mar 27 1995
BLATNER, DAVID
Frey, M. Cyberspace [Book Review]. F KUNST n144:65-66 1994
BLAUE LICHT, DAS v (Blue Light, The d Riefenstahl, Leni 1932 Ger)
Reviews
DeBartolo, J. Video tape reviews. credits port stills CLASSIC n237:12+ [3p] Mar 1995
BLECKNER, JEFF See also SERVING IN SILENCE: THE MARGARETHE CAMMERMEYER STORY
BLINDFOLD: ACTS OF OBSESSION v (d Simeone, Lawrence 1994 USA)
Reviews
"Blindfold: Acts of Obsession." FATAL VISIONS n17:26 1994
BLOCKBUSTER ENTERTAINMENT CORPORATION
Paxman, A. B'buster bullish on expansion. stat VARIETY 358:62+ [2p] Mar 27/Apr 2 1995
Paxman, A. B'buster VideoVisa: devalued relations. il stat VARIETY 358:43-44 Feb 13/19 1995
Roberts, J.L. Chips off the Block. graphs ports still NEWSWK 125:42-43 Feb 20 1995
BLOECH, MICHAEL
Anfang, G. Mit Jugendlichen videofilmen [Book Review]. MEDIEN 38:380-381 n6 1994
BLUE, JAMES See also INVISIBLE CITY, THE; WHO KILLED THE FOURTH WARD?
Lunenfeld, P. "There are people in the streets who've never had a chance to speak": James Blue and the complex documentary. bibliog biog stills UFAJ 46:21-33 n1 1994
Blue Light, The See BLAUE LICHT, DAS
BLUM, GABRIELE CLERMONT
Blum, G.C. In memory of... Georges Delerue. il F SCORE MONTHLY n36/37:25 Aug/Sep 1993
BLUWAL, MARCEL See also MISERABLES, LES
Thomas, S. Entretien avec Marcel Bluwal. il interv AVANT-SCENE n438/439:before p1-2 [3p] Jan/Feb 1995
BOBBY, KATE
Bobby, K. NVR offers libraries alternative videos at a discount. still INDEP 18:10+ [3p] Apr 1995
BOBER, PHILIPPE
Molner, D. October buys rights to Danish "Kingdom." VARIETY 358:27 Mar 13/19 1995

COUCHOT, EDMOND
Couchot, E. Au-dela du cinema. Image et temps numeriques. CINEMAS 5:69-80
n1/2 1994
COULSON, CATHERINE
Young, P.F. Wooden perf pays off. port VARIETY 358:6 Mar 13/19 1995
COULTHARD, EDMUND See also PROMISED LAND, THE
COUTTS, DOUG
Coutts, D. All I want for Xmas is a two-buck rise. il ONFILM 11:17 n11
1994/95
Coutts, D. Whatever's next -- that's the bottom line. il ONFILM [12]:14 n2
1995
COVILLE, GARY
Coville, G. and Lucanio, P. "Flash Gordon." il ports stills F FAX
n49:62-68 Mar/Apr 1995
COWARD, PATRICIA
Coward, P. "Sight and Sound": index to volume 4; January 1994 to December
1994. S&S 5:insert [16p] Feb 1995
COWBOYS IN TELEVISION/VIDEO
    Television (broadcast)
        United States. Collections and Collecting
Slide, A. The Slide area film book notes [Book Reviews]. CLASSIC
n237:42-44+ [4p] Mar 1995
COWLEY, GEOFFREY
Cowley, G. and others. RoboDocs and mousecalls. il port NEWSWK 125:66-67
Feb 27 1995
COX, DAN
Cox, D. Al DiTolla. obit VARIETY 357:80 Jan 9/15 1995
Cox, D. "Hoop," "Forrest" make the film editors' cut. VARIETY 358:24 Mar
27/Apr 2 1995
Cox, D. IA boss won't sell West Coast Short. port stat VARIETY 357:1+ [3p]
Jan 9/15 1995
Cox, D. Robert Totten. obit VARIETY 358:54 Feb 13/19 1995
Cox, D. SAG, producers settle in a cliffhanger deal. VARIETY 358:16 Mar
27/Apr 2 1995
Cox, D. Sony corporate adds Miller to its culture. port VARIETY 358:20 Feb
13/19 1995
Cox, D. WGA, producers' pact "groundbreaking." VARIETY 358:17 Feb 6/12 1995
Cox, D. Writers Guild gains ground with new pact. VARIETY 358:18 Feb 13/19
1995
Robinson, G. and Cox, D. Power shift at Sony Corp. port VARIETY 358:15+
[2p] Mar 27/Apr 2 1995
COX, TONY
Dempsey, J. Caught in corporate crossfire, pay TV exec Cox quits Viacom.
VARIETY 358:28 Mar 20/26 1995
Dempsey, J. Viacom's shift of Cox augurs push into PPV. port VARIETY
358:198 Feb 20/26 1995
CRANDALL, REBECCA
Cowley, G. and others. RoboDocs and mousecalls. il port NEWSWK 125:66-67
Feb 27 1995
CRANE, BOB
McSherry, F.D., Jr. The murder of Bob Crane. By Robert Graysmith [Book
Review]. ARMCHAIR DET 26:117-118 n4 1993
CRAWFORD, OLIVER H.
Obituaries. obits VARIETY 358:56 Mar 13/19 1995
CREDIT
    Television (broadcast)
        United States. Directors
Reynolds, G. Credits where they're due. port DGA NEWS 19:5 n6 1994/95
CRENSHAW, MICHELLE
Abbe, E. Michelle Crenshaw. il interv ANGLES 2:12-16 n4 1995
CRIME IN TELEVISION/VIDEO
    Television (broadcast)
        United States
Williams, A. Domestic violence and the aetiology of crime in "America's Most
Wanted." il port stills CAM OBS n31:96-119 Jan/May 1993
        United States. Reality Programming
Breen, J.L. Gerald, Marc, ed. Murder plus: true crime stories from the
masters of detective fiction [Book Review]. ARMCHAIR DET 28:78 n1 1995
CRISCI, RITA
Crisci, R. Italian people shows. VERTIGO (UK) 1:7-8 n4 1994/95
CRITICISM See also THEORY
    Television (broadcast)
        United States
Jalbert, P.L. Critique and analysis in media studies: media criticism as
practical action. bibliog DISCOURSE & SOC 6:7-26 n1 1995
Croatia (since 1992) See as a subheading under individual subject headings
CROSBY, BING
Slide, A. The Slide area film book notes [Book Reviews]. CLASSIC n236:47-49
Feb 1995
CROSS-CULTURAL ANALYSIS See also CULTURAL CONTEXT
    Television (broadcast)
        Great Britain
Sinclair, J. Liebes, Tamar and Katz, Elihu. The export of meaning:
cross-cultural readings of "Dallas" [Book Review]. MEDIA INFO AUSTRALIA
n75:167-168 Feb 1995
CULLINGHAM, MARK
Obituaries. obits VARIETY 358:188-189 Feb 20/26 1995
CULTURAL CONTEXT
    Television (broadcast)
        Australia
Beale, A. Framing culture: criticism and policy in Australia. By Stuart
Cunningham [Book Reviews]. CAN J COM 19:556-559 n3/4 1994
        Canada. Aborigines in Television/Video
Fraser, F. The participation of Aboriginal and other cultural minorities in
cultural development. bibliog CAN J COM 19:477-493 n3/4 1994
        Canada. Economic Aspects
Hoskins, C. and others. The environment in which cultural industries operate
and some implications. bibliog CAN J COM 19:353-376 n3/4 1994
        Canada. Government Support
Audley, P. Cultural industries policy: objectives, formulation, and

evaluation. bibliog CAN J COM 19:317-352 n3/4 1994
        Canada. Popular Culture
Knight, G. The Beaver bites back? American popular culture in Canada. Edited
by David H. Flaherty & Frank E. Manning [Book Review]. CAN J COM 19:560-561
n3/4 1994
        Great Britain. Feminist Analysis
Thornton, E.P. On the landing: high art, low art, and "Upstairs,
Downstairs." il stills CAM OBS n31:26-47 Jan/May 1993
        Latin America
Richardson, D. Communication, culture and hegemony: from the media to
mediations. By Jesus Martin-Barbero [Book Review]. CAN J COM 19:562-563
n3/4 1994
        United States. Violence in Television/Video
Pimenoff, M. Mista syntyy vakivalta? PEILI 18:9 n2 1994
Cultural identity See NATIONAL CONSCIOUSNESS
CUNNINGHAM, STANLEY B.
Cunningham, S.B. Morals and the media: ethics in Canadian journalism. By
Nick Russell [Book Review]. CAN J COM 20:128-129 n1 1995
CUNNINGHAM, STUART
Beale, A. Framing culture: criticism and policy in Australia. By Stuart
Cunningham [Book Reviews]. CAN J COM 19:556-559 n3/4 1994
CURTIS, JAMIE LEE
Jamie Lee Curtis. biog filmog port stills STARS n21:[11-12] Winter 1995
CURTIS, RICHARD
Katz, S.B. A conversation with... Richard Curtis. il interv JOURNAL WGA
8:24-27 Mar 1995
CURTIS, TONY
Tony Curtis. biog filmog il stills STARS n21:[13-18] Winter 1995
CUSHING, PETER
Ma Latorre, J. Retrato de Peter Cushing. il stills NOSFERATU n6:70-73 Apr
1991
CUTLER, R.J. See also SEMPER FI
Thomson, P. North for Senate: the movie. il INDEP 18:32-37 Jan/Feb 1995
CYBER TRACKER v (d Pepin, Richard 1994 USA)
    Reviews
Wilt, D. "Cyber Tracker." C FANTAS 26:59 n3 1995
CYBILL v (1995- USA)
    Reviews
Loynd, R. "Cybill." credits VARIETY 357:44 Jan 2/8 1995
Taubin, A. Designing women. il VILLAGE VOICE 40:43 Jan 10 1995
Waters, H.F. Looking for sitcom saviors. ports still NEWSWK 125:60 Jan 9
1995
CYBORG II: THE GLASS SHADOW v (1994 USA)
    Reviews
Mangan, D. "Cyborg II: the Glass Shadow." FATAL VISIONS n17:27 1994
D.W. Griffith Award See AWARDS - Television (broadcast) - United States.
Directors Guild of America
DABROWSKI, WALDEMAR
Dabrowski, W. Krakow '93. REZYSER n18:1 1993
DAHL, JOHN See also LAST SEDUCTION, THE
DALLAS v (1978-91 USA)
White, M. Women, memory and serial melodrama. il SCREEN 35:336-353 n4 1994
    Cross-cultural Analysis
Sinclair, J. Liebes, Tamar and Katz, Elihu. The export of meaning:
cross-cultural readings of "Dallas" [Book Review]. MEDIA INFO AUSTRALIA
n75:167-168 Feb 1995
DANES, CLAIRE
Marvel, M. Claire Danes: start remembering her name - you're going to need
to know it. interv ports INTERV 25:68-71 Jan 1995
DARABONT, FRANK
Filmografie. biogs filmogs SEGNO n72:40 Mar/Apr 1995
Katz, S.B. A conversation with... Frank Darabont. filmog interv port
JOURNAL WGA 8:28-31 Feb 1995
DARK CIRCLE v (d Irving, Judy/Beaver, Chris 1982 USA)
    Audience Research
Roser, C. and Thompson, M. Fear appeals and the formation of active publics.
bibliog diag stat tables J COMM 45:103-121 n1 1995
DARKE, CHRIS
Darke, C. Everything is connected. stills S&S 5:28-31 Feb 1995
DART, JOHN
Dionne, E.J., Jr. Washington. bibliog il ports COMMONWEAL 122:26-39 Feb 24
1995
DASNOY, CHRISTINE
Mormont, M. and Dasnoy, C. Source strategies and the mediatization of
climate change. bibliog MEDIA CUL & SOC 17:49-64 n1 1995
DASTE, JEAN
Du Bus, O.L. Les capitaines de "L'Atalante" ont leve l'ancre... filmog
still SEQUENCES n175:50 Nov/Dec 1994
DAUDELIN, ROBERT
Jean, M. Des restes d'images non identifies. il interv stills 24 IMAGES
n75:26-32+ [8p] Dec/Jan 1994/95
DAVID, PIERRE See also SCANNER COP
DAVIDOFF, SOLOMON
Davidoff, S. Kathy Merlock Jackson, Walt Disney: a bio-bibliography [Book
Review]. ANIMATION J 3:92 n1 1994
DAVIDSON, SALLY For film reviews see author under the following titles: SCANNER
COP; TIME RUNNER
DAVIES, DAVID STUART
Davies, D.S. Jeremy Brett. stills SCARLET STREET n17:95-96 Winter 1995
DAVIS, MARK H.
In memoriam. biog il obit AMCIN 76:94 Feb 1995
DAVIS, TOM
Weiner, R. Partner at the periphery. port VARIETY 358:5 Mar 20/26 1995
DAWIDZIAK, MARK
Sullivan, D. Grave secrets. Mark Dawidziak [Book Review]. SCARLET STREET
n17:97 Winter 1995
DAWTREY, ADAM
Dawtrey, A. Dueling honors at new media fest. VARIETY 357:57+ [2p] Jan 9/15
1995
Dawtrey, A. Euro majors gather in lobby. VARIETY 358:34 Feb 6/12 1995

Dawtrey, A. Gilbert, Samuelsons ink Miramax pic pact. il ports VARIETY 358:14+ [2p] Mar 20/26 1995

DAY ONE v (1993- USA)
Lawsuits
Robins, J.M. Webs stop singing when smoke gets in their eyes. stat VARIETY 358:7 Feb 20/26 1995

DAYAN, DANIEL
Scannell, P. Media events [Book Review]. bibliog MEDIA CUL & SOC 17:151-157 n1 1995

DE BERNARDINIS, FLAVIO
De Bernardinis, F. Il bacco di Bergman. stills SEGNO n71:76-77 Jan/Feb 1995

DE GRAZIA, EDWARD
De Grazia, E. Sex de jure [Book Reviews]. NATION 260:242-249 Feb 20 1995

DEAN, PETER
Dean, P. Wind up. still S&S 5:70 Jan 1995

DEANDREA, WILLIAM L. For film reviews see author under the following titles: BURKE'S LAW

DEBARTOLO, JOHN For film reviews see author under the following titles: BLAUE LICHT, DAS; MAN FROM BEYOND, THE; RAVEN, THE; STEAMBOAT BILL, JR.

DEBATES
Television (broadcast)
United States. Public
Denniston, L. Who can join public television debates? port AM JOUR REV 17:50 n1 1995

DEBNEY, JOHN
Rixman, J. John Debney. il interv F SCORE MONTHLY n38:8-9 Oct 1993

DELERUE, GEORGES
Blum, G.C. In memory of... Georges Delerue. il F SCORE MONTHLY n36/37:25 Aug/Sep 1993

DELGADO, RAY
Delgado, R. Medio making multiple moves. port VARIETY 358:40 Mar 13/19 1995

DELON, ALAIN
Alain Delon. biog filmog il stills STARS n21:[19-24] Winter 1995

DEMARCO, MARIO
DeMarco, M. Colonel Tim McCoy. il CLASSIC n236:8 Feb 1995

DEMPSEY, JOHN
Dempsey, J. Cable embraces off-net hours. il VARIETY 358:197 Feb 20/26 1995
Dempsey, J. Cable gives wings to net longruns. stat table VARIETY 358:29-30 Mar 13/19 1995
Dempsey, J. Caught in corporate crossfire, pay TV exec Cox quits Viacom. VARIETY 358:28 Mar 20/26 1995
Dempsey, J. Conservative inspiration for a station. stat VARIETY 358:49+ [2p] Feb 27/Mar 5 1995
Dempsey, J. Disaccord daunts double-run device. VARIETY 358:29+ [2p] Feb 13/19 1995
Dempsey, J. Family feature films get a familiar ring. il VARIETY 358:1+ [2p] Mar 27/Apr 2 1995
Dempsey, J. Film nets casting for indie jones. VARIETY 358:23-24 Mar 20/26 1995
Dempsey, J. Is TCI's TV! cable barker friend? Foe? VARIETY 357:37+ [2p] Jan 2/8 1995
Dempsey, J. "Jenny" incident raises specter of control. VARIETY 358:36 Mar 13/19 1995
Dempsey, J. Mid-size cable nets dial drop-dead deals. VARIETY 358:193+ [2p] Feb 20/26 1995
Dempsey, J. (Nineteen ninety-four) 1994 good to basic cablers. stat table VARIETY 357:39+ [2p] Jan 9/15 1995
Dempsey, J. Off-net strips ratings, but coin remains king. stat table VARIETY 358:39-40 Mar 6/12 1995
Dempsey, J. Viacom's shift of Cox augurs push into PPV. port VARIETY 358:198 Feb 20/26 1995
Dempsey, J. and Flint, J. Telcos take topper for TV turf tussle. il port VARIETY 358:1+ [2p] Feb 27/Mar 5 1995
Flint, J. and Dempsey, J. Liberty makes move to grow PPV. VARIETY 358:29+ [2p] Mar 27/Apr 2 1995

DENNISTON, LYLE
Denniston, L. Who can join public television debates? port AM JOUR REV 17:50 n1 1995

DENSKI, STAN For film reviews see author under the following titles: TALES OF THE RAILS

DENTINGER, JANE
Simpson, D. Dead pan. By Jane Dentinger [Book Review]. ARMCHAIR DET 26:102 n3 1993

D'ERASMO, STACEY For film reviews see author under the following titles: OFFICE, THE

DERTENO, ROBERT C. See also PIN-DOWN GIRL

Detective series See SERIES, DETECTIVE

DETECTIVES IN TELEVISION/VIDEO
Television (broadcast)
United States
Breen, J.L. Haining, Peter, ed. The television detectives' omnibus: great tales of crime and detection [Book Review]. ARMCHAIR DET 27:223 n2 1994
United States. Adaptations
Gallagher, B. It's a print!: detective fiction from page to screen. Edited by William Reynolds and Elizabeth A. Trembley [Book Review]. MICHIGAN ACADEMICIAN 27:229-231 n2 1995
United States. History
Farrell, S. The American detective: an illustrated history. Jeff Siegel [Book Review]. SCARLET STREET n17:99 Winter 1995

DI NUBILA, DOMINGO
Di Nubila, D. Abel Santa Cruz. obit VARIETY 358:54 Feb 13/19 1995

DIAZ, CAMERON
Hensley, D. Buenos Diaz. interv port MOVIELINE 6:18 Mar 1995

DIBBELL, JULIAN
Dibbell, J. The whole world-wide. VILLAGE VOICE 40:46 Feb 28 1995

DICK TRACY (fictional character)
Hoppenstand, G. Dick Tracy and American culture: morality and mythology,

text and context. By Garyn G. Roberts [Book Review]. ARMCHAIR DET 27:236-237 n2 1994

DICKINSON, MARGARET
Chanan, M. and Dickinson, M. The mind of a commissioning editor. interv VERTIGO (UK) 1:53-56 n4 1994/95
Dickinson, M. Editorial. il stills VERTIGO (UK) 1:2-4 n4 1994/95

DICTIONARIES AND ENCYCLOPEDIAS
Television (broadcast) and Video (non-broadcast)
Clements, M. The medium needs a message. il PREM 8:52-53 Mar 1995
United States
Thal, O. Cinemania '94 - der interaktive Kinofuehrer. MEDIEN 38:369-373 n6 1994
Webster, E. The motion picture guide [Book Review]. il VARIETY 358:42-43 Mar 13/19 1995
Video (non-broadcast)
Norway
Lochen, K. Filmleksikon pa diskett [Book Review]. still F&K n7:41 1993
United States
Af Geijerstam, E. Inte bara for kalenderbitare [Book Review]. il CHAPLIN 36:61 n6 (n255) 1994/95
Dykyj, O. Cinemania 1995. il SEQUENCES n175:55-56 Nov/Dec 1994
Kemp, P. Discworld [Book Review]. still S&S 5:34 Apr 1995

DIECKMANN, KATHERINE
Dieckmann, K. Frost me. still VILLAGE VOICE 40:49-50 Jan 3 1995

DIEDRICH, TRACY
Pfau, M. and others. Influence of communication modalities on voters' perceptions of candidates during presidential primary campaigns. bibliog diag stat tables J COMM 45:122-133 n1 1995

Digital See as a subheading under individual subject headings (e.g. SOUND SYSTEMS - Television (broadcast) and Video (non-broadcast) - Digital)

Digital compact discs See COMPACT DISCS

DILLARD, WILLIAM
Obituaries. obits VARIETY 358:58-59 Mar 20/26 1995

DILLMAN, BRADFORD
Weiner, R. Dillman takes Giants step. port VARIETY 357:4 Jan 2/8 1995

DINOSAUR ISLAND! v (d Wynorski, Jim/Ray, Fred Olen 1994 USA)
Videodiscs
Frumkes, R. Laserdiscs: from the sublime to the ridiculous. il FIR 45:28-30 Nov/Dec 1994

DIONNE, E.J., JR.
Dionne, E.J., Jr. Washington. bibliog il ports COMMONWEAL 122:26-39 Feb 24 1995

DIRECTING
Television (broadcast)
United States
Yonover, N.S. Mick Garris takes "The Stand." filmog il interv port DGA NEWS 19:26-28 n2 1994
United States. Conferences, Institutes, Workshops, etc.
Behrend, J. News, serials, commercials. il DGA NEWS 19:8-9 n3 1994

DIRECTORIES
Television (broadcast) and Video (non-broadcast)
Austria
Frey, M. Oesterreichischer forschungsstaettenkatalog [Book Review]. F KUNST n144:76-77 1994
Television (broadcast)
Who's screening at Monte Carlo. table VARIETY 358:44 Feb 6/12 1995

DIRECTORS See also names of directors; PROGRAM DIRECTORS
Television (broadcast)
United States
Behrend, J. "Sometimes you took off, sometimes you crashed and burned." il DGA NEWS 19:12-13 n2 1994
United States. Collections and Collecting
Behlmer, R. Directors' paper trails. table DGA NEWS 19:50+ [3p] n6 1994/95
United States. Credit
Reynolds, G. Credits where they're due. port DGA NEWS 19:5 n6 1994/95
United States. Health
Elrick, T. Stamina on the set. DGA NEWS 19:10-11+ [3p] n3 1994

DIRECTOR'S CONTROL
Television (broadcast) and Video (non-broadcast)
United States. Conferences, Institutes, Workshops, etc.
Behrend, J. DGA goes indie at IFFM. il DGA NEWS 19:24-25 n6 1994/95

DIRECTORS GUILD OF AMERICA
Conferences, Institutes, Workshops, etc.
Behrend, J. DGA goes indie at IFFM. il DGA NEWS 19:24-25 n6 1994/95

Directors, women [Prior to V16, 1988 use DIRECTORS, WOMEN] See WOMEN DIRECTORS

DIRECTV LATIN AMERICA
Paxman, A. Hughes, trio unveil new pan-Latin net. stat VARIETY 358:45 Mar 13/19 1995

Disabled in television/video See PHYSICALLY HANDICAPPED IN TELEVISION/VIDEO

DISCOVERING WOMEN v (1995 USA)
Reviews
Rich, A. "Discovering Women." credits VARIETY 358:38 Mar 27/Apr 2 1995

Discs, compact See COMPACT DISCS

DISNEY, WALT
Davidoff, S. Kathy Merlock Jackson, Walt Disney: a bio-bibliography [Book Review]. ANIMATION J 3:92 n1 1994

DISNEY, WALT, CO.
Lowry, B. Disney braces with Wind Dancer trio. VARIETY 358:45 Mar 6/12 1995
Of Mickey Mouse and men. port ESQUIRE 123:39 Mar 1995
History
Canemaker, J. Vladimir Tytla - master animator. biog il ANIMATION J 3:4-30 n1 1994
Personnel
Benson, J. and Flint, J. Disney hunts for Telco topper. VARIETY 358:6 Mar 20/26 1995
Lowry, B. Frank out at Disney. ports VARIETY 358:68 Mar 13/19 1995

DISTRIBUTION See also ADVERTISING; EXHIBITION; MARKETING; PIRATING; SYNDICATION
Video (non-broadcast)
Australia. Economic Aspects
Woods, M. Distribs find Oz video market is child's play. stat VARIETY

358:35 Feb 6/12 1995
    Brazil
Paxman, A. In Brazil, video market "Snow"-balls. stat VARIETY 358:59-60
  Feb 27/Mar 5 1995
    Finland. Pornography and Obscenity
Tuominen, S. Pornoa matkalla aikuisuuteen. still PEILI 18:10-11 n4 1994
    Great Britain. Videodiscs
Brownlie, T. Laser Disc beginning to make its mark. il FILM 4:31 n1 [1995]
    Italy. Television/Video Lists
Fittante, A. Gli inediti dell'anno. il SEGNO n63:79-86 Sep/Oct 1993
    Norway
Lochen, K. S er alternativet. still F&K n1:13 1994
    United States
Bobby, K. NVR offers libraries alternative videos at a discount. still
  INDEP 18:10+ [3p] Apr 1995
    United States. Economic Aspects
Lerman, L. Sell-through booming as video rentals linger. stat still
  VARIETY 358:bet p88 and 173 [pA5+ (2p)] Feb 20/26 1995
    United States. Films Shown on Television/Video
Koszarski, R. The movies come home. il stills F COM 31:10-12+ [5p] Mar/Apr
  1995
Sanjek, D. Home alone: the phenomenon of direct-to-video. stills CINEASTE
  21:98-100 n1/2 1995
DITOLLA, AL
Cox, D. Al DiTolla. obit VARIETY 357:80 Jan 9/15 1995
DIVA TV2
Juhasz, A. So many alternatives. stills CINEASTE 21:37-39 n1/2 1995
DIXON, WHEELER WINSTON
Dixon, W.W. Lacan, Jacques. Television: a challenge to the psychoanalytic
  establishment [Book Review]. UFAJ 46:58-59 n2 1994
Dixon, W.W. Twilight of the empire: the films of Roy Ward Baker part III.
  interv stills CLASSIC n236:bet p32 and 33 [pC12+ (4p)] Feb 1995
(DOCTOR) DR WATKINS
    Television/Video Lists
Dr Watkins. REZYSER n19:8 1993
(DOCTOR) DR. WHO v (1963-89 Gt Br)
    Music
Szpirglas, J. (Thirty) 30 years of "Doctor Who" and its music. discog F
  SCORE MONTHLY n39:14 Nov 1993
DOCUMENTARY See also ANTHROPOLOGICAL TELEVISION/VIDEO
    Television (broadcast) and Video (non-broadcast)
      Techniques
Albert, M. Solo flyers. il stills INDEP 18:24-28 Mar 1995
    Television (broadcast)
      Canada
Nicks, J. Peter Steven. Brink of reality: new Canadian documentary film and
  video [Book Review]. CAN J F STUD 3:104-107 n2 1994
      Canada. Theory
Jacquinot, G. Le documentaire, une fiction (pas) comme les autres. bibliog
  stills CINEMAS 4:61-81 n2 1994
      France
Bourelly, R. The European documentary: second in a three-part series. il
  stills DOC BOX 3:8-11 1993
      Great Britain
Chanan, M. The European documentary: third in a three-part series. stills
  DOC BOX 4:13-16 1993
      Japan
Gerow, A.A. Documentarists of Japan (second in a series). biog interv port
  stills DOC BOX 3:12-18 1993
      United States. Theory
Lunenfeld, P. "There are people in the streets who've never had a chance to
  speak": James Blue and the complex documentary. bibliog biog stills UFAJ
  46:21-33 n1 1994
DOES TV KILL? v (d McLeod, Michael 1995 USA)
    Reviews
Lowry, B. "Frontline." credits VARIETY 357:46 Jan 9/15 1995
DOLL PARTS v (d Bayer, Samuel 1994 USA)
Dieckmann, K. Frost me. still VILLAGE VOICE 40:49-50 Jan 3 1995
DOLLAR, STEVE
Dollar, S. "Buried in Light." il still INDEP 18:16-18 Apr 1995
DOMALIK, ANDRZEJ See also NOCNE PTAKI
DONALD, ANABEL
Mowery, D. An uncommon murder. By Anabel Donald [Book Review]. il ARMCHAIR
  DET 26:97-98 n3 1993
DONDUREI, DANIIL
Film, TV, video in Russia - 1994. Ed: Daniil Dondurei [Book Review]. il
  KINO(GF) n56:30 Nov 1994
DORAN, ANN
Randisi, S. Lifetime contract. il port stills F FAX n48:76-81+ [8p]
  Jan/Feb 1995
Valley, R. Ann Doran. il interv port stills SCARLET STREET n17:42+ [9p]
  Winter 1995
DOUBLE RUSH v (1995 USA)
    Reviews
Everett, T. "Double Rush." credits VARIETY 357:44 Jan 2/8 1995
Leonard, J. They know how to sitcom. still NEW YORK 28:54-55 Jan 9 1995
Waters, H.F. Looking for sitcom saviors. ports still NEWSWK 125:60 Jan 9
  1995
DOUGLAS, SUSAN J.
Robinson, L.S. Will you love me tomorrow? [Book Review]. NATION 260:138-141
  Jan 30 1995
DOVEY, JON
Dovey, J. Camcorder cults. il stills VERTIGO (UK) 1:5-7 n4 1994/95
Drama into television/video See ADAPTATIONS
DREAM ON v (1990- USA)
Farina, A. Invisibile Landis. il SEGNO n72:78 Mar/Apr 1995
DREAMWORKS SKG
Corliss, R. Hey, let's put on a show! il ports TIME 145:54-60 Mar 27 1995
Flint, J. HBO, troika in output deal. stat VARIETY 358:36 Mar 13/19 1995
Lowry, B. Goldberg's "Champs" answers opening bell for DreamWorks. VARIETY

358:45 Mar 6/12 1995
DRINNAN, JOHN
Bisset, B. Letters: Blue Book piece was half right. ONFILM 11:10-11 n11
  1994/95
Drinnan, J. Blue Book blues dog TVC shoots. ONFILM 11:3 n11 1994/95
Drinnan, J. Cash-carrot offers for key TV staff. stat ONFILM [12]:1 n2
  1995
Drinnan, J. Fee share up for nets. stat ONFILM [12]:9 n2 1995
Drinnan, J. Good manners maketh Asia. ONFILM 11:8 n11 1994/95
Drinnan, J. Hollings brings schedules oomph to 3. ports ONFILM [12]:1+
  [2p] n2 1995
Drinnan, J. Holmes safe, 3's Brown: no more Mr Nice Guy. ONFILM [12]:3 n2
  1995
Drinnan, J. Letters: John Drinnan responds. ONFILM 11:11 n11 1994/95
Drinnan, J. Minister endorses TV status quo, retreats on Channel 2 selloff.
  ONFILM 11:1+ [2p] n11 1994/95
Drinnan, J. Musivids march to different tune. stat ONFILM [12]:20 n2 1995
Drinnan, J. NZ On Air gets a B+... (but). stat ONFILM [12]:20 n2 1995
Drinnan, J. Only scraps for indies as local TV era dawns. port stat ONFILM
  [12]:7 n1 1995
Drinnan, J. Payola adds fizz to TV funding. stat ONFILM [12]:1+ [2p] n1
  1995
Drinnan, J. Pete & Pio shape up. port stat ONFILM [12]:5 n1 1995
Drinnan, J. TVNZ signals shift in equity stance. stat ONFILM 11:3 n11
  1994/95
DRYBURGH, STUART
Dryburgh, S. Letters: open letter from a film technician on the subject of
  lunch. ONFILM 11:11 n11 1994/95
DU BUS, OLIVIER LEFEBURE
Du Bus, O.L. Les capitaines de "L'Atalante" ont leve l'ancre... filmog
  still SEQUENCES n175:50 Nov/Dec 1994
DUIGAN, JOHN
Filmografie. biogs filmogs SEGNO n72:40 Mar/Apr 1995
DUNCAN, JAMES
Fry, K. Place/culture/representation. By James Duncan & David Ley (eds.)
  [Book Review]. bibliog J COMM 45:173-177 n1 1995
DUPLICATORS AND DUPLICATION
    Video (non-broadcast)
      New Zealand. Sony Sprinter
Mother of a Sprinter. il ONFILM 11:20 n11 1994/95
DURANTE, JIMMY
Slide, A. The Slide area film book notes [Book Reviews]. CLASSIC
  n237:42-44+ [4p] Mar 1995
DURSIN, ANDY
Dursin, A. Four by Basil Poledouris. F SCORE MONTHLY n36/37:32 Aug/Sep 1993
DUTCHAK, PHILIP
Dutchak, P. Multimedia and the cultural statement. il stat stills C PAPERS
  n102:32-35 Dec 1994
DWYER, TIM
Dwyer, T. Open & shut? bibliog MEDIA INFO AUSTRALIA n75:89-91 Feb 1995
DYBCZYNSKI, JAN
Sendecka, M. Oryginalnosc wyroznia. interv REZYSER n18:6-7 1993
DYKYJ, OKSANA
Dykyj, O. Cinemania 1995. il SEQUENCES n175:55-56 Nov/Dec 1994
DYMNA, ANNA
Slodowski, J. Anna Dymna. filmog still FSP 40:11 n11 (n765) 1994
E! ENTERTAINMENT TELEVISION INC.
    Economic Aspects
Flint, J. After five-year fight, E! strikes black ink. il port stat
  VARIETY 358:25+ [2p] Feb 6/12 1995
ER v (1994- USA)
    Asian-Americans in Television/Video
Lee, E. The adventures of super-Asian. VILLAGE VOICE 40:44 Mar 21 1995
    Export Market
Guider, E. "ER" series a smooth operator overseas. VARIETY 358:49 Mar 6/12
  1995
EASTMAN, SUSAN TYLER
Eastman, S.T. and Newton, G.D. Delineating grazing: observations of remote
  control use. bibliog stat tables J COMM 45:77-95 n1 1995
EBY, DOUGLAS
Eby, D. "Demon Knight." stills C FANTAS 26:12-13 n2 1995
ECONOMIC ASPECTS See also COPYRIGHT; EMPLOYMENT; FINANCING; INDUSTRY; TAXES
    Television (broadcast) and Video (non-broadcast)
      Austria
Frey, M. Kulturstatistik 1992 [Book Review]. F KUNST n144:75-76 1994
      United States
Peers, M. Is Milken mulling moguldom? VARIETY 358:1+ [2p] Mar 13/19 1995
    Television (broadcast)
      Canada. Marketing
Finn, A. and others. Marketing, management, and competitive strategy in the
  cultural industries. bibliog CAN J COM 19:523-550 n3/4 1994
      Latin America. Pay
Major U.S. investments in Latin American pay TV systems. stat table VARIETY
  358:72 Mar 27/Apr 2 1995
      New Zealand
Drinnan, J. Fee share up for nets. stat ONFILM [12]:9 n2 1995
      United States
Peers, M. Pension fund bets on the biz... VARIETY 358:6 Mar 6/12 1995
      United States. Networks and Networking
Robins, J.M. Star-struck webs wow admen. VARIETY 358:1+ [2p] Mar 27/Apr 2
  1995
      United States. Public
Goetz, T. The corporation for private broadcasting. il VILLAGE VOICE 40:46
  Mar 14 1995
    Video (non-broadcast)
      Australia. Distribution
Woods, M. Distribs find Oz video market is child's play. stat VARIETY
  358:35 Feb 6/12 1995
      United States
Weiner, R. Pirates up, profits are down in '94. graph stat VARIETY 358:bet

ECONOMIC ASPECTS
    Video (non-broadcast)
    (continued)
    p88 and 173 [pA2+ (2p)] Feb 20/26 1995
        United States. Distribution
Lerman, L. Sell-through booming as video rentals linger. stat still
    VARIETY 358:bet p88 and 173 [pA5+ (2p)] Feb 20/26 1995
Eddies See AWARDS - Television (broadcast) - United States. American Cinema
    Editors
EDELMAN, ROB
Edelman, R. "Jupiter's Wife." port INDEP 18:14-15 Jan/Feb 1995
Edgar Awards See AWARDS - Television (broadcast) - United States. Mystery
    Writers of America
EDITING, ELECTRONIC, EQUIPMENT
    Television (broadcast) and Video (non-broadcast)
        Adobe Premiere 4.0.1
Hamilton, J.C. Leaving the trim bin further behind. il INDEP 18:42-45
    Jan/Feb 1995
    Television (broadcast)
        United States
Solman, G. Sound advice for editing, playback. il DGA NEWS 20:12-13 n1
    1995
EDMUNDS, MARLENE
Edmunds, M. Belgian b'caster focus of probe. VARIETY 357:49 Jan 9/15 1995
Edmunds, M. Broadcasting sponsorship law near. VARIETY 358:43 Feb 13/19
    1995
Edmunds, M. Company answers its call to the small screen. VARIETY 358:44
    Mar 20/26 1995
Edmunds, M. Dutch channel ready to go. stat VARIETY 358:51 Feb 27/Mar 5
    1995
Edmunds, M. Dutch Kids' TV expiring. VARIETY 358:60 Mar 6/12 1995
Edmunds, M. Dutch web talks wane. VARIETY 358:175 Feb 20/26 1995
Edmunds, M. Holland goes commercial. stat VARIETY 358:45 Feb 13/19 1995
Edmunds, M. Leading the pack. il still VARIETY 358:37 Mar 20/26 1995
Edmunds, M. New cable venture gets greenlight. stat VARIETY 357:50 Jan
    9/15 1995
Edmunds, M. New web's creation a legal tangle. VARIETY 358:49 Mar 6/12 1995
Edmunds, M. Nordic b'casters set for battle, on prowl for product. VARIETY
    358:46 Feb 6/12 1995
Edmunds, M. Philips calls restructuring a success. stat VARIETY 358:57 Feb
    27/Mar 5 1995
Edmunds, M. SBS firing up its cable web. VARIETY 358:34 Mar 20/26 1995
Edmunds, M. Svensk adds Wegelius to its crown. VARIETY 357:56 Jan 2/8 1995
Edmunds, M. Vid slice lands firm in first place. graphs stat stills
    VARIETY 358:46 Mar 20/26 1995
Edmunds, M. VT4's monopoly-buster spurs suits. VARIETY 358:32 Feb 6/12 1995
Educational uses See INSTRUCTIONAL USES
EDWARDS, HILTON See also ORSON WELLES' GHOST STORY
EFFECTS OF TELEVISION/VIDEO See also INFLUENCE OF TELEVISION/VIDEO
    Television (broadcast) and Video (non-broadcast)
        United States. Pornography and Obscenity. Audience Research
Allen, M. and others. Exposure to pornography and acceptance of rape myths.
    bibliog stat tables J COMM 45:5-26 n1 1995
Gunther, A.C. Overrating the third-person perception and
    support for censorship of pornography. bibliog stat tables J COMM 45:27-38
    n1 1995
    Television (broadcast)
        Finland. Programming for Children
Lehtonen, V.-P. Hiljaa, isa lukee lehtea! PEILI 18:2 n4 1994
        Russia (since 1992). News Coverage. War
Birchenough, T. TV has role in Chechnya war. VARIETY 358:59-60 Feb 27/Mar 5
    1995
        United States
Salminen, K. "Beavis ja Butt-head" vastaan Amerikka. bibliog il PEILI
    18:10-13 n2 1994
        United States. News Coverage. Science. Audience Research
Priest, S.H. Information equity, public understanding of science, and the
    biotechnology debate. bibliog diag stat table J COMM 45:39-54 n1 1995
        United States. Political Campaigns. Audience Research
Pfau, M. and others. Influence of communication modalities on voters'
    perceptions of candidates during presidential primary campaigns. bibliog
    diag stat tables J COMM 45:122-133 n1 1995
        United States. Social Issues. Audience Research
Roser, C. and Thompson, M. Fear appeals and the formation of active publics.
    bibliog diag stat tables J COMM 45:103-121 n1 1995
    Video (non-broadcast)
        Finland. Popular Culture
Lammio, H. Video: utopia uudesta kuvakulttuurista. still PEILI 17:10-11 n3
    1993
EFFECTS ON FILM
    Television (broadcast)
        Japan
Oshima, N. Mes idees actuelles sur le cinema japonais. stills POSITIF
    n407:47-52 Jan 1995
EFFECTS ON TELEVISION/VIDEO See also INFLUENCE ON TELEVISION/VIDEO
    Television (broadcast) and Video (non-broadcast)
        United States. Networks and Networking
Ehrlich, E.M. Virtual companies, walled cities, and the right-brained
    economy: cinematographers on the information highway. AMCIN 76:96 Mar 1995
    Television (broadcast)
        United States. Reruns. Cable
Dempsey, J. Cable gives wings to net longruns. stat table VARIETY
    358:29-30 Mar 13/19 1995
        United States. Syndication
Dempsey, J. Off-net strips ratings, but coin remains king. stat table
    VARIETY 358:39-40 Mar 6/12 1995
        United States. Trial Coverage
Benson, J. O.J. coverage tries syndie rates. VARIETY 358:40 Mar 6/12 1995
EFFI BRIEST v (d Luderer, Wolfgang 1970 E Ger)
Gruber, E. Une reprise impossible? "Effi Briest" et la question de ses

reecritures filmiques. CINEMAS 4:59-71 n1 1993
Egypt See as a subheading under individual subject headings
[EGYPTIAN RADIO & TV UNION]
Warg, P. "Kamera," "Thieves" hold captive aud during Ramadan. VARIETY
    358:60 Feb 27/Mar 5 1995
EHRLICH, EVERETT M.
Ehrlich, E.M. Virtual companies, walled cities, and the right-brained
    economy: cinematographers on the information highway. AMCIN 76:96 Mar 1995
Eight mm See as a subheading under individual subject headings
EITZEN, DIRK See also TALES OF THE RAILS
ELAM, REGINA
Marriott, M. and others. Flight of the digital dish. il NEWSWK 125:61 Jan
    9 1995
Electronic editing equipment See EDITING, ELECTRONIC, EQUIPMENT
ELFMAN, RICHARD See also SHRUNKEN HEADS
ELISBERG, ROBERT J.
Elisberg, R.J. There's no place like ohm. JOURNAL WGA 8:45 Feb 1995
ELLEY, DEREK For film reviews see author under the following titles: NAKED NEWS
Elley, D. China: trick or treaty? VARIETY 358:1+ [2p] Mar 6/12 1995
Elley, D. Donald Pleasence. obit VARIETY 358:85 Feb 6/12 1995
Elley, D. Nigel Finch. obit VARIETY 358:58 Mar 20/26 1995
Elley, D. Robert Bolt. obit VARIETY 358:78 Feb 27/Mar 5 1995
ELLIS, JOHN
Hendrykowski, M. R jak Routledge [Book Reviews]. il KINO 27:41-42 Jul 1993
ELLISON, JOE
Ellison, J. A taxing encounter. JOURNAL WGA 8:30 Mar 1995
ELRICK, TED
Elrick, T. Sargent reenlists for "World War II." il interv DGA NEWS 19:8-9
    n2 1994
Elrick, T. Scott Brothers' work showcased for UK/LA. il DGA NEWS 19:26 n6
    1994/95
Elrick, T. Stamina on the set. DGA NEWS 19:10-11+ [3p] n3 1994
Elrick, T. The televiolence debate: shoot-out at the fantasy factory. il
    DGA NEWS 19:14-16 n3 1994
Elrick, T. Violence should be decried, not glorified. interv port DGA NEWS
    19:16-17 n3 1994
Yonover, N.S. and others. Artists Rights Symposium: three days of
    discussion. DGA NEWS 19:26-27+ [3p] n3 1994
ELY, JAMES W., JR.
Trager, R. Entangled values: the First Amendment in the 1990s [Book
    Reviews]. bibliog J COMM 45:163-170 n1 1995
EMHARDT, ROBERT
Lentz, H., III. Obituaries. biogs filmogs obits ports CLASSIC n237:57-59
    Mar 1995
EMMERICH, ROLAND See also UNIVERSAL SOLDIER
EMMERS, TARA
Allen, M. and others. Exposure to pornography and acceptance of rape myths.
    bibliog stat tables J COMM 45:5-26 n1 1995
EMORD, JONATHAN W.
Trager, R. Entangled values: the First Amendment in the 1990s [Book
    Reviews]. bibliog J COMM 45:163-170 n1 1995
EMPEROR JONES, THE v (d Murphy, Dudley 1933 USA)
    Reviews
Guerrero, E. "The Emperor Jones." still CINEASTE 21:100-101 n1/2 1995
EMPLOYMENT See also CONTRACTS; ECONOMIC ASPECTS; RESIDUALS AND FEES
    Television (broadcast)
        New Zealand
Drinnan, J. Cash-carrot offers for key TV staff. stat ONFILM [12]:1 n2
    1995
Encyclopedias See DICTIONARIES AND ENCYCLOPEDIAS
ENDINGS
    Television (broadcast)
        United States. Humorous Essays
Thonson, T. The happiness of an unhappy ending. JOURNAL WGA 8:46 Dec/Jan
    1995
ENVIRONMENTAL PROTECTION
    Television (broadcast)
        Great Britain
Video power. il stills VERTIGO (UK) 1:12-15 n4 1994/95
EPSTEIN, MEL
Lentz, H., III. Obituaries. biogs filmogs obits ports CLASSIC n237:57-59
    Mar 1995
EPSTEIN, RICHARD A.
Trager, R. Entangled values: the First Amendment in the 1990s [Book
    Reviews]. bibliog J COMM 45:163-170 n1 1995
Equipment, camera [Prior to V16, 1988 use either CAMERA ACCESSORIES or
    EQUIPMENT, CAMERA] See CAMERA EQUIPMENT
Equipment, editing, electronic See EDITING, ELECTRONIC, EQUIPMENT
Equipment exhibitions See TRADE FAIRS
Equipment, post-production [Prior to V16, 1988 use EQUIPMENT, POST-PRODUCTION]
    See POST-PRODUCTION EQUIPMENT
Equipment, satellite communications [Prior to V16, 1988 use EQUIPMENT, SATELLITE
    COMMUNICATIONS] See SATELLITE COMMUNICATIONS EQUIPMENT
Equipment, virtual reality See VIRTUAL REALITY EQUIPMENT
ERGAS, JOSEPH
Obituaries. biogs obits VARIETY 358:86-87 Mar 27/Apr 2 1995
ERIC OU L'OISEAU BLEU v (d Riga, Jean-Claude 1983 Belg)
Jacquinot, G. Le documentaire, une fiction (pas) comme les autres. bibliog
    stills CINEMAS 4:61-81 n2 1994
ERSGARD, JACK See also INVISIBLE: THE CHRONICLES OF BENJAMIN KNIGHT
ES IST DOCH NAEHER DRAN... v (d Leiprecht, Rudolf/Willems, Erik 1994 Neth)
    Reviews
Koehler, M. "Es ist doch naeher dran..." MEDIEN 38:364 n6 1994
ESBJORNSON, MARY
Esbjornson, M. Media arts madness. il stills INDEP 18:6-7+ [3p] Jan/Feb
    1995
ESCAPE FROM TERROR: THE TERESA STAMPER STORY v (1995 USA)
    Reviews
Leonard, J. "Somebody" to love. port still NEW YORK 28:60-61 Jan 23 1995

ESTRADA, RICHARD
  Meltzer, J. "The Illegal Interns." il INDEP 18:15-16 Jan/Feb 1995
ETHICS
    Television (broadcast)
      Canada. Mass Media
  Cunningham, S.B. Morals and the media: ethics in Canadian journalism. By
    Nick Russell [Book Review]. CAN J COM 20:128-129 n1 1995
      United States. News Programming
  Lissit, R. Gotcha! ports AM JOUR REV 17:16-21 n2 1995
  Revah, S. It's a jungle out there in cyberspace. il port AM JOUR REV
    17:10-11 n2 1995
      United States. Talk Shows
  Benson, J. Talkshows rate murder case an ethical dilemma. il port VARIETY
    358:23+ [2p] Mar 20/26 1995
ETHNICITY See also MINORITIES
    Television (broadcast)
      Australia. Research
  Bell, P. Jakubowicz, Andrew, Goodall, Heather, Martin, Jeannie, Mitchell,
    Tony, Randall, Lois and Seneviratne, Kalinga, Racism, ethnicity and the
    media [Book Review]. MEDIA INFO AUSTRALIA n75:165-166 Feb 1995
ETHNOGRAPHY
    Television (broadcast)
      United States. Audience Research
  Suoninen, A. Televisio - arkea ja yhteiskuntaa. bibliog port PEILI 18:19
    n3 1994
European Community Commission See COMMISSION OF THE EUROPEAN COMMUNITIES
EVANGELISTS See also names of evangelists
    Television (broadcast)
      United States
  Televangelism reconsidered: ritual in the search for human community. By
    Bobby Alexander [Book Review] CHR CENT 112:66 Jan 18 1995
EVANS, GREG
  Evans, G. Confirmation of new N.Y. pic commish still pending. VARIETY
    358:36 Feb 27/Mar 5 1995
  Evans, G. GLAAD honcho blasts talkers at awards. VARIETY 358:10 Mar 20/26
    1995
  Evans, G. "Gump's" glory continues. VARIETY 358:24 Mar 27/Apr 2 1995
  Evans, G. Random act opens can of bookworms. il VARIETY 358:1+ [3p] Mar
    6/12 1995
  Evans, G. Showbiz is psyched for cybermalls. VARIETY 358:1+ [2p] Mar 27/Apr
    2 1995
EVERETT, TODD For film reviews see author under the following titles: DOUBLE
    RUSH; HOPE & GLORIA; WHOLE NEW BALLGAME, A
EVERSON, SIMON See also TIME STANDS STILL
EXHIBITIONS
    Video (non-broadcast)
      France. Paris
  Julich, S. Voxel-Man. diags F HAFTET 22:55-57 n3 (n87) 1994
EXPERIMENTAL TELEVISION/VIDEO See also INDEPENDENT TELEVISION/VIDEO; VIDEO ART
    AND ARTISTS
    Video (non-broadcast)
      United States. Women Directors
  Klein, J. Transgressive tapes. stills AFTERIMAGE 22:12-13 Jan 1995
EXPORT FILM SERVICES AUSTRALIA
  Woods, M. Giving Australia a push. still VARIETY 358:61+ [2p] Feb 27/Mar 5
    1995
EXPORT MARKET
    Television (broadcast) and Video (non-broadcast)
      United States
  Elley, D. China: trick or treaty? VARIETY 358:1+ [2p] Mar 6/12 1995
      United States. Politics and Government
  Wharton, D. Gingrich vows to promote U.S. film interests. port VARIETY
    358:20 Mar 20/26 1995
    Television (broadcast)
      Latin America. Soap Operas
  Levine, F. and Paxman, A. But will it play Beijing? port stat still
    VARIETY 358:44 Mar 27/Apr 2 1995
      New Zealand
  Drinnan, J. Good manners maketh Asia. ONFILM 11:8 n11 1994/95
      United States. Markets
  Guider, E. Loyal U.S. distribbers counting on Monaco to give them the
    business. port VARIETY 358:37+ [2p] Feb 6/12 1995
      United States. Syndication
  Flint, J. Int'l cash cow on critical list for syndies. ports VARIETY
    357:52 Jan 2/8 1995
EYE TO EYE WITH CONNIE CHUNG v (1993- USA)
  Goldstein, R. Yoo-hoo, Mrs. Gingrich! il VILLAGE VOICE 40:8 Jan 17 1995
EYQUEM, OLIVIER
  Eyquem, O. Filmographie de John Carpenter. credits filmog il POSITIF
    n409:19-21 Mar 1995
FCC See FEDERAL COMMUNICATIONS COMMISSION (United States)
FTC See FEDERAL TRADE COMMISSION (United States)
FAIRY TALES
    Television (broadcast) and Video (non-broadcast)
      Finland. Adaptations
  Kylmanen, M. Zuumi muumibuumiin. bibliog still PEILI 17:10-13 n4 1993
FALLEN ANGELS v (1993- USA)
    Reviews
  Meyers, R. The crime screen. port stills ARMCHAIR DET 27:207-209 n2 1994
FALLER, JAMES M. For film reviews see author under the following titles: UNBORN
    II
FALLING FOR YOU v (d Till, Eric 1995 USA)
    Reviews
  Scott, T. "Falling for You." credits VARIETY 358:199 Feb 20/26 1995
FALUDI, SUSAN
  Faludi, S. "I'm not a feminist but I play one on TV." il MS 5:30-39 n5
    1995
FALWELL, JERRY
  Falwell challenged on anti-Clinton tapes. CHR CENT 112:166-167 Feb 15 1995

FAMILIES IN TELEVISION/VIDEO See also MOTHERHOOD IN TELEVISION/VIDEO
    Television (broadcast)
      United States
  Heide, M.J. Gender and generation: the case of "thirtysomething." bibliog
    STUDIES POP CULT 17:75-83 n1 1994
  Henry, M. The triumph of popular culture: situation comedy, postmodernism
    and "The Simpsons." bibliog STUDIES POP CULT 17:85-99 n1 1994
  Williams, A. Domestic violence and the aetiology of crime in "America's Most
    Wanted." il port stills CAM OBS n31:96-119 Jan/May 1993
FARINA, ALBERTO
  Farina, A. Invisibile Landis. il SEGNO n72:78 Mar/Apr 1995
FARRELL, SEAN
  Farrell, S. The American detective: an illustrated history. Jeff Siegel
    [Book Review]. SCARLET STREET n17:99 Winter 1995
FASCINATO, JACK
  Lentz, H., III. Obituaries. biogs filmogs obits ports CLASSIC n237:57-59
    Mar 1995
FASCISM
    Television (broadcast)
      Germany (until 1949)
  Wilhelm, W. Fernsehen Unterm Hakenkreuz [Book Review]. F KUNST n144:66-67
    1994
FEDDERSON, DONALD
  Lentz, H., III. Obituaries. il obits ports CLASSIC n236:57-59 Feb 1995
  Obituaries. biog obits VARIETY 357:83-84 Jan 2/8 1995
Federal aid See GOVERNMENT SUPPORT
FEDERAL COMMUNICATIONS COMMISSION (United States)
  Auletta, K. Selling the air. biog il NEW YORKER 70:36-41 Feb 13 1995
  Flint, J. Peacock backs off from Fox. VARIETY 358:200 Feb 20/26 1995
  Peers, M. and Flint, J. Probe may stall Fox TV affil goal. port VARIETY
    358:23+ [2p] Mar 20/26 1995
  Wharton, D. Murdoch & Co. do D.C. shuffle. VARIETY 358:29+ [2p] Feb 13/19
    1995
      Cable Television
  Thierer, A.D. Why cable TV rate regulation failed. stat table CONS RES MAG
    78:15-18 Feb 1995
      Programming for Children
  Wharton, D. Kidvid education hour urged. VARIETY 358:39 Feb 13/19 1995
      Syndication
  Slocum, C.B. FISR fallout. JOURNAL WGA 8:35 Feb 1995
      Taxes
  Flint, J. Minority deal ordeal. VARIETY 358:64 Mar 20/26 1995
FEDERAL TRADE COMMISSION (United States)
  Peers, M. and Wharton, D. FTC approves TCI-Comcast bid for QVC. VARIETY
    358:27 Feb 6/12 1995
Fees See RESIDUALS AND FEES
FELDSTEIN, AL
  Mallory, M. Al Feldstein. il interv port SCARLET STREET n17:23+ [2p]
    Winter 1995
FEMINISM
    Television (broadcast) and Video (non-broadcast)
      United States. Pornography and Obscenity
  Kershaw, S. Against pornophobia. port NEW YORK 28:20+ [2p] Jan 16 1995
    Television (broadcast)
      United States
  Faludi, S. "I'm not a feminist but I play one on TV." il MS 5:30-39 n5
    1995
    Video (non-broadcast)
      United States. Audience, Women
  Petzall, J. Want to see more work by independents? still ANGLES 2:6-7 n4
    1995
FEMINIST ANALYSIS
    Television (broadcast)
      Australia. Sports Broadcasting. Men in Television/Video
  Yeates, H. The league of men. bibliog MEDIA INFO AUSTRALIA n75:35-45 Feb
    1995
      Finland. Soap Operas
  Huhta, K. Saippuaoopperan teoriaa [Book Review]. il PEILI 18:28 n4 1994
      Great Britain. Soap Operas. Spectatorship
  White, M. Women, memory and serial melodrama. il SCREEN 35:336-353 n4 1994
      United States
  Robinson, L.S. Will you love me tomorrow? [Book Review]. NATION 260:138-141
    Jan 30 1995
  Tashiro, C.S. Ann Gray. Video playtime: the gendering of a leisure
    technology [Book Reviews]. SCREEN 35:411-415 n4 1994
      United States. Cultural Context
  Thornton, E.P. On the landing: high art, low art, and "Upstairs,
    Downstairs." il stills CAM OBS n31:26-47 Jan/May 1993
    Video (non-broadcast)
      Great Britain. Video Games
  Tashiro, C.S. Ann Gray. Video playtime: the gendering of a leisure
    technology [Book Reviews]. SCREEN 35:411-415 n4 1994
FERGUSON, ALLYN
  Theiss, K. The film music of Allyn Ferguson, vol. 1. il SCN 14:18 Mar 1995
FESTIVALS See also AWARDS; MARKETS
    Television (broadcast) and Video (non-broadcast)
      Poland. Cracow
  Malatynska, M. Koniec wieku. REZYSER n18:1-2 1993
      Poland. Cracow 1993
  Sendecka, M. Oryginalnosc wyroznia. interv REZYSER n18:6-7 1993
  Sendecka, M. Swieto reklamy. interv REZYSER n18:4-5 1993
      Poland. Cracow 1993. Awards
  Komu Tytany. REZYSER n18:5-6 1993
      Switzerland. Geneva 1992
  Krajewski, P. Kino sprute i zszyte na nowo. stills KINO 27:16-19 May 1993
    Television (broadcast)
      Germany (Federal Republic, since 1990). Munich 1994
  Tuormaa, J. Lasten ja nuorten televisiomaailmat kohtaavat. il PEILI
    18:28-29 n3 1994

FESTIVALS
    Television (broadcast)
(continued)
        Italy. Rome 1994
De Bernardinis, F. Il bacco di Bergman. stills SEGNO n71:76-77 Jan/Feb 1995
        Monaco. Monte Carlo 1995. Television/Video Lists
Programs in competition. table VARIETY 358:41 Feb 6/12 1995
    Video (non-broadcast)
        Finland. Oulu 1993
Kantola, M. Oulun kansainvalinen lastenelokuvafestivaali. still PEILI 17:40-41 n4 1993
        Finland. Pori 1993
Juurikkala, K. Latautumassa minun elokuvanifestivaaleilla. il PEILI 17:25 n3 1993
        Finland. Pori 1994
Lehtonen, V.-P. Alkaa ampuko, tehkaa videoita! il PEILI 18:27 n3 1994
        Great Britain. Bradford 1993
Salli, O.-P. Festivaalivieraan paivakirjasta. il PEILI 17:25-26 n3 1993
        Italy. Pisa 1995
Salvetti, S. I colori delle note. stills SEGNO n72:76 Mar/Apr 1995
        United States. New York, New York 1994
Larsen, E. Letters: Ernest Larsen responds. INDEP 18:2 Apr 1995
Larsen, E. Little orphan video. il stills INDEP 18:28-31 Jan/Feb 1995
McGann, N.L. True lives. stills AFTERIMAGE 22:4-5 Dec 1994
Reid-Pharr, R. Mix-defying. il stills AFTERIMAGE 22:3-4 Jan 1995
Weiss, B. Letters: veni, vidi, video. INDEP 18:2 Apr 1995
FICTION ABOUT TELEVISION/VIDEO
    Television (broadcast)
        United States
Benson, J. Thyme of death. By Susan Wittig Albert [Book Review]. ARMCHAIR DET 26:109 n2 1993
Gardner, B.W. The seventh enemy. By William G. Tapply [Book Review]. il ARMCHAIR DET 28:219 n2 1995
Meyers, R. Columbo: the grassy knoll. By William Harrington [Book Review]. ARMCHAIR DET 27:105-106 n1 1994
Mowery, D. An uncommon murder. By Anabel Donald [Book Review]. il ARMCHAIR DET 26:97-98 n3 1993
Silet, C. L.P. I'll be seeing you. By Mary Higgins Clark [Book Review]. ARMCHAIR DET 26:116-117 n4 1993
Simpson, D. Dead pan. By Jane Dentinger [Book Review]. ARMCHAIR DET 26:102 n3 1993
Simpson, D.G. A reconstructed corpse. By Simon Brett [Book Review]. ARMCHAIR DET 27:492 n4 1994
Simpson, D.G. Paper doll. By Robert B. Parker [Book Review]. il ARMCHAIR DET 27:112-113 n1 1994
Uram, S. Trek memories. il C FANTAS 26:19 n2 1995
Fiction into television/video See ADAPTATIONS
FIFIELD, GEORGE
Fifield, G. "Chinese Cucumbers." il port INDEP 18:18-19 Apr 1995
Fifield, G. The video service bureaus of the future. INDEP 18:25-27 Apr 1995
FILM COMMENT
    Indexes
Batty, L. Index to volume 30, 1994. F COM 31:insert [5p] Mar/Apr 1995
Filmmakers See groups (e.g. WOMEN DIRECTORS); names of individuals (e.g. HEMION, DWIGHT); types of television/video programs (e.g. SERIES)
FILMS CHANGED FOR TELEVISION/VIDEO
    Television (broadcast) and Video (non-broadcast)
        United States. Laws and Legislation
Wharton, D. Scorsese plugs for artists' rights on Hill. port VARIETY 358:20 Mar 20/26 1995
FILMS SHOWN ON TELEVISION/VIDEO [Prior to V16, 1988 use PROGRAMMING, FILMS]
    Television (broadcast)
        France. Youth
Amiel, V. Tous les garcons et les filles de leur age. filmog stills POSITIF n406:32-35 Dec 1994
        Great Britain
Medhurst, A. Box of delights. stills S&S 5:23 Jan 1995
        Great Britain. Television/Video Lists
The BBC 100. il stills S&S 5:16-23 Jan 1995
        Italy
Serravalli, L. La RAI-TV massacra Pier Paolo Pasolini per la seconda volta. C SUD 33:54 Jul/Aug/Sep (n113) 1994
        United States. Mystery Film
Meyers, R. The crime screen. port stills ARMCHAIR DET 26:59-61 n4 1993
    Video (non-broadcast)
        United States. Collections and Collecting
Cherchi Usai, P. The Library of Congress video collection: rare silent film with piano scores composed and performed by Philip Carli. GRIFFITHIANA n51/52:262-263 Oct 1994
Cherchi Usai, P. The Library of Congress video collection: rare silent films with piano scores composed and performed by Philip Carli. J F PRES n49:74-75 Oct 1994
        United States. Compact Discs
And if you win, an angel gets his wings. VARIETY 357:34 Jan 9/15 1995
        United States. Horror Film
Slide, A. The Slide area film book notes [Book Reviews]. CLASSIC n236:47-49 Feb 1995
Slide, A. The Slide area film book notes [Book Reviews]. CLASSIC n237:42-44+ [4p] Mar 1995
        United States. Videocassettes. Distribution
Sanjek, D. Home alone: the phenomenon of direct-to-video. stills CINEASTE 21:98-100 n1/2 1995
        United States. Videodiscs
O'Steen, K. Videodisc format focus of CES talk. VARIETY 357:36 Jan 9/15 1995
FILMVILAG
    Indexes
"Filmvilag": tartalomjegyzek, 1994. il F VILAG 38:insert [8p] n1 1995

FINANCING
    Television (broadcast) and Video (non-broadcast)
        United States
Seigel, R.L. At last: an alternative to limited partnerships. il INDEP 18:10-11 Mar 1995
    Television (broadcast)
        New Zealand
Drinnan, J. Payola adds fizz to TV funding. stat ONFILM [12]:1+ [2p] n1 1995
FINCH, MARK
Mark Finch: 1962-1995. biog obit INDEP 18:12 Mar 1995
FINCH, NIGEL
Elley, D. Nigel Finch. obit VARIETY 358:58 Mar 20/26 1995
FIND YOUR LOVING PARTNER v (1995 USA)
    Reviews
Golden, E. The wrong way to Mr. Right. still MOVIELINE 6:79 Apr 1995
Finland See as a subheading under individual subject headings
FINN, ADAM
Finn, A. and others. Marketing, management, and competitive strategy in the cultural industries. bibliog CAN J COM 19:523-550 n3/4 1994
Hoskins, C. and others. The environment in which cultural industries operate and some implications. bibliog CAN J COM 19:353-376 n3/4 1994
FINNKINO OY
Young, D. Financially strapped Finnkino shakes up top management. VARIETY 358:45-46 Feb 13/19 1995
FIORENTINO, LINDA
Palminteri, C. The fire in Fiorentino. il interv port INTERV 25:88-91 Mar 1995
FIRESTONE, CHARLES M.
Loo, E. Browne, Donald R., Firestone, Charles M., Mickiewicz, Ellen, eds. Television/radio news and minorities [Book Review]. MEDIA INFO AUSTRALIA n75:157-158 Feb 1995
FIRST NATIONS FILM AND VIDEO WORLD ALLIANCE
Masayesva, V., Jr. Notes on the Native American Producers Alliance and the First Nations Film and Video World Alliance. biog il DOC BOX 4:4-7 1993
FISCHER, DENNIS For film reviews see author under the following titles: PHANTASM III: LORD OF THE DEAD
FISHER, MICHAEL
Fisher, M. "Medio Magazine"; "substance.digizine" [Book Review]. il VARIETY 358:42 Mar 13/19 1995
FISKE, JOHN
Zook, K.B. Test patterns [Book Reviews]. il VILLAGE VOICE 40:64 Jan 10 1995
FITTANTE, ALDO
Fittante, A. Gli inediti dell'anno. il SEGNO n63:79-86 Sep/Oct 1993
FLACK, TIM
Obituaries. obits VARIETY 358:56 Mar 13/19 1995
FLAHERTY, DAVID H.
Knight, G. The Beaver bites back? American popular culture in Canada. Edited by David H. Flaherty & Frank E. Manning [Book Review]. CAN J COM 19:560-561 n3/4 1994
FLANDERS, ED
Milestones. obit port TIME 145:39 Mar 13 1995
Obituaries. biogs obits VARIETY 358:74-75 Mar 6/12 1995
Transition. obit still NEWSWK 125:81 Mar 13 1995
FLASH GORDON v (1953-54 USA)
Coville, G. and Lucanio, P. "Flash Gordon." il ports stills F FAX n49:62-68 Mar/Apr 1995
FLEMING, CHARLES
Fleming, C. and Marin, R. Same stuff, twice the testosterone. il still NEWSWK 125:68-69 Jan 16 1995
Marin, R. and Fleming, C. Late night unplugged. stills NEWSWK 125:63 Jan 23 1995
Reibstein, L. and others. Live, from Nielsen heaven. il NEWSWK 125:49 Jan 30 1995
FLINT, JOE
Benson, J. and Flint, J. Disney hunts for Telco topper. VARIETY 358:6 Mar 20/26 1995
Dempsey, J. and Flint, J. Telcos take topper for TV turf tussle. il port VARIETY 358:1+ [2p] Feb 27/Mar 5 1995
Flint, J. A ghost of a chance. ports stills VARIETY 357:51+ [3p] Jan 9/15 1995
Flint, J. After five-year fight, E! strikes black ink. il port stat VARIETY 358:25+ [2p] Feb 6/12 1995
Flint, J. Ameritech vid dialtone OK'd by FCC. VARIETY 357:41 Jan 2/8 1995
Flint, J. As time goes by, reality bites. il ports VARIETY 357:54 Jan 9/15 1995
Flint, J. Bad "Newz" for Col TriStar: $ missing. il VARIETY 358:49+ [2p] Feb 27/Mar 5 1995
Flint, J. Comp coin captures devotion of affiliates. port VARIETY 357:39+ [2p] Jan 9/15 1995
Flint, J. Cop trend unabated in new rosters. il port table VARIETY 357:51+ [2p] Jan 9/15 1995
Flint, J. Costner to helm HBO "Cycle" mini. VARIETY 358:36 Mar 13/19 1995
Flint, J. Deregulation: chaos calling? stat VARIETY 358:29+ [2p] Feb 13/19 1995
Flint, J. Eye catchers topping casters' lists. il port still VARIETY 357:48 Jan 2/8 1995
Flint, J. HBO, troika in output deal. stat VARIETY 358:36 Mar 13/19 1995
Flint, J. Int'l cash cow on critical list for syndies. ports VARIETY 357:52 Jan 2/8 1995
Flint, J. Minority deal ordeal. VARIETY 358:64 Mar 20/26 1995
Flint, J. No make-up necessary for QVC's Briggs. stat VARIETY 358:29-30 Mar 13/19 1995
Flint, J. O.J. trial bites into syndies. stat VARIETY 358:34 Mar 13/19 1995
Flint, J. Peacock backs off from Fox. VARIETY 358:200 Feb 20/26 1995
Flint, J. Peacock swaggers for Multimedia. VARIETY 358:68 Mar 13/19 1995
Flint, J. Squeeze time for TV exciters. stills VARIETY 357:47-48 Jan 2/8 1995

masters of detective fiction [Book Review]. ARMCHAIR DET 28:78 n1 1995
GERARD, JEREMY
  Gerard, J. Warren Caro. obit VARIETY 357:80 Jan 9/15 1995
GERBNER, GEORGE
  Pimenoff, M. Mista syntyy vakivalta? PEILI 18:9 n2 1994
Germany (Federal Republic, 1949-1990) See as a subheading under individual
  subject headings
Germany (Federal Republic, since 1990) See as a subheading under individual
  subject headings
Germany (until 1949) See as a subheading under individual subject headings
GEROLMO, CHRIS See also CITIZEN X
GEROW, A.A.
  Gerow, A.A. Documentarists of Japan (second in a series). biog interv port
    stills DOC BOX 3:12-18 1993
GHETTONAUT v (d Buhr, Andreas 1993 FR Ger)
    Reviews
  Koehler, M. "Ghettonaut." MEDIEN 38:364 n6 1994
GHOULIES IV v (d Wynorski, Jim 1994 USA)
    Reviews
  Wilt, D. "Ghoulies IV." C FANTAS 26:59 n3 1995
GIER, RUDOLF
  Anfang, G. Mit Jugendlichen videofilmen [Book Review]. MEDIEN 38:380-381 n6
    1994
GIERY, MARY A.
  Allen, M. and others. Exposure to pornography and acceptance of rape myths.
    bibliog stat tables J COMM 45:5-26 n1 1995
GIFFORD, FRANK
  Lupica, M. Going the distance. port ESQUIRE 123:30-31+ [3p] Jan 1995
GILBERT, BRIAN
  Dawtrey, A. Gilbert, Samuelsons ink Miramax pic pact. il ports VARIETY
    358:14+ [2p] Mar 20/26 1995
GILDAY, KATHERINE See also ANATOMY OF LOVE
GILTZ, MICHAEL
  Giltz, M. Oh, lucky guy. port NEW YORK 28:72 Jan 23 1995
GINGRICH, NEWT
  Wharton, D. Gingrich vows to promote U.S. film interests. port VARIETY
    358:20 Mar 20/26 1995
GIVEN, JOCK
  Given, J. Red, black, gold to Australia. bibliog MEDIA INFO AUSTRALIA
    n75:46-56 Feb 1995
GLAAP, DIETER
  Anfang, G. Mit Jugendlichen videofilmen [Book Review]. MEDIEN 38:380-381 n6
    1994
GLADIAATTORIT v (1994- Finl)
  Salakka, M. Gladiaattorit. stills PEILI 18:26-28 n2 1994
GLATTER, LESLI LINKA
  Zaniello, T. Hitched or Lynched: who directed "Twin Peaks"? bibliog filmogs
    STUDIES POP CULT 17:55-64 n1 1994
GLOBAL TELEVISION NETWORK
  Groves, D. Production facilities pact goes to Global. VARIETY 358:66 Feb
    27/Mar 5 1995
GODWIN, NICK See also PROMISED LAND, THE
GOETZ, THOMAS
  Goetz, T. (Fifty-seven) 57 channels (and "Nova's" on). il VILLAGE VOICE
    40:42 Feb 21 1995
  Goetz, T. School of hard-right knocks. VILLAGE VOICE 40:46-47 Feb 7 1995
  Goetz, T. The corporation for private broadcasting. il VILLAGE VOICE 40:46
    Mar 14 1995
GOLDBERG, GARY DAVID
  Lally, K. "Bye Bye Love" sees funny side of divorce. il still FJ 98:16+
    [2p] Mar 1995
  Lowry, B. Goldberg's "Champs" answers opening bell for DreamWorks. VARIETY
    358:45 Mar 6/12 1995
GOLDEN, EVE For film reviews see author under the following titles: FIND YOUR
  LOVING PARTNER
Golden Globes See AWARDS - Television (broadcast) - United States. Hollywood
  Foreign Press Association
GOLDSTEIN, RICHARD
  Goldstein, R. Yoo-hoo, Mrs. Gingrich! il VILLAGE VOICE 40:8 Jan 17 1995
GOMERY, DOUGLAS
  Gomery, D. Dinosaurs who refuse to die. port AM JOUR REV 17:48 n2 1995
GONDRY, MICHEL See also LUCAS WITH THE LID OFF
  Weisel, A. Day of the Lucas. still ROLLING STONE n694:37 Nov 3 1994
GOOD OLD BOYS, THE v (d Jones, Tommy Lee 1995 USA)
    Reviews
  Taylor, J. "The Good Old Boys." credits still VARIETY 358:55-56 Feb 27/Mar
    5 1995
GOODALL, HEATHER
  Bell, P. Jakubowicz, Andrew, Goodall, Heather, Martin, Jeannie, Mitchell,
    Tony, Randall, Lois and Seneviratne, Kalinga, Racism, ethnicity and the
    media [Book Review]. MEDIA INFO AUSTRALIA n75:165-166 Feb 1995
GORDON, KEITH See also WILD PALMS
Government and politics See POLITICS AND GOVERNMENT
GOVERNMENT INVESTIGATION
    Television (broadcast)
      United States
  Wharton, D. Murdoch & Co. do D.C. shuffle. VARIETY 358:29+ [2p] Feb 13/19
    1995
GOVERNMENT REGULATION [Prior to V16, 1988 use REGULATION]
    Television (broadcast) and Video (non-broadcast)
      Europe, Western. Audience. Youth
  Brudny, W. Jugendmedienschutz in Europa. table MEDIEN 38:376-377 n6 1994
      Europe, Western. National Consciousness
  Attali, J. Hollywood vs. Europe: the next round. il JOURNAL WGA 7:26-27
    Feb 1994
      United States. Networks and Networking
  Hadden, S.G. and Lenert, E. Telecommunications networks are not VCRs: the
    public nature of new information technologies for universal service.
    bibliog graph stat tables MEDIA CUL & SOC 17:121-140 n1 1995

      United States. Telecommunications
  How to get better phone service. CONS RES MAG 74:11-15 Dec 1991
    Television (broadcast)
      Asia. Satellite Television
  Thomas, A.O. Asean television & pan-Asian broadcast satellites. bibliog
    MEDIA INFO AUSTRALIA n75:123-129 Feb 1995
      Canada. Telecommunications
  Winseck, D. Power shift?: towards a political economy of Canadian
    telecommunications and regulation. bibliog stat tables CAN J COM 20:81-106
    n1 1995
      Europe, Western. National Consciousness
  Stern, A. France, EC in quota spat. VARIETY 358:32+ [2p] Feb 6/12 1995
  Stern, A. and Schuman, J. French fried in quota quibble. il VARIETY
    358:173-174 Feb 20/26 1995
  Williams, M. EU's TV quota directive in state of confusion. VARIETY 357:48
    Jan 9/15 1995
  Williams, M. and Stern, A. Quotas find Brussels muscle. il VARIETY 358:39+
    [2p] Mar 27/Apr 2 1995
      New Zealand
  Drinnan, J. Minister endorses TV status quo, retreats on Channel 2 selloff.
    ONFILM 11:1+ [2p] n11 1994/95
      Russia (since 1992). Commercials
  Birchenough, T. State TV's ad ban worries other webs. stat VARIETY 358:59
    Feb 27/Mar 5 1995
      United States
  Auletta, K. Selling the air. biog il NEW YORKER 70:36-41 Feb 13 1995
  Flint, J. Deregulation: chaos calling? stat VARIETY 358:29+ [2p] Feb 13/19
    1995
      United States. Programming for Children
  Wharton, D. Kidvid education hour urged. VARIETY 358:39 Feb 13/19 1995
      United States. Syndication
  Slocum, C.B. FISR fallout. JOURNAL WGA 8:35 Feb 1995
    Video (non-broadcast)
      Finland
  Salminen, K. Vallaton video, raiskatut sielut. bibliog il PEILI 18:14-15
    n1 1994
GOVERNMENT SUPPORT
    Television (broadcast) and Video (non-broadcast)
      Australia. Multimedia
  Brown, P. Cargo cults & technofetishism. MEDIA INFO AUSTRALIA n75:87-88 Feb
    1995
  Dutchak, P. Multimedia and the cultural statement. il stat stills C PAPERS
    n102:32-35 Dec 1994
      United States
  Bart, P. Newtering the arts. il VARIETY 358:6+ [2p] Feb 6/12 1995
  Nicholson, J. (Two) 2% solution. stat AFTERIMAGE 22:3 Dec 1994
      United States. Media Arts
  Esbjornson, M. Media arts madness. il stills INDEP 18:6-7+ [3p] Jan/Feb
    1995
  Shapiro, M. Tough cookies. il ports INDEP 18:6-8 Mar 1995
    Television (broadcast)
      Belgium
  Bilan 1994 de la Commission de Selection des Films du Ministere de la
    Communaute Francaise. stat tables MONITEUR n127:5-6 Jan 1995
  Qui s'occupe (encore) de la politique culturelle audiovisuelle en Communaute
    francaise? MONITEUR n126:11 Dec 1994
      Canada
  Acheson, K. and Maule, C.J. International regimes for trade, investment, and
    labour mobility in the cultural industries. bibliog CAN J COM 19:401-421
    n3/4 1994
      Canada. Cultural Context
  Audley, P. Cultural industries policy: objectives, formulation, and
    evaluation. bibliog CAN J COM 19:317-352 n3/4 1994
      Europe, Western
  Williams, M. and Stern, A. EC wants to double financial support for film,
    TV. VARIETY 358:43-44 Feb 13/19 1995
      Germany (Federal Republic, since 1990). Programming for Children
  Molner, D. German pubcasters seek federal cash for kidweb. VARIETY 358:29+
    [2p] Mar 27/Apr 2 1995
      United States. Public
  Goetz, T. School of hard-right knocks. VILLAGE VOICE 40:46-47 Feb 7 1995
  O'Gara, G. Biting the handout that feeds me. port NEWSWK 125:16 Feb 27
    1995
  Walsh, T. Beltway bumps rattle pubcasting. il stat VARIETY 357:39+ [2p]
    Jan 9/15 1995
  Walsh, T. Pubcasters fear GOP fund-slash. port stat VARIETY 357:37-38 Jan
    2/8 1995
  Zoglin, R. Mom, apple pie and PBS. il TIME 145:56 Jan 23 1995
    Video (non-broadcast)
      United States. Networks and Networking
  Osborn, B. B. Infobahn greenbacks and the invisible arts. il INDEP
    18:24-25 Apr 1995
GOYOAGA, BEATRIZ V.
  Goyoaga, B.V. Futbol's been very good to Avila. port VARIETY 358:46+ [2p]
    Mar 27/Apr 2 1995
GRADOWSKI, KRZYSZTOF
  Gradowski, K. Jutro Krakow. REZYSER n18:1 1993
GRANADA TELEVISION LTD.
  Bond, S.R. and Bond, S. Report from 221B Baker Street. il ARMCHAIR DET
    28:70-72 n1 1995
GRANGER, DOROTHY
  Lentz, H., III. Obituaries. biogs filmogs obits ports CLASSIC n237:57-59
    Mar 1995
GRANT, DANIEL
  Grant, D. Art instruction by book and videocassette. il CONS RES MAG
    75:29-30+ [3p] Dec 1992
GRANT, JOHN
  Wharton, D. Lawson ankles PBS position. port VARIETY 358:198 Feb 20/26
    1995

GRANTS
Television (broadcast)
   Australia. Research
   Telecom Australia fund. MEDIA INFO AUSTRALIA n75:151-153 Feb 1995
GRAY, ANN
   Tashiro, C.S. Ann Gray. Video playtime: the gendering of a leisure
      technology [Book Reviews]. SCREEN 35:411-415 n4 1994
GRAYSMITH, ROBERT
   McSherry, F.D., Jr. The murder of Bob Crane. By Robert Graysmith [Book
      Review]. ARMCHAIR DET 26:117-118 n4 1993
GRBIC, BOGDAN
   Grbic, B. Meine persoenlichen Grenzueberschreitungen. BLIMP n30:68 Winter
      1994
Great Britain See as a subheading under individual subject headings See BRITISH
   BOARD OF FILM CLASSIFICATION; BRITISH BROADCASTING CORPORATION; BRITISH FILM
   INSTITUTE. NATIONAL FILM AND TELEVISION ARCHIVE (London); INDEPENDENT
   TELEVISION (ITV)
GREAT DAY IN HARLEM, A v (d Bach, Jean 1995 USA)
   Reviews
   Chesire, G. "A Great Day in Harlem." credits VARIETY 358:74 Feb 20/26 1995
GREAT DEFENDER, THE v (d Wallace, Rick 1995 USA)
   Reviews
   Scott, T. "The Great Defender." credits VARIETY 358:56 Feb 27/Mar 5 1995
Greece See as a subheading under individual subject headings
GREENE, DAVID See also CHILDREN OF THE DUST
GREENE, JAY
   Greene, J. Rights squabble begins over new media explosion. VARIETY 357:4+
      [2p] Jan 2/8 1995
GREENPEACE
   Video power. il stills VERTIGO (UK) 1:12-15 n4 1994/95
GREENWALD, ROBERT See also WOMAN OF INDEPENDENT MEANS, A
GREER, DABBS
   Valley, R. Dabbs Greer. il interv port stills SCARLET STREET n17:43+ [6p]
      Winter 1995
GREMILLION, JEFF
   Gremillion, J. Star school. il ports COL JOUR REV 33:32-35 Jan/Feb 1995
GRIBBISH, IRVING
   Gribbish, I. "The Danes don't call it quality anymore." il FATAL VISIONS
      n17:24 1994
GRIDO, IL v (d Antonioni, Michelangelo 1957 It/USA)
   Reviews
   Porton, R. "Il grido." still CINEASTE 21:101 n1/2 1995
GRIFFIN, NANCY
   Griffin, N. New kid in town. il PREM 8:64-69 Feb 1995
GRIFFITHS, KEITH
   Griffiths, K. Anxious visions. il stills VERTIGO (UK) 1:47-52 n4 1994/95
GRODIN, TOM
   Marin, R. and Fleming, C. Late night unplugged. stills NEWSWK 125:63 Jan
      23 1995
GROVES, DON
   Groves, D. Continental cable in co-venture to build web in Japan. VARIETY
      358:34 Mar 20/26 1995
   Groves, D. Field pared to pair. VARIETY 358:44 Mar 13/19 1995
   Groves, D. It's bizzy down under. il stat stills VARIETY 358:61+ [2p] Feb
      27/Mar 5 1995
   Groves, D. Pay TV web a mixed bag for viewers. VARIETY 358:32 Mar 20/26
      1995
   Groves, D. Probert heads BVHV/Hong Kong. port VARIETY 358:46 Feb 13/19
      1995
   Groves, D. Production facilities pact goes to Global. VARIETY 358:66 Feb
      27/Mar 5 1995
   Groves, D. Star TV to launch 30 more channels. il VARIETY 357:56 Jan 2/8
      1995
   Groves, D. Trio jostle for position in battle for Oz pay TV. stat VARIETY
      357:50 Jan 9/15 1995
   Groves, D. Two to tangle over territory. VARIETY 358:173-174 Feb 20/26 1995
   Groves, D. and Woods, M. Homegrown kidvid thrives in land of Oz. VARIETY
      358:59 Mar 6/12 1995
   Groves, D. and Woods, M. Paper tigers: Murdoch, Packer fight over Fairfax.
      ports stat VARIETY 358:57-58 Feb 27/Mar 5 1995
   Woods, M. and Groves, D. B'casters explore hazards of peddling more vid to
      kids. VARIETY 358:54 Mar 6/12 1995
GRUBER, EBERHARD
   Gruber, E. Une reprise impossible? "Effi Briest" et la question de ses
      reecritures filmiques. CINEMAS 4:59-71 n1 1993
GRUNDY WORLDWIDE LTD.
   Peers, M. Grundy to sell 40% of his firm. VARIETY 358:32 Mar 20/26 1995
GRUNIG, J.
   Roser, C. and Thompson, M. Fear appeals and the formation of active publics.
      bibliog diag stat tables J COMM 45:103-121 n1 1995
GRUPO MEXICANO DE VIDEO
   Paxman, A. B'buster VideoVisa: devalued relations. il stat VARIETY
      358:43-44 Feb 13/19 1995
GUARD, CANDY
   Guard, C. Rough humour. still S&S 5:69 Jan 1995
GUENTZEL-LINGNER, BERND
   Anfang, G. Mit Jugendlichen videofilmen [Book Review]. MEDIEN 38:380-381 n6
      1994
GUERRERO, ED For film reviews see author under the following titles: EMPEROR
   JONES, THE
GUIDER, ELIZABETH
   Guider, E. "ER" series a smooth operator overseas. VARIETY 358:49 Mar 6/12
      1995
   Guider, E. Fremantle freewheeling in Asia's largest TV market. VARIETY
      357:57 Jan 2/8 1995
   Guider, E. Loyal U.S. distribbers counting on Monaco to give them the
      business. port VARIETY 358:37+ [2p] Feb 6/12 1995
   Halligan, F. and Guider, E. Murdoch's STAR TV on rise. VARIETY 358:44 Feb
      13/19 1995
Guides See STUDY GUIDES

GULLO, JIM For film reviews see author under the following titles: MIRACLES AND
   OTHER WONDERS
   Gullo, J. The road to hellville. il PREM 8:146 Apr 1995
GUNTHER, ALBERT C.
   Gunther, A.C. Overrating the X-rating: the third-person perception and
      support for censorship of pornography. bibliog stat tables J COMM 45:27-38
      n1 1995
GUSINSKY, VLADIMIR
   Remnick, D. The tycoon and the Kremlin. il NEW YORKER 71:118-120+ [15p]
      Feb 20/27 1995
GUSTAFSSON, ANDERS See also I NATT GAR JORDEN UNDER
   Nodfors, M. Tonsaker estet. port CHAPLIN 36:12-13 n6 (n255) 1994/95
GYNGELL, BRUCE
   Woods, M. PBL profits rise; Nine exec quits. stat VARIETY 358:48 Mar 6/12
      1995
HBO See HOME BOX OFFICE
HDTV See HIGH-DEFINITION TELEVISION/VIDEO
HAAS, PHILIP See also MUSIC OF CHANCE, THE
HACKER, DONALD
   Weiner, R. Roll out the barrel. port VARIETY 358:10 Feb 6/12 1995
HADDEN, SUSAN G.
   Hadden, S.G. and Lenert, E. Telecommunications networks are not VCRs: the
      public nature of new information technologies for universal service.
      bibliog graph stat tables MEDIA CUL & SOC 17:121-140 n1 1995
HAGER, MARY
   Cowley, G. and others. RoboDocs and mousecalls. il port NEWSWK 125:66-67
      Feb 27 1995
HAILE, MICHAEL
   Haile, M. Reminting "Schindler's" gold. il stills BOXOFFICE 131:66+ [4p]
      Apr 1995
HAINING, PETER
   Breen, J.L. Haining, Peter, ed. The television detectives' omnibus: great
      tales of crime and detection [Book Review]. ARMCHAIR DET 27:223 n2 1994
HAKE, TED
   Slide, A. The Slide area film book notes [Book Reviews]. CLASSIC
      n237:42-44+ [4p] Mar 1995
Half-inch See as a subheading under individual subject headings
HALL, CAROL
   Gates, D. and Hall, C. Will Fry come in from the cold? port NEWSWK 125:69
      Mar 13 1995
HALLIGAN, FINN
   Halligan, F. and Guider, E. Murdoch's STAR TV on rise. VARIETY 358:44 Feb
      13/19 1995
HALLIGAN, FIONNUALA
   Halligan, F. Asia launch. port VARIETY 358:61 Mar 6/12 1995
   Halligan, F. Expats to get Portuguese fare. VARIETY 358:31 Mar 20/26 1995
   Halligan, F. In Asia, it's battle of the broadbands. VARIETY 358:46-47 Mar
      13/19 1995
   Halligan, F. Satcaster Chua follows Disney lead. port still VARIETY
      358:61-62 Mar 6/12 1995
HAMILL, MARK
   Weiner, R. Spaced out. port VARIETY 358:9 Feb 27/Mar 5 1995
HAMILTON, JONATHAN C.
   Hamilton, J.C. Leaving the trim bin further behind. il INDEP 18:42-45
      Jan/Feb 1995
HAMPTON, HENRY
   Eyes on Henry Hampton. biog NEW YORKER 70:29-30 Jan 23 1995
HAMSUN, KNUT
   Jensen, J. This Knut's a hot media ticket in Scandinavia. VARIETY 358:47
      Mar 13/19 1995
HAND, DAVID See also SNOW WHITE AND THE SEVEN DWARFS
HANDELMAN, DAVID
   Handelman, D. The birth of the uncool. il stills PREM 8:84-88 Mar 1995
Handicapped in television/video See PHYSICALLY HANDICAPPED IN TELEVISION/VIDEO
HANKISS, ELEMER
   Hankiss, E. Holding the pass. NEW HUNGARIAN Q 35:84-99 n135 1994
HANNULA, MIKA
   Hannula, M. "Kauniit ja Rohkeat" vastaan "Pikku Kakkonen." ports PEILI
      18:8-9 n1 1994
   Hannula, M. "Lastenohjelman pitaa olla iloinen." il port PEILI 18:4-5 n2
      1994
   Hannula, M. "Nukkumatin" kolme vuosikymmenta." stills PEILI 17:8-9 n4 1993
HAPPY DAYS v (1974-84 USA)
   Heiskanen, O. Villit fiftarit? credits still PEILI 18:24-25 n4 1994
HARA, KAZUO
   Gerow, A.A. Documentarists of Japan (second in a series). biog interv port
      stills DOC BOX 3:12-18 1993
HARD DRIVE v (1994 USA)
   Reviews
   "Hard Drive." FATAL VISIONS n17:25 1994
HARDESTY, MARY
   Hardesty, M. Defying gravity in the Bonneville Salt Flats. credits il
      AMCIN 76:75-76 Feb 1995
   Hardesty, M. Filming 27 stories up. credits AMCIN 76:73-74 Mar 1995
   Hardesty, M. Jaguar spots light up L.A. credits AMCIN 76:75-76 Jan 1995
   Yonover, N.S. and others. Artists Rights Symposium: three days of
      discussion. DGA NEWS 19:26-27+ [3p] n3 1994
HARKONEN, RITVA-SINI
   Wuorisalo, J. Suomalaista teoriapohjaa mediavalistukselle [Book Review]. il
      PEILI 18:31 n2 1994
HARLIN, RENNY See also SAINT, THE
HARMON, JIM
   Breen, J.L. Harmon, Jim. Radio mystery and adventure and its appearances in
      film, television and other media [Book Review]. ARMCHAIR DET 26:78-79 n3
      1993
HARRINGTON, WILLIAM
   Meyers, R. Columbo: the grassy knoll. By William Harrington [Book Review].
      ARMCHAIR DET 27:105-106 n1 1994
HARRIS, CHRIS
   Obituaries. obits VARIETY 358:188-189 Feb 20/26 1995

HARRIS, JUDITH For film reviews see author under the following titles: ALIEN
  NATION: DARK HORIZON; HIDDEN II, THE; PUMPKINHEAD II: BLOOD WINGS;
  SHRUNKEN HEADS; SPACE PRECINCT
HARRIS, LESLEY ELLEN
  Harris, L.E. A roadmap for writers' rights on the information superhighway.
    il JOURNAL WGA 8:20-23 Feb 1995
  Harris, L.E. Intellectual property on the infobahn. INDEP 18:21-23 Mar 1995
HARTZELL, JAMES
  Video power. il stills VERTIGO (UK) 1:12-15 n4 1994/95
HARVEY, JOHN F.
  Harvey, J.F. Blue hearts, a novel. By Jim Lehrer [Book Review]. ARMCHAIR
    DET 26:104 n4 1993
HAUNTING, THE v (d Wise, Robert 1963 USA/Gt Br)
    Reviews
  Holt, W. G. "The Haunting." il stills F FAX n49:30+ [2p] Mar/Apr 1995
HAUPT, CLYDE V.
  Slide, A. The Slide area film book notes [Book Reviews]. CLASSIC n236:47-49
    Feb 1995
HAYNES, LAURA
  Haynes, L. Breast-feeding the nation. il JOURNAL WGA 8:36 Mar 1995
HAZMAT v (unrealized project 1989 USA)
  Clinch, C. Dancing on the truth. JOURNAL WGA 8:29 Mar 1995
HEALTH See also AIDS
    Television (broadcast)
      United States. Directors
  Elrick, T. Stamina on the set. DGA NEWS 19:10-11+ [3p] n3 1994
      United States. News Coverage
  How scientists view science news reporting. stat tables CONS RES MAG
    76:31-33 Oct 1993
  Media coverage of health care reform. graphs stat tables COL JOUR REV
    33:1-8 Mar/Apr sup 1995
HEALTHY AGING v (1995 USA)
  Gullo, J. The road to hellville. il PREM 8:146 Apr 1995
HEARN, GREG
  Hearn, G. and Mandeville, T. The electronc superhighway. bibliog table
    MEDIA INFO AUSTRALIA n75:92-101 Feb 1995
HEART FOR OLIVIA, A v (d Klein, Jonathan 1995 USA)
    Reviews
  Leonard, J. "Somebody" to love. port still NEW YORK 28:60-61 Jan 23 1995
HEBERT, PIERRE
  Jean, M. Des restes d'images non identifies. il interv stills 24 IMAGES
    n75:26-32+ [8p] Dec/Jan 1994/95
HEIDE, MARGARET J.
  Heide, M.J. Gender and generation: the case of "thirtysomething." bibliog
    STUDIES POP CULT 17:75-83 n1 1994
HEINTZ, KURT See also CHINESE CUCUMBERS
  Fifield, G. "Chinese Cucumbers." il port INDEP 18:18-19 Apr 1995
HEISKANEN, OUTI
  Heiskanen, O. Villit fiftarit? credits still PEILI 18:24-25 n4 1994
HELL'S ANGEL v (d Hitchens, Christopher 1994 Gt Br)
  Hitchens, C. Mother Teresa and me. port still VANITY FAIR 58:36+ [4p] Feb
    1995
HENDERSON, CRAIG
  Hardesty, M. Defying gravity in the Bonneville Salt Flats. credits il
    AMCIN 76:75-76 Feb 1995
HENDRYKOWSKI, MAREK
  Hendrykowski, M. R jak Routledge [Book Reviews]. il KINO 27:41-42 Jul 1993
HENRY, MATTHEW
  Henry, M. The triumph of popular culture: situation comedy, postmodernism
    and "The Simpsons." bibliog STUDIES POP CULT 17:85-99 n1 1994
HENSLEY, DENNIS
  Hensley, D. Buenos Diaz. interv port MOVIELINE 6:18 Mar 1995
HERCULES: THE LEGENDARY JOURNEYS v (1995- USA)
  Szebin, F.C. The new adventures of Hercules. il stills C FANTAS 26:46-48+
    [4p] n2 1995
    Special Effects
  Szebin, F.C. The special effects of Hercules. il stills C FANTAS 26:49-50+
    [3p] n2 1995
HERSHEY, LAURA
  Hershey, L. False advertising. MS 5:96 n5 1995
HERSHMAN, ROBERT
  Obituaries. obits VARIETY 358:58-59 Mar 20/26 1995
HERSKOWITZ, MICKEY
  Hickey, N. Dedicated Dan [Book Review]. il COL JOUR REV 33:68-69 Mar/Apr
    1995
HESTON, CHARLTON
  Errata/addenda. STARS n21:[2] Winter 1995
HEURING, DAVID
  Heuring, D. Real life through the lens. AMCIN 76:28-30 Jan 1995
HEWITT, PETER See also WILD PALMS
HEYMAN, KAREN
  Heyman, K. The Internet: interactivity. il JOURNAL WGA 8:34-35 Mar 1995
  Heyman, K. The Internet: untimely tips. JOURNAL WGA 8:35 Dec/Jan 1995
Hi-8 See as a subheading under individual subject headings
HICKEY, NEIL
  Hickey, N. Dedicated Dan [Book Review]. il COL JOUR REV 33:68-69 Mar/Apr
    1995
HIDDEN II, THE v (d Pinsker, Seth 1994 USA)
    Reviews
  Harris, J. "The Hidden II." credits C FANTAS 26:59 n2 1995
HIETALA, VEIJO
  Hietala, V. Kasvattajat irti paatoksesta [Book Review]. PEILI 18:29 n4 1994
HIFT, FRED
  Hift, F. Asian TV survives without U.S. aid. il VARIETY 358:62 Mar 6/12
    1995
  Hift, F. Hong Kong in 1997. VARIETY 358:62 Mar 6/12 1995
HIGH-DEFINITION TELEVISION/VIDEO
    Television (broadcast) and Video (non-broadcast)
      United States. Computer Software
  Beacham, F. HDTV comes to the desktop PC. AMCIN 76:64-65 Mar 1995

    Television (broadcast)
      United States. Standards and Recommended Practices
  A new beginning. CONS RES MAG 76:6 Jul 1993
HIGHTOWER, DENNIS
  Lowry, B. Frank out at Disney. ports VARIETY 358:68 Mar 13/19 1995
HILDAGO, FRANCES
  Hildago, F. Canadian network gives women a voice. still INDEP 18:13 Apr
    1995
HIRSCH, DAVID
  Hirsch, D. "Quantum Leap." F SCORE MONTHLY n39:12 Nov 1993
HISTORY OF ROCK 'N' ROLL, THE v (d Solt, Andrew 1995 USA)
    Reviews
  Gallo, P. "The History of Rock 'n' Roll." credits VARIETY 358:46 Mar 6/12
    1995
HISTORY OF TELEVISION/VIDEO
    Television (broadcast) and Video (non-broadcast)
      1990-96. Belgium. Television/Video Lists
  Bilan 1994 de la production et de la coproduction belge. MONITEUR n126:12-21
    Dec 1994
    Television (broadcast)
      Great Britain
  Brownlie, T. All our yesterdays [Book Review]. il still FILM 4:24 n1
    [1995]
      Scandinavia
  De Bernardinis, F. Il bacco di Bergman. stills SEGNO n71:76-77 Jan/Feb
    1995
      1990-96. Hungary
  Hankiss, E. Holding the pass. NEW HUNGARIAN Q 35:84-99 n135 1994
HITCHCOCK, ALFRED
  Zaniello, T. Hitched or Lynched: who directed "Twin Peaks"? bibliog filmogs
    STUDIES POP CULT 17:55-64 n1 1994
HITCHENS, CHRISTOPHER See also HELL'S ANGEL
  Hitchens, C. Mother Teresa and me. port still VANITY FAIR 58:36+ [4p] Feb
    1995
HOBERMAN, PERRY
  Malden, K. Checking in to the bar code hotel. il still INDEP 18:18-19 Mar
    1995
HOFFMAN, DICK
  Fox, M. In the program director's chair. il ports INDEP 18:30-32 Mar 1995
HOFFMANN, DEBORAH See also COMPLAINTS OF A DUTIFUL DAUGHTER
  Blackwell, E. "Complaints of a Dutiful Daughter." still INDEP 18:14-15 Mar
    1995
HOGAN, DAVID J. For film reviews see author under the following titles: AELITA;
  LSV FLOOR SWEEPINGS TAPE, THE; PIN-DOWN GIRL; STECKLER INTERVIEWS,
  VOL 1: THE MAKING OF "THE STRANGE CREATURES"
HOGUE, PETER
  Hogue, P. Flickers. F COM 31:13 Mar/Apr 1995
HOLLAND MEDIA GROUP
  Edmunds, M. Dutch channel ready to go. stat VARIETY 358:51 Feb 27/Mar 5
    1995
  Edmunds, M. New web's creation a legal tangle. VARIETY 358:49 Mar 6/12 1995
HOLLINGS, BETTINA
  Orinnan, J. Hollings brings schedules oomph to 3. ports ONFILM [12]:1+
    [2p] n2 1995
HOLLYWOOD KIDS
  Hollywood Kids. Andrew Stevens: Q&A. interv port MOVIELINE 6:32 Mar 1995
Holmes, Sherlock See SHERLOCK HOLMES (fictional character)
HOLT, WESLEY G. For film reviews see author under the following titles:
  HAUNTING, THE; INVADERS FROM MARS
HOLTER, TOM
  Fox, M. In the program director's chair. il ports INDEP 18:30-32 Mar 1995
HOME BOX OFFICE
  Flint, J. HBO, troika in output deal. stat VARIETY 358:36 Mar 13/19 1995
HOME IMPROVEMENT v (1991- USA)
    Syndication
  Benson, J. and Walsh, T. "Home" enters original syndie to duel "Seinfeld."
    stills VARIETY 358:29+ [2p] Mar 27/Apr 2 1995
HOME SHOPPING NETWORK INC.
  Shopping by television. il stills CONS REP 60:8-9+ [4p] Jan 1995
HOME SHOPPING PROGRAMMING [Prior to V16, 1988 use PROGRAMMING, HOME SHOPPING]
    Television (broadcast)
      United States
  Shopping by television. il stills CONS REP 60:8-9+ [4p] Jan 1995
HOME VIDEO SYSTEMS See also MONITORS; RECEIVERS; VIDEORECORDERS AND
  VIDEORECORDING
    Television (broadcast) and Video (non-broadcast)
      United States
  Before you buy. diags il CONS REP 60:164-165 Mar 1995
      United States. Testing and Measurement
  How we test the gear. diag il CONS REP 60:166-167 Mar 1995
Home videos See AMATEUR PRODUCTION
HOMER, STEVE
  Homer, S. DVD not among players at German CeBit. VARIETY 358:39 Mar 13/19
    1995
  Homer, S. Philips mulls DVD bow at Germany's CeBIT. VARIETY 358:69+ [2p]
    Feb 6/12 1995
HOMICIDE: LIFE ON THE STREET v (1993- USA)
    Reviews
  Meyers, R. The crime screen. ports still ARMCHAIR DET 26:63-64 n3 1993
HOMOSEXUALITY
    Television (broadcast)
      United States
  Gay activist arrested for trespassing at CBN. CHR CENT 112:263 Mar 8 1995
    Video (non-broadcast)
      Experimental Television/Video. Festivals
  Reid-Pharr, R. Mix-defying. il stills AFTERIMAGE 22:3-4 Jan 1995
HOMOSEXUALS IN TELEVISION/VIDEO
    Video (non-broadcast)
      United States
  Russo, C.J. Images in the dark: an encyclopedia of gay and lesbian film and

INTERTEXTUAL ANALYSIS
    Television (broadcast)
        Canada
    Wees, W.C. From the rearview mirror to twenty minutes into the future: the
        video image in "Videodrome" and "Max Headroom." CAN J F STUD 1:29-35 n1
        1990
INTERVIEWS
    Television (broadcast)
        United States
    Rosenstiel, T. Yakety-yak. il ports COL JOUR REV 33:23-27 Jan/Feb 1995
INTL. INC
    Shopping by television. il stills CONS REP 60:8-9+ [4p] Jan 1995
INVADERS FROM MARS v (d Menzies, William Cameron 1953 USA)
    Reviews
    Holt, W.G. "Invaders From Mars." il still F FAX n48:24+ [2p] Jan/Feb 1995
INVISIBLE CITY, THE v (d Blue, James/Santos, Adele 1979 USA)
    Lunenfeld, P. "There are people in the streets who've never had a chance to
        speak": James Blue and the complex documentary. bibliog biog stills UFAJ
        46:21-33 n1 1994
INVISIBLE: THE CHRONICLES OF BENJAMIN KNIGHT v (d Ersgard, Jack 1994 USA)
    Reviews
    Wilt, D. "Invisible: the Chronicles of Benjamin Knight." C FANTAS 26:59 n2
        1995
Iran See as a subheading under individual subject headings
IRAQ-KUWAIT CRISIS, 1990-1991
    Television (broadcast)
        United States. Ideological Analysis
    Castonguay, J. Seeing through the media: the Persian Gulf War. By Susan
        Jeffords and Lauren Rabinovitz, eds. [Book Review]. DISCOURSE n17.1:169-172
        Fall 1994
Ireland, Northern, in television/video See NORTHERN IRELAND IN TELEVISION/VIDEO
IRONY
    Television (broadcast)
        United States
    Handelman, D. The birth of the uncool. il stills PREM 8:84-88 Mar 1995
IRVING, JUDY See also DARK CIRCLE
Israel See as a subheading under individual subject headings
ISRAEL, NEAL
    Ciapara, E. "Surfujacy Ninja." credits filmogs still FSP 40:9 n4 (n758)
        1994
ISTO, KAISU
    Isto, K. Cartoon Forum 1993. il PEILI 17:36-37 n4 1993
ITALIA 7
    Rooney, D. Most recent TV upstart sputters. VARIETY 357:49 Jan 9/15 1995
Italy See as a subheading under individual subject headings See RADIOTELEVISIONE
    ITALIANA
JA TO WIDZIALEM v (d Lachnit, Ewa 1993 Poland)
    Lubelski, T. "Ja to widzialem." port KINO 27:37 May 1993
JACKSON, KATHY MERLOCK
    Davidoff, S. Kathy Merlock Jackson, Walt Disney: a bio-bibliography [Book
        Review]. ANIMATION J 3:92 n1 1994
JACKSON, WENDY
    Jackson, W. Cecile Starr: a pioneer's pioneer. biog port ANIMATION J
        3:40-43 n2 1995
JACOBSEN, CAROL
    Shapiro, M. Carol Jacobsen. still INDEP 18:44 Mar 1995
JACOBSON, RICK See also UNBORN II
JACQUINOT, GENEVIEVE
    Jacquinot, G. Le documentaire, une fiction (pas) comme les autres. bibliog
        stills CINEMAS 4:61-81 n2 1994
JAKUBOWICZ, ANDREW
    Bell, P. Jakubowicz, Andrew, Goodall, Heather, Martin, Jeannie, Mitchell,
        Tony, Randall, Lois and Seneviratne, Kalinga, Racism, ethnicity and the
        media [Book Review]. MEDIA INFO AUSTRALIA n75:165-166 Feb 1995
JALBERT, PAUL L.
    Jalbert, P.L. Critique and analysis in media studies: media criticism as
        practical action. bibliog DISCOURSE & SOC 6:7-26 n1 1995
JAMES, EDWARD
    Obituaries. biogs obits VARIETY 358:86-87 Mar 27/Apr 2 1995
JAMES, PEDR See also MARTIN CHUZZLEWIT
JANICKA, BOZENA
    Janicka, B. and others. Telewizja rzetelna. il interv KINO 27:20-21+ [3p]
        Jul 1993
JANSSON, TOVE
    Kylmanen, M. Zuumi muumibuumiin. bibliog still PEILI 17:10-13 n4 1993
Japan See as a subheading under individual subject headings
JEAN, MARCEL
    Jean, M. Des restes d'images non identifies. il interv stills 24 IMAGES
        n75:26-32+ [8p] Dec/Jan 1994/95
JEFFORDS, SUSAN
    Castonguay, J. Seeing through the media: the Persian Gulf War. By Susan
        Jeffords and Lauren Rabinovitz, eds. [Book Review]. DISCOURSE n17.1:169-172
        Fall 1994
JEFFREY, LISS
    Jeffrey, L. Rethinking audiences for cultural industries: implications for
        Canadian research. bibliog stat tables CAN J COM 19:495-522 n3/4 1994
JENKINS, SUE
    Jenkins, S. Rugby & romance a winning team. il ONFILM 11:7 n11 1994/95
JENNINGS, KAREN
    Cook, J. and Jennings, K. "Live and Sweaty." bibliog MEDIA INFO AUSTRALIA
        n75:5-12 Feb 1995
JENNY JONES v (1991- USA)
    Peyser, M. Making a killing on talk TV: is Jenny to blame for a guest's
        death? ports still NEWSWK 125:30 Mar 20 1995
JENSEN, JORN
    Jensen, J. This Knut's a hot media ticket in Scandinavia. VARIETY 358:47
        Mar 13/19 1995
JHALLY, SUT
    Seaton, B. The codes of advertising: fetishism and the political economy of
        meaning in the consumer society. By Sut Jhally [Book Reviews]. CAN J COM

20:116-120 n1 1995
    Wark, M. Jhally, Sut and Lewis, Justin, Enlightened racism: "The Cosby
        Show," audiences, and the myth of the American dream [Book Review]. MEDIA
        INFO AUSTRALIA n75:166 Feb 1995
JIANG, SHAN
    Chen, R. Jiang Shan, a rising star in music and film. il ports CHINA
        SCREEN n4:36-37 1994
JIMMY HOLLYWOOD v (d Levinson, Barry 1994 USA)
    Reviews
    Romney, J. "Jimmy Hollywood." credits S&S 5:56 Apr 1995
JOANOU, PHIL See also WILD PALMS
JOHANSSON, PEIK
    Johansson, P. Rasistista nalkaviihdetta. il PEILI 18:20-21 n3 1994
JOHN CARPENTER PRESENTS BODY BAGS v (d Carpenter, John/Hooper, Tobe 1993 USA)
    Reviews
    Mangan, D. "Body Bags." il FATAL VISIONS n17:28 1994
JOHNSON, KENNETH See also ALIEN NATION: DARK HORIZON
JOHNSON, QUENDRITH
    Johnson, Q. Meet the nominees: television dramatic specials. ports DGA
        NEWS 19:18+ [5p] n2 1994
JOJOLA, TED
    Jojola, T. Absurd reality: Hollywood goes to the Indians... filmog F&HIST
        23:7-16 n1/4 1993
JON STEWART SHOW, THE v (USA)
    Stone, L. Going to bed with Jon Stewart. port VILLAGE VOICE 40:40-42 Mar 7
        1995
JONES, TOMMY LEE See also GOOD OLD BOYS, THE
JORDAN, GLENN See also MY BROTHER'S KEEPER
JOST, FRANCOIS
    Jost, F. Direct, narration simultanee: frontieres de la temporalite.
        bibliog CINEMAS 5:81-90 n1/2 1994
JUHASZ, ALEXANDRA
    Juhasz, A. So many alternatives. stills CINEASTE 21:37-39 n1/2 1995
JULICH, SOLVEIG
    Julich, S. Voxel-Man. diags F HAFTET 22:55-57 n3 (n87) 1994
JUNTUNEN, MAX
    Juntunen, M. Tunnekasvatusta videon avulla? still PEILI 17:34-35 n4 1993
JUPITER'S WIFE v (d Negroponte, Michel 1994 USA)
    Edelman, R. "Jupier's Wife." port INDEP 18:14-15 Jan/Feb 1995
JUSTMAN, ROBERT H.
    Uram, S. Roddenberry's legacy. il stills C FANTAS 26:34-39 n2 1995
    Uram, S. Trek memories. il C FANTAS 26:19 n2 1995
JUURIKKALA, KAIJA
    Juurikkala, K. Kuka saa katsoa ja mita. still PEILI 18:24-25 n1 1994
    Juurikkala, K. Kylla piirroshahmot elavat oikeastikin, vai mita aiti? il
        PEILI 17:42 n4 1993
    Juurikkala, K. Latautumassa minun elokuvanifestivaaleilla. il PEILI 17:25
        n3 1993
    Juurikkala, K. Lyhyt johdatus lyhytelokuvan sielunmaisemaan. stills PEILI
        17:4-5 n3 1993
KAGAN, JEREMY See also ROSWELL
KAIN, JACKIE
    Fox, M. In the program director's chair. il ports INDEP 18:30-32 Mar 1995
KALB, JONATHAN
    Kalb, J. Screenings. port VILLAGE VOICE 40:76 Jan 31 1995
KALIN, TOM
    Juhasz, A. So many alternatives. stills CINEASTE 21:37-39 n1/2 1995
KANTOLA, MAIKKI
    Kantola, M. Oulun kansainvalinen lastenelokuvafestivaali. still PEILI
        17:40-41 n4 1993
KAPLAN, JONATHAN
    Calderale, M. Filmografie. biogs il filmogs SEGNO n71:40 Jan/Feb 1995
KAROL, DARCIE
    Kimmel, D. Darcie Karol. obit VARIETY 358:58 Mar 20/26 1995
KATU ON MUN KOTI v (d Tuura, Tikke 1993 Finl)
    Salakka, M. "Tama tyo on ollut tahanastisista raskain." il PEILI 17:12-13
        n3 1993
KATZ, ELIHU
    Scannell, P. Media events [Book Review]. bibliog MEDIA CUL & SOC
        17:151-157 n1 1995
    Sinclair, J. Liebes, Tamar and Katz, Elihu. The export of meaning:
        cross-cultural readings of "Dallas" [Book Review]. MEDIA INFO AUSTRALIA
        n75:167-168 Feb 1995
KATZ, SUSAN BULLINGTON
    Katz, S.B. A conversation with... Frank Darabont. filmog interv port
        JOURNAL WGA 8:28-31 Feb 1995
    Katz, S.B. A conversation with... Richard Curtis. il interv JOURNAL WGA
        8:24-27 Mar 1995
KATZENBERG, JEFFREY
    Corliss, R. Hey, let's put on a show! il ports TIME 145:54-60 Mar 27 1995
KAUFMAN, BEN L.
    Kaufman, B.L. Cincinnati's morality squad targets Pasolini. il INDEP
        18:9-11 Jan/Feb 1995
KAUFMAN, PATTI
    Evans, G. Confirmation of new N.Y. pic commish still pending. VARIETY
        358:36 Feb 27/Mar 5 1995
KAUPPILA, JEAN L.
    Slide, A. The Slide area film book notes [Book Reviews]. CLASSIC
        n237:42-44+ [4p] Mar 1995
KEATON, DIANE
    Zaniello, T. Hitched or Lynched: who directed "Twin Peaks"? bibliog filmogs
        STUDIES POP CULT 17:55-64 n1 1994
KEEPNEWS, PETER
    Keepnews, P. Letters: one froggy error. VILLAGE VOICE 40:6 Feb 21 1995
KELLEHER, RAY
    Kelleher, R. "American Values." port INDEP 18:16-17 Mar 1995
KELLY, BRENDAN
    Kelly, B. Cable leaves Canada with an int'l appetite. table VARIETY 358:46
        Feb 6/12 1995

KEMP, PHILIP
   Kemp, P. Discworld [Book Review]. still S&S 5:34 Apr 1995
KENTUCKY CYCLE, THE v (d Costner, Kevin project 1995- USA)
   Flint, J. Costner to helm HBO "Cycle" mini. VARIETY 358:36 Mar 13/19 1995
Kenya See as a subheading under individual subject headings
KERSHAW, SARAH
   Kershaw, S. Against pornophobia. port NEW YORK 28:20+ [2p] Jan 16 1995
KIM-GIBSON, DAI SIL See also SA-I-GU
KIMMEL, DAN
   Kimmel, D. Darcie Karol. obit VARIETY 358:58 Mar 20/26 1995
   Kimmel, D. PBS cuts could squeeze Brit fare. VARIETY 358:58 Feb 27/Mar 5
      1995
KING, BURTON See also MAN FROM BEYOND, THE
KING WORLD ENTERTAINMENT
   Peers, M. and Flint, J. Will King World join Turner team? VARIETY 358:9 Mar
      27/Apr 2 1995
         Economic Aspects
   Flint, J. and Peers, M. King World for a buyer - or strategic alliance.
      VARIETY 358:23-24 Mar 20/26 1995
KING, ZALMAN See also RED SHOE DIARIES
Kingdom, The See RIGET
KINGFISH: A STORY OF HUEY P. LONG v (d Schlamme, Thomas 1995 USA)
   Scott, T. "Kingfish: a Story of Huey P. Long." credits still VARIETY
      358:37 Mar 13/19 1995
   Tomasky, M. It's good to be the Kingfish. VILLAGE VOICE 40:44 Mar 21 1995
KIRSH, ESTELLE F.
   Krasilovsky, A. Estelle F. Kirsh. interv port ANGLES 2:14-17 n4 1995
KLEIN, JENNIE
   Klein, J. Transgressive tapes. stills AFTERIMAGE 22:12-13 Jan 1995
KLEIN, JONATHAN See also HEART FOR OLIVIA, A
KLEINWAECHTER, WOLFGANG
   Kleinwaechter, W. From the mountains of visions to the valleys of reality:
      new legal frameworks for broadcasting in Eastern and Central Europe. CAN J
      COM 20:25-44 n1 1995
KLUTE v (d Pakula, Alan J. 1971 USA)
   Atkinson, M. Jane Fonda in "Klute." still MOVIELINE 6:82 Apr 1995
KNIGHT, GRAHAM
   Knight, G. The Beaver bites back? American popular culture in Canada. Edited
      by David H. Flaherty & Frank E. Manning [Book Review]. CAN J COM 19:560-561
      n3/4 1994
KOEHLER, MARGRET For film reviews see author under the following titles: BIETE
   NIERE - SUCHE HERZ; ES IST DOCH NAEHER DRAN...; GHETTONAUT; RISKANTE
   SPIELE ZWISCHEN LEBEN UND TOD
KOENIG, WALTER
   Uram, S. Chekov makes Captain. stills C FANTAS 26:32-33 n2 1995
KOHL, HELMUT
   Molner, D. Hot Kohl fuels public TV feuding. VARIETY 358:33 Feb 6/12 1995
Kolchak, Carl See CARL KOLCHAK (fictional character)
KOLODYNSKI, ANDRZEJ
   Janicka, B. and others. Telewizja rzetelna. il interv KINO 27:20-21+ [3p]
      Jul 1993
KOLSKI, JAN JAKUB See also POGRABEK
KONDRAT, MAREK
   Slodowski, J. Marek Kondrat. filmog still FSP 40:13 n11 (n765) 1994
KONINCK STUDIOS LTD.
   Griffiths, K. Anxious visions. il stills VERTIGO (UK) 1:47-52 n4 1994/95
Korea (Republic) See as a subheading under individual subject headings
KOSZARSKI, RICHARD
   Koszarski, R. The movies come home. il stills F COM 31:10-12+ [5p] Mar/Apr
      1995
KOTUKU PRODUCTIONS
      Projects
   Wakefield, P. New adventures for Kotuku in wake of Enid Blyton project.
      ONFILM [12]:6 n2 1995
KRACHER, JEANNE
   Lopez, C. and Kracher, J. Media activism. interv ANGLES 2:3+ [2p] n4 1995
KRAJEWSKI, PIOTR
   Krajewski, P. Kino sprute i zszyte na nowo. stills KINO 27:16-19 May 1993
KRASILOVSKY, ALEXIS
   Krasilovsky, A. A sharper image. il port ANGLES 2:10-11 n4 1995
   Krasilovsky, A. Estelle F. Kirsh. interv port ANGLES 2:14-17 n4 1995
   Krasilovsky, A. Kelly Elder McGowen. interv ANGLES 2:11-13 n4 1995
KREMSKI, PETER
   Kremski, P. Film als Schule des Sehens. il interv stills F BUL 36:53-59 n6
      (n197) 1994
KROLL, JACK For film reviews see author under the following titles: PROMISED
   LAND, THE
KRUEGER, UDO MICHAEL
   Amort, F.M. Programmprofile im dualen Fernsehsystem 1985-1990 [Book Review].
      F KUNST n144:69-70 1994
KRUSCHKE, DOUG
   Brown, C. Gee, Officer Kruschke... il PREM 8:54-55+ [3p] Apr 1995
KULTAINEN AASI v (d Taanila, Mika 1993 Finl)
   Taanila, M. Mielihyvakupolin avajaiset. credits filmog il stills PEILI
      17:8-9 n3 1993
KUMMELI v (1990?- Finl)
   Lehtonen, V.-P. Amatoorit tekevat sketsiviihdetta. il stills PEILI
      18:18-19 n1 1994
KURTWELL, EDITH
   Hoover, S.M. Media and the moral order in postpositivist approaches to media
      studies [Book Reviews]. bibliog J COMM 45:136-146 n1 1995
KUTZERA, DALE
   Kutzera, D. "Star Trek: Voyager." il C FANTAS 26:28-29 n2 1995
   Kutzera, D. "X-Files." stills C FANTAS 26:52-53 n2 1995
Kuwait-Iraq crisis, 1990-1991 See IRAQ-KUWAIT CRISIS, 1990-1991
KYLMANEN, MARJO
   Kylmanen, M. Zuumi muumibuumiin. bibliog still PEILI 17:10-13 n4 1993
LSV FLOOR SWEEPINGS TAPE, THE v (1994 USA)
      Reviews
   Hogan, D.J. "The LSV Floor Sweepings Tape." il F FAX n49:20+ [3p] Mar/Apr

1995
LA ROCHELLE, REAL
   La Rochelle, R. Le combat du cineaste contre l'opera. discog filmog stills
      24 IMAGES n75:17-19 Dec/Jan 1994/95
   La Rochelle, R. Mythe du "That's Entertainment" ou creation d'un nouveau
      filmopera? filmog stills 24 IMAGES n76:50-52 Spring 1995
LACAN, JACQUES
   Dixon, W.W. Lacan, Jacques. Television: a challenge to the psychoanalytic
      establishment [Book Review]. UFAJ 46:58-59 n2 1994
LACHNIT, EWA See also JA TO WIDZIALEM
LAFFERTY, ELAINE
   Lafferty, E. Getting a work in edgewise. il port still TIME 145:64-65 Feb
      6 1995
LAGADERE GROUP
      Multimedia
   Weiner, R. MGM, Lagadere ink interactive pact. VARIETY 358:26 Feb 13/19
      1995
LAHR, JOHN
   Lahr, J. Bedazzled ports NEW YORKER 70:80-85 Jan 23 1995
LALANDE, J. GUY
   Lalande, J.G. Glasnost, perestroika and the Soviet media. By Brian McNair
      [Book Reviews]. CAN J COM 20:124-125 n1 1995
LALLY, KEVIN
   Lally, K. "Bye Bye Love" sees funny side of divorce. il still FJ 98:16+
      [2p] Mar 1995
LAMMIO, HARRI
   Lammio, H. Video: utopia uudesta kuvakulttuurista. still PEILI 17:10-11 n3
      1993
LANDSCAPE
      Television (broadcast) and Video (non-broadcast)
         Theory
   Fry, K. Place/culture/representation. By James Duncan & David Ley (eds.)
      [Book Review]. bibliog J COMM 45:173-177 n1 1995
Laptop videorecorders See VIDEORECORDERS AND VIDEORECORDING
LARA, CONCEPCION
   Paxman, A. Lara fine-tunes plan for Fox Latin channel. port VARIETY 358:44
      Mar 27/Apr 2 1995
LARSEN, ERNEST
   Larsen, E. Letters: Ernest Larsen responds. INDEP 18:2 Apr 1995
   Larsen, E. Little orphan video. il stills INDEP 18:28-31 Jan/Feb 1995
   Weiss, B. Letters: veni, vidi, video. INDEP 18:2 Apr 1995
LARSON, JAMES F.
   Rowe, D. Larson, James F. and Park, Heung-Soo. Global television and the
      politics of the Seoul Olympics [Book Review]. MEDIA INFO AUSTRALIA
      n75:84-85 Feb 1995
LARSON, KARLA M.
   Pfau, M. and others. Influence of communication modalities on voters'
      perceptions of candidates during presidential primary campaigns. bibliog
      diag stat tables J COMM 45:122-133 n1 1995
LARSON, RANDALL D.
   Larson, R.D. Music for Japanese animation: interview with Hiroshi Miyagawa.
      il interv port SCN 14:28-31 Mar 1995
Laserdiscs See VIDEODISCS
LAST SEDUCTION, THE v (d Dahl, John 1994 USA)
   Palminteri, C. The fire in Fiorentino. il interv port INTERV 25:88-91 Mar
      1995
LASTER, ARNAUD
   Laster, A. Les miserables sur les ecrans de cinema et de television.
      credits filmog il stills AVANT-SCENE n438/439:81-91 Jan/Feb 1995
LATE LATE SHOW WITH TOM SNYDER, THE v (1995- USA)
      Reviews
   Whitehead, C. Prisoners of talk. il VILLAGE VOICE 40:46-47 Feb 7 1995
LATE SHOW WITH DAVID LETTERMAN v (1993- USA)
   Schruers, F. Man of the year. il ROLLING STONE n698/699:30-34+ [7p] Dec
      29/Jan 12 1994/95
LAUGHTON, CHARLES See also NIGHT OF THE HUNTER, THE
Laurel Awards See AWARDS - Television (broadcast) - United States. Writers
   Guild of America
LAW & ORDER v (1990- USA)
   Lowry, B. NBC orders 2 more years of "Law." VARIETY 358:39 Feb 13/19 1995
LAWS AND LEGISLATION See also CENSORSHIP; CONTRACTS; LOBBYING
      Television (broadcast) and Video (non-broadcast)
         United States. Films Changed for Television/Video
   Wharton, D. Scorsese plugs for artists' rights on Hill. port VARIETY
      358:20 Mar 20/26 1995
         United States. Taxes
   Flint, J. Minority deal ordeal. VARIETY 358:64 Mar 20/26 1995
      Television (broadcast)
         Europe, Eastern
   Kleinwaechter, W. From the mountains of visions to the valleys of reality:
      new legal frameworks for broadcasting in Eastern and Central Europe. CAN J
      COM 20:25-44 n1 1995
         Germany (Federal Republic, since 1990). Programming for Children.
         Advertising
   Tuormaa, J. Mainoskatkot pois lastenohjelmista Saksassa. PEILI 18:7 n3 1994
         Greece
   Quinn, P. Greece nears b'cast law to regulate TV. VARIETY 358:60 Feb 27/Mar
      5 1995
         Greece. Advertising
   Quinn, P. Bill to limit "media shops" in the works. VARIETY 358:34 Mar
      20/26 1995
         Iran. Satellite Communications Equipment
   Warg, P. Iran's ban on dishes doesn't wash with public. VARIETY 358:34 Feb
      6/12 1995
         Netherlands. Advertising
   Edmunds, M. Broadcasting sponsorship law near. VARIETY 358:43 Feb 13/19
      1995
         United States
   Trager, R. Entangled values: the First Amendment in the 1990s [Book
      Reviews]. bibliog J COMM 45:163-170 n1 1995

MEDIA STUDIES
    Television (broadcast)
    (continued)
    United States
    Jalbert, P.L. Critique and analysis in media studies: media criticism as practical action. bibliog DISCOURSE & SOC 6:7-26 n1 1995
MEDICAL USES
    Television (broadcast) and Video (non-broadcast)
    United States. Interactive
    Spencer, P.L. Calling all consumers: the future of telemedicine. CONS RES MAG 76:38 May 1993
    Television (broadcast)
    United States
    Cowley, G. and others. RoboDocs and mousecalls. il port NEWSWK 125:66-67 Feb 27 1995
MEDICINE BALL v (1995 USA)
    Reviews
    Sandler, A. "Medicine Ball." credits VARIETY 358:38 Mar 13/19 1995
MEDIO MAGAZINE
    Fisher, M. "Medio Magazine"; "substance.digizine" [Book Review]. il VARIETY 358:42 Mar 13/19 1995
MEDIO MULTIMEDIA
    Delgado, R. Medio making multiple moves. port VARIETY 358:40 Mar 13/19 1995
MEHTA, DEEPA
    Vasudev, A. Deepa Mehta. il interv still CINEMAYA n25/26:68-71 Autumn/Winter 1994/95
MEIGHAN, HOWARD S.
    Obituaries. biogs obits VARIETY 358:86-87 Mar 27/Apr 2 1995
MELTZER, JULIA
    Meltzer, J. Real estate as art: CD-ROM artist Nancy Buchanan. il INDEP 18:23-24 Apr 1995
    Meltzer, J. "The Illegal Interns." il INDEP 18:15-16 Jan/Feb 1995
MEMORY
    Television (broadcast)
    Therien, G. L'effet paradoxal des images. bibliog CINEMAS 4:57-72 n3 1994
MEN IN TELEVISION/VIDEO
    Television (broadcast)
    Australia. Sports Broadcasting. Feminist Analysis
    Yeates, H. The league of men. bibliog MEDIA INFO AUSTRALIA n75:35-45 Feb 1995
MENZIES, WILLIAM CAMERON See also INVADERS FROM MARS
MERCHANDISING SPIN-OFFS
    Television (broadcast) and Video (non-broadcast)
    United States. Interactive. Contracts
    O'Steen, K. Interactive rights give studios clause. VARIETY 358:18 Mar 20/26 1995
    Television (broadcast)
    Japan. Animation
    Niskanen, E. Pienia pyoreaksvoisia tyttoja. il stills PEILI 17:20-21 n4 1993
MERCHANDISING TIE-INS
    Television (broadcast) and Video (non-broadcast)
    United States
    Evans, G. Showbiz is psyched for cybermalls. VARIETY 358:1+ [2p] Mar 27/Apr 2 1995
MERGERS
    Television (broadcast)
    United States. Cable
    Peers, M. Cablers' merger era hits dusk. VARIETY 358:39+ [2p] Mar 6/12 1995
MERRICK, GEOFFREY
    Merrick, G. and Bradley, G. Letters: more "Mystery!" ARMCHAIR DET 26:4-5 n4 1993
METRO-GOLDWYN-MAYER ENTERTAINMENT, INC.
    Multimedia
    Weiner, R. MGM, Lagadere ink interactive pact. VARIETY 358:26 Feb 13/19 1995
Mexico See as a subheading under individual subject headings
MEYER, PAUL
    Calderale, M. Filmografie. biogs il filmogs SEGNO n71:40 Jan/Feb 1995
MEYERS, RIC For film reviews see author under the following titles: FALLEN ANGELS; HOMICIDE: LIFE ON THE STREET; MYSTERY!; NYPD BLUE; PICKET FENCES
    Merrick, G. and Bradley, G. Letters: more "Mystery!" ARMCHAIR DET 26:4-5 n4 1993
    Meyers, R. Columbo: the grassy knoll. By William Harrington [Book Review]. ARMCHAIR DET 27:105-106 n1 1994
    Meyers, R. The crime screen. port stills ARMCHAIR DET 26:59-61 n4 1993
MICHAELS, ERIC
    Braman, S. Bad aboriginal art: tradition, media and technological horizons. By Eric Michaels [Book Review]. J COMM 45:178-179 n1 1995
MICHIGAN G. FROG (fictional character)
    Keepnews, P. Letters: one froggy error. VILLAGE VOICE 40:6 Feb 21 1995
MICKIEWICZ, ELLEN
    Loo, E. Browne, Donald R., Firestone, Charles M., Mickiewicz, Ellen, eds. Television/radio news and minorities [Book Review]. MEDIA INFO AUSTRALIA n75:157-158 Feb 1995
MICROSOFT CORPORATION
    Animation
    Weiner, R. Microsoft goes after animation mavens. stat VARIETY 357:87 Jan 2/8 1995
MILCHAN, ARNON
    Bart, P. Building bridges. il VARIETY 358:4+ [2p] Mar 13/19 1995
MILKEN, MICHAEL
    Peers, M. Is Milken mulling moguldom? VARIETY 358:1+ [2p] Mar 13/19 1995
MILLER, DENNIS
    Cox, D. Sony corporate adds Miller to its culture. port VARIETY 358:20 Feb 13/19 1995
MILLER, MARK
    Reibstein, L. and others. Live, from Nielsen heaven. il NEWSWK 125:49 Jan

30 1995
MILLER, STUART
    Miller, S. ABC seals season win with lame Bowl. stat VARIETY 358:28 Feb 6/12 1995
    Miller, S. CBS sweeps loss wasn't by Eyelash. stat VARIETY 358:42 Mar 6/12 1995
    Miller, S. Most web rookies prove light hitters. stat VARIETY 358:32+ [2p] Mar 27/Apr 2 1995
    Miller, S. Movies, telepix falter in sweeps. stat VARIETY 358:40-41 Feb 13/19 1995
    Miller, S. Peacock preens over sweeps wins. stat VARIETY 358:50 Feb 27/Mar 5 1995
    Miller, S. Plenty of "Hope" for replacements. stat VARIETY 358:26 Mar 20/26 1995
    Miller, S. Primetime enters post-sweep slump. stat VARIETY 358:32 Mar 13/19 1995
    Miller, S. Sweeps pix keep up disappointing pace. stat VARIETY 358:194 Feb 20/26 1995
    Miller, S. Warmth, holidays sap ratings race. stat VARIETY 357:41 Jan 2/8 1995
    Miller, S. Webs score with sked shuffles. stat VARIETY 357:40-41 Jan 9/15 1995
MILLER, SUSAN
    Cowley, G. and others. RoboDocs and mousecalls. il port NEWSWK 125:66-67 Feb 27 1995
MINISTERE DE LA COMMUNAUTE FRANCAISE. COMMISSION DE SELECTION DES FILMS (Belgium)
    Bilan 1994 de la Commission de Selection des Films du Ministere de la Communaute Francaise. stat tables MONITEUR n127:5-6 Jan 1995
MINKOFF, ROB See also LION KING, THE
MINORITIES See also ABORIGINES; ASIAN-AMERICANS; BLACKS; ETHNICITY; INDIANS, AMERICAN; RACE
    Television (broadcast)
    United States. Taxes. Laws and Legislation
    Wharton, D. Minority tax break quashed by House. VARIETY 358:52 Feb 27/Mar 5 1995
MIRABELLA, ALAN
    Mirabella, A. TV's magazine shakeout. il COL JOUR REV 33:11 Mar/Apr 1995
MIRACLES AND OTHER WONDERS v (1995 USA)
    Reviews
    Gullo, J. Miracle drugged. il PREM 8:92 Feb 1995
MISERABLES, LES v (d Bluwal, Marcel 1972 Fr)
    Thomas, S. Entretien avec Marcel Bluwal. il interv AVANT-SCENE n438/439:before p1-2 [3p] Jan/Feb 1995
    Teleplays
    "Les Miserables" de Marcel Bluwal: scenario original, d'apres l'oeuvre de Victor Hugo. credits scenario stills AVANT-SCENE n438/439:3-80 Jan/Feb 1995
MITCHELL, TONY
    Bell, P. Jakubowicz, Andrew, Goodall, Heather, Martin, Jeannie, Mitchell, Tony, Randall, Lois and Seneviratne, Kalinga. Racism, ethnicity and the media [Book Review]. MEDIA INFO AUSTRALIA n75:165-166 Feb 1995
MIYAGAWA, HIROSHI
    Larson, R.D. Music for Japanese animation: interview with Hiroshi Miyagawa. il interv port SCN 14:28-31 Mar 1995
MOHAMMED, JUANITA
    Juhasz, A. So many alternatives. stills CINEASTE 21:37-39 n1/2 1995
MOLNER, DAVID
    Molner, D. CME signs programming deal. stat VARIETY 358:57 Feb 27/Mar 5 1995
    Molner, D. German pubcasters seek federal cash for kidweb. VARIETY 358:29+ [2p] Mar 27/Apr 2 1995
    Molner, D. Germans making a public appearance. VARIETY 358:31-32 Mar 20/26 1995
    Molner, D. Germany's high-speed test drive. stat VARIETY 358:43 Mar 13/19 1995
    Molner, D. Hot Kohl fuels public TV feuding. VARIETY 358:33 Feb 6/12 1995
    Molner, D. Kindernets looming on German horizon. VARIETY 358:60 Mar 6/12 1995
    Molner, D. Media giants on prowl for digital pay TV partners. VARIETY 358:45 Feb 13/19 1995
    Molner, D. MTV, Viva set launch dates for spinoffs. VARIETY 358:46 Mar 13/19 1995
    Molner, D. October buys rights to Danish "Kingdom." VARIETY 358:27 Mar 13/19 1995
    Molner, D. With marks and airtime to burn, German nets stay close to home. VARIETY 358:44 Feb 6/12 1995
    Molner, D. Zelnick looking to boost BMG's RCA label, pump up core business. port VARIETY 357:47-48 Jan 9/15 1995
Monaco See as a subheading under individual subject headings
MONDALE, ELEANOR
    Hooper, J. Q and Eleanor. port ESQUIRE 123:16 Jan 1995
MONDINO, JEAN-BAPTISTE
    Tee, E. Die synthetische Sinnlichkeit des Jean-Baptiste Mondino. stills BLIMP n30:28-31 Winter 1994
MONETTE, PAUL
    Obituaries. obits VARIETY 358:188-189 Feb 20/26 1995
MONITORS See also RECEIVERS
    Television (broadcast) and Video (non-broadcast)
    United States
    Cohen, J. Making sense of new electronics products. il CONS RES MAG 74:34-36 Dec 1991
MOORE, DANIEL S.
    Moore, D.S. Taming the tube. il still VARIETY 358:53+ [2p] Mar 6/12 1995
MOORE, MARY TYLER
    Mary, Mary, slightly contrary. port NEW YORKER 70:32 Feb 13 1995
MOORE, RICHARD A.
    Obituaries. obits VARIETY 358:54 Feb 13/19 1995
MOORHOUSE, JOCELYN
    Moorhouse, J. Enduring. still S&S 5:61 Apr 1995

NATIONAL CONSCIOUSNESS
(continued)
    Television (broadcast)
        Conferences, Institutes, Workshops, etc.
    Yonover, N.S. and others. Artists Rights Symposium: three days of
        discussion. DGA NEWS 19:26-27+ [3p] n3 1994
        Europe, Western. Government Regulation
    Stern, A. France, EC in quota spat. VARIETY 358:32+ [2p] Feb 6/12 1995
    Stern, A. and Schuman, J. French fried in quota quibble. il VARIETY
        358:173-174 Feb 20/26 1995
    Williams, M. and Stern, A. Quotas find Brussels muscle. il VARIETY 358:39+
        [2p] Mar 27/Apr 2 1995
NATIONAL COUNCIL OF CHURCHES (United States)
    National Council quits anticensorship coalition. CHR CENT 112:41 Jan 18 1995
NATIONAL EMPOWERMENT TELEVISION
    Bellafante, G. The network that Newt built. il TIME 145:30 Jan 9 1995
    Meacham, J. Surfing on Newt's network. stills NEWSWK 125:36 Jan 30 1995
NATIONAL ENDOWMENT FOR THE ARTS (United States)
    Nicholson, J. (Two) 2% solution. stat AFTERIMAGE 22:3 Dec 1994
    O'Steen, K. Jane tells it plain. stat VARIETY 358:12 Feb 27/Mar 5 1995
    Ramos, D. Jane's addiction. port NEW REPUB 212:23+ [2p] Jan 9/16 1995
        Media Arts
    Esbjornson, M. Media arts madness. il stills INDEP 18:6-7+ [3p] Jan/Feb
        1995
National Film and Television Archive (London) See BRITISH FILM INSTITUTE.
    NATIONAL FILM AND TELEVISION ARCHIVE (London)
NATIONAL FOOTBALL LEAGUE (NFL, United States)
    Walsh, T. Rams outfoxed in bid to relocate to St. Louis. VARIETY 358:25 Mar
        20/26 1995
National identity See NATIONAL CONSCIOUSNESS
NATIONAL TELECOMMUNICATIONS AND INFORMATION ADMINISTRATION (United States)
    Osborn, B.B. Infobahn greenbacks and the invisible arts. il INDEP 18:24-25
        Apr 1995
NATIONAL VIDEO RESOURCES INC.
    Bobby, K. NVR offers libraries alternative videos at a discount. still
        INDEP 18:10+ [3p] Apr 1995
NATIVE AMERICAN PRODUCER'S ALLIANCE (United States)
    Masayesva, V., Jr. Notes on the Native American Producers Alliance and the
        First Nations Film and Video World Alliance. biog il DOC BOX 4:4-7 1993
Nazism See FASCISM
NEGROPONTE, MICHEL See also JUPITER'S WIFE
    Edelman, R. "Jupier's Wife." port INDEP 18:14-15 Jan/Feb 1995
NESSELSON, LISA For film reviews see author under the following titles:
    CATHERINE THE GREAT
Netherlands See as a subheading under individual subject headings
NETWORK AFFILIATES See also names of network affiliates
    Television (broadcast)
        United States
    Flint, J. Comp coin captures devotion of affiliates. port VARIETY 357:39+
        [2p] Jan 9/15 1995
Network Ten Australia See TV AUSTRALIA
NETWORKS AND NETWORKING See also names of networks
    Television (broadcast) and Video (non-broadcast)
        United States. Copyright
    Harris, L.E. A roadmap for writers' rights on the information superhighway.
        il JOURNAL WGA 8:20-23 Feb 1995
        United States. Effects on Television/Video
    Ehrlich, E.M. Virtual companies, walled cities, and the right-brained
        economy: cinematographers on the information highway. AMCIN 76:96 Mar 1995
        United States. Government Regulation
    Hadden, S.G. and Lenert, E. Telecommunications networks are not VCRs: the
        public nature of new information technologies for universal service.
        bibliog graph stat tables MEDIA CUL & SOC 17:121-140 n1 1995
    Television (broadcast)
        United States
    Auletta, K. The race for a global network. il NEW YORKER 71:53-54+ [7p]
        Mar 6 1995
    Gomery, D. Dinosaurs who refuse to die. port AM JOUR REV 17:48 n2 1995
    Hughes, R. Why watch it, anyway? il NY R BKS 42:37-42 Feb 16 1995
    Zoglin, R. Network crazy! il ports TIME 145:68-72 Jan 16 1995
        United States. Comparison With Television/Video
    Dibbell, J. The whole world-wide. VILLAGE VOICE 40:46 Feb 28 1995
        United States. Economic Aspects
    Robins, J.M. Star-struck webs wow admen. VARIETY 358:1+ [2p] Mar 27/Apr 2
        1995
        United States. Government Regulation
    Slocum, C.B. FISR fallout. JOURNAL WGA 8:35 Feb 1995
        United States. News Broadcasting
    Robins, J.M. Net newscasts diverge in quest for viewers. il VARIETY
        358:29+ [2p] Feb 13/19 1995
        United States. Residuals and Fees
    Lowry, B. Webs wheeze over license fees. graph il stat VARIETY 358:1+ [2p]
        Feb 20/26 1995
    Video (non-broadcast)
        Australia. Political Analysis
    Hearn, G. and Mandeville, T. The electronc superhighway. bibliog table
        MEDIA INFO AUSTRALIA n75:92-101 Feb 1995
        New Zealand. Influence on Television/Video
    Reynolds, P. The fast lane to the future. il ONFILM [12]:13 n1 1995
        United States
    Beacham, F. Magic link: E-mail to go. il AMCIN 76:63-64 Mar 1995
        United States. Applications
    Solman, G. New twists in video assists. il DGA NEWS 19:10-11+ [3p] n2 1994
        United States. Audience Research
    Braman, S. Cyberia: life in the trenches of hyperspace. By Douglas Rushkoff
        [Book Review]. J COMM 45:177-178 n1 1995
        United States. Government Support
    Osborn, B.B. Infobahn greenbacks and the invisible arts. il INDEP 18:24-25
        Apr 1995

        United States. Intellectual Property Rights
    Harris, L.E. Intellectual property on the infobahn. INDEP 18:21-23 Mar 1995
NEW TELEVISION v (1985- USA)
    Taubin, A. New (television) haven. VILLAGE VOICE 40:43 Jan 31 1995
NEW WORLD COMMUNICATIONS GROUP
    Benson, J. New World closes on Cannell. VARIETY 358:35 Mar 27/Apr 2 1995
NEW YORK MAYOR'S OFFICE OF FILM, THEATRE, AND BROADCASTING (New York, New York)
    Evans, G. Confirmation of new N.Y. pic commish still pending. VARIETY
        358:36 Feb 27/Mar 5 1995
NEW YORK TIMES COMPANY, THE
    Peers, M. Times' timing on cable raises eyebrows. stat VARIETY 357:42 Jan
        9/15 1995
New Zealand See as a subheading under individual subject headings See NEW
    ZEALAND ON AIR
NEW ZEALAND FILM & VIDEO TECHNICIANS' GUILD INC.
    Bisset, B. Letters: Blue Book piece was half right. ONFILM 11:10-11 n11
        1994/95
    Drinnan, J. Letters: John Drinnan responds. ONFILM 11:11 n11 1994/95
    Dryburgh, S. Letters: open letter from a film technician on the subject of
        lunch. ONFILM 11:11 n11 1994/95
    Howard, C. Letters: get your act together. ONFILM 11:12 n11 1994/95
NEW ZEALAND ON AIR
        Economic Aspects
    Drinnan, J. NZ On Air gets a B+... (but). stat ONFILM [12]:20 n2 1995
        Financing
    Drinnan, J. Musivids march to different tune. stat ONFILM [12]:20 n2 1995
NEWELL, MIKE
    Calderale, M. Filmografie. biogs il filmogs SEGNO n71:40 Jan/Feb 1995
NEWS BROADCASTERS See also names of news broadcasters
    Television (broadcast)
        United States. Professional Education
    Gremillion, J. Star school. il ports COL JOUR REV 33:32-35 Jan/Feb 1995
NEWS BROADCASTING See also WEATHER BROADCASTING
    Television (broadcast)
        Theory
    Jost, F. Direct, narration simultanee: frontieres de la temporalite.
        bibliog CINEMAS 5:81-90 n1/2 1994
        United States. Networks and Networking
    Robins, J.M. Net newscasts diverge in quest for viewers. il VARIETY
        358:29+ [2p] Feb 13/19 1995
NEWS CORPORATION LTD.
    Wharton, D. FCC bigwig rethinks Fox. VARIETY 358:88 Feb 27/Mar 5 1995
        Economic Aspects
    Peers, M. News Corp. 2nd qtr. better than expected. stat VARIETY 358:38
        Feb 13/19 1995
        Government Investigation
    Peers, M. and Flint, J. Probe may stall Fox TV affil goal. port VARIETY
        358:23+ [2p] Mar 20/26 1995
NEWS COVERAGE
    Television (broadcast)
        Race Relations
    Loo, E. Browne, Donald R., Firestone, Charles M., Mickiewicz, Ellen, eds.
        Television/radio news and minorities [Book Review]. MEDIA INFO AUSTRALIA
        n75:157-158 Feb 1995
        Finland. Audience, Children
    Anttila, A.H. Estonia muistuttaa Persianlahden sodasta. bibliog il PEILI
        18:12-13 n4 1994
        Russia (since 1992). War
    Watson, R. and others. Russia's TV war. il NEWSWK 125:30-32 Feb 6 1995
        Russia (since 1992). War. Effects of Television/Video
    Birchenough, T. TV has role in Chechnya war. VARIETY 358:59-60 Feb 27/Mar 5
        1995
        Rwanda
    Johansson, P. Rasistista nalkaviihdetta. il PEILI 18:20-21 n3 1994
        United States. Health
    How scientists view science news reporting. stat tables CONS RES MAG
        76:31-33 Oct 1993
    Media coverage of health care reform. graphs stat tables COL JOUR REV
        33:1-8 Mar/Apr sup 1995
        United States. Influence of Television/Video. Health
    Ward, B. Crossing the line? port AM JOUR REV 17:12-13 n1 1995
        United States. Science. Effects of Television/Video. Audience Research
    Priest, S.H. Information equity, public understanding of science, and the
        biotechnology debate. bibliog diag stat table J COMM 45:39-54 n1 1995
News media See MASS MEDIA
NEWS PROGRAMMING [Prior to V16, 1988 use PROGRAMMING, NEWS]
    Television (broadcast)
        Great Britain. Ideological Analysis
    Wortham, S. Simon Cottle, TV news, urban conflict, and the inner city [Book
        Review]. bibliog DISCOURSE & SOC 6:143-144 n1 1995
        United States. Ethics
    Lissit, R. Gotcha! ports AM JOUR REV 17:16-21 n2 1995
    Revah, S. It's a jungle out there in cyberspace. il port AM JOUR REV
        17:10-11 n2 1995
        United States. Ideological Analysis
    Jalbert, P.L. Critique and analysis in media studies: media criticism as
        practical action. bibliog DISCOURSE & SOC 6:7-26 n1 1995
        United States. Networks and Networking
    Mirabella, A. TV's magazine shakeout. il COL JOUR REV 33:11 Mar/Apr 1995
NEWSRADIO v (1995- USA)
        Reviews
    McCarthy, J. "NewsRadio." credits still VARIETY 358:30 Mar 20/26 1995
NEWTON, GREGORY D.
    Eastman, S.T. and Newton, G.D. Delineating grazing: observations of remote
        control use. bibliog stat tables J COMM 45:77-95 n1 1995
NEWZ, THE v (1994-95 USA)
    Flint, J. Bad "Newz" for Col TriStar: $ missing. il VARIETY 358:49+ [2p]
        Feb 27/Mar 5 1995
NICHOLS, NICHELLE
    Uram, S. Beyond Uhura. stills C FANTAS 26:31 n2 1995

NICHOLSON, JUDITH
    Nicholson, J. Facets African American video guide. Compiled by Patrick Ogle
        [Book Review]. il AFTERIMAGE 22:15 Jan 1995
    Nicholson, J. (Two) 2% solution. stat AFTERIMAGE 22:3 Dec 1994
NICKENS, DARYL G.
    Nickens, D.G. Back to basics. port JOURNAL WGA 8:2 Dec/Jan 1995
NICKS, JOAN
    Nicks, J. Peter Steven. Brink of reality: new Canadian documentary film and
        video [Book Review]. CAN J F STUD 3:104-107 n2 1994
NIDEROST, ERIC
    Niderost, E. Victor Mature: the "Beefcake King" and underrated actor. port
        stills CLASSIC n237:16+ [4p] Mar 1995
NIELSEN, RAY
    Nielsen, R. Ray's way: Ruth Warrick. il interv port CLASSIC n237:13 Mar
        1995
NIGHT EYES 3 v (d Stevens, Andrew 1994 USA)
        Reviews
    Mangan, D. "Night Eyes 3." FATAL VISIONS n17:28 1994
NIGHT OF THE HUNTER, THE v (d Laughton, Charles 1955 USA)
    Moorhouse, J. Enduring. still S&S 5:61 Apr 1995
NIGHT STAND v (1995- USA)
    Benson, J. Worldvision takes "Stand" on big ticket. port VARIETY 358:193+
        [2p] Feb 20/26 1995
NIGHTLINE v (1980- USA)
    Ledbetter, J. ABC nukes itself. VILLAGE VOICE 40:9 Jan 3 1995
NIKUNEN, KAARINA
    Nikunen, K. Lukottomat siveysvyot. il PEILI 18:6-7 n4 1994
NILESAT
    Warg, P. Arab TV satellite is in the works. VARIETY 358:47 Mar 13/19 1995
Nineteen mm See as a subheading under individual subject headings
NISKANEN, EIJA
    Niskanen, E. Pienia pyoreakasvoisia tyttoja. il stills PEILI 17:20-21 n4
        1993
    Niskanen, E. Shakespearea animaation keinoilla. PEILI 17:43 n4 1993
NOCNE PTAKI v (d Domalik, Andrzej 1993 Poland)
        Reviews
    Maniewski, M. Noc Iwaszki ewiczowska. credits still KINO 27:22-23 Jul 1993
NODFORS, MAGNUS
    Nodfors, M. Tonsaker estet. port CHAPLIN 36:12-13 n6 (n255) 1994/95
NOEL, JACQUES
    Noel, J. Les grandes series americaines des origines a 1970. Par Alain
        Carraze & et Christophe Petit [Book Review]. il GRAND ANGLE n176:40 Nov
        1994
NOLAN, WILLIAM F.
    Bradley, M.R. Nolan's "Run." biog il interv stills F FAX n48:42-48+ [8p]
        Jan/Feb 1995
NOONAN, PEGGY
    Wolcott, J. Beyond the values of the supervixens. il NEW YORKER 70:89-91
        Feb 13 1995
NORCEN, LUCA
    Norcen, L. Uno, nessuno e centomila. il stills SEGNO n72:15-16 Mar/Apr
        1995
Northern Ireland See Great Britain
NORTHERN IRELAND IN TELEVISION/VIDEO
        Television (broadcast)
            Great Britain
    Bennett, R. Telling the truth about Ireland. il stills VERTIGO (UK)
        1:24-29 n4 1994/95
Norway See as a subheading under individual subject headings
Novels about television/video See FICTION ABOUT TELEVISION/VIDEO
Nuclear war See WAR
ORT
    Birchenough, T. Fate of Russian TV up in air. VARIETY 358:39 Mar 27/Apr 2
        1995
Obituaries See names of individuals
Obscenity See PORNOGRAPHY AND OBSCENITY
OCTOBER FILMS
    Molner, D. October buys rights to Danish "Kingdom." VARIETY 358:27 Mar
        13/19 1995
O'DONOGHUE, MICHAEL
    Aykroyd, D. Michael O'Donoghue. port ROLLING STONE n698/699:84 Dec 29/Jan
        12 1994/95
OEHRENS, EVA-MARIA
    Anfang, G. Mit Jugendlichen videofilmen [Book Review]. MEDIEN 38:380-381 n6
        1994
OFFICE, THE v (1995 USA)
        Reviews
    D'Erasmo, S. On the Rhodagain. still VILLAGE VOICE 40:44 Mar 21 1995
O'GARA, GEOFFREY
    O'Gara, G. Biting the handout that feeds me. port NEWSWK 125:16 Feb 27
        1995
OHMER, SUSAN
    Ohmer, S. Index to "Cineaste," vol. XX. CINEASTE 21:89+ [2p] n1/2 1995
OLD CURIOSITY SHOP, THE v (d Connor, Kevin 1995 USA)
        Reviews
    Scott, T. "The Old Curiosity Shop." credits VARIETY 358:37 Mar 13/19
        1995
OLIN, KEN See also IN PURSUIT OF HONOR
OLIVER, GORDON
    Obituaries. biogs obits VARIETY 358:74-75 Mar 6/12 1995
OLYMPIC GAMES
        Television (broadcast)
            Political Uses
    Given, J. Red, black, gold to Australia. bibliog MEDIA INFO AUSTRALIA
        n75:46-56 Feb 1995
OLYMPIC GAMES, 1988 (Seoul, South Korea)
        Television (broadcast)
            Korea (Republic). Political Analysis
    Rowe, D. Larson, James F. and Park, Heung-Soo. Global television and the
        politics of the Seoul Olympics [Book Review]. MEDIA INFO AUSTRALIA

n75:84-85 Feb 1995
ON VALUES: TALKING WITH PEGGY NOONAN v (1995 USA)
    Carson, T. Vita brevis, Shelley Longa. still VILLAGE VOICE 40:27 Feb 14
        1995
        Reviews
    Browning, D. Chastening liberalism. CHR CENT 112:121-124 Feb 1/8 1995
    McConnell, F. The values thing. COMMONWEAL 122:16-17 Mar 10 1995
ONCE WERE WARRIORS v (d Tamahori, Lee 1994 New Zealand)
        Ratings
    Wakefield, P. Censor's new broom cleans up "Warriors." ONFILM [12]:9 n1
        1995
One Inch See as a subheading under individual subject headings
One-quarter inch See as a subheading under individual subject headings
O'NEILL, JAMES
    Slide, A. The Slide area film book notes [Book Reviews]. CLASSIC n236:47-49
        Feb 1995
OPEN-ARCHITECTURE
        Video (non-broadcast)
            United States
    Stalter, K. It's all in the cards. il VARIETY 358:69+ [2p] Feb 6/12 1995
OPERA
        Television (broadcast)
            Adaptations
    La Rochelle, R. Le combat du cineaste contre l'opera. discog filmog stills
        24 IMAGES n75:17-19 Dec/Jan 1994/95
OPPENHEIMER, JEAN
    Oppenheimer, J. Investigating "Incident at Deception Ridge." diag il AMCIN
        76:26-28+ [5p] Feb 1995
ORANGE
    Smith, P. Who'll pay to peel this Orange? ONFILM 11:8 n11 1994/95
ORSON WELLES' GHOST STORY v (d Edwards, Hilton 1991 USA)
        Reviews
    Persons, D. "Orson Welles' Ghost Story." C FANTAS 26:59 n2 1995
OSBORN, BARBARA BLISS
    Osborn, B.B. Dana Atchley's digital campfire stories. il INDEP 18:26-27
        Jan/Feb 1995
    Osborn, B.B. Infobahn greenbacks and the invisible arts. il INDEP 18:24-25
        Apr 1995
OSHIMA, NAGISA
    Oshima, N. Mes idees actuelles sur le cinema japonais. stills POSITIF
        n407:47-52 Jan 1995
Ostankino See ROSSIISKAIA GOSUDARSTVENNAIA TELERADIOKOMPANIIA "OSTANKINO" (Russia)
O'STEEN, KATHLEEN
    O'Steen, K. Film, interactive marketeers uncoordinated. VARIETY 358:34 Feb
        27/Mar 5 1995
    O'Steen, K. "Gump," "Fiction" take over Globes. il stills VARIETY 357:32+
        [2p] Jan 2/8 1995
    O'Steen, K. Interactive rights give studios clause. VARIETY 358:18 Mar
        20/26 1995
    O'Steen, K. Jane tells it plain. stat VARIETY 358:12 Feb 27/Mar 5 1995
    O'Steen, K. Videodisc format focus of CES talk. VARIETY 357:36 Jan 9/15
        1995
    O'Steen, K. Vidgame battle afoot. VARIETY 358:6 Mar 13/19 1995
OSTERHOLM, J. ROGER
    Slide, A. The Slide area film book notes [Book Reviews]. CLASSIC n236:47-49
        Feb 1995
OTHER SIDE, THE v (1994- USA)
    Marin, R. and Posner, A. Channeling alien babies. still NEWSWK 125:68 Mar
        20 1995
OUTER LIMITS, THE v (1995- USA) See also SANDKINGS
        Reviews
    Scott, T. "The Outer Limits." credits VARIETY 358:30 Mar 20/26 1995
OWEN, ALUN
    Lentz, H., III. Obituaries. il obits ports CLASSIC n236:57-59 Feb 1995
PBS See PUBLIC BROADCASTING SERVICE (United States)
P.O.V. See COMPLAINTS OF A DUTIFUL DAUGHTER
PACKAGING
        Video (non-broadcast)
            United States. Compact Discs
    Weiner, R. Plump CD-ROM packages squander space. port VARIETY 357:61 Jan
        9/15 1995
PACKER, KERRY
    Groves, D. and Woods, M. Paper tigers: Murdoch, Packer fight over Fairfax.
        ports stat VARIETY 358:57-58 Feb 27/Mar 5 1995
PAGANO, PENNY
    Pagano, P. Eleventh annual the best in the business. il ports AM JOUR REV
        17:30-39 n2 1995
PAGLIA, CAMILLE
    Paglia, C. When Camille met Tim. interv ports ESQUIRE 123:68-73 Feb 1995
Paid programming See COMMISSIONED TELEVISION/VIDEO
PAIETTA, ANN C.
    Slide, A. The Slide area film book notes [Book Reviews]. CLASSIC
        n237:42-44+ [4p] Mar 1995
Painters and painting See ART AND ARTISTS
PAKULA, ALAN J. See also KLUTE
PALLY, MARCIA
    De Grazia, E. Sex de jure [Book Reviews]. NATION 260:242-249 Feb 20 1995
PALMINTERI, CHAZZ
    Palminteri, C. The fire in Fiorentino. il interv port INTERV 25:88-91 Mar
        1995
PALMISANO, MARCELLO
    Rooney, D. Marcello Palmisano. obit VARIETY 358:188 Feb 20/26 1995
PALUMBO, DENNIS
    Palumbo, D. The pitch. JOURNAL WGA 8:37 Feb 1995
PAPIROWSKI, MARTIN See also RISKANTE SPIELE ZWISCHEN LEBEN UND TOD
PARAMOUNT TELEVISION GROUP
        Advertising
    Lowry, B. Par TV Group ads up for Procter & Gamble. VARIETY 358:39+ [2p]
        Mar 6/12 1995

PARK, HEUNG-SOO
  Rowe, D. Larson, James F. and Park, Heung-Soo. Global television and the
    politics of the Seoul Olympics [Book Review]. MEDIA INFO AUSTRALIA
    n75:84-85 Feb 1995
PARK, SHARON For film reviews see author under the following titles: SA-I-GU
PARKER, IAN
  Parker, I. Son of Rumpole. biog port NEW YORKER 71:78-86 Mar 20 1995
PARKER, ROBERT B.
  Simpson, D.G. Paper doll. By Robert B. Parker [Book Review]. il ARMCHAIR
    DET 27:112-113 n1 1994
PARMET, DAVINA
  Parmet, D. Moved to tears. il PREM 8:93 Mar 1995
PASOLINI, PIER PAOLO See also SALO O LE CENTOVENTI GIORNATE DI SODOMA
  Serravalli, L. La RAI-TV massacra Pier Paolo Pasolini per la seconda volta.
    C SUD 33:54 Jul/Aug/Sep (n113) 1994
Pasolini's 120 Days of Sodom See SALO O LE CENTOVENTI GIORNATE DI SODOMA
PAXMAN, ANDREW
  Levine, F. and Paxman, A. But will it play Beijing? port stat still
    VARIETY 358:44 Mar 27/Apr 2 1995
  Levine, F. and Paxman, A. Telemundo's new destiny. VARIETY 358:68 Mar
    27/Apr 2 1995
  Paxman, A. A media blitzed. il stat VARIETY 357:47-48 Jan 9/15 1995
  Paxman, A. B'buster bullish on expansion. stat VARIETY 358:62+ [2p] Mar
    27/Apr 2 1995
  Paxman, A. B'buster VideoVisa: devalued relations. il stat VARIETY
    358:43-44 Feb 13/19 1995
  Paxman, A. Cisneros views world as oyster. VARIETY 358:46 Mar 27/Apr 2 1995
  Paxman, A. Globo relies on Projac for lift. still VARIETY 358:43+ [3p] Mar
    27/Apr 2 1995
  Paxman, A. Hughes to bow pan-Latin sat network. VARIETY 358:47 Mar 6/12
    1995
  Paxman, A. Hughes, trio unveil new pan-Latin net. stat VARIETY 358:45 Mar
    13/19 1995
  Paxman, A. In Brazil, video market "Snow"-balls. stat VARIETY 358:59-60
    Feb 27/Mar 5 1995
  Paxman, A. Investment grade. VARIETY 358:70 Mar 27/Apr 2 1995
  Paxman, A. Lara fine-tunes plan for Fox Latin channel. port VARIETY 358:44
    Mar 27/Apr 2 1995
  Paxman, A. Latest Latin multichannel boom: blame it on Rio. stat VARIETY
    358:173+ [2p] Feb 20/26 1995
  Paxman, A. Mexican pay TV growing despite peso devaluation. VARIETY 358:49
    Mar 6/12 1995
  Paxman, A. Televisa holds its own. port stat VARIETY 358:66 Mar 27/Apr 2
    1995
  Paxman, A. VideoVisa springs forward as peso falls back. stat VARIETY
    358:35 Feb 6/12 1995
  Paxman, A. Weak peso slashes Mex market. stills VARIETY 358:44 Feb 6/12
    1995
PAY TELEVISION See also CABLE TELEVISION
    Television (broadcast)
        Australia
  Groves, D. Field pared to pair. VARIETY 358:44 Mar 13/19 1995
  Groves, D. Pay TV web a mixed bag for viewers. VARIETY 358:32 Mar 20/26
    1995
  Groves, D. Trio jostle for position in battle for Oz pay TV. stat VARIETY
    357:50 Jan 9/15 1995
  Woods, M. Pay TV is gradually entering Oz equation. still VARIETY 358:66
    Feb 27/Mar 5 1995
  Woods, M. Philips offshoot PPV gets OK on 20 non-sat licenses. VARIETY
    358:174 Feb 20/26 1995
        Australia. Sports Broadcasting
  Correy, S. Who plays on pay? interv MEDIA INFO AUSTRALIA n75:80-82 Feb
    1995
        Brazil
  Paxman, A. Latest Latin multichannel boom: blame it on Rio. stat VARIETY
    358:173+ [2p] Feb 20/26 1995
        Latin America. Economic Aspects
  Major U.S. investments in Latin American pay TV systems. stat table VARIETY
    358:72 Mar 27/Apr 2 1995
        Mexico
  Paxman, A. Mexican pay TV growing despite peso devaluation. VARIETY 358:49
    Mar 6/12 1995
Pay-per-view See PAY TELEVISION
PAYSAGE IMAGINAIRE v (d Widart, Nicole 1992 Belg)
  Jacquinot, G. Le documentaire, une fiction (pas) comme les autres. bibliog
    stills CINEMAS 4:61-81 n2 1994
PEARSON, BRYAN
  Pearson, B. SABC plan to trim Afrikaans use draws protest. VARIETY 358:48
    Mar 6/12 1995
PEARY, HAROLD
  Bowman, D.K. The great Gildersleeve. il port stills F FAX n49:69-72
    Mar/Apr 1995
PEERS, MARTIN
  Flint, J. and Peers, M. King World for a buyer - or strategic alliance.
    VARIETY 358:23-24 Mar 20/26 1995
  Peers, M. Cablers' merger era hits dusk. VARIETY 358:39+ [2p] Mar 6/12 1995
  Peers, M. Grundy to sell 40% of his firm. VARIETY 358:32 Mar 20/26 1995
  Peers, M. Is Milken mulling moguldom? VARIETY 358:1+ [2p] Mar 13/19 1995
  Peers, M. Multimedia moves on. stat still VARIETY 358:49+ [2p] Feb 27/Mar
    5 1995
  Peers, M. News Corp. 2nd qtr. better than expected. stat VARIETY 358:38
    Feb 13/19 1995
  Peers, M. Pension fund bets on the biz... VARIETY 358:6 Mar 6/12 1995
  Peers, M. Time Warner tactic has Street edgy. graph port stat VARIETY
    358:1+ [3p] Feb 13/19 1995
  Peers, M. Times' timing on cable raises eyebrows. stat VARIETY 357:42 Jan
    9/15 1995
  Peers, M. Turner deal cooking. VARIETY 358:8 Feb 27/Mar 5 1995
  Peers, M. and Flint, J. Multimedia mulling major modifications. stat
    VARIETY 358:25-26+ [3p] Feb 6/12 1995

  Peers, M. and Flint, J. Probe may stall Fox TV affil goal. port VARIETY
    358:23+ [2p] Mar 20/26 1995
  Peers, M. and Flint, J. Run on nation's stations. il VARIETY 358:193+ [2p]
    Feb 20/26 1995
  Peers, M. and Flint, J. Will King World join Turner team? VARIETY 358:9 Mar
    27/Apr 2 1995
  Peers, M. and Wharton, D. FTC approves TCI-Comcast bid for QVC. VARIETY
    358:27 Feb 6/12 1995
PELKA, BARBARA
  Pelka, B. Marzena Trybala. filmog stills FSP 40:12-13 n10 (n764) 1994
PELTIER, MELISSA JOY See also SCARED SILENT: EXPOSING AND ENDING CHILD ABUSE
PEPIN, RICHARD See also CYBER TRACKER
PERCEPTION
    Television (broadcast) and Video (non-broadcast)
        Theory
  Stonehill, B. The debate over "ocularcentrism" [Book Reviews]. J COMM
    45:147-152 n1 1995
        Video (non-broadcast)
  Kremski, P. Film als Schule des Sehens. il interv stills F BUL 36:53-59 n6
    (n197) 1994
PERELLI, LUIGI See also PIOVRA VII, LA
PERIODICALS See also titles of periodicals; PROGRAM GUIDES
    Television (broadcast) and Video (non-broadcast)
        Europe, Western
  Zielinski, S. Mediale Grenzueberschreitungen: Audiovisionen einer
    Zeitschriftenlandschaft. BLIMP n30:66-67 Winter 1994
        Europe, Western. Conferences, Institutes, Workshops, etc.
  Grbic, B. Meine persoenlichen Grenzueberschreitungen. BLIMP n30:68 Winter
    1994
        Video (non-broadcast)
        United States. Interactive
  Samiljan, T. See me, hear me, touch me, read me. il INDEP 18:19-21 Mar
    1995
PERKINS, ANTHONY
  Errata/addenda. STARS n21:[2] Winter 1995
Persian Gulf War, 1991 See IRAQ-KUWAIT CRISIS, 1990-1991
Persistence of vision See PERCEPTION
PERSONS, DAN For film reviews see author under the following titles: ORSON
WELLES' GHOST STORY
PESONEN, SAULI
  Pesonen, S. Kiellettyja iloja? il PEILI 17:42 n4 1993
PETE & PIO v (1994- New Zealand)
  Drinnan, J. Pete & Pio shape up. port stat ONFILM [12]:5 n1 1995
PETERS, HANS PETER
  Peters, H.P. The interaction of journalists and scientific experts:
    co-operation and conflict between two professional cultures. bibliog stat
    tables MEDIA CUL & SOC 17:31-48 n1 1995
PETERS, MICHAEL
  Lentz, H., III. Obituaries. il obits ports CLASSIC n236:57-59 Feb 1995
PETIT, CHRISTOPHE
  Noel, J. Les grandes series americaines des origines a 1970. Par Alain
    Carraze & et Christophe Petit [Book Review]. il GRAND ANGLE n176:40 Nov
    1994
PETRIE, DANIEL, JR.
  Petrie, D., Jr. The long and winding road. port JOURNAL WGA 8:2 Mar 1995
PETRIKIN, CHRIS
  Petrikin, C. and McQuillan, D. Intermedia set to play S.F.'s Moscone Center.
    VARIETY 358:71 Feb 6/12 1995
PETZALL, JILL
  Petzall, J. Want to see more work by independents? still ANGLES 2:6-7 n4
    1995
PEYSER, MARC
  Peyser, M. Making a killing on talk TV: is Jenny to blame for a guest's
    death? ports still NEWSWK 125:30 Mar 20 1995
PFAU, MICHAEL
  Pfau, M. and others. Influence of communication modalities on voters'
    perceptions of candidates during presidential primary campaigns. bibliog
    diag stat tables J COMM 45:122-133 n1 1995
PHANTASM III: LORD OF THE DEAD v (d Coscarelli, Don 1994 USA)
    Reviews
  Fischer, D. "Phantasm: Lord of the Dead." C FANTAS 26:60 n3 1995
PHANTOM OF THE MOVIES' VIDEOSCOPE, THE
  "The Phantom of the Movies' Videoscope" [Book Review]. FATAL VISIONS n17:31
    1994
PHENOMENOLOGY
    Television (broadcast)
        Australia
  Wilson, T. Horizons of meaning. bibliog MEDIA INFO AUSTRALIA n75:130-138
    Feb 1995
PHILIP MORRIS
    Lawsuits
  Robins, J.M. Webs stop singing when smoke gets in their eyes. stat
    VARIETY 358:7 Feb 20/26 1995
PHILIPS NV
  Edmunds, M. Philips calls restructuring a success. stat VARIETY 358:57 Feb
    27/Mar 5 1995
PHYSICALLY HANDICAPPED IN TELEVISION/VIDEO
    Television (broadcast)
        United States. Advertising
  Hershey, L. False advertising. MS 5:96 n5 1995
PICKET FENCES v (1992-96 USA)
    Reviews
  Meyers, R. The crime screen. port stills ARMCHAIR DET 27:207-209 n2 1994
Picture monitors See MONITORS
PIERCE, ELLISE
  Marriott, M. and others. Flight of the digital dish. il NEWSWK 125:61 Jan
    9 1995
PIKKU KAKKONEN v (1989?- Finl)
  Salakka, M. Ransu on lasten ykkonen. il still PEILI 18:4-5 n4 1994

Ruggles [Book Review]. CAN J COM 20:126-128 n1 1995
Prix Jeunesse See FESTIVALS - Television (broadcast) - Germany (Federal
Republic). Munich
Prizes See AWARDS
PROBERT, GREG
Groves, D. Probert heads BVHV/Hong Kong. port VARIETY 358:46 Feb 13/19
1995
PROBST, CHRIS
Probst, C. "Roswell": the truth is elusive. il stills AMCIN 76:58-60+ [7p]
Feb 1995
PROCTER & GAMBLE
Lowry, B. Par TV Group ads up for Procter & Gamble. VARIETY 358:39+ [2p]
Mar 6/12 1995
PRODUCERS See also names of producers
Television (broadcast)
Great Britain
Cottle, S. Producer-driven television? [Book Review]. bibliog MEDIA CUL &
SOC 17:159-166 n1 1995
Producers, independent See INDEPENDENT PRODUCERS
Product licensing See MERCHANDISING TIE-INS
Product placement See MERCHANDISING TIE-INS
PRODUCTION See also AMATEUR PRODUCTION; LOCATION PRODUCTION; POST-PRODUCTION
Television (broadcast) and Video (non-broadcast)
Techniques
Frey, M. Film production [Book Review]. F KUNST n144:67-68 1994
Video (non-broadcast)
Hi-8
Wright, T. The Hi8 mystique. INDEP 18:29 Mar 1995
Super-VHS
Wright, T. The Hi8 mystique. INDEP 18:29 Mar 1995
Germany (Federal Republic, since 1990). Youth. Techniques
Anfang, G. Mit Jugendlichen videofilmen [Book Review]. MEDIEN 38:380-381 n6
1994
United States. Forecasting
Fifield, G. The video service bureaus of the future. INDEP 18:25-27 Apr
1995
Production, location See LOCATION PRODUCTION
PROFESSIONAL EDUCATION See also STUDY AND TEACHING
Television (broadcast)
New Zealand
May, S. Blue Sky breaks through. ONFILM 11:1+ [2p] n11 1994/95
United States. News Broadcasters
Gremillion, J. Star school. il ports COL JOUR REV 33:32-35 Jan/Feb 1995
PROFESSIONNELS DE LA CREATION ET DE LA PRODUCTION AUDIOVISUELLES, LES (PRO
SPERE, Belgium)
Qui s'occupe (encore) de la politique culturelle audiovisuelle en Communaute
francaise? MONITEUR n126:11 Dec 1994
Program clearance See STANDARDS AND RECOMMENDED PRACTICES
PROGRAM DIRECTORS See also names of program directors
Television (broadcast)
United States. Public
Fox, M. In the program director's chair. il ports INDEP 18:30-32 Mar 1995
PROGRAM GUIDES See also titles of program guides
Television (broadcast)
United States
Whitehead, C. Looking for Langstons. still VILLAGE VOICE 40:51-52 Mar 28
1995
PROGRAMMING See also DEBATES; DOCUMENTARY; DRAMA; GAME SHOWS; NEWS PROGRAMMING;
REALITY PROGRAMMING; RERUNS; SOAP OPERAS; SPORTS PROGRAMMING; TALK SHOWS;
TRIAL COVERAGE
Television (broadcast)
China (People's Republic, since 1949)
Zha, J. Killing chickens to show the monkey. il S&S 5:38-40 Jan 1995
Egypt
Warg, P. "Kamera," "Thieves" hold captive aud during Ramadan. VARIETY
358:60 Feb 27/Mar 5 1995
France
Schuman, J. "Columbo" leads the way through French primetime. stat VARIETY
358:46 Feb 6/12 1995
Germany (Federal Republic, since 1990)
Amort, F.M. Programmprofile im dualen Fernsehsystem 1985-1990 [Book Review].
F KUNST n144:69-70 1994
Italy
Rooney, D. As Italo ratings plummet, broadcasters search for life. VARIETY
358:40 Feb 6/12 1995
Rossini, F. TV: non piu di tutto e di piu bensi "di poco e di meno." C SUD
33:55-56 Jul/Aug/Sep (n113) 1994
Poland
Janicka, B. and others. Telewizja rzetelna. il interv KINO 27:20-21+ [3p]
Jul 1993
United States
Whitehead, C. Then came Bronco. il VILLAGE VOICE 40:45 Jan 3 1995
United States. Schedules
Dempsey, J. Disaccord daunts double-run device. VARIETY 358:29+ [2p] Feb
13/19 1995
Programming, films [Prior to V16, 1988 use PROGRAMMING, FILMS] See FILMS SHOWN
ON TELEVISION/VIDEO
PROGRAMMING FOR ADULTS
Television (broadcast)
United States
Robins, J.M. and Lowry, B. Gen X marks the spot. il VARIETY 358:1+ [2p]
Mar 20/26 1995
PROGRAMMING FOR CHILDREN
Television (broadcast)
Conferences, Institutes, Workshops, etc.
Moore, D.S. Taming the tube. il still VARIETY 358:53+ [2p] Mar 6/12 1995
Woods, M. Kids TV summit hammers out but can't nail charter. ports VARIETY
358:31+ [2p] Mar 20/26 1995
Woods, M. and Groves, D. B'casters explore hazards of peddling more vid to
kids. VARIETY 358:54 Mar 6/12 1995

Australia
Groves, D. and Woods, M. Homegrown kidvid thrives in land of Oz. VARIETY
358:59 Mar 6/12 1995
Benelux
Edmunds, M. Dutch Kids' TV expiring. VARIETY 358:60 Mar 6/12 1995
Finland
Naranen, P. Reunamerkintoja Ronnbergin lapsikuvasta. bibliog il PEILI
18:14-15 n2 1994
Savinen, A. Lastenohjelmat muuttumassa viihteellisemmiksi. il stills PEILI
18:10-13 n1 1994
Finland. Effects of Television/Video
Lehtonen, V.-P. Hiljaa, isa lukee lehtea! PEILI 18:2 n4 1994
Finland. Schedules
Hannula, M. "Kauniit ja Rohkeat" vastaan "Pikku Kakkonen." ports PEILI
18:8-9 n1 1994
*Germany (Federal Republic, since 1990). Advertising. Laws and
Legislation*
Tuormaa, J. Mainoskatkot pois lastenohjelmista Saksassa. PEILI 18:7 n3 1994
Germany (Federal Republic, since 1990). Government Support
Molner, D. German pubcasters seek federal cash for kidweb. VARIETY 358:29+
[2p] Mar 27/Apr 2 1995
Germany (Federal Republic, since 1990). Networks and Networking
Molner, D. Kindernets looming on German horizon. VARIETY 358:60 Mar 6/12
1995
Great Britain
Clarke, S. Brit nets elbow for room in kiddie market. VARIETY 358:58 Mar
6/12 1995
Italy
Zecchinelli, C. Italians expand kidvid. still VARIETY 358:60 Mar 6/12 1995
United States
Dempsey, J. Family feature films get a familiar ring. il VARIETY 358:1+
[2p] Mar 27/Apr 2 1995
United States. Government Regulation
Wharton, D. Kidvid education hour urged. VARIETY 358:39 Feb 13/19 1995
United States. Markets
Walsh, T. Gotham goes to kids. stat VARIETY 358:193+ [2p] Feb 20/26 1995
Video (non-broadcast)
Festivals
Kantola, M. Oulun kansainvalinen lastenelokuvafestivaali. still PEILI
17:40-41 n4 1993
Finland. Short Video
Juurikkala, K. Lyhyt johdatus lyhytelokuvan sielunmaisemaan. stills PEILI
17:4-5 n3 1993
Programming, home shopping [Prior to V16, 1988 use PROGRAMMING, HOME SHOPPING]
See HOME SHOPPING PROGRAMMING
Programming, news [Prior to V16, 1988 use PROGRAMMING, NEWS] See NEWS
PROGRAMMING
Programming, religious [Prior to V16, 1988 use PROGRAMMING, RELIGIOUS] See
RELIGIOUS PROGRAMMING
Programming, sports [Prior to V16, 1988 use PROGRAMMING, SPORTS] See SPORTS
PROGRAMMING
PROJECTS
Television (broadcast)
New Zealand
Wakefield, P. Boom year ahead. stat ONFILM [12]:1+ [2p] n1 1995
PROJETO JACAREPAGUA
Paxman, A. Globo relies on Projac for lift. still VARIETY 358:43+ [3p] Mar
27/Apr 2 1995
PROMISED LAND, THE v (d Coulthard, Edmund/Godwin, Nick 1995 USA/Gt Br)
Reviews
Kroll, J. and Cohen, A. When heaven turned to hell. il NEWSWK 125:84 Feb
13 1995
Scott, T. "The Promised Land." credits still VARIETY 358:30 Feb 6/12
1995
Zoglin, R. When Chicago was heaven. il TIME 145:75 Feb 13 1995
Promotional television/video See COMMISSIONED TELEVISION/VIDEO
PROPERTIES, LITERARY
Video (non-broadcast)
United States. Copyright
Evans, G. Random act opens can of bookworms. il VARIETY 358:1+ [3p] Mar
6/12 1995
PROTAZANOV, IAKOV See also AELITA
PRYLINK, IURII
Robinson, G.J. Media in transition: from totalitarianism to democracy.
Edited by Oleg Manaev & Yuri Prylink [Book Review]. CAN J COM 20:122-123 n1
1995
PSYCHOANALYTIC ANALYSIS
Television (broadcast)
France
Dixon, W.W. Lacan, Jacques. Television: a challenge to the psychoanalytic
establishment [Book Review]. UFAJ 46:58-59 n2 1994
United States
Martin, N.K. "Red Shoe Diaries": sexual fantasy and the construction of the
(hetero)sexual woman. bibliog still UFAJ 46:44-57 n2 1994
PSYCHOLOGICAL ANALYSIS
Television (broadcast)
Canada
Therien, G. L'effet paradoxal des images. bibliog CINEMAS 4:57-72 n3 1994
PUBLIC ACCESS TELEVISION
Television (broadcast)
United States
Lopez, C. and Kracher, J. Media activism. interv ANGLES 2:3+ [2p] n4 1995
PUBLIC ATTITUDES See also CENSORSHIP; POPULAR CULTURE
Television (broadcast)
Europe, Western. Climatic Changes
Mormont, M. and Dasnoy, C. Source strategies and the mediatization of
climate change. bibliog MEDIA CUL & SOC 17:49-64 n1 1995
PUBLIC BROADCASTING SERVICE (United States)
Goetz, T. (Fifty-seven) 57 channels (and "Nova's" on). il VILLAGE VOICE
40:42 Feb 21 1995

RAVEN, THE v (d Brabin, Charles J. 1915 USA)
  Reviews
  DeBartolo, J. Video tape reviews. credits port stills CLASSIC n237:12+
    [3p] Mar 1995
RAY, FRED OLEN See also DINOSAUR ISLAND!
REALITY
    Television (broadcast)
        Canada. Documentary
  Jacquinot, G. Le documentaire, une fiction (pas) comme les autres. bibliog
    stills CINEMAS 4:61-81 n2 1994
REALITY PROGRAMMING
    Television (broadcast)
        United States
  Flint, J. A ghost of a chance. ports stills VARIETY 357:51+ [3p] Jan 9/15
    1995
  Flint, J. As time goes by, reality bites. il ports VARIETY 357:54 Jan 9/15
    1995
  Flint, J. Cop trend unabated in new rosters. il port table VARIETY 357:51+
    [2p] Jan 9/15 1995
  Williams, A. Domestic violence and the aetiology of crime in "America's Most
    Wanted." il port stills CAM OBS n31:96-119 Jan/May 1993
        United States. Crime in Television/Video
  Breen, J.L. Gerald, Marc, ed. Murder plus: true crime stories from the
    masters of detective fiction [Book Review]. ARMCHAIR DET 28:78 n1 1995
REBEL HIGHWAY v (1994 USA)
  Barajas, V. "Rebel Highway." il stills SCARLET STREET n17:32+ [3p] Winter
    1995
REBELLO, STEPHEN
  Rebello, S. Fans of bad Susan Hayward films will thank the fools behind "I
    Thank a Fool." il MOVIELINE 6:80 Apr 1995
  Rebello, S. The crown princess of young Hollywood. ports MOVIELINE
    6:48-52+ [7p] Mar 1995
RECEIVERS See also MONITORS
    Television (broadcast) and Video (non-broadcast)
        United States. Maintenance
  How to get your TV or VCR repaired. il CONS RES MAG 77:26-29 May 1994
        United States. Product Guides
  Receivers. graph il stat tables CONS REP 60:188-191 Mar 1995
    Television (broadcast)
        United States. Product Guides
  Television sets. graphs il stat tables CONS REP 60:168-174 Mar 1995
RED SHOE DIARIES v (d King, Zalman 1992- USA/Fr)
    Psychoanalysis
  Martin, N.K. "Red Shoe Diaries": sexual fantasy and the construction of the
    (hetero)sexual woman. bibliog still UFAJ 46:44-57 n2 1994
REDE GLOBO
  Paxman, A. Globo relies on Projac for lift. still VARIETY 358:43+ [3p] Mar
    27/Apr 2 1995
REDOTTEE, HARTMUT W.
  Kremski, P. Film als Schule des Sehens. il interv stills F BUL 36:53-59 n6
    (n197) 1994
REED, PEYTON See also COMPUTER WORE TENNIS SHOES, THE
REFERENCE BOOKS
    Video (non-broadcast)
        United States
  Webster, E. International Filmarchive CD-ROM. VARIETY 358:70 Feb 6/12 1995
REGIONAL TELEVISION
    Television (broadcast)
        New Zealand
  Drinnan, J. Only scraps for indies as local TV era dawns. port stat ONFILM
    [12]:7 n1 1995
Regulation [Prior to V16, 1988 use REGULATION] See GOVERNMENT REGULATION
REIBSTEIN, LARRY
  Reibstein, L. and others. Live, from Nielsen heaven. il NEWSWK 125:49 Jan
    30 1995
REID-PHARR, ROBERT
  Reid-Pharr, R. Mix-defying. il stills AFTERIMAGE 22:3-4 Jan 1995
REISMAN, DAVID
  Reisman, D. Delphine Seyrig 1932-1990. biog obit port MILLENNIUM n25:76
    Summer 1991
REISNER, CHARLES F. See also STEAMBOAT BILL, JR.
RELIGION
    Television (broadcast)
        United States
  Dionne, E.J., Jr. Washington. bibliog il ports COMMONWEAL 122:26-39 Feb 24
    1995
  Maniscalco, F.J. Postscript. il COMMONWEAL 122:49-52 Feb 24 1995
  New York. il ports COMMONWEAL 122:40-48 Feb 24 1995
  Steinfels, P. Chicago. il ports COMMONWEAL 122:14-25 Feb 24 1995
  Televangelism reconsidered: ritual in the search for human community. By
    Bobby Alexander [Book Review] CHR CENT 112:66 Jan 18 1995
RELIGIOUS ASPECTS
    Television (broadcast)
        Egypt. Influence on Television/Video
  Warg, P. Islamic clergyman blasts TV fare aired during Ramadan. VARIETY
    358:45 Feb 13/19 1995
RELIGIOUS PROGRAMMING [Prior to V16, 1988 use PROGRAMMING, RELIGIOUS] See also
  EVANGELISTS
    Television (broadcast)
        Egypt
  Warg, P. Right-wingers on media's case. VARIETY 358:34 Feb 6/12 1995
REMNICK, DAVID
  Remnick, D. The tycoon and the Kremlin. il NEW YORKER 71:118-120+ [15p]
    Feb 20/27 1995
REN & STIMPY SHOW, THE v (1991- USA)
  Gribbish, I. "The Danes don't call it quality anymore." il FATAL VISIONS
    n17:24 1994
REPUBLICAN NATIONAL CONVENTION v (1996 USA)
  Wharton, D. Senate panel votes to back Big Bird. VARIETY 358:36 Mar 27/Apr
    2 1995

RERUNS
    Television (broadcast)
        United States. Cable
  Dempsey, J. Cable embraces off-net hours. il VARIETY 358:197 Feb 20/26
    1995
        United States. Cable. Effects on Television/Video
  Dempsey, J. Cable gives wings to net longruns. stat table VARIETY
    358:29-30 Mar 13/19 1995
RESEARCH See also AUDIENCE RESEARCH; GRANTS
    Television (broadcast)
        Talk Shows. Audience
  Tolson, A. Sonia Livingstone and Peter Lunt, Talk on television: audience
    participation and public debate [Book Review]. bibliog MEDIA CUL & SOC
    17:172-174 n1 1995
        Australia
  Bell, P. Jakubowicz, Andrew, Goodall, Heather, Martin, Jeannie, Mitchell,
    Tony, Randall, Lois and Seneviratne, Kalinga. Racism, ethnicity and the
    media [Book Review]. MEDIA INFO AUSTRALIA n75:165-166 Feb 1995
        Australia. Grants
  Telecom Australia fund. MEDIA INFO AUSTRALIA n75:151-153 Feb 1995
RESIDUALS AND FEES
    Television (broadcast)
        United States
  Nickens, D.G. Back to basics. port JOURNAL WGA 8:2 Dec/Jan 1995
        United States. Networks and Networking
  Lowry, B. Webs wheeze over license fees. graph il stat VARIETY 358:1+ [2p]
    Feb 20/26 1995
RESTORATION [Prior to V18, 1990 use PRESERVATION] See also PRESERVATION
    Television (broadcast) and Video (non-broadcast)
        Australia
  Research in progress. bibliog MEDIA INFO AUSTRALIA n75:173-182 Feb 1995
RETIREMENT
    Television (broadcast) and Video (non-broadcast)
        United States
  Post, T. Age doesn't matter, unless you're cheese. port DGA NEWS 19:68 n6
    1994/95
Return of Sherlock Holmes, The See SECOND STAIN, THE
REUTERS HOLDINGS PLC
  Clarke, S. Reuters teams with Sky News. VARIETY 358:34 Feb 6/12 1995
REVAH, SUZAN
  Revah, S. It's a jungle out there in cyberspace. il port AM JOUR REV
    17:10-11 n2 1995
Reviews See titles of television/video programs
REYNOLDS, BRIAN
  Sokolsky, M. Letters: "NYPD" clarification. AMCIN 76:10 Feb 1995
REYNOLDS, GENE
  Reynolds, G. Credits where they're due. port DGA NEWS 19:5 n6 1994/95
  Reynolds, G. Directors, writers need cooperation not competition. port DGA
    NEWS 19:3 n3 1994
REYNOLDS, PAUL
  Reynolds, P. The fast lane to the future. il ONFILM [12]:13 n1 1995
REYNOLDS, WILLIAM
  Gallagher, B. It's a print!: detective fiction from page to screen. Edited
    by William Reynolds and Elizabeth A. Trembley [Book Review]. MICHIGAN
    ACADEMICIAN 27:229-231 n2 1995
RHEA, MARJI
  Rhea, M. The rise of stock footage companies. AMCIN 76:14+ [3p] Jan 1995
RHODES, STEVE
  Marriott, M. and others. Flight of the digital dish. il NEWSWK 125:61 Jan
    9 1995
RIAZANOV, EL'DAR
  Birchenough, T. Director to head anti-piracy org. VARIETY 358:59 Feb 27/Mar
    5 1995
RICH, ALAN For film reviews see author under the following titles: DISCOVERING
  WOMEN
RICHARDS, MICHAEL
  Slonim, J. To the angst antenna, Jerry Seinfeld. still INTERV 25:28 Apr
    1995
RICHARDSON, DON
  Richardson, D. Communication, culture and hegemony: from the media to
    mediations. By Jesus Martin-Barbero [Book Review]. CAN J COM 19:562-563
    n3/4 1994
RICKI LAKE SHOW, THE v (1993- USA)
  Zoglin, R. Talking trash. il ports still TIME 145:76-78 Jan 30 1995
RIEFENSTAHL, LENI See also BLAUE LICHT, DAS
RIFF-RAFF v (d Loach, Kenneth 1991 Gt Br)
  Guard, C. Rough humour. still S&S 5:69 Jan 1995
RIGA, JEAN-CLAUDE See also ERIC OU L'OISEAU BLEU
RIGET v (Kingdom, The d Trier, Lars von 1994 Denmk/Swed/FR Ger/Fr)
    Export Market
  Molner, D. October buys rights to Danish "Kingdom." VARIETY 358:27 Mar
    13/19 1995
RISKANTE SPIELE ZWISCHEN LEBEN UND TOD v (d Papirowski, Martin 1992 FR Ger)
    Reviews
  Koehler, M. "Riskante Spiele zwischen Leben und Tod." MEDIEN 38:364 n6 1994
RIVERS, JOAN
  "She's funny! She's real!" NEW YORKER 70:33-35 Jan 30 1995
RIXMAN, JOE
  Rixman, J. John Debney. il interv F SCORE MONTHLY n38:8-9 Oct 1993
ROBERTS, COKIE
  Dionne, E.J., Jr. Washington. bibliog il ports COMMONWEAL 122:26-39 Feb 24
    1995
ROBERTS, GARYN G.
  Hoppenstand, G. Dick Tracy and American culture: morality and mythology,
    text and context. By Garyn G. Roberts [Book Review]. ARMCHAIR DET
    27:236-237 n2 1994
ROBERTS, JOHNNIE L.
  Roberts, J.L. Are they jackin' The Box? ports stills NEWSWK 125:42-43 Jan
    23 1995
  Roberts, J.L. Betting the house on cable. graph ports NEWSWK 125:40 Feb 6

1995

Roberts, J.L. Changing channels. il port stills NEWSWK 125:40-41 Mar 6 1995

Roberts, J.L. Chips off the Block. graphs ports still NEWSWK 125:42-43 Feb 20 1995

Roberts, J.L. Goliath goes Hollywood. il ports NEWSWK 125:44-46 Mar 27 1995

Roberts, J.L. NBC and Turner: here they go again. port NEWSWK 125:49 Feb 13 1995

Roberts, J.L. Time-Warner: the peddling of Turner. port NEWSWK 125:46 Feb 20 1995

ROBERTSON, MICHAEL

Urban, A.L. Michael Robertson's "Back of Beyond." il stills C PAPERS n102:12-18 Dec 1994

ROBERTSON, PAT

Gay activist arrested for trespassing at CBN. CHR CENT 112:263 Mar 8 1995

Purvis, A. Jewels for Jesus. il port TIME 145:30 Feb 27 1995

ROBINS, J. MAX

Robins, J.M. CBS entices telcos. il VARIETY 358:1+ [2p] Feb 13/19 1995

Robins, J.M. Have-nots crave slots. VARIETY 357:1+ [2p] Jan 2/8 1995

Robins, J.M. Net newscasts diverge in quest for viewers. il VARIETY 358:29+ [2p] Feb 13/19 1995

Robins, J.M. Shows litter limbo land. il VARIETY 358:39-40 Mar 6/12 1995

Robins, J.M. Star-struck webs wow admen. VARIETY 358:1+ [2p] Mar 27/Apr 2 1995

Robins, J.M. TV's new hue: true "Blue." il VARIETY 358:1+ [2p] Mar 13/19 1995

Robins, J.M. Webs stop singing when smoke gets in their eyes. stat VARIETY 358:7 Feb 20/26 1995

Robins, J.M. and Lowry, B. CBS waters choppy for Lund. ports VARIETY 358:49+ [2p] Feb 27/Mar 5 1995

Robins, J.M. and Lowry, B. Gen X marks the spot. il VARIETY 358:1+ [2p] Mar 20/26 1995

Robins, J.M. and Wharton, D. Riled by regs, TV biz begs to be Newtered. il VARIETY 357:1+ [2p] Jan 9/15 1995

ROBINSON, GERTRUDE J.

Robinson, G.J. Media in transition: from totalitarianism to democracy. Edited by Oleg Manaev & Yuri Prylink [Book Review]. CAN J COM 20:122-123 n1 1995

ROBINSON, GWEN

Robinson, G. Leave the driving to U.S. il VARIETY 358:32-33 Feb 6/12 1995

Robinson, G. NBC axes "Gaijin." stat VARIETY 358:4 Mar 13/19 1995

Robinson, G. and Cox, D. Power shift at Sony Corp. port VARIETY 358:15+ [2p] Mar 27/Apr 2 1995

ROBINSON, LILLIAN S.

Robinson, L.S. Will you love me tomorrow? [Book Review]. NATION 260:138-141 Jan 30 1995

Rock video See MUSIC VIDEO

RODDENBERRY, GENE

Uram, S. Roddenberry's legacy. il stills C FANTAS 26:34-39 n2 1995

ROGERS, ADAM

Rogers, A. Through a glass, darkly. il NEWSWK 125:52 Jan 23 1995

ROGERS, PATRICK

Reibstein, L. and others. Live, from Nielsen heaven. il NEWSWK 125:49 Jan 30 1995

ROGERS, R.

Roser, C. and Thompson, M. Fear appeals and the formation of active publics. bibliog diag stat tables J COMM 45:103-121 n1 1995

ROLAND, FRITZ

Roland, F. Embracing the concept of color correction. AMCIN 76:22+ [3p] Jan 1995

ROMANEK, MARK See also BEDTIME STORY

ROMNEY, JONATHAN For film reviews see author under the following titles: JIMMY HOLLYWOOD

RONNBERG, MARGARETA

Naranen, P. Reunamerkintoja Ronnbergin lapsikuvasta. bibliog il PEILI 18:14-15 n2 1994

RONY, FATIMAH TOBING

Rony, F.T. Victor Masayesva, Jr., and the politics of "Imagining Indians." il stills FQ 48:20-33 n2 1994/95

ROONEY, DAVID

Rooney, D. As Italo ratings plummet, broadcasters search for life. VARIETY 358:40 Feb 6/12 1995

Rooney, D. Back to business for Berlusconi? stat VARIETY 357:56+ [2p] Jan 2/8 1995

Rooney, D. Marcello Palmisano. obit VARIETY 358:188 Feb 20/26 1995

Rooney, D. Most recent TV upstart sputters. VARIETY 357:49 Jan 9/15 1995

Rooney, D. "Octopus" grabs Italo headlines. VARIETY 358:46 Mar 13/19 1995

ROSE, MANDY

Rose, M. "Video Nation." il VERTIGO (UK) 1:9-10 n4 1994/95

ROSENSTIEL, TOM

Rosenstiel, T. Not necessarily the news. il ports ESQUIRE 123:76-83 Jan 1995

Rosenstiel, T. Yakety-yak. il ports COL JOUR REV 33:23-27 Jan/Feb 1995

ROSER, CONNIE

Roser, C. and Thompson, M. Fear appeals and the formation of active publics. bibliog diag stat tables J COMM 45:103-121 n1 1995

Ross, Edward See BRAZZI, ROSSANO

ROSSIISKAIA GOSUDARSTVENNAIA TELERADIOKOMPANIIA "OSTANKINO" (Russia)

Birchenough, T. Ostankino takes a leap forward with tapping of new CEO. stat VARIETY 358:176 Feb 20/26 1995

Commercials

Birchenough, T. State TV's ad ban worries other webs. stat VARIETY 358:59 Feb 27/Mar 5 1995

ROSSINI, FRANCA

Rossini, F. TV: non piu di tutto e di piu bensi "di poco e di meno." C SUD 33:55-56 Jul/Aug/Sep (n113) 1994

ROSWELL v (d Kagan, Jeremy 1994 USA)

Cinematography

Probst, C. "Roswell": the truth is elusive. il stills AMCIN 76:58-60+ [7p]

Feb 1995

ROUSSEAU, YVES

Rousseau, Y. Contre la culture du consensus. stills 24 IMAGES n75:12-13 Dec/Jan 1994/95

Rousseau, Y. Musique pub. still 24 IMAGES n76:22-23 Spring 1995

ROWE, DAVID

Rowe, D. Larson, James F. and Park, Heung-Soo. Global television and the politics of the Seoul Olympics [Book Review]. MEDIA INFO AUSTRALIA n75:84-85 Feb 1995

Rowe, D. Wall-to-wall world of sport. MEDIA INFO AUSTRALIA n75:3-4 Feb 1995

Rowe, D. and Stevenson, D. Negotiations & mediations. bibliog MEDIA INFO AUSTRALIA n75:67-79 Feb 1995

RUBIN, SAM

Rubin, S. Sam Rubin's classic clinic: the Hollywood West has changed, but it ain't real! il CLASSIC n237:47-48 Mar 1995

RUGGLES, MYLES ALEXANDER

Pritchard, D. The audience reflected in the medium of law: a critique of the political economy of speech rights in the United States. By Myles Alexander Ruggles [Book Review]. CAN J COM 20:126-128 n1 1995

RUOHO, IIRIS

Ruoho, I. Kuningatarmehilaisen tyttaret. bibliog stills PEILI 18:6-8 n2 1994

RUSH LIMBAUGH v (1992- USA)

Barnhart, A. After hours. il VILLAGE VOICE 40:47 Feb 7 1995

RUSHKOFF, DOUGLAS

Braman, S. Cyberia: life in the trenches of hyperspace. By Douglas Rushkoff [Book Review]. J COMM 45:177-178 n1 1995

Rushkoff, D. Host hogs. ports table ESQUIRE 123:32 Feb 1995

RUSHTON, RACHEL

Rushton, R. Get it write. ONFILM [12]:15 n2 1995

RUSSELL, NICK

Cunningham, S.B. Morals and the media: ethics in Canadian journalism. By Nick Russell [Book Review]. CAN J COM 20:128-129 n1 1995

RUSSERT, TIM

Dionne, E.J., Jr. Washington. bibliog il ports COMMONWEAL 122:26-39 Feb 24 1995

Russia (since 1992) See as a subheading under individual subject headings See ROSSIISKAIA GOSUDARSTVENNAIA TELERADIOKOMPANIIA "OSTANKINO" (Russia)

RUSSO, CHRISTINE J.

Russo, C.J. Images in the dark: an encyclopedia of gay and lesbian film and video. Compiled by Raymond Murray [Book Review]. il AFTERIMAGE 22:16 Jan 1995

RUTHERFORD, PAUL

Seaton, B. The codes of advertising: fetishism and the political economy of meaning in the consumer society. By Sut Jhally [Book Reviews]. CAN J COM 20:116-120 n1 1995

Rwanda See as a subheading under individual subject headings

RYSHER ENTERTAINMENT

Benson, J. Hours lose power in syndie market. port stat VARIETY 357:39+ [2p] Jan 9/15 1995

Brodie, J. Rysher sets to make splash into pic pool. stat VARIETY 358:13+ [2p] Mar 6/12 1995

SBS

Edmunds, M. SBS firing up its cable web. VARIETY 358:34 Mar 20/26 1995

SBS Television See SPECIAL BROADCASTING SERVICE

SF BROADCASTING

Peers, M. and Flint, J. Probe may stall Fox TV affil goal. port VARIETY 358:23+ [2p] Mar 20/26 1995

STAR-TV

Groves, D. Star TV to launch 30 more channels. il VARIETY 357:56 Jan 2/8 1995

Halligan, F. and Guider, E. Murdoch's STAR TV on rise. VARIETY 358:44 Feb 13/19 1995

SAAB, JOCELYNE

Thoraval, Y. Jocelyne Saab's Beirut. stills CINEMAYA n25/26:14-16 Autumn/Winter 1994/95

SAID ABDALLAH, AMED, ET LES AUTRES v (d Lentini, Giovani 1982 Belg)

Jacquinot, G. Le documentaire, une fiction (pas) comme les autres. bibliog stills CINEMAS 4:61-81 n2 1994

SA-I-GU v (d Kim-Gibson, Dai Sil/Choy, Christine 1993 USA)

Reviews

Park, S. "Sa-I-gu." AMERASIA J 19:161-163 n2 1993

SAIJA, PAULIINA

Saija, P. Adolf Born on kuuluisimpia animaation tekijoita Tsekinmaassa. port still PEILI 18:17-18 n3 1994

Saija, P. Tsekkilasten nukkumatti on pyoreapainen pikkupoika. il PEILI 18:16-17 n3 1994

(SAINT) ST. PETERSBURG'S CHANNEL 5

Birchenough, T. It's Veltsin Democrats vs. hard-liners for Ch. 5. VARIETY 357:49 Jan 9/15 1995

SAINT, THE v (d Harlin, Renny project 1991- USA)

Breen, J.L. Barer, Burl. The Saint: a complete history in print, radio, film and television of Leslie Charteris' Robin Hood of crime, Simon Templar, 1928-1992 [Book Review]. ARMCHAIR DET 27:222-223 n2 1994

SALAKKA, MATTI

Salakka, M. Gladiaattorit. stills PEILI 18:26-28 n2 1994

Salakka, M. Onko Muranen Rambon inkarnaatio? PEILI 18:26 n4 1994

Salakka, M. Playmate on pehmea ja turvallinen. il still PEILI 18:8-9 n4 1994

Salakka, M. Ransu on lasten ykkonen. il still PEILI 18:4-5 n4 1994

Salakka, M. Roskavideot pursuavat zombiehahmoja ja kotipornoa. il PEILI 18:26 n3 1994

Salakka, M. "Tama tyo on ollut tahanastisista raskain." il PEILI 17:12-13 n3 1993

Salakka, M. Televisio lasten elamassa [Book Review]. PEILI 17:45 n4 1993

SALLI, OLLI-PEKKA

Salli, O.-P. Festivaalivieraan paivakirjasta. il PEILI 17:25-26 n3 1993

SALMIJARVI, JYRKI

Salmijarvi, J. Namusetien nayteikkunat. bibliog port PEILI 18:16-17 n2 1994

SALMINEN, KARI
   Salminen, K. "Beavis ja Butt-head" vastaan Amerikka. bibliog il PEILI
      18:10-13 n2 1994
   Salminen, K. Vallaton video, raiskatut sielut. bibliog il PEILI 18:14-15
      n1 1994
Salo, 120 Days of Sodom See SALO O LE CENTOVENTI GIORNATE DI SODOMA
SALO O LE CENTOVENTI GIORNATE DI SODOMA v (Salo, 120 Days of Sodom d Pasolini,
Pier Paolo 1975 It/Fr)
      Censorship
   Kaufman, B.L. Cincinnati's morality squad targets Pasolini. il INDEP
      18:9-11 Jan/Feb 1995
SALVETTI, STEFANO
   Salvetti, S. I colori delle note. stills SEGNO n72:76 Mar/Apr 1995
SALVI, DEMETRIO
   Salvi, D. Un bel sacco di Verdone. il C FORUM 34:86 Oct (n338) 1994
SAMFILM
   Edmunds, M. Leading the pack. il still VARIETY 358:37 Mar 20/26 1995
      Cable Television
   Edmunds, M. Company answers its call to the small screen. VARIETY 358:44
      Mar 20/26 1995
      Distribution
   Edmunds, M. Vid slice lands firm in first place. graphs stat stills
      VARIETY 358:46 Mar 20/26 1995
      History
   Sam Film chronology. VARIETY 358:38 Mar 20/26 1995
SAMILJAN, TOM
   Samiljan, T. See me, hear me, touch me, read me. il INDEP 18:19-21 Mar
      1995
SAMPLES, KEITH
   Brodie, J. Rysher sets to make splash into pic pool. stat VARIETY 358:13+
      [2p] Mar 6/12 1995
SAMUELSON, MARC
   Dawtrey, A. Gilbert, Samuelsons ink Miramax pic pact. il ports VARIETY
      358:14+ [2p] Mar 20/26 1995
SAMUELSON, PETER
   Dawtrey, A. Gilbert, Samuelsons ink Miramax pic pact. il ports VARIETY
      358:14+ [2p] Mar 20/26 1995
SAMUELSSON, ARNI
   Edmunds, M. Leading the pack. il still VARIETY 358:37 Mar 20/26 1995
SANDKINGS v (1995 USA)
   Winikoff, K. "Outer Limits." stills C FANTAS 26:6-7+ [3p] n3 1995
      Reviews
   Marin, R. Tripping in the fantasy zone. stills NEWSWK 125:70 Mar 13 1995
SANDLER, ADAM For film reviews see author under the following titles: HOUSE OF
BUGGIN'; MEDICINE BALL; SLIDERS
   Sandler, A. David Cole. obit VARIETY 358:58 Mar 20/26 1995
   Sandler, A. "Lion" vid wows with huge sales numbers. VARIETY 358:26 Mar
      13/19 1995
   Sandler, A. MPAA reports banner year for nabbing pirates. stat VARIETY
      358:24 Feb 13/19 1995
   Sandler, A. Warner confirms new Media arm. port VARIETY 358:67 Mar 13/19
      1995
SANDLER, KATHE See also QUESTION OF COLOR, A
[SANDMANN] v (1959-77? E Ger)
   Hannula, R. "Nukkumatin" kolme vuosikymmenta." stills PEILI 17:8-9 n4 1993
SANGER, JONATHAN See also WHERE THE ELEPHANT SITS
SANJEK, DAVID
   Sanjek, D. Home alone: the phenomenon of direct-to-video. stills CINEASTE
      21:98-100 n1/2 1995
SANTA CRUZ, ABEL
   Di Nubila, D. Abel Santa Cruz. obit VARIETY 358:54 Feb 13/19 1995
SANTOS, ADELE See also INVISIBLE CITY, THE
SARGENT, JOSEPH See also MY ANTONIA; WORLD WAR II: WHEN LIONS ROARED
   Elrick, T. Sargent reenlists for "World War II." il interv DGA NEWS 19:8-9
      n2 1994
SATELLITE COMMUNICATIONS EQUIPMENT [Prior to V16, 1988 use EQUIPMENT,
SATELLITE COMMUNICATIONS]
      Television (broadcast)
         Digital. RCA Digital Satellite System
   Marriott, M. and others. Flight of the digital dish. il NEWSWK 125:61 Jan
      9 1995
         Iran. Laws and Legislation
   Warg, P. Iran's ban on dishes doesn't wash with public. VARIETY 358:34 Feb
      6/12 1995
         United States
   Testing the new small-dish satellite systems. il CONS REP 60:161 Mar 1995
SATELLITE TELEVISION
      Television (broadcast)
         Asia. Government Regulation
   Thomas, A.O. Asean television & pan-Asian broadcast satellites. bibliog
      MEDIA INFO AUSTRALIA n75:123-129 Feb 1995
         Germany (Federal Republic, since 1990). Pornography and Obscenity
   Tuormaa, J. Euroseksin taivas. PEILI 18:11 n4 1994
Saturday Night Live See NBC'S SATURDAY NIGHT LIVE
SAVAGE PLAY v (d Lindsay, Alan in production 1995- Gt Br/New Zealand)
   Jenkins, S. Rugby & romance a winning team. il ONFILM 11:7 n11 1994/95
SAVALAS, TELLY
   Telly Savalas. biog filmog il stills STARS n21:[35-38] Winter 1995
SAVAN, LESLIE
   Savan, L. Assault and batteries. still VILLAGE VOICE 40:47 Mar 14 1995
   Savan, L. I want to sell you. still VILLAGE VOICE 40:45 Feb 21 1995
SAVATER, FERNANDO
   Savater, F. Escalofriantemente suyo, Christopher Lee. ports stills
      NOSFERATU n6:66-69 Apr 1991
SAVINEN, ARI
   Savinen, A. Lastenohjelmat muuttumassa viihteellisemmiksi. il stills PEILI
      18:10-13 n1 1994
SAWYER, DIANE
   Rosenstiel, T. Not necessarily the news. il ports ESQUIRE 123:76-83 Jan
      1995

SCACE, NORMAN
   Lentz, H., III. Obituaries. il obits ports CLASSIC n236:57-59 Feb 1995
SCANNELL, PADDY
   Scannell, P. Media events [Book Review]. bibliog MEDIA CUL & SOC
      17:151-157 n1 1995
SCANNER COP v (d David, Pierre 1994 USA)
      Reviews
   Davidson, S. "Scanner Cop." FATAL VISIONS n17:25 1994
SCARED SILENT: EXPOSING AND ENDING CHILD ABUSE v (d Peltier, Melissa Joy 1992
USA)
   Champagne, R. Oprah Winfrey's "Scared Silent" and the spectatorship of
      incest. bibliog DISCOURSE n17.2:123-138 Winter 1994/95
SCHLAMME, THOMAS See also KINGFISH: A STORY OF HUEY P. LONG
SCHONE, MARK
   Schone, M. Black hour at black rock. VILLAGE VOICE 40:51-52 Mar 28 1995
SCHROBSDORFF, INGALISA
   Shapiro, M. and Schrobsdorff, I. It's showtime! stills INDEP 18:7+ [3p]
      Apr 1995
SCHRUERS, FRED
   Schruers, F. Man of the year. il ROLLING STONE n698/699:30-34+ [7p] Dec
      29/Jan 12 1994/95
SCHUETZ, JOHANNES
   Schuetz, J. Zuschauen kann ich nicht. F KUNST n144:35-42 1994
SCHUMAN, JOSEPH
   Schuman, J. "Columbo" leads the way through French primetime. stat VARIETY
      358:46 Feb 6/12 1995
   Schuman, J. Projects down the pike. VARIETY 358:41 Mar 13/19 1995
   Schuman, J. Speeding to l'infopike. VARIETY 358:39+ [2p] Mar 13/19 1995
   Stern, A. and Schuman, J. French fried in quota quibble. il VARIETY
      358:173-174 Feb 20/26 1995
SCHWARTZ, SHERWOOD
   Bellafante, G. The inventor of bad TV. ports TIME 145:111 Mar 13 1995
SCHWARZENEGGER, ARNOLD
   Arnold Schwarzenegger. biog filmog il stills STARS n21:[39-40] Winter 1995
SCHWOCH, JAMES
   Schwoch, J. Manaus: television from the borderless. PUBLIC CULT 7:455-464
      n2 1995
SCIENCE
      Television (broadcast)
         Germany (Federal Republic, since 1990)
   Peters, H.P. The interaction of journalists and scientific experts:
      co-operation and conflict between two professional cultures. bibliog stat
      tables MEDIA CUL & SOC 17:31-48 n1 1995
         United States. News Coverage. Effects of Television/Video. Audience
      Research
   Priest, S.H. Information equity, public understanding of science, and the
      biotechnology debate. bibliog diag stat table J COMM 45:39-54 n1 1995
SCORSESE, MARTIN See also RAGING BULL
   Wharton, D. Scorsese plugs for artists' rights on Hill. port VARIETY
      358:20 Mar 20/26 1995
SCOTT, RIDLEY
   Elrick, T. Scott Brothers' work showcased for UK/LA. il DGA NEWS 19:26 n6
      1994/95
SCOTT, TONY (AUTHOR) For film reviews see author under the following titles:
   AMAZING GRACE; CADFAEL; FALLING FOR YOU; GEORGE WENDT SHOW, THE; GREAT
   DEFENDER, THE; HOW THE WEST WAS LOST; MARTIN CHUZZLEWIT; OLD CURIOSITY
   SHOP, THE; OUTER LIMITS, THE; PROMISED LAND, THE; SOLOMON & SHEBA; TAD;
   TEXAS JUSTICE; WOMAN OF INDEPENDENT MEANS, A
   Scott, T. "Kingfish: a Story of Huey P. Long." credits still VARIETY
      358:37 Mar 13/19 1995
SCREEN ACTORS GUILD (United States)
   Cox, D. SAG, producers settle in a cliffhanger deal. VARIETY 358:16 Mar
      27/Apr 2 1995
      Contracts
   Seigel, R.L. Wanted: Guild actors at a discount. il INDEP 18:38-41 Jan/Feb
      1995
SCREEN (periodical)
      Indexes
   Cumulative index: "Screen" 1982-1989 (volumes 23-30). SCREEN 35:419-433 n4
      1994
   Index of books reviewed, volume 35. SCREEN 35:434 n4 1994
   Index of books reviewed, volumes 23-30. SCREEN 35:435-436 n4 1994
   Index to volume 35. SCREEN 35:417-418 n4 1994
Screen Writers Guild See WRITERS GUILD OF AMERICA
Screenplays See TELEPLAYS
Screenwriters See WRITERS
Screenwriting See WRITING
SEAMAN, BARRETT
   Seaman, B. The future is already here. il TIME 145:30-33 Spring 1995
SEATON, BETH
   Seaton, B. The codes of advertising: fetishism and the political economy of
      meaning in the consumer society. By Sut Jhally [Book Reviews]. CAN J COM
      20:116-120 n1 1995
SECOND STAIN, THE v (d Bruce, John 1986 Gt Br)
   Valley, R. Better Holmes and Watson: the Granada series reviewed. il stills
      SCARLET STREET n17:62-63 Winter 1995
SEGNOCINEMA
      Indexes
   Zanolin, D. Indici di "Segnocinema" 1994 (nn. 65-70). SEGNO n72:bet p40 and
      41 [8p] Mar/Apr 1995
SEIGEL, ROBERT L.
   Seigel, R.L. At last: an alternative to limited partnerships. il INDEP
      18:10-11 Mar 1995
   Seigel, R.L. Wanted: Guild actors at a discount. il INDEP 18:38-41 Jan/Feb
      1995
SEINFELD v (1989- USA)
      Influence on Television/Video
   Zoglin, R. Friends and layabouts. stills TIME 145:74 Mar 20 1995
      Syndication
   Benson, J. and Walsh, T. "Home" enters original syndie to duel "Seinfeld."

Great Britain
Blain, N. Garry Whannel. Fields in vision [Book Review]. MEDIA CUL & SOC
17:169-172 n1 1995
United States
Walsh, T. TV exex say baseball scabs don't rate. stat VARIETY 358:39 Feb
13/19 1995
United States. Ratings
Walsh, T. Fox, NBC declare NFL wins. stat VARIETY 357:41 Jan 2/8 1995
United States. Strikes
Walsh, T. Replacement baseball drives stations batty. VARIETY 358:25 Mar
20/26 1995
SPORTS IN TELEVISION/VIDEO
Television (broadcast)
Australia
Rowe, D. and Stevenson, D. Negotiations & mediations. bibliog MEDIA INFO
AUSTRALIA n75:67-79 Feb 1995
SPORTS PROGRAMMING [Prior to V16, 1988 use PROGRAMMING, SPORTS]
Television (broadcast)
Australia. Women in Television/Video
Cook, J. and Jennings, K. "Live and Sweaty." bibliog MEDIA INFO AUSTRALIA
n75:5-12 Feb 1995
SPUMCO
Gribbish, I. "The Danes don't call it quality anymore." il FATAL VISIONS
n17:24 1994
STALTER, KATHARINE
Stalter, K. Infopike leads right to Milia. il port VARIETY 357:57+ [2p]
Jan 9/15 1995
Stalter, K. It's all in the cards. il VARIETY 358:69+ [2p] Feb 6/12 1995
STANDARDS AND RECOMMENDED PRACTICES [Prior to V15, 1987 use BROADCASTING
STANDARDS AND PRACTICES]
Television (broadcast)
United States
Hughes, R. Why watch it, anyway? il NY R BKS 42:37-42 Feb 16 1995
United States. Advertising
Robins, J.M. TV's new hue: true "Blue." il VARIETY 358:1+ [2p] Mar 13/19
1995
United States. High-definition Television/Video
A new beginning. CONS RES MAG 76:6 Jul 1993
United States. Talk Shows
Dempsey, J. "Jenny" incident raises specter of control. VARIETY 358:36 Mar
13/19 1995
Video (non-broadcast)
Videodiscs. Digital
Robinson, G. Leave the driving to U.S. il VARIETY 358:32-33 Feb 6/12 1995
United States. Videodiscs. Digital
Weiner, R. Sony stands firm on its digital disc format. VARIETY 358:26 Feb
27/Mar 5 1995
STANLEY, JOHN
Slide, A. The Slide area film book notes [Book Reviews]. CLASSIC
n237:42-44+ [4p] Mar 1995
STAR TREK v (1966-69 USA)
Uram, S. Roddenberry's legacy. il stills C FANTAS 26:34-39 n2 1995
STAR TREK: THE NEXT GENERATION v (1987-94 USA)
Beeler, M. Feature vs. series. il still C FANTAS 26:24-25 n2 1995
Beeler, M. Keep on trekkin'. stills C FANTAS 26:41 n2 1995
Bond, S.R. and Bond, S. Report from 221B Baker Street. il ARMCHAIR DET
26:72-73 n3 1993
Manttari, T. Star Trek valloittaa korpimaita. filmog il PEILI 18:4-5 n1
1994
Uram, S. Roddenberry's legacy. il stills C FANTAS 26:34-39 n2 1995
Actors and Actresses
Beeler, M. The Star Trek curse. stills C FANTAS 26:26 n2 1995
STAR TREK: VOYAGER v (1995- USA)
Leonard, J. The next next generation. stills NEW YORK 28:82-83 Jan 30 1995
To boldly go where seven movies and 300-plus TV shows have gone before. il
TIME 145:15 Feb 27 1995
Reviews
Whitehead, C. Phasers on stun. still VILLAGE VOICE 40:45 Feb 28 1995
STAR WARS TRILOGY: THE DEFINITIVE COLLECTION v (d Lucas, George 1993 prod
1977-83 USA)
Reviews
Caron, A. Le coffret "Star Wars." il still SEQUENCES n175:49-53 Nov/Dec
1994
STARR, CECILE
Jackson, W. Cecile Starr: a pioneer's pioneer. biog port ANIMATION J
3:40-43 n2 1995
Stars See ACTORS AND ACTRESSES
STARS (periodical)
Indexes
Index cumulatif. STARS n21:[51] Winter 1995
STEAMBOAT BILL, JR. v (d Reisner, Charles F. 1928 USA)
Reviews
DeBartolo, J. Video tape reviews. credits port stills CLASSIC n237:12+
[3p] Mar 1995
STEBINGER, JIM
Stebinger, J. Preservation '95. CLASSIC n236:5 Feb 1995
STECKLER INTERVIEWS, VOL 1: THE MAKING OF "THE STRANGE CREATURES" v (1994 USA)
Reviews
Hogan, D.J. "Steckler Interviews, Vol 1: the Making of 'The Strange
Creatures'." il stills F FAX n48:18 Jan/Feb 1995
STEIN, MICHAEL
Stein, M. "Zacherley" solid resin figure, sculpted by Jon Wang. il F FAX
n49:28 Mar/Apr 1995
STEINFELS, PETER
Steinfels, P. Chicago. il ports COMMONWEAL 122:14-25 Feb 24 1995
STERN, ANDY
Stern, A. France, EC in quota spat. VARIETY 358:32+ [2p] Feb 6/12 1995
Stern, A. and Schuman, J. French fried in quota quibble. il VARIETY
358:173-174 Feb 20/26 1995
Williams, M. and Stern, A. EC wants to double financial support for film,

TV. VARIETY 358:43-44 Feb 13/19 1995
Williams, M. and Stern, A. Quotas find Brussels muscle. il VARIETY 358:39+
[2p] Mar 27/Apr 2 1995
STEVEN, PETER
Nicks, J. Peter Steven. Brink of reality: new Canadian documentary film and
video [Book Review]. CAN J F STUD 3:104-107 n2 1994
STEVENS, ANDREW See also NIGHT EYES 3
Hollywood Kids. Andrew Stevens: Q&A. interv port MOVIELINE 6:32 Mar 1995
STEVENS, ROBERT See also I THANK A FOOL
STEVENSON, DEBORAH
Rowe, D. and Stevenson, D. Negotiations & mediations. bibliog MEDIA INFO
AUSTRALIA n75:67-79 Feb 1995
STEWART, JON
Q & A: Jon Stewart. interv port ROLLING STONE n700:26 Jan 26 1995
Stone, L. Going to bed with Jon Stewart. port VILLAGE VOICE 40:40-42 Mar 7
1995
STEWART, MATTHEW
Stewart, M. Receptions of war: Vietnam in American Culture. By Andrew Martin
[Book Review]. WAR LIT & ARTS 6:83-86 n2 1994
STEWART, PATRICK
Beeler, M. Two captains. il still C FANTAS 26:18 n2 1995
STEWART, ROY
Wharton, D. FCC bigwig rethinks Fox. VARIETY 358:88 Feb 27/Mar 5 1995
STOCK SHOTS
Television (broadcast) and Video (non-broadcast)
United States
Rhea, M. The rise of stock footage companies. AMCIN 76:14+ [3p] Jan 1995
STODDARD, BRIAN
Lowry, B. Stoddard to ankle as ABCP prez. VARIETY 358:36 Mar 27/Apr 2 1995
STONE, GEOFFREY R.
Trager, R. Entangled values: the First Amendment in the 1990s [Book
Reviews]. bibliog J COMM 45:163-170 n1 1995
STONE, LAURIE
Stone, L. Going to bed with Jon Stewart. port VILLAGE VOICE 40:40-42 Mar 7
1995
STONEHILL, BRIAN
Stonehill, B. The debate over "ocularcentrism" [Book Reviews]. J COMM
45:147-152 n1 1995
STORARO, VITTORIO
Gentry, R. Writing with light. il interv stills FQ 48:2-9 n2 1994/95
STOSSEL, JOHN
Ward, B. Crossing the line? port AM JOUR REV 17:12-13 n1 1995
STRIKES
Television (broadcast) and Video (non-broadcast)
France
Williams, M. Unions suspend dubbing strike. VARIETY 357:49 Jan 9/15 1995
Television (broadcast)
United States. Sports Broadcasting
Walsh, T. Replacement baseball drives stations batty. VARIETY 358:25 Mar
20/26 1995
STRINGER, HOWARD
Dempsey, J. and Flint, J. Telcos take topper for TV turf tussle. il port
VARIETY 358:1+ [2p] Feb 27/Mar 5 1995
Roberts, J.L. Changing channels. il port stills NEWSWK 125:40-41 Mar 6
1995
STRODE, WOODY
Lentz, H., III. Obituaries. il obits ports CLASSIC n236:57-59 Feb 1995
STROSSEN, NADINE
De Grazia, E. Sex de jure [Book Reviews]. NATION 260:242-249 Feb 20 1995
Kershaw, S. Against pornophobia. port NEW YORK 28:20+ [2p] Jan 16 1995
Sunstein, C.R. Porn on the Fourth of July [Book Review]. NEW REPUB
212:42-45 Jan 9/16 1995
STUDY AND TEACHING See also MEDIA STUDIES; PROFESSIONAL EDUCATION; STUDY GUIDES;
TELEVISION STUDIES
Television (broadcast)
Finland
Wuorisalo, J. Suomalaista teoriapohjaa mediavalistukselle [Book Review]. il
PEILI 18:31 n2 1994
STUDY GUIDES
Television (broadcast)
Great Britain
Hietala, V. Kasvattajat irti paatoksesta [Book Review]. PEILI 18:29 n4 1994
United States. Television Studies
Williams, T. College course file: television studies/television theories -
series and mini-series. bibliog UFAJ 46:43-60 n1 1994
Stunt cinematography See SPECIAL EFFECTS
STYLE
Television (broadcast)
United States
Zaniello, T. Hitched or Lynched: who directed "Twin Peaks"? bibliog filmogs
STUDIES POP CULT 17:55-64 n1 1994
SUBJECTIVITY
Television (broadcast) and Video (non-broadcast)
Great Britain
Dovey, J. Camcorder cults. il stills VERTIGO (UK) 1:5-7 n4 1994/95
Subsidies See GOVERNMENT SUPPORT
SUBSTANCE.DIGIZINE
Fisher, M. "Medio Magazine"; "substance.digizine" [Book Review]. il
VARIETY 358:42 Mar 13/19 1995
SUGHRUE, JOHN
Obituaries. obits VARIETY 358:58-59 Mar 20/26 1995
SULIK, BOLESLAW
Janicka, B. and others. Telewizja rzetelna. il interv KINO 27:20-21+ [3p]
Jul 1993
SULLIVAN, DREW
Sullivan, D. Grave secrets. Mark Dawidziak [Book Review]. SCARLET STREET
n17:97 Winter 1995
SULLIVAN, RANDALL
Sullivan, R. Unreasonable doubt: part 1. biog ROLLING STONE n697:77-78+
[10p] Dec 15 1994

Sullivan, R. Unreasonable doubt: part 2. ROLLING STONE n698/699:130-133+ [17p] Dec 29/Jan 12 1994/95
SUMARNO, MARSELLI
   Sumarno, M. Sudsers said to clean out the Indonesian workplace. VARIETY 357:57 Jan 2/8 1995
SUNDANCE FILM CHANNEL
   Dempsey, J. Film nets casting for indie jones. VARIETY 358:23-24 Mar 20/26 1995
   Shapiro, M. and Schrobsdorff, I. It's showtime! stills INDEP 18:7+ [3p] Apr 1995
SUNSTEIN, CASS R.
   Sunstein, C.R. Porn on the Fourth of July [Book Review]. NEW REPUB 212:42-45 Jan 9/16 1995
   Trager, R. Entangled values: the First Amendment in the 1990s [Book Reviews]. bibliog J COMM 45:163-170 n1 1995
SUONINEN, ANNIKKA
   Salakka, M. Televisio lasten elamassa [Book Review]. PEILI 17:45 n4 1993
   Suoninen, A. Televisio - arkea ja yhteiskuntaa. bibliog port PEILI 18:19 n3 1994
Super-VHS See as a subheading under individual subject headings
Super-VHSC See as a subheading under individual subject headings
Surfing See CHANNEL SURFING
Surveys See POLLS AND SURVEYS
SURVIVORS OF THE SHOAH VISUAL HISTORY FOUNDATION (Los Angeles, California)
   Haile, M. Reminting "Schindler's" gold. il stills BOXOFFICE 131:66+ [4p] Apr 1995
SUTTON, GLORIA
   Sutton, G. Stript-o-caucus neA. AFTERIMAGE 22:3 Jan 1995
SUZUKI, SHIROYASU
   Abe, M.N. Documentarists of Japan (second in a series). biog il interv stills DOC BOX 2:9-16 1993
SVENSK FILMINDUSTRI AB
   Edmunds, M. Svensk adds Wegelius to its crown. VARIETY 357:56 Jan 2/8 1995
SWACKHAMER, E.W.
   Lentz, H., III. Obituaries. il obits ports CLASSIC n236:57-59 Feb 1995
Sweden See as a subheading under individual subject headings
Switzerland See as a subheading under individual subject headings
Symposia See CONFERENCES, INSTITUTES, WORKSHOPS, ETC.
SYNDICATION
      Television (broadcast)
         United States
   Benson, J. Hours lose power in syndie market. port stat VARIETY 357:39+ [2p] Jan 9/15 1995
   Benson, J. and Walsh, T. "Home" enters original syndie to duel "Seinfeld." stills VARIETY 358:29+ [2p] Mar 27/Apr 2 1995
         United States. Effects on Television/Video
   Dempsey, J. Off-net strips ratings, but coin remains king. stat table VARIETY 358:39-40 Mar 6/12 1995
         United States. Export Market
   Flint, J. Int'l cash cow on critical list for syndies. ports VARIETY 357:52 Jan 2/8 1995
         United States. Government Regulation
   Slocum, C.B. FISR fallout. JOURNAL WGA 8:35 Feb 1995
         United States. Ratings
   Benson, J. "Simpsons" tops syndie race. stat VARIETY 358:29 Feb 6/12 1995
   Benson, J. Syndicated hours shine thanks to Simpson trial, Clinton talk. stat VARIETY 358:41 Feb 13/19 1995
   Benson, J. Syndie shows slow out of gate. stat VARIETY 358:195 Feb 20/26 1995
   Benson, J. Syndie talk off, mags up post-sweeps. stat VARIETY 358:34 Mar 27/Apr 2 1995
   Benson, J. Syndies slip despite sweeps boost. stat VARIETY 358:43 Mar 6/12 1995
   Benson, J. Trial coverage crimps syndies. stat VARIETY 358:53-54 Feb 27/Mar 5 1995
   Benson, J. Trial's tribulations dog field of syndies. stat VARIETY 358:27-28 Mar 20/26 1995
   Flint, J. O.J. trial bites into syndies. stat VARIETY 358:34 Mar 13/19 1995
SZEBIN, FREDERICK C.
   Szebin, F.C. The new adventures of Hercules. il stills C FANTAS 26:46-48+ [4p] n2 1995
   Szebin, F.C. The special effects of Hercules. il stills C FANTAS 26:49-50+ [3p] n2 1995
SZNAJDERMAN, MONIKA
   Sznajderman, M. Trzecie zycie kina. stat still KINO 27:46 May 1993
SZPIRGLAS, JEFF
   Szpirglas, J. (Thirty) 30 years of "Doctor Who" and its music. discog F SCORE MONTHLY n39:14 Nov 1993
TV!
   Dempsey, J. Is TCI's TV! cable barker friend? Foe? VARIETY 357:37+ [2p] Jan 2/8 1995
TV AUSTRALIA
   Woods, M. Network Ten sells off studio center. stat VARIETY 358:175 Feb 20/26 1995
TV EYE
   "TV Eye - the Journal of Classic Australian Television [Book Review]. il FATAL VISIONS n17:31 1994
TV NATION v (1994 USA)
   Rousseau, Y. Contre la culture du consensus. stills 24 IMAGES n75:12-13 Dec/Jan 1994/95
TV3 NEW ZEALAND
      Personnel
   Drinnan, J. Hollings brings schedules oomph to 3. ports ONFILM [12]:1+ [2p] n2 1995
TVC
   Drinnan, J. Blue Book blues dog TVC shoots. ONFILM 11:3 n11 1994/95
TVNZ See TELEVISION NEW ZEALAND
TAANILA, MIKA See also KULTAINEN AASI
   Taanila, M. Mielihyvakupolin avajaiset. credits filmog il stills PEILI

17:8-9 n3 1993
TABULA RASA
   "Tabula Rasa" [Book Review]. FATAL VISIONS n17:31 1994
TAD v (d Thompson, Rob 1995 USA)
      Reviews
   Scott, T. "Tad." credits still VARIETY 358:30 Feb 6/12 1995
TAJIMA, RENE
   Tajima, R. To be Asian American. filmog CINEMAYA n25/26:44-45 Autumn/Winter 1994/95
TALES FROM THE CRYPT v (1989- USA)
   Eby, D. "Demon Knight." stills C FANTAS 26:12-13 n2 1995
   Mallory, M. Al Feldstein. il interv port SCARLET STREET n17:23+ [2p] Winter 1995
TALES OF THE RAILS v (d Eitzen, Dirk/Tetzlaf, David 1989 USA)
      Reviews
   Denski, S. "Tails of the Rails." UFAJ 46:54-56 n3 1994
TALK SHOWS
      Television (broadcast)
         Audience. Research
   Tolson, A. Sonia Livingstone and Peter Lunt, Talk on television: audience participation and public debate [Book Review]. bibliog MEDIA CUL & SOC 17:172-174 n1 1995
         Germany (Federal Republic, since 1990)
   Hueltner, R. Reden und reden lassen. ports MEDIEN 38:366-368 n6 1994
         Italy
   Crisci, R. Italian people shows. VERTIGO (UK) 1:7-8 n4 1994/95
         United States
   Bellafante, G. Playing "get the guest." il stills TIME 145:77 Mar 27 1995
   Marin, R. and Fleming, C. Late night unplugged. stills NEWSWK 125:63 Jan 23 1995
   Zoglin, R. Talking trash. il ports still TIME 145:76-78 Jan 30 1995
         United States. Ethics
   Benson, J. Talkshows rate murder case an ethical dilemma. il port VARIETY 358:23+ [2p] Mar 20/26 1995
         United States. Hosts
   Rushkoff, D. Host hogs. ports table ESQUIRE 123:32 Feb 1995
         United States. Standards and Recommended Practices
   Dempsey, J. "Jenny" incident raises specter of control. VARIETY 358:36 Mar 13/19 1995
TAMAHORI, LEE See also ONCE WERE WARRIORS
   Lewis, B. Lee Tamahori's "Once Were Warriors." port stills C PAPERS n102:4-8 Dec 1994
TAPPLY, WILLIAM G.
   Gardner, B.W. The seventh enemy. By William G. Tapply [Book Review]. il ARMCHAIR DET 28:219 n2 1995
TASHIRO, CHARLES SHIRO
   Tashiro, C.S. Ann Gray. Video playtime: the gendering of a leisure technology [Book Reviews]. SCREEN 35:411-415 n4 1994
TAUBIN, AMY For film reviews see author under the following titles: CYBILL; WOMEN OF THE HOUSE
   Taubin, A. New (television) haven. VILLAGE VOICE 40:43 Jan 31 1995
TAXES See also ECONOMIC ASPECTS
      Television (broadcast) and Video (non-broadcast)
         United States
   Ellison, J. A taxing encounter. JOURNAL WGA 8:30 Mar 1995
         United States. Laws and Legislation
   Flint, J. Minority deal ordeal. VARIETY 358:64 Mar 20/26 1995
      Television (broadcast)
         United States. Laws and Legislation
   Wharton, D. Senate panel bollixes Viacom deal. VARIETY 358:28 Mar 20/26 1995
         United States. Minorities. Laws and Legislation
   Wharton, D. Minority tax break quashed by House. VARIETY 358:52 Feb 27/Mar 5 1995
TAXICAB CONFESSIONS v (1995 USA)
      Reviews
   Whitehead, C. The first family. il VILLAGE VOICE 40:37 Jan 17 1995
TAYLOR, ELIZABETH
   Elizabeth Taylor. biog filmog il stills STARS n21:[41-44] Winter 1995
TAYLOR, JONATHAN For film reviews see author under the following titles: CITIZEN X; GOOD OLD BOYS, THE; SERVING IN SILENCE: THE MARGARETHE CAMMERMEYER STORY
Teaching practices See INSTRUCTIONAL USES
TEAGUE, LEWIS See also TOM CLANCY'S OP CENTER
TECHNOLOGY
      Television (broadcast) and Video (non-broadcast)
         Digital. Conferences, Institutes, Workshops, etc.
   Beacham, F. Digital artists: reinventing electronic media. il AMCIN 76:59-60+ [3p] Mar 1995
         United States. Telecommunications
   Seaman, B. The future is already here. il TIME 145:30-33 Spring 1995
TEE, ERNIE
   Tee, E. Die synthetische Sinnlichkeit des Jean-Baptiste Mondino. stills BLIMP n30:28-31 Winter 1994
Teenagers in television/video See YOUTH IN TELEVISION/VIDEO
TELECOM AUSTRALIA
      Grants
   Telecom Australia fund. MEDIA INFO AUSTRALIA n75:151-153 Feb 1995
TELECOMMUNICATIONS See also CABLE TELEVISION; NETWORKS AND NETWORKING; SATELLITE COMMUNICATIONS
      Television (broadcast) and Video (non-broadcast)
         Projects
   Schuman, J. Projects down the pike. VARIETY 358:41 Mar 13/19 1995
         United States
   Dempsey, J. and Flint, J. Telcos take topper for TV turf tussle. il port VARIETY 358:1+ [2p] Feb 27/Mar 5 1995
         United States. Government Regulation
   How to get better phone service. CONS RES MAG 74:11-15 Dec 1991
         United States. Technology
   Seaman, B. The future is already here. il TIME 145:30-33 Spring 1995

Personnel
Dempsey, J. Caught in corporate crossfire, pay TV exec Cox quits Viacom.
VARIETY 358:28 Mar 20/26 1995
VIDEO ART AND ARTISTS See also names of video artists
Video (non-broadcast)
Festivals
Salvetti, S. I colori delle note. stills SEGNO n72:76 Mar/Apr 1995
Croatia (since 1992). Zagreb
Darke, C. Everything is connected. stills S&S 5:28-31 Feb 1995
United States. Women
Klein, J. Transgressive tapes. stills AFTERIMAGE 22:12-13 Jan 1995
VIDEO DIARIES
Television (broadcast)
Great Britain
Dickinson, M. Editorial. il stills VERTIGO (UK) 1:2-4 n4 1994/95
Video (non-broadcast)
United States
Aufderheide, P. Vernacular video. il still COL JOUR REV 33:46-48 Jan/Feb
1995
VIDEO GAMES
Video (non-broadcast)
Great Britain. Feminist Analysis
Tashiro, C.S. Ann Gray. Video playtime: the gendering of a leisure
technology [Book Reviews]. SCREEN 35:411-415 n4 1994
United States
Brandt, J.B. "Street Fighter." il stills C FANTAS 26:56-57 n2 1995
Bryan, J. Joystruck. il PREM 8:89-90 Feb 1995
O'Steen, K. Vidgame battle afoot. VARIETY 358:6 Mar 13/19 1995
United States. Adaptations
Weiner, R. Vidgames won't play by Hollywood's rules. VARIETY 358:1+ [2p]
Mar 20/26 1995
Video, music See MUSIC VIDEO
VIDEO NATION v (Gt Br)
Dickinson, M. Editorial. il stills VERTIGO (UK) 1:2-4 n4 1994/95
Rose, M. "Video Nation." il VERTIGO (UK) 1:9-10 n4 1994/95
VIDEO WATCHDOG
Livio, J. "Video Watchdog: the Perfectionist's Guide to Fantastic Video"
[Book Review]. GRIFFITHIANA n51/52:267 Oct 1994
VIDEODISC PLAYERS
Video (non-broadcast)
United States. Formats (Technical)
Weiner, R. Zenith takes a stand in the videodisc battle. VARIETY 358:10 Mar
20/26 1995
VIDEODISCS
Video (non-broadcast)
Digital. Philips
Homer, S. Philips mulls DVD bow at Germany's CeBIT. VARIETY 358:69+ [2p]
Feb 6/12 1995
Digital. Standards and Recommended Practices
Robinson, G. Leave the driving to U.S. il VARIETY 358:32-33 Feb 6/12 1995
Trade Fairs
Homer, S. DVD not among players at German CeBit. VARIETY 358:39 Mar 13/19
1995
United States. Digital. Standards and Recommended Practices
Weiner, R. Sony stands firm on its digital disc format. VARIETY 358:26 Feb
27/Mar 5 1995
VIDEOGRAPHE, LE (Montreal, Canada)
Cloutier, M. La troisieme fenetre. il SEQUENCES n175:53 Nov/Dec 1994
Videography See CINEMATOGRAPHY
VIDEORECORDERS AND VIDEORECORDING
Television (broadcast) and Video (non-broadcast)
United States
Cohen, J. Making sense of new electronics products. il CONS RES MAG
74:34-36 Dec 1991
United States. Product Guides
VCRs. graphs il stat tables CONS REP 60:175-179 Mar 1995
Video (non-broadcast)
United States. Maintenance
How to get your TV or VCR repaired. il CONS RES MAG 77:26-29 May 1994
VIDEOTAPE
Video (non-broadcast)
United States. Product Guides
Which videotape? il CONS REP 60:180 Mar 1995
VIDEOTHEQUE DE PARIS (France)
Thomas, J. La Videotheque de Paris. J F PRES n49:19-20 Oct 1994
VIDEOVISA
Paxman, A. B'buster VideoVisa: devalued relations. il stat VARIETY
358:43-44 Feb 13/19 1995
Paxman, A. VideoVisa springs forward as peso falls back. stat VARIETY
358:35 Feb 6/12 1995
VIETNAMESE CONFLICT, 1961-1975
Television (broadcast) and Video (non-broadcast)
United States
Stewart, M. Receptions of war: Vietnam in American Culture. By Andrew Martin
[Book Review]. WAR LIT & ARTS 6:83-86 n2 1994
VIOLENCE IN TELEVISION/VIDEO
Television (broadcast)
Finland. Audience, Children
Salakka, M. Onko Muranen Rambon inkarnaatio? PEILI 18:26 n4 1994
United States
Elrick, T. The televiolence debate: shoot-out at the fantasy factory. il
DGA NEWS 19:14-16 n3 1994
Elrick, T. Violence should be decried, not glorified. interv port DGA NEWS
19:16-17 n3 1994
Williams, A. Domestic violence and the aetiology of crime in "America's Most
Wanted." il port stills CAM OBS n31:96-119 Jan/May 1993
United States. Cultural Context
Pimenoff, M. Mista syntyy vakivalta? PEILI 18:9 n2 1994
VIRTA, TEIJA
Huhta, K. Saippuaoopperan teoriaa [Book Review]. il PEILI 18:28 n4 1994

VIRTUAL REALITY [Prior to V20, 1992 use INTERACTIVE]
Television (broadcast) and Video (non-broadcast)
Austria
Frey, M. Cyberspace [Book Review]. F KUNST n144:65-66 1994
Video (non-broadcast)
Julich, S. Voxel-Man. diags F HAFTET 22:55-57 n3 (n87) 1994
VIRTUAL REALITY EQUIPMENT
Video (non-broadcast)
United States
Rogers, A. Through a glass, darkly. il NEWSWK 125:52 Jan 23 1995
Visual perception See PERCEPTION
VIVA II
Molner, D. MTV, Viva set launch dates for spinoffs. VARIETY 358:46 Mar
13/19 1995
VLAAMSE TELEVISIE MAATSAHAPPIJ
Government Investigation
Edmunds, M. Belgian b'caster focus of probe. VARIETY 357:49 Jan 9/15 1995
VOLONTE, GIAN MARIA
Lentz, H., III. Obituaries. il obits ports CLASSIC n236:57-59 Feb 1995
VOYEURISM
Television (broadcast) and Video (non-broadcast)
Great Britain
Dovey, J. Camcorder cults. il stills VERTIGO (UK) 1:5-7 n4 1994/95
VUOKKO, PIRJO
Vuokko, P. Televisiomainonta - tarinoita, unelmia ja mielikuvia. il PEILI
18:10-11 n3 1994
WB NETWORK, THE
Flint, J. and Benson, J. WB, Par weblets square off. il stat VARIETY
357:37+ [2p] Jan 2/8 1995
Keepnews, P. Letters: one froggy error. VILLAGE VOICE 40:6 Feb 21 1995
Zoglin, R. Network crazy! il ports TIME 145:68-72 Jan 16 1995
Blacks in Television/Video Industry
Zook, K.B. Warner bruthas. il VILLAGE VOICE 40:36-37 Jan 17 1995
Programming
Fleming, C. and Marin, R. Same stuff, twice the testosterone. il still
NEWSWK 125:68-69 Jan 16 1995
Martel, J. Networst. stills ROLLING STONE n704:131-132 Mar 23 1995
Whitehead, C. The tao of poop. il VILLAGE VOICE 40:42-43 Jan 31 1995
WAKEFIELD, PHILIP
Wakefield, P. Boom year ahead. stat ONFILM [12]:1+ [2p] n1 1995
Wakefield, P. Censor's new broom cleans up "Warriors." ONFILM [12]:9 n1
1995
Wakefield, P. New adventures for Kotuku in wake of Enid Blyton project.
ONFILM [12]:6 n2 1995
WALLACE, RICK See also GREAT DEFENDER, THE
WALLNER, MARTHA
Wallner, M. Chicago mediamakers get organized. INDEP 18:58 Apr 1995
WALSH, JOHN
Williams, A. Domestic violence and the aetiology of crime in "America's Most
Wanted." il port stills CAM OBS n31:96-119 Jan/May 1993
WALSH, THOMAS
Benson, J. and Walsh, T. "Home" enters original syndie to duel "Seinfeld."
stills VARIETY 358:29+ [2p] Mar 27/Apr 2 1995
Walsh, T. Beltway bumps rattle pubcasting. il stat VARIETY 357:39+ [2p]
Jan 9/15 1995
Walsh, T. Fox, NBC declare NFL wins. stat VARIETY 357:41 Jan 2/8 1995
Walsh, T. Fox puckers up for hockey. il stat VARIETY 358:29+ [2p] Mar
13/19 1995
Walsh, T. Gotham goes to kids. stat VARIETY 358:193+ [2p] Feb 20/26 1995
Walsh, T. Pubcasters fear GOP fund-slash. port stat VARIETY 357:37-38 Jan
2/8 1995
Walsh, T. Rams outfoxed in bid to relocate to St. Louis. VARIETY 358:25 Mar
20/26 1995
Walsh, T. Replacement baseball drives stations batty. VARIETY 358:25 Mar
20/26 1995
Walsh, T. TV exex say baseball scabs don't rate. stat VARIETY 358:39 Feb
13/19 1995
WALTON, BRIAN
Walton, B. Let's make a deal: Brian Walton on the state of the Guild. il
JOURNAL WGA 8:10-13 Mar 1995
WANG, ZHIWEN
Chu, H. Wang Zhiwen, a new star bursts onto the scene. il ports CHINA
SCREEN n4:14-15 1994
WAR See also POLITICS AND GOVERNMENT; VIETNAMESE CONFLICT, 1961-1975
Television (broadcast)
Russia (since 1992). News Coverage
Watson, R. and others. Russia's TV war. il NEWSWK 125:30-32 Feb 6 1995
Russia (since 1992). News Coverage. Effects of Television/Video
Birchenough, T. TV has role in Chechnya war. VARIETY 358:59-60 Feb 27/Mar 5
1995
WARD, BUD
Ward, B. Crossing the line? port AM JOUR REV 17:12-13 n1 1995
WARG, PETER
Warg, P. Arab TV satellite is in the works. VARIETY 358:47 Mar 13/19 1995
Warg, P. Filmmakers cry foul, charge U.S. with piracy. stat VARIETY 358:50
Mar 6/12 1995
Warg, P. Iran's ban on dishes doesn't wash with public. VARIETY 358:34 Feb
6/12 1995
Warg, P. Islamic clergyman blasts TV fare aired during Ramadan. VARIETY
358:45 Feb 13/19 1995
Warg, P. "Kamera," "Thieves" hold captive aud during Ramadan. VARIETY
358:60 Feb 27/Mar 5 1995
Warg, P. Right-wingers on media's case. VARIETY 358:34 Feb 6/12 1995
WARING, RICHARD
Lentz, H., III. Obituaries. biogs filmogs obits ports CLASSIC n237:57-59
Mar 1995
WARK, MCKENZIE
Wark, M. Jhally, Sut and Lewis, Justin, Enlightened racism: "The Cosby
Show," audiences, and the myth of the American dream [Book Review]. MEDIA
INFO AUSTRALIA n75:166 Feb 1995

ZHANG, XUAN
  Zhu, A. Zhang Xuan and Qin Zhiyu. il ports stills CHINA SCREEN n4:22-23
    1994
ZHU, ANNA
  Zhu, A. Zhang Xuan and Qin Zhiyu. il ports stills CHINA SCREEN n4:22-23
    1994
ZIELINSKI, SIEGFRIED
  Zielinski, S. Mediale Grenzueberschreitungen: Audiovisionen einer
    Zeitschriftenlandschaft. BLIMP n30:66-67 Winter 1994
ZIMBALIST, ANDY
  Correy, S. Who plays on pay? interv MEDIA INFO AUSTRALIA n75:80-82 Feb
    1995
ZMARZ-KOCZANOWICZ, MARIA
  CD [author]. "Kraj swiata." biog credits filmog still FSP 40:13 n4 (n758)
    1994
ZOGLIN, RICHARD For film reviews see author under the following titles:
  PROMISED LAND, THE; WOMEN OF THE HOUSE
  Zoglin, R. Friends and layabouts. stills TIME 145:74 Mar 20 1995
  Zoglin, R. Mom, apple pie and PBS. il TIME 145:56 Jan 23 1995
  Zoglin, R. Network crazy! il ports TIME 145:68-72 Jan 16 1995
  Zoglin, R. Talking trash. il ports still TIME 145:76-78 Jan 30 1995
ZOOK, KRISTAL BRENT
  Zook, K.B. Test patterns [Book Reviews]. il VILLAGE VOICE 40:64 Jan 10
    1995
  Zook, K.B. Warner bruthas. il VILLAGE VOICE 40:36-37 Jan 17 1995
ZOOMAN v (d Ichaso, Luis 1995 USA)
  Cordero, C.K. Bullets over Brooklyn. il stills PREM 8:92 Mar 1995
ZWEITES DEUTSCHES FERNSEHEN
      Programming for Children
  Molner, D. German pubcasters seek federal cash for kidweb. VARIETY 358:29+
    [2p] Mar 27/Apr 2 1995